D1161599

THE IDEA
OF SOCIAL JUSTICE

THE MACMILLAN COMPANY
NEW YORK · BOSTON · CHICAGO · DALLAS
ATLANTA · SAN FRANCISCO

MACMILLAN & CO., LIMITED
LONDON · BOMBAY · CALCUTTA
MELBOURNE

THE MACMILLAN CO. OF CANADA, LTD.
TORONTO

THE IDEA OF SOCIAL JUSTICE

A Study of Legislation and Administration and the Labour Movement in England and France between 1900 and 1926

BY

CHARLES W. PIPKIN

SOMETIME RHODES SCHOLAR AT EXETER COLLEGE, OXFORD
ASSOCIATE PROFESSOR OF GOVERNMENT AT
LOUISIANA STATE UNIVERSITY

WITH AN INTRODUCTION BY

W. G. S. ADAMS

GLADSTONE PROFESSOR OF POLITICAL THEORY
AND INSTITUTIONS, OXFORD

New York
THE MACMILLAN COMPANY
1927

Set up and printed.
Published January, 1927.

Printed in the United States of America by
J. J. LITTLE AND IVES COMPANY, NEW YORK

To

C. W. AND G. T.

who would join with them in
this dedication our friends
of the Oxford Years'
One and Two and
Three

Every state is a community of some kind, and every community is established with a view to some good; for mankind always act in order to obtain that which they think good. But, if all communities aim at some good, the state or political community, which is the highest of all, and which embraces all the rest, aims, and in a greater degree than any other, at the highest good.

ARISTOTLE, *Politics*, I.1

INTRODUCTION

WHAT is Social Justice? The question is as old as history and generations to come will repeat the question. Justice is in its nature social, for it consists in the right relation of individuals one to another. But when we speak of Social Justice we are thinking of the collective expression given to the idea of justice through the laws and customs, the orders and the social provisions which express the will of the community. To find the answer to what is Social Justice, we must try to form a complete idea of the community, seeing the manifold relations within it, each of which contributes to the sum of Social Justice. The Republic of Plato has given the world for all time a wonderful picture of the State as expressing the idea of justice. Others have from time to time presented in their pictures of Utopia the semblance of an answer to the question of what is Social Justice. There is value in these efforts to present the ideal. Their concrete forms challenge the question how far they express what is necessary to the progress of human society. But they are only a first step in the search for Social Justice. Mankind goes on striving to enrich and enlarge the answer and to bring into the picture of organised society the manifold elements in the developed form of Social Justice.

Now it is by the patient analysis of the experience of society in its various types and by critical reflection on the evidence before us that we can make more complete the picture of the Community as the expression of Social Justice. In doing so, the question has to be repeated constantly, 'Does this or that measure contribute something which is necessary to a just order of society? We have come to a stage in history when the materials of social evidence are accumulating so rapidly that a large number of workers is needed to sift out, classify and compare the data for the guidance of public policy. In particular, we must examine what is taking place in the most highly developed states of the modern world. For we can see the nature of a thing best, as Aristotle said, in its most completely developed form. And it is by examining the very highly developed communities in the modern world that we can see farthest into the problem. The complexity of the times in which we live adds to the difficulty, but gradually the eye begins to see order in our changing social system. And as we compare one State with another, and mark their common elements and distinctive features, the concept of Social Justice grows steadily more complete. But we must seek to see the question steadily and to see it as a whole. And while we examine the development of the idea in this or that State, we must not forget that it is only through an international order that the full conception of Social Justice can be realised.

Social Justice, it may be said, has been the aim of every age. How far is this true? It is difficult to answer because it is so hard to recapture the temper and feeling of bygone ages. We may have before us the annals of history and yet how far we are from being able to judge the well-being not simply of the ruling class but of the whole society! Some bygone periods seem in their simpler order of life, in the closer personal relationships between classes, in the more easy provision of at least subsistence for their more limited population to present a sense of Social Justice which contrasts favourably with the conditions of our modern society. But despite its many shortcomings and its often glaring inequalities our age marks a growingly conscious pressure towards a universal realisation of a just order. This age is often said to be very material, yet in it there is also great spirituality and there are wide and deep movements of public 'feeling after justice.'

The significance of each generation lies in the effort it makes towards the realisation of a higher measure of justice among its members. There are dead periods—winter and night—in history, as well as times of light and quickening. We live in a period of great change. It is far more complex than everything that has been before, and far more difficult of interpretation and of direction. But that which alone can give order and cohesion to the efforts of society is the controlling idea of Social Justice.

We cannot yet discern with certainty the character of our own times. We can see them more or less darkly against the ages which have gone before, but we can only dimly speculate how they will compare with those which are to come. Yet it may well be that our generation is one in which the struggle of forces is alike more complex and more uncontrolled than will be that of the future, that gradually the experience of years will guide Society to a clearer, calmer, steadier way of life, that there will be seen more plainly the true nature, structure and method of Society, and that this period in which we live and move will be looked back on as great in its dark struggle and giving birth to a new order of justice which will gain more and more complete acceptance throughout the world. If such be in any way the case how full of significance must be the study of our times, and the attempt to mark and measure the movement which is going on! The very ebb and flow of debate reflected in this volume, often seeming to show so little headway, has its own significance in revealing how gradually and with great labour opinion is being formed in the public mind. "The ideal is the truth of the actual." The task of winning this is one of great difficulty. The present volume, based on patient investigation of the main sources of evidence, is the first attempt by a comprehensive survey to examine how the idea of Social Justice is finding new forms of expression in two of the great States of the world, and it deserves a generous welcome.

W. G. S. ADAMS.

PREFACE

THE opportunity to write this book was offered by the appointment to Oxford as a Rhodes Scholar. My debt to the Rhodes Trust is gratefully acknowledged, a feeling made personal by the kindness of the splendid friends of all Rhodes Scholars, Mr. and Mrs. F. J. Wylie of Oxford and President Frank Aydelotte of Swarthmore. As an American student I am happy to express my appreciation to the Rector and Fellows of Exeter College, of which college I have the honour to be a member. To Professors T. N. Carver and James Ford of Harvard University and J. L. Stocks of the University of Manchester, I am indebted for their continuing interest in this study. The study of the idea of Social Justice was first suggested to me by Professors Carver and Ford during my work at Harvard. The privilege of three years of study under the Gladstone Professor of Political Theory and Institutions at Oxford has made me feel deeply the obligation I owe to him. Professor Adams by his *Introduction* has honoured this book and increased my obligation to him beyond any hope of adequate expression. My appreciation to these former teachers of mine would not be recorded if they could in any way be held responsible for the errors and misjudgments of this book, but I owe to them an immense debt for their friendship and encouragement.

It is good to be able to put here an expression of abiding appreciation to my friends Mr. C. Wesley Travers of Lincoln College, Professor R. K. Gooch of the University of Virginia, Mr. W. C. Greene, Jr., of the Massachusetts Institute of Technology, Mr. R. L. Hyatt of Balliol College, and Mr. Paul Vincent Carpenter of Lincoln College, and I should like to join with them Mr. W. D. P. Carey, Mr. A. L. Golnick, Mr. Malcolm Fooshee, of Christ Church College, Mr. A. Thomson of Trinity College, Mr. Ben Prescott and Mr. W. H. Peal of Exeter College. No one can find in this study the story of the days at Günterstal and the Kühlen Krug in the Black Forest or the Oxford years, but it is here. The best of Oxford is with the friends.

To my father and mother I owe more than to all others for the confidence and encouragement which they have always given me. And to my colleague and my friend Colonel A. T. Prescott, with whom I am privileged to work at Louisiana State University, I am indebted for his interest in the bringing out of this study. In the final work of preparing this study for publication Professor Robert Kent Gooch has most generously helped, and I wish to especially thank him. I am unwilling to leave unrecorded the more than formal interest of the editorial department of The Macmillan Company.

This study can be only partial. It is a beginning. I am all too conscious of the defects of style and material; yet my hope is that it can be the basis of work better done when the hand is more skillful and the mind more ready for the task. Many students must add their part to the problem of interpretation of the social politics of this century. To go even a little way with those who have thought about the good life and the good society is recompense enough for any student. I shall be grateful for corrections of errors from any who may read this book.

C. W. P.

Baton Rouge, 1926.

CONTENTS

BOOK II

BOOK I

THE IDEA OF SOCIAL JUSTICE

CHAPTER I

INTRODUCTORY

I

THIS study attempts to estimate the strength of certain forces at work in England and France which are helping to create a better social order for the individual. The danger of isolating any period of history is obvious, though to do so may help to bring into better perspective the continuous story of human effort and social progress. Therefore this study, though it deals primarily with a definite number of years, provides at first a survey of the history of the Labour movement in England and France down to 1900; and the growth of industrial legislation in each nation is indicated. Some effort is thus made to show the preparation of each country for the important developments of democratic progress in this century. Following the historical survey is a review of the legislation of the first twenty-five years of this century in England and France, dealing with social and industrial problems, which will indicate what conditions the State attempted to remedy and the means taken to enforce its will. Where it has been possible the reasons that Governments gave for their action have been set forth at length, for it is with the purpose of the responsible lawmakers and the aims of the legislature that this study is most concerned. When a law has been passed the means of administration have been given in each case, for often this is as important in estimating the advance of good will as the statute itself. Social justice, it is taken, must finally depend on the expansion of the democratic idea; and the administration of labour legislation through responsible democratic agencies can insure an authority for the good purpose of the State.

It is impossible to provide detail of the many laws passed, and there is no effort to do so; yet it is hoped that the spirit often expressed in the passing of an Act will be made plain. When the progress of legislation and administration has been outlined, the Labour movement in England and France is considered with special attention directed to the problem of State action. Also for England the political crisis caused by the famous Budget of 1909 has been utilized so far as it helps to illustrate the importance of social politics in the parliamentary debates, and with somewhat of the same purpose a good deal of attention has been given to Industrial Unrest in England and French Syndicalism.

The chief purpose in giving so much attention to the political aspect of the Labour and Socialist movement is, that the writer has sought to point out definitely that the recognized leaders, supported by an increasing number of the electorate, depended on political action playing an important part in bringing about desired changes in the life of the nation. This has value in a study of social justice, for it shows a faith in the working machinery of democracy. The economic organization is not underestimated, but for this study it is important to indicate how political interest has deepened the consciousness of all parties within the State, preparing the way for a surer rule of justice. It is thus apparent that the range of possible interests which could be considered in a study of social justice makes the selection of material a most important one, and much must be only suggested or entirely omitted that would throw light on the whole problem of how the good life has commanded from the modern community its best thought. Recognizing the wealth of material, in itself an indication of the ideal we wish to set forth, this present study is necessarily limited to the problem of State action with regard to industrial legislation and labour organization. The intention is to find out what men thought of the social system about them and what was done to direct its progress and to improve its working.

II

The indictment of the social order of the twentieth century began before 1914. It has been added to by post-war criticism, which has had the advantage of judging a period that is definitely at an end. The pre-war indictment provides a background of France and England between 1900 and 1914, in which the conflicts of the present and the future, the aims of control, the method of conquest by economic and political groups have become fairly well defined. The interlude of the war hardly proved anything more than a period of suspicious neutrality between forces in society capable of producing great social good or of causing untold social ill. It has been necessary to get back to the old problems, taking up the work of social peace where it was laid aside in 1914. For France, Professor Sait records that

the structure and processes of French Government show no permanent effects of the war; they remain to-day substantially what they were in 1914. The changes which are impending will come not so much as the result of the war, as of tendencies already set in motion before the war, held in suspension during its course, and now given a new impetus, an accelerated pace.[1]

The effect of the war on the organization of modern democracies was not overlooked by Viscount Bryce, who may have had England especially in mind. He believed that there was a continuity in the processes of trial and error by which modern States sought to attain economic and political ends. The war might divert but it could not materially change the course marked out by the industrial organization of the century. The tendency toward reform and control will continue, working itself out anew in the changed world after the war, profoundly affecting problems of government. This distinguished critic, after the war, looked back over a long period of democratic change. He saw that the absorption of men's minds with ideas and schemes of social reconstruction had directed attention from the problems of free government which occupied men's minds when the flood-tide of democracy was rising seventy or eighty years ago. That generation, he thought, was busied with institutions, this generation was bent rather upon the purposes which institutions may be made to serve. The conclusion was that, if any of the bold plans of social reconstruction after the war were put into practice they would

[1] Edward M. Sait, *Government and Politics of France* (1921), "Introduction," p. xi.

apply new tests to democratic principles and inevitably modify their working.[2] Bryce believed that

the old question,—what is the best form of government? is almost obsolete because the centre of interest has been shifting. It is not the nature of democracy, nor even the variety of the shapes it wears, that are to-day in debate, but rather the purposes to which it may be turned, the social and economic changes it may be used to effect.[3]

Even at this time, 1926, there is much difficulty in estimating the forces which were at work in the pre-war social movement. But it may be taken for granted that in England and France the war did not alter materially the conditions under which the social movement works nor did it achieve the end it seeks to realize.[4]

[2] Cf. James Bryce (Viscount Bryce), *Modern Democracies,* 2 vols., 1921, Vol. I, "Preface," pp. xi-xii.

[3] *Op. cit.,* p. 4. J. A. Hobson in his *Free Thought in the Social Sciences* (1926) reflects this point of view. He says, "If we are right in holding that the most urgent business of our age is to devise better laws of conduct in the arts of human government, within and beyond the limits of nationality, success depends upon stimulating in as many spots as possible the largest number and variety of independent thinkers, constructing and maintaining among them the best conditions of free intercourse and co-operation and finally enabling their creative thought to play freely in criticism and reform upon the existing modes of political and economic life." Professor McDougall's *Ethics and Some Modern World Problems* (1924), is suggestive, especially Lectures III and IV; and in Mr. Wells' *Outline of History* (1920 ed.), Book IX, Vol. II, chap. XLI, there is a stimulating discussion on "The Possible Unification of the World into One Community of Knowledge and Will." Cf. R. L. Buell, *International Relations* (1925), Part III; and P. B. Potter, *International Organization* (1925), Part VII.

[4] With special regard to the Labour-Socialist movement see the Introduction to the 1917 and 1919 editions of G. D. H. Cole's *The World of Labour* (1st ed. 1913), also his *Organised Labour* (1924), pp. 1-13; and compare Sidney and Beatrice Webbs' Introduction to the 1920 edition of *The History of Trade Unionism.* Besides French sources given later a convenient survey of post-war programs in France is the *Manuel des partis politiques en France* (1924), by MM. J. Carrère and G. Bourgin, which supplements the far abler work of M. Léon Jacques, *Les partis politiques sous la IIIe République* (1913), see also the new edition (1924) of Edouard Guyot's *Le socialisme et l'evolution de l'Angleterre contemporaine (1880-1914)* (1913); Paul Louis, *Histoire du socialisme en France depuis la Revolution jusqu'a nos jours* (1925), chap. XI, "The War and After the War," pp. 343-407; and Charles Rappoport, *Jean Jaures, L'Homme, Le Penseur, Le Socialiste* (1st ed. 1916, 3d ed. 1925), chap. VI, pp. 344-363, "Socialist Participation in Power."

Progress has come back to its old course: "in Germany toward State paternalism, in England toward autonomous organization, in France toward political intervention."[5] In his preface to the first edition of *Greater European Governments* (1918), President Lowell wrote that the general traits of the political systems portrayed ten and twenty years before in his *Government of England* and his *Governments and Parties in Continental Europe* had altered little. The Preface of the 1925 edition gave Mr. Lowell the opportunity to say that "while the war was raging, and every belligerent was putting forth its utmost efforts in military force, the governments were necessarily far more autocratic than in normal times; and after peace was restored some of them were profoundly altered, while others reverted to their former political traditions. This last has been the case in England and France where the general nature and working of the governments are much the same that they were before the war." Professor James Harvey Robinson has written of the new perspective of the past that the last twenty years have given us. The years which, so he believes, "have witnessed a more startling accumulation of human information, more astounding applications of ingenuity, and, at the same time, a more tragic indictment of approved human institutions than any of the stately eras into which we are wont to divide history." It is no wonder then that political history had become somewhat discredited before the World War. But the war brought the problems of the State to the fore once more and raised to a place of supreme importance justice within the State and peace among States. Yet so much has transpired since the war that it is a problem to estimate the validity of pre-war adjustments, especially with regard to trade union and syndicate organization, the inner program of parties and the force of public opinion. All reacted on the State's duty with regard to social control and reform. But the study can be made with materials that are now a part of the body of economic history, and however partial or premature any general survey must necessarily be, it is not too early for an effort to be made to estimate the significance of some of the important events of this epoch. The years since the war have proved how far from a true understanding of the causes of rebellion some pre-war judgments

[5] Professor Georges Scelle, *Le droit ouvrier* (1922), pp. 205-206.

were, and the violent outbursts in France and England after the armistice indicated how deeply laid are the grievances of the mass of the people against the order in which they live.

By 1914 these grievances had been plainly put, over and over again. With regard to the State the insistence was plain, that where the social costs of industry were undermining the sources of strength in national life social control should begin. A whole period of reform was summed up by Mr. Hobson in a study[6] which made the claim that the future citizen would see a growing social control over those occupations where routine counts for much. On the basis of general industry, State-controlled and paying a full living wage, it was believed by this economist that a nobler industrial service could be rendered by all within the State, and this spirit would extend to those forms of service over which the State cannot so fittingly exercise so direct a control. Professor MacGregor wrote that Mr. Hobson's indictment was "the fullest reasoned plea for human values that has been contributed to social study for some time"; although he added that "such a plea need not have been put forward as a protest against current economic science."[7] This statement may be taken to mean that economic science had fully realized what Professor Alfred Marshall termed "the uncertain permanence of our present social ideals," or else it must be taken to be part of a general unwillingness to have the science accept its share of the collective responsibility for the condition of England. One who had helped to formulate a "practical solution" for industrial unrest[8] declared, however, that he was convinced that to future generations the era of unrestricted competition, with its recurring crises, will seem like a malady of childhood. Professor Ashley said further that he had no sort of doubt that the State will be compelled after a time to step in and subject monopoly

[6] J. A. Hobson, *Work and Wealth: A Human Valuation* (1914). The Labour and Trade Union demands are considered later, and they indicate the progress of this movement since the war. Mr. Hobson has written that he considers J. H. Smith's *Collectivist Economics* (1925, London), the best thought out scheme of collectivism that has yet appeared.

[7] Professor D. H. MacGregor in a review of "Work and Welfare," the *Economic Journal,* December, 1914, pp. 560-563.

[8] See *Industrial Unrest, A Practical Solution: The Report of the Unionist Social Reform Committee,* Introduction by F. E. Smith (1914). The committee members were W. J. Ashley, J. W. Hills and M. Wood.

prices to a certain public supervision and, if need be, control, just as the English State already sets limits upon the charges of railway companies. "What we have to do is to see to it that the modern State is as competent as may be to discharge its delicate but ultimately unavoidable task."[9] This conviction can be added to the pitiful question against economic science implied in the calm statement of 1913 of those who were in no way committed to radical change, that

> upwards of one-third of our people are living on the border line of bare physical subsistence, never for a single day free to direct their minds from the sordid problem of the next meal and next Monday's rent . . . Millions of English people feel that they have no place and no stake in their country. Their independence and their character are rotting for want of security and responsibility; for security and responsibility must go together.[10]

It was believed that

> intimately coupled with the conception of national production, and the protection of national production, is its natural correlative, the conception of a national minimum below which no citizen should be allowed to fall.[11]

Thus very definitely the demand for a national minimum showed the extent to which politics became concerned with the social results of industry, and it marked the progress of an ideal of justice for all members of the community. It further showed with regard to the industrial movement the close relation of the development of legal protection and control.[12]

The expansion of social control is taken as an expression of aims of social justice,[13] and in the body of this study legislation

[9] W. J. Ashley, *The Economic Organisation of England* (1914), p. 189; the chapter on "Joint Stock and the Evolution of Capitalism," an idea more popular in pre-war economics than to-day.

[10] Harry Roberts, *Constructive Conservatism*, with an Introduction by L. S. Amery, M. P. (1913), p. 15.

[11] *Op. cit.*, p. 5 (Amery).

[12] See D. H. MacGregor, *The Evolution of Industry* (1911), chaps. III-IV, pp. 93-117, suggesting a somewhat different view of economic science from the earlier quotation above.

[13] Cf. W. W. Willoughby, *Social Justice* (N. Y., 1900), Part. II, chap. VIII, "The Right of Coercion," pp. 215-268; Stephen Leacock in his *The Unsolved Riddle of Social Justice* (1920) sees "a progressive movement

is considered in illustration of the major tendencies toward this social control in England and France between 1900 and 1925. The attempt is also made to provide some background of opinion on the aims of the State and of groups within the State with regard to proposed changes that social control might bring about. It is here only necessary to note that issues were defined; after the war all sides have had an opportunity to be better informed and more intelligently critical of party programs. The public too have had a chance of knowing the way that party policy is tending and the means that are being used to attain desired objectives. There is, in spite of many contradictory and contravening circumstances, a basis for believing that a theory of progress for democracy, such as the ideal of social justice interprets, can be sustained. It is certain that democracy has an increasing capacity to recover from its illusions and also a will to learn from experience. Above all there has not been lost what Bryce declared was all important, *Hope.*[14] By an appeal to the trend of political events and by judging the expanding social consciousness of the industrial movement one finds warrant for believing that democracy can express its will to power, even if wrongly at times, for mankind has been decided and articulate on some very real political and economic problems since 1918.

III

Though this study is necessarily limited to the efforts which were made to express the ideal of communal good in the action of the legislature, in the expansion of the corporate activity of groups, and the ever-increasing function of voluntary organization in community life, it is intended to make clear one large hope of democratic progress: That in the same manner and by the same means through which a man becomes good he will frame

of social control"; and Professor Carver, *Essays in Social Justice* (1915), chaps. I-VI. Professor A. Loria in his *Verso la giustizia sociale* (1st ed. 1904, 2nd 1908), asks the question, Is there such a thing as social justice? A suggestive view is given in H. E. Barnes' *The New History and the Social Studies* (1925), Preface and chap. VIII, pp. 470-518, and a creative study of intelligent social attitudes is James Harvey Robinson's *The Mind in the Making* (1921).

[14] *Op. cit.*, Vol. II, chap. LXXX, pp. 656-670.

a State which will be truly good. Thus, in this study social justice is a definitely chosen ethical ideal of relationships existing between the State and individuals. By this ideal the England and France of to-day is judged, and the question asked is: Has the good life been made definitely a purpose of the community and of individuals in the efforts which have been made to bring about conditions which make the good life possible?

At the same time that the ideal of the good life is set forth we would join with it the ideal of the good society, believing that there is a necessary relationship between them which becomes increasingly significant as mankind accepts higher standards of action. The study of politics is not discredited because "the perfect State" is described as one in which the good man is absolutely the same as the good citizen, "whereas in other States the good citizen is only good relatively to his own form of government."[15] By the acceptance of this ideal the moral growth of democratic thought is reflected, and it becomes clearer that the State has an ethical basis which binds together the individuals of a community and provides for all groups an ideal of unity. It is thus to the citizen that the demands of justice have the widest appeal and the most authentic claim. Service from the individual is commanded by the State upon this basis, the ethical insistence of which increases as the State determines that its major duty to those who give it their best allegiance is to insure that conditions of justice obtain for all. Then is true "that the virtue of the good man is necessarily the same as the virtue of the citizen of the perfect State"; the social significance being, that "in the same manner, and by the same means through which a man becomes truly good, he will frame a State which will be truly good."[16]

It is then always a worth-while task to measure the actual achievements of the political community by referring to this ideal. Men are set to thinking about fundamentals. The aim is that this ideal finding expression in government, which aims at best of sharing with citizens the purpose of achieving the highest good, shall direct the purposes of democracy. For when

[15] Aristotle's *Politics,* translated by Benjamin Jowett, with "Introduction," "Analysis" and "Index" by H. W. C. Davis (1920), IV 6.
[16] *Politics,* III, 18.

the end of the good life is more generally the will of private citizens, it is truer that political society exists for the sake of noble actions.[17] This ideal of social justice, based upon the realization of the good life in the good society, gives larger meaning to the relationship between justice and goodness, which means that as men understand their own natures better they begin to seek a fairer way of living with all other men in a community which approaches as a common rule this ideal. It is natural that good men should desire a good State; that their government, which is the means of making their desire come true, should be a good government, though it may imperfectly represent the will for the common good. This will for the common good is essentially the will of good men, constantly expressing itself in the demand for justice through political organization. Searching for a juster way of living is moreover a positive ideal for the good man, the good citizen. Compulsion is inner, directed by the strong purpose of creating conditions of life which make for the best expression of personality. The good man wills the good. He knows that at the end painstaking critics of democracy when they come to "repress the pessimism of experience," consider the saddest memories of political life moments "at which one had to stand by when golden opportunities were being lost, to see the wrong thing done when it would have been so easy to do the right thing." [18] Yet the good citizen can know that the sharing of a common purpose becomes to more men a determining social motive.

The value of this common purpose depends upon the ideals which men hold together and the ends they have in mind when they work together. It is this sharing of a common purpose that gives importance to the politics of the social movement of this century. And though the organization of justice among free citizens must always largely depend upon the individual and his character, yet the growth of group interests with political power

[17] *Politics,* III, 9.

[18] Bryce, *op. cit.,* Vol. I, Preface, pp. ix-x. Compare this with Mr. Justice Oliver Wendell Holmes' "Ideals and Doubts" in *Collected Legal Papers* (N. Y., 1920), pp. 303-307. He says, "consciously or unconsciously we all strive to make the kind of a world that we like . . . there is every reason for doing all that we can to make a future such as we desired" (p. 305).

has given a large place in the State to them. So it has become important in this century to make industrial organization a means of social justice, which cannot be done if group rights are considered distinct from the rights of the community as a whole. There has been accordingly the necessity of establishing new and broad criteria for industrial organization in the modern State. But there is a grave danger to the political community in its aim of the highest good if a solution is sought through the specious hope that it is possible that administrative government will supersede political government and that the idea of society will take rank over the idea of the State.[19] In the attitude of the groups within the State, which we shall later consider, there is the important question of whether they tended to increase the freedom of the individual and the security of the group, and at the same time found new reasons for loyalty to and confidence in the political community, to which they were willing to confide the standards of the good life and to aid in an interpretation of the common will for the highest good.

[19] Cf. Maurice Hauriou, *Principes de droit public* (2nd ed. 1916), pp 42 ff. and pp. 617-619, for a sharp statement on this point.

CHAPTER II

A SURVEY OF THE ENGLISH SOCIAL MOVEMENT

PART I

REFORM OF BRITISH INSTITUTIONS

(a) *Industrial Legislation.*

THE nineteenth century saw "the slow and sure reform of British institutions."[1] It was a century in which men were attempting to live together in a new civilization, testing whether security and happiness could be found in an industrial society which was gradually changing the purpose and the character of all institutions which the State had called into being. Security in the daily work of making a living became the increasing concern of more and more people; their happiness and welfare finally had to be one of the major concerns of the State. It was then that the slow and sure reform of British institutions began. The deepening spirit of unity in democracy began to enforce all the efforts of reform and give them meaning; and the ideal of human good which has constantly become more insistent has changed the very structure of old institutions when it has not found expression in new ones. A common aim has unified democracy when the ideal of social justice has been most clearly seen; and this common aim shared by an increasing number of men of good will has been the abiding hope of democracy.

It is ninety-nine years from the beginning of factory legislation in England, with the passing of the Health and Morals Act, 1802,[2] down to the Factory and Workshop Act, 1901;[3] which seems a fairly long time, but it is a continuous development of the principle of security within the State for the individual. It is

[1] G. M. Trevelyan, *British History in the Nineteenth Century, 1782-1901* (1922), p. 182.

[2] 42 Geo. III. c. 73.

[3] 1 Edw. VII. c. 22.

institutional change expressed in the growth of labour legislation and in the extension of the ideals of collectivism. Behind this whole movement of evolution it may be difficult to find a hard and fast interpretation which will at all satisfy with even an approach to completeness, but a change of law and a change of spirit separate the year 1802 and the year 1901. The difference in both is vital to an understanding of the work which men have tried to do with the institutions the century made possible, and the power which these great social and political organizations have had in the lives of men.

It has been said that the Act of 1802 was not based on any general principle, but "sprung from the needs of the moment, and owed nothing either to the advance of democracy or socialism";[4] contrasting strangely to the long and often dull Committee work on the law of 1901, in which all parties gave their aid and experience. But the law of the twentieth century had its beginning with the law which was a response to the humanitarian impulse of the time, in that instance especially connected with the epidemic in Manchester among the apprentices in the cotton mills. The Act provided for the cleansing and ventilation of cotton mills and factories, hours of labour, and the religious education of the apprentices employed therein; and to compare its scant provisions with the hundreds of clauses in the Act of 1901 is to gain a fairly accurate impression of the contrast in the centuries. This English Act corresponds to the French law of March 22, 1841;[5] both were protests against cruelty, and the State interfered through legislation to protect a class of workers. Yet the good intent of the lawmaker produced practically no effect because of the absence of any serious administrative control.[6] The enforcement of the Act of 1802 was in the hands of inspectors or visitors who were appointed by the justices of the peace, while the Act of 1841 was useless because there was an absence of any penal sanction. The inadequacy of enforcing measures was true of the enactments of a similar char-

[4] A. V. Dicey, *Law and Opinion in England* (1st ed. 1905, 2nd 1914), p. 110.

[5] Cf. Charles Gide, *Les institutions de progrès social (cinquième édition, 1921)*, pp. 197-198.

[6] Cf. Paul Pic, *Traité élémentaire de législation industrielle, Les lois ouvrières* (cinquième édition, 1922), p. 79; Dicey, *op. cit.*, p. 110.

acter which followed the Health and Morals Act, 1802; the Acts of 1819,[7] 1825,[8] 1829,[9] and 1831.[10] Even though there was this failure to provide administrative enforcement, in both France and England the Acts were the basis of further legislation. Certain of the authors of the French law hoped that the new rules would have the effect of reducing indirectly the hours of labour for all workers;[11] it became the basis of the law of September 9, 1848, maintaining the principle of the legal limitation of the hours of work for all of the workers;[12] and the law of May 19, 1874, further extended the principle by raising the age limit for children to twelve.[13] But the value of this law was lessened by the decrees of March 27, 1875, and March 7, 1877, which allowed children of ten years of age to work half a day (six hours) in fourteen industries. The delay in administration and the virtual destruction of a law by special permissive decree has been a common thing in France, while no such experience has cursed the progress of English legislation and administration.

From 1819 to 1856, in England, Acts were passed regulating the safety, hours, meal times and holidays of children, young persons and women. The first important Factory Act was in 1833, and in the 1844 Act, protection of women was further extended; while in 1856, the Fencing of Machinery Act was the first Act which gave any specific protection to adult males. This legislation affected only textile or allied industries, but Acts passed in 1864 and 1867 included for the first time non-textile factories and workshops. In 1875 a Royal Commission studied the whole subject of the law as to factories and workshops, which at that time consisted of a great number of regulations contained in nineteen different statutes. The Report of the Commission, published in 1876, led to the Factory and Workshop Act, 1878.[14] Additional legislation in 1883, 1889, 1895, and 1897 "re-

[7] 39 Geo. III. c. 66.
[8] 6 Geo. IV. c. 63.
[9] 10 Geo. IV. c. 51.
[10] 1 and 2 Will. IV. c. 39.
[11] Cf. Raoul Jay, *La protection légale les travailleurs* (2nd ed. Paris 1910), p. 108.
[12] Jay, *op. cit.*, p. 110.
[13] Perhaps the most important fact about the law of 1874 was that it created the *Commission Supérieure du Travail*, to see that the provisions of the law were carried out; the reorganization of this Commission was a part of the law of Nov. 2, 1892, on the work of women and children.
[14] 41 and 42 Vict. c. 16.

stored the old state of chaos and rendered it necessary to do the work of 1878 over again."[15] This was done by the Act of 1901,[16] the existing labour code, which consolidated the whole line of Factory Acts, and which has been altered by subsequent statutes. The Parliamentary Committee of the Trade Union Congress, 1901, considered it a most important landmark in legislation, advocating consolidation along the same lines of such Acts as the Mines Regulation Acts and the Education Acts.[17] The contrast of this Act with that of 1802 obviously marks the development of the nation away from the theories which dominated in the earlier time.[18] From the Act of 1802 which "owed nothing either to the advance of democracy or socialism," to the Act of 1901, which the same eminent authority considered "the most notable achievement of English Socialism,"[19] is a period which cleared the way for the common will of the people to make the effort to gain security for the individual. The larger conceptions of freedom and welfare necessarily developed as the possible chances of good living increased. But the last century was mostly concerned with gaining a living, not in the winning of happiness. If the pioneer work was mostly negative, it was necessary; if it was materialistic, there was ground work to be done.

The list of Factory Acts extending from 1802 to 1901,[20] is partly an answer that men did see what was to be done, and the slow growth of legislation through the century shows clearly that men were attempting to bring about an adjustment in the social condition of England.[21] "After 1815 thoughtful men must have perceived the existence of a want of harmony beween changing

[15] Cf. *Redgrave's Factory Acts* (12th ed. London 1916), by Charles F. Lloyd, revised by W. Peacock, pp. xxv-xxvi.

[16] I Edward VII. c. 22.

[17] Cf. London *Times,* Sept. 3, 1901, p. 9, Parliamentary Committee Report.

[18] Cf. A. L. Lowell, *The Government of England* (1st ed. 1908, new ed. 1917), Vol. II, pp. 526-527.

[19] Dicey, *op. cit.,* p. 328.

[20] The Schedule of the Acts provides a quick survey of progress of legislation. See for list of Factory Acts, extending from the Health and Morals Act, 1802, to the Factory and Workshop Act, 1901, Hutchins and Harrison, *History of Factory Legislation* (1903), p. 323; Karl Marx's *Capital,* pp. 214-288, for his interesting survey of Factory legislation.

[21] Cf. Sidney and Beatrice Webb, *History of Trade Unionism* (1920), pp. 310-313.

social conditions and unchanging laws,"[22] and yet the political theory and the economic theory of the long years of expanding industrial life in England seemed closely joined with a doctrine of social and economic fatalism.[23] The first decided triumph of the movement which began in 1802, was in the factory legislation embodied in the Ten Hours Act, "which recognized the principle that the regulation of public labour is the concern of the State and laid the basis for a whole system of Government inspection and control."[24] Legislative opinion had gone some distance from the 1802 Act. The Reform Act of 1832 had been passed; the Combination Laws of 1799 and 1800 had been repealed in the Combination Act, 1824,[25] which was itself replaced by the Combination Act of 1825;[26] the Poor Law Amendment Act in 1834 had sought to cure obvious evils, and in 1846 the Corn Laws were repealed. "The State of England" question was before the people. Public opinion was at work; legislation was in turn pointing the way to further progress and the efficacious value of the intervention of the State was seen as well as the limitations of its efforts.

Such a change had taken place in England by 1875 that the Combination Act of that year,[27] Conspiracy and Protection of Property Act, has been taken to represent in the main "the combined influence of democracy and collectivism—an influence, however, which was still balanced or counteracted by ideas belonging to individualistic liberalism."[28] It was an individualism largely based on the social philosophy of Bentham, but after 1880 the *laissez-faire* creed had less and less authority.[29] The movement behind legislation was too powerful, the needs too acute. By 1901 there were principles of labour law and administration embodied in the statute books, which had logically developed from the extension of the movement of reform since 1800, but which would not have been accepted by the most ardent advocates of change

[22] Dicey, *op. cit.*, p. 115.

[23] Cf. J. L. and Barbara Hammond, *The Town Labourer (1760-1832), The New Civilization* (1917), pp. 194-220; and their *The Rise of Modern Industry* (1925), Part III.

[24] Dicey, *op. cit.*, p. 239.

[25] 5 Geo. IV. c. 95.

[26] 6 Geo. IV. c. 129.

[27] 38 and 39 Vict. c. 86.

[28] Dicey, *op. cit.*, p. 272.

[29] Cf. Ernest Barker, *Political Thought in England from Spencer to To-Day* (1915), pp. 203-204.

at that earlier time. The progress of industrial legislation, the interference of Parliament in the industrial life of the nation, was a test of how far the State conceived its functions of control and regulation to go, and the effort to change its functions to meet the vastly more complicated structure of modern society.[30]

In discussing the relation of democracy and legislation, Professor Dicey asked,[31] "Does not the advance of democracy afford the clue to the development of English law since 1800?" It is only necessary to note the fact that between 1804 and 1900 there was small part of the English Statute book that had not been changed in form or in substance. This shows a close and immediate connection which exists in modern England between public opinion and legislation, and helps to explain that throughout the nineteenth century every permanent change of a constitutional character had been in a democratic direction. The advance of society in the democratic direction had by 1900 transformed the English Constitution into something like democracy; it had extended the electorate to a point where parliamentary and other institutions had come to have a direct relation to the democratic sentiment. Yet it is well to keep in mind that the growth of England's democracy has been greatly influenced by the traditions of the aristocratic government out of which it has developed, and this has had its share of influence in the social theory of the Labour leaders.[32] Trevelyan writing in an age in which he believes the law of perpetual and rapid change is accepted as inevitable, and the difficulty is to obtain progress without violence, thought there may be profit in the story of a statesman who, after a period of long stagnation and all too rigid conservatism, initiated in "our country a yet longer period of orderly democratic progress, and at the critical moment of the transi-

[30] Cf. Frank Tillyard, *The Worker and the State* (1923), p. 3. J. A. Hobson in his *The Evolution of Modern Capitalism* (1902), illustrates the lines along which State protection of labour advanced in the 19th century by four laws of development; (1) Movement along the line of strongest human feeling; (2) Protective legislation moves from the highly organized to the less highly organized structures of industry; (3) Growing complexity of aims and of legislative machinery; (4) Increased effectiveness of legislation with growth of centralized control (p. 321).

[31] Dicey, *op. cit.*, p. 48.

[32] Cf. J. Ramsay MacDonald, *The Socialist Movement* (1911), p. 235; Dicey, *op. cit.*, p. 58.

tion averted civil war and saved the State from entering on the vicious circle of revolution and reaction." [33] He believes to understand Lord Grey of the Reform Bill and his paramount influence in the Britain of 1830-1832 is to understand the world of that transition period.

It is to understand the position and outlook of these liberal-minded autocrats peculiar to the history of our island, whose existence was one of the reasons why the political traditions and instincts that the English have inherited differ so profoundly from those of Germany, of France, or even of America.[34]

The beginnings of the advance towards democracy in the nineteenth century were largely political; and it is remarkable that at the beginning of the twentieth century the Labour party of England were at work upon the problems which political democracy had forced upon them, with perhaps more emphasis on the means that such power gave them than on the development of economic organization. The reactions of opinion throughout the nineteenth century, and even so far in the years of this century, have indicated that there is an abiding conflict, and a continuing ebb and flow, between the political and economic method.

The Reform Act of 1832 indicated that the Parliamentary system of Government, which since 1689 was essentially the English system, would become more democratic and more representative of the cross-currents of English politics and social thought.[35] As a legislative machine it would bring more fully into effective expression the will of the people; this is indicated in the subsequent legislation of 1867, of 1872, of 1884-5,[36] the Parliament Act of 1911 and the Representation of the People Act, 1918. Modern democratic government can be taken as starting in England with

[33] G. M. Trevelyan, *Lord Grey of the Reform Bill* (1919), Preface, p. viii.

[34] *Op. cit.*, p. 368.

[35] Cf. Sir John A. R. Marriott, *The English Constitution in Transition, 1910-1924*, Oxford (1924), for a recent study of the evolution of the ever-changing Constitution; see especially, pp. 16-27, "The Legislature and the Electorate." Cf. George Burton Adams, *Constitutional History of England* (1922), "Introduction," pp. 1-3, and chap. xx, pp. 486-503, "The Recent Years."

[36] The Representation of the People Act, 1884, 48 Vict. c. 3; The Distribution of Seats Act, 1885, 48 and 49 Vict. c. 23.

the passing of the Reform Act of 1832, which gave predominant power to the middle classes and to the manufacturers. In 1867 the workers in town were given the parliamentary suffrage, further extending the "democratic system" into which England was passing and which was made more comprehensive in 1884-5. Parliamentary democracy has from 1832 more and more tended to put the emphasis on the really great common interests of the nation, and this most important development has been the work of the two great political parties of the nineteenth century. The rise of a Labour party under a discipline administered by the two-party system has had a great deal of influence on the leaders of that party, and even in England there has been the hope that if it were to continue over a long period of time, that a three-party system would tend to raise the level of parliamentary responsibility. It is from this point of view that the parliamentary Labour group in France has suffered greatly; the stability and permanence of legislative procedure which the English system has found in its party divisions have done much to make it possible for Labour to have a responsible share in Government.[37] The larger effect of this on the nation has been considerable, and over a considerable period of time it must work for the diminution of the class struggle in the politics of democracy. The achievement of this good thing is surely one of the ideals of social justice. Parliamentary democracy slowly educates the electorate. It has thus come about that in the growth of the English parliamentary system to meet the problems of industrial expansion and the

[37] Lowell, *The Government of England,* Vol. I, p. 452. Professor J. T. Shotwell's oft-quoted article, "The Political Capacity of the French," has this interesting point of view: "Now if one looks back over the history of the Third Republic since it has been under republicans, one will find a more logical development of reform, a more regular and consistent line of legislation, than can be matched where the English system prevails," *Political Science Quarterly,* March, 1909, p. 120. Professor W. B. Munro in his *The Governments of Europe* (1925), records that there are those who find satisfaction in telling the world that parliamentary government has failed in France, that ministerial responsibility has become ministerial anarchy, and that the instability of her cabinets has made France a will-o'-the-wisp among the nations. He believes that "law and order are better maintained in France than in the United States; justice is more fairly and more efficiently administered; the work of administration is carried on more economically; there is no spoils system, no Tammany Hall, no gerrymandering, no pork barrel" (pp. 430-431).

extension of governmental powers by legislation and administration, there has been "the greatest contribution of the nineteenth century to the art of government—that of a party out of power which is recognized as perfectly loyal to the institutions of the State, and ready at any moment to come into office without a shock to the political traditions of the nation." [38] This fact has greatly figured in the history of the parliamentary struggles of Labour in England, where "a degraded House of Commons really means a degraded democratic authority," and where Labour has learned that "parliamentary government without the constitutional instinct or habit is an impossibility." [39]

The faith in parliamentary government which has steadily increased in the modern Labour movement has had a constant influence on the movements of agitation. The earliest movement of agitation of the nineteenth century which went on in "the period of old Toryism," 1800-1830, was based on deep and abiding grounds of protest; for "sensible men perceived that the state of England would soon necessitate a choice between revolution and reform." [40] The major problem then, and at all times, was the adoption and changing of the political system to the new conditions in the social and industrial life of England. But the temper of the lawmakers and the dominant idea of the place of the State, is indicated in the purpose of the reactionary legislation, the same in France and in England. Chief among these restrictive laws were the Combination Act, 1800,[41] and the Act of 1817,[42] for the prevention of seditious meetings. But from the Reform Act of 1832 there was a deliberate attempt to bring the political system into accord with the life of the nation. It is by this continuous effort of reform and remaking of the law of the land that the democratic tradition was strengthened, providing an opportunity for a Labour movement to develop, freed from the embittered political philosophy of Marxism, nor bound to futile philosophies of social determinism. How important this tradition is can be seen in the history of the political parties in England during the nineteenth century; for the evolution of the

[38] Lowell, *op. cit.*, Vol. I.

[39] J. Ramsay MacDonald, *Socialism and Government* (1910, 3rd ed.), pp. 116-118.

[40] Dicey, *op. cit.*, p. 124. [41] 40 Geo. III. c. 19. [42] 57 Geo. III. c. 19.

social and political philosophy of the parties attests to the commanding importance of the idea of democracy. For some time it was the function of the party, which took soon after the Reform the name of Liberal, to extend the franchise, especially in the industrial centres; to reform the Poor Law, the criminal law, municipal government and the civil service; pass laws for the improvement of public health; establish general elementary education; give greater freedom to trade unions; remove grievances of Dissenters; disestablish the Church in Ireland; enlarge the local government and create a system of central control. When the Conservatives won their victory at the election of 1874, the period of Liberal domination had for a time come to an end, because they had worked out their chief problems, "they had brought the State in its most important aspects into accord with modern conditions." [43]

That was the task of democracy, and no party could withstand the slow-moving pressure from the people. The Conservative party under the leadership of Disraeli had been advocating progressive measures, and the Reform Act of 1867 was brought in under a Conservative Ministry. But Disraeli's efforts to bring about an alliance of his party with the newly enfranchised working class electors was not especially successful, for up until 1868 only a small number of workingmen were voters, while a majority were still unenfranchised in 1884. Political apathy, on the part of a great number, followed the collapse of the Chartist movement in 1848, combined with the normal tendency of large numbers toward political non-participation. When the struggle for legalizing the trade unions went on, 1859-1875, the Labour movement was weak numerically and financially. The first Gladstone Ministry of 1868-1874 did not affect to any appreciable extent the problems which faced the mass of the workers. It was not until Mr. Gladstone returned to power in 1880, after the fall of the Disraelian Government, that the full force of the Irish question brought out a definite, settled policy of social reform and remedial legislation.[44] The agitation for land legislation and the

[43] Cf. Lowell, *op. cit.*, Vol. II, p. 103 and pp. 116-117.

[44] In the first year of the triumphant Gladstonian Government of 1880-1885, Mr. Gladstone wrote to Lord Rosebery, that "What is outside Parliament seems to me to be fast mounting—nay to have mounted—to an importance much exceeding what is inside."

policy which Gladstone pursued, gave an opportunity for the development of the tendencies which grew into the English Labour movement of the modern period. There has as yet been no adequate appreciation of the influence that the land question has had on the English Labour movement, for at each period of a crisis the re-direction of the movement has come from this source. The same powerful influence has inevitably affected all parties, and, as much as any other factor, determined that "the state of England question" be raised to the level of a national problem. This influence has had a far more fundamental importance than any political far-sightedness of Fabianism, which plainly saw that the class struggle in economics or in politics would corrupt and degrade all social life. "The community of interest" has been fully set forth in all industrial countries, but nowhere with the same moral and social appeal as in England, against the narrow dogmatism of social determinism. In the land question this appeal has had its most complete statement.

Educational reform and the extension of political democracy have been questions which have widened the conception of "the community of interest." By 1884 the progress of socialism or collectivism had begun to be felt and to influence legislative opinion. The last Parliament elected under the Reform Act of 1832 came to an end on July 31, 1868. A new spirit in legislation became evident as the democratic movement of 1866-1884 made plain that the doctrine of individualistic liberalism or *laissez-faire* was at an end.[45] In France this doctrine continued longer and with much stronger force, continuing into this century. M. Hauriou believes that it was not until the passing of the law of July 1, 1901, the Law of Liberty of Association and Associations, that there came to an end the period of the individualism of the French Revolution.[46]

[45] The Earl of Wemyss on July 31, 1885, in the House of Lords made a speech deploring the advancement of state interference in business, and gave in his speech a résumé of Acts of Parliament from 1870 to 1885 which showed the progress of socialism. Again on May 19, 1890, he warned that body of approaching danger. Cf. W. H. Mallock's *Social Equality* (1884), and *Property and Progress or a Brief Inquiry into Contemporary Social Agitation In England* (1884), especially pp. 167-248. H. M. Hyndman's *England For All* (1881) and the Social Democratic Federation's *Socialism Made Plain* (1883), are also of interest.

[46] *Principes de droit public,* p. 550 n.

It is well to note that the rise of modern British Socialism from 1880 on had a much freer and fuller release from dogma than French Socialism; and at the same time that the doctrine of *laissez-faire* was being undermined, a similar growth of freedom was beginning in the English Labour movement.[47] About the same time that the program of Marseilles was directly deduced from orthodox Marxism,[48] 1879, there was in England a revival of Socialism under the inspiration of Henry George.[49] This period began the definite break from the Marxian influence;[50] and from this freedom there came about a positive suspicion of theory among the English working class which has not always been to its advantage,[51] but has made it possible for its leader to say, that "a reply to Marxian dogma is not a reply to Socialism."[52] There has been far more talk about Marx in the anti-Socialist controversy since the Great War than can be found in the literature of British Socialism before 1914; and it must be often taken for granted that the critics understand neither the theory of Marx nor the history of the Labour movement in England. Marx's influence on the political theory of the English Labour leaders has been very scant, while his economic theory and method has been much more persuasive in its influence.[53] The

[47] Cf. M. Beer, *History of British Socialism* (1920), Vol. II, p. 202; this author holds that "the rise of modern socialism in Great Britain, as well as the whole Labour unrest since 1907, so far as their leaders have been attempting to give them a theoretical foundation, are inseparably linked with Marxism" (p. 202). One page 345, he contradicts this.

[48] Paul Louis, *Histoire du socialisme Français* (1901), pp. 306-307.

[49] See Appendix I, by G. B. Shaw, in Edward R. Pease, *History of the Fabian Society* (1916; new edition 1925).

[50] Pease, *op. cit.*, pp. 23-24, and p. 236. The author says that none of the earlier Fabians had read Marx (pp. 23-24).

[51] Cf. J. Ramsay MacDonald, *Socialism and Society*, London (1905).

[52] Cf. J. Ramsay MacDonald, *The Socialist Movement*, p. 93.

[53] See H. W. B. Joseph, *The Labour Theory of Value in Karl Marx* (1923), pp. 1-28 and 148-174, for a recent study of certain implications drawn from Marx by Labour writers and theorists. The volume by the Master of Balliol, *Karl Marx's 'Capital'* (Oxford Press, 1926), has been eagerly awaited by all who heard his lectures on Ethics, Economics, and Politics. Mr. Lindsay has centred attention on some fundamental problems in our thinking of the individual and the good State. He has splendidly pointed out that the idealistic view of human society rests on all that makes for community of purpose in a people. The individual is not to be the sport of economic forces—not to be the slave to coal, iron, steam, or to the caprice of others. Freedom in society rests on collective control

legislative and social reform of this period of revival indicates the progress in the Labour movement from the democratic ideas of Chartism, 1838-1848. The older democratic revolt sought largely only political change, but, in common with the time, there was a revolutionary spirit in the propaganda of that struggle. It is a remarkable fact that the new democracy seeking to more adequately interpret democracy in social institutions and to insure a larger freedom in industrial relationships was moderate in temper and method. There was no definite plan of legislation like the Chartists' points, but the working class were inspired by a vague and general program for the reconstruction of society under collectivist or socialist ideals. In the second Fabian tract in 1884, George Bernard Shaw, in the concluding affirmation, said that "we had rather face a Civil War than such another century of suffering as the present one has been."[54] But just twenty-four years later the mellow view of retrospection perhaps more accurately saw the past events, and Shaw wrote, that in 1885 "we set ourselves two definite tasks: first to provide a parliamentary program for a Prime Minister converted to Socialism as Peel was converted to free trade; and secondly, to make it as easy and matter-of-course for the ordinary respectable Englishman to be a Socialist as to be a Liberal or Conservative."[55]

From the beginning of the Labour movement two influences of distinctly English genius have been at work, modifying and complementing each other. The one is the sturdy enthusiasm and

of the elementary conditions of life. The place of Marx is then suggested: "He sets in sharp contrast two stages of social development, one in which the economic conditions control the political, the other the society of the future where the political factors, in the form of social control, will master economic conditions." It is needless to say that Mr. Lindsay's interpretation of Marx is taken by some to be too kindly a view.

[54] *Op. cit.*, quoted also by Pease, *op. cit.*, p. 43.

[55] Cf. Shaw's Introduction to the 1908 edition of *The Fabian Essays in Socialism*," p. xv (American edition). The "political inadequacy of the human animal" has been a doubt which Shaw says has grown on him "during my forty years' public work as a Socialist" (p. 9, Preface to *Back to Methuselah*). This Preface of seventy-two pages is illuminating for a history of the Socialist movement, and suggests a contrast with the great literary figure of French Socialism, M. Anatole France. See Archibald Henderson, *George Bernard Shaw* (1911), chap IV, pp. 89-118. Mrs. Sidney Webb's *My Apprenticeship* (1926) has many interesting comments on the period above.

unfailing belief of the workingman in political change, and the other is the steady play of the intellectuals in their criticism of the naïve faith of their brethren; together the two influences defy the bitter denunciation which has come upon the "intellectuals" from the Socialist movement,[56] and also protect the English workingman from the charge of political disingenuousness. In 1874, for the first time, two Labour members were returned to Parliament, Alexander MacDonald and Thomas Burt. That was seventeen years after George Jacob Holyoake was parliamentary candidate for the constituency of Tower Hamlets, in 1857. It was, he said, the first claim ever made to represent Labour in Parliament.[57] His conclusion in the campaign address to the voters, dated March 23, 1857, is interesting: "All progress is a growth, not an invasion. Legislation can do little more than enable the poor people to help themselves. But this help, given with personal knowledge of their wants, and in a spirit free from the temerity which would precipitate society on an unknown future, and free from the cowardice which is afraid to advance at all, may do much." Such a characteristic statement must always remain one of the proud possessions of the democratic movement.

The movement for Labour representation in the House of Commons,[58] which meant at that time the sending of workingmen to Parliament, was helped by the formation in 1868 of the Trade Union Congress. Before the assembly of Trade Union Congresses there was no regularly constituted body to promote or initiate legislation.[59] The Congress in 1869 first declared itself in favour

[56] Cf. Karl Kautsky, "Whether Class Antagonism is Softening Down," pp. 114-134, in R. C. K. Ensor, *Modern Socialism* (3rd ed. 1910), for Marxian statement on the Intellectuals; for a French pronouncement see "Le Mouvement Socialiste," May 15, 1908, pp. 389-397, the review by Edouard Berth of Werner Sombart's sixth edition of *Sozialismus Und Soziale Bewegung* (Jena, 1908). Berth and Sorel were stung to the quick by being called by Sombart "gourmets of social theory"; Berth said he meant to be more biting, thinking of them as the "esthetes of social theory" (p. 392).

[57] Cf. George Jacob Holyoake, *Sixty Years of an Agitator's Life* (London, 1893).

[58] Cf. Humphrey, *A History of Labour Representation* (1912), for an account of the progress made; F. W. Soutter, *Recollections of a Labour Pioneer*, London (1923), pp. 25-53; A. Watson, *A Great Labour Leader, Being the Life of the Rt. Hon. Thomas Burt, M. P.* (1908).

[59] Cf. George Howell, *Trade Unionism, New and Old* (1900, 3rd ed.), p. 468.

of the direct representation of Labour in Parliament, and in that year the Labour Representation League was formed. The prospectus of the League is fairly interpretative of the point of view of the Labour leaders.[60] In 1871 the Trade Union Congress expressed the notion "that the direct representation of Labour is a necessity, not only in the interests of the working men as a class, but also in the interests of the nation at large." It was in this year that Mr. Gladstone, in speaking on the Elections Bill, declared the great blot on their representative system was that they had not been able to bring workingmen within those walls. When the Reform Act of 1867 was passed, so largely increasing the constituents, there were few honourable members who did not hope that one result of that change would be that they would have the pleasure of welcoming, in the House, some of their fellow citizens of the working class. Nearly forty years later Mr. Keir Hardie, in a memoir of the great leader, while appreciating the love of freedom which was a positive quality in Gladstone, held that "the modern Labour movement and the conditions which have called it forth, he never understood, and there was no Labour party to evidence the fact that there was a Labour movement in existence. Surely, however, this cannot be imputed as blame to him. The fault lies elsewhere."[61] Yet another generous critic,[62] has written that "constructive legislation coping with pauperism, sweating, unemployment, old-age destitution, or engaging the State in constructive work for the development of the productive resources of our land and labor lay outside his (Gladstone's) conception of practical or even legitimate politics." A political revolution was a necessary condition for the realization of a radical economic policy.

[60] For this prospectus see Humphrey, *op. cit.*, pp. 187-190, Appendix I.

[61] Cf. *The Labour Leader*, May 28, 1908. In October, 1897, Mr. John Morley (as he then was) wrote in his diary: "When will some man arise to lead and command Labour? I doubt if he will come from their class. Some man with Mr. Gladstone's genius, devoted to social ends" (*Recollections*, 1917, Vol. II, p. 76). Of Mr. Keir Hardie, he wrote in a letter in 1907: "He is an observant, hard-headed, honest fellow, but rather vain and crammed full of vehement preconceptions, especially on all the most delicate and dubious parts of politics. Perhaps it is only the men with these unscrupulous preconceptions—knocking their heads against stone walls—who force the world along" (*ibid.*, p. 235).

[62] J. A. Hobson, *The Crisis of Liberalism* (1909).

Three Labour members were elected to the House of Commons in 1880, eleven in 1885, ten in 1886, fifteen in 1892, twelve in 1895, and in 1900 ten. In 1886, eighteen years after the first Trade Union Congress, the Labour Electoral Association was organized with the aim of returning Liberal-Labour men to Parliament. Mr. H. Broadhurst, for fifteen years the secretary of the Trade Union Parliamentary Committee, in his *Autobiography*, says that the Parliamentary Committee fulfilled the function of the Radical wing of the Liberal party, exerting itself not merely for the working classes, but on behalf of the community at large. The main work of the Committee up to 1875 was to further legislation for the complete legalization of the trade unions and the protection of their funds.[63] In the seventies and early eighties the work of the Committee was largely spent on the Trade Union Bill of 1871, the Mines Regulation Act, 1872, and the Nine Hours Bill, 1871. It was also interested in the reform of jury laws, the amendment of the Summary Jurisdiction Act, and the Shipping and Patent Laws. The Committee fought for the codification of the criminal laws; drafted a Bill dealing with boiler explosions; and Broadhurst drew up a Bill for the abolition of property qualifications for membership in local governing bodies, which was introduced by A. J. Mundella in 1876, becoming a law two years later. The Committee drew up a Workmen's Compensation Law, which was subsequently read a second time and referred to a Select Committee, and also used its influence to secure the Act consolidating the Factory and Workship Laws, and the protective clauses for Labour in the Shipping Act of 1883.[64] However much the opposition of the old-line trade union officials kept the Labour movement from developing into a distinct political party, and whatever the drawbacks of this policy were,[65] there was all the time going on in the ranks of the Labour leaders practise and discipline in the

[63] From 1873 an official Report of the Trade Union Congress has been issued. W. J. Davis has done for the Congress what Léon Blum did for the Workers' and Socialist Congresses of France, written its chronological record in *A History of the British Trades Union Congress* (Vol. I, 1910; Vol. II, 1916).

[64] See Humphrey, *op. cit.*, pp. 72-73, for a summary of the activities of the Parliamentary Committee of the Trade Union Congress.

[65] Cf. Sidney and Beatrice Webb, *History of Trade Unionism*, pp. 680-682.

parliamentary struggles. In the thirty-three years from 1868 to 1901, over sixty Acts of Parliament directly affecting Labour were passed.[66] Political change through this period was indicated in the increasing demand for legislation favourable to Labour.[67] As early as April, 1873, the Federation of Employers was organized to combat the growing parliamentary influence of Labour. In a Manifesto, dated December 11, 1873, the Federation outlined its purpose, and pointed out that the growing strength of the trade unions made it possible for them to bring unusual pressure to bear on Parliament.[68]

Political power brought on the increasing demand for new Factory legislation, and at the same time directly affected the organization of the trade union world. Since 1868 there were organized such exclusive political trade union organizations as the United Textile Factory Workers' Association, such a predominantly political association as the Miners' Federation of Great Britain, together with the formation of a general political machinery throughout the trade union world, in the form of Trade Councils, the Trade Union Congress and the Parliamentary Committee. In spite of the increasing recognition of how useful in the House of Commons was direct representation of Labour, it was not until 1899 that the Trade Union Congress decided for *independent* Labour representation. A resolution was passed then, instructing the Parliamentary Committee "to invite the co-operation of all co-operative, socialistic trade unions and other working class organizations as may be willing to take part to devise ways and means for the securing of an increased number of Labour members in the next Parliament."

A special committee was appointed, composed of delegates from the Congress, the Independent Labour Party, the Social Democratic Federation and the Fabian Society, to prepare the agenda for the Conference. The task of drafting the constitution for the proposed Labour Party was given to Mr. J. Ramsay MacDonald, by the delegates. Of this committee of ten members,

[66] Cf. George Howell, *op. cit.*, pp. 469-472, for a list of these Acts.

[67] Cf. Sidney and Beatrice Webb, *Industrial Democracy* (1897 ed.), p. 351.

[68] See Frank H. Rose, *The Coming Force: The Labour Movement* (Manchester 1909), *Appendix*, for extracts from this *Manifesto*. A recent history of Labor from Chartism to present time is Keith Hutchinson, *Labor in Politics* (1925), Labor Publishing Company, London.

four were from the Parliamentary Committee of the Trade Union Congress, and two from each of the Socialist organizations. The Special Conference on Labour Representation was held at the Memorial Hall, London, February 27-28, 1900. Of this Memorial Hall meeting one qualified to judge has written that there had come

> some to bury the attempt in good-humoured tolerance, a few to make sure that burial would be its fate, but the majority determined to give it a chance.[69]

The close connection between the economic and the political Labour movement is seen by the fact that the chairman of the Trade Union Congress, Mr. J. T. Chandler, opened the proceedings. But not being a member of the Conference, he was succeeded by Mr. W. C. Steadman, who in his opening remarks said that although he had only been a member of Parliament for a short time, he had been there long enough to see that "every interest was represented and protected except the interests of Labour." The former chairman had set forth the objects of the Conference, and the Resolution of the 1899 Congress had defined the purpose of Labour representation in Parliament.

The task of the Labour leaders was to direct the increasing influence they had in Parliament, and to secure this they had to build up a sure and safe electorate throughout England. This spirit was evidenced in the proceedings of the Memorial Hall Conference of 1900, in the first resolution that was offered and in the opposition which it inspired. The resolution declared,

> That this Conference is in favour of the working class being represented in the House of Commons by members of the working class as being most likely to be sympathetic with the aims and demands of the Labour movement.

This resolution was described by Mr. John Burns as a "narrow and exclusive proposal," and to proclaim in favour of working class candidates only would be bad enough, but to give a definition to the candidates would be infinitely worse. He said he was "getting tired of working class boots, working class trains, working

[69] MacDonald, *The Socialist Movement*, p. 235.

class houses, and working class margarine." He voiced the idea of the democratic advance of the Labour movement in politics when he pleaded that they should not be "prisoners of class prejudice, but should consider parties and policies apart from class organization."[70] The amendment to the resolution moved and seconded by Mr. G. N. Barnes and Mr. Burns, was passed by a vote of 102 to 3, and was also amended further to include the co-operators. The resolution was,

> That this Conference is in favour of working class opinion being represented in the House of Commons by men sympathetic with the aims and demands of the Labour Movement, and whose candidatures are promoted by one or other of the organised movements represented by the constitution which this Conference is about to frame.

The dissensions between the Social Democratic Federation[71] and the opportunist delegates, by far the majority, who had a definite idea of what could be accomplished by the tactics of "progressive politics," were seen in the resolution of the Social Democratic Federation, when they proposed, through Mr. James MacDonald, that the representation of the working class movement in the House of Commons form there a

> distinct party . . . separate from the capitalist parties, based upon the recognition of the class war, and having for its ultimate object the socialisation of the means of production, distribution and exchange.

It was said in the discussion on this resolution that nothing would be more unfortunate for the Conference than for it to "label across its front 'Class War.'" An amendment to this resolution was offered by the veteran leader Hardie, president of the Independent Labour Party, which was unanimously decided

[70] Cf. *Report of Conference,* published by Labour Representation Committee, 1900.

[71] Cf. H. M. Hyndman, "La Crise Socialiste en Europe," *Le Mouvement Socialiste,* October 15, 1901, pp. 449-455, on no compromise in the class struggle. The general statement with reference to the industrial organization is much better given in *Tom Mann's Memoirs* (1923), which provides a readable account of this most interesting period.

upon and which outlined the independent policy of the Labour Party which was to be formed, and which really came into being with the Labour Representation Committee, which carried on the first fights of the Labour Party during the general election of 1900.[72] The Hardie Resolution read:

This Conference is in favour of establishing a distinct Labour Group in Parliament who shall have their own Whips and agree upon their policy, which must embrace a readiness to co-operate with any party which, for the time being, may be engaged in promoting legislation in the direct interest of Labour, and be equally ready to associate themselves with any party in opposing measures having an opposite tendency; and, further, members of the Labour Group shall not oppose any candidate whose candidature is being promoted in terms of Resolution I.[73]

The Social Democratic Federation in 1901 brought forward the resolution pledging the candidates to recognize the class war, but it was lost, and in August of that year the Social Democratic Federation withdrew from the Representation Committee.

The Executive Committee of the Representation Committee numbered twelve, composed of seven members from the Trade Union Congress, two each from the Independent Labour Party and the Social Democratic Federation, and one from the Fabian Society. The Labour Representation Committee had only been formed eight months when Parliament was dissolved in September, 1900, and it was not prepared to face the election; but fifteen candidates were run under the auspices of the Committee, of whom two were returned, Keir Hardie and Richard Bell. The formation of the Labour Representation Committee was the determined effort to initiate an independent political movement; and the third annual Conference held in 1903, in Newcastle-on-Tyne, definitely set forth the independent political principle:

In view of the fact that the Labour Representation Committee is recruiting adherents from all outside political forces, and also, taking into consideration the basis upon which the Committee was inaugurated, this Conference regards it as being abso-

[72] Cf. MacDonald, *Socialism and Government,* Vol. II, p. 25, n. 2.
[73] The Barnes Resolution.

lutely necessary that the members of the Executive Committee should strictly abstain from identifying themselves with or promoting the interests of any section of the Liberal or Conservative parties, inasmuch as if we are to secure the social and economic requirements of the industrial classes, Labour representatives in and out of Parliament will have to shape their own policy and act upon it regardless of sections in the political world; and that the Executive Committee report to the affiliated associations or bodies any such official acting contrary to the spirit of the constitution as hereby amended.[74]

This Conference also established a Parliamentary Fund for the payment of Labour members and for election charges.[75] The years 1903-1905 witnessed the most carefully planned and enthusiastic period of political organization in the history of the British Labour Movement, so it is no wonder that when the general election took place in 1906, of the fifty candidatures of the Representation Committee, twenty-nine were returned. A compact and coherent Labour group was formed, which had its own officers and Whip, and acted independently of the other parties in Parliament. The name of the Labour Representation Committee was changed to that of the Labour Party. It was natural that the progress of the political Labour movement would cause hopes to run unusually high.

The appearance of the Labour Party as a definite element in British politics and as an unmistakable indication of the democratic tendencies of the time, resulting in the definite establishment of a Parliamentary Labour party in the House of Commons, made a great stir in the political world, and the "Condition of the People" question at last secured attention.[76]

The entrance of the Labour Party as a definite party group just at the time when the Government was pledged to a full social

[74] *The Labour Year Book,* 1916, pp. 306-307.

[75] In 1904 the Labour Party submitted a motion for debate on payment of members of Parliament, by Mr. A. Henderson. The vote against being 221-155; for debate: Hansard 4 S. H. C., 1904, Vol. 134, pp. 1105-1129. The Resolution adopted August 10, 1911, provided for the payment of members, which the Committee on Supply allowed in the appropriations of that year.

[76] *The Labour Year Book,* 1916, p. 307.

program makes the consideration of the legislation affecting Labour and the social politics of the Government a most interesting study, a survey of which will follow.

(b) *The Expansion of the Labour Movement*

The progress of labour legislation and industrial organization since the great mass of the people have had political representation provides a basis for the study of the working out of Labour ideas and ideals. It also gives an opportunity for seeing how far the organization of industry has kept pace with the development of public opinion along the line of social welfare and the protection of the individual. Periods of reaction apparently occur with such regularity that cynicism on one hand results for the more sophisticated members of society; for others a disillusion and distrust which brings no good. This arises from the real obstacle to the progress of sound social legislation and wise social policy, by the great difference between what is known of the mechanical and inventive side of modern industry and what is known of its control and direction. In discussing the sharing of control within the works, as a suggested approach to the problem of industrial democracy, Mr. William Wallace said that "mechanically we are two hundred years ahead of what we are socially." [77] There has been a marked progress in bridging the gap between the mechanical and social development of modern society, both in the recognition of the value that State interference would have through wise legislation and effective administration, and also in the common duty which must be shared by the State with Labour and Capital—and the Public, to help adjust the problems arising in the world of industry. The indictment of the industrial system has compelled all parties to unite on certain common grounds of interest and to judge the progress of society by more comprehensive values.

This compulsion of social interest has helped to discipline the political Labour movement, and has done much to bring the light of criticism upon the useless cost in life and happiness of the industrial system. It has not only been in the ranks of organized

[77] Cf. *Report of the Industrial Conference,* Balliol College, April 6-10, 1922, p. 18.

labour and in the propaganda of political groups that the social aspects of the economic system have been stressed. Professor Marshall in his treatment of the doctrine of Welfare in economic theory, together with Professor Pigou, and able writers like Hobson, Hobhouse, Tawney, and Wallas, have put the emphasis on the side of social organization and social costs. The demand of Labour has fortunately coincided with the development of the theory of present-day thinkers who have been most concerned in a fairer and juster distribution of the wealth of the nation.[78] These men in turn have given back to the Labour movement the challenge of a most real question: What shall be the aim of this individual and social ideal of happiness and welfare?

The English Labour movement naturally taking its development from the democratic nature of the State has sought to broadly interpret the social ideal of Labour, to establish the sanction of the ideal of democracy. In the history of the New Unionism of 1833-1834 and that of 1889-1890, in England, the effect of political conditions upon the direction of the Labour movement is clearly seen. The Owenism of the former period largely rejected political action, but the leaders of the New Unionism of 1889-1890,

> aimed, not at superseding existing social structures, but at capturing them all in the interests of the wage-earners. Above all, they sought to teach the great masses of undisciplined workers how to apply their newly acquired political power so as to obtain, in a perfectly constitutional manner, whatever changes in legislation and administration they desired.[79]

The New Unionists found ready for their use an extensive and all-embracing Democratic structure, which it was impossible to destroy and would have been foolish to attempt to ignore.[80]

The trade union leaders from the time of the passing of the Trade Union Acts of 1871 and 1875, legalizing private collective bar-

[78] Cf. Edwin Cannan, *Theories of Production and Distribution* (3rd ed., 1920). He believes social reform in England derives no strength from Marxian doctrines but is "now chiefly dependent upon the popular belief that greater equality in the distribution of wealth is desirable" (pp. 404-405).

[79] Sidney and Beatrice Webb, *The History of Trade Unionism*, p. 474

[80] *Ibid.*

gaining, underwent a process of political instruction in dealing with the two established parties which stood them in good stead when the time came in this century for straight effective political action, due to the Taff Vale decision and the Osborne judgment. The development of the method of Collective Bargaining has gone hand in hand with the increase in political power of the Labour movement, reaching a crisis in its development in the post-war industrial agreements. Industrial disputes have nowadays come to constitute less and less landmarks of Trade Union history as the steps, often statutory or political in character, by which the Movement advances in public influence and in a recognized participation in the government of industry, have been taken, which in the present century has followed the action of Trade Unionism on legislation, and of legislation on Trade Unionism. This action has been incessant and reciprocal.[81]

The democratic nature of the State has thus stamped the principle of progress by assent on the English Labour movement. To look for the fountain head of the schools of English theory either in Germany or France, or more lately in Moscow, is to neglect the profoundly significant fact of the ever-changing spirit of British Socialism. Its whole tendency has been different from that found in other countries. The political tendency in undemocratic countries of the Labour movement, and especially in the Socialist movement, has been "to be more numerous, united, doctrinaire, and imposing, and in democratic countries to be fewer, less united, less uncompromising, but more constructive and more influential."[82] The influence of the democratic spirit at work on the political Labour movement has even largely inspired the changing conceptions of the place of trade unions in the social and industrial life of England, and their greatest claim to common usefulness has been that they are "schools of democracy."

The development then of the political Labour movement in France and England affords an opportunity of judgment on the will and the capacity of the two movements to further the aims of good-will in democracy. The appeal to the electorate necessarily implies that there is a willingness to persuade, to refer to the opinion of other men, and to abide by the decisions of the

[81] *Op. cit.*, pp. 557-561, 561-575.
[82] R. C. K. Ensor, Introduction to 1903 edition, *Modern Socialism*, p. xxi.

ballot box. The progressive widening of the point of view and the basis of appeal on which the political Labour movement stakes its claim for suffrage, has been a gradual democratization of the Labour movement. There has gone on what Shaw vaguely described as "the democratization of democracy."[83] Old formulæ were given up; the middle class man had about been converted to the collectivism which necessarily grew out of the economic order, and there had been a constantly deepening consciousness of the duty of society maintaining the Standard of Life. Where this has meant the State protecting the employee, the child worker or the woman at home, the average man has fully agreed that Parliament be the instrument to bring about industrial and economic change.

In both countries, France and England, the growth of political democracy by the close of the nineteenth century had given the electorate a control over the government. There was an increasing confidence on the part of the people that they could use this power to direct the development of the industrial system and to ensure a fairer and juster economic order. The range of social legislation undertaken by the modern State shows how rapid was the rise of the wage-earning class, and how quickly the nineteenth century factory system brought about the most serious problems in administration and social control. Social legislation was the way the State found to adjust itself to the new order in industry. Employers' liability, child welfare, old age pensions, fiscal reform, trade unions, national insurance, town planning, urban and rural housing, extension of education, and many other agencies of reform were discussed and put in use, or were matters of agitation by large groups in the State and found their exponents in the legislative assemblies.

The England of 1900 had already recognized the problems before the modern State and had set about to meet them. The factory laws, the oldest and best developed of any nation, were an indication that legislation had been a means to protect labour and to minimize the costs of industrial progress. The strength of the trade unions, the power of the co-operative movement, the extension of municipal trading and the capital that it represented, the recognition of the needs of a large group of the employed by

[83] Cf. Pease, *op. cit.*, Shaw's *Appendix*, p. 267.

the fixing of a standard of life in wage clauses in public contracts, and the effort of labour and capital to settle its disputes by conciliation and arbitration, all indicated that England began to understand the problems of this century.

The political schemes by which England has sought to adjust her social ills have been affected very little by the remedies used on the Continent, although she owes more to Germany than perhaps to any other nation for the helpfulness which earlier experiments and mistakes in social insurance gave to her own attempts. Social purpose has taken form from the very needs of the British people, directed by men often close to the soil, and the nightmares of Socialist theory and the futile Utopias of dreamers are not and cannot be of the history of the Labour movement in England. Not that we have not had "the kingdom of heaven according to Mr. Sidney Webb," [84]—from the beginning,—and even at times black clouds of revolution, but for the one there has been always the genial laughter even of the Fabians; and always for the other the concern of the wisest leaders of England has been that there were fellow countrymen so perplexed and so battled to the ground by necessity that revolution seemed the only road away from ruin. That is the essential distinction between the Government leaders in France and the leaders in England; the debates in the Chamber of Deputies have been at such times charged with hatred and suspicion, the oldest members would mock the efforts of the hated Government and the youngest from the Left would welcome the fullest debacle. Compare similar debates in the House of Commons, when in the midst of impending social conflict, leaders were intent on finding a way out by peaceful understanding and forbearance,—giving up traditional claims,—but always going on, nor seeking any joy in the embittering of class feelings.

Such facts give strong support in England to the political ideal of social justice which demands that no class conscious Parliament shall create a prejudiced State. Social progress has depended much on legislative enactment, and there is no indication that, so long as political jurisdictions remain, it will be less. It is thus an ever insistent necessity that the ideal of the community

[84] The famous jibe of *Punch* and its happy coinage "sidneywebbicalism," is likely to remain.

of interest be kept before the people. Here the moral claim of democracy and the State is fixed, and its growth through the nineteenth century has been a proof of its power to hold the faith and allegiance of men. That England gave the solid background to its expanding influence is only a natural thing, for its life is the parliamentary system depending upon the will of the people being expressed.

"The reformed legislature, and the reformed organs of administration which it had created," Trevelyan says, "were helping on the general social improvement and the movements by which the new Britain was striving to remedy the evils attendant on the Industrial Revolution—Co-operation, Factory Laws, Trade Unionism, Free Trade—were all like the Industrial Revolution itself, British in conception and origin." [85]

The originality in conception and origin of the attitude of England toward social reform has often made the British Labour movement a seeming contradictory thing to the Continent, and the history of parliamentary interference a confused story of compromise. In social problems, Mr. Lowell says,

the Englishman of to-day is sanguine, impatient, eager to attack the evils he perceives, and very willing to try experiments in the process. If there is overcrowding in the cities, he builds at once a few dwelling-houses. If the agricultural labourers are not well off, he passes a law whereby some of them may be furnished with plots of land. If neither of these things proves to be a serious remedy, he builds a few more houses, and makes some ineffective amendment to the Allotment Act. If the mortality among babies is large, he has in some boroughs even provided a supply of municipal milk.[86]

This able writer follows the observation of Viscount Bryce on modern democracies, applying it especially to England:

In striking contrast with the ideas dominant threescore years ago, political interest in England at the present day seems to be greater in the distribution than in the production of wealth, and this in spite of the many business men in the House of Commons.[87]

[85] Trevelyan, *op. cit.*, p. 278.
[86] Lowell, *op. cit.*, Vol. II, p. 526. [87] *Ibid.*

This interest accounts for the growth of paternalistic legislation, an effort of the State to grapple with modern industrial organization, and for the interference of the Government in industry which has gone on in every State. Business men in the House of Commons were as impotent before the march of industrialism as University representatives were of the spread of popular education, and the tacit assumption of President Lowell would give a reason for the class conscious conception of political activity, a view which he does not hold but which is supported by his strictures on the Labour Party as a perverted instrument of the popular will. The peculiar dangers of paternalistic legislation "that are not lessened by the English form of Government," [88] is only part of the indictment of the world of democracy which is in a hurry and demands results and rapid successes, therefore, has taken to the subterfuge of short cuts.

For the purposes of this study it is only worth while to suggest whether the political Labour movement has helped to increase this danger or not? Whether it is an inevitable tendency of democracy to imperil parliamentary government by the support it gives to class conscious minorities or majorities? President Lowell believed

> with the prevailing tone of thought and the rapid changes of party in popular governments, such a tendency to deal with symptoms rather than causes is a characteristic of modern democracies; but owing to the concentration of power in the hands of the ministry it is especially pronounced in the case of England.[89]

This tendency of democracy may as well be attributed to its growing pains as to the inherent prejudiced state of the democratic mind; if any tendency of democracy which does not fit into accepted molds of thought is to be ascribed to "diseased mind," the future of self-government is a delusion. If the growth of Labour's political power is just another symptom of democratic decadence there can never be much faith in the purging power of parliamentary experience. The heritage of centuries of class conscious rule cannot be shaken off in a few decades, nor can the social and political ideals of democracy be realized in a world

[88] *Op. cit.*, Vol. II, p. 528. [89] *Ibid.*, p. 530.

that is only just now beginning to realize the tremendous peril and opportunity of trying to live together.[90] It is hopeful that the political organization of the economic world has revived the age-old problem of the State and the good life, and that millions of men and women with the zeal of crusaders look to the ballot box for an expression of the will of the nation; in such circumstances vitality is given to the belief that the average man is the hope of good government. He may yet be the despair of it, but to rouse the average citizen to political interest, is a social blessing; it is then that there is an opportunity for the second blessing of thought and conviction to do their work. That is beyond the sphere of politics but the aid of politics is essential in the school of citizenship.

Citizenship is no narrow conception of the place of the individual in the State, but it is an experience that must be directed and must be informed. These two necessary conditions have been greatly helped by the growth of the English Labour movement, which has brought to the attention of the workingman the outstanding problems of modern life, and his life has been linked up with the whole "state of England question." Citizenship has not and cannot convince men that salvation is to be got by means of the ballot box, but its wider duties have been brought home to the consciousness of men when they have been called on to render their individual opinion on men and measures, and to accept the general opinion when it has been expressed. It is only necessary to instance in England the education question. At the same time that it came before the Trade Union Congress the president of the British Association declared that one reason for lack of progress was "our false notions of the limitations of State functions in relation to the conditions of modern civilization." [91]

In this connection there is a most interesting contribution that the agitation for better school facilities made to the whole social problem of the early years of this century. The great concern of Labour with regard to the question of education indicated a healthy progress within the ranks of the working

[90] Cf. A. F. Pollard, *The History of England* (1912), chap. IX, pp. 225-247, for an interesting statement of this thought.

[91] Presidential Address of Sir Norman Lockyer at the 1903 meeting of the British Association, p. 8, the London *Times,* Sept. 10, 1903.

class. Each party gave its faith. The future of the nation was seen to be staked on the State and its relation to educational policies.[92] The belief of many was given by Haldane.

There is a Liberalism which some of us believe to be the Liberalism of the future. It holds that the faith which it has made its own cannot stand still, but must advance with the advancing needs of new generations.[93]

Twelve years later this was reaffirmed, but with a more definite emphasis that the State was to play a larger part in the destiny of the individual and the community.

Democracy is becoming a reality. The possessors of new and increasing political powers are finding their feet, not less abroad than in this country. The Democracy cannot be driven. It can only be supplied with the knowledge and training which may guide it to seek its own salvation in a better State with higher ideals.[94]

How this was given form in Working Class Education has been expressed in a faith that is only just beginning to be shared bv Labour itself, but the ideal was held by the pioneers of the growing movement of to-day. It does not matter if the failures have been many and tragic, the ideal has been set forth and it has humanized much of the work of the modern university. Education cannot be "Labour" any more than religion or art or music, but the common ideal which in the sharing makes the finest contribution to well-being and happiness is a possession which increases in value as more men claim it for their own and for others. However unhappy some results of working class education have been, it is well to note a hopeful effort in such a statement as follows:

We shall take men at Ruskin College, who have been merely condemning our institutions, and will teach them instead to transform them, so that in place of talking against the world, they

[92] See the address of Lord Haldane, then a member of Parliament, before British Association, p. 7, the London *Times,* Sept. 12, 1903.

[93] R. B. Haldane, *Education and Empire* (London, 1902), p. viii.

[94] See Haldane's "Introduction" to C. K. Ogden's translation of George Kerschensteiner's *The Schools and the Nation* (London 1914), pp. xv-xxiv.

will begin methodically and scientifically to possess the world, to refashion it and to co-operate with the power behind evolution in making it the joyous abode of, if not a perfected humanity, at least a humanity earnestly striving towards perfection.[95]

A faith expressed in these words is a growth, it is social.

The part that Labour played in the elections for the London County Council in 1904 is significant. 100,000 copies of the circular, *Education, Trade Unionism, and the Forthcoming London County Council Election* were broadcast. It said that "among trade unionists there is a steadily growing feeling that the great reasons for the workers' slowness in learning (in the words of William Morris) 'to know their own, to take their own, and to use their own,' is the lack of education, and there is every reason to believe that with the increasing strength of the Labour movement, it will be no longer possible to disregard the demand of the trade unionists' organizations for better educational opportunities for the nation's children. . . . It is for trade unionists to claim, what the well-being of the nation demands, that secondary, technical and higher education be placed within the reach of all the 'hands' of the great industrial army, no less than the 'captains of industry.' By taking an intelligent interest in the election, the trade unionists of the metropolis can do much to secure the further development (on the intellectual, social and recreative sides) of the evening continuation schools, which, under the popularly elected School Board, have furnished so useful an object lesson of the uses to which the people's schools can be put. The education of the children being a matter of great public importance, the meetings of the Education Committee should be open to the public as the meetings of the popularly elected School Boards have always been."[96] Such an interest not only

[95] Cf. Arthur Mansbridge, *An Adventure in Working-Class Education* (Being the Story of the Workers' Education Association, 1903-1915), (London, 1920), pp. 7-8, and his *University Tutorial Classes* (1913); also T. W. Price, *The Story of the Workers' Educational Association* (1903-1924), with an Introduction by R. H. Tawney (1924). The chapters on "Education" in the *Labor Year Book*, 1924, 1925, 1926, should be read for a commentary on Labour and Education to-day.

[96] See *Report of the Trade Union Congress* (1904), pp. 68-69, for a copy of this Circular.

in the principle of education but in the effective agency whereby administration is carried on, means a sane social advance in the trade union spirit; and from the first law which provided "religious instruction" for young children who worked sixteen hours, it represents a tremendous moral advance in the aims of the common people.

Citizenship and social progress rely on a change in the spirit of men, and that is the reason that in this connection the attitude of Labour toward Education is significant. Behind all of the agitation was a very sure conviction: Labour had gained an influence, and this influence was finding one means of expression through political channels, in the effort to make the State an instrument of control and protection for interests which are social. Professor MacGregor has pointed out [97] that "a hundred years elapsed between the beginning of modern industry about 1770, and the beginning of modern public education and the public franchise about 1870," but in so short a time citizenship in the trade union world demanded that education cease to be class conscious, and that the "hands" of the industrial army be not dispossessed of their right to know and learn and study. There can be no surer test of the progress of the workingman from the "economic bent" of his daily work toward a more inclusive ideal of human good, than in the intelligent interest and concern with which he has viewed great social questions like that of Education, the Liquor Trade and World Peace. It is for other large and influential groups in society to question themselves, seeing if the ideal of social justice has been freed from the curse of class consciousness and class bondage and greed, in proportion to their opportunity.

However Socialism might "merge more and more into ordinary progressive politics," [98] or, as the French determinists feared, become "invaded by Radicalism" [99] and "undone by Ministerial-

[97] Cf. *Report of the Industrial Conference,* Balliol College, April 6-10, 1922, p. 32.

[98] Cf. *Labour Annual, 1900,* p. 105, "The Future of Socialism—A Forecast," George Bernard Shaw.

[99] Cf. "Congrès General des Organisations Socialists Françaises," Paris, *Compte Rendu,* 1899, the speech of M. Vaillant, pp. 88-95.

ism,"[100] it was concerning itself with every problem that had to do with the lives of the working class, and the very close contact of the Labour movement to the lives of the people was the means whereby it educated the less unsocial qualities of its members. The forecast of Shaw's was largely true of the first fourteen years of this century, and it was thoroughly in keeping with the spirit of the parliamentary leaders of Labour, who saw that the same thing was happening to Socialism that happened to Benthamism.[101] "A positive State actively co-operating with the individual, owning and controlling property, building up a communal organization in which the individual is to find liberty and self-realization, is becoming an axiom in legislation."[102] But with this change there had come a difference in the attitude of Labour representatives who may at first in the earliest days of Labour successes have held a narrow and short-sighted view of their parliamentary duties.[103] Not any more so than many of the elected representatives of other parties, but a like change has taken place among the members of Parliament, it is believed, in all parties. Parliament is not the place for political purists, and there are few places where special knowledge and actual experience can be more serviceable when given to the State, and it is certain that Labour representation has helped to broaden the conception of the work of Parliament. It is doubtful if at any time class bitterness or class consciousness has been materially increased by the presence of the Labour representative in any constituency. But, on the other hand, there is much reason for the belief that their years of work have actually lessened these two curses of democracy. Bringing Government home to the people may have

[100] Cf. "Deuxième Congrès General des Organisations Socialistes Françaises," Paris, 1900, the speech of Vaillant, pp. 208-223, *Compte Rendu;* "Socialisme ou Democratie," H. Lagardelle, *ibid.,* April 12, pp. 673-687; "Socialisme ou Democratie," H. Largardelle, *ibid.,* April 12, pp. 673-687; No. 88, April 19, pp. 720-781, "Ministerialisme et Socialisme," H. Lagardelle; also by same author in Nos. 89 and 91 (April 26 and May 10) "Socialisme ou Democratie," pp. 774-781, 889-897. The above is a thorough survey of the internal development of French Socialism in the period, and remains perhaps the best statement of the revolutionary attitude against Jaurès.

[101] Cf. MacDonald, *Socialism and Government,* Vol. II, pp. 5-7.

[102] *Ibid.*

[103] See *The Quarterly Review,* "The Labour Party," April, 1923.

at times resulted only in disillusion, but more often it has helped to convince the voter that it is at most only an expression of the good and the bad in the community. The magical element has departed, the useful and sane and ordinary have often remained.

This fact was well expressed by the Prime Minister of England, Mr. Baldwin, when commenting on the political situation in 1926. He said, "that many of those who seemed to be running most wild in their political views were men led astray by insufficient education or inexperience, but were truly desirous of bettering their country." He went on to say that he had found the study of the various types in the House of Commons a very interesting occupation. He found there, "especially among the Labor party, men who fifty years ago would have gone into the Christian ministry. They have been brought into political life from a deep desire to help the people. Such were common in all parties to-day. They were facts which relieved the darkness of the outlook." [104]

Part II

Changing Opinion Reflected in the Aims of Political Organization

The effect of applying in legislation democratic doctrines has been the creation of political and economic ideals of social justice, establishing in new forms with larger meaning the ancient ideals of justice and liberty.[105] The political extension has been slow, especially in England, but it has laid the basis for the responsibilities of democracy to be shared by all, and has called to the work of the State the energies and capacities of every citizen. This has insured for the State a sound public opinion upon which it can build more comprehensive schemes of protection and reform; it more surely wins to its allegiance the good-will of the people as they are prepared to accept social responsibility. On the political side there is no better test of the progress of this spirit than in the question of the Budget, which is the State,[106]

[104] Quoted in *Manchester Guardian Weekly,* February 26, 1926.

[105] Cf. Maurice Hauriou, *Leçons sur le mouvement social,* (Paris, 1899), Preface, p. viii, and p. 56.

[106] Cf. M. Compère-Morel, *Pourquoi nous sommes socialistes* (Paris, 1913), p. 449, and all of chap. VII. "Political Concentration," pp. 449-476;

one has said, and which indicates in every modern society how impossible it is to separate the social movement and the political movement. All schemes of social insurance, of nationalization and the aid of the State in subsidies, are linked with the Budget, and recent years have seen a development of the theory of the Budget [107] which early or even late nineteenth century chancellors would hardly have believed possible. Yet in no sphere of the State's service to the community has there been a more general acceptance of the principles which underlie its action; it has a social importance which makes it always a lively subject of politics. M. Jèze has succinctly put it:

> The budget of expenditures is nothing more than a list of credits demanded by the Government and accorded by the political party which has a majority in Parliament for the realisation of a certain programme of political action. To deny the *essential* political character of the Budget, seems to me to deny the facts. On the other hand, it is necessary to find the means of paying the expenditures. Here appears the problem of income, of taxation, distribution of charges among individuals. It is a problem essentially political for it concerns itself with knowing *who* pays, in *what measure* of payment, *what manner* of payment. Here appears at the beginning the political concepts of social justice, true equality, national solidarity.[108]

On the multifold problems of the social adjustment of the Budget and the claims of industrial legislation, the modern democratic States of England and France have had to evolve a

this is a volume in the *Enclopedie Socialiste Syndicale et Coopérative de L'Internationale Ouvrière,* published under the editorship of M. Compère-Morel.

[107] Cf. Bernard Mallet, *British Budgets, 1887-1913* (1914), note "Preface"; J. Watson Grice, *National and Local Finance* (1910), "Preface" by Sidney Webb.

[108] Gaston Jèze, *Cours de science des finances et de législation financiere Française* (Paris, 6th ed., 1922); "Preface," p. ii; author's own italics. It is interesting to note Professor Dicey on the Finance (1909-1910) Act, 1910, which he stated, "is a law passed not merely to raise the revenue necessary for meeting the wants of the State, but also for the attainment of social ends dear to collectivists. It sets a precedent for the use of taxation for the promotion of political or social ends." (p. lii.) Cf. Sidney Webb, Preface to Grice, *op. cit.,* p. v: "The enforcement of 'the National Minimum' in the conditions of existence without which the nation itself cannot permanently survive," is a first duty for the State.

democratic theory of solidarity, avoiding the anti-social peril of class exploitation. The intervention of the State has been necessary to equalize the cost of industry and the dangers of progress, of establishing justice in the community, whether it is by balancing the bargaining power of groups or of placing the duty of taxation where it belongs. When the social possibilities for good or evil of the legislative and administrative program of the State have been more clearly seen, including this problem of equitable taxation, the menace of class legislation and the political power it represents has become less, although the organized political power of Labour, and its combined economic power, have become greater. The fear that the State is to suffer the most disastrous policies of class legislation, resulting in a full denial of faith in organized democracy, has not been justified in the tendencies of the Labour movement in England and France as expressed in parliamentary action. This fear has been held by two distinguished writers who have seen in the further progress of collectivism the "peril that English legislation may combine disastrously the defects of Socialism with the defects of democratic government," [109] the peculiar structure of which makes the danger more liable in England.[110] But the alliance of the social movement and the political movement, directing legislation in modern Parliaments, has not proved a corrupting agency in democracy. Revolt in the Labour movement in France and England in the years of this century has shown again that there are deeper resources of change in the working class mind than are to be expressed in political form alone. Distrust of Government must go deeper than fear of the parliamentary Labour movements in democracy. Political scepticism is equally shared at both ends of the social scale, for about the same reasons.

The accepted fact of social progress, so far as democratic method goes, has made the social and political and economic movements allies. Now that democracy has had some years to get down to work on the problems which arise when people live together in communities, the thinking behind social reform becomes more evident and more necessary. It has often been crude and immature, shallow and full of mischance, but there has been the serious

[109] Dicey, *op. cit.*, p. lxxxvii; also lxxxvii-xciv.
[110] Lowell, *op. cit.*, Vol. II, pp. 122 f.; also pp. 519 f.

intention, as Bryce points out, of trying to put democracy to work. In this century when the political force of democratic faith and purpose has had some chance to be expressed in legislation and administration, an unreasonable fear of the consequences on the State and the established institutions has been created. But both in England and France the application of democracy to industrial and social problems has had its classic exposition in the literature of reform and revolt. In England it was Bentham insisting that law and politics were perpetual experiments in promoting "utility" or happiness, and it was Cobbett who held firmly to the view that the only way to control economic change was to speed along political change until it had caught up with the furious pace set by the Industrial Revolution.[111] The Labour movement in France, under German influence, began with a faith in political action, while by 1896 the authoritative word had been spoken at Saint-Mande, and the conquest of political power was the definite goal. The Trade Union Leaders in England and the Fabians, as well as the two old parties, have held out for years the program of legislative and administrative reform by Parliament. Just when an intelligent electorate is in the process of being a great instrument of democratic progress there has come a renewed indictment of the will to power on the part of the common people. And it is remarkable that the most sustained attack both from the Labour movement and from the capitalist class against the State, has been on the incapacity of the State to understand the economics of present-day civilization.[112] The State is both a corrupt and

[111] Trevelyan, *op. cit.*, p. 187; cf. G. D. H. Cole, *William Cobbett* (1925), and his *Robert Owen* (1925).

[112] See the *Fabian News*, Vol. XXXIV, no. 5, May, 1923, "Germany's Experiment in an Industrial Parliament," pp. 18-19, for a characteristic statement of a definite Fabian attitude toward Economic Councils and the fear of them that the political parties have, because of jealousy for their authority; the problem is discussed in relation to English political institutions in H. Finer's *Representative Government and a Parliament of Industry* (1923). In French may be noted Adolphe Delemer's *Le bilan de l'étatisme*, with a "Preface" by M. Jacques Bardoux (1922); Albert Schatz, *L'enterprise gouvernementale*" (1922), chap. IV, pp. 103-121, "Administrative Decline and the Problem of Government"; and H. Chardon, *Le pouvoir administratif* (1912). Also Gaston Raphael's *Walther Rathenau, ses idées et ses projets d'organisation économique* (1919), can be compared profitably with chap. V, pp. 212-257, of Delemer, *op. cit.*, "French Reconstruction and the New Economic Régime."

prejudiced defender of things as they are, and at the same time an inefficient blunderer in the field of business. Yet the most severe attack against the State demands political confidence that the economic structure may be rebuilt.[113]

It is difficult to determine just what would satisfy the Labour movement and the industrialists, who in turn call upon the State to redress the balance in the world of economic relationships. In such a circumstance the State can demand a clean bill from each litigant, and also demand a co-operation that has heretofore only been given in the stress of national emergency. If it is true that the State—the political government—cannot organize the economic life, and that power must pass to the dictatorship of economic organizations, it is a reversion to economic feudalism, as Esmein says, and the hopes and purposes of democracy will certainly be retarded and temporarily defeated.[114] But in France, and especially in England, there are strong indications that the Labour movement can give great vitality and reality to the political organization of democracy; and there is wisdom surely in directing its enthusiasm for local government and district administration. The human interest there forever prevents the theory of "professional bodies before political bodies," [115] from gaining control; and in the training of local government there will come a confidence in the ideal of the common good which will make for the good society.[116] The State cannot abdicate in favour of any economic organization of society, which has no power above nor no motive behind it save its own conscious will to exist and control.

The slow and sure reform of institutions has gone on because

[113] Cf. *Le bilan de la XII législature (1919-1924)* (Paris, 1924), pp. xviii-xxx, published by the *Société d'Etudes et d'Informations Économiques.*

[114] Cf. Adhéimar Esméin, *Éléments de droit constitutionel français* (7e éd., 2 vols., 1921, Paris), p. 49.

[115] Cf. Hauriou, *op. cit.*, pp. 616-619.

[116] Cf. John J. Clarke, *Social Administration Including the Poor Laws* (1922), "Introduction" and Part V; also his *Local Government of the United Kingdom* (1922), and *Outlines of Local Government* (4th ed., 1920); and G. D. H. Cole, *The Future of Local Government* (1920). Also the Labor Party *Yearbook,* 1916, 1919, 1924 and 1925, chapters on Local Government are very valuable, as well as the *Handbook of Local Government for England and Wales,* issued by the Labor Party in 1920.

there is the increasing capacity of democracy to organize its political and economic life; the "economic man" and the social determinism of the nineteenth century have slowly given way, because they could not last in a world that cared for a better society. An influence in England, that of Bentham,[117] in the shaping of methods and means of reform has been given grateful due. His belief that both law and politics were perpetual experiments in promoting "utility" or happiness, has helped to broaden the conception of social purpose, and to-day finds an expression in the "reaction from the juristic pessimism of the historical school and the juristic inertia of the latter generations of the analytical school." [118] To-day

> *the pressure of new and unsecured interests, of new and insistent human claims,* is compelling us to revise our juristic creeds. Projects for "restatement of the law" are in the air. Jurists are becoming more confident of the efficacy of intelligent effort to improve the law. . . . To make of our received legal materials, as systematized by the legal science of the last century, *a living instrument of justice in the society of to-day and of to-morrow.* Such a natural law will not call upon us to turn treatises on ethics or economics or sociology directly into institutes of law. But it will not be content with a legal science that refuses to look beyond or behind formal legal precepts and so misses more than half of what goes to make up the law.[119]

It is in the conception of social purpose that the individual has found himself and that society has been given a new meaning

[117] Dicey, *op. cit.,* Lecture VI, pp. 126-210, "The Period of Benthamism or Individualism"; and Lecture IX, pp. 303-310, "The Debt of Collectivism to Bentham."

[118] Roscoe Pound, *Law and Morals* (1924), University of North Carolina Press, p. 87; cf. W. W. Willoughby, *The Fundamental Concepts of Public Law* (1924), Part I, chap. I-IV; and Benjamin N. Cardozo, *The Nature of the Judicial Process* (1921), especially Lecture II. Of significant value in connection with the above is Sir Frederick Pollocks' *History of the Science of Politics* (1st ed. 1890), esp. chap. IV, "Modern Theories of Sovereignty and Legislation."

[119] Pound, *op. cit.,* pp. 87-88; my italics. Cf. Robert S. Rait, *Memorials of Albert Venn Dicey. Being Chiefly Letters and Diaries* (1925), and W. Jethro Brown, *The Underlying Principles of Modern Legislation* (1st ed. 1910, 6th ed. 1920).

for that individual.[120] What Bentham did for his generation[121] has been done for this age by many who have believed that the conditions for the good life can be increased and that institutions can be made to serve that purpose.

"Bentham impressed upon his countrymen," Mr. Trevelyan says, "the notion that existing institutions were not to be taken for granted, but to be judged by their results, and perpetually re-adjusted so as to produce 'the greatest happiness for the greatest number.' He did not invent that useful formula, which he had taken from Priestly, but he drove it into men's minds, and by reiterating it for half a century with a thousand different applications, he undermined the easy acceptance of chartered inefficiency and corruption, characteristic of the eighteenth century. Parliamentary, municipal, scholastic, ecclesiastical, economic reform all sprang from the spirit of Bentham's perpetual inquiry, 'what is the use of it?'—his universal shibboleth, that proved in the end the real English antidote to Jacobinism."[122]

Professor Graham Wallas in his two special studies, *Human Nature in Politics* (1908) and *The Great Society* (1914), has carried forward the criticism which was made that Bentham's system failed because of the mechanical nature of its psychology, which misrepresented the multifarious workings of the human mind. When the system of Bentham failed there was hope that the real human individual would be found, that his needs and his wants and his desires could all be better known and understood;

[120] See Sir Paul Vinogradoff, *Outlines of Historical Jurisprudence* (1920), Vol. I, chap. VIII. "Modern Tendencies in Jurisprudence," pp. 147-160. "There are signs of the appearance of a new *constructive* [his italics] point of view. It is suggested forcibly by the great social crisis on which the world is evidently entering now. The individualistic order of society is giving way before the impact of an inexorable process of socialisation, and the future will depend for a long time on the course and the extent of this process." (p. 149, *op. cit.*)

[121] President Lowell, *op. cit.*, Vol. II, p. 528, says that "The scientific tone of thought at the present day leads men to rely upon an inductive rather than a deductive process of reasoning, to judge of theories by their effects rather than by some inherent rational quality," and that "the Benthamite doctrine of utility has fortified this attitude in England." Cf. *Political Theories, Recent Times* (1924), Merriam, Barnes and others, esp. chaps. I, II, III, IV, VI, VIII; Raymond G. Gettell, *History of Political Thought* (1925); and H. E. Barnes, *Sociology and Political Theory* (1923).

[122] Trevelyan, *op. cit.*, p. 182.

that the individual would find his place in the great community a secure and happy one, and that he would help to insure a protection and happiness for all. It was here that the politics of democracy in this century have had a chance. The advent of democracy undermined the old individualism; the progress of democracy has made possible a new individualism.

Professor Wallas, it has been said:

> showed remorselessly how the optimistic democratic theory of the early nineteenth century Radicals was vitiated by their intellectualism, by their neglect of the part played in man's nature by half-conscious emotional forces, easily exploited for evil ends;

and

> how the transformation of the external conditions of civilised life by the inventions of the last hundred years have produced a political situation which is "without precedent in the history of the world;" how, for all our inventions, the dominant fact of modern politics is the insecurity of the Great Society and the general failure of mankind to control the conditions they have themselves created.[123]

This general failure has brought men close to the real needs of society, and has placed the individual once more at the centre of politics. Many ways of reform have been accepted but all seek a unifying purpose in the common good which serves the happiness of the ordinary human being. If escape from the terror and insecurity of social unrest by the application of psychology to politics has done nothing more, the individual has been brought out in the open. This suggests that in a great deal of the writing of economists and social psychologists and political theorists that deals with social reform, there is a similarity with the early Radicals in their analysis of the roots of unrest and discord.[124] It is an individualism with a great difference, yet there is the common bond of sympathy. When there is the

[123] Cf. A. D. Lindsay's review of "The Great Society, a Psychological Analysis," in the *Political Quarterly*, September, 1914, pp. 201-204; it may be mentioned that the above quotations are not in direct sequence, but refer both to *Human Nature in Politics* and *The Great Society*.

[124] Cf. Pease, *op. cit.*, p. 262, *Appendix I.* George Bernard Shaw, and the *Lives* of Owen and Cobbett (1925) by G. D. H. Cole, two valuable volumes.

desire to bring "the knowledge which has been accumulated by psychologists into touch with the actual problems of civilised life," there is a kinship in spirit with William Cobbett who sought in his writings to point the way for the working man to look for relief, the way of parliamentary reform. Economic change has determined the major task of politics.[125] It has pointed to the way of parliamentary reform as one method of bringing security to the individual. Politics and economics have each done their plain duty in this century, and have attempted to organize helpfully the life of the community.

The purpose of this organization is the real concern of the State, the aim of the labour associations and of every group in the community. When the aims of groups within the State have been expressed it is plainer just what kind of society and just what standards of living people want. That the growth of these groups should destroy the power of the State or render its central authority less necessary seems impossible, for in the slow development of social purpose is revealed a new relation between these groups and the State.[126] It is the agency whereby the common aim of all the groups can be furthered; its duty is to see that the ordinary human being is not forgot. That is the stable element in reform and reconstruction. While human nature changes slowly, all the better opportunity is offered for an understanding of the purpose behind political organization. The life of the community, and the relation of the State with it, in the maintenance and furtherance of conditions of the good life, remain the fundamental concern. In it all the individual is to be understood and known, his relation with the community a reasoned and helpful one. This problem has been stated by Mr. Lindsay:

[125] See Charles A. Beard *The Economic Basis of Politics* (1922), for clear statement of this point.

[126] Cf. A. D. Lindsay, "The State in Recent Political Theory," *The Political Quarterly*, No. I, 1914, pp. 128-145; also his "The Political Theory of Mr. Norman Angell," No. 4, 1914, pp. 127-145; cf. Ernest Barker, *op. cit.*, No. 2, 1914, "The Rule of Law," pp. 117-140, and No. 5, 1915, pp. 101-121, "The Discredited State." "The facts, then, are not," said Mr. Lindsay, "that political forces are being superseded by economic, but that the new industrial situation has called into being new political organisations" (p. 145). For Mr. Barker "the discredit of the State is a sign that it has done its work well and is doing its work well" (p. 121).

> Human nature is not, of course, independent of Society, but nevertheless it remains very much the same through all changes of political organisation. The new conditions of life are continually calling for new responses, but the new responses cannot be organic. The process of organic development is much too slow. Human nature is much the same now as it was a hundred or five hundred or a thousand years ago; political problems are quite different; and the new situation must be met not by organic change but by organisation. . . . Knowledge of the ordinary human being then is the foundation-stone of politics. Any political schemes which ignore his limitations are foredoomed to failure, as any that do not serve his happiness are useless.[127]

This study attempts to find an unifying ideal in the efforts made to organize the will and the thought and the happiness of the people;[128] to see how far the political organization of democracy gives authority to this social purpose, and to what extent this purpose is shared in the State. The necessity for political interference has depended upon the closeness of men's relations with one another, and the ethical claim since 1914 has become even more sure. One who attempted before 1914 to estimate the forces at work could in 1920

> dream that in Europe and in America a conscious and systematic discussion by the young thinkers of our time of the conditions of a good life for an unprivileged population may be one of the results of the new vision of human nature and human possibilities which modern science and modern industry have forced upon us. . . . Within each nation, industrial organisation may cease to be a confused and wasteful struggle of interests, if it is consciously related to a chosen way of life for which it offers to every worker the material means.[129]

[127] Lindsay, *op. cit.*, pp. 202-203. "Happiness is often a better basis for social analysis than Wealth, or Thought, or Will" (Wallas).

[128] Cf. Wallas, *The Great Society*, Part II, chaps. XI-XIII.

[129] Graham Wallas, *Human Nature in Politics*, pp. xi-xii. Preface to 3rd ed. 1920; also Part II, chaps. 1-4, "Possibilities of Progress." Professor Wallas' *Our Social Heritage* (1920) is a suggestive study.

CHAPTER III

A SURVEY OF THE FRENCH SOCIAL MOVEMENT

PART I

From the Revolution to 1871

THERE has been a close relationship in modern France between the growth of the Labour movement and the periods of great political upheaval which have marked the history of France since 1789. Any survey of the progress of the working class in that nation begins most naturally with the first Revolution. The development from that date has been largely conditioned by the great national events in constitutional and democratic evolution toward a stable and acceptable government. The reaction on the Labour movement has been direct and continuous of the revolutionary epochs of 1831 and 1848, the days of the Commune and the parliamentary crisis in the last years of the nineteenth century, directly affecting not only the organization of the working-class movement but having an effective influence in defining what should be the problems of the leaders. The tendency inevitably has been to give prominence to matters of theory, a fact which helps to account for the many divisions in the labour organizations and the continuous conflict in ideas and methods which has taken place in the attempt to work out a common basis for the unity of the Socialist party. The problem of labour organization has been neglected while the energies of the working class have been largely spent in endless congress debates. The leaders have divided the followers into warring camps.

This is in striking contrast to the manner in which the trade union movement has grown in political and industrial power in England, providing a strong basis for the expansion of the Labour Party with a national appeal. In France the same period affords no such example of the building up of a strong industrial organization combined with effective administration of internal affairs. The definite goal of trade union activity which characterized the English movement gave it a healthy freedom from the entanglements of national politics while at the same time it brought to its service the two great parties, each committed to the principle of parliamentary interference. It is this progressive influence of political liberty on social questions in England which has often attracted the most thoughtful men in France to a consideration of the constitutional history of a nation which in so many instances has had to be the first to make an effort to direct the political and social revolutions of democracy.

In a period of history in both countries, which was a definite crisis for the Labour movement in each, a French critic saw how unfortunate it was

> that social questions have been stirred up with us at periods of great political crises, just at the most unfavourable moment for their solution, when minds are disturbed, passions inflamed, and material prosperity rudely shaken.[1]

For a lesson to his distracted country he turned to the example of England:

> "In showing the influence of political liberty on social questions in England," Louis Philippe d'Orleans wrote, "we believe that we have brought forward an encouraging example for those who are interested in the future of the same question in France. Would it be wise to neglect a parallel lesson, under the pretext that the peculiar characteristics of the British Constitution do not permit us to profit by the experiments made under its protection? We think not, and that this would be exaggerating the importance of the ancient and complicated machinery of which it is composed. Constitutions, however artfully framed, are invariably governed by one ruling power; one, in which real and opposite influences stood exactly balanced against one another would be shattered by their shock, like a machine subjected to contrary forces. It is not any particular clause, unknown elsewhere, which has sustained the English Constitution in the midst of all the political and social revolutions of our age; it is the

[1] Louis Philippe d'Orléans, *Les associations ouvrièrs en Angleterre* (1869), pp. 317-318.

power which is destined to wield sovereign authority in all free countries, and that power is public opinion. However much the constitutions, by means of which the power of opinion makes itself felt, may vary in all these countries, they may be compared to translations of one and the same thought in different languages. Why should we French, and we alone, be condemned to have no terms in our language by which to express it? We are not more excluded than others from the political liberty to which every race and every country have a right. The remedy afforded by political liberty against the dangers arising out of social questions is equally effectual among all nations, who are competent to apply it; and no people, jealous of maintaining its rank in the world, can now with impunity treat this liberty, the highest attribute of civilised man, as a mere ornament to be worn to-day, and on the morrow to be cast aside with disdain." [2]

His conclusion was that:

in the midst of the uncertainty which envelopes the future of France, we cannot take too frequent soundings in the track of our neighbours, whose course is beset by the same dangers as ours.[3]

This commentary on the progress of France made eighty years after the Revolution of 1789 only indicated that the conceptions of the former era were no longer dominant. Reaction brought crisis after crisis, yet it would be a mistake to assume that the crises through which the Labour movement has gone made its history an entirely accidental and discontinuous record of working class achievement. The great forces which came out of the Revolution of 1789, conditioning a new order of society, continued with strength and power. From the beginning the French proletariat, it is said, possessed a tradition already old; [4] and the Declaration of Rights with its emphasis upon political democracy has preserved an authority, not only in its influence on the develop-

[2] D'Orléans, *op. cit.*, pp. 319-321. *The Trade Unions of England,* by L. Le Comte de Paris, translated by Nassau J. Senior and edited by Thomas Hughes, is the London edition of 1869; the above quotation is pp. 237-238 in English edition.

[3] *Op. cit.*, p. vii of Author's Preface; p. v. English edition.

[4] See Preface to Paul Louis' *Histoire du socialisme français* (1901), pp. v-vii.

ment of the common stock of ideas in democratic France,[5] but has been held to be binding upon the constituent law maker and the ordinary law maker.[6] The methodical and uninterrupted force of economic organization making for a new society went on in France under the more noticeable revolutionary political movement of the time, and its beginnings in 1789 were carried on through the proletariat uprisings from 1831 to 1871.

Revolution is *not* all the recorded events of the years over which it is extended, *but* the French people's deep and instinctive sense of the need of certain changes, and their efforts, beneath certain easily distinguished distractions to accomplish them.[7]

From the Revolution of 1848 the French Labour movement recognized a body of common principles and looked back upon June 1848 as an heroic period in the struggle of the workers.[8] Political reaction could not defeat the new spirit which was born. An enthusiasm continued among the working class which was expressed in the co-operative movement and which provided a hope for the reorganization of the Labour movement after the Commune. In a great many minds the June of 1848 and the Commune were linked, were a rallying point for the leaders.[9] De Tocqueville defined the new revolutionary idea when on January 29, 1848, in the Chamber of Deputies he declared that "their passions are no longer political but social."

The tradition of the revolutionary movements has provided a common background for the Labour movement in its march toward parliamentary representation. But the political and economic doctrines which were behind the development of the institutions of the State had to undergo a radical change. The

[5] Cf. Jaurès' Report for the Commission on Declaration of Principles, Congress of Tours, 1902, *Compte Rendu Quatrième Congrès Général du Parti Socialiste Français,* pp. 245, 246, 249.

[6] Cf. Léon Duguit, *Le droit social, le droit individuel et la transformation de l'état* (1st ed. 1908, 3rd ed. revised and with a new preface, 1922), pp.33-40.

[7] Godfrey Elton, *The Revolutionary Idea in France, 1789-1871* (1923), Foreword, p. iv: Author's italics.

[8] Cf. *Compte Rendu du Congrès Général des Organisations Socialistes Françaises,* Paris, 1899, pp. 321, 323.

[9] Cf. Louis, *op. cit.,* pp. 99-100.

individualism of the Assembly and the "political anti-democracy" of the First Empire did not in any way understand what social legislation was necessary to meet the demands of the new economic order which was emerging from the industrial expansion of France.[10]

The legislation of the Assembly was based upon the conceptions of the economic liberalism of the time, and there was an absence of law rather than any definite effort toward control or regulation.[11] From 1789 to 1841 is an unbroken period where the idea of the individualistic organization of production dominated. The non-intervention of the State, the prohibitions of coalition, the liberty of work (*liberté du travail*), were the accepted principles.

The guilds were abolished[12] by the decree of March 2–17, 1791, which proclaimed the principle of *liberté du travail,* inaugurating the era of competition in France.[13] By this change from the old *régime corporatif* to that of *libre concurrence* a fundamentally new condition of economic organization was introduced.[14] The Constituent Assembly passed June 14-17, 1791, the *Loi Chapelier,*[15] forbidding "all kinds of corporations of the same estate and of the same trade."[16] It imposed penalties on persons taking part in strikes or lock-outs, or becoming members of trade unions.[17] This law indicated that the individualistic legislation was directed against the meetings, associations and coalitions of the workingmen, for all coalition of the workers was declared "an attempt against liberty and the Declaration of the Rights of Man."[18]

"This law which, by means of State compulsion confined the struggle between capital and labour within limits comfortable

[10] Cf. Pic, *op. cit.*, pp. 72-74.

[11] Cf. E. Levasseur, *Histoire des classes ouvrières et de l'industrie en France de 1789–1870* (1st ed. 1867; 2nd ed. Vol. I, 1903, Vol. II, 1904), Chap. 1, Vol. II.

[12] Art. 2 et suiv.

[13] Art. 7.

[14] Pic, *op. cit.*, p. 67-68, 72, 151, p. 211 seq.

[15] Cf. "Les associations professionelles ouvrières," *Office Bureau du Travail,* Vol. I (1899), pp. 10-15, for the *Le Chapelier* Report.

[16] Art. 1 et 2.

[17] See Pic, *op. cit.*, pp. 72, 179.

[18] Art. 4.

for capital," Marx said, "has outlived revolutions and changes of dynasties." [19]

The pretext for this bourgeois *coup d'état* was characteristic, thought Marx.

"Granting," said Chapelier, the reporter of the Select Committee on this law, "that wages ought to be a little higher than they are . . . that they ought to be high enough for him that receives them to be free from that state of absolute dependence due to the want of the necessities of life, and which is almost that of slavery." [20]

After the law was passed by the Assembly, Le Chapelier added:

none of us intend to prevent the merchants from discussing their common interests. I therefore propose to insert into the proceedings the following clause: "The National Assembly, considering that the law which it has just passed does not concern the Chambers of Commerce, passes to the order of the day." [21]

This intention was further defined in legislative enactment by the law of April 12, 1803, against coalitions, compelling all workmen to have at all times a special certificate (*livret*) which placed them under police control.[22] In 1810 the law of 1803 was replaced by articles 414-416 of the Code Pénal, which prohibited and punished all kinds of coalitions either of masters or of workmen. Articles 291-294 of the Code Pénal declared illegal all societies or associations of more than twenty persons, and by the law of April 10, 1834, associations of even twenty persons were prohibited if they were branches of a larger association.[23]

It is necessary briefly to sketch this history of early antagonism between the State and the worker in France, a period in which

[19] Karl Marx, *Capital,* Translated from the Third German Edition, by Samuel Moore and Edward Aveling and Edited by Frederick Engels (17th ed. 1920, London), pp. 765-766.

[20] Buchez et Roux, *Histoire Parlementaire,* t. x., p. 195, qt. by Marx, *op. cit.,* p. 766.

[21] Cf. *Les associations professionnelles ouvrières,* Vol. I, pp. 14-15; see also chap. I, pp. 5-89, for a very excellent summary by the official historian of the *Office du Travail* of workers' legislation in France.

[22] Pic, *op. cit.,* pp. 817-821.

[23] Cf. Levasseur, *op. cit.,* t. I, II, III, Vol I, for a survey of legislation during the Revolution, the Consulate and the Empire and the Restauration.

the State was determined to prevent collective action on the part of the workingmen,[24] because it explains to a great extent the bitter struggle between the employers and the workers on one hand, and aids in the interpretation of the attitude in the early years of the century toward State interference with the combination law. Working class organization had not only to contend with restrictive legislation, for the combination law of France was till 1849 not even nominally equal between men and masters,[25] but with the disadvantage which lack of bargaining power caused.[26] Even in the *Conseils de Prud'Hommes* up until 1848, the official historian of the Office du Travail records, the workers were in an inferior position.[27]

From bondage to their own weakness and the antagonistic legislation of the State, the Revolution of 1848 was a means of freedom. The importance in the history of the French Labour movement lies not in its positive achievements but in the expression of new ideas [28] and in the organization among the workers of institutions of mutual aid and assistance.[29] The idea of a solidarity of interests and the necessity of organizing for the protection of their claims was a real contribution to the cause of the workers.[30]

The provisional Government was favourable to the workers, and though the carrying out of the organization of work, *L'Organisation du Travail,* failed, yet the Government which followed had to reckon with and make concessions to the increasing power of the working class.[31] The provisional Government on February 25, 1848, promised to recognize the right to work, *droit du travail,* and the right of free association. A committee

[24] Cf. *Les associations professionnelles ouvrières,* p. 14, Vol. I.

[25] Cf. Dicey, *Law and Opinion in England,* p. 469; Appendix, Note I, pp. 467-476, comparison between the development of combination law in France and in England during the nineteenth century.

[26] Cf. *Les associations professionnelles ouvrières,* Vol. I, chap. II, pp. 90-282, for a thorough treatment of the history of French working class organization down to 1900 from 1791; pp. 280-282, summary.

[27] *Op. cit.,* p. 280.

[28] Cf. Levasseur, *op. cit.,* t. IV, Vol. II; also Maxime Leroy, *La coutume ouvrière, Syndicats, Bourses du Travail, Fédérations Professionnelles, Cooperatives, Doctrines et Institutions,* Vols. I and II (Paris, 1913).

[29] Gabriel Hanotaux, *Contemporary France,* Vol. II, p. 699 (translated by J. C. Tarver, London, 1903-9).

[30] Louis, *op. cit.,* pp. 158-160.

[31] Pic, *op. cit.,* p. 78.

was appointed to make a special study of workers' questions and to bring forward remedies for the solution of the problems of labour. The social legislation of the Republic[32] included the decree of March 2, limiting the working day in Paris to ten hours and in the provinces to eleven; the decree of May 27, that the *Conseils de Prud'Hommes* should include an equal number of the representatives of the employers and the employees; and free employment agencies were created replacing the repressed employment bureaux.[33]

The National and Legislative Assembly were not so favourable to the working class. But for the second time in the history of French social legislation the principle of State intervention in industry was set forth, in the law of September 3, 1848, succeeding the decree of March 2, declaring the maximum working day in France to be twelve hours. Very many exceptions to this law were authorized by the decrees of May 17, 1851, and January 31, 1866; it was not until the law of February 16, 1883, that the inspectors of labour were charged with carrying out the provisions and reviving the penalties of this law. The law of February 22, 1851, on the conditions of the contract of apprenticeship, was another law that was openly violated because no special authority was charged with carrying out its provisions. The necessity of making legislation effective by strong administration and the supervision of inspectors with enforcing authority had not yet been recognized. It is now and has always been a weakness in the French system of industrial legislation.

The Government of Napoleon III began as a movement of reaction.[34] Very quickly the old restrictive laws against association were in effect; the decree of March 25, 1852, on the employment bureaux, the law of March 1, 1853, on the *Conseils de Prud' Hommes* and the law of June 22, 1854, with reference to workingmen's cards (*livrets d'ouvriers*), clearly demonstrated the reactionary purposes of the Government and the influence of the Right. But the Government were forced to consider the rising

[32] Cf. Pic, *op. cit.*, 77-78; Louis, *op. cit.*, pp. 178-185.

[33] Cf. *Les associations ouvrières encouragées par la deuxième Républic* (Décret du 5 Juillet, 1848), (Paris, 1915), Vol. IV of studies edited by *Comité des Travaux Historiques, Scientifiques;* see Introduction, pp. 1-13.

[34] Cf. Levasseur, *op. cit.*, t. VI, Vol. II; Pic, *op. cit.*, pp. 78-79.

tide of opposition and to conciliate their opponents by valuable concessions.[35]

The most important economic legislation was the law of May 25, 1864, giving to workers and employers the right of free association.[36] The right to strike was recognized, temporary combinations for the purpose of raising or lowering wages, or, strikes and lock-outs, ceased to be punishable. This law was official recognition that the legislation of the Revolution, especially the principle of liberty of work, had failed to protect the interests of the worker. Continued opposition from the working class had resulted in the gaining of an advantage for themselves which would be the basis of further attempts to win immunity from restrictive enactments.[37] It was the beginning of the repudiation of the economic system organized by the Revolution, which was finally to be discredited in the passing of legislation founded on the principles of protection for the worker and a safeguard against the dangers of industrial warfare.[38] On the 30th of March, 1868, the Minister of Commerce and Public Works declared that the policy of the Government toward the working men's organizations would be the same as toward the associations of employers. The status of the syndicates remained unchanged from this time on down to the law of 1884, which brought special protection to the professional associations. This law abrogated the law of June 14-27, 1791, and article 416 of the Penal Code; article I of this law further declared that articles 291-294 of the Penal Code and the law of April 10-18, 1834, were not applicable to the professional syndicates.[39]

While the first decade of the Second Empire was a period of persecution and antagonism against the organizations of working men, the influence of the Labour movement in the second decade surpassed that achieved by the working class in France at any previous time. During this period the co-operative movement

[35] Cf. René Foignet and Emile Dupont. *Manuel élémentaire de législation* (4th ed. 1921), p. 29.

[36] Cf. Pic, *op. cit.*, p. 181.

[37] Articles 414 and 415 of the Penal Code were repealed.

[38] Cf. Georges Bry, *Les lois du travail industriel et de la prévoyance sociale, législation ouvrière* (6th ed. Revised by E.-H. Perreau, 1921), pp. 558-560; Foignet & Dupont, *op. cit.*, p. 29.

[39] Dalloz, *Code du travail et de la prévoyance sociale* (1923 Edition), pp. 74-76.

under the inspiration of Louis Blanc became popular with the workers and united them in a common cause.[40] From 1830 there had been the growing spirit among the working people, not definitely separating itself from other Republicans, but seeking to use a democratic republic as an engine for economic change.[41]

The solidarity of the workers, which was the aim of the leaders, was furthered by the progress of secret trade groups such as the *Sociétés de Résistance,* and in 1864 there was an outward expression of it in the founding in Paris of the Internationale.[42] The ideas of Proudhon dominated for the first few years of its life, the central thesis of which was *mutuellisme* as developed in his *De la Capacité Politique Des Classes Ouvrières.*[43] From this early date an opposition by Blanqui to this tendency in the French Labour movement foreshadowed the long drawn out conflict between the collectivist program of Marxian Socialism and the revolutionary program of Blanqui and his followers.

The French Labour movement by 1871, had gained much ground; and to a great extent the tendencies which were later to become more definite and to furnish the controversial fuel for many congresses had formed themselves. The work of organization was the major problem after 1871. The right to strike had been recognized, and there was no longer the struggle to establish the right of free association of working men. The slow progress of the Labour movement from 1789 had done no more than establish the principles and tendencies which the Third Republic had to develop and apply.

Part II

From 1871–1896

(a) *Political Development of the Social Movement.*

The period from the overthrow of the Commune in 1871 to the year 1878 has been described as "one of the most mournful,

[40] M. Louis, *op. cit.,* p. 127, believes that Blanc had the same effect by his *L'organisation du travail,* as was produced by Henry George's *Progress and Poverty.* The emphasis of Blanc on the State, of course, was the counterpart of Proudhon's theory.

[41] Bryce, *op. cit.,* Vol. II, p. 245; Elton, *op. cit.,* chap. VI, pp. 108-131.

[42] Cf. Louis, *op. cit.,* chap. V, pp. 114-157,, "From Blanc to Proudhon."

[43] Louis, *op. cit.,* pp. 126-127.

most discouraging, of the social struggle in France."[44] The Labour movement which had grown up before 1871 was almost entirely destroyed in its organization, and the continued persecution made the leaders very cautious in rebuilding the old structure. There was the heritage of experience bequeathed to the working men, but there was no leader either for the political or economic organization of the working class movement. The leadership of working class thought had passed to Germany; France produced no strictly original thinker for the direction of affairs.

There were a few of the leaders of the old Internationale and the independent republican journalist J. Barberet, who "deplored the horrible repression of 1871," and set about the task of building up the labour organizations.[45] The associations of employers were stronger after the war than before, and the general organization, *L'Union Nationale du Commerce et de l'Industrie,* having no workers' association to face, "fixed at will the wages and duration of work."[46] At this time the condition of existence for working class organization was to abstain from any criticism of the Government and its laws.

The disastrous days of 1871 and the years following showed how necessary it was to build up loyalty for the Republic and its institutions. It was essential that everything be done to diminish the struggle of the classes, for the Republic could not withstand the ravages of social warfare.[47] Social peace was the condition for the continuance of the Republic.[48] On this necessity the Labour

[44] Paul Louis, *Histoire du parti socialiste en France, 1871–1914* (1922), p. 7.

[45] F. Pelloutier, *Histoire des Bourses du Travail* (1902), p. 35, Chap. I, "Après la Commune," pp. 32-49, is useful for the period.

[46] Pelloutier, *op. cit.,* p. 35.

[47] Cf. H. A. L. Fisher, *The Republican Tradition in Europe* (1911), chaps. VIII and IX. The danger of class warfare increased in France from the beginning of the nineteenth century because of the very individualism behind the legislation of the Revolution, which was not, as in the case of the combination law, "a measure of class warfare, but a corollary from the Declaration of the Rights of Man." J. L. and Barbara Hammond, *The Town Labourer,* 1760-1832, p. 326.

[48] Cf. Charles Seignobos, *L'Evolution de la 3rd République, 1875–1914* (1921), pp. 1-19, Vol. VIII, *Histoire de France contemporaine depuis la Révolution jusqu' à la Paix de 1919,* Ernest Lavisse, editor.

movement of the Third Republic was constituted and on this principle legislation of the Republic was based.[49]

Barberet, who was very prominent in the reconstituting of the syndicates, was convinced that the Second Empire had fallen because of the general strike movement of 1868-70.[50] He held that the strike was a "crime of lèse-démocratie," that the progress of the working class was menaced by its use and that it was dangerous for the political institutions of the country. The spirit in which Barbaret planned for the rebuilding of the Labour movement can be seen in the program which he outlined for the syndicates.

They were to watch over the loyal fulfilment of contracts of apprenticeship; to organise employment bureaux; to create boards of conciliation composed of an equal number of delegates from employers and working men for the peaceful solution of trade disputes; to found libraries and courses in technical education; to utilise their funds not to foment strikes, but to buy raw materials and instruments of labour; and finally, to "crown these various preparatory steps" by the creation of co-operative workshops "which alone would give groups of workingmen the normal access to industry and commerce" and which in time would equalize wealth.[51]

The syndicates were reconstituted under this influence, and in August, 1872, the various Syndicates organized the *Cercle de l'Union Ouvrière,* as the counter force to the employers' *L'Union Nationale du Commerce et de l'Industrie*.[52] The *Cercle* was dissolved by the Government, although it is said that the leaders carefully avoided the discussion of politics and the policies of M. de Broglie. Its aim was stated to be the "realization of concord and justice through study," and to convince public opinion "of the moderation with which workingmen claim their

[49] Pic, *op. cit.,* 79.
[50] Cf. A. Sauliere, *La Grève Générale: de Robert Owen à la doctrine Syndicaliste* (1913), for a survey of the early period in France.
[51] Cf. J. Barberet, *Monographies Professionelles* (1886), Vol. I, pp. 20-25, quoted by Louis Levine, *Syndicalism in France* (2nd revised edition, New York, 1914), p. 46.
[52] J. Barberet, *La bataille des intérêts,* p. 301, qt. by Pelloutier, *op. cit.,* p. 35.

rights." The workers' syndicates by 1875 numbered in Paris 135, liable to the articles 291-294 of the Penal Code, the law of April 10, 1834, and the decrees of March 23 and of April 2, 1852.

The strength of the Labour movement was represented by the increase of the professional syndicates, in the agitation for labour representation in the Chamber, in the co-operative movement, in the workers' congresses and in the workingmen's delegations from the syndicates attending the various international expositions.[53] The sending of the French delegates to the Philadelphia Exposition in 1876 suggested to certain leaders of the Labour movement that it would be a good thing to hold a workers' congress in Paris after the return of the delegates, to "discuss the bases of a common Socialist program," and that such a congress would have "considerable influence on the economic emancipation of all the French proletariat." [54] The proposition was taken up by the workers and on October 2, 1876, at the Ecoles, rue d'Arras, the first French Labour Congress was organized.[55]

The Committee which had in charge the programs of the Congress submitted eight subjects, and it is interesting to note what the French Labour Congress considered the important questions for workers: (1) the work of women; (2) syndicates; (3) Councils of Prud'Hommes; (4) apprenticeship and technical education; (5) direct representation of the working class in Parliament; (6) co-operative associations; (7) old-age pensions; (8) agricultural associations and the advantage of relations between the agricultural and the industrial workers.[56]

The Congress was conservative,[57] largely under the influence of Barberet, and the majority of the 360 delegates, 255 from Paris and 105 from the provincial towns, were *co-opérateurs* and

[53] The indispensable history of the French Labour movement with the documentary story of working class organizations is in the four official volumes of the *Office du Travail, Les Associations Professionnelles,* Vol. I, 1899, Vol. II, 1901, Vol. III, 1903, Vol. IV, 1904; see Paul Louis, *Histoire du mouvement syndical en France,* 1789-1910 (2nd ed. 1911), chap. VIII, pp. 132-154, for period from Commune to the law of 1884.

[54] Pelloutier, *op. cit.,* p. 37, qt. *Le Journal,* June 19, 1876.

[55] Cf. *Les associations professionnelles ouvrières,* Vol. I, pp. 239-242.

[56] Cf. *Séances des Congrès ouvriers de France,* 1876, Paris, 1877.

[57] Cf. Louis, *op. cit.,* p. 137.

mutuellistes.[58] The collectivists were also represented, not hesitating to put forward their theories and making a very lively protest against the presence of Barberet at the Congress.[59] But the conservative tendency was clearly given expression in the official condemnation from the organization committee of leaders like Varlin, César de Paëpe, Emile Aubry and Albert Richard, who had been active in the work of the Internationale and in the propagation of its doctrines.

The first congress of the French Labour movement was not unlike the congresses of the first years of this century, especially from that at Paris in 1899 to that at Tours in 1902, when the question of method and tactics and the fundamental divergencies in doctrine among Guesdists, Allemanists and Blanquists, made the annual meetings great debating arenas. The evolution of syndical conceptions was dominated during the period from 1871 to 1884 by the debates of the first workers' congresses, and

the penetration of the new doctrines (collectivism and communism) coincided with a marked transformation in the program of the professional groups.[60]

Emphasis upon syndical action was the chief contribution of the Allemanists [61] who countered the effort of Jules Guesde with a more pronounced political program. The influence of the first is recorded in the programs of the workingmen's organizations at the Paris Exposition of 1889, indicating the progress of ideas and the expansion of the workers' industrial horizon,[62] while the political expression was given in the *La Petite République* in 1891 in a published program of reforms common to the parties of the Left, signed by Goblet, Peytral, Millerand, Lockroy and Jaurès. This program included measures for the protection of women and children and adults by the legal limitation of the working day; arbitration of disputes; old-age pensions; protection of working

[58] Cf. Louis, *Histoire du Socialisme Français,* p. 286.

[59] Pelloutier, *op. cit.,* p. 38.

[60] Louis, *Histoire du mouvement syndical en France, 1789-1910,* pp. 136-137.

[61] Cf. Victor Griffuelhes, *L'Action Syndicaliste* (1908), pp. 4-5; yet at the first Congress of the Allemanists in 1892 the legislative program adopted contained twelve distinct economic reforms sought; see this program in *Les Allemanistes,* Maurice Charnay (1912), pp. 104-107.

[62] Cf. Charles Gide, *op. cit.,* pp. 3, 13-17.

conditions with reference to health; a more comprehensive law on accidents; and a law making it obligatory for the employer to recognize workers' associations.[63]

The second Labour Congress[64] held in Lyons, January 28 to February 8, 1878, was in all important respects of the same character as the Paris Congress. But the Congress of Marseilles[65] in October, 1879, marked the victory of Socialism, of collectivism, and the end of the "Barberetists." In 1877, Guesde began the publication of *Égalité,* and from that time exerted an influence of effective leadership on the French Socialist movement, Guesdism being considered by some as the perfect form of political Socialism.[66] At the 1879 Congress the *Parti Ouvrier* was formed, and the political and economic program of the Labour movement was elaborated. The political program[67] was based largely on the example of the German Labour movement, for both Jules Guesde and Paul Lafargue were influenced by Karl Marx and Engels. The lack of originality and independence in adapting the workers' political movement to the actual needs of France and in accordance with French temperament was shown at the very beginning.

The program for the conquest of political power included the abolition of all laws infringing on the freedom of the press, of coalitions and associations; the repeal of the law on workingmen's cards; the refusal of the budget on the Church, the public debt and armaments; and in the sphere of local government the commune master of its administration and police. The economic and the political program were of course based on the collectivist theory of the State and the economic organization of society. The preamble was:

[63] Cf. Scelle, *op. cit.,* p. 35.

[64] Cf. *Les associations professionnelles ouvrières,* Vol. I, pp. 242-244.

[65] *Op. cit.,* pp. 244-248.

[66] Cf. Edouard Berth, *Les derniers aspects du socialisme* (1923), Revised Edition of *Les nouveaux aspects du socialisme* (1908), p. 43; also, *ibid.,* pp. 8-9.

[67] "Le Programme Du Parti Ouvrier, Ses Considérants, Ses Articles," by Guesde & Lafargue, was published in June, 1880, in *Revue Socialiste, Egalité* and in *Prolétaire.* The regional congress of the *Parti Ouvrier Français* in Paris, July, 1880, adopted it, and in November at Havre the National congress. It was amended at the congress of Roanne, after the split at Saint-Etienne.

Considering that the emancipation of the producing class is that of all human beings, without distinction of race or sex, that the producer will not be free until he has possession of the means of production . . . the French workers having for their end the political and economic expropriation of the class and the return to a collectivism of all the means of production, have decided, as the method of organisation and struggle, to enter into the elections, with the following immediate programme.[68]

The reduction of the hours of work; a weekly rest day; the fixation of a minimum wage; the forbidding payment by employers of foreign workmen of a lower wage than to the French workers; scientific and professional training for all children by the State; the abolition of all indirect taxation and a progressive income tax on all revenue, constituted the economic demands.

This Congress marked the rebirth of the French Labour movement, but the unity which Guesde aimed for in the ranks of the working class was broken in 1882, when at the Congress of Saint-Etienne a majority of the *Parti Ouvrier Français* resigned. Under the leadership of Paul Brousse the *Fédération des Travailleurs Socialistes* [69] was formed, which in 1890 was divided by a minority under Allemane forming a new party, the *Parti Ouvrier Socialiste Révolutionnaire*.[70] There was yet the *Parti Socialiste Révolutionnaire,* sometimes called the *Comité Révolutionnaire Central*.[71] a revolutionary anarchist group under the direction of Vaillant.

But the most influential and the most brilliant of the Socialist groups at the beginning of the century was the Independent or Reform Socialists, who did not constitute a distinct class party.[72] It was not until 1899 when the *Comité d'Entente* was organized that the Independents became a national group, forming the *Confédération des Socialistes Indépendants*.[73] The beginning of this

[68] Cf. Paul Louis, *Histoire du parti socialiste en France, 1871-1914,* pp. 13-14.

[69] The history of the French Socialist groups has been written under the editorial direction of Alexandre Zévaès, of which *Les Possibilistes,* Sylvain Humbert (Paris, 1911), is one; cf. *Le Socialisme en France depuis 1871,* A. Zévaès (1908), for a general friendly survey.

[70] Maurice Charnay, *Les Allemanistes* (1912).

[71] Charles Da Costa, *Les Blanquistes* (1912).

[72] Cf. A. Orry, *Les Socialistes Indépendants* (1912).

[73] The Confédération divided into the *Fédération des Indépendants* and the *Fédération des Révolutionnaires Indépendants.*

group was in the "Society for Social Economy" which was founded in 1885 by Benoit Malon, who was once a member of the Internationale. The monthly journal of this society was *La Revue Socialiste,* in which the theory of French Socialism was fully debated and written about, under the successive editorship of Malon, George Renard, Rouanet and Fournière. *Le Socialisme Intégral,*[74]—thanks to which book, wrote Eugene Fournière, "Socialism is no longer a dry economic doctrine based on necessity, it is the normal expansion of humanity going on toward the justice of the future" [75]—was first printed in *La Revue Socialiste.* In 1893, *La Petite République* was founded, becoming the leading organ of the Independents. Among the most prominent of this group of eclectics were Jaurès, Millerand, Viviani and the editors of the *Revue Socialiste.* Toward the electorate and parliamentarianism they held that the first duty of Socialism was to bring about constitutional stability.[76] The development of this doctrine was given its classic exposition by M. Millerand at the Banquet of Saint-Mande, where the chief tenets of the Independents were set forth: the gradual nationalization of public services, protective laws for labour, evolutionary and parliamentary progress toward the collectivist ideal.

(b) *Industrial Legislation and Administrative Commissions*

The political development of the Labour movement in France had been up until 1896 largely an effort to apply the doctrines of collectivism to the industrial problems of the nation. There had been no distinctly original approach to the peculiar conditions of French life nor had there been any solution brought forward with especial reference to the needs of France's working class and her expanding commercial activities. But the political movement had popularized the tenets of Socialism, the principles of

[74] B. Malon, *op. cit.,* Vol. I (1890), Vol. II (1894), Cp. Maurice Bourguin, *Les systemes socialistes et l'evolution économique* (1904), pp. 91-94, for a criticism of Malon's Socialist theory. Cp. A. Fouillée, *La democratie politique et sociale en France* (2nd ed. 1910).

[75] *La Revue Socialiste,* September 15, 1890; Appendix I. *Le Socialisme Intégral,* Vol. I, pp. 405-418, for this review and other interesting reviews of the Socialist movement of the period. M. Fournière dedicated to Malon his *Les théories socialistes au XIX siècle* (1904).

[76] B. Malon, *op. cit.,* vol. I, pp. 377-381.

which have always had a wider acceptance in France than any party which directly represented their application. It can be said with much truth that in France Socialism is a principle rather than a party;[77] to which fact the legislation of the Third Republic is ample proof.

One of the first laws which expressed the new social movement after the establishment of the Third Republic, that of May 19, 1874, on the work of women and children, marks for the first time in French industrial legislation the adequate organization of inspection to insure the application of a law. This law commences uninterrupted parliamentary activity in development of protective legislation for the workers, and is the real beginning of French Labour legislation.[78] By 1890 the majority in Parliament were definitely interventionists.[79] The necessity for the State, considered as the supreme organ of the law "to intervene to fix the just limits of industrial necessities,"[80] was clearly established. From this period an increasing number of laws favourable to the working class were put on the statute books;[81] and the effective organization of industry became a major concern of law makers.

In 1881 the liberty of association was won, being more fully interpreted for the professional syndicates in the law of 1884, which legalized all professional associations having for their object the promotion and the protection of the interest of any profession or trade.[82] All earlier laws restricting freedom of action were repealed, including articles 291-294 and 416 of the Penal Code. This law was the most important of the Third Republic down to 1900. The likeness between the combination law of France since 1884 and the combination law of England since 1875 has been often suggested.

The law is intended to allow to employers and employed as unlimited a right of combination as is compatible with the respect

[77] Thomas Kirkup, *History of Socialism,* 5th ed. revised and largely rewritten by Edward R. Pease (1913), p. 329.

[78] Pic, *op. cit.,* p. 79; Foignet and Dupont, *op. cit.,* p. 30.

[79] George Scelle, *op. cit.,* p. 34.

[80] Cf. M. Berthiot, *Cours de legislation du travail et motions de législation ouvrière et industrielle,* Vol. I, *Lois appliquées par les inspecteurs du travail* (2nd ed. 1921), p. 6.

[81] Cf. Dicey, *op. cit.,* p. ix, Preface to the First Edition.

[82] *Law,* March 21, 1884, art. 3.

due to the freedom of individuals, whether masters or workmen. In each country strikes and lock-outs are lawful; in each country a trade union is a lawful society; in neither country does a trade union need for its legal existence the sanction of the Government. In each country masters and workmen stand, as regards their right to combine, on a complete equality; in each country the law allows combinations for the purpose of regulating the terms of the labour contract.[83]

The conclusion naturally follows

that the combination law of France and the combination law of England not only bear a great similarity to one another, but have at last reached exactly the same goal.[84]

These laws are not only very important in themselves but they indicate the development of the industrial life of the nations and the attitude that the State took toward the organizations which primarily were concerned with the economic interest of the worker Within the State these bodies came to have large influence upon the political movement, which increasingly had to take note of the position of the wage earner. With M. Lockroy as Minister of Commerce the emphasis on social problems became marked, and deputies of all parties asked that two sittings of the week be given exclusively to the consideration of social legislation.[85]

The scope of social legislation has gradually been extended until the danger of perilous class legislation getting on the statute book has largely disappeared. A rapid survey of legislation in France and England since 1880 reveals the fact that nearly all phases of the working life of the people have been considered. During 1880-1890 in France, laws were passed which directly affected the agricultural development of the country; the inspection of working conditions; the protection of rural workers and children; and the development of councils in the agricultural and mining occupations was the purpose of several enactments.

[83] Cf. Dicey, *op. cit.*, p. 472.
[84] *Ibid.* A recent study of interest is that of A. A. Al-Sanhoury, *Les Restrictions Contractuelles à la Liberté de Travail dans la Jurisprudence Anglaise* (Paris, 1925).
[85] Cf. Scelle, *op. cit.*, pp. 34-35.

It is true that the wider scope of workers' legislation and progressive extension into the field of industry as a whole has been slowly realized in France, compared with Germany or with England; but there was progress between 1890-1900, and in this century this ideal has been important in all agitation for an extension of labour legislation and the perfecting of administration of existing law. Germany was the first nation fully to grasp the fact that the problem of the wage earner and his protection was a nation-wide one; that the worker on the farm, in the home and in the store should have the same adequate protection and benefit as the more hazardous employments of the mine and of manufacturing. It has been often a very healthy indication of the value of protection for any class of worker, that very soon class benefits are extended to larger and more inclusive groups. Class legislation it is, but its social and economic consequences are of the highest importance for the general interests of the community and industry.

This fact is interpreted in France in the law of December 27, 1892, on conciliation and arbitration between employer and employee; of January 12, 1895, on the attachment of the wages of workers; of the laws of November 2, 1892, and March 30, 1900, bringing special protection for women and children; the health and security of the workers were increased by the laws of June 12, 1893, June 29, 1894, for the miners, and May 24, 1899, on accident insurance; and by the law of January 30, 1899, rural workers came under the protective provisions of the law of April 9, 1898, on accidents to workmen.

The last years of the nineteenth century witnessed the rapid expansion of the part that administration was to have in meeting the problems of industrial organization. The use by Governments of special decrees and the necessarily increased power given to institutions of administration and agencies of control and inspection, indicate the magnitude of the undertaking which the State had begun with hardly any forethought and very little appreciation of what the consequences were to be. Chief among the official signs of this movement in France were the laws of January 22, 1891, constituting the *Conseil Supérieur du Travail;* of July 21, 1891, instituting the *Office du Travail,* the functions of which were set forth in the decrees of August 19-21,

1891, and February 4-5, 1892;[86] and the law of December 7, 1895, on the administrative control of the *Bourse du Travail de Paris.* The further extension of earlier legislation to meet new demands of industrial growth is seen in the law of December 27, 1892, on the *Conseils de Conciliation et d'Arbitrage,* and by the decree of July 3, 1894, a *Commission Consultative Permanente,* composed of twenty-five members was created to make more effective the work of the *Conseil Supérieur du Commerce et de l'Industrie.* On the one hand there was the increase of laws dealing with the control of industry, which made it necessary to unify the administration of such legislation, in the application to establishments and trades, and at the same time it was imperative that principles of administration be clearly worked out by bodies which were competent to deal with the many-sided problems of modern industry. It was necessary that the State should have the best means of knowing the direction in which expansion of the ordinary economic life of the nation was leading. The passing of specific laws was only one method of State intervention; it was useless unless there was a definite aim toward the realization of which the State had brought all its powers.

It thus came about that in France, outside the departmental councils and committees, special commissions were appointed to consider industrial legislation and administration. It is necessary to mention here only those established between 1890-1900; the *Comité Consultatif des Chemins de Fer;*[87] the *Commission Consultative des Caisses Syndicales et Patronales de Retraits, de Secours et de Prévoyance;*[88] the *Conseil Supérieur des Habitations à Bon Marché;*[89] the *Conseil Supérieur des Caisses d'Epargne;*[90] the *Conseil des Sociétés de Secours Mutuels;*[91] and the *Commission Consultative d'Hygiène Industrielle.*[92] By such bodies of consultation and inquiry the State sought to bring together the common experience of the industrial world to guide its own industrial legislation. The transformation of the State into an active partner in the settlement of social and economic in-

[86] Cf. Bry, *op. cit.*, pp. 698-699; Pic, *op. cit.*, pp. 113-117.
[87] Decree of September 18, 1893.
[88] Law of December 27, 1895, and decree of January 10, 1896.
[89] Law of November 30, 1894.
[90] Law of July 30, 1895.
[91] Law of April 1, 1898.
[92] Decree December 11, 1900.

justice with the aid of the two ancient enemies, capital and labour, made necessary the development of the consultative and extra-departmental commissions. Parliament tried to bring the democratic method into actual use through this means, and its use is even now one of the great experiments of the community trying to find a way out of its industrial discords and social maladjustments. The effort of the State in the beginning of this century is especially worth noting in France, where the attempt was part of a general program of social reconstruction. In England it has an older and more successful history, but the lessons which it has taught have been much the same.

The history of the French syndicalist movement and the French Socialist parties bear out the same general interpretation that has been traced in the English movement. It must be understood of course that any generalizations are only approximately true, and that in the movements of France and England there are at every period differences and divergences. The French public, it appears, were for a long time much more interested in the trade unionism of England than in their own syndicalist organization.[93] The former was more attractive to the French historian than the latter, naturally so for the student of history who delights in the slow, continuous full development of an institution. The historian of the French syndicalist movement is amused, perhaps rightfully so, that the French publicists for so long a time studied the English Trade Union movement that they might find lessons in it with which to instruct their own workers.[94] They assumed the success of the English method as an argument for their side in the fight against State Socialism.[95] M. Louis convicts these

[93] Cf. Paul Louis, *Histoire du mouvement syndicalist en France, 1789-1910* (Paris, 2nd ed. 1911), p. vi. Preface to 1901 edition; compare the two Prefaces; note the 1867 Preface of M. E. Levasseur to his *Histoire des classes ouvrières et de l'industrie en France 1789 à 1870,* compared with the Preface to the second edition, 1903-4. The first preface is found in Vol. I (1903), pp. vii-xix. The same author's Preface to *Questions ouvrières en France sous la troisième République* (Paris, 1907), pp. v-xvii, offers an opportunity for a comparative view over a good number of years.

[94] An interesting letter from M. Le Comte de Paris to Mr. A. J. Mundella, is in the Barnett House Library (Oxford), in volume cited above.

[95] Cf. M. G. De Molinari, *Le mouvement socialiste et les reunions publiques avant la révolution du 4 Septembre 1870* (Paris, 1872), Part III, pp. 131-172, "Trade Unions in England," being articles reprinted from

writers of gross ignorance, for failing to see that each period of English Trade Union history was a decided advance in the direction of the principle of direct action, either through the method of the strike or through parliamentary representation.[96] They could not understand what the German critic believed he understood; that

> the English workingman cares nothing for "principles"; he is too much of an "inconsistent opportunist." He likes to be left in peace, he likes to eat his apple pie undisturbed. But if anything should happen to rob him of his peace, he is quite ready to adopt any means, even that of political warfare, that are likely to give him back his peace and his apple pie.[97]

An even later critic [98] has emphasized the historical mission of the workingman in bringing in Socialism, believing that his place in the history of ideas in England has been unappreciated by his own historian, Mr. Sidney Webb. At any rate in England the workingman has kept a closer march on the political movement than in any other country, and the structure of his economic organization reveals far fuller appropriation of the benefits of democratic institutions. No doctrine of the dictatorship of the "conscious minority" has ever had any appreciable influence in the history of trade union theory, and this is the backbone of the revolutionary syndicalist philosophy in France. This is one of the most interpretative points of difference between the two Labour movements, which is likely to obtain for some time. However blind the publicists of the French nation were, it is evident that the leaders of the French Labour movement were not far wrong on the progress of Trade Unions in England. In the famous debate from June 11-27, 1896, in the Chamber of Deputies, on the limitation of the hours of work, MM. Guesde and Vaillant used effectively the example of England for a defence of

the *Journal des Débats,* July 27 and August 5, 9 and 13, 1869, explaining "why socialism makes no progress in England." See same author's article "1899," in the *Journal des Economistes,* January 15, 1900, bringing his strictures up to date.

[96] Cf. Louis, *op. cit.,* Preface to 1901 edition.

[97] Sombart, *op. cit.,* p. 244.

[98] Beer, *op. cit.,* Vol. II, pp. 277-284.

their argument.[99] At the International Congress for the Legal Protection of Workers, 1900, held at the Musée Social, the example of the administration and effective enforcement of the laws relating to women and children in England was cited as proof that such laws were practicable.[100] It is also clear from the Amsterdam Congress of 1904, that the parliamentary struggles in France, as they centred about Millerand and Jaurès, were exciting a lively interest from the leaders of the Labour movement in England, who believed that the Labour and Socialist movements in the two countries had been too long isolated.[101] This belief was strengthened by the fact that the two leaders, M. Jaurès and Mr. J. Ramsay MacDonald, were strangely alike in their philosophy and in their method, the former exercising an influence upon the latter, acknowledged after his death in the tribute that M. Jaurès "was the greatest democratic personal force in Europe—even in the world." [102] The influence of English governmental policy in the formulation of the measures of M. Millerand is clearly seen, being often acknowledged in official reports. At that time the parliamentary successes of the Labour movement were forcing the French and English working class leaders to consider "Socialist methods under Parliamentary Government." It was significant that the English leader did not look to Germany.

Owing to the fact that the Reichstag is not the Parliament of a democratically governed people, the parliamentary successes of Socialism have not forced it to adapt itself to the parliamentary method of organic change,[103]

he studied the tactics of M. Jaurès and the French Socialists.

[99] Cf. Paul Jacquier, *La limitation légale de la journée de travail en France* (1902), pp. 58-64.

[100] Cf. Rapport Barthou, *Compte Rendu du Congrés pour la Protection Légale des Travailleurs* (1900), M. Raoul Jay, one of the most active supporters of the protective laws and the development of administration, was fully informed on the progress of the laws of England; see his *La protection légale des travailleurs* (2nd ed. 1910). The authority of MM. Pic and Bry is often quoted in this present study.

[101] Cf. Jean Jaurès, *Studies in Socialism,* Editor's Note by J. Ramsay MacDonald, p. xiv, E. T. by Mildred Minturn (1906).

[102] Cf. Margaret Pease, *Jean Jaurès,* Introduction by J. Ramsay MacDonald (1916), p. 12.

[103] Cf. Minturn, *op. cit.,* p. xiii, Editor's Note.

It is natural that the political movements of France and England during the nineteenth century should have many points in common, and that the progress of democratic ideas in each nation should at various times react with directness upon each people, both seeking to use a democratic State as an engine for economic change.[104] The Revolution from 1770 most influenced England; and from 1789 (with special reference to France), for both nations the slow, methodical and uninterrupted development of economic forces was making for a new[105] society. It cannot be said that 1830 was the beginning of modern democratic government in France, as Dicey takes 1832 for England,[106] and Bryce 1867 and 1884-5,[107] but it did mark the definite break of French social philosophy with the Revolution of 1789;[108] "the period of the bourgeois struggle ended, the period of the proletariat struggle began."[109] The days of 1831 revealed the strength in the workers' ranks, and, although the demands of the Republican party in 1831 were limited, their demands and the march of democratic ideas widened as their power became more manifest. What the Revolution of 1789 had not conceived and had not made possible, became increasingly more real from the Revolution of 1830, the June of 1848, and the March of 1871. Out of 1830 came "the idea of society," of that society being controlled for the highest good of all, and the creation of "a new society founded on the transformation of property."[110] Under the superficial calm of the Orleanist régime the most exceptionally creative period of revolution was going on, which brought in the Second Republic and made its first few weeks most spectacular. Through all economic change and expansion the idea of society was gaining a hold on the imagination of the nation, and in spite of an unfriendly political system was making headway.

This is seen in a striking way by contrasting the beginning of the nineteenth century in France and England with the opening of the new century, taking in point the Combination Act of 1800, which represented the public opinion of that time in Eng-

[104] Bryce, *op. cit.*, Vol. II, p. 245.
[105] Cf. Louis, *Histoire du socialisme francais*, pp. 51-52.
[106] *Op. cit.*, p. 128.
[107] *Op. cit.*, p. 351.
[108] *Op. cit.*, p. 92; see also Elton, *op. cit.*, chap. 6, pp. 108-131.
[109] Louis, *op. cit.*, p. 83.
[110] Louis, *op. cit.*, pp. 106-111.

land, and the Code Napoléon of 1804, which embodied the ideas of French revolutionists or reformers, and was "as strongly opposed to trade combinations, whether among employers or workmen, as the Combination Act, 1800." [111] M. Louis believes that the definition of the Webbs of a Trade Union,[112]

a continuous association of wage-earners for the purpose of maintaining or improving the conditions of their working lives,

would apply to the early professional societies of France, but at the beginning of this century would not apply to the present form of syndicalism which demands the "destruction of the capitalist régime." [113]

At the beginning of the nineteenth century workers' action was timid and cautious, while at the beginning of the twentieth century, it aspired to construct a new world on the debris of the old.[114]

It was in this spirit that M. Augagneur, in opening the Lyons Congress of 1901, said:

You will allow me to remind you that we are at the dawn of the twentieth century, that we think the twentieth century will be the century of Socialism, that we hope before the half of that century is past, the Socialist movement will have attained such power, that it will be so strong, that it will have brought us near to the ideal of justice and well-being which we all desire.[115]

The century which was ended had been largely in France a record of political development toward Republicanism. Under the Second Republic the democratic movement had little time to express itself in a constitutional way, and through the Second Empire the forces of reaction proved too strong. But in 1876,

[111] Dicey, *op. cit.*, p. 102; also Pic, *op. cit.*, pp. 74-75.

[112] Webbs' *Trade Unionism*, p. 1; see difference of definition by G. D. H. Cole, *Organized Labour* (1924), p. 1, "an organized working class movement for defence and aggression against the dominant capitalist system." That to Mr. Cole is what the 19th century developed.

[113] Paul Louis, *Histoire du mouvement syndical en France*, pp. 1-2.

[114] Louis, *op. cit.*, p. 17.

[115] Cf. "Troisième Congrès Général des Organisations Socialistes Françaises," *Compte Rendu* (1901), p. 4.

after the adoption of the Constitution of 1875, "the moment had come when the French people might, peacefully and according to Constitutional regulations, make its will known." [116] Yet this Constitution was held

> so defective that there will be no political peace or true Socialist progress in France until there is a serious and sincere democratic revision which will clear the horizon.[117]

Thus the problems which faced the leaders in the organization of the new régime proved almost too much for the French nation.[118] But the time had come when the Republican forces seemed to be able to unite for long enough to give the democratic spirit of the nation an opportunity to express itself. The year 1871 had been the dividing line very definitely for the Labour movement.[119] When it was reconstituted there was "the return of the revolutionary tradition established in 1830," [120] and, "in spite of the penetration of the social philosophies from across the Rhine the respect for traditional idealism." [121]

The Commune had been a bitter lesson to the French working class, but it taught the most valuable lesson that the political upheavals had yet given the leaders. From that time to the *Cas Millerand* the period was crowded with efforts toward organization, diffusion of ideas, internal development of the political program of Socialism, and the working out of the differences in theory and method in the Labour movement. The continual conflict between the partisans of Syndicalism, adherents of Proudhon, and the Collectivists, dominated by the dogma of the complete transformation of the State, went on speedily from the Congress of 1879, forming the two intellectual currents which have divided the workers' world in France down to the present time.[122] The same characteristics which were evident in 1882, were especially in prominence between 1899-1901, and 1906-1910.

[116] Cf. G. Hanotaux, *op. cit.,* Vol. III, p. 420.

[117] Cf. Malon, *Le Socialisme Intégral,* pp. 381-382; see chap. VIII. "The Evolution of the State and of Socialism," pp. 357-404, for a general survey from the best early study. For a list of 26 Constitutions, p. 381.

[118] Cf. Charles Seignobos, *L'Evolution de la 3rd République,* pp. 1-19.

[119] See Sombart, *op. cit.,* p. 157. [120] Seignobos, *op. cit.,* pp. 48-50.

[121] Louis, *Histoire du socialisme français,* p. 298.

[122] Cf. Louis, *op. cit.,* pp. 270-273, 284-285.

The first early warning to both the political and economic Labour movement in France after the Commune was given by Marx and Engels, who saw that one thing especially was proved by the Commune, viz., that the working class cannot simply lay hold of the ready-made State machinery, and wield it for its own purposes.[123] An acceptance of this fact accounts for the Broussistes and Guesdistes (after the Congress of 1882) defending equally the struggle of the classes and the emancipation of the workers by the workers themselves.[124] But from the early crudity of the political Marxism they accepted to the Socialist position as stated in the Saint-Mande Programme there is an interesting evolution of theory and practise. It is a study of reaction to actual necessities of industrial organization and the acceptance of the State as an expression of the growing idea of justice and right from which has developed what Jaurès called "the ideal of humanity." This ideal, he thought, was becoming incorporated in reality, becoming the motive power in the idea of progress, of the right, of the ideal, whereby unity and conciliation would be realised, because men willed it; and this conception of history was in harmony with all the powers that were making for right and justice in the world.[125] This was a faith which made possible the politics of the new French Socialism. There was a great gulf fixed between Jaurès and M. Lafargue, who held that "Justice and morals change from one historical epoch to another, according to the interests and needs of the dominant class." [126] The same interpretation is possible for M. Lagardelle's fear in 1901 of "the Radicalization of Socialism," because of the policy of the Millerand ministry interpreted at Saint-Mande.[127]

A new spirit behind the old words of revolution and the jargon of the platform attests to the vitality of Labour politics. England

[123] German Preface to a reissue of the Communist Manifesto, 1872.

[124] Louis, *op. cit.*, p. 272.

[125] A year before the Saint-Mande Programme, MM. Jaurès and Lafargue had a debate in the Latin Quarter which attracted unusual notice; see *Idéalisme et matérialisme dans la conception de l'histoire,* Conference of Jean Jaurès and reply by Paul Lafargue, held in Paris, January 12, 1895 (Lille, 1901), pp. 5-20.

[126] *Ibid.*, pp. 33-34; pp. 21-45 for Lafargue's full reply.

[127] Cf. "Troisième Congrès Général des Organisations Socialistes Françaises," *Compte Rendu* (1901), pp. 91-96; see pp. 77-91, for reply of Jaurès.

fortunately had never been so fully in bondage to the phrases of propaganda, so did not have to suffer the penalty of political disillusion so heavily as did the Labour movement in France.[128] In France it was a common possession of all the groups, largely because "the Republic from 1871-1914 was that of men of a certain political position rather than a social republic." [129] The legislature of 1893-1898 was the first to give any strong support to the legislative functions of the Republic. M. Lockroy said in the Chamber of Deputies, November 23, 1893, "it seems that this Chamber begins a new era"; [130] it was an era convincing men of the truth of what M. Waldeck-Rousseau had said ten years before in the same place, that men were thinking less of "being able to transform our social state by the means or magic of a word or a formula." [131] Yet it did not mean that there was less thought for a "new order of society," nor less belief in its possibility. There had come a fuller appreciation of the democratic idea and the method of its attainment. With a recurring power of interpretation Millerand faced the issues of his day, giving to the struggles of 1893-1902, a vigour of straightforward statement that at times confused his enemies and alienated his friends. No one better stated the cause of Republicanism at the end of the last century in France. In speaking of the problems before society and the Republican parties, he said, July 13, 1898:

Our problem is to prepare and to make easier the inevitable transition from the society of to-day to the society of to-morrow. Republicans above all, we shall combat with our last strength the continuation of the policy of the Right, which is nothing more than a policy of the betrayal of democracy. Sent here by our pledges for Republican and Socialist work, we have taken our position, we have marked our frontiers, we have defined our line of conduct before all the world. It is not in the increase of poverty, it is in the continuous progress, it is in the unceasing amelioration

[128] Cf. Elton, *op. cit.*, for a different view.

[129] Cf. Guy de la Batut and George Friedmann, *A History of the French People,* Introduction by Henri Barbusse (1923), p. 286.

[130] Cf. Paul Detot, *Le socialisme devant les chambres françaises* (1903), pp. 1-5.

[131] Cf. Waldeck-Rousseau, *Discours parlementaires de Waldeck-Rousseau,* speech April 16, 1883, in Chamber of Deputies, pp. 446 seq. qt. by Detot.

of the lot of the workers, that we look for the definite triumph of our ideas.[132]

The evolution of the political ideals of Socialism directly produced the period of Revisionism, which marked the passing of Socialism "from the forum into the Senate." [133] In France the case for the Revisionists was stated by M. Millerand, perhaps better than anyone else, because he had personally to carry out the program that such a policy made inevitable. The period in which his influence began, and in which M. Jaurès came to power, was the middle of the Revisionist struggle.[134] There was the necessity of separating the essential and scientific from that which clung to revolutionary tradition and political preoccupation in the Labour movement.[135] What would be the mechanism of victory for the working class, now that the working class spirit was expressing itself in the modern democratic State? The bankruptcy of scientific socialism had been well nigh declared; but the problem remained as to the method whereby the working class movement was to triumph, and how it was to free itself from the barnacles of an overworked Marxism.[136] Beyond this task was the larger one of interpreting in its parliamentary activities the idealism which has at all times been a part of the movements which have liberalized institutions and made more generous the sympathies of mankind. That was certainly the problem of the French Socialists of the last ten years of the century, above any other besetting obstacle of their progress and development.[137] The history of the parliamentary Socialists of France away from the dogmatic intransigeance of their earlier days, to the wider acceptance of the obligations of political life fully testifies to the break which occurred in French collectivist thought from any early bondage to German social theory, while the activity of the Socialist and Labour members of the 1893-1898 Chamber of Deputies indicated the growing strength of the economic appeal to the Labour movement in France. This fact is to be taken

[132] Detot, *op. cit.*, p. 8.

[133] Cf. Jean Jaurès, *Studies in Socialism,* editor's note, pp. xv-xvii (MacDonald).

[134] Detot, *op. cit.*, p. 8.

[135] Sombart, *op. cit.*, pp. 116-119.

[136] Cf. Jean Jaurès, *Etudes Socialistes* (1908), Introduction on Marx.

[137] Detot, *op. cit.*, p. 177.

together with the emergence of the Neo-Marxism of MM. Sorel and Berth and the eclipse of the political movement over a period of years. From this point of view M. Georges Sorel endeavoured to re-direct the Labour movement in the time of transition when the economic factors and the political were at useless enmity; [138] an enmity which was a part of the Revisionist struggle in France most of all, but very evident in Italy and Germany, and with minor significance in England.[139] While Sorel placed the entire emphasis on the economic side, it was Jaurès who kept insisting on the whole-rounded view of social progress; believing in

> the development of social justice which will abolish the iniquities of nation to nation, as well as the iniquities of individual to individual.[140]
> "But that social emancipation," he held, "that economic emancipation suppose a free working class, educated, informed; suppose in consequence a democracy organised and aggressive preparing for the new order. That is why we are doubly attached to the Republic, as Republicans and as Socialists, and that is why we are doubly attached to the politics of reform, as democrats and as Socialists." [141]

French Socialism had accepted the State, as an instrument of economic change; the problem for the Labour movement was to fulfil its duty in making the agency of the State serviceable for the protection and furtherance of the common good.

[138] Cf. Saverio Merlino, *Formes et essence du socialisme* (Paris, 1898), with a Preface by M. Sorel; this is the French translation of *Pro e contro il socialismo,* from the Italian. Note also Sorel's Preface to N. Colajanni's *Le Socialisme,* translated from the Italian by M. Tacchella (Paris, 1900). M. Colajanni was an Italian deputy. This Preface is published in Sorel's *Matériaux d'une théorie du prolétariat* (2nd ed. Paris, 1921), pp. 175-200. Yet another Preface, written in 1901, for G. Gatti, deputy in the Italian Parliament, for his *Le socialisme et l'agriculture,* published in translation in Paris 1902, and included by Sorel, *op. cit.,* pp. 201-237.

[139] Cf. Edward R. Pease, *op. cit.,* who writes of the Fabian Society: "Its first achievement was to break the spell of Marxism in England. . . . The Fabian Society freed English Socialism from this intellectual bondage, and freed it sooner and more completely than Revisionists have succeeded in doing anywhere else" (p. 236).

[140] Chamber of Deputies, March 7, 1895.

[141] Chamber of Deputies, November 14, 1899.

Part III

The Saint-Mande Programme and the Effort for Socialist Unity, 1896-1900

The unity which Guesde hoped to establish in 1880 in the French Labour movement by following the method of close discipline and political organization of the German type, was brought about in 1896 among the representatives of the Reform, the Marxian and the Revolutionary Socialists in Parliament. This unity among the Socialists in the Chamber of Deputies has been the reason for the progress of the party and for the great influence, often far out of proportion to their numbers, that they have exercised. They have acted as one disciplined body and have gained much by working as a voting unit.[142] The internal political struggles of France between 1877-1889, caused largely by the deputies of the Right,[143] gave the first opportunity of the Socialist members to profit by the mistakes of their opponents. In the twenty-five years from 1889 to 1914 the unity of the Socialist-Radical group, with the Socialists nearly always in alliance, gave to that bloc the domination of the Chamber of Deputies.[144] While the Radical-Socialist group has often been very loosely held together, the Socialists have nearly always been able to maintain an effective unity in the face of the opposition.[145]

This unity has been greatly affected by the political success of Socialism in France and by the necessity, recognized by the leaders, that the party had a definite work to do in maintaining a faith in representative institutions. In the beginning of the political movement there was an enthusiasm which the Radical parties of the various industrial countries have always brought at the first to the game of politics. The success which the Socialist parties obtained in 1893, the first general election at which the

[142] Cf. Bryce, *op. cit.*, Vol. I, pp. 245, 284.

[143] Cf. M. Hauriou, *Precis de droit constitutionnel* (1923), pp. 374-375.

[144] Hauriou, *op. cit.*, p. 377.

[145] Cf. J. O. C. of D. July 1, 1910. *Abbé Lemire:* "If I address myself to you, Socialists, it is because you alone are unified. But when I address myself to the others, to the Radical-Socialists for example, I do not know where that party begins." *M. Aynard (President of Commission):* "One knows less where it ends."

Socialists formed a distinct political party, was described by Guesde to his supporters at Roubaix, as a "true revolution, the beginning of the revolution which will make free men of you." [146] It followed upon the successes gained at the municipal elections of 1888 and 1892 and the legislative election of 1889. The *Parti Ouvrier Français* had had a minimum general program for 1880,[147] which was successively elaborated by the municipal program at the congress of Marseilles in 1892 and Nantes in 1894, and the maritime program developed at the congress of Rouilly in 1895 and at Lille in 1896.[148]

The fact that a definite program of immediate reforms had been put before the country compelled the party constantly to enlarge and popularize its method of appeal to the working class, whom they hoped to win to the general acceptance of the Socialist party as the political means for the gaining of reforms which the Labour movement demanded. The Parliamentary Socialist group numbered about fifty in 1893; some were doubtful followers of the full party program, but each success that was gained made more imperative the unity of the Socialist group. This was also made necessary by the unusual influence of the Labour and Socialist members in the legislature from 1893 to 1898,[149] due largely to the skilled talents of MM. Millerand, Jaurès and Viviani as parliamentarians. In this group the two veterans Guesde and Vaillant have a valued place, for day in and day out they put on record the often dull and dry history of social legislation in all countries, demanding from the State active participation in the remedying of industrial ills.[150] It was the interpellation of Jaurès and Millerand on November 21, 1893, that led to the downfall of the Dupuy ministry.[151] M. Charles Dupuy had ex-

[146] Cf. A. Zévaès, *Les Guesdistes* (1911), pp. 86-87, qt. message of Guesde in *L'Autorité,* September 25, 1893.

[147] *Ibid.,* pp. 9-11, for this program.

[148] *Ibid.,* pp. 73-84, for these programs.

[149] Cf. P. Detot, *Le socialisme devant les chambres françaises* (1902) for one of the best and earliest surveys of the period.

[150] Besides the programs which represent the growing tendency toward emphasis on universal suffrage and parliamentary struggle the debates are instructive; see especially Jules Guesde, *Quatre ans de lutte de classe à la chambre* (1893-1898), two volumes (1901).

[151] Cf. Albert Orry, *Les Socialistes Indépendants* (1911), p. 22.

pressed strong opposition to Socialism,[152] Jaurès denounced the attack made by the Government on the Socialist party, declaring that such a policy could not be carried out save by the desertion of republican principles.[153] For the defence and support of these principles the Parliamentary Socialist party was committed. The election of 1893 had been fought on the social question, said Millerand;[154] and the general rule of the Socialists in their activity in Parliament and in the elections was the constant and rigorous practise of republican discipline.[155] During the sixth legislature the Socialists gave unwavering support time after time to the Bourgeois Ministry when it was in power.[156] The party deputies had attained a pivotal place under this leadership, helping to maintain the republican majority.[157] Under these favourable circumstances a common tactical basis was essential, and the basis of the unity for the Parliamentary bloc was given by M. Millerand at the Banquet of Saint-Mande on May 30, 1896, following the municipal election successes of that year.[158]

For an understanding of the support which the Socialists in Parliament gave to the ministry of Waldeck-Rousseau the Saint-Mande Programme is a most useful document, besides being the classic exposition in France of Parliamentary Socialism.[159] It is important also because it provided the basis for the union of the Parliamentary bloc, and even went farther, offering a minimum program upon which the French Socialist movement was based. It

[152] See J. O., November 26, 1893, for the long debate on the ministerial declaration.

[153] Cf. A. Zévaès, *Le socialisme en France depuis 1871*, p. 155.

[154] Cf. A. Orry, *op. cit.*, p. 20, for Millerand's Address to the electors.

[155] Cf. J. L. Breton, *L'Unité Socialiste* (1912), p. 54.

[156] Breton, *op. cit.*, pp. 55-57.

[157] Cf. Léon Blum, *Les Congrès Ouvriers et Socialistes Français*, vol. II, 1886-1900 (1901), p. 157; see also *Quatrième Congrès Général du Parti Socialiste Français, Compte Rendu*, Tours, 1902, p. 213; and *Compte Rendu, Deuxième Congrès Général des Organisations Socialistes Françaises*, Paris, 1900, Report of the Parliamentary Group, pp. 88, 95-98.

[158] Cf. A. Orry, *op. cit.*, pp. 18-32.

[159] The Saint-Mande Program has been compared with a closely contemporary English program, the Report on Fabian policy which was presented to the London International Congress of June, 1896, Fabian Tract No. 70; see R. C. K. Ensor, *Modern Socialism* (3rd ed. London, 1910), p. 48. The Fabian Tracts provide a fairly good commentary on economic and political problems in England since 1884.

is essential for the interpretation of the Labour movement of the first years of the twentieth century.

The audience before which it was given was composed of the leaders of all the larger Socialist groups in France, including Jaurès, Guesde and Edouard Vaillant, and the provincial leaders of the political labour movement. All gave their unanimous approval to the program set down by Millerand,[160] which was the common ground of Socialist union when the projects of republican defense were put forward from 1898-1899. Most important of all this program was the declaration of principles of the first Socialist minister of France, and of the first outstanding parliamentary leader of the modern Labour movement that had been called to take part in the Government of his country. It was the complete statement of his belief in evolutionary or parliamentary Socialism. While in office Millerand stated that his policy was based upon the Saint-Mande Programme; that the Ministry of Commerce and Industry attempted to put into practice the objectives of that declaration.[161]

The Saint-Mande Programme laid down the minimum program of Socialism:

"At the stage of development which the Socialist party has reached," M. Millerand said, "I consider it to be its interest as well as its duty to define its frontiers with all possible precision. Whither is it going? By what paths does it propose to attain its end? Is it true that it has for its aim the suppression of liberty and confiscation of property, for its means the recourse to force? These are the traits on which our opponents of every kind usually agree in delineating the Socialist party. Yet does it not appear on the face of it that all the points of this pretended definition—suppression of property, recourse to force—form the crudest antithesis, the most brutal contradiction, to our doctrines as well as our facts? Is not the Socialist idea completely summed up in the earnest desire to secure for every being in the bosom of

[160] Cf. M. A. Briand's speech at Lyons Congress, *Compte Rendu Troisième Congrès Général Organisations Socialistes Françaises* (Lyons, 1901), pp. 301-325, one of the best statements on the period.

[161] Cf. Millerand's speech at Lens, October 7, 1900, in A. Lavy's *L'Oeuvre de Millerand, Un Ministre Socialiste* (Juin 1899-Janvier, 1902) (1902), pp. 409-415, also A. Millerand, *Politique de Réalisations* (1911), pp. 288-301, on the "XXe Anniversaire Du Mandat Législatif," before his constituents.

society, the unimpaired development of his personality? That necessarily implies two conditions, of which one is a factor of the other: first individual appropriation of things necessary for the security and development of the individual, *i.e.*, property; secondly, liberty, which is only a sounding and hollow word if it is not based on and safeguarded by property."

The description of the anarchy of capitalism was characterized by stating that under it there was no security for anyone. Farmers, merchants, manufacturers, intellectuals as well as manual workers, were the prey of every chance. Collectivism was the escape from this excess of ill which led to a new

feudal class being set up, which is accumulating in its hands the ownership of the instruments of production, to become by a slow but implacable progress the absolute master of the economic, political and moral life of the whole people, reduced by it to the modern form of slavery called the wages system.

The most exact Marxian interpretation was followed by M. Millerand so far as he outlined the development of capitalistic society which replaced "individual property, the condition and safeguard of liberty, by the tyrannous monopoly of a minority." Collectivism

does not rebel against this observed fact; it bows before it. It does not pretend to retrace the course of the centuries, nor decree the transformation of mankind; on the contrary, it adapts itself to its rules. Since it is a law of sociological evolution that all the means of production and exchange pass from the form of individual property to that of capitalistic property, withers and dies, in that proportion social property should replace capitalistic.

However valuable the contribution of the Marxian emphasis it is certain that its deterministic philosophy has not provided the highest motives for social transformation, and the definitive materialism of such a statement of M. Millerand's (so marked in much of French Socialistic writing), helps to explain the revolt of the younger men in the revolutionary syndicalist movement. The sterility of the merely Collectivist solution of the industrial break-down, and the appeal to the necessarily slow and experimental aid of Parliament, became increasingly evident as the complex problems of business and trade organization were more clearly understood and men were convinced that the State alone could not be the means of saving the social and economic order. But Millerand's appeal indicates the reliance that was put in the State.[162] His program demanded much faith in the power of Socialism:

"If Socialism to-day," he said, "dominates and overshadows every party, if it attracts and retains the passionate interest of every cultivated mind, if it thrills every generous heart, it is because in its large synthesis it embraces every manifestation of life, because nothing human is alien to it, because it alone offers to-day to our hunger for justice and happiness an ideal purely human and apart from all dogma."[163]

For the realization of this ideal there was only one way, universal suffrage, for social transformation could be got from no rebel minority but from a majority with a purpose.

Resort to force?—for whom and against whom? Republicans before everything, we do not indulge the crazy idea of appealing to a pretender's sham prestige or a dictator's sword to secure the triumph of our doctrines. We appeal only to universal suffrage. It is the voter that we want to set economically and politically free. We claim only the right of persuading him. I do not suppose that anyone will credit us with the absurd intention of taking revolutionary steps against the Senate, which a Radical

[162] An interesting contrast to the point of view of Millerand and a definite statement of a well-defined English point of view is found in J. Shield Nicholson's *Historical Progress and Ideal Socialism* (London, 1894), an evening discourse delivered to the British Association at Oxford in the Sheldonian Theatre, 13th August, 1894. This was the first occasion on which the section of Economics and Statistics had been called upon for one of the evening discourses.

[163] It is worth while noting the aloofness of Millerand's social philosophy, "purely human and apart from all dogma," as he called it, and the attitude of such theorizing purists as Sorel and Berth. The contrast with certain English thinkers is suggested later. See Guido De Ruggiero, *Modern Philosophy,* translated by A. Howard Hannay and R. G. Collingwood (London, 1921), pp. 219-224; for a much more extended account see J. Alexander Gunn, *Modern French Philosophy: A Study of the Development Since Comte,* with a Foreword by Henri Bergson (New York, 1922).

Ministry, had it vacillated less, would have sufficed to have restored to reason. No, to realise the immediate reforms capable of relieving the lot of the working class, and thus fitting it to win its own freedom, and to begin, as conditioned by the nature of things, the socialisation of the means of production, it is necessary and sufficient for the Socialist party to endeavour to capture the Government through universal suffrage.[164]

Such a faith in the efficacy of political control indicated a belief in the constructive power of the Labour movement.[165] The Saint-Mande Programme had its counterpart in the famous *Circulaire* of August 25, 1884, issued by M. Waldeck-Rousseau, while Minister of Interior in the Jules Ferry Cabinet. This Circular made known the views of the Government on the application of the law of March 21, 1884,[166] expressing the policy of Waldeck-Rousseau as Minister of Interior in 1884,[167] and the views of the leader of the French nation at the beginning of the twentieth century when the Republic was beset by military intrigue and social anarchy. It is worth while noting that from 1884, the "syndical period of legislation," a great deal had been done to make possible the alliance which was an effective force in the ministry of M. Waldeck-Rousseau during the critical period of 1898-1902. The Saint-Mande Programme and the Circular of Waldeck-Rousseau form together a working commentary on the ideas and spirit of the two leaders whose definite task when called to power was the maintenance of republican institutions.

The *Circulaire* explained the serious change in the status of the syndicates. In emphasis on the duty of the Prefects and the formulation of means and methods of carrying out the provisions of the law a turning point is marked in the adminstrative

[164] For the Saint-Mande Programme, see A. Lavy, *op. cit.*, pp. 426-438; for English translation see R. C. K. Ensor, *op. cit.*, pp. 48-55.

[165] Cf. Millerand's address of July 12, 1900, before the co-operative societies on the "workers' century," to create and direct as they will, Lavy, *op. cit.*, pp. 404-408; see also M. Duboin, "La Législation Sociale à la Fin du XIXe Siècle" (1900), pp. 9-13, with regard to Millerand's official efforts.

[166] Cf. J. O. C. of D., August 28, 1884, for this ministerial circular; also *Bull. Off. Ministry of Interior* (1884), p. 409.

[167] Cf. Henry Leyret, *De Waldeck-Rousseau à la C. G. T. La Société et les Syndicats* (2nd ed. Paris, 1921), Introduction, pp. 27-38; "the syndicalism of 1920 was in the law of 1884."

development of French labour legislation. For the first time the problem of administration was put to the forefront and made the basis of the successful working out of a law. Professor Pic takes the passing of the law of May 19, 1874, which carried with it the means of effective supervision and inspection, as the beginning of French Labour legislation, but the law of 1884 went even farther in laying down positive instructions on administration and defining the spirit behind the law.[168]

The Prefects were reminded of their "most serious duty"; that though the State in its rôle was to see that the law was strictly observed, the Prefects could do much "to favour the spirit of association" and to stimulate and make easier the use of "this law of liberty," because among the workingmen there were difficulties and inexperience which had arisen because this liberty had not existed before. The dominant purpose of the Government and the Chambers in the elaboration of the law had been the development among workingmen of the spirit of association. In fact the legislators had gone farther than that in their thought, for they hoped that these professional associations would be "less a weapon of struggle than an instrument of material, moral and intellectual progress"; legal protection and recognition had been given them "to carry on to a higher degree of usefulness their beneficent activity." The institutions which had produced among the people such splendid results must be made more useful and should be multiplied, such as old-age pension funds, mutual credit banks, libraries, co-operative societies, bureaux of employment, statistics and wages, etc. It was the wish of the Government and of the Chambers to see the development in the largest possible measure of the trade associations and of the institutions which they were destined to create.

Urging the Prefects to aid in bringing about the fullest usefulness of the law, Waldeck-Rousseau stated that in passing the law the Government and the Chambers did not let themselves be frightened by the hypothetical peril of an anti-social federation of all the workers, but hoped that the "new liberty" which had

[168] *Op. cit.*, pp. 77-79; see also the speech of M. Waldeck-Rousseau in the Senate, February 2, 1884, on article 5 of the law, permitting union of syndicates, an early settlement of his doctrine of *Solidarité* (pp. 217-230, Leyret, *op. cit.*)

been given to the workers in full confidence of the wisdom which they had so many times shown, would initiate in the minds of the most humble a conception of the great problems of economics and society.

It was further added that the Government felt the obligation of administration in making the law effective, and that the Prefects should give "active assistance in the organization of syndicates and syndical institutions," keeping always in mind that "the rôle of republican administration consisted in aiding and not in complicating." [169]

Such was the attitude of one of the many English and French statesmen who have been each called "the last of the Liberals"; [170] and there would have been little more than the accustomed opposition to the support of the Socialists for the Government which he formed had not the Ministry included General de Galliffet, against whom there was an undying hatred on the part of many in the Labour movement for his connection with the suppression of the Commune.[171] But when Millerand decided to accept office under Waldeck-Rousseau, he was supported by Jaurès, Briand, Viviani and Fournière; their common agreement was that the country was in peril, but for Guesde and Vaillant the entrance of a Socialist in a bourgeois Government violated the principle of the class struggle. The *Comité d'Entente* considered the question the 23rd of June, 1899, but went no further than passing a resolution that it was only on his own responsibility that a deputy of the party had entered the new ministry. The national council of the *Parti Ouvrier Français* met the next day and declared that there was nothing in common between the representatives of the party and a ministry which counted among its number "le fusilleur de Mai." [172] In the Chamber the Socialist deputies were divided

[169] Compare with this early policy the development of the idea in M. Paul-Boncour's *Le Fédéralisme Economique* (Paris, 1900), to which M. Waldeck-Rousseau added a Preface, and his *Les syndicats de fonctionnaires* with Preface by Anatole France (1905), chap. III.

[170] Cf. Paul Reynauld, *Waldeck-Rousseau* (Paris, 1913). Herbert Lagardelle wrote in *Le Mouvement Socialiste* that Waldeck-Rousseau would remain the last type of the French Liberals.

[171] Cf. *La République de Galliffet, La République de Millerand* (Paris, 1899), an eight page pamphlet indicating popular feeling at time; also Breton, *op. cit.*, p. 58.

[172] Cf. Orry, *op. cit.*, p. 42.

on the vote of confidence in the new Ministry; some voting for the ministerial declaration,[173] others abstaining.

President Loubet charged M. Waldeck-Rousseau with the duty of constituting a Cabinet of "Republican Defense," when the third ministry of Dupuy fell. France needed the strong hand of a master. From 1896 the forces of reaction and conspiracy had grown in power and effrontery, reaching a climax in the rioting at Auteuil when President Loubet was assaulted. "The year of hatred," as 1899 was called, made France a victim of the mobs of Paris and the intrigues of the Nationalists, the Clericals and the Militarists.[174]

The phrase "a Cabinet of Republican Defense," suggests the resolution that forced out of office M. Méline and his Government of Moderates, when the Chamber declared that the Government should depend upon "an exclusively Republican majority." M. Brisson with his Republican-Concentration Cabinet,[175] preceded the ministerial crisis of 1899 when Waldeck-Rousseau decided to follow the counsel of republican leaders who saw the only hope of the Republic in an "alliance of the bourgeoisie and of the working class." [176] This condition was seen much earlier by Gambetta as a condition of maintaining the Republic.[177] And at this time the

[173] Cf. *Les Déclarations Ministérielles et les Ministères* (du 4 Septembre, 1870, au Ier Janvier, 1914), Guy Lavaud (1914), pp. 95-96, for the declaration; see also J. O., 27 June, 1899.

[174] An English philosopher viewed the dangers besetting the French Republic (December, 1898) as tests applied to the strength of the national idea. "If the idea cannot maintain itself, we must reluctantly suppose that it ought not—that the common life has not the necessary depth." In 1919 he added, "The question seems to have answered itself." See Bernard Bosanquet, *The Philosophical Theory of the State* (3rd ed. 1920), pp. 299 n 1. Cf. A. Hassall, *The French People* (1902), pp. 363-377.

[175] Cf. Parl. Doc. *Les Déclarations Ministerielles et les Ministères,* pp. 86-94, for this period.

[176] Cf. G. Hanotaux, *op. cit.,* Vol. II, p. 181; it may be mentioned that M. Hanotaux was a member of the second Dupuy Ministry (May 30, 1894, to January 26, 1895); the third Ribot Ministry (January 26 to November 1, 1895); and the Meline Ministry (April 29, 1896, to June 28, 1898).

[177] Cf. Paul Mantoux, *Lectures on the History of the Nineteenth Century* (Cambridge, 1902); no. ix, pp. 171-192, "Two Statesmen of the Third Republic" (Thiers and Gambetta); "Waldeck-Rousseau as a political pupil of Gambetta and his democratic tradition," pp. 191-192; and H. A. L. Fisher, *op. cit.,* pp. 280-301.

Socialist leader Paul Brousse, who had led the opposition which caused the first rupture in French Socialism, at the Saint-Etienne Congress in 1882, could write in *La Petite République,* that

> the safety of the country is the supreme law. When it is in danger, it is necessary to exhaust all measures of defense, equally the legal arms as well as the revolutionary means.[178]

The address[179] of M. Paul Deschanel, who had been re-elected President of the Senate, opening the Chamber on January 11, indicated that the movement of anti-parliamentarianism had only revealed more plainly the need of orderly constituted Government, and the "respect for justice which is the foundation of the State." His concern was that France should guard the "principle of justice which she has always represented in the world"; her *raison d'être* was the defence of the "rights of the human person and respect for the forms of justice." M. Deschanel declared that

> during the last twenty years the essential rules of parliamentary government and the very spirit of the constitution have received blows from which the country suffers, and a consequence is that certain ills are imputed to parliamentary institutions when they are the result of a misapplication of those principles.

Yet he felt it was given to France at the end of the nineteenth century to show to the world, in the International Exposition, "the glorification of labour, the encyclopædia of the efforts accomplished to ameliorate human life, the picture of the conquests of universal genius."

The day before, January 10, M. Léon Bourgeois at a dinner given by the Committee of Action for Republican Reforms, had warned against the subversive forces from the Right and the extremes of reaction which threatened the Government on all sides; which fear was again emphasized when on January 12, in receiving the office-bearers of the Chamber, President Loubet urged the union of all Republican deputies in defence, with him,

[178] August 7, 1899, quoted by Sylvain Humbert, *Les Possibilistes* (1911), p. 80.

[179] J. O. C. of D., Jan. 12, 1900, pp. 5-6.

of the Constitution and of the parliamentary system.[180] To an outside political observer it appeared that

the Republic exists because it exists. It exists because the great mass of the people have rallied to it, and ask nothing better than to preserve it, but it wishes to preserve the Republic in peace, and it cannot be counted upon at moments of supreme crisis when the Republic has to be defended, otherwise than by simple adhesion and vote. What the Nationalists are looking for is a man, and everyone knows what this word means; a Boulanger, a Roget, who consents, a general ready to risk his head to obtain the supreme place.[181]

The Ministry of Waldeck-Rousseau began its work of defense and social pacification under such a condition of affairs.[182] The fact that M. Millerand was asked to take office as Minister of Commerce and Industry, indicated a reliance upon the Left, and the increasing power and influence of this group.[183] Up until 1905 when the Socialists refused to co-operate with bourgeois Governments, the Union of the various groups of the Left with the Radicals was the condition of maintaining a ministerial majority.[184] M. Waldeck-Rousseau resigned office June 6, 1902, after

[180] It should be kept in mind that often certain official phrases are used after they cease to have their original meaning, but the bitter and cruel struggle of this period must have a real place in an understanding of the parliamentary history of the French people at the beginning of the century; it is especially to be kept in mind when one reflects that no such crisis could have occurred in England.

[181] London *Times,* January 3, 1900, p. 6, Paris correspondent of *Times.*

[182] Bryce has emphasized the "difference in preparation of France and England for a Parliamentary democracy" (Vol. I, pp. 327 ff.), finding "since the death of Gambetta no single leader of dominating personality" (p. 298). Under hard conditions Waldeck-Rousseau held office longer than any premier since 1875. Commenting on the state of France one critic declared that "the elections of 1898 sent to the Palais Bourbon the most turbulent chamber of any that the Third Republic had produced. In its usurpation of judicial and executive functions it has treated the principle of the separation of powers after the manner of a convention and not of a Parliament." (J. E. C. Bodley, *France,* 1900 edition, p. xxiv.)

[183] Cf. Seignobos, *L'Evolution de la 3rd République,* pp. 211-216 and p. 288.

[184] Cf. A. Zévaès, *Le parti socialiste de 1904 à 1923* (1923), pp. 13-46; also J. L. Breton, *op. cit.,* pp. 54-87, for one of the best criticisms of the class struggle in Parliament by a careful writer with much experience of what he recounts and interprets.

winning a general election, when his Ministry had a majority of more than fifty votes. He was succeeded by M. Coombs, 1902-1905, who largely lacked the capacity of effective leadership,[185] or the ability to direct the republican forces against the combined reactionary tendencies of his opponents.[186] The problem of maintaining democratic institutions was to the fore in all of the political and economic struggles of the Government.[187]

In the face of such serious political crises as beset the French Labour movement it is remarkable that the effort for unity and a common organization of forces could have gone on with so much of success. But the very difficulties which beset the nation seemed to make more determined the will of the most thoughtful leaders. Although unity among the representatives of the various Socialist groups in Parliament preceded by two years the forming of a committee of the parties for joint action (October, 1898), the *Parti Ouvrier Français,* under the skilful direction of Jaurès, at the Congress of the party at Montlucon in September, 1898, opened the way for Socialist unity. This Congress held that the crisis which the clericals and nationalists had brought upon the country demanded an unitary organization of the working class, and approved a project which would unite the five Socialist organizations, expressing the concerted action of the militant and revolutionary workers.[188] The resolution which was passed at

[185] Cf. Parl. Doc., *Les Déclarations Ministerielles et les Ministères,* pp. 95-102.

[186] Cf. Ernest Dimnet, *France Herself Again* (1914) (Tr.), for a partisan criticism against M. Coombs, with some degree of bitterness; the Church controversy and the split in the Socialist ranks were more to account for the lack of persistent policy, both of which M. Dimnet overlooks. If Jaurès had had a united backing Coombs would have been stronger; his entire administration was a very critical one.

[187] The stormy parliamentary sessions of 1905 can be instructive; see especially the two days' debate on the Vazeille interpellation on the general policy of the Government: J. O. C. of D., January 14, 1905, S. O., pp. 11-23; J. O., January 15, 1905, S. O., pp. 27-52. These pages cover the chief speeches of the Left for the Government; Zévaès (pp. 19-21); Vaillant (pp. 22-23); Jaurès (pp. 46-48); and the survey from 1902 of M. Coombs (pp. 31-39); note the chief opposition speech, M. Paul Deschanel (pp. 16-19), who said Coombs had "abdicated." The Government carried the order of the day by a majority of ten, pp. 289-279, but M. Coombs declared he could not carry on under the circumstances.

[188] Cf. Léon Blum, *Les Congrès Ouvriers et Socialistes Français,* Vol. II, pp. 166-169.

the Congress stated that the central organization for proletariat defence and for the Republic would include the *Parti Ouvrier Français*, the *Comité Révolutionnaire Central*, the *Fédération des Travailleurs Socialistes*, the *Parti Ouvrier Socialiste Révolutionnaire* and the *Socialistes Indépendants*.[189] The Independents were unorganized, but were to form a national group and take the Saint-Mande Programme as their base.[190] Delegates from each of the five groups would constitute the representative committee of the *Union Centrale*.[191] These organizations formed at the first meeting the *Comité de Vigilance*.[192] This Committee adopted a motion declaring that the revolutionary forces were united and resolute against all eventualities; it protested against the attacks on the liberty of the workers and made a strong appeal to all of the working class to join together in the defence of the republic. This appeal was signed by two representatives of the five organizations and the delegates from the Socialist press. Among those who signed the appeal were Guesde, Vaillant, Brousse, Jaurès, Briand, Millerand and Viviani.[193] It is interesting to note that in this group were three future Premiers and a president of the Republic, an interpretative commentary on the Socialist movement of France at the beginning of the century.[194] It also represented the leadership of the entire Socialist party at the end of the nineteenth century, and indicates the tremendously high feeling which characterized all of the activities of the Labour movement in France at the beginning of the new era. Out of the many proposals and debates which follow closely on this period one can understand how the working class movement attempted to meet the issues, and how the Republic sought to

[189] Article 1. [190] *Ibid.* [191] Article 2.

[192] At this meeting the *Parti Ouvrier Français* had 25 mandates; the *Parti Socialiste Revolutionnaire*, 15; the *Parti Ouvrier Socialiste Revolutionnaire*, 12; the *Federation Des Travailleurs Socialistes*, 5; *L'Alliance Communiste*, 8; the *Federation Republicaine Socialiste de la Seine*, 5; the *Coalition Revolutionnaire*, 5 (Briand held one of these); and the Socialist press 5, two of these including Millerand and Jaurès.

[193] Cf. *Le Mouvement Socialiste*, January, 1899, for the full plan and program of Socialist unity by Jaurès.

[194] Cf. Etienne Fournal, *Le Modern Plutarque ou les Hommes Illustres de la IIIe République* (1923), pp. 151-174, for a study of M. Briand, which is also an estimate on the forces which influenced his political life.

maintain that social compromise which the legislation of the period very fully represents.[195]

The *Comité de Vigilance,* in November, 1898, decided in favour of a permanent central organization of the Socialist groups, which was formed December 11, 1898, and named the *Comité d'Entente.* It included the five Socialist organizations named above, taking the Saint-Mande Programme as the base. The substitution of the collectivist for the capitalistic régime, the conquest of political power, and the international entente of all workers, were the major principles held in common. The decisions of the Committee were required to be unanimous, so it is easily understood why the deliberations would become tedious and often sterile.[196] But soon there was an opportunity for the *Comité d'Entente* to be useful. The entrance of Millerand in the Waldeck-Rousseau Cabinet was the signal for the French Labour movement to divide;[197] those who regarded the action of Millerand as a repudiation of the idea of class warfare joining with Guesde and Vaillant, while Jaurès, Brousse and the Independants defended the policy of participation. So acting on the proposal of Jaurès to Guesde and Vaillant, the *Comité d'Entente* called for a congress in Paris of the French working class, where the whole of the French Labour movement would be represented. The *Cas Millerand* was the most grave event which had taken place since 1871 in the history of the French working class; it was the dividing of the world of the worker and the revolutionary into two parts—deciding in effect if French Socialism should remain bound by the limitations of the movement which was represented by the Communist Manifesto of 1848 and the *Parti Ouvrier Français* in 1880, or, if participating in bourgeois Government, it would become a political faction, a neo-radicalism, a wing of the Republican party.[198]

The Congress which was called begins the direct study of the Labour movement of this century, and is the logical turning point in the historical development of the ideas and organization of the French working class.

[195] Cf. Scelle, *op. cit.*, p. 13.

[196] Cf. Paul Louis, *Histoire du parti socialiste en France,* 1871-1914, p. 20.

[197] Cf. Paul Louis, *Histoire du socialisme français,* pp. 272-273.

[198] *Ibid.*

CHAPTER IV

SOCIAL LEGISLATION IN ENGLAND, 1900-1925

DURING October, 1900, the fifteenth and last Parliament of Queen Victoria was elected. It was also the first Parliament of Edward VII. The number of general Acts placed on the Statute Book by the 1900 (63 & 64 Vict.) session was 63, five more than in the session of 1899; and in the 1901 (64 Vict. & I Edw. VII) Parliament about 300 Bills were introduced, 40 receiving Royal assent. The ever increasing work [1] of the House of Commons can be readily seen in the volume and the scope of the Bills submitted to it, even though the first two Parliaments of this century were largely engaged in the business of carrying the military activities of the nation to a successful finish. From 1900 to 1914 the duties of "the omnicompetent Parliament" did not become less. The Report of the Select Committee on Procedure in 1914 stated that the problem was not a new one nor confined to the House of Commons, presenting itself

> in almost every more or less popularly elected legislative assembly in all countries where modern views as to the duties of the State are finding expression, and the vastly complicated social, industrial and commercial problems of our time are pressing for solution.[2]

It was increasingly evident that the effort by democracy to control legislation was creating entirely new parliamentary conditions,

[1] See volumes of Public Acts. From 1909 to 1914 may be noted: 9 Edw. VII, 1909, 49; 10 Edw. VII & 1 Geo. V, 1910, 38; 1 & 2 Geo. V, 1911, 58; 2 & 3 Geo. V, 1912-13, 31; 3 & 4 Geo. V, 1913, 38; 4 & 5 Geo. V, 1914, 91.

[2] *Parliamentary Papers of the House of Commons* (1914), No. VII, p. 599. Cf. Sir Courtenay Ilbert's *The Mechanics of Law Making* (N. Y., 1914), chapters I and IX, "The Legislature and the Draftsman" and "Some Characteristics of Modern Legislation" and his *Legislative Methods and Forms* (1901, Oxford), chapter on Parliament as a legislative machine.

and that some means would have to be found to satisfy the demand for democratic control and at the same time give Parliament a necessary freedom from the slavery of detail. The incongruous position forced upon the members of Parliament of voting in less than five hours £42,000,000,[3] and then for days considering Bills dealing with Boiler Registration and Inspection, is just as pertinent commentary on the Parliament of 1900[4] as the Report of the Select Committee on Procedure. Direct control of legislation made both possible.

The 1900 election had been fought mainly over the issue of the South African War. The embittered feelings of the time were expressed in the extended debate on the Address, finding an outlet in personal bitterness and recrimination. Members of the Government had especially to look to their financial connections, and at the same time to hear that it was "no excuse for presumptuous ignorance that it is directed by insolent passion."[5] The leader of the Opposition centred attack on the Government on war policies and failure to adequately meet the internal problems of the country. He claimed the full right of criticism; it was "the very time for effective criticism," if the nation was to understand the issues of the day. The Address[6] had omitted any reference to measures dealing effectively with overcrowded and insanitary dwellings and old-age pensions, the two great social

[3] June 19, 1900; a few days before the close of the session of 1904, the sum of £28,000,000 was voted *en bloc* without discussion, adds Sir Sidney Low. See *The Governance of England,* Revised Edition 1914 (1st ed. 1904), p. 90n, also 90-94.

[4] Cf. James F. Hope, *History of the 1900 Parliament* (1908).

[5] Hansard, 4 S., Vol. LXXVIII, 1900, p. 787; Mr. John Burns quoting Burke.

[6] Hansard, *op. cit.,* p. 4. The official statement of the Government on the internal affairs of the country was: "The time is not propitious for any domestic reforms which involve a large expenditure. Amendments are required in the laws which govern limited liability companies and those which relate to agricultural tenancies. Measures for amending the law of ecclesiastical assessments, and in regard to education in Scotland, and for the relief of tithe-rent payers in Ireland, will also be laid before you. Your attention will also be invited to proposals for better enabling local authorities to aid secondary and technical education in England and Wales; for controlling the contracts of money lenders; for the amendment of the Factory Law, of the Law of Lunacy, and of the Housing of the Working Classes Act."

questions that the people were concerned with most intimately.[7]

Criticism against the Government on the ground of its failure to consider the insistent claims of social reform was particularly a feature of the debates on the Mines (Eight Hours) Bill, the Housing of the Working Classes (1890) Amendment and the Old Age Pensions Bill. The Government were reminded time and time again that the pledges of 1895 were to be honoured; that they were responsible for the great majority which the Government received in that election. In the debate on the Sale of Intoxicating Liquors to Children, it was declared that

> their great majority was given to the Government in 1895 for a specific purpose, and that was to devote their attention to matters of social legislation for this country.[8]

The Government accepted this point of view. In the debate on the Old Age Pensions Bill, a Government supporter[9] stated that "in the general election of 1895 prominence was given to subjects of social character," and that "the promise of social amelioration in their program had very much to do with the return of the Unionist party at the general election of 1895." It was added that the great majority of the promises had been fulfilled.

It was to be expected when such an issue as the Khaki Election centred upon was predominantly to the front that "democratic control over legislation" would be slight.[10] Nevertheless it was impossible for the Government to be unmindful of the imperative problems of keeping the machinery set up by past legislation functioning and the necessity of bringing the administration of the laws constantly into touch with actual needs. There were parliamentary achievements in the years 1900-1901 which meant progress in industrial legislation by extension and application of principles of State interference which had before been accepted. Within this period were passed the Mines (Prohibition of Child

[7] The two chief speeches of Sir Henry Campbell-Bannerman, leader of the Opposition, on the Address were on January 30, Hansard, Vol. LXXVIII, pp. 79-111; and February 6, *ibid.*, pp. 803-814.

[8] Hansard, Vol. LXXX, p. 521 (Mr. John Wilson).

[9] *Ibid.*, pp. 312-313 (Sir J. Fortescue Flannery).

[10] Cf. J. Ramsay MacDonald, *Socialism and Government*, Vol. II, pp. 7-8; and Hope, *op. cit.*, pp. 1-7.

Labour Underground) Act,[11] an enlarged Workmen's Compensation Act,[12] the Railway Employment (Prevention of Accidents) Act,[13] the Merchant Shipping (Liability of Shipowners and others) Act,[14] and the epochal Factory and Workshop Act, 1901.[15] From 1901 to 1905 the Government had much more definitely a hard problem of social politics in dealing with the rights of the Trade Unions and with the whole Government policy toward social reform.

With regard to social reform there was a spirit of compromise and agreement upon many principles. But in 1900 in debate Mr. Bryce (as he then was) stated that

we are in a perpetual dilemma between Government interference on the one hand and the danger of removing individual responsibility on the other. I don't believe it will ever be possible to find a general principle to guide us satisfactorily between the two extremes of this dilemma. All we can do is, in each case, to try and reconcile individual responsibility with so much Government interference as is necessary to deal with the evil. If we look back fifty or sixty years it will be found that we have always had to accept the doctrines of both sides and endeavour to steer between them.[16]

Yet the country became restive under such counsel, for it wanted bolder, larger schemes of action. The War brought bitter weariness to many, while it encouraged cautious plans for leaders. One who had studied his century honestly and had thought much upon his changing time wrote to an American friend:

The prospect of coming to an end is sometimes cheered for me by the thought that at any rate I shall hear no more of preferential tariffs and protection.[17]

On the other hand the veteran Labour leader, J. Keir Hardie, could appeal to Mr. John Morley to cut himself adrift from the

[11] 63 & 64 Vict. c. 21.
[12] 63 & 64 Vict. c. 22.
[13] 63 & 64 Vict. c. 27.
[14] 63 & 64 Vict. c. 32.
[15] 1 Edw. VII, c. 22.
[16] Hansard 4 S. H. C. 1900, Vol. LXXX, pp. 306-308.
[17] Leslie Stephen in letter to Charles Eliot Norton, October 12, 1903, in F. W. Maitland's *The Life and Letters of Leslie Stephen* (1906), p. 485.

"Rosebery-Asquith" section of Liberalism, and give a lead to democracy. An open letter to Mr. Morley declared that

a section of very earnest Liberals are thoroughly ashamed of modern Liberalism and are anxious to put themselves right with their own consciences. Working class movements are coming together in a manner, for a parallel to which we require to go back to the early days of the Radical movement. Already, 212,000 have paid affiliation fees to the Labour Representation Committee. What is wanted to fuse these elements is a man with the brain to dare, the hand to do, and the heart to inspire. Will you be that man?[18]

Of the Trade Union Congress at Leicester in 1903 one wrote that

The enthusiasm and earnestness for Labour Representation are most marked. One feels as if at last one could almost see the masses becoming articulate and determined to look after themselves and improve themselves by united action instead of grumbling about what the people they elect, who have other points of view from themselves, do or don't do.[19]

It could be said that even in 1903 some thought that it was possible for Parliament to help individuals in building the City of God in this world, dwelling upon dwelling, street upon street.[20]

The beginning of the century, April 23, 1901, saw the first complete Socialist declaration made in the House of Commons by J. Keir Hardie, who unluckily was last on the private members' ballot. One wrote that the Prime Minister was drawn there by the metaphysical curiosity of the Scot to amuse himself by hearing what a brother Scot had to say on Socialism.[21]

Twenty minutes before midnight Hardie offered his resolution:

That considering the increasing burden which the ownership of land and capital is imposing upon the industrious and useful classes of the community, the poverty and destitution and general

[18] *J. Keir Hardie: A Biography,* by William Stewart, with an Introduction by J. Ramsay MacDonald (1921), quoted p. 161. Hardie later made the same appeal to Mr. Lloyd George.

[19] Margaret Ethel MacDonald, quoted by J. Ramsay MacDonald in his book of this title (1st ed. 1912, 5th ed. 1920), pp. 182-183.

[20] *Ibid.*

[21] Stewart, *op. cit.,* p. 181.

moral and physical deterioration resulting from a competitive system of wealth production which aims primarily at profit-making, the alarming growth of trusts and syndicates, able by reason of their great wealth to influence governments and plunge peaceful nations into war to serve their own interests, this House is of opinion that such a state of matters is a menace to the well-being of the Realm and calls for legislation designed to remedy the same by inaugurating a Socialist Commonwealth founded upon the common ownership of land and capital, production for use and not for profit, and equality of opportunity for every citizen.

"Socialism," Hardie concluded, "by placing the land and the instruments of production in the hands of the community, will eliminate only the idle and useless classes at both ends of the scale. The millions of toilers and of business men do not benefit from the present system. We are called upon to decide the question propounded in the Sermon on the Mount, as to whether we will worship God or Mammon. The last has not been heard of this movement either in the House or in the country, for as surely as Radicalism democratised the system of government politically in the last century, so will Socialism democratise industrialism of the country in the coming century."

Whether or not this period will be regarded as marking the end, and therefore also the beginning of a new era in political thought,[22] when there was an appeal to economic facts and needs and to new social ethics,[23] it is important in marking the sure and steady turn toward the great upheaval of 1906 in British politics. The year 1904 [24] has been taken as an especially good

[22] Cf. L. T. Hobhouse, *Democracy and Reaction* (1904, 2nd ed. 1909), p. 3; also *Social Evolution and Political Theory* (New York, 1913), esp. chap. IX, pp. 185-206; and *Liberalism* (1911).

[23] Cf. M. Beer, *History of British Socialism* (Vol. I, 1916, Vol. II, 1920), Vol. II, p. 345.

[24] Dicey, *op. cit.*, pp. 295 ff. The temper of the 1904 Parliament can be seen in the prolonged debate on the Address; the lengthy debates on the fiscal question, the Education and Licensing Bills did not stop the flood of new Bills which are noted later. For Address see Hansard 4 S. H. C. 1904, Vol. 129, pp. 1-5; pp. 106-118 for the Government; pp. 118-138, Campbell-Bannerman; pp. 138-147, Chamberlain; and pp. 199-237, Redmond. Cf. J. A. Spender, *The Life of the Rt. Hon. Sir Henry Campbell-Bannerman* (1923), chaps XXV-XXVI. Vol. I, pp. 136-187, for years 1904-1905, and view of changing political forces. And John Morley, *Recollections,* Vol. II, pp. 140-145.

example of the trend of sentiment in England. Surveying the year 1904 one writer said it would be memorable in history as the year in which the vested interests first began openly to flaunt their power over the Legislature. The struggle was one between the people and the Interests. What was doubtful was the duration and character of the conflict and the final form of victory. If the enthusiasm of the people was slow to be aroused, if the leaders quarrelled amongst themselves, if the great majority of the well-educated, well-meaning, moderate men and women were content to allow themselves to drift into the camp of the Interests the struggle would be long and bitter, the final result bear the spirit of revenge. But if the people responded quickly to the call, if the leaders were strong and unselfish, if moderate men and women frankly took sides with the people, the struggle would come almost without conflict, and the inevitable result be achieved in merciful justice. But clear insight would be necessary to choose correctly and high moral courage to abandon cherished prejudices.[25]

The Government Program of 1905 stated that legislation would be submitted for the establishment of authorities to deal with the question of unemployment, a Bill for the amendment and extension of the Workmen's Compensation Act, and a proposal for establishing a Ministry of Commerce and Industry.[26] At the end of the session the *Times* stated that "the session of Parliament which comes to an end to-day, leaves behind it a record of futile debate and disappointing achievement." [27] The chairman of the Labour Party said at the London Conference in 1906 that "from the legislative aspect of our work the last session

[25] Cf. F. W. Pethick Lawrence, in "Preface" to *The Reformers' Year Book,* 1905. The party literature of the period is interesting. See especially *Nine Years' Work,* issued by the Central Conservative Office, a review of the legislation and administration of the Government from 1895-1904; *Ninth Year of Tory Government,* being speeches and party leaflets by the leading Liberal members of Parliament; *The Liberal View,* with Preface by Earl Spencer, being articles on current politics by the '80 Club. Also J. A. Spender, *A Modern Journal: A Diary for the Year of Agitation* (1903-4); and B. Villiers, *The Opportunity of Liberalism* (1904).

[26] Hansard 4 S. 1905, Vol. 141, pp. 1-5. The Ministry of Commerce and Industry Bill, introduced by Mr. Sinclair was House Bill No. 151, 1905.

[27] August 11, 1905.

of Parliament was undoubtedly the most barren in modern history." [28] For another critic the session was "a burning national scandal and a dire disaster." [29] But no more sweeping condemnation was given than by the leader of the Opposition, Sir Henry Campbell-Bannerman, in the debate on the address. At that time he declared that

a situation so unthinkable as that of the Government at the present time is unknown in our Parliamentary history. The feeling of the country has been demonstrated beyond all doubt or dispute. The political situation to-day is of such ingrained falsity, it is so fraught with danger to the public interest, that to prolong it is a betrayal and usurpation of power. A Parliamentary majority is, no doubt, a great instrument and a necessary instrument for the Executive Government, but it is not everything. There is something behind any Parliament or any majority in any Parliament from which both Parliament and the majority derive their power. That is the public conscience. The public conscience is greater than any constitutional machinery, and no man can say in this case that the public conscience is vague.[30]

Very soon a new Government came into power,[31] after the Unionist Party had been in office for over twenty years, with a brief exception—the Rosebery and Fourth Gladstone Ministries. England had faced the severest struggles of a democracy attempting to administer an Empire, and at the same time making an

[28] Arthur Henderson, Chairman's Address in the *Report of the 6th Annual Conference of the Labour Party,* London, 1906, p. 42, pp. 39-42 entire.

[29] *The Reformers' Year Book 1906*, p. 62.

[30] Hansard, *op. cit.*, pp. 120-141, speech entire.

[31] Social legislation promised in the Address of 1906 (Hansard 4 S. H. C., 1906, Vol. 152, pp. 21-24) were Bills dealing with the law of Trade Disputes, Workmen's Compensation and for amending the Unemployed Workmen Act; note speeches of the Prime Minister, pp. 164-179; Mr. Joseph Chamberlain, pp. 149-164; and for Labour Mr. Hardie, pp. 193-201, and Mr. Barnes, pp. 259-265. The Prime Minister declared that underlying every proposal of his Government would be a policy of social reconstruction looking toward a greater equalization of wealth, and the destruction of the oppressive monopolies of land and liquor. Mr. Asquith, succeeding to the leadership of the Commons, declared that the injustice of the existing social system rendered a popular attack upon it inevitable. He said, "Property must be associated in the minds of the masses of the people, with the ideas of reason and justice."

effort to direct the democratic movement at home.[32] In the years which the Conservative Party governed the principles upon which the State interfered in the organization of industry were definitely expressed and greatly enlarged. The years from 1890 to 1905 were a background for that wider and more expansive movement which in this century has sought to bring in the democratic state.[33] From 1905 to 1914 the Liberal Party was to have the opportunity to govern, aided and urged to action by a Labour Party, with as much freedom and as complete a parliamentary majority as their opponents had possessed from 1885. The country was ready for a change, and to the new work which had to be done the Liberal and the Labour parties were dedicated. It is well to directly consider now the social and industrial legislation of the century, and in its later developments some attention will again be given to the relationship of politics, so far as there is anything to be gained from party controversies with regard to social politics.

Part I

The State and Legislation Dealing with Children and Young People

The conditions imposed by the State on the employment of young persons and children is a history of continuous progressive legislation. From the Health and Morals of Apprentices Act, 1802, to the Acts passed in the early years of this century, is an unbroken record of the effort of the community to insure conditions for the young that would increase the opportunities

[32] The first public and private speeches of Mr. Balfour, retiring Prime Minister, provide a review of his long period of service and his interpretation of them; on Dec. 9, 1905, at Manchester, the *Times*, Dec. 11, p. 6; on December 18, at Leeds, the *Times*, Dec. 19, p. 7. See also the long editorial survey "1905," the *Times*, Dec. 30, 1905, pp. 9-11. The Albert Hall speech of Campbell-Bannerman, December 21, the *Times*, Dec. 22, p. 7, also at Perthshire, Nov. 30, the *Times*, Dec. 1, may be compared with Mr. Balfour's speeches. These are interesting because the changing tendencies of the time are well expressed by the official leaders. They provided the cues for parties.

[33] Cf. John Morley, *Life of Gladstone* (1903), Vol. III, chaps. VII-X, pp. 490-552; also J. A. Spender, *op. cit.*, Vol. II, chap. XXVIII, on formation of first Liberal Ministry.

for their realizing the good life. The 1900 Act was an extension of long established principles of State interference. It was enacted that a boy under the age of thirteen should not be employed in or allowed to be for the purpose of employment in any mine below ground;[34] that sections four and five of the Coal Mines Regulation Act, 1887,[35] and section four of the Metalliferous Mines Regulation Act, 1872,[36] should read and have effect as if for the word "twelve" the word "thirteen" were substituted. By 1900 the number of boys affected by the Act was only 3,000[37] (and there were kind-hearted legislators who wanted them to be allowed to work), but the number was sufficient to compel the State to say positively that it would see that they did not work underground. This same regard for the value of human life and the problem of legislating for small groups found expression in 1900 in the three Bills and the one Government measure for the Inspection and Registration of Boilers. The mover of the second reading of the Bill said that

> it may be, and probably will be contended during the course of this debate that the loss of life and injury to persons from such a cause is very small compared with the number of steam boilers in use, but be the loss and injury small or great, if we can prove, as I believe we can, that such loss and suffering arise from preventable causes, then I contend we shall have made out a case for further intervention on the part of the legislature in the interests of the general community.[38]

There was this common bond between much of the restrictive legislation, for the purpose was protection of the individual, and the close relationship between measures of social reform became more evident in the administration of industrial and social legislation.[39]

[34] Section I of the Act of 1900 (Mines Prohibition of Child Labour Underground) (63 & 64 Vict. c. 21).

[35] 50 & 51 Vict. c. 58.

[36] 35 & 36 Vict. c. 77.

[37] Hansard, 4 S. Vol. LXXX, 1900, p. 463; also 4 S. Vol. LXXXI, 1900, p. 148 (Sir Charles W. Dilke).

[38] Hansard, 4 S. Vol. LXXX, 1900, pp. 266-267 (Fenwick). Cf. *Report of the Departmental Committee on the Night Employment of Male Young Persons in Factories* (Cd. 6533), 1912, *Evidence* (Cd. 6711), 1913.

[39] On this point see Irene Osgood Andrews' *Economic Effects of the War upon Women and Children in Great Britain* (1918), in the Carnegie Series, Preliminary Economic Studies of the War.

Perhaps the most obvious example is the field of legislation now under survey, that dealing with children and young persons. The gradual raising of the age at which employment of young persons and children became legal went steadily on from the passing of the Education Act of 1870.[40] This Act was the outcome of the Report of the Duke of Newcastle's Commission on Elementary Education, which had reported in 1861 that only two-thirds of the children of the working classes attended any school at all, and that so small a proportion remained long enough to receive any permanent benefit that it could be said that only about one child in seven was getting satisfactory instruction. From the Education Act of 1870 to the Education Act of 1918 is only 48 years, but in that short time the conviction had found Parliamentary endorsement that the proper place for the child was in the school, and that the emphasis should not be on the number of hours spent in the factory and workshop, but in the school. From 1867 education and factory legislation were making comparatively quick strides and marching side by side,[41] and both were profiting by Parliament passing a new kind of "class legislation." The lack of an effective Education Act kept back factory legislation as regards children.

And it is rather interesting to notice the mutual reaction of the two causes; education is made the motive and object of restricting children's hours of work, and then the factory inspectors in their turn become promoters or furtherers of State education, because they realise that only thereby can the restriction of hours become effective.[42]

There is no danger of "class legislation," fully proved in the history of Factory Legislation and Education Acts,[43] when the

[40] 33 & 34 Vict. c. 75; the 1876 Act, 39 & 40 Vict. c. 79. Cf. Frederick Keeling, *Child Labour in the United Kingdom: A Study of the Development and Administration of the Law Relating to the Employment of Children* (1914).

[41] Cf. Frank Tillyard, *op. cit.*, p. 114. Two recent studies are *Unemployment Among Boys* (1925, London), by W. McG. Eager and H. A. Secretan, and *The Employment and Welfare of Juveniles* (1925, London), by O. Bolton King.

[42] Hutchins & Harrison, *History of Factory Legislation*, p. 79.

[43] Cf. Education Act of 1918 (8 & 9 Geo. V, c. 39), Sections 13-16, on children's rights; sections 17-25, on the extension of powers and duties

cumulative value of social legislation in any special field helps in time to bring the lessons of that side of the common problem of the community to bear on the needs of every class in the nation. This is certainly one of the most worth while results of experiment in industrial legislation, what Jevons called a matter of practical work, creating human institutions.

The intervention of the State was much more drastic in the Employment of Children Act, 1903,[44] dealing with the whole question of child labour outside factories, workshops and places of public entertainment. The administration provisions of this Act were almost equally important, for large powers were given to local authorities, to make by-laws for regulating the employment of children.[45] Any local authority was given power to make by-laws prescribing for all children, or for boys and girls separately, and with respect to all occupations or to any specified occupation, (a) the age below which employment is illegal; and (b) the hours between which employment is illegal; and (c) the number of daily and weekly hours beyond which employment is illegal. Further power was given to make by-laws "prohibiting absolutely or permitting, subject to conditions, the employment of children in any specified occupation." [46] Besides these special powers given to local authorities the general restrictions on employment of children were comprehensive. A child could not be employed between the hours of nine in the evening and six in the morning; a child under eleven could not be employed in street trading; and it was forbidden to employ a child in any occupation likely to be injurious to life, limb, health or education, regard being had to the physical condition of the child worker.[47] The State went so far in its protective capacity that it held both the employer and the parent of the child liable to a fine

within the Act. This law is the best commentary with regard to laws on child life.

[44] 3 Edw. VII, c. 45.

[45] See *Report of the Departmental Committee on the Hours and Conditions of Employment of Van Boys and Warehouse Boys* (Cd. 6886), 1913, *Minutes of Evidence* (Cd. 6887), 1913, for progress of administration powers by by-laws. The Committee recommended that powers should be given to local authorities to frame by-laws regulating the employment of all van boys under 18.

[46] Act of 1903, Sect. 1.

[47] Act of 1903, Sec. 3.

when the Act was contravened.[48] It declared that society had rights in child life that only the State could adequately protect; that where a parent through carelessness or through necessity allowed these rights to be disregarded it was a duty for the State to penalize.

By-laws made under this Act could apply either to the whole of the area of the local authority or to any specified part thereof;[49] and it was also provided that by-laws made under the Prevention of Cruelty to Children Act, 1894[50] should be made by the same authority and confirmed in the same way as by-laws under this Act. The Prevention of Cruelty to Children Act, 1904,[51] practically re-enacted, with a few modifications, the Act of 1894. Legislation becoming uniform was having beneficial effects in unifying administration.

The Acts of 1900 and 1903 and 1904 definitely confirmed the principle of State intervention for the welfare of children, indicating that the Government was prepared to place unusual powers in the hands of local authorities. The Education (Provision of Meals) Act, 1906,[52] established a new principle of State action. The attitude of the Government toward the Bill was given by the President of the Board of Education who stated that the Government considered that the Bill "was in the first place an education question."[53] It was significant that the Government had directed its Minister of Education to handle the Bill, an indication of the common bond of human interest which was an important part of all social legislation.[54] The source of the Bill was interesting, having been first introduced for the Labour Party by Mr. W. T. Wilson, February 22, 1906,[55] but it had its real beginning in the steady policy of agitation which had been skil-

[48] Act of 1903, Secs. 5 and 6.

[49] Sec. 4 covers general provisions for by-laws.

[50] 57 & 58 Vict. c. 41.

[51] 4 Edw. VII, c. 15.

[52] 6 Edw. VII, c. 57; amended by the Education (Provision of Meals) Act, 1914 (4 & 5 Geo. V, c. 20).

[53] Hansard, 4 S., Vol. 152, 1906, pp. 1440-1443.

[54] Professor Dicey held that the statesmen who passed the Education Act of 1870 might not have passed the Act of 1891, relieving parents from the necessity of paying for any part of their children's elementary education, and it is certain that they would have opposed the Act of 1906 (*op. cit.*, p. L).

[55] The Act of 1906 was based on House Bills Nos. 10, 331 and 366, 1906.

fully carried on in unsuccessful Bills, yet which gained in April, 1905, the Resolution by the Government on the feeding of school children.

The Bill provided that local education authorities might supply food for any children attending a public elementary school who might be unable through want of food to take full advantage of the education offered;[56] it also proposed to sanction the provision of food for other children and enable the authorities to recover the cost from the parents or guardians. The provision of food was not to be deemed parochial relief.[57] which meant that the father of a child who was fed by the State retained the right of voting for a Member of Parliament. This caused one learned critic to say, "Why a man who first neglects his duty as a father and then defrauds the State should retain his full political rights is a question easier to ask than answer."[58]

The debates on the second and third readings of this Bill indicated the main dividing issues which were constantly to appear in the debates on the social measures of the Government. It was maintained by the Labour leaders "that the late Government recognized that there was an evil and a public responsibility for finding a remedy for that evil," and that "the principle had been admitted in past sessions of Parliament by all sections of the House."[59] Several of the speeches indicated the danger of socialism, but for the great majority of the members of Parliament the Act was a good step toward wider protective enactments which would include the whole interests of the child and the family.[60] The Parliament of 1906 had very little sympathy for a doctrinaire individualism, especially when the victims

[56] See Act of 1906, sect. 3. [57] *Ibid.*, sect. 4.

[58] Dicey, *op. cit.*, *Introduction to the Second Edition*, p. L.

[59] Hansard, 4 S. Vol. 152, 1906, pp. 1394-1399 (A. Henderson). Two Education (Provision of Meals) Bills, based on the Report on Physical Deterioration, 1904, were introduced in 1905 by Mr. Henderson (House Bills of 1905, Nos. 132 and 196); and two Elementary Education (Feeding of Children) Bills (House Bills of 1905, Nos. 126 and 197), meet the same fate of being withdrawn or dropped. The tendency of legislation and the public interest were manifest.

[60] Hansard, 4 S. Vol. 152, 1906, pp. 1390-1447, second reading debate; committee stage and the numerous amendments by opponents of the Bill, chiefly Mr. Harold Cox and Sir H. (now Lord) Banbury, Hansard, 4 S., Vol. 166, 1906, pp. 1273-1291, and pp. 1315-1465. Note pp. 1440-1443, 1446-1447 for Government statement.

of its logic were children; and it was alleged that the leader of the opposition "had put his opposition to the Bill on the peculiarly arid ground of individualistic dogmatism." [61] This feeling was not shared by any party in the House of Commons, for after the Government had accepted and sponsored the Bill the third reading was passed without division.[62] In the Select Committee the Government accepted another Labour measure, the Education (Provision of Meals) (Scotland) Bill,[63] yet when the Bill was given back to the lower House, Scotland was omitted from the working of the Act.[64] But among the first Bills of the 1907 session was the reintroduction of the Scottish Bill,[65] supported by the Parliamentary Secretary of the Local Government Board, Dr. MacNamara, who had given aid to the 1906 Bill. The opposition remained the same small minority. Though the question of party alignment was not present with regard to this Bill, which was not at all true of the contentious legislation of the following years, it is well to note that the same course was followed by the Government of accepting and sponsoring Labour Bills in the sessions of 1906 and 1907. There was a real effort on the part of the Government to keep the Labour Party in full confidence of its friendship, for valuable concessions were made in accepting amendments and in making the provisions of Acts more comprehensive. The Education (Provision of Meals) Act, is a good example. "This issue formed one of the chief demands of the Labour movement in 1906," wrote J. Keir Hardie, and "the political independence of the Party was thus justified in its very first attempt at industrial legislation." [66]

It would be difficult to place too much emphasis on the new principle of State action which the Education (Provision of Meals) Act implied, for in a nation jealous of individual rights and proud of its conservative instincts it was nothing less than

[61] Hansard, 4 S. Vol. 152, 1906, p. 1435.

[62] Hansard, 4 S. Vol. 167, 1906, pp. 722-780.

[63] House Bill, No. 92, 1906, introduced by Mr. Barnes.

[64] For course of this Bill through the House of Lords, which caused longer debate, and apparently more interest, than the Trade Disputes Act, 1906, see Hansard, 4 S., Vol. 167, 1906, pp. 1473-1482, pp. 1629-1670. Parts of two days were given for a discussion of all stages, which was unusual for a Bill in the House of Lords.

[65] House Bill, No. 14, 1907 (J. Ramsay MacDonald).

[66] J. Keir Hardie, *The Case for the Labour Party* (1909), p. 106.

a revolutionary principle. Thirty-six years after the passing of the Elementary Education Act, 1870, Parliament had declared that the same necessity which gave the State the duty of educating its children also demanded that there should be provision for the hungry and the underfed. It was not the fault of the children that they were undernourished,

and if the parents through force of circumstances were unable to feed them properly the State should see that they were fed. If the parents were unable to pay they should not be pauperised by accepting such assistance.[67]

The State believed it was the part of wisdom to meet the need through the agency of the educational authorities, though in some ways the Act was "industrial legislation," as the Labour leader suggested. This again proved that progress was slowly being made in social legislation toward the ideal of the common and inter-related life of the whole community as the aim of all enactments and their administration.[68]

The Education (Provision of Meals) Act was only the beginning of legislation affecting children. The carrying out of the recommendations of the Report [69] of the Interdepartmental Commission on Physical Deterioration, a large proportion of which dealt with child life, was demanded by public opinion stirred by a survey of the awful cost childhood was being called on to pay in both city and country. There was agreement by all parties with the Prime Minister who said in his Budget speech, April 18, 1907, that "there is nothing that calls so loudly or so imperiously as the possibilities of social reform." [70] The Education Act [71] of

[67] Hansard, 4 S. Vol. 152, 1906, pp. 1390-1393.

[68] In 1912 Mr. Lansbury asked the Prime Minister if he would arrange for sufficient time being given to allow the House to pass the necessary amending Bill to the 1906 Act to enable feeding of the children during holiday time. Mr. Asquith's reply was: "I am not aware that any Bill for this purpose is before the House. The Government are, however, prepared to give favourable consideration to the principle." (Hansard, 5 S. H. C., Vol. 35, 1912, p. 379.)

[69] Published July 28, 1904, Cd. 2175, 2210, 2186. Contained fifty-three recommendations by which physical deterioration could be diminished.

[70] Hansard, 4 S. Vol. 172, 1907, pp. 1189-1193 (Asquith).

[71] 7 Edw. VII, c. 40; also The Education (Administrative Provisions) Act, 1907 (7 Edw. VII, c. 43).

that year reflected this sentiment, containing provisions for play centres, vacation schools and for free medical inspection of children. To decrease the alarming infant mortality rate and secure proper medical care for young children, Lord Robert Cecil introduced a Bill on April 23, 1907,[72] which was eventually enacted as the Notification of Births Act.[73] Just a year before Hardie said in the debate on the Address that "property was secured in England but life was a thing of no account." "Why was it," he asked, "that amongst the children of the poor in our great cities 66 per 1000 died before they reached one year of age, while only 18 per 1000 of the children of the class who sat in Parliament died before attaining one year?"[74] Only a year before in the debate which caused the downfall of the Coombes Ministry, M. Dejeante, answering the taunt of the Centre Party against the Socialists for supporting the Government, gave the death rate in France among children as the specific proof of a class struggle—6 per 100 among the rich, and 60-70 per 100 among the poor.

"The world of labour," he said, "does not accept any more than you the theory of the class struggle, but protests on the contrary with the greatest energy against the practice of the class struggle carried on without scruple and without pity against the working class, a struggle which the bourgeois republicans have only increased in alarming proportions." [75]

It is evident then in the Labour movement of France and England that any legislative Act which would protect the child would help to decrease the bitterness of social outlook which the above typical quotations represent in a sober way. Herein lies the great value of such legislation in a survey of legislation and its relation to social justice, for it tends to remove a peculiarly malignant source of class warfare and helps to free the energies of the community from futile hatreds.

[72] Hansard, 4 S. Vol. 172, 1907, pp. 1572 sqq.

[73] 7 Edw. VII, c. 40. In this year the Probation of Offenders Act (7 Edw. VII, c. 53) was passed, dealing with juvenile offenders along reformatory rather than punitive lines. The first Act was extended by the Act of 1915 (5 & 6 Geo. V, c. 64), with which compare the Maternity and Child Welfare Act, 1918 (8 & 9 Geo. V, c. 29), and the Local Education Authorities (Medical Treatment) Act, 1909 (9 Edw. VII, c. 13).

[74] Hansard, 4 S. Vol. 152, 1906, p. 200; pp. 193-201, entire speech.

[75] J. O. C. of D., January 15, 1905, p. 27; pp. 27-31, entire speech.

The Government introduced February 10, 1908, the Children's Act,[76] which dealt with practically every phase of infant and child life, protection and treatment of children in reformatories and industrial schools, the question of juvenile crime, children's courts and probation officers.[77] The Housing and Town Planning Act, 1909,[78] considered the health and general welfare of child life,[79] in the nation as well as the adults; the Labour Exchanges Act, 1909, made special provisions for juvenile employment, and in addition the Board of Trade co-operates with committees appointed by various local education authorities in England and Wales in accordance with schemes approved by the Board of Education under the Education (Choice of Employment) Act, 1910,[80] and with Scotland under the Education (Scotland) Act, 1908.

The State has taken upon itself unusual responsibilities for young people until they reach the age of eighteen, and this legislation is not only important in itself but it often provides the basis of the more advanced enactments dealing with adults.

[76] 8 Edw. VII, c. 67; amended by 1910 Act (10 Edw. VII & 1 Geo. V, c. 25); Hansard, 4 S. Vol. 183, 1908, pp. 1432 sqq., for speech of the Under-Secretary of the Home Department, Mr. Herbert Samuel; this Bill passed third reading in the House of Commons, October 19, and in the House of Lords, November 30. The Act of 1908 consolidated 38 previous Acts.

[77] See the Carnegie Report on *The Physical Welfare of Mothers and Children, England and Wales,* Vols. I and II (Liverpool, 1917), especially pp. 87-112, Vol. I for abstract of legislative enactments in operation in England and Wales. This is a comprehensive survey of the legislation under discussion, showing the inter-relationship of the social legislation of this century and giving the pertinent provisions of the major Acts. Cf. *The Labour Year Book,* 1916, pp. 297-302, on State interference, and Tillyard, *op. cit.,* Section 3, chap. II, pp. 117-153.

[78] 89 Edw. VII, c. 37.

[79] See speech of the President of the Local Government Board (Mr. Burns), on introducing the Bill of that year, May 12, 1908 (Hansard, 4 S., Vol. 188, pp. 947-968) and his remarks on the Bill of 1909 on second reading, 9 (Hansard, 5 S., pp. 733 sqq.).

[80] 10 Edw. VII and 1 Geo. V, c. 37; cf. The Children (Employment Abroad) Act, 1913 (3 & 4 Geo. V, c. 7). See Parl. Deb. H. L. 5 S. 1911, Vol. 7, pp. 780-807, and Vol. 8, pp. 277-298, 831-834, for the committee discussion of the Employment of Children Act (1903) Amendment Bill, 1911; and Vol. 36, 1912, pp. 759-834, for second reading debate of same Bill, which passed without division.

Part II

The State and Compensation Legislation

The Workmen's Compensation Act [81] of 1897 introduced a new principle into English legislation, that an employer must, subject to certain limitations, insure his workmen against the risks of their employment. Until that time the employee had the same right to compensation when injured through the negligence of fellow workers as a stranger, but the law of that year provided that compensation for accidents should be paid without the application of the test of negligence. For proof of the employer's negligence there was substituted proof that personal injury by accident, arising out of and in the course of employment had been caused to the workman seeking compensation.[82] This principle was extended to include agricultural labourers in 1900,[83] and was given wider application in the Workmen's Compensation Act, 1906, and the Health Insurance part of the National Insurance Act, 1911. The Act of 1900, unlike the Act of 1897, was not a Government measure, but it became a law without serious opposition in either the House of Commons or the House of Lords. The Act was short, consisting of one operative section only:

> The Workmen's Compensation Act, 1897, shall apply to the employment of workmen in agriculture by any employer who habitually employs one or more workmen in such employment.[84]

This Bill was not a party question and was one of the most important of the 1900 session in extending the protective arm of legislation.[85] Before considering the important new principle which the Act of 1906 introduced, it is well to note the administrative features of the Railway Employment (Prevention of Accidents) Act, 1900.[86]

[81] 60 & 61 Vict. c. 37; compare law of April 9, 1898, France.
[82] Cf. Tillyard, *op. cit.*, p. 30.
[83] 63 & 64 Vict. c. 22; compare French law of June 30, 1899.
[84] Sect. I.
[85] Hansard, 4 S. Vol. LXXXII, 1900, pp. 490-493, and Vol. LXXXIV, pp. 1211-1213, on extension of Act to naval and military workers.
[86] 63 & 64 Vict. c. 27.

This Act was passed on the recommendation of a Royal Commission and gave the Board of Trade extensive powers of making rules for the control of risks and the reducing of accidents in railway service. It was provided that

the Board of Trade may, subject to the provisions of this Act, make such rules as they think fit with respect to any of the subjects mentioned in the schedule of this Act, with the object of reducing or removing the dangers and risks incidental to railway service. Where the Board of Trade consider that avoidable danger to persons employed on the railway arises from any operation of railway service (not being a matter in respect to which rules may be made under the foregoing provisions of the section), whether that danger arises from anything done or omitted to be done by the railway company or any of its officers or servants, or from any want of proper appliances or plant, they may, subject to the provisions of this Act, after communicating with the railway company, and giving them a reasonable opportunity of reducing or removing the danger of risk, make rules for that purpose.[87]

The schedule of the Act enumerated twelve subjects with respect to which the Board of Trade might make such rules as they saw fit and necessary. The first Rules under this Statute were made in 1902;[88] in 1906 the Notice of Accidents Act[89] substituted a much more stringent set of provisions as to notice of accidents, especially with regard to certain "dangerous occurrences," even though no bodily injury is caused by them; and later substantial change was made in the passing of new rules, known as the Prevention of Accident Rules, 1911.[90] When the original Bill came up for second reading Mr. Bryce spoke of the gratifying unanimity with which it was received.

"Everybody feels," he said, "that the State has now completely established its rights to intervene in matters of this kind, and we

[87] Sect. I, clauses 1 and 2 of the Act of 1900.

[88] S. R. and O. 1902, No. 616.

[89] 6 Edw. VII, c. 53; this Act repealed Section 19 of the Act of 1901, and is one of the seven statutes which came into force in the fourteen years after the Factory and Workshop Act, 1901, affecting the law relating to factories and workshops.

[90] S. R. and O. 1911, No. 1058.

have scarcely heard any of the old arguments in favour of the *laissez-faire* attitude with which we used to be favoured." [91]

This Act is one of the best examples of how far Parliament was willing to go in giving large administrative power to the central inspectorate of the Board of Trade. A new staff of inspectors were attached to the Board of Trade to carry out the provisions of the Act of 1900, which extended to the railway service the principles before recognized in the Mining Code administered by the Home Office and the mining inspectors.

There was constant legislative attempt to extend the Workmen's Compensation Act. The Address of 1905 [92] included three important proposals: the Trade Unions and Trade Disputes Bill, the Workmen's Compensation Bill, and the Unemployed Workmen Bill. The failure of the Government to pass the Workmen's Compensation Bill, a much-needed and non-controversial social measure, increased the outcry against the "legislative scandal of 1905." The Home Secretary, moving the second reading, [93] enumerated the additional classes of workmen whom it was now proposed to bring within the scope of the Act of 1897. They included workers in workshops where five persons or more were employed; persons employed in the care and management of horses and locomotives, including farriers; persons employed on buildings less than 30 feet in height and on which no machine or scaffolding was used; and persons employed on tramways and private railways and sidings. The aim of the Bill, the Government said, was to simplify and make less expensive its working, and also to remove as far as possible the temptation to litigation. The Bill would have introduced a great improvement in the law

[91] Hansard, 4 S. Vol. LXXXI, 1900, pp. 1307-1308.

[92] Hansard, 4 S. H. C. 1905, Vol. 141, pp. 1-5; see following speeches: the Prime Minister (Balfour), pp. 153-167; Campbell-Bannerman, pp. 120-121; Asquith, pp. 178-190; A. Chamberlain, pp. 190-209. They indicate the politics of the session. The Trade Union Workmen's Compensation Bill had been introduced in 1904 by Mr. R. Bell (House Bill No. 122, 1904); this was introduced in 1906 by Mr. Shackleton (House Bill No. 84, 1905), and another by Lord Belper (House Bill No. 31, H. L. and Hansard 4 S. 1905, Vol. 144, pp. 263-284 for debate).

[93] Hansard, 4 S. H. C. 1905, Vol. 144, pp. 263-284; the Bill (House Bill No. 31, 1905), was introduced in the Lords on April 4 and was disposed of by them on May 29; the second reading in House of Commons was moved by Home Secretary, Mr. Akers-Douglas, June 5.

of compensation, it was said, "and the failure to carry it through indicates a wanton disregard on behalf of the Government for the hopes and needs of Labour." [94] The attitude of the Trade Union Congress was indicated by the resolution passed, which called for the inclusion of all workmen, including every person who has entered into, or works, whether by way of manual labour or otherwise, under a contract of service anywhere in the United Kingdom. Also that the employer be compelled to register an agreement in the county court. The provision of some system of State compulsory insurance was demanded, to secure that employers should have paid the necessary funds to compensate for all accidents or injuries arising out of any employment.[95]

The most important development with regard to the law on accidents was the Workmen's Compensation Act, 1906,[96] introduced [97] by the Government March 26, 1906. The historical stages in the growth of the idea of compensation were noted by the Home Secretary to be the Employers' Liability Act of 1880 and the Workmen's Compensation Acts of 1897 and 1900.

"The Government now think," he announced, "that the time has arrived for a wide extension of the Act of 1897 to every class of labour, and in the Bill a new principle is adopted which differentiates it from the Act of 1897. That Act excluded all classes of workmen who were not directly and expressly included; and it is now proposed to reverse this, and, subject to the definition of a workman in the Bill, all be included who are not expressly excluded." [98]

[94] *The Reformers' Year Book,* 1906, p. 66.

[95] *Report of the Parliamentary Committee at the Trade Union Congress,* Leeds 1904, pp. 53-82, full survey; also pp. 47-53, the President's remarks on the Bill and the Labour amendments.

[96] 6 Edw. VII. c. 58; compare French law of April 12, 1906, and Decree Feb. 18, 1907.

[97] The Act on 1906 was based on House Bills 1906, Nos. 123, 272, 365. See Hansard 4 S. Vol. 154, 1906, pp. 886-895, for the Government exposé of their Bill; first reading debate, pp. 886-934; second reading debate, *ibid.,* Vol. 155, pp. 523-578, and 1191-1219; third reading debate, *ibid.,* Vol. 167, pp. 693-722. The Report stage of the Bill is interesting, for which see Vol. 166, pp. 321-392, 781-860, 974-1059, 1204-1271. The Bill was referred to the Standing Committee on Law.

[98] Hansard, 4 S. Vol. 154, 1906, pp. 886-887.

This Act thus began the series of Acts dealing with the protection of other than manual workers of all kinds, for under the inclusive clause a workman meant any person who has entered into or works under a contract of service or apprenticeship with an employer, whether by way of manual labour, clerical work or otherwise.[99] Almost equally important was the statement that while most of the proposals of the Bill were based fully or in part on the recommendations of the Departmental Committee over which Sir K. Digby presided, that the Government on its own initiative proposed to extend workmen's compensation to include industrial diseases. "That involves a new departure," the Home Secretary added.

This experiment was to extend to only six scheduled diseases, but the Home Secretary was authorized to extend the list by Order,[100] and as early as May, 1907, eighteen minor industrial diseases had been included. It was on this last feature that the former Home Secretary felt that there was any objection to the Bill; the principle had been firmly established and extension was a logical development of the experience gained by the preceding Acts.[101] Further legislation was foreshadowed by the statement of the Home Secretary that "the ultimate solution of the whole question is probably to be found in a scheme of compulsory insurance."[102] With this, Labour was in agreement,[103] believing with Sir Charles W. Dilke that compulsory insurance in some form or other lay at the root of all improvement, and that France had given a good example in this regard, in her compulsory system.[104]

The third reading and the report stage of this Bill were indicative of the great interest in the principle of the measure. It was shown definitely that the new Labour Party was determined to use the Parliamentary machine for its full worth, and to profit by their influence at the time with the Government. Their faith too was fresh enough to keep them close to the dull detail of their

[99] Sect. 13, 1906 Act.

[100] See 1906 Act, sect. 8 for application to industrial diseases; compare French law of October 25, 1919.

[101] Hansard, 4 S., Vol. 154, 1906, pp. 895-900; as Home Secretary he had introduced a similar Bill, not including industrial diseases, the year before.

[102] *Ibid.*, p. 889.

[103] *Ibid.*, pp. 900-906 (Barnes).

[104] *Ibid.*, pp. 906-908; also *ibid.*, Vol. 155, pp. 526-527.

duties, and their contribution to the success of the Bill was enough to cause them to credit this Act as one of the Labour Party's achievements. When introduced in 1906 the Government Bill was so limited in extent, wrote Hardie, that it only applied to about 2,000,000 workers. When it passed it applied to 6,000,000. The Government first of all excluded shop assistants, but after pressure from the Labour Party agreed to their inclusion when the number employed was more than three. The party declined this compromise, and in the end the Government gave way. The Government proposed that compensation should not be payable until a week had elapsed from the date of accident. The Labour Party carried an amendment in committee that it should begin in three days. At a later stage this was altered by agreement with the Party, so that if the incapacity of the injured workman lasts longer than two weeks, compensation shall date from the day of accident. The Party also succeeded in carrying an amendment that an illegitimate child or the parent or grandparent of an illegitimate child, if dependent upon the workman, should rank as a dependent. The Party sought without success to add a clause providing that where an injured workman has sufficiently recovered to be able to perform some slight and less remunerative employment, reduced compensation shall not take place unless he is able to obtain such employment. The Government only proposed to schedule six "diseases of occupation" for the purpose of the Act, but the Labour Party secured a pledge that this would be increased.[105]

From such testimony it is easily deduced that there was belief in England among the working class that Parliament could be responsive to the needs of the nation. That is one of the strong forces by which come political ideals of social justice, inspiring a devotion to democratic institutions which causes men to spend hours in the drudgery of Committee that some clause may be added that will have a beneficial effect. This was the decision given between 1900-1914 by France and England on parliamentary Government, attesting to the growth of a democratic political consciousness among the people, who came to believe more cer-

[105] Hardie, *op. cit.*, p. 110; also pp. 111-113, for his summary of what "Labour did in Parliament," 1906-1908, by raising questions, Committee Work and Bills, being fuller than the Trade Union Congress Reports.

tainly that they had in their own hands the instrument whereby wrongs could be righted. The ideal of industrial legislation was including the whole nation's welfare, and the progressive extension of the Workmen's Compensation Act is a practical example. When the Act was first passed in 1897 protection was given to 6,000,000 workers, which in 1900 was granted to 1,000,000 more, and the Home Secretary in his concluding speech on the Bill pointed out that by its new provisions 6,000,000 additional workers would receive like benefits.[106] The Act besides extended the benefits of industrial legislation to a large number of non-manual workers, for the Act included all non-manual service the remuneration of which did not exceed £250 a year.[107] The contractual capacity of workmen and masters was cut down, and "in the background stands the State, determining in one most important aspect the terms of the labour contract." [108] Yet it was a principle given far wider effectiveness in the National Insurance Act, 1911. The principle was much more than compensation, for the Act gave

> a new and a national status to the British worker—a status founded upon the recognition that, whether in public or private employment, he is playing a truly national part, and that his welfare and independence are a truly national concern.[109]

If such a principle can become the possession of a democratic industrial nation it will mean substantial progress toward the realization of the aims of social justice, and it will mean that the Parliament of the people has not been unmindful of the work it can do to make these aims come true.

A natural consequence of the development of labour law dealing with workmen's compensation in France and England was the Workmen's Compensation (Anglo-French Convention) Act, 1909,[110] granting to French citizens employed in the United Kingdom the same rights under the Act of 1906 that the English worker possessed. This Convention allowed to British subjects meeting with accidents arising out of their employment in France, and persons entitled to claim through or having rights derivable

[106] Hansard, 4 S. vol. 167, 1906, pp. 693-695.

[107] Act of 1906, sect. 13.

[108] Dicey, *op. cit.*, pp. 283-284.

[109] G. C. Cope, "Workmen's Compensation Act," in *Reformers' Year Book, 1908*, p. 157.

[110] 9 Edw. VII. c. 16.

from them, the benefits of the compensation and guarantees secured to French citizens by the legislation in force in France.[111] The survey of the legislation of each nation shows a parallel development of legislation dealing with accidents and its extension to include non-manual workers and industrial diseases. The movement of thought was much the same in both countries, inspired by similar necessities which directed each to a common end. This treaty was an early illustration of what is, and will increasingly be, one of the most important developments of a new international social order in this century.[112] France and England, two democratic industrial nations, recognized the international nature of the labour problem, and this treaty suggested problems which are worthy of the diplomacy that democratic nations can use most effectively for the good of all the peoples.[113] It is well to note that the French have taken the keenest interest in the development of these international labour treaties.[114]

It is only necessary to note the passage since the war of the Workmen's Compensation (Illegal Employment) Act, 1918,[115] which allows compensation even though the worker with or without his knowledge is illegally employed; the Workmen's Compensation (Silicosis) Act, 1918,[116] a further extension of the principle of professional diseases; and the Workmen's Compensation Act, 1923,[117] bringing up to date the provisions of the principal Act. The two Workmen's Compensation (War Addition) Acts, 1917-1919,[118] were repealed.

[111] Art. I of Convention.

[112] Cf. Bry, *op. cit.*, pp. 265-267, for a summary and an interpretation of the new social treaties of this century; also B. E. Lowe, *The International Protection of Labour* (1921), and H. J. W. Hetherington, *International Labour Legislation* (1920). An early survey is one prepared by M. Albert Métin in 1908, who at that time was head of the staff in the French Ministry of Labour, *Les Traités ouvriers: Accords internationaux de prévoyances et de travail,* and a recent study is by M. Albert Vabre, *Le droit international du travail.* Mr. E. Beddington Behrens of the London office of the International Labour Office has written a very valuable book, *The International Labour Office (League of Nations). A Survey of Certain Problems of International Administration* (1924).

[113] Cf. Pic, *op. cit.*, pp. 100-101.

[114] Note bibliography in Bry and Pic.

[115] 8 and 9 Geo. V. c. 8.

[116] 8 and 9 Geo. V. c. 14.

[117] 13 and 14 Geo. V. c. 42.

[118] 7 and 8 Geo. V. c. 42 and 9 & 10 Geo. V. c. 83. The 1917 and 1919 Amendment Acts undertook to relieve the situation produced by changes

An administrative feature of the 1923 Act is interesting, providing for reciprocity with foreign countries by orders in council instead of by statute as formerly. This is an extension of the principle of the Anglo-French Convention of 1909. Also if the Secretary of State finds, from the number and nature of accidents in any factory or class of factories, that special safety provisions should be made, he may by order require such equipment or supervision to be made.

In view of the fact that the liability to pay compensation is imposed by act of Parliament, the Government has always kept in mind the question whether or not a more economical system of insurance could be established. The Secretary of State for the Home Department appointed in May, 1919, a committee to inquire into the present system of the payment of workmen's compensation, to consider the desirability of establishing a system of insurance under the control or supervision of the State, and to recommend such alterations as might seem desirable to remedy defects which experience had disclosed or to give effect to their recommendations.[119] The matter of State control was considered under two general heads: First, whether or not a State fund should be established, either exclusive or competitive, or again by a system of mutual insurance; or, secondly, whether State control of commercial companies and supervision of mutual associations and self-insurers would afford sufficient security.

Speaking generally, the witnesses representing the trade unions were in favor of a monopolistic State fund, mainly on the ground that the money which goes in profits to the insurance companies would be available for the workmen. On the other hand, the employers and their representatives were unanimous against a monopolistic State fund, urging that it would be more expensive

in the value of currency and in the cost of living. The Act of 1923 however provides for considerable increase in benefits, and also extends the scope of the law with regard to salaried persons not engaged in manual labour, the wage limitation being raised from £250 ($1,216.63 par) to £350 ($1,703.28 par), thus permitting non-manual employees up to the higher range of salaries to receive the benefit of the law.

[119] See *Departmental Committee on Workmen's Compensation. Report to the Rt. Hon. the Secretary of State for the Home Department.* (London, 1920.)

than the present system and would not work so efficiently or satisfactorily in any respect.

The 1923 Act, which came into effect January 1, 1924, was preceded by an agreement between the Government and the accident insurance companies, and while there will be no interference with the carrying on of the business by insurance officers, there has been an agreement reached whereby the cost of insurance is materially reduced.

Part III

The State and the Factory Acts, the Shop Acts and the Mining Regulations Acts

Section A. The special significance of the Factory and Workshop Act, 1901,[120] has been pointed out in this study; it is necessary now to briefly outline its administrative principles and their contribution to the idea of social justice in England. In this study it should be kept in mind that the aim with regard to the administration of labour law is to see how far the control and management is directly in the hands of the people or their responsible agents. That is the important factor in the development of administration, for it is no new idea that Government should be for the good of the whole people, but the remarkable contribution of democratic thought in politics and economics is, that the machinery of control and direction should be also the people's. Local authorities, local government, self-government, decentralization, indicate this aim.

The Act of 1901 consolidated with Amendments all previously existing Factory Acts, especially the Factory and Workshop Act, 1878,[121] and the Amending Acts of 1883,[122] 1889,[123] 1891,[124] 1895,[125] and 1897.[126] The Standing Committee on Trade fused two Bills introduced in the House of Commons, the one an Amending Bill, the other a Consolidating Bill. The Act contained

[120] 1 Edw. VII. c. 22.

[121] 41 & 42 Vict. c. 16.

[122] 46 & 47 Vict. c. 53.

[123] 52 & 53 Vict. c. 62.

[124] 54 & 55 Vict. c. 75.

[125] 58 & 59 Vict. c. 37.

[126] 60 & 61 Vict. c. 58 (The Cotton Cloth Factories Act). With the exception of several sections in the Acts of 1891 and 1895, the six Acts were repealed.

10 parts and 163 sections. The headings of the 10 parts indicate the wide scope of the Act: Part I, Health and Safety; II, Employment; III, Education of Children; IV, Dangerous and Unhealthy Industries; V, Special Modifications and Extensions; VI, Home Work; VII, Particulars of Work and Wages; VIII, Administration; IX, Legal Proceedings; and the last part deals with the application and definitions of the Act. This Act with its modifications and the subsequent legislation which has carried its principles to every phase of the industrial life of England is often referred to in this survey of legislation. For this reason the protective and humanitarian features of the Act can be passed over without definite enumeration.[127] Part VIII of the Act, dealing with Administration, can now be outlined.

The appointment, powers and duties of factory inspectors and certifying surgeons are given first,[128] then the powers of the local authorities are defined,[129] together with the procedure of Special Orders by which the Home Secretary can extend or curtail the application of the Act to particular industries.[130] Remaining sections definitely set forth the duties of occupiers of factories and workshops with regard to the Act, and the duties which are required of district councils and their medical officers.[131] Where the general provisions of the Act are not sufficient to meet the needs, the Home Secretary is given power to make regulations:

Where the Secretary of State is satisfied that any manufacture, machinery, plant, process, or description of manual labour, used in factories or workshops, is dangerous or injurious to health or dangerous to life or limb, either generally or in the case of women, children or any other class of persons, he may certify that manufacture, machinery, plant, process or description of manual labour, to be dangerous; and thereupon the Secretary of State may, subject to the provisions of this Act, make such regulations as appear to him to be reasonably practicable, and to meet the necessity of the case.[132]

[127] See Redgrave's *Factory Acts* (12th ed. Revised by W. Peacock, 1916) for a complete commentary on this Act, pp. 1-244, and Introduction.

[128] Sects. 118-124.

[129] Sect. 125.

[130] Sect. 126.

[131] Sects. 127-134.

[132] See Act, 1901, Part IV, Sect. 79.

The great majority of Special Regulations under the power given to the Home Secretary have been made with reference to the health and safety of the worker. It is well to note that there is a difference in the Special Rules under the Act of 1891, which had to be made for each separate factory or workshop, whereas under the 1901 Act Special Regulations apply to every factory and workshop of the class specified.[133] This was a change in administrative enforcement which has been carried into other Acts. Special Regulations were made by the Home Secretary in 1905, 1906, 1907 and 1909, largely dealing with means for the prevention of accidents. There were in 1913 under Regulations or Special Rules, 68,432 works or departments.[134]

Parliament further made it possible for the Home Secretary to extend the workings of this Act by giving power of legislating by Special Order. This was in keeping with the spirit of Parliament of late years to settle principles and to leave detailed decisions and the working out of extensions to "other bodies," creating inferior bodies to whom law-making powers have been delegated.[135] This power was given in the Particulars section of the 1901 Act, which is as follows:

> The Secretary of State, on being satisfied by the report of an inspector that the provisions of this section are applicable to any class of non-textile factories or to any class of workshops, may if he thinks fit, by Special Order, apply the provisions of this section to any such class, subject to such modifications as may in his opinion be necessary for adapting those provisions to the circumstances of the case. He may also by any such order apply those provisions, subject to such modifications as may, in his opinion, be necessary for adapting them to the circumstances of the case, to any class of persons of whom lists may be required to be kept under the provisions of this Act relating to outworkers, and to the employers of those persons.[136]

[133] Cf. 1901 Act, ss. 80-85 (Regulations for Dangerous Trades); the earlier procedure is found in ss. 8-10 of the 1891 Act, amended by ss. 12, 24 (3), and 28, of the Act of 1895. Different texts are usually compared.

[134] Cf. Tillyard, *op. cit.*, pp. 167-169.

[135] Cf. "Non-Parliamentary Industrial Legislation," *Economic Journal*, September, 1915, pp. 360-361. The most recent comprehensive study is by H. A. Mess, *Factory Legislation and Its Administration, 1891-1924* (London, 1926).

[136] 1901 Act, Sect. 116, subsect. 5.

Under the power to extend the provisions of the Particulars section, which originally included only textile factories and workshops, to non-textile works, the Home Secretary by 1903 had brought under this section more than 3,000 factories and workshops, and by 1913 this number was increased to 27,000. The industries to which Special Orders have been made applicable have constantly increased,[137] and 19 Special Orders have been issued to suit the special circumstances of the industries under the control of this section.[138] The principle Parliament recognized by passing an Act has been extended as experiment and effective inspection have shown its usefulness. It is convincing proof that administration is legislation in action, and emphasizes the value of delegating the working out of labour regulations to responsible departmental heads after Parliament has laid down the general principle of action. When the Factory Extension Act, 1867, and the Workshop Regulation Act, 1867, were passed, statutory orders were first introduced. At that time a division of work between Parliament and the Departments of State was set up, and has constantly increased.[139] The Factory and Workshop Act, 1901, expressly defined it with regard to factory legislation, and the provisions as to Special Orders by the Secretary of State is of such importance as to be especially noted.

The Order shall be under the hand of the Secretary of State and shall be published in such manner as the Secretary of State thinks best adapted for the information of the persons concerned. The Order may be temporary or permanent, conditional or unconditional, and whether granting or extending an exception or prohibition, or directing the adoption of any special means or provision, or rescinding a previous Order, or affecting any other thing, may do so either wholly or partly. The Order shall be laid as soon as may be before both Houses of Parliament, and if either House of Parliament, within the next forty days after the rder has been so laid before that House, resolves that the Order ought to be annulled, it shall after the date of that Resolution be of no effect, without prejudice to the validity of anything done in the meantime under the Order or to the making of a new

[137] Special Orders have been made in the case of about 40 trades.
[138] Cf. Tillyard, *op. cit.*, pp. 83-87.
[139] Cf. Hutchins and Harrison, *op. cit.*, Appendix A.

Order. The Order while it is in force, shall, so far as is consistent with the tenor thereof, apply as if it formed part of the enactment which provides for the making of the Order.[140] The power to make Orders is relevant to 45 sections of the Factory Act, and has been exercised in regard to 33 of these sections.

The powers of local authorities and their officers for the purpose of their duties with respect to workshops and workplaces under this Act of 1901 and under the law relating to public health[141] were that they should have, without prejudice to their other powers, all such powers of entry, inspection, taking legal proceedings, or otherwise, as an inspector under this Act.[142] The term local authority for the purpose of this Act includes city and town councils, urban and rural district councils acting as the local authority for public health purposes.[143]

The labour code known as the Factory and Workshop Act, 1901, has been added to by nine statutes besides the two already mentioned, the Employment of Children Act, 1903, and the Notice of Accidents Act, 1906. The Census of Production Act, 1906,[144] authorizing a small alteration in the time for sending in returns of persons employed, is the least important, but the remaining six indicate the steady progress of State control in administering the provisions of the Act and in extending it to include more workers. The Factory and Workshop Act, 1907,[145] brought "commercial laundries" under the general law, and applied the Act, subject to modifications, to work such as needlework, embroidery and laundry work carried on in charitable and reformatory institutions, unless the institution was already under Government inspection. The work of women was further pro-

[140] Act of 1901, sect. 126, subsections 1-4.

[141] The Public Health Act, 1875, sect. 91, is the basis for provisions with regard to sanitary conditions of workshops and domestic factories, but the Factory and Workshops Act, 1901, extended that section so as to make provisions for sanitation in factories and workshops, with two minor differences, practically identical—see ss. 1-2, Part I, 1901 Act.

[142] Act of 1901, Part VIII, sect. 125.

[143] Act of 1901, sect. 154.

[144] 6 Edw. VII. c. 49.

[145] 7 Edw. VII. c. 39. As early as 1904 Bills were presented for substantial changes in the Factory Acts: see the Factory and Workshops Act (1901) Amendment Bill (House Bill No. 61, 1904), by Mr. Tennant, and the Accidents (Mines and Factories) Bill, by Mr. Cochrane (House Bill, No. 73, 1905).

tected by the Employment of Women Act, 1907,[146] repealing section 57 of the Act of 1901 which allowed unrestricted labour by women in flax mills, in order to bring the law of the United Kingdom into conformity with the rules of the 1906 Berne Convention. A further international agreement found expression in the White Phosphorus Matches Prohibition Act, 1908,[147] prohibiting the use of yellow phosphorus in the manufacture of matches or in the sale or importation of matches so made. Parliament again gave authority to the Secretary of State to legislate in the Factory and Workshop (Cotton Cloth Factories) Act, 1911,[148] which superseded sections 90-94 and Schedule IV of the Act of 1901, for the Secretary of State could make regulations as regards cotton cloth factories, which he did in the Regulations of 1912. The systematic growth of industrial regulation is noted in these Acts, and their development seemed only a natural outcome of the State's duty of protection. There was no particular comment when it was decided by Parliament how a laundry should be ventilated, nor did it appear an unwarranted interference when certain industries were forced by law to change their method of manufacture or go out of business.

The Employment of Women, Young Persons and Children Act, 1920,[149] carried out four conventions agreed to at the Washington Conference in 1919. They were conventions (1) fixing a minimum age for admission of children to industrial employment; (2) concerning night work of young persons employed in industry; (3) concerning the night work of women employed in industry; and (4) the fixing of minimum age for admission of children to employment at sea. The administration of the Act is under the Factory and Workshop Act, 1901-1920, to which it is the most recent addition, together with the Women and Young Persons (Employment in Lead Processes) Act, 1920.[150]

[146] 7 Edw. VII. c. 10. [147] 8 Edw. VII. c. 42. [148] 1 & 2 Geo. V. c. 21.

[149] 10 & 11 Geo. V. c. 65. A child is one under 14 years of age, a young person is one under 18, and at 18 a woman reaches her industrial age, 12 years before her political privilege of voting (Sect. 4). A study of interest with regard to women workers is that of Barbara Drake, *Women in Trade Unions,* Labor Research Department, Trade Union Series, No. 6 (1920), and *Margaret Bondfield* (1925), by Iconoclast (Mary Agnes Hamilton).

[150] 10 & 11 Geo. V. c. 62. An International Labour Convention.

Constant changes and continued agitation are making for a new Factory Act, to the bringing in of which the Government of Mr. Baldwin is pledged. It is certain to be an extended work for the House of Commons. From the Act of 1901 to 1926 is the most important period of England's administrative history with regard to factory legislation; any Act passed will demand a tremendous amount of legislative effort and departmental research.

Section B. The tendency toward unifying labour laws, of which the Factory Act is the pre-eminent example, is indicated in the Shop Hours Act, 1904.[151] In that year three Bills on the question of shops and early closing were introduced,[152] which brought a warning from Sir Francis Powell and Sir Frederick Banbury that it was "very hazardous to pass legislation having for its object the limitation of adult labour."[153] However this argument seemed to have little effect on the majority of the members of Parliament, especially those who looked back to 1847 to the beginning of the passing of legislation dealing with adults. There was hardly an important debate between 1900-1914 when from one side or another a member did not confess that an opponent's speech could just as well have been made three-quarters of a century before. So it was in this debate. Professor Dicey commenting on the Act was moved to say that

the time is rapidly approaching when the State will, as regards the regulation of labour, aim at as much omnipotence and omniscience as is obtainable by any institution created by human hands.[154]

Yet there has been no tendency to be less interested in the detail of regulation, and the Home Department in asking for a Select

[151] 4 Edw. VII. c. 31. This Act was cited as the Shop Hours Act, 1904, the Shop Hours Acts, 1892 to 1895, and the Seats for Shop Assistants Act, 1899 (62 & 63 Vict. c. 21), and altogether as the Shops Regulation Acts 1892 (55 & 56 Vict. c. 62) to 1904 (Sect. 10, Act of 1904).

[152] House Bills of 1904, Nos. 24, 31, and 165; the last (Cochrane's) becoming by adoption of Government the Act of 1904.

[153] Hansard, 4 S. H. C. 1904, Vol. 132, p. 802; pp. 794-802 for the second reading debate on the Dilke Shops Bill.

[154] *Op. cit.*, p. 290.

Committee in 1911 indicated the progress that had been made since the first Committee on the subject was appointed in 1886.[155]

The administrative principle of the Shops Acts has remained the same: county and borough councils, and urban district councils, in districts with a population over 20,000 can by order, confirmed by the central authority, fix the hours on the several days of the week at which all shops or shops of specified class are to be closed for serving customers.[156]

The Act of 1904 determined that the hour fixed by a closing order of a local authority must not be earlier than seven o'clock in the evening on any day of the week, except on one day it may be as early as one o'clock in the afternoon.[157]

Section C. The general principle of regulation can be well illustrated further in the Coal Mines Regulation Act, 1908,[158] generally known as the Eight Hours Act, and the Coal Mines Act, 1911,[159] comparable to the Factory Act of 1901. On the second reading debate of the first Bill in 1900, Sir Charles W. Dilke stated that the demand for the Bill was the demand of Labour, and the one upon which Labour was most agreed. Of all the suggested proposals put before Parliament by the trade unions in the ten years before this was the one which had received the largest support from Labour.[160] On the second reading debate in 1901 it was stated that the trade unions were turning more and more against strikes, and demanded the regulation of these

[155] Parl. Deb. 5 S. H. C. 1911, Vol. 23, pp. 1685-1695 (Masterman); the Committee was allowed by a vote of 262-21; Vol. 32, pp. 1773-1874, Committee Report, third reading and passing of the Shops Regulations Act, 1911 (1 & 2 Geo. V. c. 54), *op. cit.*, pp. 2796-2808, consideration of Lords' amendments. Since the Select Committee of 1886, there had been one in 1892, 1895, and 1901. In 1912 was passed the consolidating Shops Regulations Act, 1892-1912 (2 Geo. V. c. 3).

[156] See section I on the 1904 Act, and sections 5 & 6 of the 1912 Act on procedure for closing orders.

[157] Act of 1904, section 2. The Shops (Early Closing) Act, 1920, continued in force till December, 1921, an administrative order requiring shops to close not later than eight o'clock every day except Saturday. This Act was again renewed at the end of 1921.

[158] 8 Edw. VII. c. 57.

[159] 1 & 2 Geo. V. c. 50.

[160] Hansard, 4 S. H. C., 1900, Vol. LXXIX, p. 1329; pp. 1309-1318 (Sir James Joicy, in opposition to Bill because the miners of Durham and Northumberland were opposed); and the footnotes give the references to the second readings of this Bill since 1892.

things, wherever possible, by law.[161] It was very much better that the public through their representatives legislate upon matters which affected the public at large than that a section of the population belonging to one particular trade, without conferring with others and without obeying what is the obvious desire of the public, should assert by voluntary effort what might be opposed to the interests of the others. In other words, Parliament was a legislative machine for the purpose of giving effect to what was believed to be not merely for the interest of any particular class, but what is believed to be for the interest of the community at large.[162] The amount paid in wages in reference to the question of profit caused one member to say that

the very same arguments which are used to-day about the destruction of trade were used as far back as 1847, and if anyone will take up Hansard for that year he will find that practically he might be reading the very debate which is taking place in the House now.[163]

Defeated on second reading in 1900 by 24 votes, in 1901 by 13 votes, the Miners' Eight Hours Bill continued each year to be introduced.[164] When it was presented [165] in the 1906 session the author,[166] who had introduced the 1892 Bill, stated that it was drawn up on the example of the French Act dealing with that problem, that is a gradual reduction of working hours extending over a number of years. This was the seventh introduction of the Bill, it having been rejected four times and carried three times on second reading. The Government asked for a

[161] Hansard, 4 S. H. C., 1901, Vol. LXXXIX, p. 1365 (Yoxall).

[162] Hansard, *op. cit.*, pp. 1380-1381 (Atherley-Jones). Mr. J. Keir Hardie used the Home Office Report on the output of coal to answer attack of the opponents of the Bill on its unfair distribution cost (*op. cit.*, p. 1384).

[163] Hansard, *op. cit.*, p. 1382 (Atherley-Jones).

[164] Two Dilke Bills of 1904 may be mentioned: the Coal Mines Regulation Bill (House Bill No. 42, 1904), to amend the law relating to coal mines, and the Coal Mines (Employment) Bill (House Bill No. 57, 1904), to amend the Coal Mines Regulations Acts; and in 1905 the Coal Mines (Employment) Bill (House Bill No. 4, 1905), presented by Mr. Jacoby, reported before Committee and dropped.

[165] House Bill No. 11, 1906.

[166] Hansard, 4 S. H. C. 1906, Vol. 157, pp. 41-45 (Brunner); pp. 41-95, debate.

Committee on Inquiry, promising if it were done to take care of the Bill.[167] The next year the Coal Mines (Eight Hours) Bill[168] was introduced again by Mr. Walsh for the Labour Party and the Miners' Federation. He referred to the fact that for 19 years it had been presented as a distinct Bill for the limitation of the hours of labour in mines, coming from the House in that form in 1889, and for two years before that it took the form of the amendment of measures which were before the House. "There was a satisfaction in knowing that, after all," he said, "the matter has never been looked upon as a purely Party question."[169] The Home Secretary supported[170] the Bill, asking that it go before the Committee on Trade; and though the second reading of the Government Bill was not reached in the 1907 session, the Address of 1908 promised the Bill's introduction, and on June 21 it was presented[171] and by a vote of 204 to 89 became law that year.

The Coal Mines Regulation Act, 1908, prohibited a workman from being below ground in a mine for the purpose of his work, and of going to and from his work, for more than eight hours during any consecutive twenty-four hours.[172] The passing of this Act was the first definite statutory regulation of hours for adult male labour. The Factory and Workshop Act, 1901, did not

[167] Hansard, *op. cit.*, pp. 59-61 (Gladstone). The Coal Mines Regulation Bill (House Bill No. 16, 1906), introduced by Mr. Compton-Rickett, was dropped; and in this year the Labour Bill on the Hours of Railway Servants (House Bill No. 211, 1906), was introduced by Mr. Crooks (see Hansard 4 S. H. C. 1906, Vol. 157, pp. 552-581, debate).

[168] House Bill No. 13, 1907; Hansard, 4 S. H. C. 1907, Vol. 172, pp. 501-556, second reading debate.

[169] Hansard, *op. cit.*, pp. 501-502.

[170] Hansard, *op. cit.*, pp. 536-545 (Gladstone). The Walsh Bill provided that working hours below ground in coal mines be limited to nine in 1908, eight and one-half in 1909, and eight thenceforward. Dropped after report of Committee when Government Bill was prepared, Coal Mines (Eight Hours) Bill (No. 2), (House Bill No. 295, 1907).

[171] Hansard 4 S. H. C., 1908, Vol. 190, pp. 1343-1362 (Gladstone), pp. 1343-1456, debate, then Vol. 191, pp. 1261-1344, further debate; note speeches of President of Board of Trade, pp. 1325-1354 (Churchill), and Hardie (1281-1288) Report stage: Vol. 198, pp. 517-608, 779-907, 942-1098; third reading, pp. 1285-1361; consideration of Lords amendments, pp. 2269-2294. For House of Lords: second reading, pp. 1418-1528; Committee, pp. 2006-2040; third reading, pp. 2198-2205.

[172] **Act of 1908, sect. 1.**

directly interfere with the hours of adult male labour, but the same beneficial experience that Millerand sought in the limitation of hours of work for women and children, that it would by inspection and enforcement materially affect the working conditions of men, was true in England. But by the passing of the Act of 1908 Parliament began the interference with the right of a workman of full age to labour for any number of hours agreed upon between him and his employer. The contravention of this Act by the workman himself imposes a penalty upon him,[173] and if the workman is below ground for a longer period during any consecutive twenty-four hours than the time fixed in the Act he shall be deemed to have been below ground in contravention of this Act unless the contrary is proved.[174] The passing of this Act made more certain the fact that the State was considered to be the protector of the life of the whole family, for legislation with regard to the adult male is in keeping with that faith. It was a long way from the Act of 1802. Post-war legislation is considered later but it may be stated that the Coal Mines Act, 1919, is a direct continuation of the Act of 1908, for it established the principle of a seven hour day.[175]

In announcing the Government measure which became the Coal Mines Act, 1911,[176] the Home Secretary said that it was based on the report of the Royal Commission appointed in 1906, with further provisions recommended by departmental experience and by recent colliery disasters. The legislation sought was essentially that of safety, it was said, and since 1887 there had been Acts dealing with specific points, but there was no further safety legislation.[177] The Bill as passed contained 127 sections,[178] being debated in committee for thirty days, in contrast

[173] *Ibid.*, sect. 7. [174] *Ibid.*, sect. 7, sub-sec. 3.

[175] Act of 1919, sect. I, 9 & 10 George V, c. 48.

[176] 1 & 2 Geo. V. c. 50.

[177] The beginning was the Coal Mines Regulations Act, 1887 (50 & 51 Vict. c. 58), then the Act of 1896 (59 & 60 Vict. c. 43), and the amending Act for 1887 of 1903. In connection should be taken the Coal Mines (Check Weighers) Act, 1894 (57 & 58 Vict. c. 52), the Coal Mines (Weighing of Minerals) Act, 1905 (5 Edw. VII. c. 9), and the Checkweighing in Various Industries Act, 1919 (9 & 10 Geo. V. c. 51), providing protection for rights of the worker. Certain of the Factory Acts also applied.

[178] Part I ss. 1-28 dealt with Management; Part II ss. 28-75, with Safety; Part III ss. 76-79, Provisions as to Health; Part IV ss. 80-85, Provisions

to the 1887 Act, which was discussed only four days in committee.[179] At the time the Act was passed the number of workers employed was 1,049,000, of whom 848,000 worked below ground, and their safety was the main consideration of the Government from first to last in the Bill.[180] The Home Department pointed out that in two recent mining disasters the loss of life had been more than in any battle fought in the South African War. The administration of the Act again entrusted large powers to the central authority, for the Secretary of State was given the right to make general regulations and special regulations as well as power by special orders.[181] In the vote on Account, March 21, the Government promised 30 working class inspectors of mines in that year.[182] This fact together with the advance in protective provisions made the Act one of the most constructive passed by Parliament for the safety of the worker. It was no party question and it was passed without division. A minor amending Act was passed in 1914;[183] and post-war legislation has only completed the comprehensive nature of the earlier Act. Post-war legislation has also increased the powers of the central authority; a good example of this tendency being the Check Weighing in Various Industries Act, 1919,[184] an Act which applies primarily to the coal mining industry, but it is provided that the provisions of this Act may be extended by regulations made by the Secretary of State to any other industry where payment is made by weight.

as to Accidents; Part V ss. 86-90, Regulations; Part VI ss. 91-95, Employment (Boys, Girls and Women); Part VII s. 96, Wages; Part VIII ss. 97-100, Inspectors; Part IX ss. 101-127, Supplemental.

[179] Parl. Deb. H. C. 5 S. 1911, Vol. 22, pp. 2646-2652 (Churchill), pp. 2646-2674, second reading debate entire; Vol. 31, pp. 1392-1524, 1544-1629, consideration of Standing Committee's amendments; Vol. 32, pp. 1233-1363, Report and third reading.

[180] Parl. Deb., *op. cit.*, pp. 1361-1362 (Masterman).

[181] See section 86 for procedure; also Schedule Second (Part I), for general regulations, and (Part II) special regulations. Cf. section 19 of the Mining Industry Act, 1920.

[182] In 1912 there were 205 inspectors and assistants, 18 of whom were women, administration costs being about £100,000. See *Annual Report of the Chief Inspector of Factories and Workshops for the Year 1912* (Cd. 6852), 1913.

[183] 4 & 5 Geo. V. c. 22.

[184] 9 & 10 Geo. V. c. 51.

Part IV

The State and the Housing of the People

Two important aspects of State action between 1900 and 1925 are dealt with in this section on the Housing of the Working Classes, and in the section which follows on Old Age Pensions. The State, in the first, has intervened after the breakdown of private enterprise to supply a public need; and in the second, the State has established the civil right of a citizen for a pension. A standard of life in each instance has been affirmed, for which the State stands as a guardian for the whole community, and, with regard to certain classes, undertakes on its own responsibility to make possible. This standard of life is determined for the community and for the individual; the common bond between them being recognized in the statutes which aim to protect both from falling below a certain minimum.[185] The constant reinterpretation of a satisfactory standard and the consequent effect on legislation is a remarkable feature of Housing and Old Age Pensions enactments. It is a reflection of a developing social and personal standard of life in the community as well as a test of how far the State will go in helping to promote that standard by laying down from time to time a progressive minimum of existence. Just as a higher standard of working class houses made private speculation insufficient and its failure a social menace, so a better security of a personal standard of living under modern conditions compelled the State to consider the needs of over half of its old age population.

The Housing of the Working Classes Acts provide a continuous history of Parliamentary action on an important social problem. The debates of 1900 reviewed the history of the Acts passed the fifty preceding years, beginning with Lord Shaftesbury's Labouring Classes Lodging Houses Act, 1851,[186] continuing with

[185] Cf. H. W. Macrosty, *Trusts and the State* (1901). "To the organised State alone can we entrust the guardianship of the standard of living" (p. 309). See Hugh Dalton, *Public Finance* (1923), for fresher statement of this principle.

[186] 14 & 15 Vict. c. 34. A summary of the Acts repealed in 1890 follows: Dwelling Houses (Scotland) Act, 1855, (18 & 19 Vict. v. 88); Labouring Classes' Dwelling Homes Act, 1866 (29 & 30 Vict. c. 28); Artizans' and

the Torrens Acts of 1868-1882, the Cross Acts of 1875-1882, the consolidated Housing of the Working Classes Act, 1885,[187] and the Housing of the Working Classes Act, 1890,[188] which repealed all previous legislation. Lord Salisbury moved in the House of Lords in 1884 for a Royal Commission on Housing, and in that year Mr. Gladstone appointed the Commission whose Report, a Labour member believed,[189] was responsible for Salisbury and his party being in power in 1890. The Act of that year based on the Report represents the progress of public and legislative opinion.

The period included between the Labouring Classes Lodging Act, 1851, and the Housing of the Working Classes Act, 1900,[190] marks the development of modern public administration in Great Britain.[191] The expansion of central and local authority is obvious in the Housing Acts. A growth of sentiment which made it possible for the Act of 1890 to empower local authorities to purchase (with right of compulsion) land on which they could build houses for sale to private individuals, was only another indication of the creation of administrative agencies to meet the necessary legislation which resulted from the spread of collectivist doctrine.[192] Before 1890 the local authority had little power with regard to house building, but the Act of that year

Labourers' Dwellings Act, 1868 (31 & 32 Vict. c. 130); Labouring Classes' Lodging Houses and Dwellings (Ireland) Act, 1866, (29 & 30 Vict. c. 44); Artizans' and Labourers' Dwellings Improvement Act, 1875, (38 & 39 Vict. c. 36); for Scotland, 1875 (38 & 39 Vict. c. 49); Artizans' and Labourers' Dwellings Improvement Act, 1879 (42 & 43 Vict. c. 63); for Scotland, 1880 (43 Vict. c. 2); Artizans' and Labourers' Dwellings Act (1868) Amendment Act, 1879 (42 & 43 Vict. c. 64); and Amending Act same year, 1879 (43 Vict. c. 8); and, finally, Artizans' Dwellings Act, 1882 (45 & 46 Vict. c. 54). All repealed except sections 3, 7, 8, 9, and except section 10 so far as it relates to by-laws authorized by those sections, by 1890 Act. Sections mentioned are yet active and can be used.

[187] 48 & 49 Vict. c. 72. [188] 53 & 54 Vict. c. 70.

[189] Hansard, 4 S. H. C., 1900, Vol. LXXXII, pp. 1274-1287 (Steadman),

[190] 63 & 64 Vict. c. 59.

[191] Cf. F. W. Maitland, *The Constitutional History of England,* edited by H. A. L. Fisher, Cambridge University Press (1908), Period V. Sketch of Public Law at the Present Day, 1887-8, sect. H. "Social Affairs and Local Government," pp. 492-506.

[192] See Sidney Webb, *Socialism in England* (1890); cf. W. G. Towler, *Socialism in Local Government* (1908), and A. W. Kirkaldy, *Economics and Syndicalism* (1914), chapters 3 and 5.

gave large powers of buying up insanitary areas, of demolishing insanitary dwellings, of letting out land to contractors under conditions as to the rebuilding of dwellings for the poor and of selling to private persons the houses erected. Municipalities were allowed to build additional houses on land not previously built upon, and to erect, furnish and manage lodging houses.

The advocates of Housing reform throughout the debates of 1900 sought to place foremost their contention that greater opportunities should be given to the local authorities to grapple with the areas for which they were responsible. The debates on Local Taxation [193] that year were an interesting commentary in point, and the fact was emphasized by Mr. Lloyd George that "during the course of the last 25 years there were 119 purposes for which local taxation had been authorized by Parliament." [194] The discussions on Municipal Trading [195] which preceded the appointment of a Select Committee on that subject bear also upon the unusual growth of the powers of local authorities. The large administrative powers given to district councils under the Housing of the Working Classes Acts and the Factory and Workshop Act, 1901, are proof of the progress made up to that time. Subsequent legislation down to 1914 carried forward very quickly and in a comprehensive manner this principle of State administration. For, "It should never be forgotten," Professor Dicey pointed out, "that powers given to local authorities are, no less than powers possessed by the central government, in reality powers exercised by the State." [196]

[193] Hansard, 4 S. H. C. 1900, Vol. LXXXII, pp. 441-483. Cf. Debate on Amendment to 1911 Address on Burden of Local Rates, the official Opposition Amendment (Parl. Deb. H. C. 5 S. 1911), Vol. 21, pp. 700-818.

[194] Hansard, *op. cit.*, p. 442.

[195] Hansard 4 S. H. C., 1900, Vol. LXXXI, pp. 757-776, 1343-1374.

[196] *Op. cit.*, p. 291 n 1. See *Final Report of the Royal Commission on Local Taxation,* 1900 (Cd. 638, 1900); and *The Appendix to the Final Report (England and Wales) of the Royal Commission on Local Taxation,* 1902 (Cd. 1221). Compare the *Final Report of the Departmental Committee on Local Taxation* (Cd. 7315), 1914, considering "locally administered services of a national character." . . . "The characteristic of this intermediate class of semi-national services is that while they are administered by local authorities, the State has at the same time so marked an interest in their efficiency as to justify a claim to the supervision of their administration." The Budget of 1914 (H. C. Papers No. 132) considers the changes affecting the relations of central and local taxation.

The Government in introducing [197] in 1900 their Bill to amend Part III of the 1890 Act, made it plain that they had in mind not so much fresh legislation as a more effective administration of the existing laws. The new principle they proposed to enact was that local authorities should be empowered to go outside their districts for the purpose of establishing workingmen's dwellings for those who worked inside their areas. Any council, except a rural district council, which had already complied with the earlier law was to have the power of acquiring or building lodging houses for the working classes outside their district.[198]

The debates [199] on Housing were perhaps the most illustrative for the purposes of this study in the 1900-1901 Parliament. It is oftentimes a difficult thing to judge how far members of any Parliament use the privileges of debate for party propaganda, for airing of personal bias and prejudice, or for the bringing forward of controversial issues between parties which may be used for campaign purposes. In the speeches of party leaders or private members and in the program of parties due allowances must be made for such considerations. But in the parliamentary democracies of France and England responsibility can nearly always be brought home, for the Government necessarily must define a policy and the Opposition, having always before it the possibility of becoming the Government, must assume likewise on important questions an official attitude. Often too, debates are held for no other reason than to allow a subject to be discussed from all sides and leaders given a chance to interpret party wishes. With this in mind there is a fair basis of judging the conviction of the individual member and of ascertaining the general principles for which a party stands.

The partisan emphasis and the avowal of class interest were not lacking by any side in the first debate. One Labour member declared,

[197] Hansard, 4 S. H. C., 1900, Vol. LXXIX, p. 839. The President of the Local Government Board introduced the Bill for the Government.

[198] Act of 1900, sect. 1.

[199] Hansard, 4 S. H. C., 1900, Vol. LXXXII, pp. 1260-1350, Vol. LXXXIII, pp. 427-523, and Vol. LXXXIV, pp. 923-1018, for debates which bring out full opposition to the policy of the Government because of its inadequate Bill to meet the Housing situation at beginning of century. The third reading was passed by 325 votes to 293, for which debate see Vol. LXXXV, pp. 1394-1422.

I never knew yet when the time was opportune to discuss legislation that had for its object benefit for the working classes of this country. Workingmen may be deluded by some of your promises for a short time, but they find you out. The interest of my own class is paramount with me over the interests of all other classes.[200]

The Government was able to find money to carry on the War, he said further, but for every measure of social reform there was the denial because of the expense which such reforms entailed. A member representing a working class constituency said,

When we go into the homes of the people and speak with them across the table, and not from the platform, we learn that there are two questions that profoundly interest them. They ask, "Can nothing be done to improve the housing of the working classes?" and "When are the old age pensions coming into operation?" These questions are much more interesting to them than the abolition of the House of Lords. The social policy is what claims their attention.[201]

Statements such as these provided good background for Sir Robert Reid's belief that some satisfactory way could be found, some proposal could be followed "unless the evil reaches such a stage that the people became desperate and lost their sense of justice."[202] The Prime Minister stated that the proposals brought forward heretofore had "violated some fundamental principle of equity";[203] and quoting Lord Salisbury he said that

our friends are anxious to magnify the defects of our institutions in order to destroy them; we are anxious to remedy the defects of our institutions in order to preserve them.[204]

But the proposal of the Government "whispers housing reform to the ear and breaks it to the hope of every poor workman," said one who was to be responsible in the next Government for a solution of the problem of housing.[205]

The problem was such, one member believed, that

[200] Hansard, 4 S. H. C., 1900, Vol. LXXXII, pp. 281-283 (Steadman).
[201] Hansard, 4 S. H. C., 1900, Vol. LXXXII, p. 431 (H. C. Richards).
[202] Hansard, *ibid.*, p. 436.
[203] Hansard, *ibid.*, p. 509.
[204] Hansard, *ibid.*, p. 432.
[205] Hansard, 4 S. H. C., 1900, Vol. LXXXV, p. 1417 (Burns).

no work that we can undertake can be greater or more important, but it is not a work that should be undertaken for a moment as a party work; it is merely a work of justice to our working classes. There may be points of a party character suggested as solutions, but the real question we have at heart is not a question of party at all; it is a question of the country; it is a question of everyone living in the land.[206]

The housing of the working classes "struck at conditions which made decency impossible and morality a miracle," declared Sir Walter Foster, who deplored the fact that the Government Bill in respect to rural districts did practically nothing and that it could not be looked upon as in any way an adequate method of meeting a great national emergency.[207] Any Bill which attempted to grapple with this problem ought to afford opportunities to the local authorities to reach the man who was fattening on the miseries of his fellow creatures. It should also give power to the local authorities to take over by a simpler and cheaper method all property declared to be insanitary at the bare price of land and materials; and it should further provide simple and inexpensive methods of taking land by purchase or by hire for this great public purpose in which the ordinary expense of taking land compulsorily should not be allowed. Power should also be vested in a central authority, or in a large local authority, to supervise local areas and to force local authorities to do their duty; and also means should be provided by which money should be granted at the lowest possible rate of interest for the longest period in order to enable local authorities to carry out the work of housing the people without unduly adding to the rates.[208]

It was successfully brought out in 1900 that one of the chief defects of the 1890 Act was failure to help solve the problem

[206] Hansard, 4 S. H. C., 1900, Vol. LXXXII, pp. 1293-1294 (Sir Samuel Hoare); pp. 1287-1294, speech entire.

[207] One of the final Bills to be introduced in the session of 1904 was his Housing of the Working Classes (Rural Districts) Bill (House Bill No. 207, 1904). Also a Bill introduced by Mr. Nannetti, the Housing of the Working Classes, &c., Bill (House Bill No. 92, 1904), received much support; its purpose was to amend the law relating to housing of the working classes, amend the law of rating, and to establish fair rent courts. Both reintroduced in 1905 were dropped again. Also Mr. Hutton introduced in 1904 a Cottage Homes Bill (House Bill No. 195, 1905).

[208] Hansard, 4 S. H. C., 1900, Vol. LXIX, pp. 840-841.

in rural communities, and in this connection the Small Holdings and Allotments Acts should be kept in mind. Legislation on this subject has extended over a long time; the Allotments Acts 1887 [209]-1890,[210] consolidating a long line of earlier Acts which had done comparatively small good; and in 1892 the first Small Holdings Act for England and Wales gave county councils the power to buy land and let it out in small holdings. In 1907 a new Small Holdings and Allotments Act was passed,[211] and in 1908 [212] a consolidating Act was passed which was amended in 1910.[213] County councils were given the power in 1908 to obtain land for small holdings by compelling owners to sell it to them for this purpose. The same powers were given to local authorities under these Acts as were given under the Housing Acts. Their vital significance is that, with regard to Land, definite principles of State interference and control had been established which were more comprehensively elaborated in later legislation. The various Irish Land Laws and the Land Valuation Acts have special social significance when the theory of State interference for the common good is considered.[214] People became accustomed to a State authority being exercised with

[209] 50 & 51 Vict. c. 48.

[210] 53 & 54 Vict. c. 65. A rapid survey of earlier legislation can be had from consulting the repeal schedule of these two Acts, in the General Statutes of those years. [211] 7 Edw. VII. c. 54. [212] 8 Edw. VII. c. 36.

[213] 10 Edw. VII & 1 Geo. V. c. 34. The Small Landowners Act for Scotland, 1911 (1 & 2 Geo. V. c. 49) and the 1908-1910 Acts, consolidated enactments with respect to small holdings and allotments in England, Wales and Scotland. Parl. Deb. 5 S. H. C., 1911, Vol. 26, pp. 1355-1424, second reading debate on Small Landowners (Scotland) Bill; Vol. 30, pp. 1285-1434, before Standing Committee; Vol. 31, pp. 650-656, 675-788, further Committee and third reading. Progress in House of Lords: Parl. Deb. H. L. Vol. 10, pp. 293-360, second reading; pp. 487-648, Committee. On the Small Holdings and Allotments Bill, 1911, moved by the Secretary for Agriculture see Parl. Deb. 5 S. 1911, H. L. Vol. 10, pp. 335-352, second reading; pp. 923-962, Committee, and pp. 1091-1115, third reading. In connection with this subject may be taken the Land Settlement (Facilities) Act, 1919 (9 & 10 Geo. V. c. 59), an Act to make further provision for the acquisition of land for the purpose of small holdings, amending the principal Act of 1908.

[214] The social significance of the Budget is a commonplace. For years in France and England the Treasury Ministers have remarked on this phase of their duty. The Budgets in England from 1909-1914 have special significance with regard to land taxes, and in both countries in the same period with regard to social legislation expense.

regard to the Land without at all agreeing at other times to proposals which sought to apply the same principle in other activities. A minimum wage for agricultural labourers, considered later, again provided an illustration of the far reaching effects of the land question, the Government in 1914 definitely including this principle in their program of land reform.[215]

The powers of the local authorities were being felt in many financial and administrative directions,[216] and the effect was evident in the debates of the House of Commons. The means of administration of the proposals for legislation demanded as much care and discussion as the actual needs contained in a Bill. Often the argument was advanced that those whom an Act would affect were not in favour of it, as the Miners' Bill of 1900; or, that the machinery of enforcement was inadequate and that administration would be a failure, as in the discussion of the Housing of the Working Classes Amendment of the same year. The other partner in administration had increasing recognition, which was suggested by Mr. Asquith in the debate on lead poisoning in potteries, when he said, that

> it is only by focusing public opinion in such cases that we can create the feeling of public sentiment which as everyone concerned in the administration of these laws knows is necessary for their vigilant enforcement.[217]

Public opinion played an especially strong part in the Housing agitation,[218] and it was accurately stated by a mover of an amendment to the 1900 Bill of the Government, that

[215] Cf. *The Report of the Land Enquiry Committee* (2 Vols., 1914), chap. I, Part I, Vol. II. (Urban) on ill-housing; also a most significant study is *Property: Its Duties and Rights, Historically, Philosophically, and Religiously Regarded.* Essays by various writers with an Introduction by the Bishop of Oxford (1914, 2nd ed. 1915), note papers by Mr. A. D. Lindsay and Mr. L. T. Hobhouse. Cf. H. Seebohm Rowntree, *Land and Labour: Lessons from Belgium*" (1910).

[216] See *30th Annual Report of the Local Government Board,* 1900-1901; also *Economic Journal,* June, 1902, "The Financial Control of Local Authorities," pp. 182-191; *ibid.,* "Local Authorities and the Housing Problem in 1901," by Lettice Fisher, pp. 263-271.

[217] Hansard, 4 S. H. C., 1900, Vol. LXIX, p. 988.

[218] Especially seen in the National Housing Reform Council, founded in 1900, and changed in 1910 to the National Housing and Town Planning Council. In organization and method a model of public service councils developed by individual efforts.

when people come to understand the magnitude of this evil this question will be put first in every political programme. It is a national danger in the very fullest sense. You may expand or consolidate your empire as much as you like; you may increase your defence forces; you may add to your wealth and excel in every external sign of national greatness; but if you let this question alone, if you leave it to be cured by Bills of this kind before us, you will allow the foundations of all national greatness to be sapped.[219]

Three years after the 1900 Act the Housing of the Working Classes Act, 1903,[220] gave further powers of control and administration to the local authorities. This Act defined "working class" to constitute mechanics and labourers working for wages; hawkers and others who do not employ anyone but their own family; and persons other than domestic servants whose income does not exceed 30 shillings a week. Regulations were made for the re-housing of the persons of the working class whose land was compulsorily taken, it being enacted that where houses occupied by 30 or more persons of the working class were taken, a re-housing scheme was required to be approved by the Local Government Board before any house was removed, under the penalty of a £500 fine. The Act also provided that in any letting of a working class house there should always be an implied condition that it is reasonably fit for human habitation, notwithstanding any agreement to the contrary. This Act and the Workmen's Compensation Act set up different rights than the Common Law recognized.

The progress of legislation dealing with overcrowded and insanitary living conditions had complementary aid from the Public Health Acts, represented chiefly by the Public Health Act, 1875,[221] and its amending Acts of 1890[222] and 1907,[223] and the Public Health (London) Act, 1891,[224] which gave powers to local authorities for dealing with specific nuisances and isolated

[219] Hansard, 4 S., 1900, Vol. LXXXII, pp. 1266-1273 (Robson).

[220] 3 Edw. c. 39.

[221] 38 & 39 Vict. c. 55. The system of sanitary law can be stated to have started in 1848, the main stages being marked by Acts of 1848, 1858, and 1875; and in 1919 the Ministry of Health was established.

[222] 53 & 54 Vict. c. 59. [223] 7 Edw. VII. c. 53. [224] 52 & 53 Vict. c. 50.

cases of overcrowding. These Acts are all administered by local authorities, with special powers often remaining in the hands of the Local Government Board; and the Acts enable the local councils to deal with every problem of insanitary housing accommodation which affects the worker in either an urban or a rural area.

The progress of Housing Legislation since the Royal Commission under Sir Charles W. Dilke was appointed in 1884, was best indicated in the Government Bill of 1908 [225] which was introduced by the President of the Local Government Board, who outlined the scope of the Bill and the policy of the Government.[226] "This is not a party matter," he said, "it is one in which partisanship of any kind ought not to find a place." [227] The Government purposed through the Bill

> to provide a domestic condition for the people in which their physical health, their morals, their character, and their whole social condition can be improved by what we hope to secure in this Bill. The Bill aims in broad outline at, and hopes to secure, the home healthy, the house beautiful, the town pleasant, the city dignified, the suburbs salubrious.[228]

If one is inclined to wonder at the phrasing of the Government's purpose, one can be reminded of a judgment of the time,[229] that this was a Parliament "optimistic and reforming" given a "Meph-

[225] Preceding this Bill were the Housing of the Working Classes Acts Amendment Bill (House Bill No. 9, 1906, presented by Mr. Mackarness), and the Bill of Mr. Steadman (House Bill No. 104, 1906, withdrawn). The mover of the first said the principle had been approved by all parties, and in the fifty years before 35 measures had been passed with a view to improving the condition of the rural population in this regard (Hansard 4 S. H. C., 1906, Vol. 156, pp. 131-144; pp. 131-180, and pp. 1274 ff. debate entire). The Government asked for a Select Committee, announcing that the debate had been "absolutely free from party recriminations" (*op. cit.*, p. 171, Burns).

[226] The Bill was introduced March 26, 1908, and the second reading debate was May 12, for which see Hansard, 4 S. 1908, Vol. 188, pp. 947-1063; failing to pass in that session it was re-introduced February 17, 1909, by the President of the Local Government Board, who said on second reading debate, April 5, that it was an almost exact reproduction of the Bill before the Grand Committee in 1908.

[227] Hansard, 4 S. H. C., 1908, Vol. 188, pp. 968; pp. 947-968, speech entire.

[228] Hansard, *ibid.*, p. 949.

[229] The *Nation* (London), August 31, 1907, p. 949.

istophelian touch" by the leader of the Opposition, Mr. Balfour. But the Government had seen to its facts, and the responsible Minister showed that the population was becoming urban, overcrowding was bad in the cities, the industrial areas especially, and in the counties. In Glasgow 26 per cent. of the population lived in one room, and in London 14 per cent. The Government in reintroducing the Bill in 1909 declared that "the majority of those for whose welfare this Act is designed have at present no home."[230] Class Legislation; but a necessity had to be faced. By their declarations the Government was committed to a radical program, justifying it on straightforward collectivist doctrine, for they intended for the State to do what had not been done or could not be done by private or individual effort.

The Act of 1909[231] set forth a new constructive principle, Town Planning, and extended the powers delegated to the local authority, broadly confirming this general administrative tendency which endowed with larger and more stringent powers the local government councils of England. This is made clear by the fact that the 1890 Act made it optional for the Council to build new houses in extreme instances, but the 1909 Act made it the duty of the Council to build new houses where needed. Part III of the Housing Act of 1890 was made universally applicable without adoption, so that local authorities might build new houses without getting leave from the County Council; and the Act

[230] Parl. Deb. H. C., 1909, vol. 3, p. 797 (Masterman); pp. 787-797, entire speech; pp. 733-742, entire speech of President of the Local Government Board in reintroducing Bill; and pp. 733-798, 849-871, complete second reading debate, 1909.

[231] 9 Edw. VII. c. 44. "An Act to Amend the Law relating to the Housing of the Working Classes, to provide for the working of Town Planning Scheme, and to make further provision with respect to the appointment and duties of County Medical Officers of Health, and to provide for the establishment of Public Health and Housing Committees of County Councils." A Bill to consolidate the Town Planning Acts was introduced by the Labour Government in 1924, and was passed by the House of Lords but its passage through the House of Commons was not completed. Town-planning schemes in preparation in 1925 covered considerably more than a million acres of land, and, pending the preparation and approval of the schemes, development is guided and controlled by the responsible Local Authorities over the whole of this area under Interim Development Orders issued by the Minister of Health, and subject to an appeal. All development is thus brought into conformity by the Ministry.

allowed land to be acquired compulsorily on the terms of the Small Holdings and Allotments Act, 1907.[232] The Public Works Loan Commissioners were empowered to grant loans to rural authorities for the purposes of the Bill for eighty years, the rate of interest not varying with the duration of the loan. The Act enabled the Local Government Board to authorize a borough or urban District Council to prepare a town planning scheme in or about the neighborhood of their area; to facilitate such a program various provisions were made for the exchange of land and for compulsory purchase.

This Act, besides consolidating the previous Housing Acts, made a decided step in advance in dealing with the Housing situation by making the existing law obligatory which enabled local authorities to provide houses. The first part[233] of the Act of 1909 dealt with the housing of the working classes, and the second part with town planning.[234] The Bill was subjected in the House of Lords to several amendments which were unsatisfactory to the Government.[235] The great objection to the Bill by the Lords was that it conferred too great powers on the Local Government Board, which was viewed as an increasing menace.[236] The Lords amendments when sent to the House were considered unsatisfactory,[237] and the Bill was returned for further consideration. At that time the debate centred about the increasing power which the Local Government Board might exercise, but the

[232] 7 Edw. VII. c. 54. "To consolidate the enactments with respect to small holdings and allotments in England and Wales."

[233] Parl. Deb. H. C., 1909, Vol. 6, pp. 833-906, for opening discussion on the allocation of time for Committee stage; Vol. 10, pp. 28-150, for Committee debate on Part I Housing.

[234] Pp. 187-324, for Part II Town Planning; pp. 1635-1714, consideration and third reading.

[235] Parl. Deb. H. L. 5 S., 1909, Vol. 2, pp. 1140-1184, second reading debate in House of Lords; presented by Earl Beauchamp for Government (pp. 1140-1147), supported chiefly by the Bishop of Birmingham (pp. 1157-1161) and the Archbishop of Canterbury (pp. 1165-1168). Committee stage, Parl. Deb. H. L. 5 S., 1909, Vol. 3, pp. 25-126, pp. 130-359; third reading and passed, *op. cit.*, pp. 635-712, and p. 1007.

[236] Parl. Deb. H. L. 5 S., 1909, Vol. 2, pp. 1147-1157 (Earl of Onslow).

[237] Parl. Deb. H. C. 5 S., 1909, Vol. 11, pp. 1448-1627, reconsideration; Government reasons for refusal of amendments, pp. 1448-1450 (Burns); and final reconsideration, second time, after Lords consideration of Commons amendments, Parl. Deb. H. C. 5 S., 1909, Vol. 13, pp. 445-448.

Marquess of Salisbury counselled patience and tact, for the country, he said, must be conciliated on the question of social reform and the House of Lords could not allow the impression to grow that they were opposed to measures of reform.[238] This has its significance in this study, wholly aside from the constitutional issue, because it was the same argument which had been used in 1906 by the Marquess of Lansdowne on the Trade Disputes Bill, when he counselled acceptance.

The importance of administration was emphasized in the strong objections that the House of Lords held on any extension of the powers of the Local Government Board,[239] and the Act of 1909 effectively laid down administrative discipline. It made compulsory the optional clauses of the 1890 Act with regard to inspection,[240] and every County Council was required to appoint a medical officer of health with full powers over housing and inspections. The Council of every borough or urban or rural district must cause their district to be inspected in order to ascertain whether any dwelling-house is in a state so dangerous or injurious to health as to be unfit for human habitation. The regulations made by the Local Government Board under the Act have built up a system of inspection reports that show how effectively the Act is being carried out in every administrative area, and the exact condition of the housing situation of any district can be gotten from these reports. The detailed attention given to the work of inspection and the powers of the Council to act upon the reports of the Medical Officer of Health and the Inspector of Nuisances, together with the penal power contained in the closing order of the Council, gave the Act of 1909 a comprehensiveness that no Act of social legislation had

[238] Parl. Deb. H. L. 5 S., 1909, Vol. 4, pp. 667-673; and pp. 667-728 entire debate on Commons amendments.

[239] In 1919 the duties of the Local Government Board were taken over by the Ministry of Health, an interesting commentary on the growth of State departments and their functions in England, which the transfer clause of the Act suggests. Professor Maitland years ago observed "that every reform of local government has hitherto meant an addition to the powers of the central government. These two processes have been going on side by side; on the one hand we get new organs of local government, on the other hand we get new organs of central government" (*op. cit.*, p. 498).

[240] Act of 1909, sect. 17.

had up to that time. The drastic powers as to the closing and demolition of insanitary dwellings, the clearance and rehousing powers, together with the constructive duty of providing more houses, indicate how seriously the State concerned itself with the housing of the people. By 1909 the State had definitely put forward the housing of the people as a foremost public concern.[241]

Before considering postwar legislation on housing, the program of national development which the famous Budget speech of April 29, 1909, intimated would be introduced may be considered.[242] The Chancellor of the Exchequer said the Development Bill which the Government had in mind would include such objects as the institution of schools of forestry, the purchase and preparation of land for afforestation, the setting up of a number of experimental forests on a large scale, expenditure upon scientific research in the interests of agriculture, experimental farms, the improvement of stock, the equipment of agencies for disseminating agricultural information, the encouragement and promotion of co-operation, the improvement of rural transport so as to make markets more accessible, the facilitation of all well-considered schemes and measures for attracting labour back to the land by small holdings or reclamation of wastes. That was only one side of the problem which fully illustrates the essentially serious attitude of the leaders of the Government in making legislation an instrument of service in raising the condition of the people of England. That there has been no new legislation but what has been built on the achievement of those years is proof of the constructive genius of a Parliament which passed ameliorative and protective measures a nation has used in a long struggle of war and in an equally difficult time of peace. But the spirit of the Government is more important, it is the force which gives validity to the passion for social betterment, interpreting the indictment

[241] For debate on administration of Housing Act in the Supply vote for the Local Government Board, 1912, see Parl. Deb. 5 S. H. C., 1912, Vol. 39, pp. 137-216. See also the debate on the Housing of the Working Classes Bills (I and II) of Sir A. Griffith-Boscawen, based on the French State system, it was claimed, offered as amending measures to the 1909 Act: Parl. Deb. 5 S. 1912, H. C., Vol. 35, pp. 1413-1495, and Vol. 41 (Bill No. 2), pp. 2973-2975.

[242] Parl. Deb. H. C., 1909, Vol. 4, pp. 472-548; social problems dealt with in pp. 481-494.

of countless bluebooks. One side of the problem was to remake England, no less a task than seemed fit for parliamentary endeavour then, and the other was to replenish the capital of human material.

"We have, more especially during the last sixty years," the Chancellor of the Exchequer continued, "in this country accumulated wealth to an extent which is almost unparalleled in the history of the world, but we have done it at an appalling waste of human material. We have drawn upon the robust vitality of the rural areas of Great Britain, and especially of Ireland, and spent its energies recklessly in the devitalizing atmosphere of urban factories and workshops as if the supply were inexhaustible. We are now beginning to realise that we have been spending our capital, and at a disastrous rate, and it is time we should make a real, concerted, national effort to replenish it. I put forward this proposal, not a very extravagant one, as a beginning."

On the second reading [243] of the Development Bill, the success of which had been linked with the Budget,[244] Lord Hugh Cecil, the most strenuous opponent of the Bill, quoted the words of the Labour leader Hardie, who had just written that it was "the most revolutionary measure ever introduced into Parliament, and that it endorses one of the main principles of the Right to Work Bill." [245] Two years later, 1911, the mover of the Labour Right to Work Amendment declared that

that Act (the Development Act, 1909 [246]) contains every proposal of the Labour and Socialist movement for the last 20 and 25 years, proposals about afforestation, erosion of the coast, building of light railways, and reclamation of land.[247]

There is no wonder that the chief objection in the House of Lords was that the Bill meant in the long run nationalization of land,[248]

[243] Introduced August 26, 1909, and read a second time on September 6. Parl. Deb. 5 S. H. C., 1909, Vol. 10, pp. 906-1046, second reading and passed by a vote of 137 to 17, after closure applied, and after a defeat by 105 votes to 6 of an amendment limiting the grant to one year of £500,000.

[244] Part VII, clauses 87-91, of the Finance Act, 1909, are the provisions.

[245] Parl. Deb. 5 S. H. L., 1909, Vol. 10, p. 1047.

[246] 9 Edw. VII. c. 47.

[247] Parl. Deb. 5 S. H. C., 1909, Vol. 21, p. 590 (O'Grady).

[248] Parl. Deb. 5 S. H. L., 1909, Vol. 3, pp. 291-299.

but the President of the Board of Agriculture in his explanation [249] of the six clauses on development and the other fourteen on road improvement gave no such interpretation. All efforts to amend the Bill failed,[250] which again called down condemnation from the leader of the Opposition in the House of Lords on the policy of the Government. The Development and Road Improvements Funds Act (1909) Amendment Bill which was brought forward the next year,[251] supplementary to the 1909 Act, provided an opportunity for an opponent to recall his opposition to the original Act because "it has always seemed to me," he said, "to fulfil the idea of a Socialist measure more completely than any Act which has been before Parliament." [252] The debate was interesting also because the Act was taken by Mr. Belloc as an opportunity of again showing that the party system was the curse of Parliament, and to pay his respects to the author of the Act as the chief example of the evil which he condemned.[253]

Criticism of Acts of Parliament on the grounds of their Socialistic nature, as against the Development Act, read strangely [254] now when the legislation of 1909 is considered with postwar development, conditioned necessarily by the experience of the War and the needs when peace came. Legislation after the war has extended the powers of the State with regard to Housing and the Land; the policy of State aid and control has been directly carried on and new principles confirmed. Early

[249] Parl. Deb., *ibid.*, pp. 1225-1233 (Earl Carrington); second reading debate, pp. 1225-1283—note speech of Marquess of Salisbury, pp. 1233-1242; Committee stage, Parl. Deb. 5 S. H. L., 1909, Vol. 4, pp. 200-311; amendments from Commons reported and third reading, *ibid.*, pp. 443-477.

[250] Committee stage in House of Commons, Parl. Deb. 5 S. H. C., 1909, Vol. 10, pp. 1047-1065, 1277-1279; further procedure, Vol. 11, pp. 1932-1966; report stage and third reading, *ibid.*, pp. 2204-2335, 2347-2454; consideration of Lords amendments, *ibid.*, pp. 445-448, and Vol. 13, pp. 372-445.

[251] Parl. Deb. 5 S. H. C., 1909, Vol. 17, pp. 155-183, second reading debate entire; pp. 155-157 (Lloyd George), pp. 158-161 (Sir F. Banbury); Committee stage, *ibid.*, pp. 377-399, 535-536, 581-595. All stages in House of Lords, Parl. Deb. 5 S. H. L., 1909, Vol. 5, pp. 815-817.

[252] Parl. Deb. 5 S. H. C., 1909, Vol. 17, p. 166 (Lord Hugh Cecil).

[253] Parl. Deb., *ibid.*, p. 385.

[254] Cf. Low, *op. cit.* (1914 ed.), Preface. "State Socialism has been accepted in fact if not in name; and there is no influential body of political thought which repudiates the principles, though there is much controversy as to the extent and manner of its application" (p. xxxii).

in the War the Rent Restriction Act, 1915,[255] gave Government protection against raised rents and evictions; and by the Increase of Rent and Mortgage Restrictions Act, 1923,[256] millions of working class and middle class tenants have been granted to 1926 the protection of the earlier Act. The Act of 1915, with its amendments,[257] has been continued because it has not been possible for private enterprise or State aid to establish a normal housing situation.[258] The principle already seems so securely fixed in the minds of the people, that

> though these (Rent Restriction Acts) are at present classed as Emergency Legislation, the principle of no longer leaving rent to the higgling of the market, on which they are based, has, in the opinion of many, "come to stay." [259]

The Minister of Reconstruction was convinced that the State would have to assume the major burden of providing houses for the people,[260] and in 1919 the Government confirmed completely the Act of 1909 in passing the Housing, Town Planning, etc., Act,[261] "an Act to amend the enactments pertaining to the Housing of the Working Classes, Town Planning and the Acquisition of Small Holdings." The Act made it

[255] 5 & 6 Geo. V. 1915. [256] 13 & 14 Geo. V. c. 32.

[257] The Increase of Rent and Mortgage Interest (Restrictions) Act, 1920 (10 & 11 Geo. V. c. 17), repealed all previous rent restriction Acts, including the principal Act of 1915, the Courts (Emergency Powers) Act, 1917 (7 & 8 Geo. V. c. 25), and its extension in 1919 (9 & 10 Geo. V. c. 64), the Increase of Rent and Mortgage Interest (Amendment) Act, 1918 (8 Geo. V. c. 7), the Increase of Rent (Amendment) Act, 1919. Important social principles of State control of prices and powers of investigation for "limiting the profit" were contained in the Act to Check Profiteering, 1919 (9 & 10 c. 66), continued unto May, 1921 by the Profiteering (Continuance) Act, 1919 (9 & 10 Geo. V. c. 87) and the Profiteering (Amendment) Act, 1920.

[258] The Government of Mr. Baldwin is pledged to a continuance of this State policy with regard to rent restrictions to 1928.

[259] E. F. Foa, *The Law of Landlord and Tenant* (6th ed. 1924), Preface, III-IV; pp. 911-966, for Rent Acts.

[260] See *Memorandum by the Advisory Housing Panel on the Emergency Problem in Housing,* 1918; also *The Betrayal of the Slums,* by the Rt. Hon. Christopher Addison, M. D. (1922), Minister of Reconstruction and the first Minister of Health.

[261] 9 & 10 Geo. V. c. 35; for Scotland, 9 & 10 Geo. V. c. 60.

the duty of every local authority to consider the needs of their area with respect to the provision of houses for the working classes, and within three months after the passing of this Act, and as often thereafter as occasion arises, or within three months after notice has been given to them by the Local Government Board, to prepare and submit to their Local Government Board a scheme for the exercise of their powers.[262]

Under this section 1805 local authorities were required by the central authority to submit schemes for house building in their area; a special Department of Housing was set up by the Ministry of Health, subdivided into an administrative and a technical section. The new feature of this Act was the taking over by the State of the financial loss on any unsound investment of capital by the local authorities on any scheme approved under Parts I, II, III, of the principal Act; that is, acquisition, clearance, development and rehousing; [263] and additional powers were given to alter, enlarge, repair and improve.[264] This Act was "a step which was indicated by the realization of the social necessity of house building." [265] This was further indicated in the Housing (Additional Powers) Act, 1919,[266] allowing the payment of a lump sum as a subsidy to private builders of working class houses, a completely new feature in English housing legislation. The first Act of 1919 allowed financial aid out of moneys provided by Parliament to a Public Utility Society,[267] registered under the Industrial and Provident Societies Act, 1893; [268] and the second Act of that year permitted the Ministry of Health to authorize the local authority to issue bonds for house building, town planning and other purposes of the Act. Subsidization of loss and a subsidy to private capital were the features of these two Acts. The Housing Act of 1921 [269]

[262] Act of 1919, Sect. 1.

[263] Act of 1919 (c. 35), Sect. 7. Cf. Part III of the Land Settlement (Facilities) Act, 1919, on recoupment of losses incurred by councils.

[264] *Ibid.*, Sect. 12.

[265] *European Housing Problems Since the War, 1914-1923* (Geneva, 1924), p. 87, International Labour Office; pp. 71-110, survey of Great Britain. Cf. Richard Reiss, *The New Housing Handbook* (1924); and Henry R. Aldridge, *The National Housing Manual* (1924), Parts III and IV.

[266] 9 & 10 Geo. V. c. 99.

[267] Sect. 12.

[268] 56 & 57 Vict. c. 39; amending Act, 1913 (3 & 4 Geo. V. c. 31).

[269] 11 & 12 Geo. V. c. 19.

sought to revive the Small Dwellings Acquisition Act, 1899,[270] and the same object of encouraging private enterprise is in the Housing, Town Planning, etc., Act, 1923,[271] known as the Chamberlain Act. But the essential fact of prewar legislation and its extension remains in full force, for the Minister of Health is authorized to make contributions out of moneys provided by Parliament toward any expense incurred by local authorities in promoting the building of houses by private enterprise or in providing houses itself.[272] A principle which the Housing Act of 1924[273] of the Labour Government, the Wheatley Act, extends so far as the effort to get co-operation from the local authorities is concerned. This Act provided for a 15-year local program, offering a State subsidy for houses completed before October, 1939.

In this long survey the overwhelming detail of Acts from 1851 to 1924 may obscure the important principle of State action which unifies them in aim, giving them great social value. A purpose gradually unfolds itself, becoming more clear as the standards of housing decency are raised. The State has treated housing as a public service, and while it has outlined large duties for local authorities it has vastly increased the central authority's power of control, and the purpose of it all is evident: the conditions of life must be made better for men and women and children.[274] The Housing Problem is a particular instance of the

[270] 62 & 63 Vict. c. 44. This Act was rarely used by local authorities.

[271] 13 & 14 Geo. V. c. 24. The Minister of Health was authorized to make contributions, out of monies provided by Parliament, toward any expenses incurred by a local authority in promoting or providing the construction of houses of a certain type if completed by October 1, 1925 (Section I, subsect. 1 and 2). The Act authorized the local authorities with the approval of the Minister of Health to assist private enterprises in building houses. The assistance to take the form of a lump-sum grant, the refund of rates for a specified period, or repayment of advances to a building society. The Act authorised the Metropolitan Borough Councils to provide houses themselves, instead of promoting their construction by others, and permitted the London County Council to supplement the State contribution in respect of such houses to an extent not exceeding three pounds a house each year for a period not exceeding 20 years (Sect. I. subsect. 6).

[272] Act of 1923, Sect. I, subsect. 1-2.

[273] 14 & 15 Geo. V. c. 35 (Housing (Financial Provisions)).

[274] Two recent books provide a clear statement of the belief that public enterprise must step in where private enterprise has failed, Harry Barnes, *Housing, the Facts and the Future* (1923), and A. Aayle, *The Houses of the Workers* (1924).

general principle, set out by Professor Pigou, that it is the duty of a civilized State to lay down certain minimum conditions in every department of life below which it refuses to allow its free citizens to fall. Any man or any family which fails to attain independently to any of these must be regarded as a proper subject for State action.[275]

This principle was recognized in the report of the National House Building Committee in 1924,[276] composed of building employers and employees, and a committee of manufacturers and dealers in building materials. The report plainly stated that the high cost of producing houses was such that working-class houses could not be produced on an economically satisfactory basis such as would induce the investment of capital, unless a subsidy was provided by the State. The committee said the subsidy provided in the Chamberlain Act of 1923 was proved inadequate, and the Wheatley Act of 1924 attempted to carry into effect the Committee's report. Mr. Neville Chamberlain again has charge of the national housing program in 1926, and his problem in the Ministry of Health is not less serious than it was in 1923. In one of the periodic debates in the House of Commons on the Housing situation, Mr. Chamberlain, December 18, 1925, hinted at new powers for local authorities to deal with slums. It might be necessary, he said, to give them powers compulsorily to buy slum property in preparation for future building schemes. In the meantime the property had to be made more habitable. During this housing debate, raised by the Liberal party, the Prime Minister, Mr. Baldwin, made a very important announcement of a new State Housing plan for Scotland. Mr. Baldwin stated that the Government's recent offer made to Scotland of a special subsidy of £40 a house had definitely failed in its object of encouraging local authorities to bestir themselves to deal with a national scandal. The offer, he announced, had lapsed, and the Government had decided to build itself 2,000 houses in Scotland. The Prime Minister said some persons expected the popu-

[275] Cf. B. Seebohm Rowntree and A. C. Pigou, *Lectures on Housing* (Manchester University Press, 1914); also A. C. Pigou, *Wealth and Welfare* (1912).

[276] Cmd. 2104, *National House Building Committee Report*, 1924, and also the Second and Third Interim Reports of that year (Cmd. 2310 and Cmd. 2334.

lation that lives in the infamous conditions that have made the Clyde notorious to be patient and forbearing and to admire the civilization which in these places is represented by these conditions.[277] The Prime Minister was quoted by Mr. David Kirkwood, the irrepressible Labour member from the Clyde, as saying of the conditions in the slums of Glasgow, "it is damnable." The Prime Minister looked on as he was quoted.

The housing problem is to-day more than ever a part of a larger problem—that of enabling society to control the expression and arrangements of its social life, and as Mr. Lloyd George has forcefully intimated in the Land Reports of 1925 this problem must be brought under control, even if for that purpose the interests of property have to be put second to the needs of the nation.

Part V

The State and Old Age Pensions

Long continued agitation for the State to assume a duty toward the aged poor resulted in the Old Age Pensions Act, 1908,[278] which provided that every person of British nationality who had resided within the United Kingdom for twelve years, and whose yearly means did not exceed £31. 10. 0, became entitled, as of right, on attaining the age of seventy to receive at the cost of the State a weekly pension of from one shilling to five shillings a week.[279] This large responsibility for the welfare of its citizens which the State accepted, definitely recognized that the aged poor had a claim against the community. The pensioner was not a pauper, and it was enacted that the receipt of an old age pension under this Act shall not deprive the pensioner of any franchise, right or privilege, or subject him to any disability.[280] This Act, along with certain other well-known Acts of Parliament, was taken by one learned authority as belonging in character to, and a sign of the power exercised by, the collectivist

[277] See *Report of the Committee on the Rent Restriction Acts,* Edinburgh, 1925 (Cmd. 2423), for a full account of the problem in Scotland.

[278] 8 Edw. VII. c. 40.

[279] Act of 1908, sects. 1, 2, and Schedule.

[280] Act of 1908, sect. 1, subsect. 4.

movement during the first thirteen years of the twentieth century.[281] The problem of old age pensions was before Parliament between 1896 and 1905 in no less than 37 [282] Bills, and there was no part of the social program of the Government which had received more general attention than the proposal for old age pensions.[283]

A Royal Commission on the Aged Poor appointed in 1893, presided over by Lord Aberdare, reported in 1895; [284] the following year by a Treasury Minute a Committee of nine, under Lord Rothschild, was set up "to consider any schemes that may be submitted to them for encouraging the industrial population, by State aid or otherwise, to make provision for old age." In June, 1898, the Committee reported [285] that

> after careful examination of all the schemes which seemed worthy of attention, we were very reluctantly forced to the conclusion that there was not one of them, whatever its particular merits, which would not ultimately injure rather than serve the best interests of the industrial population.[285]

The Report of the Select Committee in 1899 under the President of the Local Government Board,[286] Mr. Chaplin, stated that

[281] Dicey, *op. cit.*, pp. xxxii-xxxvi. The laws which most directly illustrate the progress of collectivism were the following Acts, taken in several cases together with the amendments thereof: The National Insurance Act, 1911; the Trade Disputes Act, 1906; the Trade Union Act, 1913; the Acts fixing a Minimum Rate of Wages; the Education (Provision of Meals) Act, 1906; the Mental Deficiency Act, 1913; the Coal Mines Regulation Act, 1908; and the Finance (1909-1910) Act. (2) For a full survey of the early schemes see the Report of the Old Age Pensions Committee, 1898, pp. 159-183; and the *Economic Journal,* March, 1909, in the article by Bertram Wilson, "Economic Legislation of 1908," pp. 130-151, gives the above number for the Old Age Pensions Bills. Each year's debates in the House of Commons from 1900 on, provide the best running commentary on the history of the agitation.

[282] Hansard, 4 S., 1900, Vol. LXXX, pp. 312-313 (Sir J. Fortescue Flannery).

[283] *Report of the Royal Commission on the Aged Poor* (Cd. 7684), 1895.

[284] *Report of the Old Age Pensions Committee* (Cd. 8911), 1898.

[285] The Report of 1898 (Rothschild), p. 9.

[286] *The Report of the Select Committee on Aged Deserving Poor,* 1899 (Cd. 296); also the *Report of the Departmental Committee on the Financial Aspects of the Proposals made by the Select Committee of the House of Commons of 1899 About the Aged Deserving Poor,* 1900 (Cd. 67).

if the State is to provide the means for the cost of pensions, the State, it seems to us, must necessarily administer the scheme, and that is a proposition which we are unable to support.[287]

Yet the numerous proposals before Parliament indicated in England, as in France, the general trend of popular and legislative opinion. The principle was becoming clearer and more fully defined as each parliamentary session passed. It had practically ceased to be a party question. The Government spokesman in 1900 said, "this question of old age pensions is one which should be placed above and beyond party politics"; and, giving broader endorsement, declared, "the elementary principle of honourable pensions for the deserving in their old age has been recognized by the community just as clearly as it has recognized the necessity for the education of our children." [288] The second reading of the Old Age Pensions Bill in that session meant an acceptance by the Government of the principle, but the matter of expense was the Government reason for not pursuing the question further at that time.[289] The mover of one of the Aged Pensioners Bills in 1904 [290] had declared that in 1902 and 1903 a Bill similar to his had reached second reading, and that the Government by allowing each year a Bill of that nature to pass second reading was committed in principle to the passing of an old age pensions scheme.[291]

The Chaplin report of 1899 said that their scheme [292] could be easily put into legislation subject to the difficulties of a financial kind being overcome. The cost of the system was to be met two-thirds by Parliament and one-third out of the county rates; and the county councils were to administer the system. It was provided that members of the Friendly Societies were to

[287] The Report of 1899 (Chaplin), p. IX; pp. III-XIII for summary and proposals of their scheme.

[288] Hansard, 4 S. 1900, Vol. LXXX, p. 315.

[289] The cost of Poor Law Relief was given for 1874 and 1897; in the former year there were 820,446 paupers in England and Wales, costing the State £7,664,959, or £9. 5. 0 per head; and in 1897 there were 814,887 paupers, kept at an expense of £10,432,189, or £12. 16. 0 each. The financial report on the Chaplin scheme revealed the wide need of a great part of the population, and yet compared with the 1919 Report to the Treasury its underestimate is patent.

[290] Public Bills of 1904, No. 17.

[291] Hansard, 4 S. H. C. 1904, Vol. 134, pp. 696-699 (Tennant).

[292] The 1899 Report (pp. iii-xiii) and the 1900 Report (p. iii).

have the right to a payment of five shillings a week at the age of 65, but that those in regular employment receiving more than that sum a week in wages or in receipt of an income of over 40 pounds were excluded.

"Let us experiment practically by some legislation," one of the Committee said, "and extend the application of the system afterwards. Make a beginning which would show the country that this House is in earnest, and which would be doing something to bring justice to the humbler workers, and remove what has been rightly described as one of the greatest scandals of the nineteenth century." [293]

The Trade Union Congress of 1900 declared in favour of the principle of old age pensions as a "civic right." But this was not the point of view of those who looked on the Report of the Select Committee as representing "the reaction in favour of the increased dependence of individuals on the State," and who saw in this reaction the main reason for the administrative failure of the poor law.[294] It had been argued by Mr. Charles Booth that the millions spent for pensions would be used as advantageously for the community in the hands of the pensioners as in those of private persons.[295] For a great many people this was a revolutionary doctrine in relief and in State protection.

"Such an argument implies socially and economically," wrote one recognized critic, "an entirely different theory from that of antecorn days, and it cannot fail to influence sentiment, as similar theories have done in the past. That the individual member of society should be under a social obligation to maintain himself is the older view which the conditions, under which the Poor Laws were enacted, were plainly intended to enforce. The new view

[293] Hansard, 4 S. H. C. 1900, Vol. LXXX, pp. 317-319 (Sir J. Fortescue Flannery).

[294] See *Economic Journal,* Vol. IX, 1899, pp. 520-540, "Old Age Pensions," by C. S. Loch.

[295] See *Economic Journal,* Vol. IX, 1899, pp. 212-223, "Poor Law Statistics as used in Connection with the Old Age Pension Question," by Charles Booth. It is hardly necessary to suggest the great influence of this author on the social problems of his time by his monumental survey of conditions among the poor. No study was cited nearly so often as his in parliamentary debates.

is that this obligation is of a very limited nature. The State and the municipality are to make grants to the individual and even to cater for his purely private and personal benefit. The principal object of these grants is not to promote the growth of well-disciplined citizenship. They are largess. That they are reserved for old age makes in principle no difference. They are the result of the same change in sentiment as during the last years has weakened the administration of the poor law, and cannot but in time lower the estimation at which prudence and self-help are held by the people. Of this change, both in sentiment and in economic theory, a new system of State finance is a necessary corollary; and a State in which classes of citizens have the social protection of special grants and government aid, is necessarily in theory and temper, and, therefore ultimately in practice, protective in the interests of class against class, and also as against other countries. It is to protection or class legislation that his report (Chaplin's) taken as an indication of public sentiment, logically leads.[296]

The foreshadowing of the Minority Report of the Poor Law Commission could be plainly seen in the tendency of Bills before Parliament in the early years of this century. Three Outdoor (Friendly Societies) Bills were introduced in the session of 1904,[297] the purpose of which was to do away with any discredit or "stigma of pauperism." The propaganda of the years had done its work, and enactments made plain the results. It is even

[296] Loch, *op. cit.*, pp. 527-528. See also his *Old Age Pensions: A Collection of Short Papers* (London, 1903). Mr. Loch was long Secretary of the London Charity Organization. William Sutherland's *Old Age Pensions in Theory and Practice* (London, 1907), gives parliamentary history and plans.

[297] The first (House Bill No. 5, 1904; Hansard, 4 S. H. C. 1904, Vol. 129, p. 854), and the third (House Bill No. 188; Hansard, 4 S. H. C. 1904, Vol. 134, p. 574), were withdrawn; but the second, introduced by Mr. Gretton (House Bill No. 106; Hansard, 4 S. H. C. 1904, Vol. 130, p. 1493), became law (4 Edw. VII, c. 32). The Outdoor Relief (Friendly Societies) Act, 1894, (57 & 58 Vict. c. 25), authorized boards of guardians, when granting outdoor relief, not to take into consideration any sum up to five shillings a week received by the applicant as member of a friendly society. The Act of 1904 made a course of action which was optional imperative. "The board of guardians shall not take into consideration any sum received from friendly society as sick pay. except in so far as such sum shall exceed five shillings a week" (Act of 1904, Sect. I, subsect. 1).

now too early for one to say just what effect this legislation has had, and to what extent the principles will be further applied. The problem became one of the first major difficulties which beset a Labour Government. In that same year, 1904, five Bills on the subject of Old Age Pensions, marked the importance of that question before Parliament.[298] In 1905 two Bills on Old Age Pensions were re-introduced,[299] and in the session of 1906 five such Bills were put before the House of Commons.[300]

The Labour party in the session of 1907 followed its policy of moving for debate on a popular subject by submitting an amendment regretting the absence from the sessional program of a measure making provision for an adequate pension for the aged poor. The Party, the mover said,[301] "approached the subject in no carping spirit of factious opposition to the Government," but that the time had been reached when the problem must be settled on "a universal plan, giving pensions not as a consequence of poverty or desert but as a civil right to every man and woman who had conformed to the laws of the country and was entitled by residential qualifications." The Chancellor of the Exchequer, Mr. Asquith, replying, said

the figure of a man or woman who, in old age, through no fault or default, is compelled to beg bread or lodging, is an eyesore

[298] Four were dropped, one withdrawn. The first two were presented by Mr. Remnant, with whom were associated several Labour and Liberal members; see Hansard, 4 S. H. C. 1904, Vol. 134, pp. 669-699, for debate on the first (House Bill No. 17); and the Old Age Pensions Bill (No. 2), (House Bill No. 23), was the first Bill re-submitted. The three remaining sponsors for Bills were, Mr. Spear (House Bill No. 24, Old Age Pensions Bill; Mr. Channing (House Bill No. 37, Old Age Pensions Bill); and Sir James Rankin (House Bill No. 108); Hansard, 4 S. H. C. 1904, Vol. 131, p. 85.

[299] Old Age Pensions Bill, House Bill No. 171, 1905 (Channing); and the Aged Pensions Bill, House Bill No. 1905 (Goulding).

[300] Aged Pensioners, House Bill No. 28, 1906 (Roberts), withdrawn; Aged Pensioners (No. 2), House Bill No. 152, 1906 (Roberts), dropped; Old Age Pensions, House Bill No. 18, 1906 (Wilson), withdrawn; Old Age Pensions (No. 2), House Bill No. 47, 1906 (Channing), withdrawn; Old Age Pensions (No. 3), House Bill No. 146, 1906 (Wilson), dropped.

[301] Hansard, 4 S. H. C. 1907, Vol. 169, pp. 216-222 (Barnes); on this amendment see speeches of Mr. Harold Cox (pp. 227-233), Sir Howard Vincent (pp. 233-238), Mr. A. Chamberlain (pp. 261-265); for Labour, Mr. Hardie (pp. 265-268), and Mr. Shackleton (pp. 256-257).

in our social system, and a standing, and, indeed, a crying reproach to our statesmanship.

He believed that when the Government could invite the House to take effective steps toward the solution of the question, it would be with the universal good will of all the parties, and confidence that they were making substantial strides in advance on the path of true social reform;[302] and that any proposal to be brought forward by the Government or other parts of the House in regard to old age pensions should be discussed on its merits apart from all party feeling.[303]

The statement of the Chancellor of the Exchequer in the Budget speech, that financial plans were being laid for an old age pension system, had been forecasted by Mr. Asquith himself, and the President of the Local Government Board expressly pledged the Government to carry forward old age pensions so far as time, means and opportunity allowed.[304] The Budget statement[305] of 1907 defined the policy of the Government on social reform, based especially on the duty of the State to the child and to the aged. Taken together with the Budget statement of 1908,[306] made by the Prime Minister himself, it is a good introduction for the social finance features of the epochal Budget of 1909. With regard to old age pensions the belief became more insistent that the State should assume the financial burden. The Lever Old Age Pension Bill of 1907[307] provided that one-tenth of the funds necessary should be supplied by local taxation funds and nine-tenths by the Exchequer. The temper of the Parliament of 1907 on the principle of old age pensions

[302] Hansard, 4 S. H. C., 1907, Vol. 169, pp. 222-227.

[303] *Op. cit.*, p. 227. The Barnes amendment, which Labour refused to support after the Government statement, forced to a vote, in which Labour abstained, was defeated by 231 votes to 61.

[304] Hansard, *op. cit.*, pp. 257-261 (Burns).

[305] Hansard, 4 S. H. C., 1907, Vol. 172, pp. 1175-1211; pp. 1189-1193, the section on social reform.

[306] Hansard, 4 S. H. C., 1908, Vol. 188, pp. 445-480.

[307] House Bill No. 17, 1907. The object of this Bill was to provide pensions for persons of 65 upwards; in the first year of operation pensions would be paid to persons of 75 and upwards; in the second year to persons of 70 and upwards; and in the third year to persons of 65 and upwards.

was indicated on the motion for second reading [308] of the Lever Bill, when a counter motion by Mr. Harold Cox,[309] seconded by Sir Frederick Banbury,[310] declaring that the House declined to proceed further with a measure which would enormously add to the national expenditure until the country had an opportunity of saying whether it was willing to bear the necessary burden of taxation, was defeated by 232 votes to 19. After the Government had said that all were agreed that something should be done and that the Government accepted the principle of the Bill,[311] the second reading was passed, and the Bill was referred to a Committee where it was finally dropped.

But the agitation for old age pensions went on unabated by the failure of the Bill of 1907. The continued discussion that centred about the Poor Law Commission helped to keep the major problems of Poor Law relief and principles of State aid before the nation. There was a determined conviction that the State should actively interfere to redress what was considered a national scandal, the lot of the aged poor.[312] At the annual conference of the Labour Party at Hull, 1908, it was urged that the Labour Party not be

> inveigled into discussing Protection, or the abolition of the House of Lords, or allowing them to be the battle cries next General Election when Old Age Pensions and the Unemployed problem need facing and dealing with. Our Party must make the social poverty problem the election cry of the future.[313]

The Labour Party considered the question of old age pensions in a special conference that year, together with a conference on unemployment.[314]

[308] Hansard, 4 S. H. C., 1907, Vol. 174, pp. 470-530, second reading debate; pp. 470-477, the author's speech; pp. 477-483, the seconder (Sir F. Channing).

[309] Hansard, *ibid.*, pp. 483-495. [310] Hansard, *ibid.*, pp. 495-501.

[311] Hansard, 4 S. H. C., 1907, Vol. 174, pp. 523-530 (Burns); the President of the Local Government Board gave the Government statement.

[312] See the *Nation* (London), March 9, 1907, pp. 104-105, editorial, "Pensions and the Poor Law," for a characteristic point of view.

[313] *Annual Report of the Labour Conference,* 1908, p. 10.

[314] *Ibid.*, pp. 83-97, for Report of these Conferences.

The inclusion in the Address [315] of 1908 of the promise that in connection with the financial arrangements of the year a proposal would be brought forward making better provision for old age fulfilled the Budget pledge of 1907, which was fully carried out in the introduction by the Chancellor of the Exchequer of the Government measure for old age pensions.[316] The principles on which the Government based their Bill were given by Mr. Lloyd George. It was non-contributory [317] because

> a workman who has contributed health and strength, vigour and skill, to the creation of wealth by which taxation is borne has made his contribution already to the fund which is to give him a pension when he is no longer fit to create that wealth.[318]

The Government had been attacked by the *Spectator* on the provisions of the Bill, and the interesting ministerial reply gives added insight into the purpose of the Government. The weekly was referred to as "the official organ of the new anarchist party which has appeared in this House. They are frankly and ruthlessly individual." [319] But the Government were not unmindful of the task before it, of legislation for a nation

> with its thronging millions, with its rooted complexities; and everyone who has been engaged in any kind of reform knows how difficult it is to make way through the inextricable tangle of an old society like ours.

The Government in their Bill were asking the House

> to sanction not merely its principle, but also its finance, having regard to the fact that we are anxious to utilise the resources

[315] Hansard, 4 S. H. C., 1908, Vol. 183, p. 4.

[316] Hansard, 4 S. H. C., 1908, Vol. 189, pp. 564-586, speech moving second reading.

[317] In contradistinction to the French system.

[318] Hansard, *op. cit.*, p. 563.

[319] Hansard, *op. cit.*, p. 584. The reference was to Mr. Harold Cox and Sir Frederick Banbury, who consistently gave similar arguments against social reform measures. For an interesting French point of view on this period and the men mentioned, as well as the typical attitude of the editor of the *Journal des Economistes,* see *Politique parlementaire et politique atavique,* M. Yves-Guyot (Paris, 1924), Book VI.

of the State to make provision for undeserved poverty and destitution in all its branches.[320]

The attitude of Labour was again plainly stated. They wanted it to be "perfectly clearly understood that the claim put forward from these benches was that old age pensions should be given as a social right without respect to any qualification." [321]

The Committee [322] stage of the Old Age Pensions Act, 1908, is especially interesting now in the light of subsequent legislation which has extended the financial provisions of the original Act. The amendments moved by Lord Cecil and Mr. Bowles, altering the wording of the first clause so as to stamp the measure as experimental, were rejected respectively by 293 votes to 55, and 341 votes to 103. An amendment by Viscount Castlereagh, embodying the principle of a sliding scale according to means, was opposed by Labour members, though they would accept a scale ranging from ten to fifteen shillings a week. Lord Robert Cecil proposed another amendment, providing that the scheme should be contributory under regulations made by the Treasury, but this was rejected by 346 votes to 86, after the Government had repeated its objections to the contributory principle. These decisive votes together with the passing of the third reading by

[320] Hansard, *op. cit.*, pp. 585-586; note also the two Government speeches, the Prime Minister (pp. 823-832) and the Secretary of State for War, Mr. Haldane (pp. 660-672). For varying points of view in opposition to the Bill of the Government see speeches of Mr. Balfour (pp. 812-823), Lord Robert Cecil (pp. 613-618), and Mr. Harold Cox (pp. 596-613).

[321] Hansard, 4 S. H. C., 1908, Vol. 189, p. 620, and pp. 618-626, entire speech; see also for Labour Mr. Barnes (pp. 804-812).

[322] The opening struggle on this Bill was the Old Age Pensions (Expenses) Motion, which was leave asked to bring in the Bill; for this see Hansard, 4 S., 1908, Vol. 189, pp. 1126-1145, 1389-1395. The second reading debate, Hansard, 4 S. H. C. 1908, Vol. 190, pp. 564-676, pp. 725-836, and pp. 889-992; Committee stage, June 23-24, *op. cit.*, pp. 1530-1636, and pp. 1737-1836; and for Committee July 6-7, Hansard, 4 S. H. C. 1908, Vol. 191, pp. 1343-1415, and pp. 1489-1592. For consideration in Committee on Supply of the vote for £910,000 for payment of old age pensions and administrative expenses in 1909, see Parl. Deb. 5 S. 1909, Vol. 1, pp. 1136-1217; pp. 1279-1312 (Resolution reported); Vol. 2, pp. 2027-2033; Vol. 3, pp. 1209-1216; for Old Age Pensions (Ireland), Vol. 4, pp. 2026-2096, pp. 2103-2131. These extended debates provide full commentary on the first year's working of the system.

315 votes to 10, sufficiently attest to the general acceptance of the principle. The leader of the Opposition defending his action and that of his party through Committee, announced that he would vote for the Bill.[323] This was a signal for Labour to bitterly attack the policy of the Opposition,[324] but the Parliamentary Secretary to the Local Government Board[325] and the Chancellor of the Exchequer[326] were both willing to end the debate for the Government, convinced that a measure was passed which had met with almost unanimous assent.

On the second reading[327] of the Bill in the House of Lords it was moved by the Earl of Wemyss that such legislation was unwise pending the Report of the Poor Law Commission.[328] Lord Rosebery, while profoundly disquieted as to the effects of the Bill,[329] urged the House of Lords not to incur the risk of a dispute with the House of Commons by rejecting a measure that was largely fiscal.[330] The leader of the Opposition, Lord Lansdowne, declared that he was opposed to the Bill, but counselled its adoption as good party tactics. So for a third time since 1906 almost identical advice had been given by two leaders, which certainly has its interest in the social politics of the period of constitutional turmoil. The rejection by the House of Lords of a Bill very dear to the Government, and upon which a

[323] Hansard, 4 S. H. C. 1908, Vol. 192, pp. 175-187 (Balfour).

[324] *Op. cit.*, pp. 193-202 (Crooks); pp. 148-158 (Snowden), also for Labour.

[325] *Op. cit.*, pp. 139-148 (Masterman).

[326] *Op. cit.*, pp. 187-193 (Lloyd George). The Bill was fought to the end by Mr. Harold Cox and Sir Henry Craik, for whose final speeches see pp. 106-123.

[327] Hansard, 4 S. H. L. 1908, Vol. 192, pp. 1335-1432, complete debate on second reading. Introduced in the House of Lords July 10, the Bill came up for second reading July 20. For all stages of this Bill following second reading, July 28-30, see Hansard 4 S. H. L. 1908, Vol. 193, pp. 1073-1164, 1438-1444, and p. 1637.

[328] Hansard, 4 S. H. L. 1908, Vol. 192, pp. 1335 ff.

[329] *Op. cit.*, pp. 1379 ff. It may be noted that the Archbishop of Canterbury and the Bishop of Ripon defended the Bill, see Hansard, *ibid.*, pp. 1389 ff.

[330] For the expression of this view from the Labour Party, see remarks of Mr. Shackleton on the Budget and Old Age Pensions, Hansard 4 S. H. C. 1907, Vol. 169, pp. 256-257.

great deal of the legislative year had been spent, the 1908 Licensing Bill, was alleged to be responsible for this last caution. At any rate the House of Commons refused to accept [331] any of the Lords amendments to the Old Age Pensions Bill, and on January 1, 1909, the Government Act became operative. Approval of the Act was evident in the policy of the Government.[332]

The Act far from being "a mortal blow to the Empire," as the Chancellor of the Exchequer quoted from the debate in the House of Lords,[333] was used as an argument for the national insurance program of the Government. Administrative improvements were made by the amending Act of 1911,[334] and continuous efforts were being made to reduce the age at which pensions were payable from 70 to 65. Besides this provision the Labour Party's Bill introduced in 1913 by Mr. Barnes, sought to provide that small pensions from friendly societies and trade unions, as well as the pensions of soldiers and sailors, should not be included in calculations of income.

At the beginning of 1914 there were 982,292 old age pensioners in the United Kingdom, and throughout the War the problem of administration became increasingly difficult.[335] A Departmental Committee [336] reported in 1919. It had been charged

[331] Hansard, 4 S. H. C. 1908, Vol. 193, pp. 1970-2000.

[332] See *Report of the Local Government Board,* 1912-1913, Part I. *Administration of the Poor Law, the Unemployed Workmen Act, and the Old Age Pensions Act* (Cd. 6980), 1913. The number of pensioners in the United Kingdom, March 28, 1913, was 967,921, made up of 363,811 men and 604,110 women. An increase from 1911-1912 of 4 per cent in England and 2.7 per cent in the United Kingdom. Cf. H. J. Hoare, *Old Age Pensions* (1915), chap. IX, pp. 163-184, a practical study.

[333] D. Lloyd George, *The People's Insurance* (1911), p. 221.

[334] 1 & 2 Geo. V. c. 16. Parl. Deb. 5 S. H. C. 1911, Vol. 25, pp. 2284-2354, second reading debate entire, moved by Hayes-Fisher (pp. 2286-2294); see speeches of Barnes, pp. 2302-2307, A. Henderson, pp. 2317-2321, and Lloyd George, pp. 2338-2339. No division on Bill (Parl. Deb. 5 S. 1911, Vol. 27, pp. 103-117); also Vol. 29, pp. 2261-2263, agreement of Lords amendments.

[335] Cf. *Administrative Concessions Made to Old Age Pensioners Since the Commencement of the War* (Cd. No. 8320, Session of 1916).

[336] *Report of the Departmental Committee on Old Age Pensions* (Cd. No. 410, Session of 1919), and *The Appendix to the Report of the Departmental Committee on Old Age Pensions* (Cd. No. 411, Session of 1919), contain the complete statistical and financial history of the system.

"to consider what alterations, if any, as regards rates of pension or qualification shall be made in the existing statutory scheme of Old Age Pensions." Reviewing the statistical history of the State system, the fact was pointed out that 56 per cent of the estimated total septuagenarian population were in receipt of Old Age Pensions, and that approximately nine-tenths of the persons were in receipt of the maximum rate. "The result is," the Report says, "that hopes of State assistance are now entertained by large sections of the community to a much greater degree than ever previously known."[337] But the inference drawn is the commentary that is significant.

The final object which we have in view is a system under which complete and adequate public assistance would be available in all cases in which it is required, whether the need arises from old age in particular, or from invalidity, unemployment or other forms of disability, and whether or not the need extends to destitution. Such a system would cover the field occupied by Old Age Pensions and National Insurance on the one side, and the Poor Law, regenerated as welfare, on the other.[338]

The development of legislation and the lessons of administration have lifted to a plane of national importance all phases of the social problem; pre-war legislation showed remorselessly the great need which the War only intensified, and, for a short time, seemed to have made possible great changes.

Post-war legislation on old age pensions is represented by the Old Age Pensions Act, 1919,[339] and the Old Age Pensions Act, 1924.[340] The first Act increased the rate[341] to 10s. a week for those whose means do not exceed £26. 5. 0 a year, and so proportionately up to the means limit of £49. 17. 6. The Act of 1924

[337] *Report of the Departmental Committee on Old Age Pensions,* 1919, p. 7.

[338] *Ibid.*

[339] 9 & 10 Geo. V, c. 102. The Blind Persons Act, 1920 (10 & 11 Geo. V, c. 49), may be considered with these Acts, for the administrative regulations are from the same central authority.

[340] See *Ministry of Health Circular No. 521,* August, 1924.

[341] Cf. S. R. & O. 1921, No. 2001, *Old Age Pensions Consolidated Regulations.*

provided that "a person will not in future be disqualified for receiving or continuing to receive an old age pension by reason of the receipt of outdoor relief," [342] and exempts from consideration in the pension scale all yearly income up to £38, or £79 for man and wife.

Plainly, then, the State has extended the principles which were established in the Act of 1908, and has already embodied nearly all of the more advanced proposals submitted at that time.[343] Beset by untoward necessities Governments have been forced to first consider a way to safety—ordinary maintenance—for the population. There has been little latitude for reconstruction. The parliamentary debates of 1924 contain no such defense of individualism nor no such hope from collective action as those of 1906-1912. It is enough that there is an Act to amend or continue, but the large hopes of pre-war legislation are expressed rarely in the Parliaments to-day. Men are more uncertain of what to do, also less willing to make unusual and experimental effort. Necessity for it has largely taken the place in the England of to-day of any theory of State action. The Government is confronted with an appalling need, and its duty is to administer the legislation of relief and protection. It is well that there were years in this century when great constructive programs of social reform could be discussed by Parliament and a basis made for the legislation of the future.

This fact was well expressed by the Minister of Health in Mr. Baldwin's cabinet, Mr. Neville Chamberlain, in moving the second reading [344] of the Widows', Orphans', and Old Age Contributory Pensions Bill, in the House of Commons May 18, 1925. This Bill was passed and received royal assent on August 7, 1925, coming into operation January 4, 1926. The Minister said he did not think that any Bill which he had introduced could be compared with the Bill which was before the House for the width of its range or for the permanence of the mark which it was likely to

[342] Circular 521, Ministry of Health.

[343] For example see the Budget of 1925 which contained proposals which went into effect from January 1, 1926. *Times,* April 29th, 1925, pp. 8-10, together with the chancellor of the exchequer's (Mr. Churchill) remarks.

[344] Debate on second reading is taken from the London *Times* of May 19, 1925, pp. 9-10. See also the *Memorandum* explanatory of the Bill (Bill No. 164, 1925) issued by the Ministry of Health (Cmd. 2405).

leave on the life of the nation or for the intensity of its human interest. The Bill, the Minister of Health continued, was in the direct succession of a long line of measures, all of which had been passed within the last 30 years and all of which had been founded on the recognition of the fact that there existed a state of society in which a large part of the population no longer themselves produced the necessaries of life, but depended upon continuous employment in other occupations to obtain the means of purchasing. A state of society of that kind involved constant menace and risk to the security of the worker, and involved, therefore, a corresponding need for providing against that risk.

The first step toward that provision was taken by the Workmen's Compensation Act which was passed in 1897, and which provided for the dependents of a man who was injured or killed by accident in the course of his trade. Then, in 1908, came the first Old Age Pension Act, which, at any rate, attempted to make some provision for the decline of earning power as old age came upon the worker, and in 1911, three years later, there came the great Insurance Act—an even more important measure, because, for the first time, it established the principle of contributions from the employer, from the worker, and from the State. Every one of those Acts had since been extended and expanded, and in particular the 1920 Unemployment Insurance Act, which very greatly increased the number of workers coming within the unemployment provision of the previous Act, so that to-day it covered something like 12,000,000 workers. Taking all these measures together, it might be said that they had effected in that short space of time a profound and almost revolutionary change in the status of the workers of this country.

The object of the Bill, it was explained,[345] was to add to the existing schemes of health insurance, unemployment insurance, and workmen's compensation a scheme of pensions for widows and dependent children, and for "old age pensions commencing at the age of 65, instead of 70, and passing, on the attainment of 70, into pensions under the Old Age Pensions Act, freed from the restrictions and disqualifications at present applied to such pensions." With regard to administration the Government con-

[345] *Memorandum of Ministry of Health,* cit., p. 2.

sidered whether they should set up a new machine to administer the scheme or attempt to link it up with one of the existing systems of insurance. For reasons of economy it was obviously undesirable to set up a new machine, and they chose to link their scheme up with health insurance, chiefly on the ground that health insurance covered so much wider a field than unemployment insurance, including something like 15,000,000 workers, against 12,000,000 workers covered by unemployment insurance. So the scheme was interlocked with the National Health Act, and was compulsory upon all workers who came under the terms of that Act.

The provisions as to pensions to widows and orphans commenced from January 4, 1926. The Act provides that the widow of a man who died at any time after that date and who had satisfied the conditions in the Act should be entitled to a pension of 10s. a week until she reached the age of 70, when she came into the old age pension, or until she remarried. If she has young children dependent upon her she receives an additional allowance of 5s. in respect of the eldest and 3s. each in respect of the others, including those under the age of 14. If the mother dies, orphan allowances are allowed at a higher scale. The provisions as to unrestricted old age pensions (i.e., pensions freed from the restrictions and disqualifications existing under the present Old Age Pensions Act), awarded to or in respect of persons over 70 on July 2, 1926, or who attain the age of 70 between July 2, 1926, and January 2, 1928, commenced from July 2, 1926. The provisions as to other old age pensions will commence January 2, 1928.[346]

The Minister of Health linked this Bill of the Government with the Rating and Valuation Bill of the Government. Different as the two Bills were in character, scope, and purpose, each of them filled its allotted place in the scheme of social reform which the Government had set before themselves and which they meant to pursue as long as they had the power and the opportunity. The policy of the Government was to use the great resources of the State not for the distribution of an indiscriminate largesse, but to help those who had the will and the desire

[346] See *Report of the Government Actuary on the Financial Provisions of the Bill* (Cmd. 2406, 1925).

to raise themselves to higher and better things. They could find that policy in the Housing Act of 1923, and in the Rating and Valuation Bill, where for the first time, they were trying to set up a standard by which they could measure the ability of the local authorities to bear their burdens, and the need they might have of assistance from the central authority. They would find it again, in the measure which he hoped to introduce next year (1926) for the reformation of the Poor Law, and for the more scientific and equitable distribution of public assistance. Pre-eminently they would find it in the present Bill, which, following on the two great schemes of insurance, combined with workmen's compensation and old age pensions under existing Acts, completed the circle of security for the worker.

On the second reading of the Bill, the Minister of Health in the MacDonald cabinet, Mr. John Wheatley, one of the most vigorous debaters that Labour commands, offered the Labour party amendment.[347] It was quite true that to-day every party in the House was in favour of the principle of widows' pensions. The Labour Party were the pioneers of this policy. In 1908, the annual conference of the Women's Labour League passed a resolution in favour of a widows' pension scheme, and at various times since conferences of trade unions and of the Labour Party had passed similar resolutions. But Mr. Lloyd George, in his speech of "helpful criticism," wisely remarked that Mr. Wheatley's quotations of Labour Party resolutions would have been more effective if the Labour Government had taken the first opportunity to carry it into effect. Yet he admitted that Mr. Wheatley had made out a strong case against a contributory scheme. The chief complaint of the militant Labour Leader was that

The Bill would not benefit more than a small fraction of the population. It would do nothing for widows, dependent children,

[347] "That this House, while it would welcome a just and generous scheme of widowed mothers' and orphans' pensions with a reduction of the age of qualification for old age pensions and the removal of the means limit, declines to give a second reading to a Bill which exacts contributions from wage earners and imposes an additional burden on industry, makes no provision for a large number of widows and orphans and families where the father is incapacitated, and, in the case of those qualified to become recipients, provides allowances which are wholly inadequate."

or orphans, and he questioned whether it would do anything in the matter of old age pensions. Its benefits were not equal to the burden that it was placing on the mass of the population and, particularly, on the struggling industries of the country. He was amazed that those who claimed to represent the capitalists should make such a great gamble on the future industrial prosperity of this country. He could only suppose that a few die-hard economists among members opposite felt it was worth taking the risk, knowing that the wages and incomes of the very poorest to a large extent determined the rate of wages, and thinking that if they were to have fuller control of the fixing of wages they must have greater control of the fixing of incomes. The only consolation he found in the whole miserable scheme was that any scheme of the kind based on the poverty of 70 per cent of the population, brought the country nearer to the end of the capitalist system.

Nor could Mr. George Lansbury, the militant veteran from Bow and Bromley, allow the opportunity to pass for a characteristic assault. He said that the Bill just gave sufficient for people to starve upon. It was a disgrace to the British Parliament that such a paltry allowance as 10s. a week should be proposed, and if he was told that there was not sufficient money to pay more he would reply that, in spite of all the taxes that had been put on, the rich were still rich and getting richer, and that profits and dividends instead of falling, were in many industries going up. He would never allow the statement to go through without protest that the expense could not be afforded at a time when the State paid an ex-Queen £80,000 without any contribution from her, £10,000 a year for Princesses, and £6000 for others, and hundreds of thousands of pounds to well-to-do people who never paid a halfpenny or did any really useful work for it. Sir John A. R. Marriott, Unionist, regarded the Bill as a really courageous, honest, and laudable attempt to advance another step toward that system of better co-ordination and more comprehensive insurance which would do something to mitigate that sense of instability and insecurity which was eating into the vitals of English industrial life. Labour again expressed objection to the contributory principle, Mr. Pethick Lawrence saying that the fundamental objection was that it picked and chose quite improperly; and Miss Wilkinson believed that the scheme bore very hardly on the single women in industry. There were from 1,500,000 to 2,000,000 women who would in the normal course of things never marry and would remain in industry all their lives. The debate was ended by the Unionist member from Oldham, Mr. Duff Cooper, quoting Mr. Wheatley as saying that as a result of the capitalist system widows had to be pensioned. Socialism was to abolish a great many things, but how or when was it to abolish widows? Widows would always be widows until a scheme was devised for the simultaneous destruction of spouses.

In a report by the Government actuary on the financial provisions of the Bill, it is stated that the estimated number of employed persons under the age of 65 coming into insurance at the beginning of the scheme are 10,170,000 men and 4,595,000 women. These numbers will increase until about the year 1960, when the estimated numbers are 11,671,000 men and 4,842,000 women. From that time onwards some reduction in the insured population between the ages of 16 and 65 is indicated by the actuary's calculations. In addition it is estimated that there will be 275,000 men and 50,000 women employed contributors between the ages of 65 and 70 in January, 1926, in respect of whom contributions will be payable between the years 1926 and 1927, so long as they are in insurable employment and still under 70. This makes a total of 15,090,000 employed persons (10,445,000 men and 4,645,-000 women) brought in as contributors at the outset. No wonder that the Act is regarded as a landmark in the history of social legislation, and under this Act every person in Great Britain already insured under the National Health Insurance scheme will be guaranteed further State protection against want and suffering, to an extent which would have been thought quite impossible a generation ago.

One source of satisfaction with regard to the Act, the London *Times* in an editorial said,[348] is that the Act is not a mere partisan measure, but "is the product of the united wisdom of Parliament," since it is the outcome of the deliberations of Parliaments wherein first Conservatives, then Labourites and then again Conservatives predominated.

[348] December 31, 1925, quoted by New York *Times* of that date.

The new pension scheme for the relief and assistance of widows and orphans and old age, is a notable landmark in our social history. The Prime Minister, the Government and Parliament as a whole may justly be proud of the results of their exertions. The Act as it stands is the coping stone on all the various measures of social insurance which have been carried on by successive Parliaments. The essence of it is that it is compulsory and contributory. It calls employers, employed and the State into co-operation as three partners in the great human work of caring for those of employed wage earners and their dependents who are less able to fend for themselves.

But the most encouraging thing about the new Government insurance scheme is the fact that sound discussion of State policy has been encouraged, and there is a clearer understanding to-day of what is demanded from the social system with regard to the minimum of security for the worker. Yet criticism has been direct and penetrating. How significant is this recent indictment.[349]

The most terrible thing about the Widows' Bill is that the Government appear to envisage a permanent state of civilization in this country in which those who have lived a life of toil and industry are unable to lay aside any adequate maintenance for their old age, and are compelled to live not on the fruits of their labour, but from the alien hands of the State. The Bill assumes that there are at present fifteen millions of persons in that condition, and the Government Actuary contemplates that in the year 1960 the number will have risen to sixteen and a half millions. It is scarcely surprising that the Socialists are not satisfied with civilization as it exists at present if this is all it has to offer. The Conservatives appear to envisage a permanent future in which the vast majority of the population are workers at a weekly wage so insufficient that they cannot make provision for their subsistence in old age and for the maintenance of their dependents. They live in rows of houses, within convenient reach of the nearest factories, built with the aid of public money, and as expensive as they look cheap. They are mulcted weekly of a part of their scanty earnings in order to provide for an entirely in-

[349] The *Nineteenth Century and After,* No. 581, Vol. XCVIII, July, 1925, "The Widows', Orphans' and Old Age Contributory Pensions Bill, W. R. Barker, pp. 19-31.

sufficient maintenance for an old age they may never enjoy and dependents who may never be attached to them. Their outings are to Blackpool and even Wembley, but not to Paris or Venice. They ride in trains, but not, as in the United States, in motor cars. Their amusements are the cinema (American) and the fringe of the football field. For intellectual recreation they can rely on the growing provision of public libraries and University tutorial classes; for outside society, on the health visitor, the school attendance officer, and the panel doctor. . . . It is a dingy prospect.

There is much to be gained from such taunts against social legislation, for it means that it is impossible to go back to the dreary argument of early parliamentary debate and the stale cries of a meaningless Individualism. State action and State aid will have done a great deal if they have helped to bring the conscience and intelligence of the community to know wherein the present organization of society has failed to create the conditions which make possible the living of the good life.

Part VI

The State and a Living Wage

(a) *Sweated Trades and the Trade Boards Act*

The conditions under which the working class lived became known by the enforcement of the Housing Act, the Factory and Workshop Acts, and the Public Health Laws. Year by year departmental reports supplemented by competent private investigation made it possible for a larger number of people to become acquainted with the "condition of England" question, and to be aware of the "startling probability" that from 25 to 30 per cent of the town population of the United Kingdom were living in poverty.[350] The low earnings in sweated trades had for many

[350] See B. Seebohm Rowntree, *Poverty: A Study of Town Life* (1901). Cf. A. L. Bowley and A. R. Burnett-Hurst, *Livelihood and Poverty* (1915), a study of four towns; S. Rowntree and May Kendall, *How the Labourer Lives* (1913), 42 Budgets of agricultural families; Mrs. Pember Reeves, *Round About a Pound a Week* (1913); and A. L. Bowley, *The Nature and Purpose of the Measurement of Social Phenomena* (1915), chap. VIII, The Standard of Living. Miss Theresa McMahon's *Social and Economic Standards of Living* (1925) is suggestive.

years been the subject of public discussion. The evil of cheap labour had been given a sound economic sanction by John Stuart Mill in a chapter "On Popular Remedies for Low Wages," in his *Political Economy;* and as early as 1889 a Select Committee under Lord Dunraven had made a report recommending better inspection and registration of outworkers in industries that depended largely on sweated labour.[351] In 1900 a Wages Boards Bill[352] was introduced, "to provide for the establishment of Wages Boards." The first introduction of such a scheme in the House of Commons was in 1898, by Sir Charles W. Dilke, who reintroduced a Bill for this purpose in 1904[353] and in 1905.[354] The Board of Trade in 1906 began a remarkable survey and census of Earnings and Hours of Employment of Workpeople in the United Kingdom.[355] The first two volumes of this series dealt with the textile trades and the clothing trades, containing appalling evidence of the industrial degradation of the nation, particularly with reference to women and girl workers.[356] The Home Office in 1907 sent Mr. Ernest Aves to study the system[357] at work in Australia and New Zealand. That year a Sweated Industries Bill[358] was introduced by Mr. Arthur Henderson; a Wages Boards

[351] Committee Reports 1890, No. 62.

[352] House Bill No. 102, 1900. Dr. MacNamara introduced in 1902 the Bill for the Workmen's National Housing Council which would have excluded outwork and sweating as allowed under the Factory Acts: see *Report of the Trade Union Congress*, 1902, pp. 81-82.

[353] House Bill No. 47, 1904. A Home Industries Bill (House Bill No. 64, 1904), was also introduced.

[354] House Bill No. 33, 1905; supported by Bell, Burns, and Trevelyan.

[355] See *Report of an Enquiry by the Board of Trade into the Earnings and Hours of Employment of Workpeople in the United Kingdom in 1906:* No. I. *Textile Trades,* Cd. 5445 (1909); No. II. *Clothing Trades,* Cd. 4844 (1909); No. III. *Building and Woodmaking,* Cd. 5086 (1910); No. IV. *Public Utility Service,* Cd. 5196 (1910); No. V. *Agriculture,* Cd. 5460 (1910); No. VI. *Metal, Engineering and Shipbuilding Trades,* Cd. 5814 (1911); No. VII. *Railway Service,* Cd. 6053 (1912); No. VIII. *Paper, Printing and Miscellaneous Trades,* Cd. 6556 (1913). The date refers to the year the Report was published; there was a similar survey in 1886, and the final Report of that study was in 1893. A summary of each Report can be found in pp. iii-iv of each volume, except Nos. II and VII.

[356] See p. vi. Vol. I and Vol. II, pp. iii-iv.

[357] See *Report on the Wages Board and Industrial Conciliation and Arbitration Acts of Australia and New Zealand,* Cd. 4167 (1908).

[358] Public Bills 1907, No. 27.

Bill [359] by Mr. E. Lamb; a Home Bill [360] by Mr. Barnes; and a Home Work Regulation Bill [361] by Mr. J. Ramsay MacDonald. The principle that the first two Bills proposed to establish was that of the minimum wage, determined by Wages Boards composed of equal numbers of employers and employees in the trades where the conditions were notoriously bad; and the last two Bills were intended to protect the home worker.

The Sweated Industries Bill was reintroduced,[362] February 21, 1908, and had for its purpose the establishment of wages boards with power to fix the minimum wage for workers in certain scheduled trades; the Home Secretary having power to add to the schedule, and payment of the minimum wage to be enforced through the factory inspectors. Sir Frederick Banbury again saw "the thin edge of a Socialist wedge," but it was accepted by the Government, the Home Secretary asking that it be referred to a Select Committee on Home Work. The Government prepared their Bill on the recommendations of this Committee, under Sir Thomas Whittaker, which issued its report in June, 1908.[363] Two Bills dealing with the problem of sweating were introduced independent [364] of the Government Bills,[365] which was introduced by the President of the Board of Trade, Mr. Churchill, on March 24.

The central principle of the Trade Board Bill was the establishment of Trade Boards in certain trades where the evils known as sweating prevailed, of fixing by those particular boards of a

[359] Public Bills 1907, No. 20. [360] Public Bills 1907, No. 158.

[361] Public Bills 1907, No. 60. The four Bills were dropped.

[362] Public Bills 1908, No. 2 (Toulmin).

[363] Committees' Reports 1908, No. 246.

[364] Mr. H. Marks, a Unionist and Protectionist, unsuccessfully moved on March 23 for leave to bring in a Bill providing that when a minimum rate of wages in any trade had been established by law or custom, it should be protected from the competition of goods produced abroad by sweated or lower-paid labour (Hansard, 5 S. 1909, Vol. 2, pp. 1642-44). On March 26, Mr. Hills, a Unionist, moved the second reading of the Dilke Wages Boards Bill, which was designed to create wage boards of employers and employed to fix a minimum wage for tailoring, dressmaking, and shirt-making, and certain other trades to be designated by the Home Secretary. The debate on this Bill was adjourned pending the second reading of the Government Bill (Parl. Deb. 5 S. H. C. 1909, Vol. 2, pp. 2061-2129).

[365] Parl. Deb. 5 S. H. C. 1909, Vol. 2, pp. 1787-1792 (Churchill).

minimum standard of wages, and the enforcement by those Trade Boards of that minimum when fixed. The Trade Boards set up under this Bill would exercise other functions besides their particular statutory functions of fixing a minimum rate of wages. They were to be a centre of information, and become the foci of organization. As centres of information they would in time be charged with some other aspects of the administration of the work of the trades, with the question of the training of workers, and also they would be able to afford information upon the subject of unemployment. They would generally be not merely boards for the purpose of fixing the minimum rate of wages, for that was their primary purpose, but boards designated to nourish, so far as possible, the interests of the worker, the health, and the state of industry of each particular trade in which they operated.

The Government statement was immediately attacked by Sir Frederick Banbury, who declared [366] the right honourable gentleman might have saved the time of the House, and made his position more clear if he had said that the principles which actuated His Majesty's Government were to be found in a complete surrender to the Socialist party. His opinion was that the Bill would put the final nail in the coffin of what was left of the trade of the country. The Parliamentary Secretary to the Board of Trade, Mr. H. J. Tennant, moved on April 28, the second reading of the Government Bill.

"Our remedy," he said, "proceeds upon lines parallel with those which have led the State to interfere with the control of the hours of labour, and the conditions of safety and sanitation. Our proposals are very limited in their application, they are limited to those plague spots of industry where, without drastic treatment, they will continue, as they have continued for three-quarters of a century, feeding upon the national wealth, supplying recruits to our hospitals, asylums, and workhouses, and swelling the ranks of the unemployable. When I am told that this legislation will subvert the foundations upon which the commercial supremacy of this country is based, I decline to believe that the commercial supremacy of this or any other country rests upon sweated labour. If I am told Capital will not stand it, I answer

[366] Parl. Deb., *op. cit.*, pp. 1792-1793.

there is another and a greater capital with greater claims upon us. It is against the drain upon this capital that we protest—I mean the life capital of the nation." [367]

The Home Secretary believed that the passing of the Bill would have a good influence on the progress of similar legislation in Europe. (So Pic agreed in France.) He thought Parliament would not only be dealing manfully with a grave social evil, but would also take another step upon that path of social organization on which we have fully entered, and along which the Parliaments of this generation of whatever complexion, willingly or unwillingly, will have to march.[368]

The second reading [369] of the Bill was passed without division. In Committee the Labour leaders fought to provide for the inclusion of other trades besides those scheduled,[370] but on this point had to be satisfied with the granting to the Board of Trade of the power to extend the Act,[371] by a provisional order, when they were satisfied that the rate of wages in certain trades or in parts of them are "exceptionally low," [372] By 1913 four new trades were included within the provisions of the Act, through the Trade Boards Provisional Orders Conformation Acts, 1913.

The Trade Boards Act, 1909, is important because it indicates plainly how far Parliamentary interference had been carried into the actual control of the industrial system. The wide powers of the Trade Boards for the establishment of minimum [373] rates of

[367] Parl. Deb. 5 S. H. C. 1909, Vol. 4, p. 351; pp. 342-351, speech entire.

[368] Parl. Deb. *ibid.*, p. 393; pp. 385-393, speech entire (Churchill).

[369] Parl. Deb., *ibid.*, pp. 341-411, second reading debate entire. The Bill went to a standing committee, and was reported to the House and read a third time July 16: Parl. Deb. 5 S. H. C. 1909, Vol. 5, pp. 961-966, 1551-1562, for finance motion; and for Committee and third reading, Vol. 7, H. C., pp. 2429-2481. The Bill was introduced in the House of Lords by Lord Hamilton, who moved the second reading on August 30: Parl. Deb. 5 S. H. L. 1909, Vol. 2, pp. 974-980; the Bill was opposed by the Marquess of Salisbury: Parl. Deb., *ibid.*, pp. 979 ff.; for entire debate, pp. 974-1015; Committee and third reading, pp. 1076-1117, September 13.

[370] *Report of the Trade Union Congress,* 1909, p. 72.

[371] 9 Edw. VII, c. 22.

[372] Act of 1909, Sect. 1, sub-sect. 2.

[373] Act of 1909, Sects. 1 and 4. Cf. *Memoranda in reference to the Working of the Trade Boards Act* (H. C. Papers 134), 1913; also the *Special Report from the Select Committee on the Trade Boards Act, Provisional Orders Bill,* etc. (H. C. Papers No. 209), 1913. It was esti-

wages meant a definite decision by Parliament that below a certain standard it was not possible for a worker to be legally employed. How that principle has been modified and extended will be considered. The Board of Trade were only empowered to apply the Act to specified trades, and by order which had to be confirmed by Parliament, to extend the Act to other trades. The trades that were in mind were the notoriously underpaid ones, the sweated and unorganized ones. The Secretary of the General Federation of Trade Unions wrote [374] in 1910, the year the Act became operative, that

> the results of the Act are not reassuring. The Trade Boards have served one useful purpose; they have assisted the Labour Exchanges to demonstrate the futility of attempting the millennium from mere Acts of Parliament.

However useful the Act would have been from that point of view alone, it was the beginning of a movement that has become increasingly important in legislation and has achieved great administrative changes in English labour organization. In the beginning it united the sympathies of great numbers of people, directing attention specifically to the social question of housing and the better enforcement of the laws of public health, made prominent a part of the investigations of the Committees and the National Anti-Sweating League.[375]

By 1909 the Government were compelled to introduce legislation on this important point of wages control, passing an Act which was "blessed by everyone, and became an Act without any vote

mated that the six Boards in the four originally scheduled trades covered 200,000 workers, of whom about 70,000 were women. These two reports provide a full account of the administration and extension of the Act of 1909.

[374] See Charles Watney and James A. Little, *Industrial Warfare, the Aims and Claims of Capital and Labour* (1912), cited pp. 235-236.

[375] See Stephen W. Gywnn and Gertrude M. Tuckwell, *The Life of Sir Charles W. Dilke* (1917), Vol. II, pp. 342-367; *Sweated Industries Exhibition Handbook* (Articles) (1906); Constance Smith, *The Case for Wages Boards* (1906); Emmeline Pethick Lawrence, "The Sweating Exhibition," the *Reformers' Year Book* (1907), pp. 160-161; Watney and Little, *op. cit.*, pp. 37-42; Canon and Mrs. S. A. Barnett, *Towards Social Reform* (1908); Gertrude Tuckwell, *Women in Industry from Seven Points of View*, with six others (1908).

on principle having been registered against it," [376] But it was the conviction, Professor Dicey declared, of English economists and social reformers up until the last quarter of the nineteenth century, "that any attempt to fix by law the rate of wages was an antiquated folly. This belief is no longer entertained by our Parliamentary statesmen." [377] The conviction had become widespread that "when the conditions of the workman's life are settled, without interference by law or trade unionism, by absolutely free contact between man and man, the workman's freedom is delusive"; and the "growing consciousness of the weakness of the wage earner in his bargaining with the great capitalist employer is to bring us, at the opening of the 20th century to the threshold of the Legal Minimum Wage for every branch of industry." [378] Public opinion had come to defend quickly any serious attack on the Standard of Life. It was necessary to get back as a community what had been lost by individuals.[379] On this basis the proposals that a minimum wage should be fixed by authority of Government below which no one may work had a wide col-

[376] *The Labour Year Book* (1916), p. 214. The following Government Reports give a comprehensive account of the industrial situation in the period of 1909-1913; taken together with the eight Reports noted above: (1) *Report of an Enquiry by the Board of Trade into Working Class Rents and Retail Prices, together with the Rate of Wages in Certain Occupations in the Principal Towns of the United Kingdom* (Cd. 6955), 1913. A similar *Report* was made in 1905, and the two *Reports* on 88 towns, London treated separately, are compared. (2) *Board of Trade Report on Changes in Rate of Wages and Hours of Labour in the United Kingdom in 1912* (Cd. 7080), 1913; and (3) a similar *Report* for 1913 (Cd. 7635) gives comparative statistics and a chart of wages, 1895-1913. In 1909 a *Report* (Cd. 4512) on France was made, of working class rents, housing and retail prices, together with the rate of wages in certain occupations, with introductory memoranda and comparison of the condition in France and England.

[377] *Op. cit.*, p. xlix.

[378] Sidney and Beatrice Webb, *Introduction* to *Problems of Modern Industry* (1902); also *Industrial Democracy*, Part III, chap. II-III, and *The Case for the Factory Acts* (1902).

[379] Webbs' *Problems of Modern Industry*, Introduction. Cf. *The Industrial Unrest and the Living Wage: Lectures Given at the Interdenominational Summer School at Swanwick, July, 1913* (1913), on significance of the progress of the ideal of a Living Wage as a revolt due to social progress, and not to abject misery. It was an achievement of the workers of conditions for the good life. Also J. Ramsay MacDonald, *The Social Unrest, Its Cause and Solution* (1913).

lective appeal, which was reflected in the belief of Professor Marshall that the minimum wage should be in many cases adjusted to the family, instead of the individual.[380] Before the Act of 1909 was passed the learned Cambridge economist declared that he had been steadily growing a more convinced supporter of social reform by State agency.[381] To escape from the degeneration caused by the cost of the industrial system, providing remedies against the dangers of modern industrialism have constituted a large part of the efforts of legislative enactments in modern democracies. To safeguard genuine freedom has been an increasing concern, and the Act of 1909 committed the State to far-reaching powers of control over the wage contract.

The Act of 1909 helped to stir the conscience of the "aristocratic" and prosperous trade unions, convincing them of the necessity of organization in all the ranks of Labour.[382] Four years after the passing of the Trade Boards Act a careful student who knew at first hand the working of the Act, said that the most important results of the Trade Boards were the spread of organization in the trades affected, which brought in for the first time the principle of collective bargaining between the employers and the workpeople in the trades scheduled in the Act.[383] Immediate extensions of Trade Union membership and improvements in Trade Union organization in the industries concerned have followed the Trade Disputes Act of 1906, the Trade Boards Act of 1908, the Coal Mines Regulation (Eight Hours) Act, 1908, the National Insurance Act, 1911, the Trade Union Act, 1913, the Corn Production Act, 1917, and the Trade Boards Extension Act, 1918.[384]

(b) *The Miners' Minimum Wage Struggle*

The power of organized Labour during 1911-12 was seen in the demand of one of the most effectively organized and com-

[380] *Principles of Economics* (8th ed. 1920), p. 715.

[381] *Economic Society Address of 1907.*

[382] See *Report of the Trade Union Congress* (1909), pp. 47-53, presidential address of Mr. D. J. Shackleton. Cf. Rt. Hon. Charles Booth, *Industrial Unrest and Trade Union Policy* (1913).

[383] Cf. R. H. Tawney, *Minimum Rates in Chainmaking Industry* (1914), and *Minimum Rates in Tailoring Trade* (1915).

[384] Sidney and Beatrice Webb, *History of Trade Unionism*, pp. 474-475; also G. D. H. Cole, *Organized Labour* (1924), pp. 144-147.

paratively higher paid trades, the Miners' Federation of Great Britain, for the establishment of a legal minimum wage for coal and iron mines. The Federation backed the demand, after negotiations between coal owners and workers had failed, by calling a general strike. Before this the Government had given to representatives of the coal owners and workers proposals which embodied the principles of the Coal Mines (Minimum Wage) Act, 1912.[385] The Government statement was:

(1) His Majesty's Government are satisfied, after careful consideration, that there are cases in which underground employees cannot earn a reasonable minimum wage, from causes over which they have no control.

(2) They are further satisfied that the power to earn such a wage should be secured by arrangements suitable to the special circumstances of each district. Adequate safeguards to be provided to protect the employer from abuse.

(3) His Majesty's Government are prepared to confer with the parties as to the best method of giving practical effect to the conclusions, by means of district conferences between the parties, a representative appointed by the Government being present.

(4) In the event of any of the Conferences failing to arrive at a complete settlement within a reasonable time, the representatives appointed by His Majesty's Government to decide jointly any outstanding points for the purpose of giving effect in that district to the above principles.[386]

The proposals of the Government were accepted by coal owners representing 60 per cent of the coal trade of the country as measured by output. The Miners' Federation answered the proposals with the following resolution:

That we agree to re-affirm the resolution passed by the Executive Committee and the 17 additional representatives from districts, and we repeat that there can be no settlement of the present dispute unless the principle of an individual minimum wage for all underground workers is agreed to by the coal owners. We are

[385] 2 Geo. V, c. 2. "An Act to provide a Minimum Wage in the case of Workmen employed underground in Coal Mines."

[386] The statement was made by Mr. Lloyd George on February 28 in the House of Commons, but the Government proposals were given on February 17: see Parl. Deb. 5 S. H. C. 1912, Vol. 34, pp. 1492-1495.

still willing to meet the coal owners at any time they desire to discuss the minimum rates of each district, as passed at special conferences of this Federation.[387]

The impassé was pointedly put by the Prime Minister when he stated at the end of the conferences with the Ministers' Executive Committee, on February 28, that the Government had made itself responsible for putting forward proposals to insure that a reasonable minimum wage should be secured for underground workers, and that these proposals had been accepted by a majority of coal owners, but that it was impossible, without discussion and negotiation between the parties, as proposed by the Government, to determine the amount of the minimum wage suitable to each district. On the other hand, the representatives of the men stated that they were not prepared to regard the amount of the minimum wage for coal getters, as revised and finally adopted on the second of February, 1912, as open to negotiations.[388]

Four days later the Prime Minister made his statement on the Coal Strike and the Minimum Wage, prefacing it by saying that the Government had taken it as a duty to intervene in the coal dispute, issuing invitations to both the interests concerned to confer separately with the Government.

"We have unanimously come to certain conclusions," he stated. "The first was that there are cases in which underground workers in the coal industry are prevented by causes over which they have no control, and for which they are not responsible, from earning a minimum wage. We came further to the conclusion, in which we were equally unanimous, that such cases ought to be met, and must be met, by the recognition and application of what, if I may use a compendious expression, I may call district minimum wages." [389]

The Government proposals had been accepted by practically all of the coal owners of England and North Wales, but rejected by those who represented South Wales and Scotland. The miners were satisfied—they had every reason to be satisfied, said the Prime Minister, adding that the Government had recognized, and

[387] Parl. Deb., *ibid.*, p. 1494. [388] Parl. Deb., *ibid.*, p. 1495.
[389] Parl. Deb., *ibid.*, pp. 39-40 (Asquith).

that 65 per cent of the owners had recognized, the principle of a minimum wage for which they had been contending.[390] But he was anxious to make it clear that he did not regard the grant of the minimum wage in the coal industry as the first step to the attainment, apparently by legislation, at any rate by some form of compulsion, of a minimum wage in all the industries of the country. "I am not in the habit," he declared, "of engaging in sly flirtations of this kind with Socialism and then trying to conceal from the public the manner in which I have been employing my time." [391]

Yet he reminded the Miners and the Labour Party that

you are now, to-day, in a position which a year ago, six months ago, six weeks ago you would have thought it would be impossible to be placed in. What have you got? You have 65 per cent of the coalowners of the country agreeing that a reasonable minimum wage must be established in your industry. You have got further than that, the representatives of the responsible Government of the country declaring they are convinced of the reasonableness and justice of that principle, and that they will take whatever means are necessary, notwithstanding the reluctance or even the resistance of what we hope and believe is a dwindling minority of owners who still take the other view, to carry out that principle throughout the coalfields of this country. You have got the principle for which you have been fighting and contending recognized practically by the employers and recognized in terms by the Government of the country.[392]

That the situation was considered most grave by the Government was evident in the closing words of the Prime Minister. He said that

the responsibility of those, who having it in their power to take any step to minimise and shorten this terrible national calamity, do not use it to the full is a responsibility which history will not measure.[393]

When he announced, on March 18, that the next day he would ask leave to introduce a Bill to provide for the payment of a

[390] Parl. Deb., *ibid.*, p. 41.
[391] Parl. Deb., *ibid.*, p. 41.
[392] Parl. Deb., *ibid.*, pp. 43-44.
[393] Parl. Deb., *ibid.*, p. 48.

minimum wage for persons employed underground in coal mines, he stated that not only the introduction, but the passing of the Bill at the earliest possible moment was very serious, and indeed, imperative.[394] The Government had left the matter until the last possible moment, Lord Hugh Cecil declared, "until the crisis is so acute and the situation so terrible that all considerations of ordinary Parliamentary procedure must be of secondary importance." [395] The consequences were not overlooked by another member who thought the Government Bill

> one of the most important measures that have ever been submitted to this House during the last twenty years—a measure changing the whole economic conditions of labour and employment in this country.[396]

The Prime Minister stated that the introduction of such a Bill by the Government, and its passing by Parliament promptly and within a very short period of time, was absolutely imperative in the best interests of the country.

> I say with perfect confidence every effort was made to bridge or circumvent, by persuasion and by argument, the chasm which divided them. As time went on it became clear at last that, by such means, that chasm was impossible. The injury not only to the actual combatants, but to the country at large, is increasing every day, both in the width of its area and the gravity of its character. In these circumstances His Majesty's Government came without hesitation to the conclusion that Parliament must be asked to intervene, and that if the parties could not agree to a settlement the State must provide a settlement for them.

The Bill was emergency legislation, a temporary measure, for according to its final clause it was to continue in force for three years, unless Parliament chose to prolong it.

"It starts with this," the Prime Minister said, "that *prima facie* it is to be a statutory term of every contract for the employment of workmen underground in a coal mine, that the employer shall

[394] Parl. Deb., *ibid.*, p. 1544; pp. 1544-1549, entire.
[395] Parl. Deb. 5 S. H. C., 1912, Vol. 35, p. 1720.
[396] Parl. Deb. cit., p. 1720 (Sir Frederick Banbury).

pay to the workingman wages of not less than the minimum rate settled under the Act and applicable to that workman. Any contract to the contrary will be void."

The administration of the Act was an advanced step toward a share in control for the worker and for the public.[397]

"We propose," the Government statement continued, "that both the rate of the minimum wage, and what I call the district rules—that is to say the rules for securing efficiency and regularity of work—should be settled by Joint District Boards, recognized as to each district, by the Board of Trade. These Joint Boards will be the existing Boards of Conciliation, or such other Boards as may be constituted and are considered by the Board of Trade to fairly and adequately represent the employers and workmen in the various districts. There will be practically equal and even representation of both parties. Each Board will have an independent chairman, who will be appointed between the two sides of the Board, or, in default of agreement, by the Board of Trade. The chairman shall have a casting vote in any case of difference of opinion between the two sides of the Board, and if it is thought desirable, three persons may be appointed to act as chairman instead of one. The Joint Boards will settle the general minimum rate for the district and the general district rules."

The Bill was to have no penal provisions,

but what the Bill says is this: a coal mine is opened for work by the employer, and if a man descends the pit to work underground,

[397] On April 10, 1912, the following Resolution was moved: "That this House having regard to the vital importance to the nation of economic power production, and recognising that the United Kingdom has a special relative advantage in regard to coal which needs to be carefully conserved, calls for the public control of the coal-mining industry and the establishment of a permanent Power Commission charged with the conservation, development, control, and distribution of power." The Government spokesman replying to Sir Leo Chiozza Money, said: "I have indicated my general assent to the line of reasoning, and taken his survey and summary as a kind of step in the evolution of society and of the world" (p. 1384). (Hansard, 5 S. H. C. 1912, Vol. 36, pp. 1367-1384, debate entire; pp. 1367-1380, Chiozza Money; pp. 1381-1384, J. M. Robertson, Under Secretary.) Cf. *Coal and Power,* The Report of an Enquiry presided over by the Rt. Hon. D. Lloyd George (1924), with Appendix on "Housing Conditions in Mining Areas," by R. A. Scott-Jones. This Report indicates the major problems and the solution of a recognized group.

it is to work, so far as the minimum wage is concerned, upon these statutory terms—the employer is liable to pay the underground worker a wage of not less than the wage fixed in the manner provided by this Bill. Owing to the special conditions of a particular trade, and the special emergency affecting the whole community in almost all its interests, the State by this Bill steps in, and with the State, after this Bill has become an Act of Parliament, both interests will have to reckon. We are asking Parliament here to make a legislative declaration of the principle of a statutory minimum wage. We are asking Parliament by this Bill to set up as a necessary accompaniment and corollary of that legislative declaration a perfectly fair, independent, and impartial machinery for the ascertainment of that wage and the conditions under which it shall be enjoyed in all the special areas of the country.[398]

The leader of the Opposition declared immediately that

Society has been held up. It is one of the greatest evils which can possibly happen to any society. It has been forced in many countries by many Governments, some of them even Socialistic Governments; but there never has been any Government which forced it in the way in which this Government does.[399]

This statement caused the leader [400] of the Labour Party to inquire from Mr. Bonar Law, "Does he mean to destroy collective bargaining, with all its consequences, or does he mean to establish paternal Government which will be Socialism in its very worst form?" He added, "I regret the Bill, I suppose we all regret the Bill"; his objection being primarily to any feature of compulsory arbitration. Lord Hugh Cecil declared that

It is absurd to treat this as a mere, ordinary labour dispute. It is really ridiculous to treat it that way. It is unquestionably an attempt to obtain control of the industries of this country by a band of men with revolutionary and anarchical theories which they recommend.[401]

[389] Parl. Deb. cit., pp. 1723-1733, Prime Minister's speech introducing the Bill, March 19, 1912; pp. 1723-1797, first reading debate entire.

[399] Parl. Deb. cit., p. 1739; pp. 1733-1742, speech entire (Bonar Law).

[400] Parl. Deb. cit., p. 1743; pp. 1742-1750, speech entire (MacDonald).

[401] Parl. Deb. cit., p. 1767; pp. 1764-1773, speech entire. The September, 1910, *The Industrial Syndicalist* and the September, 1911, *Socialist Review* were the sources quoted by Lord Hugh Cecil supporting this view.

The Labour spokesman had anticipated such a view and had said that

Syndicalism and those sort of things are not matters which emanate only from two or three gentlemen who have gone to Ruskin College, Oxford. They are created because owners, more particularly in South Wales, have taken up in these negotiations, and in what preceded these negotiations, an attitude which no body of self-respecting workmen would tolerate for a single instant. After all, men have got to be treated as human beings and not as beasts of burden or as mere profit-making machines.[402]

But Lord Cecil declared he looked to causes that were deeper, saying that

The root cause of the whole difficulty is that there is growing up, and has grown up in the past, a measure of class hostility which is a profound danger to civilization. I do not deny there are secondary causes. There is the rise in the cost of living. There are the speeches of the right honourable gentleman the Chancellor of the Exchequer, speeches which could not have been better designed if their purpose had been to stir up hatred between class and class, to encourage the rich in the oppression of the poor, and to influence the poor into resentment against the rich. Though these causes have undoubtedly increased the difficulty, I do feel that the fundamental difficulty is not due to the hostility between classes. The chief offender, in my judgment, is the wages system. (Cheers from Labour benches.) I submit that the system by which you buy the labour of a fellow creature, without any other element in it than the mere transaction of bargain and sale of another man's labour, is a thoroughly bad system. If you are going to put an end to the growing hostility which at present exists you must devise some new system of industry which shall recognise that the workingman is something more than a mere labour machine, and that doles and gifts are perfectly useless and do not touch even the fringe of the question. What you want to do is to give every man a genuine living interest in the industry in which he is engaged. I dismiss State Socialism, which has succumbed to the Syndicalist parasite which has grown upon it. It is absolutely intolerable to have the tyranny of any class—I care not whether it is the working class

[402] Parl. Deb. cit., p. 1749 (MacDonald).

or the landowning class or any other class. If the result of the transactions which have led up to this Bill, and if this Bill brings us appreciably nearer to the tyranny of the organised working classes, the trade unions organized and directed by men who are moved by the wildest economic and political theories, I am certain that that is absolutely intolerable. If you are to pass legislation in obedience or in deference to mere agitation, you must take care that it is of such a character that it will not hand over this country entirely to the domination of these Syndicalist people.[403]

The Government point of view was given by the Chancellor of the Exchequer, who did not believe Syndicalism was a real peril.

"I cannot see," he said, "men of very great weight in the Labour movement who have committed themselves to it. No men of real influence or power have committed themselves to Syndicalism. Syndicalism and Socialism are, of course, two totally different things. They are mutually destructive. As a matter of fact the Socialist would prefer to deal with the capitalist rather than the Syndicalist, for the simple reason that it is much more easy to deal with the Capitalist than the Syndicalist, because when once you hand over the whole profits of an industry merely to that industry, without any regard to the interests of the community, you raise a very formidable obstacle in the way of Socialism which is not in existence now, so that I can understand the Syndicalist as the bitterest enemy of the Socialist. Let the Noble Lord take this comfort, that the best policeman for the Syndicalist is the Socialist."

To which statement, the member referred to said, that "the best policeman for the thief is the lunatic." The Chancellor replied that

"I do not think the Noble Lord will consider that very fair, for the greatest intellects in Europe have been the greatest believers in Socialism." Adding, "I have seen the strikers; I have seen the leaders of the strike, but their position has not been the Syndicalist position. After all, the demand for the minimum wage is not a Syndicalist demand." [404]

[403] Parl. Deb. cit., pp. 1772-1773; see also speech of Mr. Stephen Walsh for the Miners, pp. 1758-1764.

[404] Parl. Deb. cit., pp. 1773-1783, speech entire (Lloyd George).

Opposition to the Bill [405] continued on the second reading; at which time Mr. Balfour, moving the reading this day six months, asked

Has any feudal baron ever exercised his powers in the manner which the leaders of this great trade union are now using theirs? This is the first formidable exhibition or display of a policy and a power, which if it be allowed unlimited sway will be absolutely destructive of society.[406]

But a Labour member declared [407] that "as a result of the Strike Syndicalism will have its death blow"; and the veteran Hardie stated that he was prepared to go farther in denunciation of the Syndicalist position.[408] The second reading of the Bill was passed by 348 votes to 225. Following Committee [409] stage, during which the Labour Party failed to secure the including of the miners' list of minimum rates as a schedule to the Bill, the Bill was passed on third reading,[410] Labour opposing, by 213 votes to 48. The close connection of the Labour Party and the Miners' Federation in the dispute was evident; and

throughout the varying course of the dispute the Parliamentary Party was in constant touch with the officials of the Miners' Federation, and all actions taken on the floor of the House were the subject of joint consultation.[411]

One writer has observed that

Organized Labour in a trade upon which the whole industrial life of the United Kingdom was dependent had forced Parliament,

[405] Public House Bills of 1912, No. 92. Second reading debate, March 21, pp. 2077-2202 entire debate; note Prime Minister's speech, pp. 2089-2097.

[406] Parl. Deb. cit., p. 2088; pp. 2077-2089, entire speech.

[407] Parl. Deb. cit., p. 2121; pp. 2120-2128, speech entire (Brace).

[408] Parl. Deb. cit., p. 2163; see p. 2164 (Lansbury). Note speeches of the Secretary for Foreign Affairs (2179-2187), Sir Edward Grey; pp. 2171-2179, Mr. A. Chamberlain.

[409] Parl. Deb. cit., pp. 2229-2427, complete; Bill reported as amended, House Bill No. 103.

[410] Parl. Deb. H. C. 5 S., Vol. 36, pp. 223-385 (Report), and pp. 385-400, third reading: Banbury (385-386); MacDonald (386-388); Lloyd George (389-391); Hardie (391-393); and S. Walsh (396-398).

[411] *Labour Year Book,* 1916, p. 330, "The Parliamentary Labour Party."

in the interests of industrial peace, to pass an Act which was more or less contrary to the opinion of the country as a whole. This is a typical example of direct action.[412]

Though Parliament by passing this Act plainly established the principle "that wages can rightly be fixed by law and not by mere haggling of the market," [413] the fact remained that in the social life of England there was nothing better than a state of economic war." [414]

(c) *Government Interference*

Before briefly bringing the survey of minimum wage legislation down to date, as affected by emergency enactments in the war time and postwar conditions, the Report of the Industrial Council may well be outlined for it belongs to the period in which the whole tendency of Labour legislation was toward approving the principle of the minimum wage. This was less true in France than in England, but there was a persistent demand in both countries for a Living Wage, and the all-round protection of the family as a working-unit,[415] as well as the individual. The Council was appointed in 1911 by the Government in order to aid in the settlement of important trade disputes, its formation resulting directly from the railway strike of that year. The "widespread industrial unrest" of 1911-12, a period in which more persons had been involved in strikes than in the previous ten years put together (and the number of days lost were far greater) forced the Government to act. The disorganization of the industry and trade of the country was a menacing and recurrent problem.[416] The railway world, the coal trade and the transport industry, the fundamental trade organizations, had been the first

[412] B. G. De Montgomery, *British and Continental Labour Policy* (1922), p. 361.

[413] Dicey, *op. cit.*, p. xlix.

[414] Cf. A. J. Carlyle, *Wages* (1912), Chap. IX-X, pp. 104-125.

[415] The *Confédération Générale du Travail* voted in 1923 against the acceptance of any scheme for a "family wage," on the grounds that it was only a new form of "wage slavery," and contrary to the principles of syndicalism.

[416] See *Board of Trade Report on Strikes and Lockouts and on Conciliation and Arbitration Boards in the United Kingdom in* 1913 (Cd. 7658). Reviewed in *Labour Gazette*, November, 1914.

to indicate that a new spirit on the part of the Government and the leaders of the organized workmen was imperatively demanded. The Prime Minister stated the view of the Government in the House of Commons, when he instructed the Industrial Council on the work of inquiry it was intended they should carry out. Taken together with the Government statements on the Port of London Strike, the attitude of the responsible Ministers was known.

The Prime Minister's statement was in part:

From the experience derived from the industrial disputes which have lately occurred, it has become evident that one of the chief difficulties in the way of peaceful and friendly relations between employers and men is the want of effective measures for securing the due observance of industrial agreements by both sides. Further, where agreements are come to between employers and workmen in regard to conditions of employment the agreement, though binding on those who are parties to it, is not binding on the whole of the trade of the district. These matters affect the employers and the workmen alike, and it seems essential to ascertain (1) What is the best method of securing the due fulfilment of industrial agreements? (2) How far industrial agreements, which are made between representative bodies of employers and workmen, should be enforced throughout the particular trade or district? The Government are anxious to have inquiry made into the matter, and to receive advice from those best qualified to give it. In these circumstances, they propose to refer the above questions to the Industrial Council, which is representative of the employers and the men in the great industries of the country; to request the Council carefully to consider the matter, to take such evidence as they may think fit, and to report to the Government any conclusions to which they may come. The view of the Government has been strengthened by the following resolution of the Industrial Council, who have considered the matter: "The question of the maintenance of industrial agreements having come before the Industrial Council, that Council are of opinion that this subject is of the highest importance to employers and Trade Unions, and work people generally, and would welcome an immediate inquiry into the matter." The resolution was agreed to unanimously. The Government are therefore requesting the Industrial Council to undertake the inquiry, and they will give the most earnest attention to any recommendation which the Council may be able to make.

The Report [417] of the Industrial Council was presented to Parliament in July, 1913. The Council expressed themselves in favour of the continued maintenance of voluntary conciliation and arbitration boards, and against compulsion, or against "any alternative based upon principles other than mutual consent." They considered that the machinery for the voluntary settlement of disputes should be strengthened by the right of appeal to some independent body or impartial individual. The Council strongly emphasized the importance of efficient organization on the part of employers and work people as one method of securing the due fulfilment of agreement.[418] The value of "moral obligation" was a strong factor, the report argued, and the pressure of moral influence should be brought to bear upon all parties in the settlement of disputes. The consideration of the second part of the reference of the Government, relating to the extension of industrial agreements, formed the most important part of the Report. Where Trade Union organization was strong, it was often possible to exert sufficient pressure on non-associated employers to induce them to observe agreements with the masters' associations. When, however, organization was imperfect, the effective maintenance of agreements was jeopardized by the existence of a section (perhaps only a minority) which was not party to, and therefore not in any sense bound by whatever agreement may be arrived at by the rest of the trade.[419] It was suggested that the Board of Trade should have power to extend agreements made by trade unions and employers' associations to the whole industry of a district, on application to the central authority by either of the parties to the agreement, provided that the Board of Trade was satisfied

[417] *The Industrial Council: Report on Enquiry into Industrial Agreements* (Cd. 6952), 1913.

[418] In the Parliamentary Committee's Report on the General Federation of Trade Unions at the Bristol Congress, it was declared as one of the reasons for the value of the Federation that "complete organization means industrial peace to the nation," *The Report of the Trade Union Congress,* Bristol, 1904, p. 77. The Reports of the General Federation of Trade Unions fully discuss this point.

[419] Cf. *Fifth Report of the General Federation of Trade Unions,* 1904.

that the associations represented by the signatories to the agreement constitute a substantial body of the employers and workmen in the trade or district, and that the agreement is a proper agreement and one that might suitably be extended.

This proposal of the Industrial Council would virtually amount, therefore, to the establishment of a legal minimum wage by trades, or sections of trades, for the agreements made by voluntarily constituted Trade Boards would be officially ratified.[420] This report indicated the extent of common agreement between the employers and the representatives of Labour with regard to State intervention. It cannot be said to have done anything more than interpret the sentiment of the time, proving that there was no strong tendency toward compulsory arbitration; but, on the other hand, there was complete willingness for the State to continue to act as a mediator, furthering the work of industrial agreement by official machinery.

The year that the Parliamentary Committee made its report on systems of conciliation and arbitration, at the 1911 Congress, a Bill[421] was introduced in the House of Commons by Mr. W. Crooks, which attempted to guarantee a settlement of trade disputes. It was supported by several of the leading Labour members, including Mr. Arthur Henderson. The provisions of the Bill were such that it could not be successful. Each workman should be liable to a fine of not less than two pounds and not more than ten pounds for each day or part of a day that he was on strike contrary to the provisions of the Bill; and the employer declaring or causing a lockout contrary to the provisions of the Bill should be liable to a fine of not less than twenty pounds and not more than two hundred pounds a day. The failure of this Bill made more evident the wisdom of building up a strong sentiment for making voluntary agreements more effective, and the Government had done this in supplementing the Conciliation Act, 1896, by the Government Memorandum of September 1st, 1908.

[420] Cf. Arthur Greenwood, article in *Economic Journal,* September, 1913, pp. 449-451; also note Supplement on Minimum Wage in the *Crusade,* June, 1912. It is impossible to even briefly consider the Reports, Minutes and Awards dealing with the Industrial Courts Act, 1919, which have carried forward in a broad way the principle of State intervention.

[421] *Public Bills,* 1911, No. 360.

This Memorandum was sent to all employers' and workmen's associations and Chambers of Commerce. It provided for the establishment of a Court of Arbitration composed of three to five members, according to the wishes of the parties. The members of the Court were to be appointed by the Board of Trade, employers and workmen to be represented in equal number. The arbitration by the Court was of a purely voluntary character.

In the Port of London (Transport) Strike the attitude of Labour was manifest in the Industrial Agreements Bill,[422] introduced June 25, 1912, "to make agreements come to voluntarily between employers and workers in the Port of London legally enforceable on the whole trade." In the Bill there was no clause relating to the legal enforcement of the agreement.[423] From the standpoint of the Labour Party the chief value of the Parliamentary discussions on the Port of London Authority Dispute was to bring pressure to bear upon the Board of Trade.[424] Earlier in the long dispute the Chancellor of the Exchequer in reply to a question raised by a Labour member,[425] declared that

I do not suppose anyone in the House will accept the view laid down by the Hon. Baronet (Sir Frederick Banbury) [426] that it is the business of the Government to stand aside and let the parties fight it out. That has been abandoned long ago.[427]

In this long drawn out dispute Labour brought forward several pronouncements; and on July 1, a motion by Mr. O'Grady was passed by 254 votes to 188,

That, in the opinion of this House it is expedient that the representatives of the employers' and the workmen's organisations

[422] *Public Bills of 1912,* No. 253; introduced by Mr. J. Ramsay MacDonald. See Parl. Deb. H. C. 5 S., 1912, Vol. 39, pp. 220-222.

[423] This was true of the Millerand decrees. For a full treatment see *Industrial Negotiations and Agreements,* Foreword by J. R. Clynes, published by the Trade Union Congress and Labour Party (1923).

[424] *Labour Year Book,* 1916, pp. 330-331.

[425] Parl. Deb. H. C. 5 S., 1912, Vol. 39, pp. 216-224 (O'Grady); pp. 216-257, debate entire. See Lloyd George (pp. 235-243); Bonar Law (pp. 244-248); MacDonald (pp. 248-255). June 6: pp. 422-428; June 12: pp. 872-996, very important debate; June 17: pp. 1316-1323; June 24: pp. 30-37, Vol. 40; June 25-26, Vol. 40, pp. 212-215, 326-330.

[426] Parl. Deb. H. C. 5 S., Vol. 39, pp. 224-230.

[427] Parl. Deb. cit., p. 236.

involved in the present dispute should meet, with the view of arriving at a settlement.[428]

The Labour motion was based on the belief that

the events of the last 12 months have surely taught us that the era of *laissez-faire* has definitely passed away, and that Governments in future must be prepared to take a regular though not necessarily an arbitrary part in all important industrial conflicts. For in every such industrial conflict the general interests of the community are directly and vitally engaged, alike in the conflict itself and in its sequel. . . . Whenever an industrial dispute takes place in which the weaker party is forced into accepting terms degrading and injurious to its standard of life, it is the manifest duty of the State to intervene.[429]

The Government too were convinced that the time had come for the reconsideration of the whole problem of the settlement of trade disputes.

"I do not believe it is possible to deal with them without some form of legislative sanction," Mr. Lloyd George said, "because you always come up against some employer or some union who will listen to no appeal, and who are perfectly indifferent to public opinion, and there mere methods of conciliation must be a failure. In a case of that kind there must necessarily be legislation, the sanction of some legislation which can be enforced. The Government have come to the conclusion that it will be necessary to deal with this problem. The weapon with which the Executive is armed is absolutely futile beyond a certain point. I am not criticising the Act of 1896, because I do not think public opinion would have justified the Government of the day going beyond legislation at that stage. But since then a great deal has happened. Therefore the Government have come to the conclusion that it will be necessary to deal with the whole problem, and to deal with it in the immediate future."[430]

[428] Parl. Deb. H. C. 5 S., 1912, Vol. 40, p. 849; pp. 849-902, debate entire on O'Grady motion; note Bonar Law (pp. 862-871); MacDonald (pp. 871-877); the Prime Minister (pp. 859-862); Barnes (pp. 882-885).

[429] Parl. Deb. cit., p. 854. In 1904 Mr. R. Bell introduced for Labour a Conciliation and Arbitration Act (1896) Amendment Bill (House Bill No. 122, 1904).

[430] Parl. Deb. H. C. 5 S., 1912, Vol. 41, pp. 1111-1120, speech entire; note appeal for settlement by Messrs. Crooks and O'Grady, July 9 and

It is well to bear in mind that upon the question of arbitration and conciliation the Government had always to be very cautious in bringing forward any measure, for the Trade Unions and the employers' associations have at no time been in agreement among themselves or between each other on what is a workable solution of the industrial disputes that are continually arising. The Bill of Mr. Crooks, while supported by some of the Labour Party, was more usually denounced; and the Trade Union Congresses of 1912 and 1913 defeated resolutions that embodied to some extent the principle of Mr. MacDonald's Bill of 1912.[431] The Report of Lord Askwith (then Sir George), Chief Industrial Commissioner of the Industrial Council, avoided making any definite recommendations, limiting its observations to the possibility of the application of the conciliatory features of the Canadian Arbitration and Conciliation Law to England.[432] The Social Reform Committee of the Unionist Party issued a report in 1914 which gave its solution of industrial unrest.[433] It recommended that officially appointed Boards should in case of industrial disputes, publish definite recommendations for a settlement. The Boards should have compulsory powers, but the recommendations were to be published for the guidance of public opinion. The second recommendation was the gradual extension of the principle of the minimum wage; and the third, a reorganization of the Board of Trade, and the improvement of its usefulness for all of industry and trade.

The three recommendations of the Social Reform Committee of the Unionist Party represented phases of a tendency in all the political parties since 1890, to round out a social program which would be self-consistent. From the miners' strike in 1893,

July 11, pp. 1843-1847, pp. 2222-2225, Vol. 40. Note also on July 23, together with the speech of the Chancellor of the Exchequer, the following: O'Grady (pp. 1079-1090); Lansbury (1090-1097); MacDonald (1104-1108); Bonar Law (pp. 1120-1123); all of which are in Vol. 41, the debate entire being in pp. 1079-1130.

[431] Cf. Parliamentary Committees' Report, *Report of the Trade Union Congress*, 1913, pp. 77-170.

[432] Cf. *Report to the Board of Trade on the Industrial Disputes Investigation Act of Canada, 1907*, by Sir George Askwith, Chief Industrial Commissioner. Cd. 6603, 1913.

[433] *Industrial Unrest, A Practical Solution: The Report of the Unionist Social Reform Committee.* Introduction by F. E. Smith (1914).

when the cry for "a living wage" was heard, to 1914 is hardly over twenty years, yet by that time in the House of Commons there was something like a real unanimity in facing the question of the minimum wage and in adjusting the disputes of industry in a peaceful fashion. The Bill introduced by Mr. Bell in 1904 and Mr. MacDonald in 1912 have a good deal in common with the first recommendation of the Unionist Committee, however long the fight might be carried on over certain interpretations in the execution of the provisions of a law. The third point, the reorganization of the Board of Trade, had been dealt with by the Labour and the Conservative parties. When the Board of Trade Amendment of the Conservative Party in 1908 was given, the Labour Party promptly offered its Amendment to the Address on a Ministry of Labour.[434] The Leicester Trade Union Congress of 1903 had also passed a resolution on the extension of the Labour department and asking for the appointment of a Minister of Labour.

The Labour motion stated that, "the era of *laissez-faire*" had definitely passed away, and it was believed then that the abandonment of the *laissez-faire* policy by the Government in regard to industrial disputes would one day come to be recognized as the most important development in economic matters in the last fifty years.[435] While part of a more complex industrial problem—the control of industry—this agitation had direct bearing upon the question of the better standard of living, which to bring about organized labour had determined to use its complete economic and political power. Brief mention of the Fair Wages Clause debate of 1909 and the General Minimum Wage Resolution of 1911, may well conclude this survey of the problem in its Parliamentary history, down to 1914.

(d) *Fair Wages Clause and the General Minimum Wage*

The most important motion brought forward by the Labour Party in the 1909 Parliament dealt with the administration of the Fair Wages Clause.[436] "We are recognizing in prospective legis-

[434] Cf. Parliamentary Committees' Report, *Report of the Trade Union Congress,* 1909, p. 25.

[435] Watney and Little, *op. cit.,* 235.

[436] Parl. Deb. H. C. 5 S., 1909, Vol. 2, pp. 415-420, pp. 415-458, debate entire.

lation," it was stated, "that the Government has a right to see to it that every willing worker has a living wage in return for the labour he performs." [437] The new Clause [438] agreed to in 1909 indicates the progress of a standard of "the fair wage" which the Government recognized:

The contractor shall, under the penalty of a fine or otherwise pay rates of wages and observe hours of labour not less favourable than those commonly recognized by employers and trade societies (or, in the absence of such recognized wages and hours, those which in practice prevail amongst good employers) in the trade in the district where the work is carried out. Where there are no such wages or hours recognized or prevailing in the district, those recognized or prevailing in the nearest district in which the general industrial circumstances are similar shall be adopted. Further, the conditions of employment generally accepted in the district in the trade concerned shall be taken into account in considering how far the terms of the fair wages clauses are being observed. The contractor shall be prohibited from transferring or assigning directly or indirectly, to any person or persons whatever, any portion of his contract without the written permission of the department. Sub-letting, other than that which may be customary in the trade concerned, shall be prohibited. The contractor shall be responsible for the observance of the Fair Wages Clauses by the sub-contractor.[439]

In the agenda of the Trade Union Congress each year the Fair Wages Clause had a place, and continual deputations kept the matter before the Government. The Prime Minister in 1905, replying to a deputation, said that the Government were determined to be model employers.[440]

[437] Parl. Deb. cit., p. 424; pp. 420-425, entire speech (Roberts); motion moved by Mr. J. Hodge.

[438] Cf. Report of the Fair Wages Committee (Cd. 4422), 1908, appointed in August, 1907, by the Treasury to consider the working of the Fair Wages Resolution of the House of Commons of February 13, 1891.

[439] Compare with the Millerand Decrees of August 10, 1899 (Dalloz, *Code du Travail,* pp. 125-128). From 1894 measures had been before the Chamber of Deputies, but M. Millerand did not wish to risk the fate of any Act on wages of employees in public works before the Senate, so his end was gained through departmental decrees.

[440] Parliamentary Committee's Report to the Trade Union Congress of 1905, *Annual Trade Union Congress Report,* 1905, pp. 67-68.

During the debate on the motion in 1909 the Government policy was outlined by the Postmaster General,[441] whose personal responsibility for the Fair Wages Clause gave his testimony of the progress made since 1891 added weight. The Fair Wages Resolution applied, he said, as a legal obligation, only to workers engaged on the Government contract in question. It would, however, not be the practice of Government departments to keep on their lists of contractors firms who obeyed the letter of the Clause by paying recognized rates on Government contracts, but who were proved to be notoriously bad employers in other directions. Still less would a department give work to a firm who took advantage of the fair wages paid in Government work, to employ those same workers at a rate even below the normal in the output of non-Government articles—a practice that had been known to exist in sweating trades. The real security in regard to this matter was that contracts were renewable from time to time, and this gave the power and the opportunity to review the conditions of labour under any contract. The Local Government Board had issued to all local authorities a Circular urging them to adopt the Fair Wages Clause as adopted by the Government in its contracts.[442] The London County Council provisions with regard to Fair Wages cover about twenty pages of the Standing Orders; Liverpool, Glasgow and other cities have adopted strict forms of contract to fully protect Trade Union and Labour rates and standards.[443] This is a field where Trade Unions have very effectively put pressure on the local authorities.[444]

The resolution moved for a General Minimum Wage, on April 26, 1911, declared:

That the right of every family of the country to an income sufficient to enable it to maintain its members in decency and comfort

[441] Parl. Deb. H. C. 5 S., 1909, Vol. 2, pp. 425-435.

[442] See A. Millerand, *Politique de Realisations,* p. 188, "the State as a model employer"; the entire debate in the Chamber of Deputies, December 15, 1910, on the railway strike, is most valuable for the survey that M. Millerand gave of the State and its attitude toward the workers, see pp. 163-190, *op. cit.*

[443] *Labour Year Book 1916,* pp. 633-641, for extracts from Fair Wages Clauses in London and other cities, and charts dealing with wages and conditions of municipal employees. See London County Council Standing Orders Nos. 281, 286, 287.

[444] See *Report of the Committee of 1908.*

should be recognised; and this House is therefore of opinion that a general minimum wage of thirty shillings per week for every adult worker should be established by law, and also declares that the Government should set an example by adopting this standard in their own workshops.[445]

The mover declared, "You do not and never will employ men for the love of God. You employ them for what you can make out of them." He effectively portrayed the tragic fact that the study of the family budgets in England revealed a destitution and poverty which were degrading, and made right living almost impossible. It was emphasized in the debate that the share of capital in the product had increased much more than that of labour.[456] The Parliamentary Secretary for the Board of Trade replied for the Government, stating that it was impossible to accept the motion; of the 3,600,000 workers of whom there were statistics 60 per cent received a wage less than 30s a week. The Fair Wages Clause of 1909 and the increased wages in Government departments, together with the Trade Boards Act, 1908, were pointed out by the Government as efforts toward raising the standards of life and work.[447] State action had shown that the nation was alive to the peril of the unfit and the underpaid.

(e) *Post-war Legislation*

The extension of the principles embodied in the Coal Mines (Minimum Wage) Act, 1912, to apply to the emergency of war-time conditions is indicated in the Munitions of War Act, 1915,[448] the Amending Act of 1916,[449] and the Munitions of War Act, 1917.[450] The Corn Production Acts, 1917[451]-1920,[452] extended

[445] Parl. Deb. H. C. 5 S., 1911, Vol. 24, pp. 1881-1924, debate entire; pp. 1881-1882, the Resolution, moved by Mr. Crooks (pp. 1881-1892); seconded by Mr. Will Thorne (pp. 1892-1895). Parl. Deb. H. C. 5 S., 1911, Vol. 26, pp. 1136-1155, pp. 1459-1498, debate on Fair Wages Clause in Government works.

[446] Parl. Deb. cit., pp. 1907-1914 (Chiozza-Money); also note Steel-Maitland (pp. 1895-1907).

[447] Parl. Deb. cit., pp. 1919-1924 (Tennant).

[448] 5 & 6 Geo. V, c. 54. Part I relating to the settlement of labour differences and the prohibition of strikes and lockouts.

[449] 5 & 6 Geo. V, c. 99.

[450] 7 & 8 Geo. V, c. 45.

[451] 7 & 8 Geo. V, c. 46; Amending Act of 1918 (8 & 9 Geo. V, c. 36).

[452] 10 & 11 Geo. V, c. 76. (Being Part I of the Agricultural Act, 1920.)

the principle of a minimum wage [453] to the key industry of agriculture, establishing Wages Boards and District Wages Committees.[454] The Corn Production Acts (Repeal) Act, 1921, abolished the Agricultural Wages Board for England and Wales, established by the Act of 1917, creating in place voluntary joint councils of employers and workmen in agriculture.[455] But the Agricultural Wages (Regulation) Act, 1924,[456] provided for the establishment [457] of an Agricultural Wages Board and Agricultural Wages Committees, with powers and duties with respect to minimum rates of wages for agricultural workers.[458] The two points most strongly debated were whether the Bill should include a legal minimum below which no district might go, and whether the local committees should have full power, or be subordinate to a central board. The Act provided that the County Committees, which consist of equal numbers of workers and employers, together with two appointed members and a chairman, have the duty of fixing statutory minimum rates of wages for agricultural workers.[459] The Agricultural Wages Board consists of equal numbers of workers and employers together with a number of appointed members not exceeding one-fourth of the total numbers of the Board. The Board has power to fix, cancel, or vary the rates fixed by the County Committees, if a County Committee does not within two months of its establishment notify the Board a minimum rate which it has fixed; if a County Committee fails to substitute a new rate for one which has ceased to operate; and if a resolution of the representative members of a County Committee requests the Board to fix, cancel, or vary a minimum rate. The Minister of Agriculture has power also to direct County Committees to reconsider their rates. The Act requires that the Minister of Agriculture establish an agricultural wages committee for each county, or for a group of counties, in England and Wales, and the Agricultural Wages Board for all England and Wales.

While no minimum rate was fixed by the Act of 1924 itself, the

[453] Act of 1917, Part II. Sections 4-7; sects. 11-13, and 17 of 1909 Trade Boards Act were applicable.

[454] Act of 1917, Part IV.

[455] Act of 1921, Section 4.

[456] 14 & 15 Geo. V, c. 37.

[457] Act of 1924, Section I.

[458] *Ibid.*, Section II, and see First Schedule.

[459] Compare Section 4 of the Corn Production Acts (Repeal) Act, 1921.

Act directed that a committee shall, so far as practicable, secure for able-bodied men such wages as are adequate to promote efficiency, and to enable a man to maintain himself and his family in accordance with a reasonable standard of comfort. By January, 1925, a great majority of the County Committees had already agreed upon minimum rates for their areas.[460]

In the report of Mr. Lloyd George's Liberal Land Committee 1923-25,[461] a minimum wage condition for agricultural workers is laid down. The suggestion is that before the fair rents are fixed in any area a minimum wage for agricultural workers shall be fixed for that area. When the fair rent is fixed for any holding, the cultivating tenant shall have a right of appeal against it on the ground that he cannot pay the minimum wage to labour at the rate fixed.

The Wages (Temporary Regulation) Act, 1918,[462] an effort to aid in restoring stable conditions in the labour market, prescribed a minimum wage,[463] and the amending Act of 1919,[464] continued its provisions for six months longer. The Trade Boards Act, 1918[465] which may be applied "if no adequate machinery exists for the effective regulation of wages throughout the trade," gave the Minister of Labour power to make a special order applying the principal Act to that trade.[466] Thus the principle of 1909 has become completely confirmed by postwar enactment. There has been a further confirmation in the Coal Industry Commission Act, 1919,[467] prescribing for the Commissioners that all investigation into the industry must take into consideration the acceptance of a "reasonable standard of living amongst the colliery workers."[468] A similar provision was contained in the terms of ref-

[460] Hansard, December 15, 1924, cols. 603-608, for first decisions as to minimum rates reached by the County Committees.

[461] *The Land and the Nation,* London, published in October, 1925, is the Rural Report; *Towns and Land* (1925) is the Urban Report.

[462] 8 & 9 Geo. V, c. 61.

[463] Act of 1918, Section I. Section II provides arbitration through Ministry of Labour.

[464] 9 & 10 Geo. V, c. 18.

[465] 8 & 9 Geo. V, c. 32.

[466] Act of 1918, Section II, and First Schedule.

[467] 9 & 10 Geo. V, c. 1.

[468] Act of 1919, Section I, full duties of investigation are set forth. The Act provided that a commission should be constituted to inquire into the position of and conditions prevailing in the industry with special

erence for the Agricultural Tribunal of Investigation, 1922, their findings having regard to "the employment of labour at a living wage." The Mining Industry Act, 1920,[469] established a new principle in industrial welfare legislation, providing a fund for "social improvement," a Mines Department of the Board of Trade, an Advisory Committee on Coal and Coal Industry, and for Pit Committees.[470]

Although a return to the principle of the 1909 Act was suggested by the Departmental Committee appointed in September, 1921,[471] under the presidency of Viscount Cave, "to inquire into the working of the Trade Boards Acts, and to report what changes, if any, are required," on the other hand there are the Whitley Reports [472] (1917-1918) and the Memorandum [473] of the Labour representatives of the Joint Industrial Council (1919) attesting to the power behind the continuing agitation for a higher standard of living among the people.[474] There is the certainty, moreover, that the ideal of a Living Wage will find expression in legislative and administrative measures based on the experience gained by the State in attempting to insure a decent minimum of existence for the workers. The State itself will be increasingly concerned to sanction by legislation the advancing standards which the com-

reference *inter alia* to wages, hours of work, cost of production and distribution, selling prices and profits, and the social condition of colliery workers. The Coal Mines act, 1919, and the Mining Industry Act, 1920, the provisions of which are noted herein, carried out recommendations of the commission.

[469] 10 & 11 Geo. V, c. 50, Part I, Sections 1-6, deal with Administration; Part II, with Regulation of Coal Mines. This does for Coal Mines what the Education Act, 1918, did for Education.

[470] Besides the Coal Mines Act, 1919 (9 & 10 Geo. V, c. 48), establishing a seven-hour day, State action may be noted in the following Acts: Coal Mines (Emergency Act), 1920 (10 & 11 Geo. V, c. 4); the Price of Coal (Limitation) Act, 1920 (5 & 6 Geo. V, c. 4); and the Coal Mines (Decontrol) Act, 1921 (11 Geo. V, c. 6), which curtailed the duration and amended the Coal Mines (Emergency) Act, 1920.

[471] The Report of the Committee was issued in April, 1922, Cd. 1645. Cf. Trade Boards Acts, 1909-1918. Statement of the Government's policy in the administration of the Acts pending legislation (Cd. 1712), 1922.

[472] Cd. 8606, Cd. 9001, Cd. 9002, Cd. 9085, Cd. 9099, and Cd. 9153.

[473] See *Report of the Provisional Joint Committee to the meeting of the Industrial Conference*, April 4, 1919 (Cd. 139).

[474] See Dorothy Sells, *The British Trade Boards System* (1923), for a careful survey and estimate of the system.

munity conscience both demands and makes possible. The national minimum wage motion brought forward in Parliament on March 4, 1924, and adopted without division is one of the recent indications of the strength of the movement in England. The following is the motion:

That in view of the practically universal acceptance of the principle that a living wage for all workers should be the first charge upon industry, and in view of the large measure of agreement with respect to the advisability of fixing minimum time rates of wages reached at the national industrial conference, this House urges the Government to proceed without delay with the Bill introduced by the Government of the day of 1919, constituting a Commission to inquire into and report upon legal minimum time rates and wages.

Part VII

The State and Wage Disputes

(a) *Extension of the Problem of a National Minimum*

The requirements of the War necessitated new powers for dealing with labour disputes with regard to wages, and Parliament did not hesitate to take the most drastic measures of control during the War period to speed up production and insure a minimum amount of stoppage of work owing to trade disputes.[475] The "Treasury Agreement" of March, 1915, entered into by the Government and the principal trade unions, proposed to limit profits and prevent strikes, and this principle was extended effectively in the Munitions of War Acts, 1915-18.[476] Yet even eight years after the War the Government is continually faced

[475] See the splendid studies in the *Economic and Social History of the War,* British Series, for a survey of the pre-war and war and post-war State organization, especially Humbert Wolf, *Labour Supply and Regulation* (1923); G. D. H. Cole, *Labour in the Coal-Mining Industry 1914-1921* (1923), and *Trade Unionism and Munitions* (1923).

[476] See the *Ministry of Labour Report,* No. 185 of 1919, which is the Twelfth Report under the Conciliation Act, 1896, and reports on arbitration under the Munitions of War Acts. Together with particulars of (1) Proceedings under the Wages (Temporary Regulation) Act, 1918, and (2) Settlements arrived at under the Coal Mines (Minimum Wage) Act, 1912. General Report 1914-1918.

with the problem of avoiding a great national crisis in the coal or the railway industry by the breakdown of the wage agreements in these important public services. It is no exaggeration to say that a war condition often obtains in these national wage disputes.

For the well-organized trades it has been felt that the Whitley Councils introduced in 1918 would meet the needs. There are now 72 Councils and 19 Interim Industrial Reconstruction Committees in existence, however the active bodies are 63 in number, 55 being Joint Industrial Councils. It is estimated that some 3,000,000 workers are now covered by Joint Industrial Councils or Interim Industrial Reconstruction Committees. The principal groups of workers outside the scope of such organizations are the miners, the iron and steel workers and the cotton workers, all of whom are well-organized groups with elaborate negotiating machinery of their own already in existence. In addition to the National and District Councils there are estimated to be over 1,000 Works Committees in existence. It is important to note that the single item which has bulked most largely in the activities of the Joint Industrial Councils has been wage negotiations. The attitude of Labour has been skeptical, and the Trade Union Congress in 1923 voted decisively against legislation of voluntary agreements. Labor has been of the opinion that employers have no intention of handing over to the workers any share in control, and the continued trade depression in England has made many workers thoroughly dissatisfied with Whitleyism.

One good result followed: Organization of the workers was greatly encouraged, and joint consultation and action between, and even amalgamation of, Unions in the same industry were stimulated by the joint activity on Whitley Councils. Otherwise Whitleyism merely typified the optimism and superficial harmony which prevailed during the period immediately following the Armistice, just as its results showed how empty and hollow these sentiments really were when brought to the test of practical application.[477]

The Whitley scheme contemplated organization by industries, each establishment of a given industry to have Works Committees, formed of representatives of employers and workers, for handling

[477] *Labour Year Book* (1924), p. 51.

the problems of the individual plant. Above these were to be District Councils, uniting the plants of a given district, and, for the industry as a whole, a National Joint Industrial Council to pass upon general questions.[478] The expansion of the Trade Boards Act made permanent some of the wage machinery in operation during the war, and in the working of this Act labour has taken a great interest. The progress since the original Act in 1909 is nothing less than phenomenal, and the history of the administration of the Act is a tribute to the Ministry of Labour and the staff of inspectors. The great strain that prolonged industrial depression has put upon the system has been recognized, and the fact that to-day over 3,000,000 workers in about forty trades are protected by the Act is significant proof of the will of the State to protect the worker. The trade boards system, as it has developed, is bipartite. Legislative power is vested in the Trade Boards, administrative and executive functions rest with the Ministry of Labour and have in practice involved four distinct features: (1) setting up of Boards, (2) confirmation of rates, (3) enforcement of legal rates, (4) decision on questions of demarcation and scope.

(b) *Control of Railway Wages*

The State has been forced to consider the wage scale in three great national services, in agriculture, in the coal mines, and in the railway system of Great Britain. The State made the epochal step with regard to the coal industry of granting a subsidy, and this has even been urged with regard to the wages of railway workers.[479] In these two instances, coal mines and the railways, the movement toward nationalization is often joined with the

[478] See *Ministry of Labour Report* (1923), on the establishment and progress of Joint Industrial Councils, 1917-1922. In all 73 Joint Industrial Councils were formed, 20 in 1918, 32 in 1919, 16 in 1920, 5 in 1921, and none in 1922. Cf. G. D. H. Cole, *Workshop Organization* (1923), chap. XIII, and *Appendices* for survey of work shop organization under the Whitley Report.

[479] In November, 1925, the National Wages Board had before it the petition of the workers on the railways for wage increase, and at the same time the owners were asking for reductions. The *Manchester Guardian Weekly's* comment was that "a decision against the unions may easily lead to trouble, and Mr. Baldwin may yet be asked to give still another subsidy." (November 20, 1925.)

problem of the wage scale. It is urged that only by taking over of the mines and the railways can the State fulfil its duty to the workers. Between the industrial and political Labour movement the chief difficulty seems to be the agreement with regard to compensation to be offered the owners of the mines and the railways.

The Ministry of Transport Act, 1919,[480] provided for the unified governmental control of all railways and other means of transportation. The Ministry was given power to improve existing lines or to construct additional facilities. Control was temporary, the law lapsing after two years, but in that time the Minister of Transport was given authority to fix railway tariffs and wages. The Act also set up an advisory panel or committee, consisting of 16 members; and the first consisted of 12 railroad managers and four representatives of the workers.[481] In 1920 the organizations of employees whose members were concerned in the negotiations with the Government for the standardization of railway wages made arrangements with the Government for dealing with questions of wages and conditions of employment during the period when the railways were under the control of the Ministry of Transport.[482] A central wage board was constituted, consisting of five railway managers and five representatives of the trade unions, and each side had the power to add a sixth member. Failing agreement by this central board, matters of dispute were referred to a national wages board, consisting of four railway managers, four railway workers (or their representatives), and four users of the railways, of whom one was to be nominated by the Parliamentary Committee of the Trade

[480] 9 & 10 George V, c. 50. [481] Section 23 of the Act of 1919.

[482] A very able study by Mr. Edward Cleveland-Stevens, *English Railways, Their Development and Their Relation to the State* (London, 1915), gives a detailed historical account of the control by Parliament of the railways in the interests of the public. His conclusion (p. 324) is interesting: "Whatever the future may bring, a strong, continuous, certain and comprehensive policy of State control must be evolved, and the outstanding lesson to be drawn from the history of English railways is the danger of entrusting control to the Legislature. The central problem, whether the railways remain in private hands or be taken over by the State, is the creation of a permanent Board of Control, and one as far removed as is possible from the interference of Parliament." It is well to note how this has been carried out with regard to the settlement of the wage contract.

Union Congress, one by the Co-operative Union, one by the Federation of British Industries, and one by the Associated Chambers of Commerce. An independent chairman was appointed by the Government. The Unions agreed that no strike would take place on account of a dispute arising on wage matters until one month after the question in dispute had been referred to the National Wages Board. Local committees were to look after the details of wage agreements.

The reorganization and the regulation of the British railways after the expiration in August, 1921, of the period of Government control was provided for in the British Railways Act, 1921. This Act provided for the amalgamation of the existing railway companies into six groups and the establishment of a tribunal to deal with the question of railway charges. The tribunal consists of three members, an experienced lawyer to act as chairman, and two members having experience, one in commercial affairs, and the other in railway business. The Minister of Transport has authority when it is considered necessary in any particular case to add two other members, one from a "railway panel" and one from a "general panel" of 36 persons, 22 of whom are nominated by the President of the Board of Trade to represent business interests 12 by the Minister of Labor after consultation with bodies representing the interests of labour and the passengers on the railways, and two by the Minister of Agriculture and Fisheries to represent agricultural interests. The Act further provided that the Central and National Wages Boards, as outlined above, were to continue at least until January 1, 1924, during which time all questions relating to rates of pay, hours of work, etc., should in default of agreement, be referred to the Central Wages Board, or upon appeal, to the National Wages Board. This provision is yet in force in 1926.[483] The Act also provided for the constitution of one or more counsels for each of the railway companies consisting of officers of the railway companies and

[483] Two recent studies of interest with regard to railways and the State are Mr. Harold Cox's *The Failure of State Railways* (1925), and A. Emil Davies, *British Railways, 1825-1924: Why Nationalisation is Inevitable* (1925). The well-known thesis of Mr. Davies is that it is only "when a vital service is publicly owned, and its administration has to come under review by the elected representatives of the nation or locality, that you can hope to obtain operation for use rather than profit."

elected representatives of the workers. Each railway company may also establish a similar conference for the police force of the company to which all questions of wages, hours, and conditions of service shall be referred which may be appealed to the central conference composed of representatives of the conferences of the separate railways. In case of disagreement an independent chairman shall be appointed who has the power to give binding decisions.

(c) *The Industrial Courts Act, 1919*

The termination of the Wages (Temporary Regulation) Act, 1918, made it necessary for Parliament to legislate into existence permanent machinery for the voluntary arbitration of trade disputes. This was done by what is known as the industrial Courts Act,[484] which became a law November 20, 1919. Under the terms of the 1918 Act wages had, since the Armistice, been maintained at a level not lower than that prevailing at that time, unless modified by agreement of the parties concerned or by awards made by the Interim Court of Arbitration, and thus there had been prevented a sudden drop in wages while industry was passing from a war to a peace basis. The Interim Court of Arbitration, established upon the passing of the Act of 1918, continued the work of the Committee on Production [485] which was created in February, 1915, and which fixed wage awards during the War. So successful had their work been that it seemed advisable to form a permanent body to which disputes could in all cases of necessity be referred for settlement. The Act provided first a permanent court of arbitration, to which industrial disputes may be referred;[486] secondly the Act provided for the appointment of a court of inquiry which shall make immediate investigation of any existing or apprehended dispute and give an impartial report of its merits to the public;[487] and thirdly the Wages (Temporary Regu-

[484] 9 & 10 Geo. V, c. 69.

[485] With the establishment of the Ministry of Munitions, 1915 (5 & 6 Geo. V, c. 54), the functions of the committee in regard to production were absorbed by the Ministry. The committee then became an arbitration body and quickly developed into the principal arbitration tribunal for the settlement of labour disputes (see Munitions of War Act, 1916 (5 & 6 Geo. V, c. 99), section 8).

[486] Part I, Act of 1919.

[487] Part II, *ibid.*

lation) Act, 1918, was continued to September, 1920.[488] The Court functions in an advisory and consultative capacity as well as judicially, and while voluntary it depends upon the honour and civic sense of the disputants to carry out the awards.

The Minister of Labour is given wide latitude in the establishment of the Industrial Court and of the Courts of Inquiry.[489] In the case of the Industrial Court he appoints the personnel, the only restriction being that it shall consist of men and women representing the public, the employers and the workers. The length of office is also fixed by him, and at any time he deems advisable it may refer matters to this tribunal for opinion. The president of the Industrial Court of Great Britain, Sir William Mackenzie, while believing that industrial arbitration is "a plant of slow growth," considers however that the Industrial Court may reasonably be expected to shape and express the increasing sense of social justice and to "establish a recognized body of principles by which industrial questions can be judged." He warns, however, "that ambition may easily overreach itself in this matter," and concludes:[490]

All law is the result of a process of crystallizing the good sense of mankind into definite rules. But what has been so slow in the matter of common and criminal law can not be effected by hasty generalizations in the sphere of industrial relationships, where the matters at issue often represent a tangle in which law, ethics, economics, and politics are inextricably woven.

In all wage disputes before the Industrial Court and in all investigations by the Courts of Inquiry due weight has been given to the necessity of preventing wages from falling below the level

[488] Part III, *ibid.* [489] Part IV, *ibid.*

[490] See article by Sir William Mackenzie in the *International Labour Review*, Geneva, July-August, 1921. The director of the International Labour Office in concluding his *Report to the Fourth Session* (Geneva, 1922) declared that the success of the I. L. O. depended on the capabilities and solidarity of labour organizations, on valuable aid from employers who are fully aware of the importance sane legislation may render to industry, and on the attitude of Governments toward social progress. Success also depended "on the active vigilance, the tact and prudence of the I. L. O.," on the authority it acquires, the confidence it inspires, and the security it affords. Above all, "success will depend on men's faith in justice."

necessary for an adequate standard of living. The operation of this Act has had to be carried on in a period during which there has been a downward trend of wages. There have been important strikes over wage disputes between 1918 and 1926, and there have been many disputes, but the fact is well stated by Labour that the extent to which some of the disputes might have developed had the Government not taken steps to see "fair play" can better be imagined than recorded in cold print.[491]

By availing themselves of the powers afforded by the Industrial Courts Act, and appointing Courts of Inquiry to investigate in public the merits of the various claims they were able to ensure the facts being impartially placed before the public, and to call upon the employers to refute the workers' claims by logical argument instead of by brute force. It was this fact that brought many of the big disputes to an end in a comparatively short time, the employers' case being shattered so soon as the workers' representatives had an opportunity of submitting their opponents' witnesses to cross-examination.

The emphasis put by Mr. Baldwin upon the spirit of industry and labour being one of mutual forbearance, and the effort of trade union leaders to find a working plan for co-operation with industry, together with the general determination in Great Britain that the standard of living of the workers must not be lowered, have all contributed to making a serious national problem less bitter. Justice will be done because nothing less can satisfy the nation.

(d) *The Nation and the Coal Mines*

The first great inquiry after the War was not conducted under the Industrial Courts Act, which had not then been passed, but under the special Act of Parliament which set up the Coal In-

[491] *Labor Year Book,* 1925, p. 78. Important Courts of Inquiry have been the Dockers' Court of Inquiry early in 1920; coal tippers and their employers concerning hours of labour (1920); engineering workers and the Engineering and National Employers' Federation concerning wages (1920); shipbuilding workers and employers concerning wages (1920); engineering workers and the Engineering and National Employers' Federation (1922); printing workers and employers (1922); and in 1924 seven important wage disputes were under Inquiry, including the Dockers' Strike, the Building Trade Strike and the Coal Mines Dispute.

dustry Commission, on which Mr. Justice Sankey was chairman. This Commission consisted of six representatives of labour (three of whom directly represented miners), six representatives of employers (three of whom represented mining interests), and the chairman. The proposals of this Commission, and those of the miners themselves as embodied in their Nationalization of the Mines and Minerals Bill, remain to-day (1926) the chief issues of this great national controversy. The chairman's Interim Report [492] advocated either nationalization or unification of the industry, and recommended that the workers should have an effective voice in the direction of the mines. The chairman's final Report [493] advocated immediate State ownership of coal royalties; the principle of the State ownership of mines, and a scheme for acquiring the mines for the State in three years' time together with a scheme for administration. Mr. Justice Sankey declared that there was "fair reason to expect that the relationship between Labour and the community will be an improvement upon the relationship between Labour and Capital in the coal fields." The main difference between the Report of the Chairman, which has overshadowed the other three Reports presented by the different members and groups of the Commission, and the Labour Report,[494] is that the Labour representatives claimed more power for the miners over the administration of the mines. Throughout the whole discussion of the relation of the State to the coal industry the problem of a decent standard of living has been kept to the front, and the emphasis has been placed at times on the question of housing and the hours of work. The Sankey Commission Reports rank among the most valuable social documents of this century, and the Commission made a most worthwhile contribution to the statement of the problem of industry and labour in modern civilization. The very topics they discussed indicate what changes

[492] *Interim Report of the Commission*, 1919, Cd. 84.

[493] Cd. 210, 1919.

[494] Cd. 201, 1919. Two Appendices of importance are attached to Mr. Cole's *Chaos and Order in Industry* (1920), the first is a *Memorandum* on the causes of and remedies for labour unrest, presented by the trade union representatives on the joint committee appointed at the National Industrial Conference, London, February 27, 1919, signed by Arthur Henderson and G. D. H. Cole; and the second is the Mines Nationalization Bill mentioned above.

have come about in the world of capital and labour. The fact that they did discuss them indicates that the effort is being made to understand what are the conditions of justice for workers.[495]

This principle is further made plain in the effort to get at a fair wage scale for the mine workers, as well as in the effort to make the coal industry of Great Britain a factor in national and industrial well being. The Miners' Federation in 1921 objected to the Government Coal Mines (Decontrol) Act, 1921, which terminated Government control of the mines. The miners and the mine owners could not agree upon a scheme for regulating wages, and in 1921 a lockout occurred in the coal industry which resulted in the pits being closed from April 1 to July 4 throughout the country. The question of the future regulation of the wage contract was definitely made one of the major points of the workers' program. By the agreement of July 1, 1921, known as the National Wages Agreement, the State affirmed most emphatically the right of the worker to a decent standard of living. That standard was to be the first charge on industry, a principle that is nothing less than a landmark in the development of social theory. Moreover the Government allocated £10,000,000 to prevent the immediate reduction of wages in certain districts, and National and District Wages Boards were set up for the industry. Wages were to be regulated on a "collective profit-sharing" principle, the first charge on the industry being standard wages at the *district* rates prevailing in 1914 plus 20 per cent. It was also provided that wages were to be fixed by the District Wages Board for low-paid workers. Thus in 1921 the miners failed to obtain the principle of the financial unification of the industry with the pooling of profits, and wages fixed upon a national basis. But the nation knew the acute situation in which the workers, and the owners, of a vital industry were placed, and the best brains of the country have tried to work out a national program for the mining industry. It is a step in advance to have the problems of the owners and the workers and the public placed on a national basis.

[495] Cf. G. D. H. Cole, *Chaos and Order in Industry* (1920), chap. V, pp. 62-85, for interesting comment on the Coal Commission and the political situation in England during the period from 1918-1920.

This was proved in 1924, when on January 17, the Miners' Federation of Great Britain gave three months' notice to the Mining Association of Great Britain to terminate the National Wages Agreement of July 1, 1921. Proposals were offered by both the miners and the mine owners. On the recommendation of the Executive of the Miners' Federation of Great Britain the Minister of Labour set up an inquiry under the Industrial Courts Act, to investigate the matters at issue between the parties. Lord Buckmaster was chairman of the court, before whom the miners put the claim of "a living wage, which should not be less than the rates obtaining in 1914." The Court of Inquiry, after the public hearings, recommended that it should be possible for the two parties to come to a new agreement. The terms of settlement finally accepted by the miners provided that the *standard profits* item was to be 15 per cent of the *standard wages* item, instead of 17 per cent. Of the *surplus proceeds* 88 per cent was to be allocated to wages instead of 83 percent. The minimum percentage payable on basis rates was increased from 20 per cent to 33 1/3 per cent above standard wages. Subsistence wages already granted in certain districts were increased one-eighth, and the proviso was added that no wage was to fall below an amount equal to 40 per cent on the standard wage of the lowest-paid class in the district. This agreement remained in force from May 1, 1924, to May 1, 1925, thereafter being terminable by a month's notice on either side. It was recognized on all sides that the year's agreement would provide little more than a truce, and that during the year the coal owners and the miners would spend much time upon the propaganda phases of the struggle between the operators and the workers. The year 1925 began with a warning from Mr. A. J. Cook, Secretary of the Miners' Federation of Great Britain, who said that there was no doubt whatever

that the purpose of the coal owners in suggesting a joint inquiry is to press the necessity for a reversion to the eight-hour day, and, probably, a revision of wage rates. It is no use blinking at the facts. The year 1925 will test the courage and solidarity of the Miners' Federation to the utmost. . . . By virtue of their dangerous calling and its importance to the community, the public should long ago have recognized the right of the miners to a living wage, and not allowed them to struggle and suffer for the smallest improvement in their miserable lot.[496]

So it was not at all surprising that the miners unanimously rejected the terms of the operators, which involved a complete change in the existing methods of wage fixing. The General Council of the Trades Union Congress clearly stated the important issue for the workers, and the significance of the principle of the minimum wage is stressed.

The terms put forward by the mining association for a revised agreement proposed drastic reductions in the already meagre wages paid to the miners, abolish the principle of the minimum wage, destroy the principle of national agreement, make the national unification of the industry an impossibility, and would, if carried to their logical conclusion, eventually lead to settlements between individual companies and their workers and cause chaos within the industry.

The principle of the minimum wage was again put to the front when Labour, refusing to appear before the Court of Inquiry, declared they would not enter any discussion in which the principle of a guaranteed minimum wage should be called into question. It was also pointed out that for the fourth time in six years the British coal industry found itself facing the prospect of a disastrous struggle between employers and employees, and that within the six years several Courts of Inquiry had been set up, the latest only a year before, and that they saw no good to be served by another of the same kind. However the Court of Inquiry was appointed on July 13, and presented its Report on July 28, 1925.[497] It is very important to record, though the miners refused to appear before it at all, that the Report gave official sanction to the view that "wages at some agreed minimum rate must in practise be a charge before profits are taken."

[496] *Daily Herald,* January 3, 1925, p. 6, from article, "Mine Owners to Attack Hours and Wages." See the Secretary's article in the *Daily Herald,* January 5, 1925, in which he discusses his proposal for a minimum wage of twelve shillings a day.

[497] *Court of Inquiry Concerning the Coal Mine Dispute,* 1925. Report. London, 1925. Cmd. 2478.

We are satisfied on one point, that the workers are justified in claiming that any wages agreement which they can be asked to accept should provide for a minimum wage. What that minimum should be is a matter for negotiation between the parties. We do not think that a method of finding wages which allows of their indefinite diminution can be regarded as satisfactory.

Also it is well to note that the Court of Inquiry considered that there were other means than a reduction of wages for improving the condition of the industry. Good-will, it was held, was an important matter in the industry, and the organization of the industry must take that factor into consideration. The Court of Inquiry could do nothing to stem the tide of high feeling, and the Government were forced to avert a national stoppage in the mining industry. The coal crisis brought to a head the tremendous feeling of insecurity with regard to the wage contract that was common among the highly organized industries of Great Britain. At the time the railwaymen and the engineers were threatened with lower wages or longer hours, and it was felt that the defeat of the miners would be a blow to their own resistance, and would be the first victory in a general campaign against wages and hours in other industries. The fight of the miners was taken up, and the railwaymen and the transport workers pledged themselves not to move coal, if a stoppage came, by land or water, for domestic or any other use. The Alliance of Unions was not perfected, but the conduct of affairs was placed in the hands of the Trade Union Congress, which was authorized to call strikes if necessary. The Trade Union Congress represented a membership of over 4,000,000, and in a time of industrial depression and widespread unrest, the Government decided that at any cost a general strike must be prevented. There was in the country something of the tense feeling of 1911 and 1913, and the National Minority Movement had helped to give a "militancy" to the workers in certain districts. The miners had in their fiery secretary a militant leader, and the Left Wing of the Labour Party added its influence to the industrial section.

On July 31, the Prime Minister announced in Parliament that an arrangement had been made with the owners, under which the notices they had given were to be withdrawn for a fortnight, during which time a permanent agreement was to be drawn up. The withdrawal was made after the Government had promised aid to the coal industry in the form of a subsidy, extending over nine months, from August 1, 1925, to May 1, 1926. During this wages to be paid on the basis of the 1924 agreement. The Treasury Memorandum issued to the House of Commons before the vote asked the House to make

> provision for a temporary subvention to enable the coal mining industry to continue the payment of wages at rates not less than those obtaining in July, 1925.[498]

The explanatory memorandum of the settlement issued on August 5, 1925, as Parliamentary Paper,[499] simply announced the continuation of the 1924 National Wages Agreement.

It can be fairly said that the settlement of the coal dispute in 1925 was not regarded with entire favour by anyone, the Government, the Labour Party, the mine owners, the workers, the general public. It is avowedly a makeshift, but what else could have been done by the Government? The comment of the leader of the Opposition, the ex-Labour Prime Minister, Mr. J. Ramsay MacDonald, was that the settlement was "an interesting chapter in the revolutionary effects of reactionary governments."[500] The vigorous old leader of many battles, Mr. Robert Smillie, told the House of Commons that it was not the threat of a general strike, but the answer of the House to the humanitarian appeal of the miners that prompted the subvention. Whatever the result may be, it is now certain that the State must carefully consider every proposal brought forward that offers a solution to one of the most important industrial problems that Great Britain now faces.

[498] When the subsidy was granted it was thought that £9,000,000 would be sufficient, but in December, 1925, Mr. Churchill, the Chancellor of the Exchequer, asked the House of Commons for nine additional millions. By May, 1926, the coal subsidy will have cost the country between £20 and £21 millions, far more than the official estimate. It is a disquieting situation.

[499] *Coal-mining Industry: Explanatory memorandum of the terms of settlement of the dispute in the coal-mining industry,* London, 1925. (Cmd. 2488.)

[500] See his article, "British Constitutionalism and the Coal Settlement," in the *Nation* (New York), August 26, 1925, No. 3138, p. 226.

There is support for this view in the fact that as part of the settlement a Government Commission was to be appointed to inquire into the whole situation in the industry, with a view to seeing whether it could not be put into a better economic position. The terms of reference of the Coal Commission were the widest possible terms:

To inquire into and report upon the economic position of the coal industry and the condition affecting it and to make any recommendations for the improvement thereon.

There is no withholding of the fact that the Government is anxiously awaiting the final Report of the Royal Commission. A former member of the MacDonald ministry believes that the subsidy has come to stay, and that the inevitable outcome is complete State ownership. He says

the issue before the British people to-day is one of principle and doctrine. We are really fighting out at home an ancient fight; the echoes of 1893, the last occasion when the miners of Great Britain fought for a living wage, are in our ears.[501]

A keen observer of the contemporary political and industrial struggle in Great Britain has recorded his impressions of what is going on in the dispute. He recently wrote:

One sees something, I believe, of what is amiss in the present position by attending a session or two of the Coal Commission. Sir Herbert Samuel is as able a chairman as one could wish to find—quick, courteous, incisive, and supremely intelligent. Sir William Beveridge is as fine a master of the art of cross-examination as I have ever seen on a Royal Commission. If attention to the economic aspect of the problem could solve it, it would, for sheer ability at getting at the facts, have been solved already. But, with all the good will possible, I do not feel that the Commission realizes that its issue is at least as much moral as it is economic. One feels that as one watches the antagonism of miner and mine owner over each minute point that arises. One grasps it even more clearly in listening to the entire inability of a great

[501] See "British Industrial Crisis," an article by Brigadier General the Rt. Hon. Lord Thomson, in *Proceedings of the Academy of Political Science,* Vol. XI (January, 1926), No. 4, pp. 163-168.

technical expert like Sir Richard Redmayne to understand why the miner seeks nationalization as a solution. And one detects, I think, a certain impatience in the Commission itself when the issue is moved from purely economic considerations. The Sankey Commission had great defects; but its chairman grasped early and never lost sight of, the root fact that there is a reserve of moral energy in the miners which the present system of ownership can never bring into play.[502]

In the light of these criticisms it is well to note the proposals that were put before the Coal Commission. The owners proposed that the industry should be left alone to seek its own salvation with the help of longer working hours, drastically reduced wages, and a large reduction in railway rates at the expense of railwaymen's wages. It has been well said that this is a plan that holds out no prospect of peace for the industry, and its economic wisdom is equally questionable. Sir Herbert Samuel, the chairman, said that the scheme meant that even if all the coal owners' expectations were fulfilled, the industry would still be unprofitable, and that it would be producing a greatly increased output of coal, which, if it were not taken up, could only bring prices down still more ruinously or throw 100,000 men out of work. The miners denounced the scheme as a wage-lowering device, and they refused to be a party to an attack on the wages of their fellow workers in more "sheltered" trades.

The miners, backed by the industrial and political Labour movement, put forward a scheme of nationalization. The scheme was considered of such importance that it was worked out as the joint policy of the whole Labour movement—that is by the Executive of the Miners' Federation, the Labour Party Executive, the Executive of the Parliamentary Labour party (members in Parliament), and the General Council of the Trade Union Congress. General agreement was quickly reached on the general principles of the scheme, which is a bold plan for combining public control with the scientific development of the industry. Difference of opinion arose on the question of compensation to royalty

[502] See article of Mr. Harold J. Laski, "Great Britain and the Communists," in the *Nation* (New York), January 6, 1926, Vol. XLV, No. 579, pp. 183-184, and his article in the same weekly, December 16, 1925, "Mr. Baldwin's First Year," for the quotation above (p. 104).

owners, and this has been a thorny question for several years between the industrial and political Labour movement. By the Labour program put before the Coal Commission, the coal industry is to become an organization for mining coal, manufacturing electrical power on a very large scale, making both coke and smokeless fuel, and producing, in addition, a large range of by-products. The transformed industry is to be nationally owned. It is to be administered by a statutory body—a power and transport commission to replace the present Electricity Commission. Below this supreme body is a national coal and power production council of technicians and workers, and below that provincial councils, pit and works committees. A consumers' council will be also set up. Exports will be dealt with by a coal export commission. Political interference is sought to be eliminated by the statutory character of the main commission. It is also intended that the industry should be self-supporting without Parliamentary subsidy. The *Manchester Guardian Weekly* editorially said that in principle the scheme adopted the main outlines of the Liberal "coal and power" scheme, but carried them very much farther, to the point of elimination of private enterprise. It added that "whatever its political future, the scheme marks an important development in modern Socialist thought." [503] This is an interesting comment, especially in the light of what has been written since 1918 by the leaders of the Labour party with regard to the reorganization of national industries. The chief argument, so it seems, is that the State must be directly concerned within the area of production upon which public welfare depends.[504] This principle was defined in the Memorandum of the Government, wherein it was stated that the

Government have recognized that the coal-mining industry as a whole is under existing conditions financially unable to continue

[503] Issue of January 15, 1926, p. 41.

[504] Cf. H. J. Laski, *A Grammar of Politics* (1925), chap. 9, "Economic Institutions," pp. 433-540, a suggestive treatment of the whole problem. The writings of the Webbs, of Tawney, of Cole, of Russell, and the numerous Labour reports and researches are invaluable in providing an indictment of the intent of the present capitalistic system. A volume published by the Fabian Research Department in 1916, edited by Sidney Webb, is interesting, *How to Pay for the War,* especially chapters II and III.

either to give employment or to produce coal on a scale which the interests of the country demand.

In bringing to a close the problem of a living wage and official sanction of the Government to the principle, it is well to note that on July 28, 1925, a committee of twelve was announced to serve as the Food Council recently recommended by the Royal Commission on Food Prices in its Report.[505] The Council is authorized to investigate and report on the supply and prices of food in general, and of the staples in particular. It is to undertake investigations when called upon to do so by the President of the Board of Trade, or when in its judgment the interests of consumers or traders require such action. Its powers are somewhat limited, but according to a statement made by the chairman these may be enlarged if necessary. One of the interesting developments of the future will be the extension of the powers and activities of this Food Council. What it is likely to become was intimated by Sir Charles Fielding, in his evidence before the Royal Commission on Food Prices. Sir Charles, who was Director of Food Production in 1918, suggested that the first Board be appointed in the same manner as the Metropolitan Water Board and the Port of London Authority, the former composed of representatives nominated by public authorities in the water area, while the Port of London Authority consists of both elected and appointed members. Sir Charles proposed that the Board should control and organize the import of wheat, the price of bread to the consumer over the baker's counter, the import of meat, and the yearly price to be paid by a municipality or Food Board Centre to the farmer for milk. The Board, he also proposed, should have power to erect flour mills, bakeries, bacon factories, and to establish a minimum guarantee for certain farm products.

Whatever the future may hold with regard to the place of the State in control of the standard of living, it is proved that the State is to be more than a co-ordinating agency. Miss Follett says the State must "appear as the great moral leader. Its supreme functioning is moral ordering." The ordering of relations, so this able writer believes, is morality in its essence and com-

[505] *Royal Commission on Food Prices,* First Report, Vol. I, London, 1925, Cmd. 2390.

pleteness. The State must gather up into itself all the moral power of its day, and because the relations of communities and individuals are widening constantly, the State must be the explorer which discovers the kind of ordering, the kind of grouping, which best expresses its intent.[506]

The ideal of a Living Wage has been shown to be the dominant ideal of social politics in the twentieth century. All parties within the State have recognized it in their programs of action. It is significant that the National Council of the Independent Labour Party puts this demand first in their new policy, outlined at the annual conference at Whitley Bay, Easter, 1926. The object the party sets before itself is "winning Socialism in our time" by a "conscious and resolute Socialist policy planned deliberately to carry us rapidly through the period of transition from the old to the new civilization." The key to the program is a "national living wage," in which the "I. L. P. sees a first demand for justice, with the power, if we follow its logic with courage, to carry us rapidly towards the realization of a Socialist State." The demand necessitates the establishment of a national banking system, with the control of credit and currency for national purposes; the nationalization of the importation of food and raw materials; the nationalization, as co-ordinated services, of railways, mines, and electrical generation; the reorganization and development of agriculture and the public ownership of land, and the national organization of the building industry and of the production of building materials.[507] This series of measures, it is declared, "would lay the foundation of the new Socialist State." It was proposed that "the whole Labour movement should at once set up a commission of its own to fix a living wage, representing the minimum standard of civilized existence which should be tolerated. It should then make the demand for this standard the key of its policy, both politically and industrially."

[506] *The New State* (1918), chap. XXXIV, "The Moral State and Creative Citizenship," pp. 333-343.

[507] Material on nationalization is abundant, but the following provide a basis of study: Sir Leo Chiozza Money, *The Triumph of Nationalization* (1920), the war proved it he says; Lord Emmett, *Nationalization of Industries, A Criticism;* Lord Haldane, *The Problem of Nationalization* (1921), with Introduction by R. H. Tawney and H. J. Laski; and A. Emil Davies and Dorthy Evans, *Land Nationalisation, The Key to Social Reform* (1921).

The party program as outlined by the National Council goes on to demand that

> the Labour party in Parliament should not be satisfied with opposing the actions of the Government, but should seek any and every opportunity of asserting the demand for a living wage and of advocating the broad Socialist program through which it alone can be realized.
>
> The I. L. P. considers that the Labour Party should make it clear that it will introduce this program whenever the opportunity to take office recurs. Immediate steps should be taken to prepare measures for the necessary economic reorganization, so that Labour may be ready to introduce them without delay.
>
> The fact that it had only a minority behind it should not deter a Labour Government from this purpose. The responsibility should be placed upon Labour's opponents of rejecting the Socialist measures proposed. By this means the issue of the poverty of the people and the proposals of constructive Socialism would be thrust into the forefront of practical politics.

The future will show how competent the Labour movement is to direct the agencies of reform, and it will be a test of the Labour party's ability to understand the parliamentary spirit of English government. Great issues are forming in the England of to-day, the future is unknown and uncertain. The parties within the State have before them a tremendous duty—the duty of earnest study of the needs of all the people and the courageous carrying out of plans of reform. It is certain that Parliament has a pre-eminent place in the life of to-day, for there is need of patriotism from all men who love England and her heritage of freedom.

CHAPTER V

THE CONSTITUTIONAL CRISIS AND THE BUDGET OF 1909 WITH REFERENCE TO SOCIAL REFORM

Part I

1907–1909

The financial policy of the State as affected by the costs of social legislation must now be briefly considered before further details of Liberal social reform can be adequately presented. The Budget of 1909 marks an epoch in the history of social reform and the State. The conflict centering about the constitutional question of the powers of the House of Lords must also be briefly outlined, in so far as it, like the Budget, provides any material for the purpose of this study. Financial and constitutional theories are outside the scope of this survey, but the controversies about the Budget and the Upper House may help to illustrate important tendencies of the time.

The 1907 Parliament opened with the certainty that the conflict between the House of Lords and the House of Commons would be one of the outstanding considerations of the year. The clause in the King's Speech dealing with the House of Lords was the most important, though Bills were announced for regulating the hours of labour in mines and for the better housing of the people.[1] The Government had gone through the hard year of 1906 and already had set in the first ebb-tide of popular feeling from a united party and Labour. Above all the Lords veto of the Education Bill of Mr. Birrell, the Licensing Bill and the Plural Voting Bill provided the Liberal Party with the necessary determination to make sure the rights and powers of the Commons. "Serious questions affecting the working of our Parliamentary system" it was said in the Speech, "have arisen from unfortunate differences between the two Houses. My Min-

[1] Hansard, 4 S. H. C., 1907, Vol. 169, pp. 1-3.

isters have this important subject under consideration with a view to a solution of the difficulty."

This announcement was enough for the Opposition to allege that the Liberal Party was repeating its mistakes, and that social reform would be neglected while the Government engaged in an effort that was contrary to the Constitution and the history of the nation.[2] The Prime Minister, openly declaring that Mr. Balfour was directing and controlling the course of Bills in the House of Lords, said,

I would have him remember what is the essential and inherent nature of the constitution of this country. It is that it is representative. But ours ceases to be a representative system if the leader of a Party who has been overwhelmingly defeated by the popular voice at the polls is to remain, directly or indirectly, in supreme control of the legislation of the country.

He added further that "the present state of things is discreditable; it is dangerous; it is demoralizing. It is demoralizing to this House." [3]

The leader of the Labour Party in his speech gave attention to the problem of social reform.[4] He regretted the omission of any reference to old age pensions and to the unemployed. He disputed the proposition that a certain amount of unemployment must exist in order to give fluidity to the industrial system. If the industrial system could only be carried on by such demoralizing means it must be so reconstructed that everybody should be given work, and poverty should be driven from the shores. He appealed to honourable members opposite and to the Government, before proceeding with highly contentious legislation, to call a truce of God in regard to all social reform touching the common people. They would go on with their fight with the Lords, they would enjoy it, and in the end they would triumph, but let them not forget those who had no share in that fight.

[2] Hansard, *ibid.*, pp. 18-31, for speech of the Marquess of Lansdowne, leader of Opposition in House of Lords, on conflict between the two Houses; pp. 62-78, for Mr. Balfour's speech, Opposition leader in House of Commons.

[3] Hansard, *ibid.*, pp. 78-89 (Campbell-Bannerman).

[4] Hansard, *ibid.*, pp. 104-111 (Hardie).

Let them think of the suffering children, the aged poor, and see to it that the claims of our common humanity were met before entering into a conflict of that kind.

The debate on the Address was given fresh life by the principal attack of the Opposition, the amendment moved by Earl Percy deploring that the social legislation declared by Ministers to be urgent should be postponed in order to effect revolutionary changes in Parliamentary control over the affairs of the United Kingdom, and in the constitutional relations between the Houses.[5] The Chancellor of the Exchequer, Mr. Asquith, made the principal speech for the Government on this amendment.[6] It was his belief that the House of Lords did not really fulfil the function of a second chamber, but that it was primarily concerned with protecting the vested interests from progressive social reform. "The deliberate opinion of His Majesty's Government," was, he declared, "that we are face to face with a caricature and a mockery of representative government."[7] Labour, through Mr. Henderson, believed that the House of Lords needed ending not mending.[8] Mr. F. E. Smith, whose remarks on the Trade Disputes Bill in 1906 had caused a member to wish "that there was a little more of Christian charity and less brilliancy,"[9] warned the Government against confounding the Liberal party with the people, and asked what signs there were in the country of public indignation against the Lords. The leader of the Opposition believed that it would be utter folly to intrust legislation to a single Chamber working under closure rules. The controversy over the Lords, he said, would postpone indefinitely all social reforms. Mr. Birrell,[10] whose ill-fated Education Bills were consuming time and Government patience, ended the debate for the Government. Parliament had listened to the chief speakers on all sides on this important question; the problem had been fully set forth. The amendment of Earl Percy was rejected by 374 votes to 111.

The Prime Minister introduced on June 24, 1907, the Resolution dealing with the relations between the two Houses of Parliament. He moved,

[5] Hansard, 4 S., 1907, Vol. 169, pp. 571-587, for remarks of Earl Percy; for debate amendment, pp. 571-667.

[6] Hansard, *ibid.*, pp. 587-597.

[7] Hansard, *ibid.*, p. 597.

[8] Hansard, *ibid.*, pp. 638-643.

[9] Hansard, 4 S., Vol 155, 1906, p. 33.

[10] Hansard, 4 S., Vol. 169, 1907, pp. 661-668.

That, in order to give effect to the will of the people, as expressed by their elected representatives, it is necessary that the power of the other House to alter or reject Bills passed by this House should be so restricted by law as to secure that within the limits of a single Parliament the final decision of the Commons shall prevail.[11]

The moving of this Resolution formally began the fight for the curbing of the power of the House of Lords which was to continue until the passing of the Parliament Act, 1911.

The motion affirmed the predominance of the House of Commons as the representative House of Parliament, and the Prime Minister submitted that in spirit and in fact that was the strictly true constitutional point of view. He affirmed that "the second Chamber was being utilized as a mere annex of the Unionist Party," and if the authority to speak for the nation was not to remain in the House of Commons, if that authority was to be usurped by the non-elective House, it followed that representative institutions must take a secondary place. It was proposed that if a Bill was sent up to the other House, and the two Houses found agreement impossible, a conference should be held between members appointed in equal numbers by the two Houses. The conference would be of small dimensions, its proceedings private, and its object would be to enable each party to negotiate and to seek for a common means of agreement which the Government might find itself able to adopt. The Prime Minister stated that the policy he had sketched would have to receive statutory definition.

It is worth while noting the trend that the Government policy was taking, and what problems affecting the life of the whole people were thrown into relief by this great political struggle. This is found on one hand in the attitude of the Labour Party, and on the other, in the rather remarkable speeches of the Ministers. Mr. Arthur Henderson moved the Labour amendment, which stated that "the Upper House, being an irresponsible part of the legislature, and of necessity representative only of interests opposed to the general wellbeing, is a hindrance to national progress and ought to be abolished." [12]

[11] Hansard, 4 S. H. C., 1907, Vol. 176, pp. 909-926.

[12] Hansard, *ibid.*, pp. 1193-1202, Henderson; pp. 941-947, Shackleton.

The Under-Secretary of State for the Colonies, Mr. Churchill, expressed in somewhat colourful manner one point of view in the debate. He stated that

in the main the lines of difference between the two parties are social and economic—in the main the lines of difference are increasingly becoming the lines of cleavage between the rich and the poor. Let that animate us in the great struggle which we are now undertaking, and in which we shall without rest press forward, confident of this, that, if we persevere we shall wrest from the hands of privilege and wealth the evil and sinister weapon of the Peers' veto which they have used so ill and so long.[13]

The speech of Mr. Lloyd George was peculiarly a setting for the struggles that he entered into two years later, for his taxation program could be deduced from the remarks that he made on property and capital.[14]

The Resolution was carried by 432 votes against 147.[15] From that time the controversy was carried forward with increasing bitterness and recrimination. Out of the political turmoil which it occasioned there will be found some contribution made to the problems with which this study is concerned.

Part II

The Budget of 1909

The Budget of 1909 was introduced on April 29, 1909, by the Chancellor of the Exchequer, Mr. Lloyd George.[16] The financial proposals submitted were under discussion in all on seventy-two Parliamentary days, including several all-night sittings. On November 4 the Budget was passed by a majority of 230 votes. The

[13] Hansard, *ibid.*, pp. 1240-1254. [14] Hansard, *ibid.*, pp. 1420-1435.

[15] Hansard, *ibid.*, for the whole discussion on the Resolution: pp. 909-1011; 1157-1254; and, 1409-1524. Note especially the speeches of Lord Robert Cecil (1176-1184); Sir William Anson (997-1003); Mr. F. E. Smith (1435-1443); and Mr. Asquith (1506-1514).

[16] Parl. Deb. 5 S. H. C., 1909, Vol. 4, pp. 472-548. The speeches made by Mr. Lloyd George in the Land campaign (1925-1926) have been often reminiscent of the Budget campaigns of 1909 and 1910.

Budget proposals were based on the common ground between the parties that the State urgently needed sixteen additional millions of money for the year. Tax expenditure on the Navy and Old Age Pensions were the major cause of the increased expenditure. The increased expenditure under both these heads, the Chancellor stated in his address, was substantially incurred with the unanimous assent of all political parties in Parliament. What is more this War Budget, as Mr. Lloyd George called it, against poverty, and social degradation, sought to make provision for old age pensions, general elementary education, labour exchanges, town planning and rural development. It had to provide for the maintenance of the whole machinery of administration set up by the social measures of the century, especially since 1905. It was this necessity that faced the Chancellor of the Exchequer. His closing words, after four and a half hours, were typical of the man and reveal the purpose of the Budget:

This, Mr. Emmot, is a War Budget. It is for raising money to wage implacable warfare against poverty and squalidness. I cannot help hoping and believing that before this generation has passed away we shall have advanced a great step towards that good time when poverty, and the wretchedness and human degradation which always follow in its camp will be as remote to the people of this country as the wolves which once infested its forests.

Old Age Pensions came first as the social measure which bore heaviest on the exchequer. For this, Mr. Lloyd George declared, "we simply honoured a checque drawn years ago in favour of the aged poor, which bore at its foot the signature of all the leaders of political parties in this country." It was only one of the pressing social problems.

What the Government have to ask themselves is this: Can the whole subject of further social reform be postponed until the increasing demands made upon the National Exchequer by the growth of armaments have ceased? Not merely *can* it be postponed, but ought it to be postponed? Is there the slightest hope that if we deferred consideration of the matter, we are likely within a generation to find any more favourable moment for attending to it? And we have to ask ourselves this further question: If we put off dealing with these social sores, are the evils which arise from them not likely to grow and to fester, until finally the loss which the country sustains will be infinitely greater than anything it would have to bear in paying the cost of an immediate remedy.[17]

That was a principle on which "the first Democratic Budget" was based. No one can mistake the humanity of the further appeal of the Chancellor.

There are hundreds of thousands of men, women and children in this country now enduring hardships for which the sternest judge would not hold them responsible; hardships entirely due to circumstances over which they have not the slightest command; the fluctuations and changes of trade, even of fashions; ill-health and the premature breakdown or death of the breadwinner. Owing to events of this kind, all of them beyond human control—at any rate beyond the control of the victims—thousands, and I am not sure millions, are precipitated into a condition of acute distress and poverty. How many people there are of this kind in this wealthy land the figures as to Old Age Pensions have thrown a very unpleasant light upon. Is it fair, is it just, is it humane, is it honourable, is it safe to subject such a multitude of our poor fellow-countrymen and countrywomen to continued endurance of these miseries until nations have learnt enough wisdom not to squander their resources on these huge machines for destruction of human life? I have no doubt as to the answer which will be given to the question by a nation as rich in humanity as it is in store.

Provision had to be made for those out of work through no fault of their own; any pauper disqualification from Old Age Pensions must be removed; voluntary and compulsory systems of insurance had to be considered; the Government pledge to deal on a comprehensive scale with unemployment had to be carried out through insurance against unemployment and a national system of labour exchanges. Mr. Lloyd George saw only one way to meet the financial demands of reform; a radical application of the principle of direct taxation—graduated income tax, super-

[17] Parl. Deb., *ibid.*, pp. 481-494, for the social reform sections.

tax, tax on the unearned increment, and tax on undeveloped property. There was also to be a readjustment of the indirect taxes, especially the licensing duties, with a view to equalizing the financial burden among the various classes in the community.

The Chancellor of the Exchequer believed that the greatest provision of all for unemployment was contained in the Land Clauses of the Budget,[18] the provisions of which "must have the effect eventually of destroying the selfish and stupid monopoly which now so egregiously mismanages the land." [19] It was this phase of the Budget with its graduation of real estate duties and income tax, its distinction between earned and unearned income, which most successfully aroused the Opposition.[20]

Old Age Pensions, Trade Boards, Labour Exchanges, Small Holdings, Housing and Town Planning, all these measures might have been overlooked, but the policy which places the control of industry in the hands of the people and provides equal opportunities for self-development, which asserts the claims of the State to a share of the unearned increment, is a policy which has aroused the Opposition, finally culminating in the revolt of the Lords and an attempt to assert their supremacy. The famous Budget of Mr. Lloyd George discriminated between income that is earned and income that is unearned.[21]

It was no wonder that Sir Frederick Banbury denounced it as "the maddest Budget ever introduced in the House of Commons," [22] saying that "for two hours we have listened to every Radical fad which I have ever heard enumerated, but which had nothing to do with the Budget Question." [23] The debate immediately after the Budget statement revealed the stunned condition

[18] Clauses 1-42, Part I, the Finance Bill, 1909.

[19] D. Lloyd George, Preface, p. xi, to *The People's Budget*, a collection of the speeches explaining and defending the provisions of the Budget. On this point see also C. F. G. Masterman, *The Condition of England* (1909), the parts dealing with rural conditions and agricultural labourers.

[20] Cf. Carlton H. Hayes, *British Social Politics* (New York, 1913), p. 19.

[21] Percy Alden, *Democratic England* (1910), p. 7. See also J. A. Hobson's *Industrial System* (1909), for a complete discussion of the relation of unearned increment and unemployment and the right of the State to the unearned surplus. Note speech of Mr. Churchill at Leicester on September 4, *Times*, September 6, 1909, p. 5.

[22] Parl. Deb. 5 S., 1909, 4 H. C., p. 589.

[23] Parl. Deb., *ibid.*, p. 583; entire speech, pp. 583-589.

of a good number of the members of Parliament. Mr. Austen Chamberlain and Mr. Balfour expressed the views of the Opposition, the latter dealing especially with the land values tax.[24] For the Labour Party Mr. Barnes declared, "we of the Labour Party will give a steady and consistent support to the Government in all the steps necessary to carry this Budget into effect."[25] The Postmaster General,[26] Mr. Buxton, spoke after Mr. Balfour, and in ending the discussion the Government was represented by Mr. Churchill.[27] How inextricably the Budget was joined with a definite purpose and program for social reorganization was expressed in his closing words:

We believe that if Great Britain is to remain great and famous in the world we can not allow the present social and industrial disorders, with their profound physical and moral reaction, to continue unabated and unchecked. We propose to you a financial system; we also unfold a policy of social reorganization which will demand sacrifice from all classes but which will give security to all classes. By its means we shall be able notably to control some of the most wasteful processes at work in our social life; and without it let the Committee be sure that our country will remain exposed to some fatal dangers against which fleets and armies are of no avail.[28]

The general principles of the Budget were debated for three days, May 3-5, at which time the major tendencies of social politics between 1900-1909 were discussed.[29] "It is Socialism and nothing else which is the foundation of this Budget," one speaker declared;[30] while Lord Hugh Cecil said he could not believe "it

[24] Parl. Deb., *ibid.*, pp. 549-566, Chamberlain; pp. 749-773, Balfour.

[25] Parl. Deb., *ibid.*, p. 795; pp. 794-806, complete speech; pp. 579-583, for speech of the Irish Nationalist leader, Mr. Redmond.

[26] Parl. Deb., *ibid.*, pp. 773-794.

[27] Parl. Deb., *ibid.*, pp. 843-854; complete discussion on presentation of Budget, pp. 472-604, and pp. 749-854.

[28] Parl. Deb., *ibid.*, p. 854; pp. 843-854 entire.

[29] Parl. Deb., *ibid.*, whole debate, May 4, pp. 907-1008; May 5, pp. 1056-1124. Main speeches besides those referred to above were: for the Government, the Attorney-General, Sir W. Robson (pp. 941-951); Masterman (pp. 1116-1123); Lloyd George (pp. 987-1005); Opposition: Austen Chamberlain (1096-1115) and Chaplain (1057-1072); see also speech of Sir Charles W. Dilke (pp. 951-960).

[30] Parl. Deb., *ibid.*, p. 908, E. G. Pretyman; pp. 929-941 entire.

is right to use taxation for the purpose of advancing the morality of temperance faddists or the prejudices of Radical politicians." [31] The speech of Mr. Snowden on May 5 was one of the strongest defences of the Budget, containing a wealth of detail relating to the social aspects of English life that the Budget touched upon.[32] It was this character of the Budget that appealed most strongly to Labour, for it presaged an increasing emphasis on social reform legislation. "There has never been a democratic government in the history of the world," Mr. Snowden said, "and we are just beginning to evolve a democratic Government in this country. We are beginning to see what the democracy is going to do to right wrong and set things right." He illustrated his attack on the social system by referring to the speech of the Home Secretary before the National Liberal Club, at which place he said "the condition of the poor in our great cities is much worse than that of naked savages in some parts of Africa." The Prime Minister gave for one of his defences of the tax on unearned increment, that it might relieve congestion in such places as Glasgow where 120,000 people were living in one-room tenements.[33]

Budget resolutions were considered from May 3-21. The progress of the Budget through to Report stage, May 24-26, was marked by repeated clashes of the partisans of the Budget and their opponents. The debates revealed the intense interest that was taken by the nation at large. The days on which the land values duties and the income tax and death duties were discussed are especially important for an understanding of the attitude of the Opposition to the Government's plan of direct taxation. Perhaps no one better defined issues and made the differences clearer than Mr. F. E. Smith (now Lord Birkenhead). In his Parliamentary speeches quotations from party propaganda and party leaders were always apt. In one of the debates, May 10, he quoted the *New Age* on the Budget, illustrating the Socialistic nature of the Government's proposals:

[31] Parl. Deb., *ibid.*, p. 950; pp. 941-951, entire.

[32] Parl. Deb., *ibid.*, pp. 1072-1084.

[33] Parl. Deb., 1096-1115. Mr. Snowden fifteen years later became the first Socialist Chancellor of the Exchequer. Two postwar books of his are *Labor and National Finance* (London, 1920), and *Labor and the New World* (London, 1921).

Mr. Lloyd George's Budget is splendid, almost as much as we should have expected from a Socialist chancellor in his first year of office. We cannot deny that the author of the present Budget is good enough statesman for Socialist support, during the next five or ten years at any rate. The Budget is not merely a Budget, but a programme; consequently it is to be regarded as Mr. Lloyd George's bid for the premiership.[34]

On the second reading[35] the Chancellor of the Exchequer referred to the taxes in France compared with those in Britain.[36] It had been stated[37] that there was no income tax in France and no death duties. Mr. Lloyd George replied that in France their death duties run up from one per cent to 20½ per cent, and that in France the equivalent of the Government Income Tax scheme was to be found in taxes on dividends, taxes on land—equivalent of Schedule A in England—and on trade.[38]

The third reading[39] passed by a majority of 230 on November 5. The final words of the Chancellor of the Exchequer were

[34] Parl. Deb., 5 S., 1909, 10 H. C., p. 1573.

[35] On May 26 the Finance Bill was introduced and read for the first time, and on June 7 the four days' debate on the second reading began. From June 21 to October 7, the Finance Bill was considered in Committee, forty-two days in all, and from October 19 to 29 in report stage. Three days, Nov. 2-4, were taken for third reading. A review of the 1909 Budget can be found in *British Budgets, 1887-88 to 1912-13,* Bernard Mallet (London, 1913), pp. 289-313; also pp. 313-323 for the 1910 Budget. See Lloyd George's summary in *Nation,* October 30, 1909.

[36] Parl. Deb., 5 S., 1909, 6 H. C., pp. 333-349.

[37] Parl. Deb., *ibid.,* pp. 19-42 (A. Chamberlain).

[38] An authoritative opinion on the crisis of 1909-1910 from the French point of view may be found in *Le Budget,* Gaston Jèze, p. 501 et seq.; also the same authority in R. S. L. F., 1910, p. 256 et seq.; 1911, p. 587 et seq.; also his *Cours de science des finances et de législation financiere française* (6th ed. 1922), pp. 45-56, on the Budget from the political point of view, with references to the 1909-10 controversy in England. A more extended comment can be found in *Le régime parlementaire,* by Professor Robert Redslob (1924), pp. 68-86. The Leader of the Opposition in the House of Lords on the second reading debate, November 22, quoted approvingly from the adverse criticism on the Budget of M. Leroy-Beaulieu, who can fairly be taken as representing the economic liberalism of his school. (Parl. Deb. 5 S., 1909, 4 H. L., p. 739.)

[39] Parl. Deb. 5 S., 1909, 12 H. C., pp. 1655-1666, Lloyd George's final speech and summary of Budget. See also the speech of Attorney-General, Mr. Robson, pp. 1666-1673, and Mr. Snowden, p. 1681 seq., both the latter speeches dealing with Socialism and the Budget.

that the Budget made adequate provision, ample and adequate, for objects which make for the security of the State and the well-being of its people. On November 22 the Earl of Crewe moved the second reading in the House of Lords without a speech. The Marquis of Lansdowne moved his resolution that the House was not justified in giving its consent to the Bill until it had been submitted to the judgment of the country.[40] The Lord Chancellor, Lord Loreburn, replied for the Government, intimating the one resource the Government possessed—the power to create peers—and declared that the attitude of the Opposition was "a step towards constitutional revolution." [41] The Earl of Halsbury intimated that the Liberal idea of the House of Lords as an "appanage of Carlton Club" was at the basis of the Ministerial action,[42] and Lord Willoughby de Broke stated that the party, "they and their Cabinet have surrendered to the forces of revolution and to the forces of Socialism." [43]

The Earl of Camperdown on November 23 quoted from the speech of Mr. J. Keir Hardie in the House of Commons on September 20, when he said,

> we are supporting this Budget well knowing that it is the first step towards the ideal which we have in mind—the absorption by the community for the use of the community of unearned incomes whether derived from land or from other sources.[44]

The Prime Minister at Birmingham, on September 17, had made one of his strongest speeches on this point, in reply largely to Lord Rosebery who thought the Budget "the end of all," representing Socialism which meant the negation of faith, of family, of property, of monarchy, of Empire.[45] Mr. Asquith declared

[40] Parl. Deb. 5 S., 1909, 4 H. L., pp. 731-750. The complete debate in House of Lords, November 22, pp. 730-820; November 23, pp. 821-923; November 24, 925-1025; November 25, pp. 1023-1116; and November 30, pp. 1233-1342.

[41] Parl. Deb. 5 S., 1909, 4 H. L., p. 755; pp. 750-760 entire.

[42] Parl. Deb., *ibid.*, pp. 750-767.

[43] Parl. Deb., *ibid.*, p. 783; pp. 775-785 entire. Note speeches of Lord Bishop of Bristol (pp. 767-770) against, and the Lord Bishop of Birmingham (pp. 799-806) in favour of Budget on grounds of social needs and social reforms; and Lord Sheffield (pp. 770-774) in support.

[44] Parl. Deb., *ibid.*, p. 855; pp. 852-861 entire.

[45] London *Times,* September 11, 1909, pp. 7-8, the Glasgow speech, note editorial, p. 11.

the Budget "pursued strictly and straightly into new territory the lines of historic Liberalism in the past. The equipoise of relations between the individual and the State could not be expressed in any scientific formula; it could only be reconciled in practice." [46] The speech of Earl Camperdown was followed by Earl Russell who said,

your Lordships have inaugurated a revolution. We live nominally, and your Lordships will find we live really, under the control of the democracy of this country, and I think your Lordships will find that democracy intends to have the expression of its will obeyed and observed.[47]

When the Earl of Rosebery spoke on November 24 he stated he spoke with a sense of the "awful gravity of the situation, by far the gravest that has occurred in my lifetime or in the lifetime of any man who has been born since 1832." [48] "The Budget threatens," he continued, "to poison the very sources of our national supremacy." Of the Government and the Lords he said,

the menaces addressed to you now come from a wholly different school of opinion (referring to former Governments' pressure on House of Lords) who wish for a single chamber and who set no value on the controlling and revising forces of a second chamber—a school of opinion which, if you like it and do not dread the word, is eminently revolutionary in essence, if not in fact.[49]

His hope was for a change which would bring a new Government: "we should then have an anti-Socialist Government, a luxury which I cannot say we possess now."

The Lord Bishop of Hereford allied himself with the Lord Bishop of Birmingham, and in his remarks stated that "you cannot expect an educated democracy and their leaders to remain content with the survivals which represent the present constitution of our society." [50] Such sentiments were constantly being

[46] London *Times,* September 18, 1909, p. 7; note editorial, p. 11.

[47] Parl. Deb., 5 S., 1909, 4 H. L., pp. 869-870; 861-871 entire.

[48] See also his Preface to the pamphlet edition of his Glasgow speech, and the *Times* editorial, "Lord Rosebery's Preface," September 17, 1909, p. 7.

[49] Parl. Deb., *ibid.,* pp. 942-954.

[50] Parl. Deb., *ibid.,* p. 1082; pp. 1080-1086 entire.

expressed all over the country, revealing underneath the great political forces of the day a conviction on English life and thought which was profoundly significant. Viscount Morley stated this phase of the question in his speech of November 25 when he charged the Lords with changing representative supremacy into oligarchic and non-representative supremacy.

"The people of this country," he said, "are either of the predatory species or they are not. If they are, it is quite certain that the success of this Parliamentary operation of your Lordships will not set up any dam or rampart or barriers against the destructive flood such as would then arise. Anyone who tells you that by passing this Amendment you are obstructing Socialism is as foolish as the courtiers of King Canute. My own view about the present aspects of Socialism is that there is a great feeling pervading quite beyond the lines of Party in this country at present of pity, of sympathy, and of horror at the miseries which our industrial system entails."

The effect of the Budget on the Continent was in Lord Morley's mind, and he made the point with an opposite intention than that with which Lord Lansdowne began the debate in the House of Lords. "For many glorious generations," Lord Morley said, "England has been the stable and far-shining model of reform, and any clouding of her position in either fiscal or constitutional policy will be a gain, and a heavy gain, on the Continent of Europe to the parties of reaction." [51]

The final day of debate in the House of Lords was enlivened by the remarks of the Lord Archbishop of York who announced that he was going to vote for the Bill. He did not agree that

[51] Parl. Deb., *ibid.*, pp. 1137-1153. He had earlier written of Gladstone's financial policy and the Continent in his *Life*. Lord Morley's account of the struggle is characteristically given in Book VI, chap. 1, of his *Recollections*. He seemed to see in the conflict a stage of the revolution from 1832, undermining steadily the old territorial aristocracy: "To-day (1910) the particular stages did not matter. What was pulling them down was the revolt of general social conscience against both the spirit and the obstinate actual working of the institution" (p. 357). Of interest is *A Speaker's Commentaries*, by the Rt. Hon. James William Lowther, Viscount Ullswater, Speaker of the House of Commons, 1905-1921 (London, 1925), and Judge Atherley-Jones' *Looking Back: Reminiscences of a Political Career* (London, 1925).

the Bill was revolutionary. The supposed revolutionary tendency behind the Bill, found in the speeches of Mr. Lloyd George, he attributed to the "tendency of the Celtic temperament to respond to environment," a tendency promoted by the mysterious Celtic *huel,* "which makes the speaker say he knows not what, and excites the audience they know not why." He said further, "the Marxian Socialist is logical, the full-blown Protectionist is logical, we may thank Providence the English people is not logical.[52] With that observation the danger of Socialism was dismissed by him. Lord Curzon declared he welcomed the coming struggle,[53] and the Earl of Crewe closed the debate for the Government.[54] The Bill was defeated by 350 votes to 75.[55]

After the rejection Mr. Asquith gave notice that he would move the next day a resolution, "That the action of the House of Lords in refusing to pass into law the financial provision made by the House for the Service of the year is a breach of the Constitution and a usurpation of the rights of the Commons." After reading the Lords debates, the Prime Minister said, "I came to the conclusion that there was not a single one of our proposed new taxes, except perhaps the duty on motor spirit, in which the keen scent of one or another of the Tory spokesmen could not detect the fatal and poisonous taint of Socialism." "We are living," he added, "under a system of false balances and loaded dice." Believing as the Ministry did that the first principles of representative government were at stake, they would ask the electorate to declare that the organ and voice of the free people of the country was to be found in the elected representatives of the people.[56] Mr. Balfour defended the action of the Lords and ridiculed the resolution as an abstract motion, and held that the Lords were within their rights in rejecting the Budget.[57]

The word "revolution" was perhaps the most used word of all in the debates of this period. The Labour leader spoke to that point. He declared that the Lords' action

[52] Parl. Deb., *ibid.*, pp. 1234-1243.

[53] Parl. Deb., *ibid.*, pp. 1243-1264.

[54] Parl. Deb., *ibid.*, pp. 1324-1342.

[55] Note two earlier articles in the *Times,* "The Deadlock," No. 1, September 9, p. 6; No. 2, Sept. 9, p. 8. Also the editorial, September 6, "The Unionists and the Budget," p. 7.

[56] Parl. Deb., 5 S., 1909, 13 H. C., pp. 546-558, Asquith; for whole debate on resolution, pp. 546-578.

[57] Parl. Deb., *ibid.*, pp. 558-571.

establishes an uncontrolled force, antagonistic to democratic thought and tendency. They are not only prepared to aid and abet revolution; they are actually daring to precipitate it. Many people in recent years have been afraid lest the demonstrations on Tower Hill and those great processions of the workless army on the Embankment might lead the people to revolt. No, the revolt is not coming from that direction. It is not the voices of the multitude of unemployed into whose souls the iron of want and suffering has eaten that has initiated this revolution. It has come from the representatives of privilege and vested interests.[58]

There was, and is, great divergence of opinion among constitutional authorities on the action of the House of Lords.[59] Sir Frederick Pollock considered the rejection of the Budget "the most audacious attempt to subvert the foundations of Parliamentary Government made since the Revolution of 1688," while other authorities of equal distinction, such as Professor Dicey and Sir William Anson, held that rejection to be perfectly legitimate.[60] Professor Dicey thought as a result of the Parliament Act of 1911 that the direct appeal from the House of Commons to the electorate by a sudden dissolution may henceforward become in England almost obsolete.[61] That with the increase of party power in the hands of political leaders the Parliament Act enabled a majority of the House of Commons to resist or overrule the will of the electors, or, in other words, the nation. "No impartial observer can therefore deny," he wrote, "the possibility that a

[58] Parl. Deb., *ibid.*, p. 574; pp. 571-574 entire. (A. Henderson.)

[59] Parliament was prorogued on December 3, 1909, and subsequently dissolved. From then until January 15, 1910, the political controversy was the dominant thing. The rejection of the Budget had opened wide the whole question of social reform, constitutional reform and Government policy. The King's Speech at the end of the 1909 session expressed regret that provision for social reform had proved unavailing. The Government were determined to put that issue to the front as its most popular appeal. On the day Parliament adjourned the Chancellor addressed a meeting at the National Liberal Club, dealing thoroughly with the rejection, declaring that "every grain of freedom is more precious than radium." (Cf. *Annual Register,* 1909, p. 258.)

[60] May-Holland, *The Constitutional History of England* (ed. 1912, 3 vols.), Vol. III, p. 358; pp. 355 ff.

[61] A. V. Dicey, *Law of the Constitution* (8th ed. 1915), p. liii. This has not been true since 1918.

fundamental change in our constitution may be carried out against the will of nation." [62]

Whatever the consequences, the Government had set out to settle the conflict between the House of Commons and the House of Lords. There was really no turning back from the day that Sir Henry Campbell-Bannerman put his Resolution to the House in 1907. The Prime Minister's resolution had passed by a vote of 349 to 134 on December 2. There was no mistaking the temper of the Liberal and Labour parties, and the four years of the 1906 Parliament had convinced them, to their own satisfaction, that the veto of the House of Lords must go. "During the four years of the Parliament of 1906 no Government measure against the third reading of which the official Opposition voted in the House of Commons passed into law." [63]

At the general election in January, 1910, the Government lost over one hundred seats, the Labour Party losing five and the Liberals ninety-nine seats. So far as Labour was concerned it had fewer numbers, yet relatively to the Government forces were more of a potent force, as Mr. Hardie declared in the presidential address at the Labour Party Conference at Newport in 1910.[64] Nor was the attitude of the Party such as to cause the Liberals to be alarmed over its desertion on the question of the Lords and their powers. For the first time in the history of the Labour Party Labour went into the election under one banner,[65] and while there were dissentient voices on the part that Labour should take in supporting the Government on the political issue the support was given. This attitude was evident in the Labour reply

[62] *Ibid.* The *Introduction* to the last edition, written in 1914, is most valuable for the judgment of one who could compare critically the constitution as it stood in 1884 with the constitution as it stood in 1914. Dicey says, "It is thus possible to take a general view of the development of the constitution during a period filled with many changes both of law and of opinion." (Pp. xvii-xviii.) He suggests comparison with the *Introduction* to the second edition of *Law and Public Opinion in England during the Nineteenth Century* (1914).

[63] May-Holland, *op. cit.,* Vol. III, p. 343. Mr. Francis Holland gives an account of the struggle over the Parliament Bill in the final chapter of his new edition. Compare Lowell, *op. cit.,* Vol. I, chap. XXII, A, pp. 423-436, on the House of Lords and the Act of 1911.

[64] *Report of the 10th Annual Conference of the Labour Party* (1910), p. 55.

[65] *Ibid.,* "Report of the Executive for 1909," pp. 3-15.

to the King's Speech at the opening of the 1910 Parliament, given by Mr. Barnes:

"Of course, we know democracy sometimes goes mad," he said, "but the House of Lords always goes mad with it. Democracy, or at all events Governments sent to represent democracy, sometimes do things in a hurry and repent them at leisure, but the House of Lords never has saved the democracy from itself." [66]

Labour was beginning to grow restive because it was not certain just what the policy of the Government would be in dealing with the House of Lords.[67] The King's Speech promised "Proposals, with all convenient speed, to define the relations between the Houses of Parliament, so as to secure the undivided authority of the House of Commons over Finance, and its predominance in legislation." [68] On February 28 the Prime Minister announced that the Government would deal with the matter at first by putting before the House Resolutions which would be the basis of the Bill which would be introduced at a later time.[69]

The Prime Minister's resolutions on the relation between the two Houses were put on the paper of the House of Commons on March 21. These resolutions declared "that the House of Lords be disabled by Law from rejecting or amending a Money Bill," and

that the powers of the House of Lords as respects Bills, other than Money Bills, be restricted by Law so that any such Bill which has passed the House of Commons in three successive sessions . . . shall become Law without the consent of the House

[66] Parl. Deb., 5 S., 1910, 14 H. C., p. 89; pp. 83-95 entire; note also Hardie, pp. 175-182.

[67] See William Stewart, *J. Keir Hardie, A Biography* (1921), pp. 290-325, on Labour and two general elections of 1910; also on the House of Lords, see J. Ramsay MacDonald, *Socialism and Government* (3rd ed. 1910), London, pp. 46-73.

[68] Parl. Deb., 5 S., 1910, 14 H. C., pp. 33-34; on King's Speech note Asquith, pp. 52-63; Balfour, pp. 40-52; F. E. Smith, 95-124; Belloc (on Party System), pp. 117-124; Churchill, pp. 132-139; Chamberlain, 214-229; Sydney Buxton, 231-239; MacDonald, J. R., pp. 252-267.

[69] Parl. Deb., *ibid.*, pp. 591-595, Asquith; Balfour, pp. 596-603; Lloyd George, pp. 632-637; Barnes, pp. 644-647; Belloc, on Party again, pp. 654-656.

of Lords on the Royal Assent being declared; provided that at least two years shall have elapsed between the date of the first introduction of the Bill in the House of Commons and the date on which it passes the House of Commons for the third time.

A final resolution added, "that it is expedient to limit the duration of Parliament to five years."

"We put them forward," Mr. Asquith said on March 29, "as the first and indispensable step to the emancipation of the House of Commons, and to preserve from something like paralysis the principles of popular government. . . . The absolute veto of the Lords must follow the veto of the Crown before the road can be clear for the advent of full-grown and unfettered democracy." [70]

The meaning of the constitutional question was expressed the next day, March 30, by Mr. J. Ramsay MacDonald, for Labour:

"The simple truth is this," he said, "that in the social class and in the social interests represented exclusively by the House of Lords, is the source of much of the evils which necessitate social reform at the present moment. So far as we are concerned this is no mere barren political issue. It is a great economic issue." [71]

The Unionists the next day put forward their resolution through Sir R. Findlay who moved an amendment to the effect that the House was willing to consider proposals for the reform of the existing Second Chamber, but declined to proceed with proposals which would destroy the usefulness of any Second Chamber, and would remove the safeguard against changes by a Government without the consent, and against the wishes of the electorate.[72] This

[70] Parl. Deb., 5 S., 1910, 15 H. C., pp. 1180-1182; pp. 1162-1182, entire; and pp. 1162-1278, complete debate on March 29, pp. 1303-1386, March 30; pp. 1471-1583, March 31, on Findlay resolution. Note speeches of Balfour, pp. 1182-1198; Barnes, pp. 1213-1222; F. E. Smith, pp. 1303-1318; Lord Hugh Cecil, pp. 1327-1342. On the Findlay motion, note speeches of Sir W. Robson, Attorney General, pp. 1491-1506; and Lloyd George, pp. 147-160, Parl. Deb. 5 S., 1910, 16 H. C. The Government resolutions were carried by 357 votes against 251.

[71] Parl. Deb. 5 S., 1910, 15 H. C., p. 1375; pp. 1363-1375 entire.

[72] Parl. Deb. 5 S., 1910, 15 H. C., pp. 1471-1494. The mover declared that "the new Liberalism was intellectually bankrupt." Mr. Lloyd George, Parl. Deb. 5 S, 1910, pp. 147-160, gave a full summary of the action of the House of Lords since 1900 on legislation passed by the Commons.

resolution called forth one of the most spirited of the Ministerial defences, Mr. Churchill claiming that the Conservatives would reduce the Liberal Party to impotency by their control of the House of Lords. He gave a justification of the Party System, which had been the favourite theme of attack for Mr. Belloc and Mr. Harold Cox.[73] When the Conservative object had been attained, Mr. Churchill said,

do not suppose, do not let honourable Gentlemen opposite suppose that thereby they will have escaped from the democratic movement. Those who are now grouped under the standard of party will re-form themselves under the standards of class. The class line must become, if the party system is shattered, the line of demarcation.[74]

The Prime Minister on April 5 moved the resolution for allocation of time on the resolutions which the Government had put before the House.[75] and the first resolution was introduced by Mr. Haldane.[76] From April 11-14, the Committee considered the rights of the House of Lords on Bills other than Money Bills, the duration of Parliament and votes on general legislation.[77] On April 14 the Parliament Bill, 1910, based on the resolutions, was introduced by the Prime Minister, who declared that if the Lords refused to accept the plan, the Government would either resign or dissolve.[78]

The death of King Edward VII on May 6 made necessary a political truce between the parties. On the reassembling of Parliament, June 8, 1910, it was announced that the Ministry were

[73] The day after Parliament met, 1910, Lord Rosebery presided at a dinner given to Mr. Cox, by the British Constitutional Association. In reply to his speech Mr. Cox attacked the tyranny of the two-party system and urged the rescue of the country from the growing despotism of the State. (*Annual Register,* 1910, p. 18.)

[74] Parl. Deb. 5 S., 1910, 15 H. C., p. 1582; pp. 1567-1583 entire.

[75] Parl. Deb. 5 S., 1910, 16 H. C., pp. 229-382, entire discussion.

[76] Parl. Deb. 5 S., 1910, 16 H. C., pp. 449-515, April 6; pp. 611-724, April 7.

[77] Parl. Deb., *ibid.,* April 11, pp. 895-1007; April 12, pp. 1082-1196; April 13, pp. 1251-1321; April 14, pp. 1425-1493; and pp. 1493-1531, on duration of Parliament, and pp. 1531-1547 votes on general legislation.

[78] Parl. Deb. 5 S., 1910, 16 H. C., pp. 1547-1548; pp. 1549-1551, Balfour's statement.

ready to propose a small private conference between themselves and the Opposition leaders. This suggestion hardly met with approval from either side, but on June 16 the Conference was formally decided upon by the leaders on both sides and the next day the first meeting was held in the Prime Minister's rooms. The Government were represented by Mr. Asquith, Mr. Lloyd George, the Earl of Crewe and Mr. A. Birrell; Mr. Balfour (A. J.), the Marquess of Lansdowne, Earl Cawdor and Mr. Austen Chamberlain represented the Opposition. On November 10, after twenty-one meetings of the conference, the Prime Minister announced the failure and stated that the Government had decided that after passing the Finance Bill for the year and a few other necessary measures, Parliament would be dissolved on November 28. The Prime Minister announced that it was useless to submit to the Lords the Parliament Bill which they were certain to reject.[79]

Lord Rosebery in 1907 had succeeded in having a Select Committee appointed to consider a reform in the composition of the House of Lords, following the first attack by Sir Henry Campbell-Bannerman. The Committee Report, published December 3, 1908,[80] proposed to distinguish between Peers and Lords of Parliament, or members of the House of Lords; and recommended that, except in case of a peer of the blood royal a peerage should not entitle one to a seat in that House. No action was taken upon that report. When Mr. Asquith met Parliament in 1910 he declared that the passing of the Budget would be insisted upon and a definite settlement of the constitutional question along the lines laid down by the Commons Resolution of 1907.[81] Lord Rosebery sought to anticipate the action of the Government and on February 24, 1910, gave notice that on March 14 he would move that the House of Lords resolve itself into Committee to consider the best means for so reforming its organization as to constitute it a strong and efficient Second Chamber. On March

[79] Parl. Deb. 5 S., 1910, 20 H. C., pp. 82-87. See also, *ibid.*, speeches of Balfour, pp. 87-93; Barnes, pp. 117-124, who introduced the subject of the Osborne judgment at this time; and Lloyd George, pp. 124-128.

[80] *Annual Register* (1908), p. 240 for summary.

[81] Parl. Deb. 4 S., 1907, 176 H. C., pp. 909-926, statement of Campbell-Bannerman; whole debate, pp. 909-1011, 1157-1254, 1409-1524.

12 a report was published of the public service of Peers.[82] This report showed that in 1909, 81 out of a total of 589 Peers, including minors and Peers kept away by their official duties or ill-health, did not attend the House of Lords, and 168 attended less than ten times.

The resolutions of Lord Rosebery were debated from March 14-25, at which time the old ground was gone over again, principally by Lord Morley for the Government, who differed diametrically from Lord Rosebery in the belief that the House of Lords could be reformed from the inside.[83] Lord Rosebery referred to his proposals in 1888 [84] and to Lord Newton's Report in 1908, as indicating what could come about from within the House itself. The Marquess of Salisbury took the opportunity to say that he thought the character and reputation and the independence of the House of Commons had decayed, believing that only in the House of Lords there was perfect independence.[85] This point is interesting with regard to similar expressions by the Earl of Rosebery, Mr. Belloc and Mr. Cox, men differing widely. The first two statesmen bridged the period of the old and the new in nineteenth century and twentieth century politics, and "possessed the greatest influence with the people," [86] wrote Mr. Lowell, at the beginning of the century; while in 1909-1910, Mr. Cox and Mr. Belloc were conspicuous, if minor figures, in the revolt against parliamentarianism and political democracy.[87]

The resolutions of Lord Rosebery were passed without division,[88] for the Government were centring their interest on the Parliament Bill and cared very little to become entangled in the efforts of the House of Lords to solve the controversy. On November 16 the leader of the Opposition asked for the Gov-

[82] Parl. Deb. 5 S., 1910, 5 H. L., pp. 114-119.

[83] Parl. Deb., *ibid.*, pp. 140-169, Rosebery; pp. 169-189, Morley; whole debate, pp. 140-228, March 14.

[84] *Annual Register,* 1888, p. 58.

[85] Parl. Deb. 5 S., 1910, 5 H. L., pp. 240-250.

[86] Lowell, *op. cit.*, p. 240.

[87] Cf. Beer, *op. cit.*, Vol. I, p. 360.

[88] Parl. Deb. 5 S., 1910, 6 H. L., pp. 232-276, March 15; pp. 277-366, March 16; pp. 371-410, March 17; pp. 413-450, March 21; pp. 459-494, March 22; pp. 683-694, March 25, cover the debate in the Lords on the Rosebery resolutions.

ernment to bring in their Parliament Bill,[89] and at that time the Earl of Crewe introduced the Government measure in the House of Lords.[90] Further debate on the reform of the House of Lords took place on the 17th of November when Lord Rosebery brought forward his resolutions again,[91] and the question of dissolution gave further opportunity for party politics, and at that time the leaders again stated the issues before the House of Lords.[92]

The Earl of Crewe, Lord Privy Seal and Secretary of State for India, on November 21, moved the second reading of the Parliament Bill in the House of Lords. He thoroughly reviewed the political situation from 1906 when the House of Lords vetoed the Education Bill of that year, and set forth the provisions of the Parliament Bill.[93] The Marquess of Lansdowne vigorously opposed,[94] and the Earl of Rosebery complained that the House was regarded simply as a condemned criminal without the usual indulgences.[95] The Lord Chancellor, Lord Loreburn, declared it was futile to expect the House of Lords to reform itself from within.[96] But the Opposition had to face the country with a program of their own, so the Marquess of Lansdowne presented to the House of Lords the scheme in the form of resolutions, November 23, and in his speech of that day he commented largely upon the value of the principle of Referendum.[97] These resolutions were passed at once, and the deadlock between the Houses and the Parties was now complete.

Parliament was prorogued preparatory to its dissolution on November 28, and from then until the election the controversy was carried on unabatingly. The result was much the same as in

[89] Parl. Deb. 5 S., 1910, 6 H. L., pp. 684-691.

[90] Parl. Deb., *ibid.*, pp. 691-697; entire debate, pp. 684-706. House of Lords Bill No. 167.

[91] Parl. Deb. 5 S., 1910, 6 H. L., pp. 714-758, entire debate.

[92] Parl. Deb. 5 S., 1910, 6 H. L., pp. 760-764, Crewe; pp. 764-769, Lansdowne; pp. 760-776 entire.

[93] Parl. Deb., *ibid.*, pp. 777-788; entire second reading debate, pp. 777-810, November 21; pp. 838-916, November 23; and pp. 924-1012, November 24.

[94] Parl. Deb., *ibid.*, pp. 788-797; see also speech of Marquess of Salisbury, pp. 798-799.

[95] Parl. Deb., *ibid.*, pp. 800 seq. [96] Parl. Deb., *ibid.*, pp. 801 seq.

[97] Parl. Deb., *ibid.*, pp. 838-849; for reply of the Earl of Crewe, pp. 849-857.

the January election, the Ministerialists with a possible 398 votes to 271 Opposition. On February 21, 1911, the Prime Minister asked leave to introduce the Parliament Bill and the next day it passed first reading by 351 votes to 227.[98] The Prime Minister made his special indictment against the Referendum and Unionist support of the principle; it was Jacobin and Napoleonic, and showed the extreme to which Toryism had come. To apply the Referendum to British conditions was infinitely more revolutionary than anything in the Bill. It would reduce a general election to a sham parade, and degrade the House of Commons to the level of a talking Club. He had faith in the representative system with all its imperfections, and the Parliament Bill was only another expression of making the will of the people effective. The Labour party leader stated "we regard the present Second Chamber purely as an economic expression," and expressed the opposition of his party to the Referendum because it was only a negative thing.[99] The Referendum was condemned by Mr. Churchill who ended the second day's debate for the Government; it led to anarchy, Jacobinism and Cæsarism. "We believe in democracy," he said, "we believe in representative institutions, we believe in democracy acting through representative institutions.[100]

The debate on the second reading of the Parliament Bill began on February 27, and four days of debate were allowed before the vote was taken and the second reading passed by 368 votes to 243.[101] The Bill was in Committee thirteen days,[102] three days

[98] Parl. Deb. 5 S., 1911, 21 H. C., pp. 1742-1851, debate February 21, and pp. 1923-2042, February 22; and pp. 1742-1752, the Prime Minister's speech.

[99] Parl. Deb., *ibid.*, pp. 1765-1773 (MacDonald).

[100] Parl. Deb., *ibid.*, pp. 2023-2038. Note the speeches of Mr. Balfour (pp. 1752-1765) and Mr. F. E. Smith (pp. 1926-1945).

[101] Parl. Deb. 5 S., 1911, 22 H. C., 1st day, pp. 45-153; 2nd, pp. 218-289, 305-331; 3rd, pp. 389-502; 4th, pp. 565-686. Note especially speeches of Mr. Austen Chamberlain (pp. 45-57); Mr. Snowden (pp. 447-456); and Mr. Balfour (pp. 565-581).

[102] Committee debates, with Labour and Opposition Amendments, are found in Parl. Deb. 5 S, 1911, 23 H. C., pp. 1815-1939, pp. 2016-2130, 2219-2350; 24 H. C., pp. 47-176, 252-392, 673-840, 1054-1241, 1369-1550, 1607-1759, 1808-1882 (on Referendum especially); 25 H. C., May 1-3, pp. 47-166, 219-397, 445-558 (Barnes Amendment). Prime Minister's speech on presenting motion for allocation of time, pp. 861-866; entire debate, pp. 861-916.

were given for consideration of amendments,[103] and on May 15 the third reading was passed by 362 votes against 241.[104] The opinion of the Opposition on this Bill was stated by the Marquess of Lansdowne during debate on the King's Speech in the House of Lords. "It is a Bill," he said, "for breaking down the barriers and admitting the full flood tide of revolution into our institutions."[105] So it was expected that attempts would be made to again put obstacles in the way of the Government, or at least offer a satisfactory alternative to their measure. The first effort was the Bill[106] introduced by Lord Balfour of Burleigh,[107] on March 2, at which time the Government reply was given by the Earl of Crewe,[108] The second reading of this Bill, March 28-29, was again only an opportunity for the Marquess of Lansdowne to plead the cause of the Referendum as the necessity for the will of the people to be known,[109] to which Lord Morley replied that it would corrupt the electorate.[110] The debate on this Bill was adjourned indefinitely.[111]

The Marquess of Lansdowne on May 8 introduced the House of Lords Reconstitution Bill.[112] Again Lord Morley[113] and Lord Loreburn brought out the now oft-told tale of what the Government position was on the Referendum, and on May 23 Lord

[103] Amendments considered, May 8-10, 25 H. C., pp. 915-983, 1045-1176, 1220-1340.

[104] Parl. Deb. 5 S., 1911, 25 H. C., Third Reading, May 15, entire debate, pp. 1658-1786. Note speeches of Mr. F. E. Smith (pp. 1658-1674); Asquith (pp. 1691-1699); Balfour (pp. 1699-1709); Churchill (pp. 1768-1776).

[105] Parl. Deb. 5 S., 1911, 7 H. L., p. 28; pp. 14-29 entire speech of Lansdowne; see reply of the Earl of Crewe, pp. 29-40.

[106] Public Bills 1911, House of Lords, No. 26.

[107] Parl. Deb., 5 S., 1911, 7 H. L., pp. 253-266.

[108] Parl. Deb., *ibid.*, pp. 266-275.

[109] Parl. Deb., *ibid.*, pp. 680-693.

[110] Parl. Deb., *ibid.*, pp. 667-680; note speech of Earl Beauchamp for Government, pp. 711-726.

[111] Parl. Deb., *ibid.*, pp. 253-288, and pp. 657-718, the entire debate on this Bill.

[112] Public Bills, 1911, House of Lords, No. 75.

[113] Parl. Deb. 5 S., 1911, 8 H. L., pp. 236-242, and pp. 376-383, his two speeches on this Bill; pp. 215-236 and 369-376, the two speeches of the Marquess of Lansdowne. For complete debate on Bill; first reading, pp. 215-242; second reading, pp. 369-434, 444-486, 489-574, 635-694 (May 8, 15, 16, 17, 22, respectively).

Morley moved the second reading of the Parliament Bill.[114] The amendments that the Lords attached to the Bill were considered unsatisfactory by the Government, and on July 24 the Prime Minister announced[115] the intention of the Government to advise the creation of enough Peers to pass the Bill, the assent of the King having been secured before the general election to the creation of peers in case of necessity. Lord Lansdowne advised his followers to abstain from voting on the Bill. The fear that "puppet peers" might be created was sufficient however for a small number of Unionists to join with the Liberals, the two Archbishops and eleven Bishops making up a majority of 131 to 114 for the Bill. A vote of censure against the Government on the policy followed (the threat of the creation of peers) was introduced in the House of Lords by Earl Curzon,[116] passing by 281 votes to 68. Introduced in the House of Commons by Mr. Balfour,[117] this resolution failed to pass by a vote of 365 to 246. The passing of the Parliament Bill into law[118] marked the end of the bitter struggle the consequences of which cannot yet be told. It served in a great measure to point out the fact that social and economic forces are making constantly for changes in the State and in the powers which the State exercises.

The Budget of 1909 and its rejection by the Lords was the challenge which brought to a head the constitutional crisis. The Government at all times declared that it was a Budget intended to meet the expenses of social reform legislation for which all parties

[114] Parl. Deb. 5 S., 1911, 8 H. L., pp. 698-708, Morley; debate May 23, pp. 698-746; May 24, pp. 748-828; May 25, 839-908; May 29, 911-967. Committee Stage, *ibid.*, pp. 1031-1118, June 28; pp. 1122-1204, June 29, Parl. Deb. 5 S., 1911, 9 H. L., Committee Stage, July 3-6, pp. 6-96, 100-192, 196-280, 283,386; Report and Third Reading, pp. 441-492, 572-620.

[115] Parl. Deb. 5 S., 1911, 28 H. C., pp. 1467-1484, consideration of Lords amendments; pp. 1470-1473, the Prime Minister's statement, and pp. 1473-1482, Balfour's reply. See also Parl. Deb. 5 S., 1911, 29 H. C., pp. 967-1116, for further consideration and final vote on Lords amendments.

[116] Parl. Deb. 5 S., 1911, 9 H. L., pp. 815-878, entire debate; pp. 815-832, Curzon; pp. 832-843, reply of the Earl of Crewe. See also pp. 833-982, 987-1077, August 9-10, the Lords consideration of the Commons reasons for disagreeing with Lords amendments.

[117] Parl. Deb. 5 S., 1911, 29 H. C., pp. 795-922, entire debate; see especially speeches of Balfour (795-807), Asquith (807-817), F. E. Smith (817-830), and Churchill (904-912).

[118] 1-2 Geo. V, c. 13.

in the State were responsible. It sets a precedent for the use of taxation for the promotion of political or social ends, Professor Dicey believed, and such taxation may easily become the instrument of tyranny. Revolution was not the more entitled to respect because it was carried through not by violence, but under the specious though delusive appearance of taxation imposed to meet the financial needs of the State.[119]

That was the principle on which the Finance (1909-10) Act, 1910[120] was based.[121] When the Budget of 1910 was presented the Chancellor of the Exchequer introduced at the same time the wider and more comprehensive program of unemployment and invalidity insurance, nothing less than a national insurance scheme.[122] The State was fully pledged by these Budgets to financial responsibility for social legislation which the Parliaments of the century had passed.

Second Chamber Reform, as the phrase is now used, is a problem of first rate importance for English statesmen. The Government of Mr. Baldwin is pledged to its consideration, and yet the subject is one that no leader of the Conservative party approaches without great caution. The Labour party stands for the complete abolition of the House of Lords and for a most strenuous opposition to any machinery for revision of legislation taking the form of a new Second Chamber, whether elected or not, having in it any element of heredity or privilege or of the

[119] Dicey, *Law and Opinion in England,* pp. lii-liii; cf. Bernard Mallet, *op. cit.,* the Preface, gives a more friendly view to the Budget and the principles on which the Chancellor of the Exchequer had to formulate his financial proposals. The needs of the State in 1845 could hardly be compared with the vast expenditure required in 1909. Professor Dicey underestimated this fact of hard necessity.

[120] 10 Edw. VII, c. 8.

[121] The 1910 Bill, changed very little from 1909, was introduced April 20; Parl. Deb. 16 H. C., pp. 1725-1838, 1903-2008, 2102-2200; second reading, April 25, Parl. Deb. 17 H. C., pp. 41-154, entire debate. Committee Stage and third reading, April 26-27, pp. 267-377, 461-530; passed by 324 votes to 231. Note speeches of Mr. A. Chamberlain (pp. 41-42) and Mr. Asquith (pp. 522-530). In the House of Lords, all stages, Parl. Deb. 5 S., 1910, 5 H. L., pp. 775-815; note speech of Lord Chancellor, Lord Loreburn, pp. 810-815.

[122] Parl. Deb. 5 S., 1910, 18 H. C., pp. 1123-1143, Lloyd George's Budget statement; note the speeches of Mr. A. Chamberlain (pp. 1143-1153) and Mr. Barnes (pp. 1160-1164).

control of the House of Commons by any party or class,[123] and the Webbs in their *Constitution for the Socialist Commonwealth of Great Britain* bluntly say, "there is, of course, in the Socialist Commonwealth no place for the House of Lords." But so long as there are believers "that the Parliament Act has put into the hands of the extremists a weapon of deadly potentiality, which will render it a simple matter to destroy the constitution, bring the country to ruin, and the Empire to dismemberment—by parliamentary procedure," [124] there will be efforts towards reform. There can be little dispute that such a condition as exists to-day, an upper house within what is virtually a Single Chamber Government, is not conducive to a sound parliamentary system. But this problem can be left to the genius of a race who put great faith in their capacity to "muddle" through.

[123] *Labour and the New Social Order* (1918).

[124] See the article in *Nineteenth Century,* Vol. XCVIII, No. 585 (November, 1925), by Brigadier-General F. G. Stone, "The Parliament Act and Second Chamber Reform," and *Second Chamber Reform,* published by National Union of Conservative and Unionist Associations.

CHAPTER VI

SOCIAL LEGISLATION IN ENGLAND 1900-1925
(*Continued*)

PART VIII

The State and Unemployment and a National Insurance System

(a) *Unemployment and Parliament*

THE aim of this survey of English legislation between 1900 and 1925 is to suggest the conditions upon which State action depended and the principles by which it was guided. The growth of humanitarian sentiment, by which civilization may be measured, Mr. Lowell believes, has certainly to be reckoned with in the history of the Factory Acts, which made a breach in the tenets of *laissez-faire*.[1] But it is not an adequate interpretation of the substance of later enactments establishing new duties for the central authority and giving to State departments by statutory rules and orders a power to exercise authority over property and rights till then almost exclusively reserved for Parliament.

A population which we have seen a hundred years ago hardened by suffering has become distinguished for compassion to misery and aversion to pain, as a new consciousness arose of the commonwealth as a whole, which must suffer from the weakness of any part.[2]

This new consciousness demanded a better State, fulfilling higher service in not only protecting but promoting the conditions favourable for the good life of its citizens. Earlier legislation represented a reaction to the blind faith in an all-wise economic law, but the continuance of State intervention inevitably made more definite a purpose behind Parliamentary action. Toynbee antici-

[1] *Op. cit.,* Vol. II, pp. 522-523.

[2] John Richard Green, *A Short History of the English People,* Revised and Enlarged with Epilogue by Alice Stopford Green (1916), Epilogue, p. 895. Cf. T. G. Williams, *The Main Currents of Social and Industrial Change, 1870-1924* (London, 1925).

pated Dicey by twenty-five years in the interpretation of Socialistic Acts "passed by Tory country gentlemen"; adding, in 1882, "I tremble to think what this country would have been without the Factory Acts." But even at that time he clearly pointed out that material inequality of men under the existing social conditions was a fact; that the poor law, factory legislation and the trade unions might lessen the pressure of the strong upon the weak, modifying and mitigating the effects of the inequality of wealth, but notwithstanding all, the fact of inequality remained, and on this fact were founded the maxims of the Radical Socialists:

First, that where individual rights conflict with the interests of the community, there the State ought to interfere; and where the people are unable to provide a thing for themselves, and that thing is of *primary social importance,* then again the State should interfere and provide it for them.[3]

A theory of the State based on these maxims meant little less than a revolution in the purpose of Government. The unfolding of that purpose and its development in Acts of Parliament is one of the chief concerns of social justice. This concern lifts the detail of countless sections of enactments to a place of vital significance daily in the lives of millions of people.

The policy of the State in dealing with the aged poor and the housing of the people developed no less a general principle of a decent standard of life, for the maintenance of which collective action became increasingly necessary, than resulted from the extended history of unemployment before the Parliament of England. The peculiar bitterness at times of the controversy has shown the importance of the subject in the minds of the people, and the long continuance of unemployment with its cumulative

[3] Arnold Toynbee, *The Industrial Revolution of the Eighteenth Century in England* (First edition, 1884), pp. 232-233 (his italics), for the Popular Address, "Are Radicals Socialists." In his *Reminiscence* of Toynbee, written in 1894, Lord Milner speaks of the striking change in the social and political philosophy of Oxford during these years. "When I went up (1873) the *laissez-faire* theory still held the field. All the recognised authorities were 'orthodox' economists of the old school. But within ten years the few men who still held the old doctrines in their extreme rigidity had come to be regarded as curiosities" (p. xxv). Lord Milner's post-war writings are interesting commentaries, see his *Questions of the Hour* (1923).

effects upon the morale of the labouring class and the efficiency of industry has constituted a menace to the nation's well-being. It is impossible to read debates in the House of Commons on this topic and not feel the intense social significance that it possesses for all parties. It is only necessary to compare the debate on unemployment in 1904 [4] in the House of Commons and in the French Chamber of Deputies to clearly find the distinction between the social politics of France and England; the former allowing far more for the play of doctrinal disputes of theory than the latter permitted for the indulgence of this brilliant and costly French habit. This may be partly accounted for on the grounds that the English Labour movement had no such orators as MM. Jaurès, Briand and Viviani, nor a Parliamentary position before 1906 which would allow free publicity for party philosophy. The Labour member in England had to content himself with a possible amendment to the Address, or a good twenty minutes to midnight to move the first Socialist resolution while an amused House looked on; and he could always engage in the unequal contest of question asking or in conducting a Trade Union deputation before chiefs of Departments.

The problem of unemployment has added significance because it has been connected in France and England with the effort for a minimum wage and the reduction of the hours of work, together with subsidiary plans for technical education and prolongation of compulsory school attendance. Unemployment has provided a frequent opportunity for the Labour and Socialist party to ascribe the major responsibility of society's ills to the system of capitalism which necessarily involves a pitiless burden of human and social cost. In the consideration of the tactics and programs of the parties the importance of this phase should be noticed. On the fourteenth day of the debate on the Address in 1904,[5] the Labour leader Hardie introduced a resolution,[6] regretting that

[4] Cf. Edouard Vaillant, *Le Chomage à la Chambre* (1905), esp. pp. 34-35. A reprint of the debate of November 30, 1904.

[5] The debate on the Budget, November 30, 1904, was the occasion for M. Vaillant offering the Socialist Resolution for the Permanent Committee of the *Conseil Supérieur du Travail* to consider the problem of Unemployment. The Chamber voted favourably.

[6] Hansard, 4 S. H. C., 1904, Vol. 130, pp. 451-506, debate entire on Hardie Amendment; Hardie (pp. 451-466), seconded by Mr. W. Crooks (pp. 466-474). The amendment was lost by 231 votes to 151.

in view of the distress arising from lack of employment your Majesty's advisers have not seen fit to recommend the creation of a Department and Minister of Labour fully empowered, *inter alia,* to deal effectively, acting in conjunction with local authorities, with such lack of employment, mainly by the execution of necessary public works, and further by encouraging an increase in the number of those employed in agricultural pursuits.

This amendment was supported by the Liberal Party,[7] and the debate served to bring light to bear on the administrative side of governmental departments with regard to unemployment. Mr. Hardie, in common with the well-informed Labour members of Parliament, was especially conversant with the powers and possibilities of local government authorities, and in this debate he quoted from a document issued by a Secretary of State in 1694 on the duties of local authorities.[8] Their importance had been stressed in the series of conferences held between 1902-1904 on unemployment, and their co-operation with the central authority was specifically a part of the Unemployed Workmen Act, 1905,[9] the one Government proposal on labour questions which was passed in the 1905 session.[10]

The Government altered in Committee stage the original Bill, so that the Act, while it provided certain machinery for dealing with the unemployed did not sanction wages being paid to them out of the rates under any circumstances whatever. The Act created throughout England and Wales a local body in each metropolitan borough and a central body for the whole of the London area dealing with the unemployed. The central authority[11] had general supervision over the local bodies, and could establish labour exchanges and employment registries. While it would be the duty of the local authorities to endeavour to obtain employ-

[7] Hansard, *ibid.*, pp. 502-505, speech of Mr. Asquith, and pp. 481-483, of Mr. S. Buxton.

[8] Hansard, *ibid.*, p. 455.

[9] 5 Edw. VII. c. 18. Introduced by the President of the Local Government Board, Mr. Gerald Balfour, April 18, 1905; second reading June 20, and passed into law August 11.

[10] Hansard, 4 S. H. C., 1905, Vol. 145, pp. 459-461, speech of President of the Local Government Board; also pp. 461-463 (S. Buxton), opposition to Bill.

[11] Act of 1905, Sect. I, subsect. 4.

ment for applicants, they were not empowered to provide work, nor could they under certain conditions and limitations, which the original Bill outlined, allow for the payment of wages to the unemployed out of the rates. The powers [12] granted the Local Government Board for making regulations for carrying into effect the Act provided the most hope for those who had long been fighting to bring the unemployment problem before the House of Commons.[13] But most of the powers were made discretionary rather than obligatory, and the amendment limiting the Act to three years tended to make the Act of less value than might otherwise have been the case.

The outstanding value of the Act of 1905 was that it put the problem of unemployment on a national basis,[14] recognizing that the nation must concern itself seriously with the peril of the unemployed and the unemployable. Parliament set up an additional authority to cope with the needs, and for this reason Labour leaders accepted the Act, giving their energies to enlarging and making effective its provisions.[15] The wisdom of the continued agitation on the unemployed problem was quickly manifest for the chaotic condition of the Poor Law was constantly brought out in the debates in Parliament and in the propaganda literature on the subject. It was no surprise when on August 2, 1905, the Prime Minister was asked whether he would consider the advisability of the appointment at an early date of a Royal Commission to inquire into the workings of the Poor Law, and the results of the borough councils in finding work for the unem-

[12] Act of 1905, Sect. 3, subsections a—m, for powers and provisions.

[13] Cf. *Report to the Board of Trade on Agencies and Methods for Dealing with the Unemployed in Certain Foreign Countries* (Cd. 2304), 1904, by D. F. Schloss, author of *Insurance of Unemployment* (1909).

[14] See Percy Alden, *The Unemployed, A National Question,* (1905), with Preface by Sir John Gorst, for a convenient summary and interpretation of the two blue books on unemployment issued by the Board of Trade in 1893 and 1904 and their bearing on the life of the people. Cf. Sir William Beveridge, *Unemployment, a Problem of Industry* (1909), for authoritative statement; also Joseph L. Cohen, *Insurance against Unemployment* (N. Y., 1921).

[15] See J. Keir Hardie, *John Bull and His Unemployed* (1905), after the Local Government Board Orders were issued, an interpretation of the law; the Independent Labour Party issued in 1905 a pamphlet on the *Unemployed Bill: What It Does and Does Not Do, but Should Be Made to Do,* and two other pamphlets dealing with the question.

ployed in pursuance of orders from the Local Government Board, in order to ascertain to what extent, if any, the existing powers of the Poor Law authorities were insufficient to meet modern industrial needs and conditions. Mr. Balfour replied that the Government were of the opinion that the time had come when a full inquiry into the subjects referred to in the question ought to be undertaken. There had been no inquiry since the great investigation of the "thirties." So late in 1905 the Government appointed a Royal Commission to "consider how far the present powers of the Poor Law Authorities are adequate to modern conditions." The scope of the inquiry to include "everything that pertains to the problem of the Poor," whether "poor through their own fault or through lack of employment." The very terms of reference for the work of the Commission indicate how far public opinion and legislative thought were removed from the Report of 1834.[16] The Unemployed Workmen Act, 1905, though unsatisfactory to Labour and the Trade Union groups, who continued agitation within and outside Parliament, had made the important distinction that unemployment-relief was not poor-relief, and that unemployment did not come under the Poor Law. Mr. Lloyd George stated the matter succinctly when he said that the Act would do very little good, but "it recognized the right of a man to call upon the State to provide him with work, to which the State replied by recognizing the right but refusing to provide the work." [17]

From the passing of the Act Labour's aim was to gain the acceptance of the principle that the State should provide the work or provide maintenance. The Prime Minister objected to this principle,[18] declaring it was one which he did not believe; the Government had put forth their policy with regard to unemployment in the passing of the Act which authorized the creation of Labour Bureaux in London,[19] the expenses of which were to be borne out of the general rates, and in the Aliens Act,

[16] Cf. Vol. I, p. 109, of the Majority Report.

[17] Hansard, 4 S. H. C., 1905, Vol. 151, p. 432.

[18] Hansard, *ibid.*, p. 434.

[19] Labour Bureaux (London) Act, 1902 (2 Edw. VII. c. 13), allowing the Council of any London Borough to establish such unemployment office. See *Poor Law Report,* 1909, Vol. I, pp. 509-510, on failure of this Act.

1905,[20] which had caused in the House of Commons bitter controversy on unemployment. The session of 1906 carried on the debate of the Aliens Act and the Unemployed Workmen Act; the Labour amendment to the Address being moved in 1906 by Mr. Hay and in 1907 by Mr. Thorne, and in both years Mr. Hardie brought forward the question on the motion for the Easter recess. The mover in 1907, regretting the absence from the speech of any proposal for dealing with unemployment, stated[21] that 5 per cent of the most highly skilled artisans were out of work and that the Unemployed Workmen Act had proved inadequate.[22] The debates on unemployment 1904-1907, on the Address, show that Parliament necessarily had to concern itself with a problem which Labour and the workers in organized trades were especially bent upon keeping to the front of discussion, and upon which every party had made important declarations. Unemployment gave a full opportunity for discussion of the fundamental questions of State responsibility, industrial organization and the evils of the day; all of which brought the "condition of England question" to a place of great Parliamentary significance, especially in the new Parliament of 1906 which showed by positive enactment in just what ways the State had accepted its share of the burden under modern conditions.

The Labour Party introduced in 1907 their Unemployed Workmen Bill,[23] but the Bill did not reach second reading. It provided for the constitution of local and central unemployment authorities with powers and duties to form schemes to provide (a) reasonable public work, and, in default, (b) public maintenance for genuine and willing workers when in need through unemployment. The Bill conferred on all authorities large powers for the compulsory acquisition of land, and definitely directed the Local Government Board to draw up schemes for employment on works of national utility and to carry them out in times of exceptional distress. Unemployment was first brought to the attention of the House of Commons in the 1908 session by

[20] 5 Edw. VII. c. 13.

[21] Hansard, 4 S. H. C., 1907, Vol. 169, pp. 923-972, debate entire on the Labour unemployment amendment, which was rejected by 207 votes to 47.

[22] See *Poor Law Report 1909*, Vol. I, pp. 490-504, and Vol. III, p. 544-546, on the failure of the Unemployed Workmen Act, 1905.

[23] House Bill No. 273, 1907

the new leader of the Labour Party, Mr. Henderson, in his reply [24] to the Address, and the Unemployment Amendment [25] was moved by Mr. J. Ramsay MacDonald, who deprecated waiting until the Poor Law Commission report because the Local Government Board already had sufficient information. Labour continued to agitate for the "right to work" principle.[26] The President of the Local Government Board declared that the Act of 1905 would be continued pending the Poor Law Commission Report, and that the Government would continue supplying funds to districts where unemployment was most distressing. The Government would do nothing, he added, that would tend to pauperize the workers who were unemployed.[27] In the division on the Labour Unemployment Amendment the Government majority fell to 49, the lowest it had experienced since it took office in 1905.

This tactical advantage was followed by the reintroduction of the Unemployed Workmen Bill,[28] the Labour Party being responsible for the "right to work clause," which they considered essential to the Bill,[29] though Mr. Wilson, who introduced the Bill for them, was willing to have that amended or deferred.[30] The Chancellor of the Exchequer announced that the Government were awaiting the Poor Law Commission Report before formulating their plans on State aid for the unemployed, and the House was asked not to sanction the principle that it was the duty of the State to provide work until the results of the Report were known. He held that the recognition of the right to work would ultimately necessitate the assumption by the State of complete control of the whole machinery of production.[31] The following

[24] Hancard, 4 S. H. C., 1908, Vol. 183, pp. 164-171.

[25] Hansard, *ibid.*, pp. 247-254.

[26] Hansard, *ibid.*, pp. 254-259 (Curran), seconder's speech.

[27] Hansard, *ibid.*, pp. 247-359, debate entire on Amendment.

[28] House Bill No. 5, 1908. The Bill was re-introduced by Mr. P. W. Wilson, a Liberal, who moved its second reading, and seconded by Mr. J. Ramsay MacDonald. It was rejected by 265 votes to 116.

[29] Hansard, 4 S. H. C., 1908, Vol. 186, pp. 19-28 (MacDonald). See also Report of the Annual Conference of the Labour Party, 1908, the Parliamentary Committee's Report on the activity of the Labour members on the unemployed question, and Appendix I, pp. 91-101, for the *Memorandum* of the Executive Committee on Unemployment.

[30] Hansard, *ibid.*, pp. 10-19 (Wilson); pp. 10-100, entire debate on Bill.

[31] Hansard, 4 S. H. C., 1908, Vol. 186, pp. 85-88 (Asquith).

resolution against the Bill was carried by 241 votes to 95; however 136 Liberals abstained from voting.

"While ready to consider any practical proposal," the resolution read, "for dealing with the evil of unemployment, this House cannot entertain a measure which, by wasting the resources of the nation, would throw out of work more persons than it could assist, and would destroy the power of organized Labour, but hopes that the Government will give immediate consideration to the recommendations as to the unemployed in the forthcoming report on the Poor Law Commission."

The Government the next year set forth its constructive program for the distribution of labour and employment in the Labour Exchanges Bill.

But the Government was forced throughout 1908 constantly to consider unemployment. On the 21st of October the Prime Minister, after a Cabinet Committee had considered the problem, made a statement [32] in the House in reply to the formal question of the Labour leader. This was of importance because he stated that in 1909 the Government would make a beginning with legislation dealing with the permanent causes of unemployment; and following a day of discussion of the statement, the official resolution, moved by Mr. Alden, welcomed the recognition of the national importance of unemployment and approved the Ministerial proposals.[33] The Labour Amendment, moved by Hardie, brought again the doctrine of the "right to work" to the attention of the House.[34] In the debate were seen the bitter feelings of Labour toward the President of the Local Government Board, who appeared to be moving more and more toward the Right.[35] The first Labour Minister of England when compared with M. Millerand had not done "for the English workers what the other Socialist Minister of our generation achieved for French in-

[32] Hansard, 4 S. H. C., 1908, Vol. 194, pp. 1160-1173 (Asquith).

[33] Hansard, *ibid.*, pp. 1631-1646 (Alden); pp. 1631-1778, entire debate on the Government Resolution and the Labour Amendment.

[34] Hansard 4 S. H. C., 1908, Vol. 194, pp. 1646-1656 (Hardie); pp. 1656-1662 (Crooks); and pp. 1695-1707 (MacDonald).

[35] Hansard, *ibid.*, pp. 1662-1679, statement of Burns. See S. D. Shallard, "Has Liberalism a Future," "The Present Ministers and Their Records" (1909), chap. 8, pp. 94-96, "The Man with the Red Flag."

dustrial law." [36] Another most interesting thing in the unemployment debates was the attention with which all parties awaited the Report of the Poor Law Commission. The Government time and again stated that their policy would have to be carried out with reference to that Report.

The Labour Party introduced again in 1909 their Unemployed Workmen or Right to Work Bill. The Bill proposed to require county and borough councils to provide work or maintenance for unemployed persons qualified by six months' residence, and provided that when the registered unemployed in a locality exceeded four per cent of the wage earners, the schemes for their benefit should be financed by monies voted by Parliament.[37] The mover of the second reading,[38] Mr. John Hodges, stated in the debate that the permanent proportion of unemployed trade unionists averaged five per cent, or 250,000; this rate applied to the whole body of workers gave a total of 750,000 continually unemployed. The Government's reply [39] to the Labour Bill was that every workman who came under it would be pauperized, and that its own proposals were dealing with the subject in better ways. The debate on the supplementary vote of £100,000 for unemployment aid, under the 1905 Act, in this same year, was seized by Labour to put forward their attack on that Act and to urge active measures through administrative reform and new legislation.[40]

The debate on the Address at the opening of the Parliament of 1909 gave the President of the Board of Trade an opportunity

[36] The *Nation* (London), August 31, 1907, p. 950.

[37] Parl. Deb. H. C. 5 S., 1909, Vol. 4, pp. 633-700, second reading debate.

[38] Parl. Deb., *ibid.*, pp. 633-638 (Hodge); pp. 685-691 (MacDonald). The Right to Work Bill was moved in 1911 by Hardie, who declared that "this Bill seeks to set up quite a new and distinct principle in modern politics" (p. 1219), but based it on a statute of Elizabeth (43 Elizabeth, c. 2). (Parl. Deb. 5 S. H. C., 1911, Vol. 25, pp. 1218-1220.)

[39] Parl. Deb., *ibid.*, pp. 691-700 (Burns). The 1908 Right to Work Bill was defeated by 265 votes to 116, the Alden Resolution being carried at 1.50 a.m. by 196 votes to 35; the 1909 Bill was rejected by 228 votes to 115. See Report of the Parliamentary Committee of the Labour Party to the Newport Congress of 1910, *Annual Report of the Labour Party Conference*, pp. 16-22.

[40] Parl. Deb. H. C. 5 S., 1909, Vol. I, pp. 1217-1223, 1312-1346, and pp. 1441-1498.

to outline the Government policy on unemployment, based upon the Poor Law Commission Report.[41] The Labour unemployment amendment had again been moved,[42] and on May 19, Mr. Pickersgill, a Liberal, calling attention to the Minority Report of the Poor Law Commission, moved a resolution declaring the urgency of steps for the decasualization of casual labour and the absorption of the surplus labour thereby thrown out of employment; also to regularize the demand for labour, to develop trade union insurance against unemployment, and to establish training colonies and detention colonies.[43] At this time the President of the Board of Trade set forth the Government scheme of labour exchanges and unemployment insurance.[44] The principle of the first was accepted heartily by the Opposition [45] which did not commit itself on the question of universal compulsory insurance, but both principles affirmed by the Government were supported by Labour.[46] The Pickersgill Resolution was withdrawn, and the next day the Government Bill was introduced.[47] The failure of the Acts of 1902 and 1905 was recognized, and the Labour Exchanges Act, 1909,[48] gave the Board of Trade power to take over such exchanges as had been set up under these Acts. Further delegated authority

[41] *Report of the Royal Commission on the Poor Laws and Relief of Distress,* Vol. I (being Parts 1-6 of the Majority Report), Part VI, chap. 4, pp. 505-565; for Minority Report statement on unemployment, see Vol. III, Part II, chap. 5, pp. 635-716.

[42] Parl. Deb. H. C. 5 S., 1909, Vol. I, pp. 98-108 (Barnes); and the Labour Party leader had made unemployment the main attack on the sessional program, for which see Parl. Deb. cit., pp. 50-56 (Henderson).

[43] Parl. Deb. H. C. 5 S., 1909, Vol. 5, pp. 484-490 (Pickersgill); the motion was seconded by Mr. Percy Alden (pp. 490-494), and supported by the Labour Party (pp. 494-499, MacDonald); pp. 484-525, debate entire.

[44] Parl. Deb. cit., pp. 499-512 (Churchill).

[45] Parl. Deb. cit., pp. 512-515 (F. E. Smith).

[46] Parl. Deb. cit., pp. 515-518.

[47] Parl. Deb. cit., pp. 579-582. Parl. Deb. H. C. 5 S., 1909, Vol. 6, pp. 994-1063, second reading debate entire; Vol. 7, H. C., pp. 747-762, 1169-1171, Committee stage; Vol. 8, H. C., pp. 1432-1437, third reading and passed. Progress in House of Lords: Parl. Deb. 5 S. H. L., Vol. 2, 1909, pp. 876-898, second reading; note the speeches of the Bishop of Birmingham (pp. 883-886), and the Marquess of Salisbury (pp. 886-892); Committee and third reading, Parl. Deb. cit., pp. 951-955.

[48] 9 Edw. VII. c. 7.

was given by Parliament in this Act, which provided that the work of the Exchanges was to be conducted under general regulations made by the Board of Trade.[49] Legislation directly to be considered with the whole problem of unemployment and compulsory insurance will indicate more fully the powers of the State departments in this regard. The Poor Law Commission Report had directed a great deal of attention to the administrative side of Poor Law Reform, and it was generally agreed that the first and most important consideration in all questions of Poor Law Reform relates to the machine created to carry out the principles of administration.[50] The fact that the Minority Report of the Commission treated under Unemployment what was known as able-bodied pauperism in 1834, suggests an entirely different method of administering State aid.[51] This no doubt was in the mind of Sir Frederick Banbury when he described the signers of the Report "as people suffering from soft hearts and soft heads, who are willing to dispose of the property of other people for the purpose of relieving distress whether the distress is owing to

[49] Act of 1909, Sect. 2.

[50] Parl. Deb. H. C. 5 S., 1911, Vol. 25, p. 2015 (Lord A. Thyme); debate on London Poor Bill; for second reading debate entire see Parl. Deb. H. C. 5 S., 1911, Vol. 26, pp. 593-670; see Burns (pp. 658-669).

[51] See debate on the Prevention of Destitution Bill, 1910: Parl. Deb., 1910, 5 S. H. C., Vol. 16, pp. 780-852; on Poor Law Administration and Reform in debate on Supply, April 27, 1911, Parl. Deb. H. C. 5 S., 1911, Vol. 24, pp. 1980-2082. The Amendment offered: "This House endorses the unanimous condemnation of the administration of the Poor Law contained in the majority and minority reports of the recent Royal Commission, and is of opinion that the present administration of the Poor Law does not meet modern requirements and demands the immediate attention of His Majesty's Government" (p. 1980). The State was administering a sum of £60,000,000 in education, in Poor Law Relief, and in Public health services, and in poor law relief was dealing with 1,700,000 people (see speech of Secretary of Local Government Board, *op. cit.*, pp. 2024-2039). Cf. speeches of Lansbury (pp. 1997-2004) and Addison (pp. 2010-2015). The vote on the Goldstone motion fell to 107-48 for the Government. See also 1912 debate on Poor Law Administration: Parl. Deb. H. C. 5 S., 1912, Vol. 35, pp. 823-890, 903-912. Cf. *Comparative Statement of Pauperism and Cost of Relief of the Poor in Certain Years from 1848-9 to 1911-12* (Cd. 6675), 1913; and the *General Consolidated Index of the Royal Commission on the Poor Laws and Relief of Distress*, Vol. XXXVII (Cd. 5443), 1913, running to 1,086 double-column folio pages, indicates the scope of the problem.

the fault of the distressed or not." [52] But the Parliamentary Committee of the 1909 Trade Union Congress reported that "if this Majority Report were carried out, the present Poor Law would merely be set up again, under a new name, without democratic control." [53]

(b) *Insurance a National Problem*

But the temper of the time made it possible to conceive great changes and with large hopes plan far-reaching improvements. The Government seemed almost pleased to accept the taunt that they were planning a new heaven and a new earth.[54] The Government program [55] outlined in the King's Speech in 1911 promised proposals for carrying out and extending the policy initiated in previous Parliaments, by securing the permanent provision of old age pensions to persons previously disqualified by reason of the receipt of poor relief; and by providing for the insurance of the industrial population against sickness and invalidity, and for the insurance against unemployment of those engaged in trades specially liable to it. In moving the formal Address the Government spokesman said that "Old Age Pensions have almost passed beyond the range of controversy," [56] and on this subject the leader of the Opposition replied that there was "no vital difference of opinion between the two sides of the House." [57] It was hoped that in the larger and more comprehensive reform which the Government had on several occasions intimated it would introduce, and which had been announced in the Budget Speech of 1910, there would be something of the same spirit of common purpose. For three years committees and experts had been considering the many problems involved in a scheme of national insurance; a revolutionary departure in social legislation by which England was to assume an unquestioned leadership in pointing the way to State action.

[52] Parl. Deb. H. C. 5 S., 1911, Vol. 26, p. 611.

[53] *Report of the 42nd Trade Union Congress,* Ipswich, 1909, p. 92.

[54] In his appeal to constituents in September, 1909, Sir Charles W. Dilke said that the Government "commanded a confident and an enthusiastic support on the part of a wider majority of people than any other movement of modern times," quoted in Gwynn and Tuckwell, *op. cit.,* Vol. II, p. 525.

[55] Parl. Deb. H. C. 5 S., 1911, Vol. 31, pp. 44-46.

[56] Parl. Deb. cit., p. 49; pp. 46-50 entire.

[57] Parl. Deb. cit., p. 62; pp. 52-64 entire (Balfour).

The National Insurance Bill

The National Insurance Bill was introduced by the Chancellor of the Exchequer on May 4, 1911, being the last important measure of social reform enacted by Parliament in the decade preceding the War. The Poor Law Commission Report had made necessary important legislation on new lines; even before its completed report the influence of the inquiry was evident. The Government in 1908 sought to find a remedy for the tragedy of the industrial worker who falls in service, by the Old Age Pensions Act, and thus dealt with one of the causes of pauperism.[58] Drink was a major cause,[59] and the Government attempted to deal with this evil in the Licensing Bill of 1908, adopted by a large vote in the House of Commons, but rejected in the upper House. Bad housing conditions and bad sanitation produced and aggravated certain of the causes which made for pauperism, the Commission reported;[60] the Government applied a remedy in the Housing and Town Planning Act, 1909. Another cause[61] to which was assigned a distinct degree of pauperism in certain occupations was "earnings habitually below what are required for healthy subsistence"; an evil the Trade Boards Act, 1909, sought to prevent. Yet considering all of these causes the Commission were of the opinion that the foremost industrial cause of pauperism was irregularity of employment. Their major recommendations were labour exchanges, vocational guidance and unemployment insurance.[62] The Labour Exchanges Act, 1909, was an effort to rid the nation of that evil, and in 1911 this effort was increased by the National Insurance Act, Part II, dealing with unemployment; and Part I dealt with another major cause of pauperism,[63] sickness. The Government had taken to

[58] Cf. *Poor Law Commission Report,* 1909, Vol. I, pp. 284-286.

[59] *Ibid.,* pp. 286-287.

[60] *Ibid.,* pp. 288-289; also the special report of the *Relation of Industrial and Sanitary Conditions to Pauperism,* made by Mr. Steel-Maitland and Miss Squire.

[61] *Poor Law Commission Report,* 1909, Vol. I, p. 291.

[62] *Ibid.,* Part VI; also Vol. III (Minority Report), Part II, chaps. IV and V.

[63] *Poor Law Commission Report,* 1909, Vol. I, Part V; Vol. III, Part I, chap. V.

the House of Commons the conclusions [64] of the Poor Law Commission: [65]

"Notwithstanding our assumed moral and material progress," the Report stated, "and notwithstanding the enormous annual expenditure, amounting to nearly sixty millions a year, upon relief, education and public health, we still have a vast army of persons quartered upon us unable to support themselves and an army which in numbers has recently shown signs of increase rather than decrease." [66]

With this report as a background the Chancellor of the Exchequer brought in the National Insurance Bill,[67] turning "from controversial questions for a moment to a question which, at any rate, has never been the subject of controversy between the parties in the State." In presenting the Bill he said that 30 per cent of pauperism was attributable to sickness. A considerable percentage would have to be added to that for unemployment. The administration of the Old Age Pensions Act has revealed the fact that there was a mass of poverty and destitution in the country which was too proud to wear the badge of pauperism, and which declined to pin that badge to its children. They would rather suffer from deprivation than do so. He was perfectly certain if that was the fact with regard to persons of seventy years of age, there must be a multitude of people of that kind before they reach that age. That was basis enough to bring forward a scheme that would attempt to remedy the major troubles which beset the working man and woman and young person. Against death, with which the Bill did not attempt to deal,

[64] A convenient summary of the Commission is in *The Poor Law Report of 1909*, pp. 24-42, by Mrs. Bernard Bosanquet, a member of the Commission; *English Poor Law Policy* (1910), Sidney and Beatrice Webb, fully presents the view of the Minority Report of the four dissenting members of the Commission.

[65] On September 15, 1909, the Lord Archbishop of Canterbury reviewed the Report of the Poor Law Commission in the House of Lords; Parl. Deb. H. C. 5 S., 1911, Vol. 2, pp. 1195-1211; the two other speakers were the Earl of Crewe (pp. 1211-1217), and the Lord Bishop of Southwark (pp. 1217-1222).

[66] *Poor Law Commission Report*, 1909, Vol. I, p. 78.

[67] Parl. Deb. H. C. 5 S., 1911, Vol. 25, pp. 609-644 (Lloyd George); complete debate on first reading, pp. 609-677, 700-720.

there were, the Chancellor stated, 42,000,000 industrial policies where the payments were weekly, monthly or quarterly; in the Friendly Societies there were 6,000,000 people who had made provision against sickness; and in the trade unions there were about 700,000 members insured for sick benefits. So far as unemployment went not one-tenth of the working classes had made any provision at all, only 1,400,000 being insured against that contingency.

That was the provision made in 1909 by the working classes: 42,000,000 policies against death, about 6,100,000 with some kind of provision against sickness, and 1,400,000 who had made some provision for unemployment. The decision of the Government to take action, the Chancellor of the Exchequer said, was due to that fact. It was not because the working classes did not consider it necessary to make provision against sickness and unemployment, but it was certain that those who stood most in need of it made up the bulk of the uninsured. "Why?" the Government asked. Because very few could afford to pay the premiums, and pay them continuously, which enabled a man to provide against those three contingencies. As a matter of fact, you could not provide against all those three contingencies anything which would be worth a workman's while, without paying at any rate 1s.6d. or 2s. per week at the very lowest. There were a multitude of the working classes who could not spare that, and ought not to be asked to spare it, because it involved the deprivation of children of the necessaries of life. Under the Government scheme 15,000,000 people would be insured; compulsory unemployment insurance would apply to the precarious trades which were liable to very considerable fluctuations and in which one-sixth of the industrial population were employed. It was a major task for the Government to institute a system whereby 15,000,000 people would be insured against the acute distress which darkened the homes of the workmen wherever there was sickness and unemployment.

The Government did not pretend that the Bill was a complete remedy.

"Before you get a complete remedy," Mr. Lloyd George said, "for these social evils you will have to cut deeper. But I think it is partly a remedy. I think it does more. It lays bare a good many of those social evils, and forces the State, as a State, to pay attention to them. It does more than that. Meanwhile, till the advent of a complete remedy, this scheme does alleviate an immense mass of human suffering, and I am going to appeal, not merely to those who support the Government in this House, but to the House as a whole, to the men of all parties to assist us to carry through a measure that will relieve untold misery in myriads of homes—misery that is undeserved; that will help to prevent a good deal of wretchedness, and which will arm the nation to fight until it conquers 'the pestilence that walketh in darkness, and the destruction that wasteth at noonday.' "

It is well to note this introductory speech. As the controversy over the Bill progressed the Chancellor of the Exchequer carried his plea to the Nation, a remarkable incident in modern social politics, and in his fighting speeches gave some of the most penetrating criticism of the social legislation of the first decade of this century. Of course it was impossible on the first reading of the Bill for any member to express a mature judgment on the Government's proposals, which had been under closest consideration for three years, but the Opposition gave its opinion on the effort "to set the foundation-stone of a work which every party desires to see carried to a successful conclusion." [68] The responsible spokesman added, "We feel that a subject so vast, so difficult, and touching such complicated matters requires the good will and assistance of all sections without regard to party, and this ought not to be made the subject of party strife." [69] The attitude of Labour was very favourable, and the opportunity was taken to stress again the principle of the Right to Work Bill.[70]

[68] Parl. Deb. cit., p. 645 (Chamberlain); pp. 644-651, entire.

[69] *Ibid.*, p. 651.

[70] *Ibid.*, pp. 654-657 (MacDonald), also Vol. 21, pp. 101-103, on the King's Speech (pp. 44-46), the principle set forth; pp. 586-659, the Labour Amendment on Right to Work or full maintenance by State. The Leicester Labour Congress (1911) directed the Party to bring a Bill in "That the State should take the responsibility directly of providing employment or maintenance for the unemployed." The Labour Amendment regretted "that no promise had been made of a Bill establishing the right to work by placing upon the State the responsibility of directly providing employment or maintenance for the genuine unemployed" (p. 586). One Labour speaker stated that "this problem of unemployment is very much a prob-

The President of the Board of Trade, Mr. Sydney Buxton, on May 24, moved the second reading [71] of the Bill.

"The idea on which it is based," he said, "is that under existing conditions the whole burden of sickness, invalidity, and unemployment over which the working man has no control, falls directly with crushing force on the individual whether he be provident or improvident, and I think the House is generally agreed that it is time that the employer and the State should enter into partnership with the working man in order so far as possible to mitigate the severity of the burden which falls upon him." [72]

It would be difficult to find a second reading debate between 1900 and 1914 which contained more explicitly a definite acceptance of the State as a leader, even a pioneer, in social reform. This philosophy behind legislation was in all of the Government speeches, and the Labour members followed their discursive example. The first Labour member to speak remarked that

With the advent of democracy to power new views regarding the duty of the State towards its individual members have come into being and find expression in this House. This Insurance Bill is the latest of a series of efforts made in the last generation to cope with the evils and miseries which have been produced by generations of class legislation in the interests of the rich.[73]

The divergences of opinion from the Government on the Bill which Labour had put forward,

but not in any factious spirit. We are very glad the Bill has been introduced. We think it marks a great step forward, because it brings many millions of workmen into direct contact

lem of the State organization of industry, and not necessarily organization of industry by the State itself, but by the State taking such action that all industry shall be regulated in such a manner as to secure work for all citizens willing to work" (Lansbury, p. 639; pp. 639-649, entire). Cf. speeches of President of Local Government Board, pp. 627-638, and Chiozza-Money, pp. 606-614, and Clynes, pp. 591-600. The O'Grady Amendment was defeated by 225 votes to 39.

[71] Parl. Deb. H. C. 5 S., 1911, Vol. 26, pp. 270-387 (May 24); pp. 451-571 (May 25); pp. 718-832 (May 29).

[72] Parl. Deb. H. C. 5 S., 1911, Vol. 26, p. 271; pp. 270-287, entire.

[73] Parl. Deb., *ibid.*, p. 300; pp. 299-303, entire (Clancy).

with the State, and is therefore going to be of immense educational value. We believe people have been too much inclined to look upon the State simply as a big policeman and this Bill will enable a great many of them to realise that the State, after all, is what they like to make it. We welcome this Bill from that point of view.[74]

The members of the Cabinet were hardly less enthusiastic in praise of the Bill than the Chancellor of the Exchequer. The Attorney General in a very carefully planned survey of the German social insurance system, said "this House has now the opportunity of placing the nation at the head of the world in social reform." [75] The Secretary of the Home Department, Mr. Churchill, had the duty of explaining the unemployment insurance features of the Bill,[76] and the First Lord of the Admiralty, Mr. McKenna, outlined the invalidity sections.[77] The former believed that

no one can measure the futile unnecessary loss which the State incurs. Unemployment and sickness will return to the cottage of the working man, but they will not return alone. We are going to send him by this Bill other visitors to his home, visitors who will guard his fortunes and strengthen his right arm against every foe.[78]

A speech such as this would most likely convince Professor Dicey that the free discretion or indiscretion of each individual was very much limited by what Mr. Lowell termed grandmotherly legislation." Before this Act, Dicey wrote, "his conduct no more concerned the State than the question whether he should wear a black coat or a brown coat." [79] But even in 1887 Professor Maitland, warning his students against taking too narrow a view of modern English law, spoke of the active duties which

[74] Parl. Deb., *ibid.*, p. 314; pp. 303-314, entire (Barnes).

[75] Parl. Deb., *ibid.*, p. 458; pp. 368-387, entire (Sir Isaac Refus). Cf. A brief study by Anne Ashley, *The Social Policy of Bismarck: A Critical Study with a Comparison of German and English Insurance Legislation* (1912), Section 12.

[76] Parl. Deb., *ibid.*, pp. 493-510.

[77] Parl. Deb., *ibid.*, pp. 566-571.

[78] Parl. Deb., *ibid.*, p. 510.

[79] *Op. cit.*, p. xxxvii.

modern statutes have cast upon Englishmen in general.[80] Yet the first distinguished critic believed that the

> statesmen who have introduced unemployment insurance by the State have, whether they knew it or not, acknowledged in principle the *droit du travail* for the sake of which socialists died behind the barricades of June, 1848.[81]

The linking of this Act [82] with the Coal Mines (Minimum Wage) Act, 1912,[83] made it certain that such was not the belief of the Prime Minister.[84] But the leader of the Labour Party found the principle one which all parties could accept, and typical of a very decided advance in public opinion.

> "If this Bill had been introduced ten years ago," he said, "it would not have found, I think, a single supporter from either of the Front Benches. The point of view which the Chancellor and the Government have taken is one which is quite new, and which marks a fundamental change of public opinion, and the most extraordinary thing for those who are sitting on these benches is to find that that point of view is not challenged by any section of this House. The old assumption upon which we used to approach questions of legislation, by which State aid and State organizations were regarded as something which ought

[80] F. W. Maitland, *The Constitutional History of England,* p. 505. "An Englishman has a child born to him; within 42 days (says an Act of 1874, 37 and 38 Vict. c. 88), he must register its birth at the proper office, if he does not he can be fined. Within three months, says an Act of 1867 (30 and 31 Vict. c. 84), he must have that child vaccinated, otherwise he can be fined. Then, says an Act of 1876 (39 and 40 Vict. c. 79), 'it shall be the duty of the parent of every child to cause such child to receive elementary instruction in reading, writing and arithmetic, and if such parent fail to perform such duty he shall be liable to such orders and penalties as are provided by this Act.'" (*Ibid.*, p. 504.)

[81] Dicey, *op. cit.,* pp. xxxviii-xxxix.

[82] 1 and 2 Geo. V. c. 55. "An Act to provide for Insurance against Loss of Health and for the Prevention and Cure of Sickness and for Insurance against Unemployment and for purposes incidental thereto."

[83] 2 Geo. V. c. 2. "An Act to Provide a Minimum Wage in the Case of Workmen Employed Underground in Coal Mines."

[84] Parl. Deb. H. C. 5 S., 1912, Vol. 35, p. 42; also Parl. Deb. H. C. 5 S., 1911, Vol. 21, pp. 627-638, the Government statement on the Right to Work Amendment of the Labour Party. Cf. Hilaire Belloc, *The Servile State* (1912) on the Insurance Act.

to be suspected by every wise man, has been thrown over, thrown over not only by those who sit in this quarter of the House, but thrown over by everybody. That is a very substantial advance, one of those advances which one finds in public opinion happening periodically about once every century, and I think it is an indication that to-day in the times that have come upon us the old political parties are largely losing their significance; and the combination which has taken place, during the last week or two, on both sides of the House, to praise this Bill and facilitate its passing is one that is welcome, at any rate, very heartily and most sincerely by those who sit with me here. For the first time in a clear, unmistakable, systematic way a Government has come before the country and has said that these breaches in the way of life are a responsibility imposed upon the Government, and an Opposition has also offered to say to the Government: 'We support you in your efforts and agree with your general position.' "[85]

The Bill passed second reading without division, following a final summing up by the Chancellor on the debate,[86] in which he again invited all parties to join with him in making the Bill what it was intended to be. The House as a Committee[87] of the Whole began consideration of the Bill on July 5, the main effort of the Labour Party in the Committee being to secure an increased contribution from the State.[88] Between the second and third

[85] Parl. Deb. H. C. 5 S., 1911, Vol. 26, pp. 718-719; pp. 718-736, entire (MacDonald).

[86] Parl. Deb., *ibid.*, pp. 756-782 (Lloyd George); note Opposition speeches of second reading: Forster (pp. 287-299), Bonar Law (pp. 511-525), and A. Chamberlain (pp. 736-756).

[87] Committee Stage: Parl. Deb. H. C. 5 S., 1911, Vol. 27, pp. 1148-1294; 1361-1390; 1483-1560; and Financial Resolution, pp. 1390-1462. Vol. 28: pp. 31-168; 207-340; 382-456; 697-840; 881-955; 993-1244. Vol. 29: pp. 37-152; 201-342; 381-542; 720-766. Vol. 30: pp. 57-105; completing 14 days in Committee, and on Oct. 25, the Government put through its motion on the Business of the House (pp. 111-267), and until November 21, 16 days were allotted: *ibid.*, pp. 307-414; 426-498; 542-660; 721-836; 878-963; 1017-1120; 1485-1590; 1667-1777; 1826-1941; 1963-2032. Vol. 31: pp. 44-155; 208-332; 389-479; 532-650; 832-984; 1030-1155; the Financial Resolution, November 15, pp. 383-389; and important report on Part II (Unemployment Insurance), Standing Committee B. November 2-16, pp. 1637-2120. Vol. 32: Report Stage, November 28 to December 4, pp. 215-329; 420-543; 599-835; 853-954; 1033-1159; allocation of time discussion, pp. 836-852.

[88] Parl. Deb. H. C. 5 S., 1911, Vol. 27, pp. 1391-1400 (Snowden); pp. 1441-1499 (MacDonald).

readings of the Bill, Mr. Lloyd George made two important speeches in defence of the measure and conducted a campaign before the people explaining the Bill,[89] with special reference to the Friendly Societies, Trade Unions and all existing institutions and agencies which would be affected by the operation of the Bill.

It must be taken into account that the Chancellor of the Exchequer had no easy task to convince the nation of the wisdom of the Insurance Bill. It is likely that his agitation and speeches on this subject did as much to arouse personal antagonism to him, and to "inflame the masses," as his opponents said, as the Budget campaign. The temper of the country in 1911 was different than 1909, and the full effect of the social policy of the Government in arousing popular interest was more in evidence in 1912. The indictment made against social evils in the first decade of this century was not more popularly put than by Mr. Lloyd George. One has only to read the Parliamentary debates with their great wealth of personal reference to understand why Mr. Clynes thought he had done more than any man of his time to reveal the ugliness of the social system, and why Lord Hugh Cecil believed he was responsible for arousing the bitterest class hatred. His speech at Birmingham may illustrate this divergence of view.

> "What is the evil of this country?" he asked. "Side by side with great and most extravagant wealth you have got multitudes of people who cannot consider even a bare subsistence as assured to them. What do I mean by a bare subsistence? I don't mean luxuries; I exclude even comforts. By a bare subsistence I mean that minimum of food, raiment, shelter, and medical care which is essential to keep human life in its tenement of clay at all." [90]

[89] Cf. *The People's Insurance,* by the Rt. Hon. D. Lloyd George (2nd ed. 1911), Part IV, pp. 175-188; Part II, replies to letters addressed to Chancellor of Exchequer before the Bill was finally amended; and pp. 33-63 contains the scheme of the Bill compiled from explanatory *Memoranda* issued by the Treasury and the Board of Trade at the time the Bill was introduced.

[90] *Op. cit.,* p. 192; for the Birmingham speech, June 10, 1911, pp. 191-204. Mr. Lloyd George's speeches on land reform, 1925-6, are reminiscent of the earlier period of his activity.

He made plain that that was not his idea of the Government's aid:

We aspire to something more. Our object, our goal ought to be enough to maintain efficiency for every man, woman, and child. The individual demands it, the State needs it, humanity cries for it, religion insists upon it.[91]

The value of this Act as a lesson in practical politics for great numbers of people was brought out fully in the debates, and with this the Government was in sympathy. Mr. George said:

There is nothing more marked in this country, in most countries, than the contrast between the relentlessness and the rigour with which the laws of property are enforced and the slackness and sluggishness with which the laws affecting the health of the people are administered. These health committees, these societies will be administered by the men themselves. It will be a great lesson in self-government. It will be the first time the workers of this country have been really federated for the purpose of administering affairs which are essential to their very happiness and comfort.[92]

The Chancellor delivered a speech at Whitefield's Tabernacle which was unusually full of the strange popular appeal, touched by humour and imagination, which made many of Mr. Lloyd George's campaign utterances seem far removed from the authoritative words of a member of the Government. These speeches were responsible ones, for which their author had to make allowance that back in the House of Commons they would have to be validated. At the late date, October, the Chancellor spoke of the effects of the Bill on the country at large:

"Next year it will be in operation," he said, "in the following year the benefits will be flowing, and the stream of benefits will get wider, greater in value—swollen year by year, and by the time the general election comes, what will be the use of misrepresentations of this Bill? Why, there will be living refutations of every falsehood springing up in every street, town, city, and hamlet of the land. There won't be a village where you cannot point to lives having been saved by the Insurance Bill. There

[91] *Op. cit.*, p. 193. [92] *Op. cit.*, p. 203.

won't be a town or hamlet where you cannot point to households saved from privation and hunger by the Insurance Bill. There will be the man who has come back from the sanatorium fit for work, strong, vigorous, who but for that Bill, would have been a poor wretched consumptive, staggering to the grave. There will be children who will be saved. There will be the slums which have defiled our great cities for generations cleansed and swept out of the way by the health provisions of this Bill. They say, 'Why not wait?' Wait for whom? Wait! For what are we to wait? Wait until the stream, that dark stream of human misery has all flowed past? Or are we to wait until it surges up and swells and breaks over the banks of law and convention which hem it in and devastates the land with its horrors. . . . This Bill was promised three years ago. It has been on the table six months, discussed and advertised in every paper. No; we will have it through. We want to get on with other work. This is not the end of social reform.[93] It is a good beginning. Some of these provisions are only palliatives until we can get deeper. But it does more than that. It amasses information, and gathers it from all sources as to social evils—analyses and collects it; and all this will be of enormous benefit when we come to deal with the great problems. I never said it would do everything. It will help, and then we will go on. I am taunted that I promised 'a new heaven and a new earth.' They seem to think that phrase was uttered by me. But I am a humble believer in it. I should like to be able in a humble way to help its advent—a new earth, where the health of the multitude would be more precious in the eyes of the law than the wealth of the few; a new earth, where the superabundance with which Providence blesses labour can be directed and controlled so that the home of the labourer shall be saved from wretchedness, penury, and privation; a new earth, and the best of all to be concentrated and organised to avert the worst from each." [94]

If one is tempted to discount the natural fervour of speaking to popular audiences, it need only be recalled that the same speaker

[93] See Parl. Deb. H. C. 5 S., 1911, Vol. 32, pp. 1433-1441, Labour's closing speech on the third reading of the Insurance Bill, by Mr. J. Ramsay MacDonald: "The great value of this Bill is not what it is going to do as a remedial measure immediately, but that it is going to compel us to face problems that we should not have faced if it had not been introduced" (p. 1440).

[94] *The People's Insurance,* pp. 222-223; pp. 205-223, entire speech.

could drive a sleepy House in the early morning hours through the almost endless drudgery of the Bill's amendments, and later in the same day begin skilfully once more to bring the Bill to completion.

Such was the statement of the responsible Minister, and it can be taken fairly for the social purpose of the Government in their program of legislation, implied by Sir Henry Campbell-Bannerman when, in his opening speech in 1906, he declared that England must be "less of a pleasure ground for the rich and more of a treasure house for the nation." [95] The Prime Minister, Mr. Asquith, on the third reading [96] of the Insurance Bill, December 6, added his authority to the principle by which politics is an instrument of service in bringing about social justice. "Political machinery," he said, "is only valuable and is only worth having if it is adapted to and used for worthy social ends," and this Bill confers "upon millions of our fellow countrymen by the joint operation of self-help and State help the greatest alleviation of the risks and sufferings of life that Parliament has ever conferred upon any people." [97] Though in effect only a short time before the War the National Insurance Act even by 1914 [98] had contributed much valuable information with regard to the condition of the people; [99] and the administration of the Act involved directly or indirectly every type of social question[100]

[95] Hansard, 4 S. H. C., 1906, Vol. 152, pp. 164-179, entire.

[96] Parl. Deb. 5 S. H. C., 1911, Vol. 32, pp. 1419-1530, third reading entire; note speeches of Forster (pp. 1419-1433), Bonar Law (pp. 1504-1518), and Lloyd George (pp. 1451-1470); see pp. 2785-2796 for Lords amendments' consideration. Progress of National Insurance Bill in House of Lords: Parl. Deb. 5 S. H. L., 1911, Vol. 10, pp. 736-765, introduced by Lord Haldane, Secretary of State for War; second reading debate entire, pp. 736-800; Committee, December 12-14, pp. 806-808, 990-1091.

[97] Parl. Deb. 5 S. H. C., 1911, Vol. 32, p. 1522; pp. 1518-1522, entire.

[98] Cf. M. B. Hammond, *British Labour Conditions and Legislation During the War,* published by Carnegie Foundation (1919), pp. 20-21.

[99] See *Report for 1912-1913 on the Administration of the National Insurance Act, Part I. Health Insurance,* Cd. 6907 (1913); and *First Report of the Proceedings of the Board of Trade under Part II. of the National Unemployment Insurance Act, 1911,* Cd. 6965 (1913).

[100] Note Budget statement of 1911 on the finances of the National Insurance Bill; Parl. Deb. 5 S. H. C., 1911, Vol. 25, pp. 1868-1870; pp. 1849-1870 entire (Lloyd George). Also the extended debate the next year on the Insurance Commissioners and the politics of the time as affected by the Insurance Act, in Civil Services (Supplementary Estimates) Com-

as well as a necessary examination of the whole machinery of enforcement.

The Act of 1911 insured compulsorily,[101] with certain exceptions, all "employed" persons, British or alien, from 16 to 70 years of age, and persons not "employed" could insure under certain conditions during the same age period, against the risk of ill-health, and in the employments specified in the Act, against unemployment. Compulsory health and unemployment insurance, with State aid and under State control, was established. Part I of the Act, Health Insurance,[102] was placed under the control of Insurance Commissioners appointed by the Treasury, to whom power was given to effectively carry out the Act by making regulations which, if not annulled became a part of the Act itself. This power to make regulations was probably the widest power of subordinate legislation ever conferred by Parliament upon any body of officials.[103] Over 100 matters were specifically left to be dealt with by regulations.[104] It was provided [105] that

> The Insurance Commissioners may make regulations for any of the purposes for which regulations may be made under this Part (I) of this Act or the schedules therein referred to, and for prescribing anything which under this Part of this Act or any such schedules is to be prescribed, and generally for carrying this Part of this Act into effect, and any regulation so made shall be laid before both Houses of Parliament as soon as may be after they are made, and shall have effect as if enacted in this Act.

The Administration of Part II of the Act, Unemployment Insurance,[106] was placed in the hands of the Board of Trade, with similar comprehensive powers [107] of making regulations for the

mittee: Parl. Deb. H. C. 5 S, 1912, Vol. 34, pp. 1558-1624; and on Estimates for 1912-13, National Insurance Act (Administration): Parl. Deb. 5 S., 1912, Vol. 37, pp. 523-600, 1108-1164, 1948-1996; Vol. 38: pp. 1943-2002; Vol. 39: pp. 257-261; Vol. 40: pp. 2173-2220; Vol. 41: pp. 1739-1774.

[101] Act of 1911, Sect. I.

[102] Act of 1911, Sects. 1-83.

[103] Dicey, *op. cit.*, p. xl.

[104] Cf. Sections 1 and 3 of the Ministry of Health Act, 1919 (9 & 10 Geo. V. c. 21). "An Act to establish a Ministry of Health to exercise in England and Wales powers with respect to Health and Local Government."

[105] Act of 1911, Sect. 65.

[106] Act of 1911, Sects. 84-107.

[107] Act of 1911, Sect. 91.

administration of the Act with regard to unemployment, and the power of adding to the number of insured trades.[108] As early as 1913 Part of the 1911 Act was amended,[109] and in 1914 Part II was amended by the law of that year;[110] both amending Acts being directed mainly to the removal of certain administrative difficulties.[111] The scope of this Act was necessarily widened during the War,[112] but legislation since that designed to meet unusual wartime conditions has steadily confirmed the principle established in the Act of 1911.

(c) *Post-war Legislation and Poor Law Reform*

The Unemployment Insurance Act, 1920,[113] carried out the Government's policy of bringing the great majority of the wage-earners of the country under a comprehensive compulsory scheme of contributory unemployment insurance, domestic servants and agricultural labourers being about the only classes excluded. An additional 8,000,000 workers were included by this Act, among them non-manual workers receiving less than £250 a year. This Act enlarged powers granted for making special orders,[114] and also provided for the placing of unemployment insurance on an "industry basis,"[115] which Labour has opposed except it be under

[108] Act of 1911, Sect. 103, and Sixth Schedule.

[109] 3 & 4 Geo. 5. c. 37. [110] 4 & 5 Geo. 5. c. 57.

[111] See *National Health Insurance, Report of Second Year's Working* (Cd. 7496, 1914) wherein the 1913 Act is fully considered along with the whole problem of administration.

[112] These Acts were: The National Insurance (Navy and Army) Act, 1914 (4 & 5 Geo. V. c. 81); The National Insurance (Navy and Army) (Session 2) Act, 1914, (5 Geo. V. c. 15); The National Insurance (Part I. Amendment) Act, 1915, providing for total disablement (5 Geo. V. c. 29); The National Insurance (Part II. Amendment), 1915 (5 Geo. V. c. 27), and 1916 (6 & 7 Geo. V. c. 20), extension to workers abroad and munition workers; The National Insurance (Temporary Employment in Agriculture) Act, 1916 (6 & 7 Geo. V. c. 53); The National Insurance (Part I. Amendment) Act, 1917 (7 & 8 Geo. V. c. 15), disablement from war.

[113] 10 & 11 Geo. V. c. 30. Between the War Acts and the principal Act of 1920 were passed the National Insurance (Unemployment) Act, 1918 (7 & 8 Geo. V. c. 63), and 1919 (9 & 10 Geo. V. c. 77), which increased the rate of unemployment benefit.

[114] Act of 1920, Sect. 36.

[115] Act of 1920, Sections 18-20. Cf. Report on the administration of Section 18 of the Unemployment Insurance Act, 1920, and on the action

State control.[116] But amending and extending Acts followed fast on the passing of this principal Act, almost as if Parliament were playing hide-and-seek with the problem of unemployment. The Unemployed Insurance (Temporary Provisions Amendment) Act, 1920;[117] the two Acts of 1921,[118] providing for an increase of the contribution rates and the period of benefit; the Unemployed Workers' Dependants (Temporary Provisions) Act, 1921,[119] and the Unemployment Insurance Act, 1922,[120] supplementing the allowance of an unemployed person; the Unemployment Insurance Act, 1923,[121] continuing for further periods the payment of unemployed benefit; and the Unemployment Insurance Act, 1924,[122] have all been superseded by the Unemployment Insurance (No. 2) Act, 1924.[123] This provides that an unemployed person may claim one week's benefit for every six contributions paid in respect of him and for periods not exceeding in the aggregate 26 weeks in a benefit year. This means that for half the year an

taken with a view to investigating the possibility of developing unemployment insurance by industries (Cmd. 1613), 1923.

[116] *The Labour Year Book 1924,* pp. 41-43.

[117] 10 & 11 Geo. V. c. 82.

[118] Unemployment Insurance Act, 1921 (11 & 12 Geo. V. c. 1); No. 2 (11 & 12 Geo. V. c. 15).

[119] 11 & 12 Geo. V. c. 62; repealed in 1922.

[120] 12 Geo. V. c. 7. In 1922 the Minister of Labour issued a Memorandum addressed to the National Confederation of Employers' Organizations and the Trade Union General Council, asking the co-operation of these bodies in considering steps which might be taken to improve the system of national unemployment insurance. It was generally agreed that the State should administer the system, the employers and the workers both agreeing to this. See *Ministry of Labour Gazette,* December, 1922, and February, 1924; and a Report for the Trade Union Congress and the Labour Party, *Social Insurance and Trade Union Membership* (1923) which discusses fully the advantages to the worker of having social insurance administered by the Government. From the workers' point of view are also two Reports, one the *Memorandum on Unemployment Insurance by Industry* (1922), issued by the National Joint Council, formed to represent the Trade Union Congress, the Labour Party Executive and the Parliamentary Labour Party, and the other *Unemployment: A Labour Policy* (1921), being the report of the joint committee on unemployment appointed by the Parliamentary committee of the Trade Union Congress and the Labour Party Executive, together with the resolutions unanimously adopted by the special Trade Union and Labour Conference in London, January 27, 1921. This report includes a copy of the Labour Party's Prevention of Unemployment Bill.

[121] 13 Geo. V. c. 2. [122] 14 Geo. V. c. 1. [123] 14 & 15 Geo. V. c. 30.

unemployed person may be legally entitled to an allowance benefit, which is fixed at 18s. a week for men, 15s. for women, 7s.6d. for boys, and 6s. for girls. That Acts of Parliament cannot solve the problem has been amply proved; but they have provided some relief against the havoc of unemployment, considered by some as equally devastating as the strain upon the nation in the days of war.

With regard to Part I (Health Insurance) of the Act of 1911, it may be noted that changes have been mainly administrative. The National Health Insurance Act, 1918,[124] sought to bring the working of the Act up to date; and the National Health Insurance Act, 1919,[125] besides altering the rates of benefit and contribution, raised the rate of remuneration for exemption from compulsory Health Insurance from £160 per year to £250, for all manual workers and those whose income fell below that amount.[126] The period of disorganization, mixed with dismay, is reflected in the National Health Insurance Acts, 1920,[127] 1921,[128] and 1922,[129] which are largely concerned with the financial provisions and their amendment. By the Ministry of Health Act, 1919,[130] the powers exercised by the Insurance Commissioners for England and Wales were transferred [131] to the Minister of Health, and in

[124] 7 & 8 Geo. V. c. 62 (Part I. Sections 1-6 for Financial Provisions).

[125] 9 & 10 Geo. V. c. 36.

[126] Act of 1919, Sect. I; the Act of 1911 included all non-manual workers, as well as manual workers, below £160.

[127] 10 & 11 Geo. V. c. 10.

[128] The National Health Insurance Act, 1921 (11 & 12 Geo. V. c. 25), and the National Health Insurance (Prolongation of Insurance) Act, 1921 (11 & 12 Geo. V. c. 66), extending temporarily the period during which persons who were unemployed might remain insured, under general provisions of the National Health Insurance Acts, 1911-1921.

[129] 12 & 13 Geo. V. c. 38.

[130] 9 & 10 Geo. V. c. 21.

[131] Act of 1919, Sect. 3. *The Report of the Inter-Departmental Committee on Public Assistance Administration* (London, 1924, Cmd. 2011) gives a useful summary of the historical development of forms of assistance, and gives recommendations for linking these services more closely together, so as to prevent failure or overlapping of assistance in case of need. The Committee was appointed to work out a system of co-ordination for administrative and executive arrangements for the grant of assistance from public funds on account of sickness, destitution and unemployment. Cf. *The Inter-Departmental Committee on Health and Unemployment Insurance, First and Second Interim Reports* (Cmd. 1644, 1922), and the *Third Interim Report* (Cmd. 1821, 1923). It is significant that the Minister of Labour gave an adverse report to a change in the present

the Ministry was set up the Insurance Department for the National Health Insurance Act. The powers and duties of the new ministry were to include the supervision and administration of the entire insurance system.[132] The Scottish Board of Health Act, 1919, gave that body control in Scotland. Co-operating with the Minister of Health is the National Health Insurance Joint Committee, consisting of representatives of England, Wales and Scotland, with the Minister of Health as chairman. The Minister, acting through the Insurance Department, takes the place of the former body called the Insurance Commissioners. The Minister may appoint such employees as are needed, has general charge of the system, and is authorized to issue regulations controlling all subordinate officers and organizations. The Acts governing National Health Insurance have all been consolidated in the National Health Insurance Act, 1924.[133] The Administration of the system of Health Insurance was fully gone into by the Royal Commission on National Health Insurance which was appointed in 1924.[134] The aim of the Commission was to make a

principle of the benefit and insurance system in his *Memorandum on the proposal to use unemployment benefit in aid of (a) wages on relief work, or (b) wages in industry* (1923). Professor Henry Clay writing in the Manchester *Guardian Commercial* in the "Reconstruction in Europe Supplement," October 26, 1922, concluded his study by saying that "finally, the community should face its obligations of maintaining its unemployed members adequately and continuously, instead of inadequately and intermittently. If it does it will realise the expense involved, and will apply itself to the problem of understanding and controlling the trade fluctuations which are the chief cause of unemployment." An unemployment study that is suggestive is Mr. Felix Morley's *Unemployment Relief in Great Britain: A Study in State Socialism* (1924), and the able Reports, *The Third Winter of Unemployment* (1923), and *Is Unemployment Inevitable? An Analysis and a Forecast* (1924).

[132] Cf. Ministry of Health, *First Annual Report,* 1919-1920. Part I—(i) Public Health; (ii) Local Administration; (iii) Local Taxation and Valuation. (Cmd. 923.) Part II—Housing and Town Planning (Cmd. 917). Part III—Administration of the Poor Law, the Unemployed Workmen Act, and the Old Age Pensions Acts (Cmd. 932). Part IV—Administration of National Health Insurance (Cmd. 913). These Reports of 1920 indicate the scope of the Ministry of Health.

[133] 14 & 15, Geo. V. c. 38.

[134] The Reports and Evidence of this Commission describe fully the present system, and are a mine of information on the whole problem of social insurance in England. A French study is one by E. Marlin, *Le chômage involuntaire et la législation anglaise* (1924, Paris).

full and impartial investigation into the working of the system set up under the Act of 1911, with a view to securing the fullest possible advantages for the fifteen million workers who are compulsorily insured under the scheme. The terms of reference for this Commission were:

To inquire into the scheme of National Health Insurance established by the National Health Insurance Acts, 1911-1912, and to report what, if any, alterations, extensions, or developments should be made in regard to the scope of that scheme and the administrative, financial, and medical arrangements set up under it.

One of the most significant of the results of public discussion and official investigation of the system of health insurance is that the Government has had the benefit of expert advice with regard to all schemes of social insurance. The Widows', Orphans' and Old Age Pensions Act, 1925, is one indication of this, and the movement for a unified system of social insurance is another.[135] In the Parliamentary debates since 1918 there have been many references to a system of unified insurance, and the Government is committed to the idea, but as yet no satisfactory scheme has been brought forward. Yet it is worth while to record that the Government has made definite proposals on the question of Poor Law Reform. And such reform has a close connection with the program of the State with regard to unemployment and health insurance. Labour held that probably the chief way in which the new Unemployment Act of 1924 operated in this connection was that it enabled the Poor Law authorities to discontinue or reduce payments in supplementation of unemployment benefit.

Poor Law Reform

The Minister of Health in December, 1925, addressed a letter to the Boards of Guardians in England and Wales, together with a Memorandum containing provisional proposals for a measure of

[135] The writings of Sir William Beveridge are especially significant in this regard, and the same may be said of the Labour and Trade Union research papers on the subject. See also Joseph L. Cohen, *Social Insurance Unified and other Essays* (1924), and Alban Gordon, *Social Insurance: What It Is and What It Might Be* (1924). The International Labour Office has issued a survey, *Studies and Reports Series C. (Employment and Unemployment), No. 10. Unemployment Insurance* (1925).

Poor Law Reform. It will be remembered that the whole question was exhaustively considered by the Royal Commission which was appointed in 1905 and reported in 1909. In July, 1917, a Committee known as the Maclean Committee was appointed by the Minister of Reconstruction

> to consider and report upon the steps to be taken to secure the better co-ordination of public assistance in England and Wales and upon such other matters affecting the system of local government as may from time to time be referred to it.

The Committee in a number of instances reconciled the majority and the minority reports of the Royal Commission of 1909. It recommended the abolition of the boards of guardians and the transfer of their functions to local authorities—normally county and county borough councils—on certain stated lines. The provisional proposals that have been put forward by the Ministry of Health are drawn on the lines proposed by the Maclean Committee. It making the proposals the Minister of Health wrote that he was in no small degree influenced by the fact that the existing organization of local government was such as seriously to detract from the value to the community of the devoted personal service rendered by so many members of boards of guardians. In case after case Parliament has recently decided to assign not to the guardians but to other authorities new social services where the work to be done was either wholly or mainly of the nature of public assistance, and the Minister believed that a single local authority should be wholly or mainly responsible for the local administration of its area. If the proposals are carried out, boards of guardians will disappear, "and with them much of the unpalatable flavour associated with the Poor Law and its administration to-day." [136] By the proposals applicable to the country generally, the objects it is sought to attain are, briefly (and apart from the reduction in the number of local elections and local administrative bodies):

1. The co-ordination and improvement of the provision made for the prevention and treatment of ill-health both institutionally

[136] Manchester *Guardian Weekly,* December 11, 1925, p. 461, editorial and also note issue of January 8, 1926, p. ii, for complete survey of the Ministry of Health's proposals.

and otherwise, and the inclusion in this provision of all public assistance required as the result of sickness, accident, and infirmity. In county boroughs a complete unification of the health services can be secured, and as regards administrative counties there is contemplated a concentration in the county council of a general responsibility for the administration of health services in the hands of borough and district councils acting within the county.

2. The co-ordination of all forms of public assistance, and especially an improved correlation between Poor Law relief and unemployment benefit.
3. The decentralization of the responsibility at present falling on the Minister of Health.
4. The simplification of the financial relations between the Ministry and the local authorities and the freeing of the local authorities from the financial restrictions in matters of comparative detail which are a necessary concomitant of the present system.
5. The correction of certain anomalies of historic origin, such as the association of the registration service (births, deaths, and marriages) with the provision for the relief of the poor.

Proposals for the reform of the Poor Law in 1926 need only be set forth to indicate the remarkable changes that have taken place in the principles of relief since the beginning of the nineteenth century. If this change means anything at all it means that human life has become of more value, that the individual is more important. It means also that the State is determined to aid in bringing in the good society in every way that it can. The moral earnestness of social effort is to-day a tremendous factor in laying the foundations of a new order in which the purposive will of the State can interpret its intent that conditions of life shall be good. A century and a quarter of progress has really given to the modern State a new citizen. This citizen believes in the State because in a great many ways the State is competent to carry out reforms and to maintain high standards of collective action. Thus, as Professor Gilbert Murray has suggested, one of the great objections to State interference in the last century—that the State did not possess enough knowledge or enough organization to do the proposed work effectively or intelligently—does not obtain.[137] Now it often does. And the conclusion is reached that the State has become a far more self-conscious unity, and where it has knowledge it can act.

[137] *Contemporary Review,* Vol. 128, No. 720 (December, 1925), p. 693, from an address to Liberal candidates on October 26, 1925, "What Liberalism Stands For," pp. 681-697.

CHAPTER VII

POLITICS OF THE ENGLISH LABOUR MOVEMENT, WITH REFERENCE TO THE TRADE UNION CONGRESS, THE STATUS OF THE TRADE UNIONS, AND INDUSTRIAL UNREST

THE chief features of social legislation in England have now been considered. This legislation showed to what extent the State made an effort to control industry by protecting the conditions of work and by advancing the standards of living for the individual. The State prescribed positive duties with regard to the health and safety of the worker, beyond this the State inaugurated a general system of social insurance based upon the principle of a minimum standard of life and security. The intervention of the State made it necessary to consider the organization of the workers within the community and the rights that could be given special recognition. It is thus of interest to see how the Trade Union Congress, the "Parliament of Labour," reflected the changing opinion of Labour which was also an important factor in the bitter controversy over the laws defining the status of trade unions. The public, though greatly concerned in that long conflict, had its case more fully presented in the Parliamentary debates on industrial unrest. The consideration of the Trade Union Congress, the status of trade unions and industrial unrest may now provide an opportunity to judge the tendency of public opinion with regard to State action.

PART I

The Trade Union Congress

The Plymouth and Huddersfield Trade Union Congresses of 1899 and 1900 can be compared with the first and second general

Congresses at Paris of the same years of the French Socialist organizations. The Labour movement of each country was making an effort to more clearly outline economic and political functions. The Congresses reflected the progress of the Labour movements of France and England, indicating that though the development of the movements had been different, common problems were faced by both countries. From two major points of view the French and English leaders at that time were not far apart. It was accepted as essential that political power through parliamentary representation must be increased, and that the Labour movement had to be reorganized and reconstituted to meet the demands of the new century. The tendency to uniformity in the Labour movements of France and England was, of course, only an expression of the general tendency toward an internationalization of the Labour movement.[1] Industrial expansion and commercial development forced modern nations to find a way out of their problems; workers' legislation was a necessity in each nation; the development of the laws relating to labour being a measure of the extent to which a country was industrialized.[2] The expected result was then that by 1900 the inner political programs of the Labour parties, and the parliamentary questions of all parties on industrial problems should be moving toward uniformity in expression and purpose.

The chairman of the Huddersfield Congress in his opening address declared there never was a time when the hearty cooperation of all the workers was more required, not only if they wished to secure a reasonable proportion of the reforms which the Congress advocated, but to preserve those rights and privileges which for years they had believed they were in full enjoyment of but which were in danger of being whittled away by recent decisions in the court.[3] The president, William Pickles, in his address assumed what had been said by an earlier speaker, that the Congress were representatives of the great democracy, and he had faith in that great democracy, but it had its destiny

[1] Cf. Sombart, pp. 178-211; for a discussion of the tendency of the French and English inner political programs toward uniformity, see pp. 211-253; also Paul Louis', *Histoire du socialisme français,* pp. 273-4, and *Histoire du mouvement syndical en France* (1789-1910), p. 13.

[2] Cf. Foignet and Dupont, *op. cit.,* 45.

[3] The London *Times,* Sept. 4, 1900, p. 10.

in its own hands. With this in mind he discussed the Trade Union method and aim from the point of view of natural science and evolution, marking a departure from the usual presidential efforts of the Congress. He purposely neglected the political and industrial phases of the Labour movement to deal with what he called the "philosophical" aspect of the Trade Union world. The president affirmed that all were convinced that a great change had taken place in the Trade Union movement, both in the minds of those who might be called the leaders of the movement and also in the character of the problem which these men had to solve. Ten years ago the problem was, "How best to determine the rights and duties of the working class in the existing social order?" But from the resolutions agreed to by the last two or three Trade Union Congresses, it could be judged that Trade Unionists had gravely decided that the existing social order was not worthy of such adjustment, for they had pledged themselves to a program which if carried into effect, would entirely sweep away the capitalistic basis of society and substitute for it a collectivist basis. The capitalist had socialized production, and the people would socialize ownership and distribution.[4] This address concluded with the famous dictum of Engels on the approaching hour when man would become master of his own social organization. The London *Times* commented at length editorially on this presidential address,[5] and it was taken by some to indicate a new spirit in the Trade Union outlook.[6]

This was further expressed by the Report of the Parliamentary Committee which urged and put forward two changes in the Standing Orders, affecting the choice of officials and the control of business, "in order to make the Congress a good practical legislative assembly." [7] These changes made clear the purpose

[4] The London *Times*, Sept. 5, 1900, p. 10.

[5] The London *Times*, Sept. 5, 1900, p. 7.

[6] J. Ramsay MacDonald, "The Huddersfield Trade Union Congress," *Economic Journal*, p. 573, Vol. X, December, 1900.

[7] The first change was that the president of the Congress should be, instead of chosen by delegates, *ex officio* the chairman of the Parliamentary Committee for the past twelve months, and that similarly the vice-chairman and treasurer of the Parliamentary Committee should be the vice-president and secretary-treasurer of the Congress. The second change gave the Parliamentary Committee authority to place on the program of the Congress only such propositions as came within the objects of and aims

of the Trade Union leaders, that the annual gatherings of representatives of the various workmen's organizations must be

> for the purpose of deciding the chief points of some practical program in legislation, and of supporting with the whole force of its affiliated membership trade union struggles of more than local or sectional importance. The other idea which a section of the Congress has of its utility is, that it is to guide and inspire the trade union aim, and that in consequence, it is its duty to take the widest possible view of what is known as "the working class movement." [8]

The report of the Parliamentary Committee presented at Huddersfield, having in mind this idea of the function of the Congress, was mainly taken up with a record of Parliamentary bills, lobbyings and divisions, deputations to Government officials; and reports on Workmen's Trains, Education, Banking, Picketing, Labour Representation, Eight Hours Bill, Federation, and Cooperation. The resolutions passed at the Congress indicate the acceptance on the part of the rank and file of the purposes of the Parliamentary Committee.

The following resolutions were among those passed at the Huddersfield Congress:

1. An eight hour day in all trades and occupations in the United Kingdom, and that this should be a test question at all parliamentary and municipal elections.
2. In favour of the principle of Old Age Pensions, and, "that the only legislation that will solve the problem presented by age and poverty in modern industrial life is that which recognises the pension as a civic right, which may be claimed by any citizen."
3. Abolition of employment of children under fifteen years of age.
4. Cheaper and better trains for workmen.
5. Increased legislation on the Housing difficulty.
6. Taxation of ground rents and values.

of trade unionism. The vote on the first was 657,000 for, 549,000 against; for the second 572,000 for, 394,000 against. There were at the Congress 386 delegates, representing 1,225,133 Trade Unionists.

[8] MacDonald, *op. cit.*

7. For Bills relating to inspection of mines and compulsory Shop half-holidays.
8. Fair Wages contracts in Government departments and by Government contractors.
9. The amendment of the Workmen's Compensation Act so as to include all workers in its provisions.
10. The extension of the right to organize to the postal employees.
11. That education be extended and that the Government assume this work as one of its chief obligations to the people.

The purpose of the Labour leaders was to devise some machinery by which the will of the Congress would become effective. That was a major duty, for there was a growing feeling that the Trade Union Congress had no definite work to do. The paralysis of the Parliament of Westminster, it was said, had been closely followed by the paralysis of Labour's Parliament. Socialist resolutions had been passed, and there the matter seemed to end—at least no particular effort was made to put them into force. Critics within and without the Labour movement were convinced that the limitations of trade unionism were more apparent. It was recognized that the Trade Unions had done great work in educating and safeguarding the workpeople, in providing "countless opportunities for men to learn the meaning of democratic government and administration," and in making plain that amongst the workpeople of Great Britain could be "found men competent to take the responsibilities of the highest offices of state."

But the methods that are available when Labour is organised and the capitalist is alone are useless when the capitalists are also organised in strong combinations. The strike has become an antiquated and clumsy method of fighting—a method, moreover, that in most cases now leaves the workmen the worse at its conclusion. As friendly societies and as co-operative fraternities the limitations of trade unionism are even more apparent. What then is to be done? The political power of the trade unionist must be brought into operation. Some common ideal—social, political, industrial—must possess the members of trade unions in this country, and for the realization of this ideal every effort must be made. It is neither likely nor desirable that all workmen will think alike on matters affecting the commonwealth. The important thing is that there should be in the Labour world some common democratic ideal of citizenship. Without this ideal there can be no future for trade unionism and no room for the palaver of a Trade Union Congress.[9]

The Parliamentary Committee was determined on that problem, for in their report it was pointed out that although the Boiler Inspection and Registration Bill and the Miners' Eight Hours Bill secured a second reading debate, neither was passed into law. This they regarded as an indication of the strength of the industrialist vote in the House of Commons. "Every effort," they urged, "should be made during the election to secure the election of members more in sympathy with the legislation required by, and the aspiration of, the working class."

The next year the presidential address at the Swansea Congress declared that matters affecting the social and industrial welfare of the masses had been disregarded during the last Parliamentary session. The fact that the Factory and Workshop Amendment Bill was placed upon the Statute Book was taken to mean a victory for the power of organization.[10] The report of the Parliamentary Committee was even more definite. The slaughtering of the Miners' Eight Hours Bill was used as an illustration of their belief that

it must be obvious to every one who has watched the proceedings of Parliament during the past few years that it is useless to expect any drastic measures of industrial reform from the House of Commons, composed as it is at the present time.[11]

Further disapproval of the Government was expressed by the Parliamentary Committee because they declared that the Government instead of helping higher grade education, had endeavoured to destroy it on every possible occasion. They had resisted to the uttermost the creation of any democratic governing body; every friend of popular education was to be vigilant, otherwise the Government would change the whole educational policy of the

[9] *The New Age,* Sept. 13, 1900; editorial article, "The Annual Trade Union Congress: Its Past, Present and Future."

[10] The London *Times,* Sept. 4, 1901, p. 5.

[11] The London *Times,* Sept. 3, 1901, p. 9.

country, to the injury, if not the destruction, of the higher interests of the people.

The consequences of the decision of the House of Lords in the Taff Vale case had just begun to be fully understood by the Trade Unionists, and at the Swansea, 1901, Congress the necessity of strict organization and reconstruction, "because of the employers' fight," was urged by the official legal counsel of the Congress. The recommendations of the Parliamentary Committee with reference to the Taff Vale case were unanimously passed. The Committee were empowered to take a test case to the House of Lords to ascertain how far picketing might be carried on without infringing the law, and rendering the funds of the societies liable for damages. A fund was created for this purpose. The day following the handing down of the Taff Vale decision the *Times* editorially remarked that it would "commend itself to the natural sense of justice of the British people." [12] But John Burns at the London Congress of 1902, which can well be compared with the Tours Congress of that year for practical results, stated the views of the Trade Unionists. While signs were not lacking, he pointed out, that their organization was regarded as a menace both politically, socially and commercially, the Trade Union Congress of 1902 must mark an epoch,

> because it registered by the unions the taking up of the challenge thrown down that Labour should be smashed and combination overthrown, so that the large aggregation in former times of wealth in the hands of unscrupulous men shall lead to the reintroduction into this country of ours of Slavery under the mask of Freedom, industrial oppression under the mask of Liberty. You must tear this mask off, the re-barbarization of industry must be opposed.[13]

The leaders of the English Labour movement and the Congress knew that another period of crisis in trade union history had been reached, corresponding to the periods of 1824-5, 1867-76, and which came again in 1911.[14] But it is not exact to say that

[12] The London *Times,* editorial article, p. 9, July 23, 1901.

[13] *Trade Union Congress Report,* London, 1902, pp. 29-30.

[14] Cf. Sidney Webb's *Preface* to *The Theory and Practise of Trade Unions,* by J. H. Greenwood (1911), pp. 5-6.

the leaders of the Labour movement had not decided upon the policy which was made more necessary by the Taff Vale crisis, and which, of course, was given great impetus by it. By the means of a strong Parliamentary Representation Committee and effective Trade Union workers the Taff Vale case was used to unify the English Labour movement. The political Labour movement, it is certain, would not have reached anywhere near the strength represented by the 1906 Parliament if it had not been for the Taff Vale decision. From 1875, when trade unions were finally legalized, political redress for their grievances was one of the major concerns of the Labour movement. It has been said that "the Socialists made rapid progress under the shadow of the Taff Vale case," [15] in the ranks of organized Labour; but one has to look much further back in Trade Union history for the growth of the collectivist idea. In 1894 the Norwich Trade Union Congress adopted a resolution in favour of the socialization of all the instruments of production. Although in 1901, it is interesting to note that the Congress changed, in the resolution calling a conference to consider a comprehensive scheme for old age pensions, the phrase "Socialist societies," to "and other societies." [16] The leaders were determined that the Trade Union movement was not to be a stumbling block in the path of the Labour movement in England.[17] The wisdom of the policy of the industrial and political movements has been vindicated, which has not been true in France nor in Germany.

The resolutions passed at the 1901 Congress further carried out the purpose of the leaders with regard to the will of the Congress becoming effective. The reconstitution of the Labour movement and the aims of its leaders in directing the affairs of the workers, while looked on by some as destructive and revolutionary, seem from this distance to have definitely marked a period where Labour took upon itself a larger share in the common task of organizing the industrial system of England. A wider view of the responsibilities of Parliamentary activity was becoming more manifest. The report of the Parliamentary Com-

[15] Walter V. Osborne and Mark H. Judge, *Trade Unions and the Law,* (1911), pp. 6-7.

[16] The London *Times,* Sept. 6, 1901, p. 6.

[17] Sombart, *op. cit.,* p. 215.

mittee on the Miners' Eight Hours Bill, the keystone to regulation of hours of labour by law, and the Factory and Workshops Acts Amendment and Consolidation Bill, set forth the fact that Labour representatives were giving themselves with vigour to all the work of the House of Commons in which their knowledge and personal equipment could be best used. The Committee in their report advocated the passing of consolidation Acts, similar to that which codified all the Acts dealing with factories and workshops, of all the other Acts affecting Labour, such as the Mines Regulation Acts, the Education Acts, etc. The Amendment and extension of the Workmen's Compensation Act, the Mines Regulation Act, and the enlargement of the powers of Factory Inspectors, were included in the report.

While often the narrower and meaningless jargon of early days was used (and this is true of all the contemporary movements), the Labour forces were approaching the problems of democracy with a less class-conscious point of view. Better organization was

being often followed by better judgment, and especially among the higher trade union officials, by a quiet determination to take an all-round, instead of a purely partizan view, of industrial relationship. This is, perhaps, a matter upon which it is rash to generalize, but the comments of trade unionists on the question of education; the wider recognition of the threatening reality of foreign competition; the prominence given to the discussion and elucidation of technical processes in some of the journals of the trade unions, and the growing tendency for the unions to become something wider than protective organizations of small sections of workers, are among the most hopeful signs of the movement; while probably at no time in the past were the unions so widely recognised as providing on the side of "labour" the machinery of pacific adjustment of difficulties that may arise.[18]

The 1901 Congress expressly instructed that the Eight Hours Day should be fought for "through various local administrative bodies" where the question of strong parliamentary opposition would not be met.[19] This same idea was expressed by John Burns

[18] *The Economic Journal,* Vol. XI, March, 1901, pp. 136-7, "Labour Notes."

[19] The Parliamentary Committee pledged themselves to support Sir Charles W. Dilke in his Shops Bill, and the 48-Hours-Week Bill.

at the 1902 Congress when he suggested copying the tolerant, practical, useful work that the Labour group of the London County Council had been able to do in combination with the sympathetic men of all religions and all views on politics on those municipal problems which did not divide them as the political problem did. He declared that a critical time was upon the Labour movement; trade was on the decline, wages were beginning to fall, the Press was more bitter, Parliament was often unsympathetic, and the law, with heavy strokes, was descending upon them, and not with strict impartiality. Public opinion was heavily against them. But their business was to head off the stream of reaction. The Congress was told that

> they must so focus their aim, so express their object and so formulate their demands that the depth of grievances and misery should be the justification for all their actions in that place, where Labour, inarticulate no longer, was determined that its grievances should be removed.[20]

The introduction of the Report of the 1902 London Trade Union Congress surveyed the progress of the Labour movement of England towards the ideals of Labour which were comprised in the terms "a living wage," "full legislative protection," and "an adequate and equal representation in Imperial Parliament and on local governing bodies." It was pointed out that in 1867 Labour's voice was almost inarticulate in Parliament, on local governing bodies, and also on the magisterial bench. In 1902 Labour's representatives were to be found by the hundred on local governing bodies, by scores on the magisterial bench, and by thirteen or fourteen direct Labour members in the House of Commons. Thirty-five years ago there was practically no Mines Regulation Act, an imperfect Factory Act, no laws regulating railways so far as safety was concerned, no Truck Act worthy of the name, and no Workmen's Compensation Act. By 1902 there were improved mining legislation, a fairly good Factory Act, moderate regulations in regard to safety on railways, a great improvement in laws in regard to "truck," a valuable instalment in reference to workmen's compensation for injuries, in addition to many other valuable reforms affecting the interests of Labour.

[20] The *London Trade Union Congress Report,* 1902, pp. 29-30.

The keynote which was sounded at the London Congress is clear and unmistakable, namely, that the primary and most important weapon that the industrial classes can use at the present time is to secure a large body of Labour representatives in the House of Commons to voice and give effect to the rising hopes of the present generation of workers, with a view of ameliorating the lot of the industrial classes. If this is done we shall soon see a radical change in regard to the laws on the Statute Book of England.[21]

The report of the Parliamentary Committee at the 1902 Congress covered the questions of Old Age Pensions, Education, Corn Tax, Steam Engines (Persons in Charge) Bill, Workmen's Compensation and Fair Wages Questions, Miners' Eight Hours Bill, Postal Questions, and the Woolwich Arsenal and Dockyard Labourers' Wages.[22]

The address of the president pointed out that much work had been done by the Parliamentary Committee, however that not a single measure of benefit to the working classes had been put upon the Statute Book during the last session; on the contrary, the Education Bill of the Government was a decidedly reactionary measure, no provisions being made in the way of elementary education. The duty of the State was clear, children should not be stunted in their physical or intellectual growth. The Bill was attacked because it abolished the School Boards, placing the schools under the municipal or borough councils, with power to nominate a given number to form a Schools Committee, they in turn having the power to co-opt other members,—this in itself being a blow to democratic representation, an interference with the right of citizenship, and public control stunted and arrested. The president believed the moral and intellectual advance of the people depended on the spirit and success with which they faced the situation, and that no measure could be regarded as satisfactory that did not provide one authority directly elected by the people for all educational purposes and free from sectarian bias.[23]

The Congress of 1901 instructed the Parliamentary Committee

[21] Introduction to *Report of the London Trade Union Congress*, 1902, pp. 27-28.

[22] *Ibid.*, 39-56, for *Parliamentary Committee Report.*

[23] *Report Trade Union Congress of London*, 1902, pp. 27-28.

to convene a national conference on old age pensions of the trade unions, co-operative, friendly and other societies. This conference was held January 14-15, 1902, at Memorial Hall, London, attended by representatives of three million working men and women. The following resolution was passed:

That this Conference urges upon the Government the urgent necessity of establishing a national system of old age pensions which shall be universal in its application to all citizens, male and female, on attaining the age of sixty years, the pension to be at the rate of at least five shillings a week, and that the entire cost of such scheme be met entirely by means of Imperial taxation.

Two other Conferences were held which indicated the interest of the Trade Union world in the affairs of the nation. The first was the Corn Tax Conference, May 27, 1902, in London, following the introduction of the Budget by the Chancellor of the Exchequer. Over a million organized workmen were represented by 170 delegates, and after the adjournment of the Conference the Chancellor of the Exchequer received a deputation from the delegates. The Education Conference was held in London, May 28, 1902, with the same representation as the Corn Tax Conference.[24] The discussion of Education in the sessions of 1900-2 ranked closely behind the questions of the Housing of the Working Classes, the Miners' Eight Hours Bill, and the Old Age Pensions Bill. Early in the first session of 1900 a resolution had been put before the House providing an opportunity for the discussion of the proposed modifications in the system of elementary education.[25]

The Resolution passed at the Education Conference was,

[24] See Speeches of Mr. Asquith and Viscount Bryce in the House of Commons, July 23, 1901, on Education Bill; also Campbell-Bannerman on the political situation and the Education Bill, a speech reported in the London *Times*, July 3, 1901, p. 10; and the London *Times*, Sept. 5, 1901, p. 10, "Education Reform—Possible or Practicable."

[25] The Jebb Resolution: "That, in the opinion of this House, the proposals contained in the Code of Regulations for Day Schools and in the Minutes of the Board of Education laid before Parliament during the present session are conducive to the interests of Education." Ayes 188, noes 105. Hansard, LXXXII, p. 596. Viscount Bryce referring to this Resolution declared that the discussion on it lacked the conventional topics of educational controversy. *Ibid.*, p. 693.

That, as the Government Bill will destroy popularly constituted bodies of education this Conference expresses its dissent to the Government policy on Education; and further it is of opinion that the abolition of School Boards will be detrimental to the interests of the education of the people, and will take away the advantages which the workers have in direct representation in the management of School Boards.[26]

The phrase "direct representation" indicates the spirit of the Congress, finding expression in the report of the Parliamentary Committee

that steps should be taken at the next Parliamentary election to secure the defeat of every member of the present House of Commons and all Parliamentary candidates who may not promise to vote for a solution of the education problem in accordance with the declared policy of the Parliamentary Committees' Report and in consonance with the expressed desire of the Trade Unionists.[27]

At the opening of the Parliament in January, 1901, Campbell-Bannerman declared, in his speech on the Address, that the social reforms of the day must be about Education, Housing and Temperance, and that a new spirit was in Education, which brought about "the dreadful dilemma" of the Unionists.

They have to please the powers of reaction and privilege, and yet they must satisfy popular sentiment and popular demands. They have trusted to the respite given to them by Royal Commissions, and they hoped that those Royal Commissions would find for them some way of reconciling the irreconcilable forces.[28]

The London Congress could not fail to take note of the controversy which had been begun in the London *Times* in a series of articles from October 7, 1901, to December 27, 1901, headed "The Crisis in the British Industries."

"Is Trade Unionism destructive of British Industry?" was taken up by the Congress, at the same time that its Parliamentary

[26] The *Report of the London Trade Union Congress,* 1902, pp. 41-2.
[27] *Ibid.*, p. 42.
[28] Hansard, Vol. LXXXIX, 1901, pp. 82-99; pp. 99-109, Prime Minister's reply (Balfour).

Committee was seriously studying the legal position of the Trade Unions. Through action of the Labour members and the aid of Sir Charles Dilke, a debate on this subject took place in the House of Commons on a motion moved by Mr. Beaumont. The Government majority on the motion was only twenty-nine. The president of the Congress defined [29] the attitude of organized Labour when he said that

> modern industrial society is based upon freedom, and it is a serious matter for our organizations that this should be now challenged by the Law Courts, as it has been in certain recent judgments. Let us face facts as we find them in a bold and honest manner and go out for an alteration in the law. In order to do this we shall have to reconstitute the House of Commons. We must build up a great Labour Party in Parliament from the ranks of the Trade Unionists, and not only make ourselves a great industrial but also a political force in the country.

For this reason the president pointed out that the Trade Unions had a moral as well as an economic effect, for by them "we are schooled and educated in thrift, self-restraint, and the practical wisdom of social politics." The duty of all was to build an empire consisting of men working together for the common good and the uplifting of its inhabitants.

The Management Committee of the General Federation of Trade Unions made a statement on the "crisis," affirming that so far from the aggregate product being less per head and decreasing, they were convinced, on the evidence of employers themselves, that greater sobriety, greater regularity, increased intelligence, and improved methods of remuneration made the manual labour of the country (irrespective of the results of machinery) far more productive than it ever was before. They further declared that at the time the influence of trade unionism as a whole, was more efficacious in increasing than in reducing the productivity of its members.[30] But to other critics "the whole system,

[29] *Report of the London Trade Union Congress,* 1902, pp. 32-36.

[30] The London *Times,* Dec. 20, 1901; also the defence of the English Trade Unions and their methods by Mr. and Mrs. Sidney Webb, the London *Times,* Dec. 6, 1901.

as now being worked, is in fact, the direct outcome of trade unionism coupled with advanced Socialism." [31] Such criticism was preceded by the conviction that whatever political leaders may or may not be able to do, there was much that employers and employed can and should accomplish, on their own initiative, in the way of putting their mutual relations on a better footing.[32] There were disinterested critics who held that the falling behind of English competition was not due to the supposed average inefficiency of British Labour or on account of trade restrictions imposed by labour organizations. The discussion on the decadence of British industry, which had been continued for some time, partook "at best of the unphilosophical character . . . while at times it degenerates into an avowed polemic against Trade Unions." [33]

The most informed of the observers of the English Labour movement at that time did perceive the fact that there would be a great expansion of the political activity of the Trade Unions. This is evident from the reports of the Congresses which have gone before. The development of a Labour Party in England having a great effect on the two older parties and under the direction of leaders like Millerand in France and Bernstein in Germany, was a not uncommon view, being emphasized at that time by certain French students of the English movement.[34] It appears to the writer to be a mistake to ascribe the growth of the Labour Party in a large measure to the "tactical craft of the astute intellectuals of the Labour Party." [35] This overlooks the solid advance toward working class representation and influence which was a phenomenon of politics in France, England, and Germany in the early years of the twentieth century. However this attitude has even lately been clearly stated by a student of English politics and institutions.

[31] E. A. Pratt, *Trade Unionism and British Industry* (1904), p. 27.

[32] Pratt, *op. cit.*, pp. 17-18.

[33] G. B. Dibblee, "The Printing Trades and the Crisis in British Industry," the *Economic Journal*, March, 1902, pp. 1-2; see also Paul Mantoux and Maurice Alfassa, *La Crise du Trade-Unionisme* (1903), Chapters II and III.

[34] Cf. Paul Mantoux and Maurice Alfassa, *op. cit.*

[35] Cf. L. L. Price, "Industrial Policy," two reviews. The *Economic Journal*, Sept., 1923, p. 357.

A clever advertising coterie, so it appears to us, has, for the time, dragged in its train, with unwilling, if it be polite, acquiescence, the less vocal, if not less statesmanlike, Trade Unionist officials of the older, soberer, more responsible type, while younger inexperienced agitators have vented defiantly their enthusiasm in glad clamorous response to the red flag held out to them of internecine enmity to Capitalists and Capitalism. Yet we must allow that we do not see how in these circumstances it was possible to consider or describe, the political Labour movement, even in this country, as not becoming more and more tightly tied outwardly to the fetishes and dogmas, the positive large overthrow and the vague negative reconstruction, for which open and avowed Socialists feel, and exhibit, a complacent but servile regard.[36]

The drift in the direction of a fighting political machine for Labour set in when the Trade Union leaders began to turn away from Gladstonian Liberalism. When it became apparent that Labour could determine the failure or success of certain measures and that direct control over legislation was possible the creation of a parliamentary party became the first duty of the hour.[37] An Act of Parliament has, the Webbs have pointed out, at all times formed one of the means by which British Trade Unionists have sought to attain their ends. The fervour with which they have believed in this particular method, and the extent to which they have been able to employ it have varied according to the political

[36] Price, *ibid.*, pp. 357-8.

[37] See the *Nation* (London) for 1907, for an indication of the force of Labour politics, and note especially the series of articles by Mr. J. A. Hobson, October 26-December 7. The books of 1907-9 provide a commentary also, see especially: A. Griffith-Boscawen's, *Fourteen Years in Parliament* (1907); J. Ellis Barker, *British Socialism: An Examination of its Doctrines, Policy, Aims, Practical Proposals* (1908); *Practical Socialism: A Remonstrance,* Edited by Mark H. Judge (1908), being Papers of the British Constitution Association; H. O. Arnold-Foster, *English Socialism of To-day* (1908); B. Villiers, *The Socialist Movement in England* (1908); Jane T. Stoddart, *The New Socialism* (1909); *The Triumphs of Liberalism,* Liberal Publication Department (1908), No. 2184; *The New Order: A Forward Policy for Unionists,* Edited by Lord Malmesbury (1908); *Towards a Social Policy: Suggestions for Constructive Domestic Reform,* by various writers, representing the conclusions of a committee consisting of Messrs. C. R. Buxton, J. L. Hammond, F. W. Hirst, L. T. Hobhouse, J. A. Hobson, C. F. G. Masterman, and others (1907); and J. Keir Hardie, *My Confession of Faith in the Labour Alliance* (1909).

circumstances of the time.[38] France and England from 1890 were splendid fighting ground for the Labour leaders who were trying to build up a parliamentary strength; the legislature of 1893-8 in France and the great victory of 1906 in England of the Labour party were well prepared for by years of planning and leadership.

This tendency toward parliamentary representation has through every period of Labour history in France and England been linked with a recognition that there were duties that the Trade Unions could not perform acceptably in the modern State. Tom Mann and John Burns of the Amalgamated Society of Engineers were among the first to insist that the Trade Unions were becoming ineffective in handling the problems that the State should look after. John Burns asserted that the

> reckless assumption of the duties and responsibilities that only the State or whole community can discharge, in the nature of sick and superannuation benefits, at the instance of the middle class, is crushing out the larger unions by taxing their members to an unbearable extent. The result of this is that all of them have ceased to be unions for maintaining the rights of labour, and have degenerated into mere middle and upper class rate-reducing institutions.[39]

This attitude became more common as the organization of Labour and its increasing influence in governmental investigations and industrial disputes forced it to assume an increasingly important rôle in arbitration. The growth of Labour in this regard is an outstanding contribution of the Trade Union movement to the slow work of building up industrial peace in England. This important work was recognized by the Royal Commission on Labour in their final report in 1894,[40] while Lecky believed "there can be little doubt that the largest, wealthiest, and best organized Trade Unions have done much to diminish labour conflicts." [41] The real value of this development of arbitration proceedings is

[38] Cf. Sidney and Beatrice Webb, *Industrial Democracy,* Vol. I, p. 247.

[39] Quoted by J. F. Rees, *A Social and Industrial History of England 1815-1918* (1920), p. 135.

[40] Cf. *Fifth and Final Report of Royal Commission on Labour,* 1894 (Cd. 7421).

[41] Lecky, *Democracy and Liberty,* Vol. II, p. 355, quoted by Webbs' *Industrial Democracy,* p. 239; cf. pp. 241 ff.

in the patient work of conciliation; and its growth is among the hopeful signs that industry will command a leadership that will save modern society from the anarchy of economic disruption and warfare.

In this connection it is worth while noting the attitude of the early Trade Union Congresses in this century toward the annual resolution brought forward on the establishment of a Court for compulsory arbitration. Compulsory arbitration in labour disputes was defeated at the 1900 Congress by 939,000 votes to 246,000; at the 1901 Congress it was rejected by 676,000 votes to 366,000; and the London 1902 Congress voted against it by a majority of 658,000 votes.[42] The majority at the 1903 Congress at Leicester was 618,000 against the resolution;[43] and at the 1904 Congress at Leeds the majority against was 486,000,[44] while the 1905 Congress at Henley the majority against compulsory arbitration was even larger.[45] The vote at the 1900 Congress was explained as due

to the suspicion which trade unionists still have of the "outsider," and it was plain from the debate that if a satisfactory method of choosing the arbitrator could be devised, the unions would accept compulsory arbitration.[46]

Just before the 1900 Trade Union Congress, Lord Avebury, president of the British Chambers of Commerce, declared in favour of joint conciliation boards to settle industrial disputes.[47] The attitude of the Government had been given by the President of the Board of Trade on December 15, 1898, when receiving a deputation of trade unionists. He pointed out the evils of industrial warfare, but believed that those evils could not be remedied by any legal enactment making arbitration in labour disputes compulsory.[48] The decision of Mr. Justice Farwell in the Taff Vale case was reflected in the attitude of the Trade Union

[42] *Report Trade Union Congress* (1902), pp. 66-68.
[43] The London *Times,* Sept. 12, 1903, p. 12.
[44] *Report of the Trade Union Congress* (1904), pp. 103-5.
[45] The London *Times,* Sept. 7, 1905.
[46] *Economic Journal,* Vol. X, Dec., 1900, p. 574 (J. Ramsay MacDonald).
[47] The London *Times,* p. 4, Sept. 6, 1900.
[48] *Economic Journal,* Vol. IX, March, 1899, p. 85.

Congress of 1900,[49] and for several sessions the Penrhyn quarries dispute tempered the arguments of the trade unionists.[50] It has been held that at the time that the 1902 resolution was submitted to the Congress "one would have indeed expected that the Taff Vale decision would have influenced the Trade Unionists strongly in favour of compulsory methods."[51] But it was not until the Sheffield Congress of 1910 that Mr. Tillett succeeded in getting the Congress to instruct the Parliamentary Committee "to prepare a report on the various existing forms of conciliation and arbitration in industrial disputes both British and foreign." The Committee carried out the instructions of the Congress, and their report was published in the Report of the Trade Union Congress, 1911. The Committee made no recommendations. However, the Congress of 1903 instructed the Parliamentary Committee to draft a Bill for the establishment of a Court which should be authorized to demand evidence compulsorily in any trade dispute in which the parties had not agreed to settlement after a month had expired since the declaration of a strike or lock-out. The power to call for an investigation was given to either of the parties or a public authority, and in the event of disagreement between the parties concerned a public report should be made. An equal number of employers' and trade union representatives should constitute the Court and should appoint a chairman, or in case of disagreement the Board of Trade should appoint a chairman. The Court should be moveable and have the power to call for Special Commissions of investigation and report. This Bill, offered as an Amendment to the Conciliation Act, 1896,[52] was presented by Mr. R. Bell in 1904.[53] No results came from this effort to follow out the recommendations of the trade unionists. The Report of the Parliamentary Committee to the Leeds

[49] See especially the speech of the Secretary of the Railway Servants, Mr. Bell.

[50] Mr. Lloyd George, as counsel for the strikers, appeared before the 1902 Congress on their behalf. He referred to the owner as one who had "feudal ideas." For his speech see p. 64 of the *Report of the Trade Union Congress.*

[51] De Montgomery, *op. cit.*, p. 338.

[52] 59 & 60 Victoria, Ch. 30. The only legal instrument dealing with the settlement of trade disputes which was in force at the beginning of this century.

[53] See *Report of the Trade Union Congress*, 1904, p. 71.

Congress, of which Mr. Bell was chairman, declared that in 1904, a year in which no greater political or industrial questions could have been before the workers, "we have been under the rule of one of the strongest reactionary Governments of modern times." [54]

Part II

The Status of the Trade Unions

In the year 1904, Sir Charles W. Dilke believed that an "extraordinary paralysis had overtaken Government legislation." [55] He brought forward on February 28 the Trade Union and Trade Disputes Bill (No. 2),[56] "to legalize conduct of Trade Disputes and to alter the law affecting the liability of Trade Union funds." Mr. Paulton on February 5 had introduced a similar Bill,[57] which was supported by Sir Robert Reid and Mr. Robert Bell, but to which the Prime Minister found very serious fault, and, while not making it a party issue, declared his opposition. The proposal to put the Bill before a Standing Committee failed.[58] The debates on this Bill indicated the struggle that was yet to come on the question of the legal status of the trade unions. The same ground had been gone over in 1903, at which time a similar Bill was before Parliament. Sir Frederick Banbury and Mr. Cripps saw in the law a revolutionary doctrine on the rights of combination on the part of the workman, while others believed that the whole progress of the organized Labour of England was at stake. The main point for this study is, that Parliament had before it several years the problem of the legal status of the trade unions, about which was centred the fullest discussion of the rights of Labour, of the community and the State.

[54] Report of the Parliamentary Committee, *Trade Union Congress Report,* 1904, p. 54.

[55] Hansard, 4 S. H. C., 1904, Vol. 132, p. 795, in debate on the Shops Bill.

[56] House Bill No. 91, 1904; Hansard, 4 S. H. C., 1904, Vol. 130, p. 574.

[57] House Bill No. 8, 1904; Hansard, 4 S. H. C., 1904, Vol. 133, pp. 958-962, for speech of Mr. Paulton on second reading of Bill, April 22.

[58] The debate on second reading: Prime Minister (pp. 974-979), Sir Robert Reid (pp. 979-984), Mr. Cripps (pp. 983-990), and Mr. Bell (pp. 990-996), Hansard, 4 S., Vol. 133, pp. 958-1008. The vote for adjournment which prevented any further proceeding of the Bill was only carried by a majority of 39 votes, 238-199. This is indicative of what was to be.

In the debate on the King's Speech in 1905 the leader of the Opposition condemned the lack of any reference to the question which above all others was on the minds of the working classes of the nation, the status of the Trade Unions. This was one of the main problems before all parties, and its history in the 1905 session "did not exhibit either the Government or the House of Commons in a very happy light." [59] On February 17, Mr. Whittaker introduced into the House of Commons the Trade Unions and Trade Disputes Bill, 1905.[60] The Bill provided that it should be lawful for the agents of a trade union to picket premises for the purpose of peacefully persuading any person to abstain from working; but a combination to do any act in furtherance of a trade dispute should not be ground for an action, if such act might be done by one person with impunity; and that an action should not be brought against a trade union for the recovery of damage sustained by reason of the action of any of its members.

The Bill was read a second time in the House of Commons on March 10, passing by a majority of 122 (252-130), and was referred to the Standing Committee on Law.[61] The mover, on second reading,[62] urged that recent judicial decisions revealed a danger to the progress of the trade unions and the industrial peace of the nation. Better conditions between the employers and workmen had prevailed during the past thirty years, mainly due to the position in which the trade unions had been put. This belief was strongly supported by Mr. Asquith, who thought there had been introduced "by a recognition of the practice of combination a sense of responsibility and of statesmanship in the conduct of industrial relations which was of equal value to employer and employee." [63] It was "not a matter of Party controversy, the general principles of which the vast majority of the House favoured." [64] He maintained that in view of the recent judicial decisions legislation was not only expedient but absolutely

[59] *Annual Register*, 1905, p. 82.

[60] Two Bills were presented: House Bills No. 2 and No. 205, both being withdrawn.

[61] The Minutes and Report of the Standing Committee are published as Report No. 154, 1905.

[62] Hansard, 4 S., Vol. 142, 1905, pp. 1054-1069 (Whittaker) for seconder (Wilson), pp. 1069-1075.

[63] Hansard, 4 S. H. C., 1905, Vol. 142, pp. 1093.

[64] *Ibid.*, p. 1097: pp. 1092-1098, speech entire.

necessary. The Attorney-General, Sir R. B. Finlay, was of the opposite opinion, believing that it would be nothing more than passing class legislation in favour of the workmen, and would not define the law but would put the trade unions above the law. The Attorney-General announced that he would vote for the rejection of the Bill, but that no pressure would be taken to put the followers of the Government in line of opposition, recognizing, on the authority of the Prime Minister, that

> a practice had grown up of regarding the second reading of private Bills as more in the nature of an abstract Resolution which had the support of the members than as a stage in legislation.[65]

The first clause of the Bill, to legalize peaceful picketing, was in Committee amended by a proviso to the effect that no picketer should

> after being requested by any person annoyed by his conduct, or by any constable instructed by such person, to move away, so act as wilfully to obstruct, insult or annoy such person.

This was, of course, unsatisfactory to the friends of the Bill, and Mr. Whittaker, who was in charge of the Bill, moved to withdraw the Bill. This was refused, by a vote of 26 to 22. It was the unanimous opinion of the Labour members and of those who represented the organized Labour of the country, that the proviso was "fatal to the Bill" and made it "an absurdity." The promoters of the Bill complained that they had received no help from the Government in the Grand Committee, and that on the contrary Ministers, particularly the Solicitor-General, Sir Edward Carson, had voted for every "destructive amendment." Sir Henry Campbell-Bannerman at the Council of the National Liberal Federation, Newcastle-on-Tyne, May 18-19, referred to the "deplor-

[65] *Ibid.*, pp. 1106-1107; pp. 1098-1108 entire. Speeches against the Bill: Sir Thomas Wrightson (pp. 1075-1080), Mr. Duke (pp. 1080-1085) and Sir W. Tomlinson (pp. 1091-2); for, Mr. Atherley-Jones (pp. 1086-1090); debate entire second reading, pp. 1054-1127. In 1904 a similar Bill passed second reading by a majority of only 39, and those who voted against it were 199. In a year the majority was increased to 122, and those voting against were 130.

able spectacle of the last few weeks" when the Trade Unions and Trade Disputes Bill, intended to revive the

original intention of Parliament, had been so mauled and maimed in the Committee under the inspiration of the Government led by their own Solicitor-General, that the Labour and Liberal Members had been obliged to leave the room.

A resolution was unanimously passed at this Council declaring that immediate steps ought to be taken "to restore to workmen the right of effective combination of which they have been deprived by recent decisions of the courts."

In its amended form the Bill was reported to the House by the Grand Committee, where the Bill was withdrawn by its friends. The Report of the Parliamentary Committee of the Trade Union Congress at Henley in September, 1905, said that

above all the past year will be remembered as the one in which the Trade Unions and Trade Disputes Bill, after passing its second reading by a large majority was finally so mutilated in the Standing Committee on Law as to render it not merely practically useless but positively harmful to trade unions.

In its conclusion the Committee recognized the great assistance of the trade unions in promoting legislation for the benefit of the workers. The time was ripe for great effort on every side. Capital was arrayed against the workers, organized as it had never been before, supported by the immense influence of an unjust state of law. It was the opinion of the Parliamentary Committee that the first and foremost need was for more Labour men to be sent to Parliament. Mr. Sexton, in the presidential address, advocated unity among all sections of the Labour party, urging the importance of securing increased independent Labour representation in Parliament. The 1905 session had taught a valuable lesson because of its fruitlessness, he believed.[66] Such determined and consistent criticism of the Government told on the nerves of the leaders of the Conservative Party, combined with the open dissensions in their own ranks. On May 5, at Birmingham, Mr. Chamberlain declared it would have been better to

[66] London *Times,* Sept. 5, 1905, p. 4; and September 6, p. 6.

have the elections sooner, and to let the people, if they wished it, change their rulers, and see how they liked their substitutes, who were "calling their political followers from every point of the compass, not to decide a policy, but as vultures come to a feast." [67]

It is difficult to overemphasize the effect that the judicial decisions in the early years of this century had on the Labour movement of England.[68] The Report of the Royal Commission on Trade Disputes and Trade Combinations,[69] appointed in 1903, reported early in 1906. The Commission had been opposed from the first by the Parliamentary Committee of the Trade Union Congress and the Labour members of Parliament, who in joint meeting on January 17, 1903, protested

> against the appointment of the Trade Disputes Commission, as being calculated to hinder the early settlement of the point at issue; and in addition to this fundamental objection, we protest against the composition of the Committee, which include a majority of members already publicly committed to a course of action in relation to the subject they have to examine and report upon, and in addition contains representatives of the organized employers, but no representatives of the organized workmen, and is therefore neither impartial nor judicial.

The Parliamentary Committee at the Leicester Congress, September 1903, recommended that no trade union or trade union official recognize or give evidence before the Trade Disputes Commission.[70] The Congress gave this mandate, and again in 1904 determined that "in consequence of its inequitable and non-representative character, no evidence or information should be supplied to it by the trade unions." [71]

The controversy centring about the legal status of the trade unions gave an opportunity for general political discussions on the

[67] *Annual Register,* 1905, p. 150.

[68] See the Authors' Introduction to the 1902 ed. of *Industrial Democracy,* Sidney and Beatrice Webb, for series of legal decisions. Also the article by Professor Geldart, *Economic Journal,* June, 1906, pp. 189-211, on the principles which have been developed by judicial decisions almost entirely since 1894. This article also reviews the Report of the Royal Commission.

[69] Cd. 2825, 1906.

[70] London *Times,* Sept. 8, 1903, p. 5.

[71] *Report of the Trade Union Congress,* Leeds, 1904, pp. 55-56.

place of politics in the Labour movement, and the necessary attitude of the organized workmen to the direct representation of Labour in Parliament.[72] The Taff Vale judgment had thrown wide open the flood gates of recrimination, on both sides, and from 1901 to the general election in January, 1906,[73] it was the centre around which the political forces of the time played. When the new Government came in, one of their first duties was to settle definitely the status of the trade unions.

(a) *Trade Union and Trade Disputes Act, 1906, and the Trade Union Act, 1913*

The Prime Minister (Sir Henry Campbell-Bannerman) in his Albert Hall address, December 21, 1905, stated the attitude of the new Government on the law of combination:

"It has been gravely affected by a series of judicial decisions," he said, "and it will be our desire with the least possible delay so to amend it as to give freedom and security to the trade unions in the pursuit of their legitimate ends." [74]

This promise was fulfilled when on March 28, 1906, the Attorney-General, Sir John Walton, introduced the Government Bill.[75] Under legal decisions, he held, a construction had been put upon the law of conspiracy, so loose and so wide that it was now impossible to tell beforehand what was the legal quality of action which a trade union might take; the right of peaceful persuasion had been seriously impaired, and provident funds had been made liable for claims founded on the acts of unauthorized officials. All this had created a feeling of insecurity and injustice and the Government had received a mandate to redress the grievance.

[72] Cf. A. W. Humphrey, *op. cit.*, chap. X, pp. 142-163; also Geoffrey Drage, *Trade Unionism* (1905), for an opposing point of view. French comments can be seen in M. Morin, *La situation juridique des Trade Unions en Angleterre* (Caen, 1907), and M. Barrault, *Le droit d'association en Angleterre* (1908).

[73] Cf. Webbs' *Trade Unionism,* chap. X, pp. 594-676, for the views of these writers on the period from 1890-1920, including of course, the Taff Vale judgment.

[74] The London *Times,* December 22, 1905, p. 7.

[75] Hansard, 4 S. H. C., 1906, Vol. 154, pp. 1295-1311, speech of the Attorney-General; pp. 1295-1352, entire debate on the first reading.

He claimed that the Bill was an honest attempt to do justice to trade unions without inflicting injustice upon the community at large and that it accorded with the mandate that the Government had received at the election. The Government Bill met with the opposition of Conservatives [76] because it set up a "class privilege" for trade unions, while Labour members declared that the Government Bill could not be accepted.[77] On second reading [78] of the Government Bill the leader of the Opposition, Mr. Balfour, attacked the Government for its surrender to Labour on the Trade Disputes Bill.[79] The Government was accused of following the dictates of Labour.[80] The second reading of the Government Bill was agreed to, and along with the Labour Party Bill[81] went before the Committee. When the Labour Party Trade Disputes Bill was being debated on the second reading, the Labour leader, Mr. Hardie, had hoped "that as the Government was pledged to the country to deal with this question they would deal with it in such a way as to remove it forever from the field of politics." [82] This point of view was expressed in the debate on the Government Bill, when a Labour member, Mr. Shackleton, declared that the problem was one that was outside of party politics and should so be treated.[83] It was from the Conservative members that chief opposition to the Hudson Bill came, both in the Committee stage and the first and second readings.[84]

The Government, in the Bill brought forward by the Attorney-General, proposed to limit the liability of trade union funds for damages to cases where the act complained of was that of the executive committee of a trade union or of its authorized agent acting in accordance with its express or implied orders, or, at

[76] Hansard, *ibid.*, pp. 1320-1328 (Sir Edward Carson); pp. 1331-1335 (Lord Robert Cecil).

[77] Hansard, *ibid.*, pp. 1328-1331, Brace; Bell, pp. 1335-1342.

[78] Hansard, 4 S. H. C., 1906, Vol. 155, pp. 1482-1496 (Sir W. Robson, Solicitor-General).

[79] Hansard, *ibid.*, pp. 1524-1536.

[80] Hansard, *ibid.*, pp. 1496-1502 (Bowles).

[81] House Bill No. 5, 1906. Reached Committee stage and withdrawn.

[82] Hansard, *ibid.*, p. 51; pp. 47-51, entire.

[83] Hansard, 4 S. H. C., 1906, Vol. 154, pp. 1311-1316.

[84] Hansard, 4 S. H. C., 1906, Vol. 155, pp. 21-83, debate on Hudson Bill; especially F. E. Smith, pp. 28-33.

least, not contravening them. The Hudson Bill would prevent trade unions being sued or their funds becoming liable for damages resulting to employers from any act of any member of the trade union. It was because the Government Bill was unsatisfactory on this point that the Labour Party pressed forward their own Bill, which was read a second time on March 30, the Government themselves voting for it. The Prime Minister, after declaring that trade unions were beneficial institutions, said he had voted two or three times previously for Bills on the lines of the Hudson Bill, and he proposed to vote for the second reading of the Bill.[85] The Prime Minister held that the difference between the Labour members' Bill and the Government Bill was one of method rather than of principle. For that reason he asked the House to pass the second reading of the Bill, and details could be arranged in Committee. The second reading passed by a vote of 416 to 66.

The strength of the Labour Party for their Bill can be seen from the vote on the clause upon which the trade unionists put the whole emphasis.[86] It is this clause which protects from liability for any tort or wrong by or on behalf of the trade union. It is section four of the Trade Disputes Act, 1906.[87]

An action against a trade union, whether of workmen or masters, or against any members thereof on behalf of themselves and all other members of the trade union for the recovery of damages in respect of any tortious act alleged to have been committed by or on behalf of the trade union, shall not be entertained by any Court; provided, that nothing in this section shall affect the liability of the trustees of such unions to be sued in the events provided for by the Trade Union Act, 1871, section 9.[88]

[85] Hansard, 4 S. H. C., 1906, Vol. 155, pp. 51-54.

[86] The appointment of a Select Committee in Housing in 1906 was the first occasion of Labour claiming a distinct right for representatives on such committees. The Government announced that "the Labour Party were entitled to have one twenty-third of the representatives on these Committees, and yet, out of seventeen Committees which had been appointed, they were represented on no fewer than thirteen" (Hansard, 4 S. H. C., 1906, Vol. 156, p. 1282 (Whitley); pp. 1383-1384 (Crooks). By a vote of 320-43 the Labour claim for a member on the specific Committee was rejected.

[87] 6 Edw. 7. c. 47.

[88] Trade Disputes Act, 1906, sec. 4, subsec. 1.

This was carried by a vote of 259 to 29 in Committee stage:[89]

The Act confers a privilege quite foreign to the fundamental principles of the Common Law, contrary to the report of the royal commission appointed to inquire into the subject, which was unanimous on this point, and contrary to the original intention of the Government. Yet in deference to the strong electoral pressure of the trade unions it was accepted by the Liberal cabinet, and passed by the Conservative House of Lords without a division, except on subsidiary amendments relating to picketing and to interests in land.[90]

It was the reversal of the Taff Vale judgment that the Labour Party wanted, and opinion upon this statute will continue to be widely different, according to the place given in industry to trade unions and the powers they are expected to exercise, with or without special privileges.[91]

The Trade Union Act, 1913,[92] was Parliamentary intervention to meet the situation created by the Osborne judgment, which decided that the Amalgamated Society of Railway Servants, a registered trade union, could not lawfully collect levies from its members for the formation of a parliamentary fund, and apply such fund for political purposes, even if a rule of the union authorizing this had been duly made in accordance with the constitution of the society.[93] When the Osborne judgment was given there were 1,153 trade unions registered at the Board of

[89] Hansard, 4 S. H. C., 1906, Vol. 162, pp. 120-204, pp. 1607-1785, for Committee consideration July 26th and August 3rd; Hansard, Vol. 163, pp. 1349-1440, pp. 1452-1520, for consideration as amended (House Bill No. 342) on Nov. 1st and 2nd; Hansard, Vol. 164, pp. 145-236, pp. 856-916, for further consideration Nov. 5th, and third reading and passing, without division, on Nov. 9th. Note especially concluding speech of Sir John Walton, Attorney-General, pp. 912-915, and Mr. Balfour, pp. 906-911. For progress in House of Lords, all stages, Hansard, Vol. 167, pp. 272-320, 810-820, 1465-67.

[90] Lowell, *op. cit.*, Vol. II, pp. 534-5.

[91] See Webbs' *Trade Unionism*, pp. 604-8; Dicey, *op. cit.*, pp. xliv-xlviii.

[92] 2 & 3 Geo. V. c. 30.

[93] See the full and clear article of the late Professor W. M. Geldart, "The Present Law of Trade Disputes and Trade Unions," *Political Quarterly*, No. 2, May, 1914, pp. 17-61, for a friendly, yet critical estimate of the changes in the law and the principles of judicial decisions. The Acts of 1906 and 1913 are analyzed at length.

Trade, with a membership of 2,350,000. Shortly after the decision a resolution [94] was moved in the House of Commons:

That, in the opinion of this House, the right to send representatives to Parliament and to municipal administrative bodies, and to make financial provision for their election and maintenance, enjoyed by trade unions for over forty years, and taken from them by the decision in the case of Osborne v. Amalgamated Society of Railway Servants, should be restored.

A Bill was introduced in that session, being withdrawn, but the Government introduced in 1911 their Bill,[95] which finally became the Act of 1913, providing that a trade union shall have power to apply its funds, without restriction, for any lawful objects or purposes (other than political objects) for the time being authorized under its constitution.[96]

(b) *Parliament, the Labour Party, and Trade Union Action*

The Acts of 1906 and 1913 represent the development of the purposes of trade union action, and in this study interpret well

[94] Parl. Deb. 5 S. H. C., 1910, Vol. 16, p. 1321; moved by J. W. Taylor, pp. 1321-1325. See speeches of Attorney-General, pp. 1349-1359 (Robson); Vivian, pp. 1337-1346; Pringle, pp. 1328-1334; and Shackleton, pp. 1356-1362.

[95] Parl. Deb. 5 S. H. C., 1911, Vol. 26, pp. 916-1026, second reading debate on Government Bill, which passed by 219 votes to 18. See speeches of Sir Rufus Isaacs, Attorney-General, the mover, pp. 916-931; MacDonald, pp. 942-952; the Secretary of the Home Department, pp. 1013-1024 (Churchill). On March 6, 1912, Mr. Claude Lowther asked the Prime Minister, "whether he would consider the introduction of legislation designed to substitute in trade unions the secret for the open ballot on questions vitally affecting the interests of the whole nation? and he further asked if he were aware that the opinions of members of trade unions are very often gotten by bullying and intimidation? Is it not the desire of the Government to obtain the opinion of the men themselves, and not that of syndicalist Socialists?" (Parl. Deb. H. C. 5 S., Vol. 35, 1912, pp. 374-375.) Mr. Asquith replied: "I am sorry the hon. gentleman should have used language of that kind. I think the methods adopted for the purpose of ascertaining the opinions of trade unions are a matter of internal regulation, and I have every confidence in the good sense and good faith of my fellow countrymen to whatever class they belong." (*Op. cit.*, p. 375.) See answer to similar question a week later, *op. cit.*, p. 1096.

[96] Act of 1913, Sect. 2. Procedure was given (Sect. 3) on the formation of a fund for certain political purposes.

the expansion of the political Labour movement.[97] How unsatisfactory was payment by trade unions to members of Parliament was plainly put by the leader of the Labour party during the Budget debate of 1911. He declared it was

an exceedingly bad thing for trade unions to provide income for the maintenance of members of Parliament. We are not trade union servants here in this House. Members of the Labour party ought to be national servants.[98]

The contrary was intimated by Mr. F. E. Smith who quoted Mr. J. Keir Hardie, when he said, "Labour representation means more than sending a member to the House of Commons. It is a means to an end, and that end is not trade unionism, but socialism." [99] This same point of view was in the resolution of the Miners' Federation at the Lambeth Congress of 1913, which asked

That the Labour Party Conference direct its attention more to urgent political questions, with a view to having adequate discussion thereon, and allow the Trade Union Congress to deal with industrial questions and all other matters affecting the Trade Unions not of a political nature.[100]

Such an attitude has been taken to represent a British compromise between social democracy and syndicalism, and Mr. Beer believes that "the Trade Unions Congress since 1915 onwards have taken up the question of control in the sense of a forward move of Labour toward a higher conception of social justice." [101] The president of the 1913 Trade Union Congress, W. J. Davis, who

[97] See *Report of the 10th Annual Conference of the Labour Party*, Newport, 1910, Appendix I, pp. 101-110, for Report of the Special Conference on the House of Lords Decision on Labour Representation. See also the Parliamentary Committee Report of the Trade Union Congress on the Trade Unions (No. 2) Bill, pp. 149-150, *Report of the 46th Trade Union Congress*, Manchester, 1913.

[98] Parl. Deb. H. C. 5 S., Vol. 25, 1911, p. 1887, pp. 1883-1888, entire (MacDonald).

[99] Parl. Deb. H. C. 5 S., Vol. 26, 1911, p. 938, pp. 931-942, entire.

[100] See *Report of the 14th Annual Conference of the Labour Party*, Glasgow, 1914 (January), p. 18.

[101] Beer, *op. cit.*, Vol. II, p. 376.

is also the historian of the Trade Union Congress, having written its history in two volumes, could say that although the Congress was the mother of the great Labour movement, the Labour party was, and should be mainly political. The political force of Labour was its greatest force.[102] The progress of Labour, Mr. J. R. Clynes said at the same Congress, was to be judged by the greatly improved outlook and higher standard of understanding which possessed the working classes, showing by the wisdom of their decisions and the calmness of their judgment, that Labour can be trusted with the destinies of the nation.[103]

The subjects of bills and motions as agreed upon at the opening of the Parliamentary Session in 1914 by the Labour party indicate the wide scope of Party action on industrial politics. Up until 1914 at the opening of each session it was the practice of the Parliamentary Labour Party to review the various resolutions of the Labour Party Conferences, which were accepted as general guidance upon Parliamentary matters. The National Executive of the Party sat with the Parliamentary Party in joint meeting at the opening of each Session for the purpose of compiling a list of Party bills and subjects for motions. Members agreed if successful in the ballot for bills to put forward the Party bills in the order or priority decided upon by the Joint Committee, but members were free to select the subject of any motion on the Party list that they preferred. The list of bills in the 1914 Parliamentary Session follows:

Prevention of Unemployment.
Education (Administrative Provisions).
Representation of the People.
Education (Provision of Meals) Amendment.
Nationalization of Mines.
Agricultural Labourers (Wages and Hours).
Agricultural Labourers (Scotland) Half-Holiday.
Prevention and Cure of Sickness and Destitution.
Provision for Minimum Wages and Maximum Hours of Labour.
Minister of Labour.
Prevention of Sickness and Destitution amongst Children.

[102] *Report of the 46th Trade Union Congress 1913,* Manchester, p. 56, pp. 55-61, entire.
[103] *Ibid.*, pp. 52-53.

Old Age Pensions (Amendment).
Compulsory Weighing.
Railway (Eight Hours).
Local Authorities (Enabling).
Abolition of Fines.
Saturday to Monday Stop.
State Aid for the Blind.
Abolition of Artificial Humidity.
48-Hour Week in Cotton Trade.
Enginemen's Certificate.
Factory and Workshop (Underground).
Hairdressers' Sunday Closing (Wales).

It is not remarkable that the Labour Party won many men and women who believed that at last in Parliament the needs of the people could be discussed. The Labour party came at a time when the industrial workers' movement could give it power, and the program of the party reflects in a direct way the influence of the highly organized trade union world of Great Britain. To the list of bills consider the list of Subjects for Motions, and together compare these with the program at the beginning of the century. One can thus gain a fair idea of the growth of the industrial and political labour movement of England. The list follows:

General 30s Minimum Wage.
Eviction of Workmen During Trade Disputes.
Atmosphere and Dust in Textile Factories.
System of Fines in Textile and other Trades.
Inclusion of Clerks in Factory Acts.
Eight-hour Day.
Truck.
Hours in Bakehouses.
Maladministration of Fair Wages Clause.
Factory Inspection.
Poor Law Reform.
Railway and Mining Accidents.
Labour Exchanges Administration.
Extension of Particulars Clause to Docks, etc.
Workmen's Compensation Act Amendment.
Railway and Canal Nationalization.
Nationalization of Hospitals.

National Factory for Municipal Clothing.
Land Nationalization.
Socialism.
House of Commons Procedure.
Day Training Classes.
School Clinics.
Commission of Inquiry into Older Universities.
Inquiry into Industrial Assurance.
Payment of Jurors.
Militarism.
Abolition of the Right of Capture of Private Property at Sea.

The British Labour Party, like the French Socialists, have always recognized the value of debates in the House of Commons as good publicity for the party. With increasing Parliamentary influence their contribution to the cause of good government has been substantial. Of the 29 members returned by the Labour party in 1906, under the auspices of the Labour Representation Committee, only four had had any previous Parliamentary experience. This was a handicap in a body skilled in legislative discipline, but Party procedure was immediately put upon a regular business basis.[104] Prior to the outbreak of the war in 1914 the Party had special Committees on the following subjects: Foreign Affairs, Electoral Reform, Unemployment, Party Policy, Municipal Affairs, Workmen's Compensation, Railway and Transit, Government Workers' Conditions, Finance, Education, and Truck.

When war came in 1914 Labour was called upon to take a responsible part in carrying on the Government and in prosecuting the work of winning against a common foe. For a time the immediate problems of work and wages and industrial organization were forgotten, but very soon in England men began to think of what the world would be like when peace came. They set forth aims, elaborated principles of reconstruction, and it is well to briefly note the political and industrial labour movement since 1918, which is done in a succeeding chapter.

[104] See *The Labour Year Book,* 1916, p. 318-319.

Part III

Industrial Unrest

The period in England from 1910-1914 has definitely come to be considered years of industrial unrest. The political activity of the trade unions from 1899 to 1910 had kept constantly before the country the major problems of industrial conflict, and the way out of the social struggle as conceived by Labour. The political labour movement could not limit the rapid expansion of the industrial movement which not only had a strong economic argument for revolutionary action in the position of the wage earner, due to the phenomena of falling prices and almost stationary wages, but there was the added strength of an intellectual revival going on in the Labour movement. There were the combined forces of the effort to reorganize the economic structure of trade unionism and to interpret the expanding consciousness of the working class by a new economic theory.

The Seamen's and Dockers' Strikes of 1911 began the definite expression of the new movement, followed by the National Railway Strike of the same year. In 1912 was the National Miners' Strike; in 1913 the Dublin strike; and in 1914 the London Building Dispute. Direct effect on the structure of trade unionism was seen in the formation of the National Union of Railwaymen in 1912-1913, "on an industrial basis, which made it to some extent the twentieth century 'new model' of Trade Union structure." [105] Then followed the Triple Industrial Alliance proposed at a conference of the Miners' Federation of Great Britain, the National Union of Railwaymen, and the National Transport Workers' Federation, held on April 23, 1914. The idea of such a conference was first brought into prominence at the Miners' Annual Conference in 1913, when a resolution was passed

That the Executive Committee of the Miners' Federation be requested to approach the Executive Committee of other big Trade Unions with a view to co-operative action and the support of each other's demands.[106]

[105] Cf. G. D. H. Cole, *The British Labour Movement* (3rd ed. 1924), p. 17.

[106] Robert Smillie, "The Triple Industrial Alliance," *The Labour Year Book 1916,* p. 103.

Action was to be confined, the president of the Miners' Federation wrote, to joint national action. Sympathetic action was no longer to be left to the uncontrolled emotions of a strike period, but it was to be the calculated result of mature consideration and careful planning. The predominant idea of the alliance was that each of these great fighting organizations, before embarking upon any big movement, either defensive or aggressive, should formulate its program, submit it to the others, and that upon joint proposals joint action should then be taken.[107] Mr. Smillie considered the Triple Industrial Alliance "one definite concrete result of the industrial unrest," made necessary by the progress of industrial development which forced capital to attack Trade Unionism and defend itself against Trade Union advance. That this attack would further the amalgamation of Trade Unions and Federations, leading to the further extension of the principle of common defence was seen by the leaders of the Triple Alliance. While the scheme at the moment was not intended to include more than the three trades referred to,[108] there was the belief that

> it may well be found advisable later on to extend the scope of the alliance in the general interests of Labour as a whole. Even now, indeed, it has already been discussed whether the Triple Alliance might not be in a position to assist our fellow workers in the textile industry if, at an adverse moment, they were threatened with a lock-out. Under such circumstances there is every probability that a stoppage of production would cause an immediate settlement. In every case the results of joint action on a large scale should be rapid and decisive, and all the suffering and loss inseparable from trade troubles of the past could be prevented in the future.[109]

The growth of the amalgamation movement in the Trade Union world was part of the unusual extension of the influence of organized Labour by an enormous increase in membership in the first years of the century. In 1899 there were 1,310 separate

[107] *Ibid.*, p. 104.

[108] The membership of the three bodies was considerable, the miners numbering 800,000, the railwaymen 270,000, and the transport workers 250,000. The miners considered that the two industries most comparable with their own were the railwaymen and the transport.

[109] Smillie, *op. cit.*, p. 104.

Trade Unions in the United Kingdom, with a total membership of 1,860,913; in 1910 there were 1,195 Trade Unions with a membership of 2,446,342. By 1914 the number of separate Trade Unions had decreased to 1,123, but having a membership of 3,959,863, which was an increase of 105.3 per cent compared with 1905. The growth of Trade Union membership was due in great measure to the industrial revival from 1910 onwards, which was characterized by the disputes which involved all of the United Kingdom, English, Welsh and Scottish miners, English railwaymen and Irish transport workers. It was due also "to the growing feeling among the workers that only by industrial organization can organized capital be combated."[110] In a group of special trades the Insurance Act was a factor in the increase, combined with the fact that the Trade Union Congress was giving more attention to the organization of the unskilled worker. It was the unusual growth of Trade Unionism[111] and the extension of the benefits of organization to include many millions more of workers and their dependents in the United Kingdom that gave to Labour politics the necessity of bringing before Parliament the question of Industrial Unrest.

The Government in 1910 was compelled to give most of its attention to the controversy between the Commons and the Lords, while the death of King Edward VII was the occasion of a general truce. But the Government had foreshadowed a comprehensive program of reform in their legislative measures, and the Ministerial declarations embodied an acknowledgment of the principles

[110] *The Labour Year Book 1916*, p. 105.

[111] *The Labour Year Book 1916*, p. 105, gives the statistics for 1910-1914:

Year	*No. at end of year*	*Membership*	*Per cent. increase (+), decrease (—)*
1910	1,195	2,446,342	+ 3.3
1911	1,204	3,018,903	+ 23.4
1912	1,149	3,287,884	+ 8.9
1913	1,135	3,987,115	+ 21.5
1914	1,123	3,959,863	— 0.7

See also for a comparison of French and English and German Trade Union membership the *Third and Fourth Abstract of Foreign Labour Statistics by the Board of Trade* (1906 and 1911), pp. xx and xxxv respectively.

of reform which had been fought for in measures which had been introduced or supported by the Government. At that time the Labour Party wanted nothing better than to debate all questions on the floor of the House of Commons. The Government was constantly aware that every important debate on social questions or industrial peace would be a review of their record from 1906.[112] It was also face to face with the problem of Trade Unionism in all of English industry and the measures of control that were made inevitable by the social reform legislation of the Government. There was a considerable change of attitude about several Government measures between 1909 and July 23, 1912, when Mr. Lloyd George spoke on the Port of London Authority Dispute. The Government was in somewhat of the same position as the Trade Union Congress and the Labour Party: the swiftly moving forces of industrial progress, the economic development of the nation, swept aside nicely laid plans and Ministerial programs. The economic movement was larger than the conception of the Trade Union Congress and the political consequences could not be adequately handled by the Government, nor was the Labour party any closer to an understanding of the unrest and revolt.

There was no conflict between the Trade Union Congress and the social program of the Government. At the Ipswich Trade Union Congress in 1909 there was special consideration of the Labour Exchanges Act [113] and the National Scheme of Unemployed Benefit,[114] and a careful reading of the Report of the Congress is convincing proof that there was no Trade Union opposition on the basic principle of the proposed social reforms which the Government had put forward.[115] There was some fear that the power and place of the Trade Unions would be injured by the remedial measures of the Government, but this feeling was not shared by the members of the Parliamentary Committee or by those Trade Union leaders who saw that the Trade Unions

[112] See *Report of the Parliamentary Committee to the Trade Union Congress*, 1913, pp. 77-170, of the Congress Report; also *Report of the Executive to the 14th Annual Conference of the Labour Party*, 1914, pp. 3-32.

[113] The *Report of the Trade Union Congress*, 1909, pp. 57-59.

[114] *Op. cit.*, pp. 55-56.

[115] The Parliamentary Report at this Congress is most interesting, covering in detail the chief questions before the Congress and Parliament of 1909; see pp. 53-106.

would more than likely have the influence of a larger share in the administration of social and industrial schemes. The period was as full of incessant turmoil and perturbation for the Labour party and Trade Unionism as for the Government, all were nonplussed by the series of economic crises that made this period a definite background in the struggle "between State Socialism and Revolutionary Trade Unionism." [116] There had to be a revision of the method of the Trade Union leaders as well as for the party in power which seemed to have reached the period in which its evolution had most fully expressed itself in a "Neo-Liberalism" or "Socialism of the State." [117]

Parliamentary debates in 1911 on labour disputes clearly revealed that all parties within the State were equally at a loss to offer a satisfactory means of adjustment, though the Labour leader could denounce the Home Secretary because he had not given in a debate "one single idea regarding the reasons why there is industrial unrest." [118] For their part, he said, they had succeeded in converting the nation at least to the great truth of individual and national prosperity, that unless a man can possess enough at the end of the week to give his individuality free play, then you can talk about your constitutional liberties as much as you like, that man cannot possibly fulfil his duties as a citizen and his responsibilities as an individual.[119] The employment of the military in Labour disputes,[120] had stirred the deepest hatred,

[116] Cf. M. Beer, Vol. ii, p. 363.

[117] Cf. Edouard Guyot, *Le Socialisme et l'Evolution de l'Angleterre Contemporaine,* 1880-1911 (1913), pp. 241-315; Chap. V, "Le Socialisme d'Etat et l'Evolution du Parti Liberal"; also Jacques Bardoux, *L'Angleterre Radicale (1905-1913), Essai de Psychologie Sociale* (1913); and André Siegfried, *L'Angleterre d'Aujourd'hui, Son Evolution Économique et Politique* (5th ed. 1924).

[118] Parl. Deb. 5 S. H. C., 1911, Vol. 29, pp. 1948-1949, pp. 1948-1959 entire; pp. 1943-1991, debate entire on August 16, during debate on Appropriation Bill; for August 17, 18, pp. 2193-2204, 2247-2250.

[119] Parl. Deb. 5 S. H. C., 1911, Vol. 29, p. 2293; debate entire, August 22, on employment of military, pp. 2282-2378. See speeches of Prime Minister (pp. 2291-2293); A. Chamberlain (pp. 2299-2301); J. H. Thomas (pp. 2301-2304); Barnes (pp. 2315-2321); Chiozza Money (pp. 2304-2309); Hardie (2333-2341); Lloyd George (pp. 2345-2354).

[120] The tactics of Mr. Churchill were compared with those of M. Briand, who made, said Captain Wedgewood, "an exactly similar speech justifying the use of the military in order to maintain the supplies of food at the time of the great strike in France a year ago." (*Op. cit.,* pp. 2341-2345.)

though the Home Secretary, Mr. Churchill, stated that he did not know "whether in the history of the world a similar catastrophe [referring to the railway strike of 1911] can be shown to have menaced an equally great community." [121] Mr. MacDonald declared that

the Department which has played the most diabolical part in all this unrest is the Home Department. This is not a medieval State, and it is not Russia. It is not even Germany. We have discovered a secret which few countries have heretofore discovered. The secret this nation has discovered is that the way to maintain law and order is to trust the ordinary operations of a law-abiding and orderly-inclined public.[122]

The Labour party in November, 1911, offered a resolution declaring that the refusal of the railway companies to carry out the Railway Conciliation Agreement of 1907 had no justification, and asked the Government for the "public interest" to bring both sides into a conference.[123] The unrest which flourished in July and August, Mr. MacDonald said in November, had a characteristic which was far more than that of a mere passing agitation. It had the characteristic of a fundamental upstirring, of fundamental discontent with everything in general, which could only let itself go in ways which were familiar with the public. All classes, rich and poor together, the capitalist class and the labouring class in those extraordinary months were seized with a sort of revolutionary spirit.[124]

This phase of the industrial unrest was suggested forcibly by Dr. Gore, Bishop of Birmingham, in a farewell diocesan letter on his transfer to the bishopric of Oxford. It was written during the railway and dockers' strike, 1911:

"There is," he said, "a profound sense of unrest and dissatisfaction among workers recently. I cannot but believe that this pro-

[121] *Op. cit.*, p. 2327, pp. 2323-2333 entire.
[122] *Op. cit.*, pp. 2296-2298.
[123] Parl. Deb. 5 S. H. C., 1911, Vol. 31, pp. 1209-1329, debate entire, November 22, on railway companies and their employees. See speeches of Prime Minister (pp. 1229-1233); Bonar Law (pp. 1233-1237); J. H. Thomas (pp. 1238-1245).
[124] *Ibid.*, p. 1211, pp. 1209-1223 entire.

found discontent is justified, though some particular exhibitions of it are not. As Christians we are not justified in tolerating the conditions of life and labour under which the great mass of our population is living. We have no right to say that these conditions are not remediable. Preventible lack of equipment for life among the young, and later the insecurity of employment and inadequacy of remuneration and consequent destitution and semi-destitution among so many people, ought to inspire in all Christians a determination to reform our industrial system."[125]

The Labour party amendment[126] on Industrial Unrest in the 1912 Parliament provided a full opportunity for a debate on the state of England question and the reform of the industrial system. The leader of the Labour party declared that there were 2,000,000 families in the nation with an income of only £45 per annum. Between 1901-1911, according to the Board of Trade returns, there was a drop of £57,500 in wages. In 1910, in the transport trade, as classified by the Board of Trade, wages were increased by the sum of £341 per week in the gross, and 3,900 were affected. In 1911, owing to strikes, that £341 per week increase became £12,270 per week, and the number of people affected rose from 3,900 to 77,000.

"You cannot shut your eyes," he said, "to the moral to be drawn from that state of things. As a matter of fact, it is because those

[125] Quoted by S. P. Orth, *Socialism and Democracy in Europe* (1913), pp. 221-222. Cf. J. W. Scott, *Syndicalism and Philosophical Realism* (1919); G. D. H. Cole, *The World of Labour* (1913), and the allied books of this writer and the Guild Socialists; Bertrand Russell, *Principles of Social Reconstruction* (1916), and *Roads to Freedom: Socialism, Anarchism and Syndicalism* (1st ed. 1918, 3rd ed. 1920), esp. chap. VIII. Mr. Scott wrote of British workmen's unrest 1910-1919, that they were "seeking something vaguer and vaster, something, they knew not what, something, as far as could be judged from their spokesmen, suggestive of fundamental alteration of the whole condition of labour, if not the abolition of the industrial system altogether." (P. 12, *op. cit.*)

[126] Parl. Deb. 5 S. H. C., 1912, Vol. 34, pp. 44-98, debate entire on Labour Amendment (p. 45). The Amendment regretted, "That, having regard to the existing industrial unrest arising from a deplorable insufficiency of wages, which has persisted notwithstanding a great expansion of national wealth, and a considerable increase in the cost of living, your Majesty's Government's speech contains no specific mention of legislation securing a minimum living wage and for preventing a continuance of such unequal division of the fruits of industry by the nationalization of railways, mines and monopolies."

men are demanding to see something better and are beginning to appreciate that width of life we all like—that enormous and unfulfilled possibility of the human mind acting in a state of freedom—that you are hearing now not the calm counsels of men who can sit and hold on, but the hasty, angry, enraged counsels of men who have got nothing to hold on to."

There was a strange lack of confidence about in everything that was reasonable. If workmen were asked to submit their case to conciliation and arbitration, they said, "We have been cheated so often we will not do it again." Mr. MacDonald said that in 1906, and before his colleagues and himself went all over the country saying "a strike is an antiquated weapon which involves suffering and pain and trouble, and in the end the side that is right does not win. Trust the House of Commons. Build up a political party." They did; they adopted conciliation. As a matter of fact, between the years when they were telling them to build up the party and the delivery of the Osborne judgment conciliation was tried as it never was before. They did more by that propaganda, it was claimed, than anything that was ever done before to persuade the workman to put his case in writing, lay it on a table, to argue it out in reason, and that he was going to get more by that method than any other he might adopt. But no sooner was the worker persuaded that peaceful methods were right than conciliation was smashed by the railway directors, and Parliamentary methods were smashed by lawyers that might or might not have been good law, but was exceedingly bad common sense and exceedingly bad and false history. As a matter of fact it was the red-tape of the lawyers that stood side by side with the red-flag of the syndicalist—the two things were absolutely the same. The type of mind that gave that decision, and that regarded that type of labour combination from the merely static and legal point of view was what had whistled up the very worst elements inside the labour movement; and so long as that judgment remained so long would the unrest and lack of confidence in civil and peaceful methods remain in the minds of the very best men in the trade union movement.

Despite any condemnation of the Labour chieftains social progress was inevitably joined with legislation. The national minimum wage was, along with trade union status, a patent illustration. Industry could only be carried on if the living minimum wage was made the first charge on an industry.

Legislation has to come; it has to embody the moral requirements which nobody can resist, and the time has come when we ought to translate these abstract moral propositions into effective Acts of Parliament. Labour unrest must be dealt with by this House. This House cannot afford to shut its eyes to it; and, if it tried, it would not be allowed to do so. Both outside and inside, this House will hear voices explaining and explaining what labour unrest means, asking for legislation, asking for administrative interference, the intention of which will be to do justice to men who are not economically strong enough to see justice is done to themselves. And that must be the intention of this House more and more. We cannot possibly allow capital and labour simply to fight out their own battles, we, standing on one side, looking on. There are three sides to every dispute; there is the side of capital, and there is the side of labour, there is the side of the general community; and the general community has no business to allow capital and labour, fighting their battles themselves, to elbow them out of consideration. This House and its officers, this Government and its administration must represent the third party, the general public.[127]

The Chancellor of the Exchequer's Birmingham speech was quoted by a Labour member.[128] Mr. Lloyd George had said that the protection of property in England was the most perfect machine ever devised by the human brain. The guardians of property patrolled every street, and if the transgressor eluded them their vigilance pursued him to the end of the earth. But compare that with the way in which the Public Health Acts and the Housing Acts were administered, asked Mr. Lloyd George. Public Health Acts the country had had for years and years, now Housing Acts on the Statute Book, and yet there was no city or town, nay not a village, but you had the reek of insanitary property.[129] Labour seemed to be content in this debate to quote from contemporary sources, and Mr. Lansbury read into the record the Lambeth Resolution of the whole College of Bishops, "That

[127] *Op. cit.*, pp. 51-52 (MacDonald).
[128] *Op. cit.*, pp. 54-56 (Clynes). [129] *Op. cit.*, p. 60.

the labourer, the workman and his wife and children, should and ought to be, from every point of Christianity and national morals, the first charge upon industry."[130] He asked the House to remember when it talked of Syndicalism, that if it refused to deal with the wrongs of the people, if ever it was powerless to deal with them, there was nothing for the people to do but to attend to the matter outside that House. For his part, while the House refused to deal with the social problem, he was going to join with all men outside who would join with him in doing what was possible to stir up and foment revolt against revolting conditions. He was going to do all he could to make the poor hate poverty, to make them hate their poverty—never mind about hating their social conditions. He did not want them to hate the rich, but to hate the idea that they and their children should live under untoward conditions. Soon after Mr. Lansbury's appeal his indictment found a response in the statement of Lord Hugh Cecil that he thought

it is true that the great sufferings and sorrows of which we are hearing so much are the fruit of the industrial system. I think it is also true that the competitive system depends upon a side of human nature which is fundamentally unchristian, and appeals to and is animated by those motives of self-interest, which are essentially inconsistent with the profession of Christianity.[131]

But profit-sharing, upon which Lord Hugh Cecil placed emphasis, was no part of the concern of syndicalism. This was evident in the debate on March 27, 1912, when a resolution was offered

That in the opinion of this House, the growth and advocacy by certain Labour agitators of an anti-social policy of Syndicalism based upon class warfare and incitement to mutiny constitute a grave danger to the State and the welfare of the community.[132]

The mover, Mr. Ormsby-Gore, referring to France as the natural home of syndicalism, believed that one of the reasons for the growth of syndicalism was the failure of the Parliamentary Labour parties of France and England to carry out their lavish promises.

[130] *Op. cit.*, pp. 80-89.
[131] *Op. cit.*, pp. 107-108, pp. 107-113 entire.
[132] Parl. Deb. 5 S. H. C., 1912, Vol. 36, p. 537; pp. 535-559 debate entire.

The Government, through the Chancellor of the Duchy of Lancaster, Mr. Hobhouse, declared [133] that Syndicalism did not create unrest in England. It was due to two reasons. First, looking back over a series of years there had been a much greater rise in the cost of living than in wages, and on the other hand, on the intellectual side, there was an increased *mental sense* of the poverty among the working classes in the country, as compared with those more fortunate than they are, which had not been accompanied by any corresponding advancement in their material welfare. Those were the two reasons if Syndicalism, or anything approaching it, had obtained a foothold in England. The Labour spokesman,[134] considering the condition of the time an inevitable form of capitalistic development, yet declared he was not a believer in the class war, nor had he sympathy with Syndicalism. If the nation were to be rid of the enemy, as Syndicalism had been called, the causes would have to be removed. The causes were poverty, low wages, and those incidental miseries which affect the working classes. The Labour party, he said, were prepared to associate themselves with any party or any section of any party who were genuinely desirous of removing the causes that brought those things about, and that curse which fell upon the working classes because of no inherent evil on their part, but because of conditions over which they had no control—the curse of undeserved poverty.

Faith that the Government could be used as a means toward understanding the causes of industrial unrest was indicated once again in the resolution [135] on May 8, 1912, in the House of Commons, which declared

That this House is of the opinion that the recent industrial disturbances show the necessity of a thorough and authoritative investigation into the causes of the present industrial unrest, and into possible remedies therefor, and, in view of the prospective recurrence of such disturbances calls upon the Government to prosecute such investigation by all appropriate means and in the speediest manner compatible with adequate inquiry into the issues involved.

[133] *Op. cit.*, pp. 552-555.
[134] *Op. cit.*, pp. 555-559 (Roberts).
[135] Parl. Deb., 5 S. H. C., 1912, Vol. 38, p. 487; pp. 487-534 debate entire.

The mover,[136] a Liberal, Mr. Crawshay-Williams, thought that the situation was serious, but that the unrest was not in itself a bad thing. It was part of a struggle for better conditions on the part of the workers of the country. It was part of a long development which began with the first Factory Act. From being a blind and groping movement it became a conscious and connected effort. Not only had Labour learned its power, but labour had obtained an ethical conviction of its causes. Unrest was part of a deliberate revolt against the untrammelled nature of wealth getting, and this in itself was not bad. It was only the symptoms which were considered bad, and it was remembered that strikes were not the unrest; they were the symptoms of unrest.

It is an idealism; it may be crude idealism; it may be blind idealism; but it is an idealism, and the cruder and blinder it is, the more it needs our guidance and assistance . . . We are in a period of change, and unless we recognise that we are in a period of fundamental change, unless we take the matter in hand to-day, not only we but those who come after us will rue it. The spirit behind this movement is a right spirit, it will prevail. Labour will get, and rightly get, a larger share of this world's goods. Our duty, as the ruling body in this great nation, is to see to it that Labour gets its due without the miseries and calamities of industrial strife.[137]

There was no lack of faith either in the attitude of the veteran Hardie,[138] who declared that Booth and Rowntree had showed facts enough, as Campbell-Bannerman in 1906 stated, and he warned the House and the Government that if any make-believe Committees were set up no single working class organization would appear before them. The working class would give no evidence. They had formulated their demands, and if the House did not satisfy the demands, so much the worse for the House. Syndicalism was the direct outcome of the apathy and indifference of Parliament toward working class questions, and he rejoiced at the growth of Syndicalism. The more Syndicalism outside, the quicker would be the pace that Parliament moved. Parliament never moved except in response to pressure, and the more pressure the more likelihood there would be of real drastic re-

[136] *Op. cit.*, pp. 487-503. [137] *Op. cit.*, p. 503. [138] *Op. cit.*, pp. 513-520.

forms, and the conditions of the workmen improved. Conditions in respect to railway wages were aptly put by Mr. J. H. Thomas, when he said [139] that in ten years there had been an increase of a halfpenny a man.

But at the close of the debate the Government were brought to the issue for their share of the responsibility in the causes of industrial unrest, because of the doctrines which underlay the legislative program of the Government since 1906. Mr. Peto specifically mentioned [140] the Coal Mines (Eight Hours) Act, 1908, the Coal Mines (Minimum Wage) Act, 1912, the Budget of 1909, and the Parliament Act of 1911. The Government [141] through the Chancellor of the Exchequer found one answer in the fact that in their indictment of the present order the Labour leader Hardie and the distinguished Conservative apologist Lord Hugh Cecil [142] were in accord. Great needs had brought men together. The "state of England question" could never more be downed.

In this survey from 1900 can be seen the beginning of a new idea in the Parliamentary activities of Labour organization. This idea is that the State cannot be the instrument of class legislation, but that the basis on which the State intervenes in economic organization is to establish a surer order of justice. The ideal of social justice began slowly to have a place in the work of Governments, its political and economic meaning becoming more clearly defined.

So much emphasis was placed on the Labour side, right of association, hours of labour, minimum wage, enforcement of existing protective measures, the conditions of work for women and children, etc., because for a long time the actual struggle had to be centred there. There had to be laborious building up of laws relating to the primary needs of the workingman. Up until 1900 agitation had largely been centred on the repeal of anti-labour and restrictive legislation; a negative policy of progress, or, at least, a defensive program. The intervention of the State from 1900 became more and more frequent in industrial organization, and the legal protection of workers was extended into all branches of economic activity. It must be noticed, too,

[139] *Op. cit.*, pp. 520-521.
[140] *Op. cit.*, pp. 532-534.
[141] *Op. cit.*, pp. 521-532.
[142] *Op. cit.*, pp. 508-513.

that most of the laws called workers' are equally favourable to employers and to workers. In truth, the laws on Labour have never been voted by the Parliamentary majority, in a hostile spirit to the employer. They have been voted, at the time, with the intention of social justice, and with the purpose of reducing the violence of conflicts in industrial relationships. The intervention of the legislator in the economic organization justifies itself fully by that intention to set right the social order.

CHAPTER VIII

THE ENGLISH LABOUR MOVEMENT AND THE TRADE UNION MOVEMENT, 1914-1925

PART I

The War, Reconstruction, and the Labour Government

A GREAT deal of ridicule has been directed against the workers' and the Socialist organizations of the world for their failure to live up to the high sentiments of brotherhood and peace to which their programs formally committed them. The war should have sufficiently humbled all men (for what creeds of religion and democracy did it not lay low?) that no one would seek mock comfort in cynicism. Mankind was disgraced and degraded. But men and women sacrificed, redeeming much that was brutal, much that seems an intolerable curse on the human spirit. And it is a matter of record in every country that the workers did their duty in the struggle which almost destroyed Europe. In England and France there was heroism which would make peace times noble if directed toward high aims for the common people. The mood is reflected in the programs which the British Labour Party and the Trade Union Congress elaborated. It was not too much to expect a new world. In a letter dated September 11, 1914, Mr. J. Ramsay MacDonald, later to be Prime Minister, well stated that incalculable political and social consequences would follow upon victory; that the quarrel was not of the people, but the end of it would be the lives and liberties of the people.

The British Labour movement has faced since the war the lively issues growing out of the difficult problem of adjusting a political party to new economic conditions.[1] Much credit is

[1] J. Ramsay MacDonald, *A Policy for the Labour Party* (1920); G. D. H. Cole, *Chaos and Order in Industry* (1920) and *Social Theory* (1920); S. G. Hobson, *National Guilds and the State* (1920); R. H. Tawney, *The Sickness of an Acquisitive Society* (1920); the Webbs' Introduction to

due the leaders of the Labour party for the way in which discipline has been achieved, at times in the face of almost overwhelming obstacles. Since 1918 no party in England has had a more united front than Labour, although often the leadership of the Party has been set some difficult internal problems to settle. The opposition press has delighted in the antics of the Labour members, has emphasized the real divergence in point of view of Mr. MacDonald and some prominent men in the Party, especially of the Left Wing, but the Labour forces have held their own in the State. They have increased their poll since 1900 by over five million votes; and from a vote in 1918 of 2,244,945, they reached the total of 5,487,620 in 1924, although they lost 40 seats in the October, 1924, election. The electoral progress of the Labour Party can be readily seen in the summarized history here given:[2] In the General Election, 1924, the total number of votes cast were 16,120,735. Of this number the Conservatives polled 7,385,139; Labour, 5,487,620; Liberals, 2,982,563; and scattering, 265,413. The state of the parties in December, 1924, was: Conservatives, 402 members, Labour 151, Liberal 41, others 9.

After the General Election of 1918, the Labour Party entered a new period of activity and influence. The election of that year was the first test of the popular hold of the party on the people

1920 edition of *Industrial Democracy;* Arthur Gleason, *What the Workers Want. A Study of British Labour* (1920).

[2] This table is taken from the *Labour Year Book 1925,* p. 189. It may be noted that the December, 1910, election was the second election in one year and fewer candidates were run by all parties. A comprehensive account of the history and policy of the Labour party is given in the recent three volume *The Book of the Labour Party* (1925, London), edited by Herbert Tracey; the first volume is history, the second a series of essays setting out its policy, and the third consists of biographical sketches of some 30 of its leaders. Of course the writing is uncritical and is written frankly from the party point of view.

General Election	*Seats Contested*	*Members Returned*	*Labour Vote*
1900	15	2	62,698
1906	50	29	323,195
1910 (January)	78	40	505,690
1910 (December)	56	42	370,802
1918	361	57	2,244,945
1922	414	142	4,236,733
1923	427	191	4,348,379
1924	514	151	5,487,620

since 1910, and the returning of 57 members to the House of Commons, representing a total electoral strength of 2,244,945 votes, gave enthusiasm to the cause of Labour. The Labour Party was the largest opposition group in attendance on Parliament, for the representatives of the Sinn Fein Party, while more numerous, did not attend at Westminster. The Party was not recognized as the official Opposition, as it wanted to be, but the procedure adopted by the Speaker was to grant precedence on all occasions of first-class importance to the Labour Party and to the Independent Liberals alternately.

The Session of 1919 of the new Parliament opened on February 11, and on the Address in answer to the King's Speech, the Labour Party moved an amendment regretting the absence of any mention of definite proposals for dealing with the causes of industrial unrest and for securing, as regards wages and working hours, conditions of labour that would establish a higher standard of life and social well-being for the people. The Labour Party brought forward a number of bills for Second Reading in 1919, being fortunate in the ballot for bills. Among these bills were the Prevention of Unemployment Bill, which was thrown out; the Women's Emancipation Bill passed through all stages, but did not become law because the Government introduced instead their own Sex Disqualification Bill, which became a law; the Checkweighing in Various Industries Bill passed all stages and became law; the Local Authorities (Enabling) Bill, which sought to extend the powers of local authorities in matters of finance and municipal trading, was rejected on Second Reading. The Party also gained from the Government, in their debate on the motion on Pensions for Mothers, an expression of agreement with the principle.

On the Address, in answer to the King's Speech in the Parliamentary Session of 1920, the Party moved an amendment expressing regret at the absence of any proposal to nationalize the coal mines of the country. This amendment, along with an amendment practically demanding a revision of the Peace Treaties, was defeated. The Labour Party Bills in this session were its Women's Emancipation Bill, introduced as the Representation of the People Bill, which received a Second Reading and went to Committee, and this stage was not concluded; the Local Authorities (Enabling) Bill came up for Second Reading and was again rejected; and the Blind (Education, Employment and Maintenance) Bill, secured a Second Reading, but the Government brought forward their own provision, the extension of Old Age Pension, and the Labour Bill was dropped.

The official Party Amendment to the Address in the Parliamentary Session of 1921, was an amendment expressing regret that in view of the serious distress consequent upon unemployment and the lack of preparedness on the part of the Government to deal with the situation, there was no legislation recognizing the right of the genuine unemployed to work or to adequate maintenance. During the year the Labour Party by motions and questions kept the important problems of housing and unemployment in the first place of legislative interest. Again in 1922 the Labour Party amendment to the Address dealt with unemployment and expressed regret, in view of the disaster to British trade, and the amount of unemployment, that there was no indication that the Government were prepared to recognize and deal effectively with the course of unemployment, or to provide the opportunity for useful productive work; and further, in view of the exhaustion of national funds provided for the assistance of local authorities, and the approaching cessation of unemployment insurance benefit, regretted that there was no apparent intention on the part of the Government to grant substantial financial aid to the local authorities who could not be expected to bear a national burden. The amendment was defeated by 270 to 78.

From 1918 to 1922 was "a cycle of profound economic disturbance and political unsettlement, marked by trade depression, falling prices, heavy wage reductions, and abnormal unemployment." [3] It was a critical phase of Labour history in which forced readjustments took place and heavy losses were sustained by the working-class movement. But the British Labour movement from 1918 has had an unfailing interest for all who study the politics of democracy. Mr. Arthur Henderson, quite qualified to judge, wrote in 1922 that this was perhaps due in a measure to two outstanding facts: (a) that the organized movement in Britain was regarded almost universally as the most powerful, highly organized, and progressive organization in the world, and (b) that the

[3] J. Ramsay MacDonald, *The Labour Year Book 1924,* "Foreword."

political labour movement was expected soon to be called upon to assume the responsibilities of national government.[4]

Professor W. G. S. Adams, Gladstone Professor of Political Theory and Institutions, Oxford, declared that a new complex of problems—constitutional, political and economic—was the result of the rapid rise of Labour since 1918. This was especially significant in a great political society with strong traditions and understandings marking out lines of natural social progress. Professor Adams' interpretation is suggestive.[5]

Temporary appearances may seem to contradict what experience and study may suggest. Yet there is a logic underlying the development of human society, and the study of what has been and of what is reveals in some measure what is to be. Even great convulsions in society, marking a new ferment of thought which leavens the whole body politic and, it may be, overthrowing a long established order, settle down into a development in which we can trace a continuity through change. England has been notably free from violent convulsions, and a characteristic steadiness has marked its long political evolution. But with this stability there has been a power of readjustment to new conditions and of further development. The English constitution has been peculiarly flexible, and with age it does not become less but rather more so. There is in it, somehow, a wonderful power of shock absorption.

On October 26, 1922, following the resignation of the Prime Minister, Mr. Lloyd George, Parliament was dissolved. The newly elected Parliament, which met on November 23, 1922, with Mr. Stanley Baldwin as Prime Minister, contained 142 Labour members, representing a Labour vote of 4,236,733. The Party made an early claim to be regarded as the Opposition, which carries with it the exclusive occupation of the Front Opposition Bench. The Speaker, however, ruled that he must take into account the existence of other parties in opposition, and it was ultimately decided that the major portion of the Front Bench should be allocated to the Labour Party, which should be regarded as the chief Opposition. At the first meeting of the

[4] In his "Introduction" to Paul Blanshard's *An Outline of the British Labour Movement* (1923), p. v.

[5] See his "England after the Election," *Foreign Affairs,* Vol. II, No. 3 (March, 1924), pp. 351-365.

Party, Mr. J. Ramsay MacDonald, regaining his hold securely on the Labour Party, was elected Chairman and Leader; Mr. J. R. Clynes and Mr. Arthur Henderson were elected Deputy-Leader and Chief Whip respectively.

The influence of the Labour Party in the House of Commons from the election of 1922 has met no serious setback, so far as losing its hold on the loyalty of its supporters. The official amendments of the Party in these years have dealt mainly with old age pensions, unemployment, housing, and questions arising out of the Peace Treaties of the Great War. These problems remain unsettled, but honest effort is continually given by the best brains of Great Britain to understanding "the state of England" question. Perhaps the attitude of the Labour Party can be well set forth in the agreed motion on the Capitalist System, offered March 20, 1923. The debate was initiated by Mr. Philip Snowden, later the Labour Chancellor of the Exchequer. The resolution read as follows:

That, in view of the failure of the capitalist system to adequately utilize and organize natural resources and productive power, or to provide the necessary standard of life for vast numbers of the population, and believing that the cause of this failure lies in the private ownership and control of the means of production and distribution, this House declares that legislative effort should be directed to the gradual supersession of the capitalist system by an industrial and social order based on the public ownership and democratic control of the instruments of production and distribution.

This was answered by an amendment by Sir Alfred Mond as follows:

To leave out from the word "That" to the end of the Question and to put instead thereof the words:

This House, believing that the abolition of private interest in the means of production and distribution would impoverish the people and aggravate existing evils, is unalterably opposed to any scheme of legislation which would deprive the State of the benefits of individual initiative, and believing that far-reaching measures of social redress may be accomplished without overturning the present basis of society, is resolved to prosecute proposals which, by removing the evil effects of monopoly and waste, will conduce to the well-being of the people.

The vote taken at the end of the second day's sitting, July 16, 1923, resulted in a vote for Socialism of 121, for Capitalism 368. The minority consisted entirely of members of the Labour Party; the majority was composed from every other party in the House.

The debate in 1923 brought very little new material together, but it did serve the function of indicating the useless waste in human life that the economic system based on exploitation demands. This indictment was just as sincere from the ranks of the Liberals and the Conservatives as from the Labour benches, and therein is the hope of the struggle for a sounder social order. Mr. Lloyd George, who is excelled by no one in indicting social waste, pointedly said that

those who are most anxious to preserve the present system ought to be the most anxious to remedy the evils which arise from it. Unless they do so, I am certain that the bulk of the workers of this country will come to the conclusion that they are evils which are inherent in the system . . . I should like . . . to point out to the House of Commons circumstances which fill me with a great deal of apprehension from the after-effects of the War. Those facts are greater than we apprehended, and I think they are more potent. If anyone doubts that the war has made a permanent impression upon the people of this country he has only got to look at one fact, that Hon. Members who challenge the existing order of things, at the last election, for the first time, polled 4,250,000 votes. The House will make a very great mistake if it goes away with the idea that everything is all right, because it has demolished an impossible proposition made by the Hon. Member for Colne Valley (Mr. Snowden), because the facts will remain. It is not his arguments, powerful as they are, but the facts that we have to consider.

Sir John Simon believed that the most important thing of all was to humanize industry:

You cannot humanize industry by the vain and dreary repetition of an arid formula. The way to humanize industry is not to put it into the straight jacket of universal Socialism; it is to use the force of public opinion, the power of Parliament, to correct the rigors of unrestricted selfishness by putting public needs and human rights before private interests, and by doing it, as I believe it can be done, without sapping the energies or undermining the liberties of the British people.

Mr. Arthur Henderson reviewed, somewhat in the fashion of Mr. Snowden, the history of the industrial and labour movement of the last thirty years in the indictment of the existing system. The war, he added, brought into operation new ideas of social possibility, of economic reconstruction, of unity, of responsibility, and of human rights. Labour indicted the capitalist system because, in its opinion, the system condemns large numbers of honest, decent, self-respecting and law-abiding citizens to long periods of undeserved and unrelieved misery, and to conditions of life which any person with a spark of human feeling would not defend as tolerable, let alone as just.

There is no one in the Labour movement who can more ably put what the opponents of its doctrines call the "metaphysics of Socialism," than Mr. J. Ramsay MacDonald. He concluded the debate in 1923, as follows:

I object to the human spirit being limited and confined in its freedom by embattled economic power such as capitalism affords to-day. Talk about liberty to-day! Why, we have not got a whiff of liberty yet. The great mass of our people are not free to choose a destiny for their own children, and to live lives that would be good lives. The great mass of our people are not free to say what they like and to think what they like. I object most strongly to this domination of materialism, which is capitalism, over life, absolutely. Moreover, what is the great problem we have all got to face? I say it is the problem of production to begin with. What is the appeal of capitalism for more production? Absolutely nothing at all. It cannot be the appeal of property. Until you can enlist the soul of your worker you are neither going to have duty coming from his heart nor amplitude coming from his efforts. Capitalists cannot lift the man up to that; they may give him big positions and managing posts, but this is gross materialism which moth and dust doth corrupt and which thieves break through and steal, and until society has discovered that fine, impalpable, spiritual effort it will never solve this great problem of production.

In a very short time this spokesman of Labour was to be called upon to form a Government, for on November 13, 1923, when the Session of 1923 was resumed, Mr. Stanley Baldwin, the Conservative Prime Minister, announced the decision of the Government to advise a Dissolution of Parliament in order that they might ask for a mandate from the country to carry out Protectionist proposals for the cure of unemployment. The action of Mr. Baldwin was bitterly censured by some of his followers, and the country was greatly surprised at the Government's policy. The events which followed have somewhat balanced the feeling of popular disapproval which at one time threatened the leadership of Mr. Baldwin.

The Labour Party put the following Motion on the Paper, and it was debated on November 15:

That this House censures the neglect of His Majesty's Government to deal with the pressing needs of the unemployed, regrets its failure to devise and pursue a national policy calculated to restore the influence of the country abroad and re-establish international peace and trade; condemns the decision of the Government to leave millions of British people in want in order to fight an election on an undisclosed scheme of tariffs and imperial preference, conceived by sections of capitalists in their own interests, and the effect of which must be to increase the cost of living and encourage the formation of anti-social trusts and combines.

This motion was defeated by 285 votes to 190. The country then awaited the General Election which took place in December. The Government returned 258 members, the Liberals 158, Independents 8, and Labour increasing its number by 149 returned 191 members in the House of Commons. The Labour total vote polled was 4,348,379.

The Conservative Prime Minister decided to meet Parliament on January 8, 1924, and on the 15th of that month Parliament was formally opened with the King's Speech prepared by the Conservative Government.[6] After two days of debate on the

[6] The Conservative Government framed the Speech knowing full well that there would be little chance of carrying out the proposals contained in it, which proposed to give effect to the recommendations of the Imperial Conference on Imperial Preference, and extension of the exist-

Speech, during which period many questions regarding foreign affairs, education, housing, unemployment, and feeding of school children were raised, the Labour Party moved the following Amendment to the Address in answer:

But it is our duty respectfully to submit to your Majesty that your Majesty's present advisers have not the confidence of this House.

This Amendment was debated for three days, and was then carried by 328 to 256, a majority of 72, the Liberals voting with the Labour Party. The following day, January 22, the Prime Minister announced the resignation of the Government, and the House was adjourned until February 12. The King called upon Mr. J. Ramsay MacDonald to form a Government, exactly twenty-four years after he had been organizing secretary of the Labour Representation Committee which met in London. Prior to the opening of Parliament, when it was almost a certainty that the Conservative Government would be defeated on the Address, the National Executive of the Party and the Parliamentary Executive met and decided in favour of the Party taking office should the opportunity offer. When Parliament reassembled on February 12, the first Labour Prime Minister made a statement of Government policy dealing with such questions as Disarmament, the League of Nations, Housing, Unemployment, Agriculture, Recognition of Russia, and the Peace of Europe. Mr. MacDonald recognized the situation that his Government was in, a position representing a new constitutional problem, for the election of 1923 left no one of the three parties in the position of having a majority, and brought into the sphere of practical politics the program of a third party. He announced that the Government would only go out on the defeat of a question of policy when the will of the House was definitely expressed.

It is unnecessary here to make any attempt to estimate the nine months of Government by the Labour Party. There is no better statement of the matter than Mr. MacDonald gave in Albert Hall, London, May 13, 1924:

ing methods of dealing with Unemployment, and Agricultural Conference, an additional bonus to Pre-war Pensioners, and legislation to deal with the discouragement of thrift operating under the Old Age Pensions Acts.

No minority ought to be asked to do the work of a majority. It is not sound democracy.

Four months before in the same place, January 8, MacDonald set forth what he thought a Labour Government might do and what its attitude to problems of the State would be. This Albert Hall address made a great impression on the country, and was enthusiastically welcomed by his followers. One thought at the time of what MacDonald in 1921 had written of Hardie:

His life was but the manifestation of the spirit, and to him "the spirit" was something like what it was to the men whose bones lay on the Ayrshire moors under martyrs' monuments. It was the grand crowned authority of life, but an authority that spoke from behind a veil, that revealed itself in mysterious things both to man's heart and eyes.[7]

MacDonald wrote of the leader:

When the great labour leader comes he must possess the power which is to purify society and expose the falseness and vulgarity of materialist possession and class distinction. The mind of the labour leader must be too rich to do homage to "tinsel show," too proud of its own lineage to make obeisance to false honour, and too cultured to be misled by vulgar display. A working class living in moral and social parasitism on its "betters" will only increase the barrenness and futility of life.[8]

The Albert Hall speech thus was well begun with a reference to the pioneers who had made the whole adventure of modern labour possible.

You and I, my friends, their successors, the heirs of their labour, must cherish with religious zeal the inspiring memories they have left behind, and guard with all the care that tender human hearts can show the lamps they lit before the altars of democracy and Socialism. We are upon a pilgrimage. We are on a journey. . . . We shall take office if we have the chance in order to try and settle the manifold and pressing difficulties that beset our nation, Europe, and the whole world at the present moment. My task, and my colleagues' task, is going to be to mobilise all men and women of good-will and sane judgment.

[7] His "Introduction" to William Stewart's *Keir Hardie.*

[8] *Ibid.*

The audience that heard the man who in a few days was to become the Prime Minister knew that he did not underestimate the difficulty of the problems at home that were equalled by the tremendous tasks of foreign policy. Europe, Russia, the League of Nations, were talked of, along with the problems of housing and unemployment. In a few days he was to be leader of the Government, and it is interesting to note Mr. MacDonald's closing passage:

I want a Labour Government so that the life of the nation can be carried on; 1924 is not the last year in God's program of creation. We shall be dead and gone and forgotten, and generation after generation will come, and still the journey will be going on, still the search for the Holy Grail will be made by knights like Hardie. The shield of love and the spear of justice will still be in the hands of good and upright men and women. And the ideal of a great future will still be in front of our people. I see no end, thank God, to these things. I see my own horizon, I see my own sky-line, but I am convinced that when my children and my children's children get there, there will be another sky-line, another horizon, another dawning, another glorious beckoning from Heaven itself. That is my faith, and in that faith I go on and my colleagues go on, doing in their lifetime what they can to make their generation contribute something substantial to the well-being and happiness and holiness of human life.[9]

The Labour rule of nine months,[10] declared Mr. Arthur Henderson, "upheld all that was best in the British Constitution," did

[9] London *Times,* January 9, 1924. The record of the Labour period is yet a matter even of party controversy, but various points of view are to be found in the *Reviews* and *Quarterlies* of England, on the Continent, and in the United States. *J. Ramsay MacDonald (1923-1925)* (1925), by Iconoclast, provides a survey, and was preceded by her *J. Ramsay MacDonald: The Man of To-morrow* (1922).

[10] With the Labour Party in office, a new situation, from the point of view of Parliamentary internal organization, arose. All the officers of the Party and many of those who served on the Executive in the previous Session of Parliament had become Ministers, and it was decided, therefore, that instead of an Executive composed mainly of the officers of the Party, there should be an Executive composed of twelve Members not in the Government, plus three Ministers, to act as a liaison committee between the Party and the Government. It was convenient to the Government to be able to consult a representative committee of the Party at short notice, and it was convenient to the Party as a whole to have a committee to make representations to the Government when considered necessary.

more in nine months to restore the peace of the world than its predecessors accomplished in as many years, and "demonstrated by its legislative and administrative record that the ability to govern can no longer be regarded as the monopoly of any one particularly privileged class." [11]

The Party bills and motions in the Labour period followed exactly the line that had been pursued by Labour from 1918. There was one very serious criticism of Labour, that they did not attempt to put into effect the reforms that very easily might have won Parliamentary support. The attitude of Labour with regard to industrial legislation is noted in the study dealing with actual statutes, and it is only worth recording that other bills of the Labour Party brought forward were the Rent Restrictions Bill, which was abandoned in Committee, the Representation of the People Bill, providing for equality in the franchise by conferring the vote upon women at the age of twenty-one, assimilating the Parliamentary and Local Government franchises, abolishing the University fee for registration, and removing the disqualification resting upon members of certain local authorities who may have received poor relief, passed Second Reading but got no farther; the Nationalization of Mines and Materials Bill, promoted by the Miners' Federation and approved by the Party, was rejected on Second Reading; and the Motions on a National Minimum Wage and Mothers' Pensions were accepted without division.

The importance of administration is again emphasized in all of the propaganda literature of the Labour Party, for since the fall of the Labour Government its supporters have cited often the sympathetic, the constructive administrative policy of the Labour Government which, so it is claimed, doubly benefited the people with regard to the provisions of old age pensions, unemployment, and housing requirements. Friends of Labour believe that the record of the first Labour Government will compare favourably with any other, and it is officially declared [12] that

if the full program for the Session had been completed in the Autumn, comprising as it would a great Housing scheme, a good working-class Budget, a welcome improvement in the Old Age

[11] Foreword, *Labour Year Book 1925*, p. iii.
[12] *Labour Year Book, 1925*, p. 155.

Pensions Scheme, a substantial amendment of the Unemployment Insurance Scheme, an agreement with Russia which, if ratified by the Parliament, would have helped considerably towards increasing the volume of employment, an Inter-Allied agreement with Germany which it is hoped may pave the way to durable peace and economic restoration of Europe, a Factories Bill which would confer great benefit upon many workers, an Eight-hour Day, Equality in the Franchise, and a national scheme of Electricity Supply, the record for the year would have been phenomenal.

All of which of course is part of the unpredictable in politics, and has no more value than any other unfulfilled promise.

The Labour Government fell after nine months of office on the issues arising out of the famous Communist prosecution, initiated against the acting editor of the *Workers' Weekly,* Mr. Campbell. The weekly is the organ of the Communist Party in Great Britain, and the Government decided to withdraw the prosecution on the ground that it would not be in the public interest to attach an entirely unwarranted importance to the seditious article in question or to those responsible for it. The action of the Attorney-General in withdrawing the prosecution was raised, and the Conservative Opposition asked for a day to discuss the matter. On October 8, 1924, the Conservatives moved a Motion of censure, to which the Liberal Party offered an amendment, which was finally accepted by both Conservatives and Liberals in order to insure the defeat of the Government. The Liberal amendment was:

That a Select Committee be appointed to investigate and report upon the circumstances leading up to the withdrawal of the proceedings recently instituted by the Director of Public Prosecutions against Mr. Campbell.

The Prime Minister said the motion demanding an inquiry by a Select Committee, practically gave the lie to the solemn assurances of the Ministers, and if carried the Government would go to the country. By a vote of 364 to 198 the Liberal amendment was carried, and the next day, October 9, 1924, the Prime Minister announced that the King had acceded to his request to dissolve Parliament.

In the General Election of 1924, which quickly followed dissolution, Labour contested 514 seats, polled 5,487,620 votes, and returned 151 members to the House of Commons. Polling over a million more votes than ever before the Party nevertheless lost 40 seats. But the coming into office of Labour gave it a prestige that has greatly strengthened the Party and its hold on the country. At the same time Labour came to grips with the disillusioning facts of politics. The Labour Party for a long time had gained much from the ardent and eager spirits of reform and revolution in England, and the season of training as a Government dealing with knotty problems of finance, trade and administration has done a good deal to clarify their thinking. The Party has a discipline now which will mean a larger and fuller share in the government of Great Britain. The future belongs to those who make no truce with economic or social injustice, but who day in and day out fight the good fight against predatory interests and privilege. In the Labour Party there are an increasing number who carry on their work in the spirit of a crusader, and their spirit is deeply moved at times by what can be called nothing less than religious zeal. This spirit, of course, insures the permanence of the Labour movement as a purifying political force in the life of England. Already the Party has compelled the Conservative Party to formulate programs of political and economic reform with which to go before the electorate; and, as at all times, the Liberal Party admirably serves the function of critic and judge of what is going on. It is to be hoped that both Labour and Liberalism will aid Mr. Baldwin's Government by at all times submitting his leadership to a keen flow of intelligent criticism. Whether or not Labour and Liberalism can be brought together will remain for some time a question of almost no consequence.

The Labour Party program was well outlined in the Election Manifesto in the General Election of 1924 issued with the united support of the Parliamentary Labour Party, the General Council of the Trade Union Congress, and the Executive Committee of the Labour Party. This Manifesto emphasized the work for international peace of the Labour Government; the Budget, the housing, education, agriculture and unemployment program of the Labour Government were indications of a new spirit at Westminster, it was affirmed. The Labour Government's Bills before

Parliament were cited as evidence of the capacity of the Party to understand the needs of the people and to use Parliament as an instrument of reform. Under the caption "The Spirit That Giveth Life," the Election Manifesto of 1924 concluded with the following:

It is along such lines as those marked out in this Appeal, and in the spirit of public service herein indicated, that the Labour Party, in conformity with its consistent public declarations, would work in Parliament towards the transformation, gradual as it must be, of the existing economic and industrial system into a genuine Commonwealth of Labour. We know the facts. We realise the difficulties. The path to our goal is long and narrow and sometimes so hard to travel that men and women faint by the way. But we have faith in humanity. We refuse to believe that there is nothing to be done but conserve the present order, which is disorder; or that the misery, the demoralization and the ruin it causes to innocent men and women and children can be remedied by the perpetual repetition of the abstract principles of Individualism.

We appeal to the People to support us in our steadfast march—taking each step only after careful examination, making sure of each advance as we go, and using each success as the beginning of further achievements towards a really Socialist Commonwealth, in which there shall at least be opportunity for Goodwill to conquer Hate and Strife, and for Brotherhood, if not to supersede Greed, at least to set due bounds to that competition which leads only to loss and death.

Such an appeal illustrates what one distinguished English critic believes to be by far the greatest asset of the Labour Party—its vision of a new political, social and economic order.[13] Of course in the great economic organization of Labour there lies ready to hand an instrument of political propaganda and social organization possessed by neither of the old parties. But Labour

has brought freshness into the rather stale atmosphere of political controversy and there is a much more widely extended sympathy with its program than would have seemed possible before the war.

[13] W. G. S. Adams, *op. cit.*, p. 355 ff.

This has been increased by a growing recognition of the essentially constitutional character of the Labour movement. In recent times the leaders of the party have taken marked pains to insist on this point. The English constitution is their possession and heritage as much as that of any other party; their allegiance to it is as true as that of any other party. They have observed the parliamentary system and have regarded it as the right means for the expression of the will of the people.[14]

What this has meant to the politics of Great Britain all serious students of affairs recognize. Parliament has again become a place where debate and discussion of great policies takes place, and here the Labour Party has made a contribution to the cause of good government.

It is however in domestic affairs that Labour marks a great departure from either of the old parties. A new school of thought is coming into power and responsibility, a school which may be called that of the socialization of national life. It is not a school of Communism, but one which seeks much more than any other party to organise community action and to control the sources of power within the nation. Responsibility for action is bound to exercise a great influence on the formulation and practical expression of this school of thought. The application of its underlying ideas in different fields of public life is taking shape in various definite proposals, the difficulties and advantages of which can now be considered, deliberately if not altogether dispassionately. Parliament will again become the great debating centre in which discussion will focus. The country will also be schooled in the same problems, and the quickening of thought in the country will react on the work of Parliament.[15]

[14] *Ibid.*, p. 355-356.

[15] *Ibid.*, p. 357. Compare the article by M. Émile Vandervelde, chief of the Socialist party in Belgium, in *Foreign Affairs,* Vol. 3, No. 4 (July, 1925), "Ten Years of Socialism in Europe," pp. 556-566. His thesis is that the workers must wrest political power from the State. "In short, the ultimate progress of socialization depends largely on the political progress of the working class, and such progress is itself a function of industrial development, of the growth of the proletariat, and of the consciousness and organization of the working class. From this standpoint there can be no doubt that the war has given a definite impulse to previously existing tendencies and has laid the way wide open to the socialist conquest of power" (p. 564). Cf. his *Le Parti Ouvrier Belge* (Brussels, 1925), for a significant study of labour politics.

Many students in the United States have studied the remarkable rise of the Labour Party to a position of strength and influence in British politics during the past ten years, and recently one of our ablest leaders in the field of government has declared that it carries lessons which might well be taken to heart by organized Labour in America.[16] One of the lessons is that the Labour movement in England has welcomed professional men, educators, even peers,—anyone who accepts its creed. It has appreciated the fact that brains, as well as numbers, are essential to success in politics. This wide appeal has been strengthened by its constructive program, and the British Labour party has acquired a unifying bond other than a common enemy. It has not spent all its energy in denouncing the ogre of capitalism, in railing at profiteers, and in scenting various conspiracies to enslave the worker. Professor Munro believes the party has produced a program which, whether you like it or not, is at least comprehensive, constructive, and arguably practicable.

And it urges the acceptance of this program, not for the benefit of the organized manual worker alone, but for the advantage of brain workers also—for virtually the whole people and for posterity. It has adopted the language of altruism, and has couched its demands in terms of nationalism, not of class warfare. It has gone on the principle that there is a fundamental harmony in all human relations and that the best interests of the wage earner are not in conflict with those of men who earn their livelihood by labour other than that of their own hands.

That quality which the Oxford scholar considers to be Labour's greatest asset is used by the Harvard scholar to direct a lesson to the labour movement of the United States. Finally, Professor Munro believes, the leaders of the British Labour party have placed their cause on a high spiritual plane.

They have not allowed themselves to become wholly absorbed in controversies over the open shop, the standard of living, the minimum wage, the use of injunctions in labour disputes, and the eight-hour day on public utilities. Rather they have devoted

[16] See Professor W. B. Munro's *The Governments of Europe* (1925), pp. 257-258.

themselves to voicing the plea of the worker for industrial democracy as a means of elevating the entire plane of his life and making him a better craftsman in the new society. In this way they have reached many thousands of generous-minded people, wholly outside the wage-earning ranks, whose emotions naturally impel them towards an ideal that is stated in human terms.

Organized labour in America thus can learn that the statement of its aims in terms of the common good is sound politics, and there may well be learned the lesson of presenting labour's cause to the whole people in the form of a constructive, democratic, spiritual ideal.

Part II

The Trade Union Movement

The reader should always keep in mind that when the British Labour Party is written of,—its program in Parliament and the electoral promises of its candidates,—the Trade Union movement can be considered to be included. The political program of Labour is backed by the highly organized industrial movement of Great Britain. The growth of the Labour party is largely due to the fact that organized Labour in England has been won over to its side. There has been no long drawn out struggle between the parliamentary and the industrial labour movements, though there has been from time to time a sharp conflict with regard to specific economic questions and the proper tactics of a united Labour party. The Syndicalist agitation before the war in England centred largely around the movement for the minimum wage, and was not the anti-parliamentary struggle that the militant Syndicalists in France carried on in the pre-war France. The National Minority Movement in England,[17] a revival of the old Syndicalist campaign led by Mr. Tom Mann, has had little more response than the similar effort in the industrial unrest of 1911 and 1912. This

[17] The writings of Mr. Harry Pollitt, Mr. Tom Mann, and Mr. A. J. Cook, in the *Labour Monthly*, provide a running account of this movement, and the insurgent spirit in trade unionism can be noted in the efforts to give larger powers to the General Council as central authority of the industrial workers.

is well illustrated in the attitude of the Labour Party in their relations with the Communist Party, whose openly avowed policy is to scrap the present methods and objects of the Labour party and to transform it into a Communist organization. At the London Conference of 1924 the chief debate at the Conference centred around the Party's attitude to members of the Communist Party, and this question again came to the place of first importance at the Liverpool Conference in October, 1925. Both of these Conferences showed that the hold of "MacDonaldism," as the National Minority like to call it, is unshaken. There is to-day a revival of the familiar discussion of the antagonism between democracy and the militant worker, but it is not likely that there will be the years of tedious, vague polemics that characterized the pre-war social movement in France. It is fairly certain whatever direction the industrial movement of the next few years goes in England, that the political Labour movement will continue to be a powerful factor in establishing ideals of public service. The Labour Party realizes that England possesses almost a wholly enfranchised adult population and a Parliament and a system of government that will respond to the direction of the working people as soon as they express intelligent desire for change through the ballot box. Mr. Sidney Webb, a member of the MacDonald Ministry, and a Labour leader of unfailing energy and freshness, declared at the Labour Party Conference in 1923 that

> Violence persuades no one, convinces no one, satisfies no one . . . violence may destroy but it can never construct. Moreover, in our practical British way we can see that by the very nature of the case violence can be much more easily and effectively applied on the conservative side, to keep things as they are because this requires only acquiescence, than on the side of change.

The Executive Committee of the Labour Party in making their recommendations to the 1924 Conference [18] to refuse affiliation to the Communist Party squarely put the issue:

[18] *Labour Year Book, 1925,* pp. 1-12, and *Report of the Labour Party Conference,* London, 1924. See also the extended report of the Executive Committee to the Labour Party Conference in 1922 when the same question was considered. The 25th Annual Conference, Liverpool, 1925, by a vote of 2,954,000 to 321,000 defeated the motion which meant the

The Communist Party believes that Parliament and other Administrative Authorities are simply machines that should only be exploited to their own destruction; that there is no hope in the masses of the people rising to the height of their political responsibilties; and, that therefore, so soon as a minority in the community feel that they are sufficiently powerful to revolutionize the present political and industrial system, they are justified in using power, armed and otherwise, to achieve that purpose. Pending the speedy conversion of the masses, should they disagree with this procedure, the correct position is that they should be held down by force, deprived of liberty of speech, organisation and Press, and such expressions in the direction of opinion will be dealt with as counter-revolutionary symptoms.

But the Labour Party differences are fundamental and unchanging, as is evident from their stated opinion that

The Labour Party holds a fundamental objection to tyranny, quite apart from the social, political, or industrial standing of the tyrant. In its opinion political intelligence wisely directed is more enduring in its results than coercion, no matter how well intentioned. It objects to the limitations at present suffered by the masses of the people, but aids and welcomes their increasing desire for a freer and a fuller social life. The advances made during its short existence form the justification for steady and continuous effort in the direction of securing the suffrages and support of the greater masses of the nation. Socialism that will secure the freedom under which men and women can develop their finest faculties and lead to a still higher social organization must essentially be based on freedom.

Thus it seems that Labour politics can be used to strengthen the constitutional guarantees of freedom, and promote conditions of good-will which will bring to the State a larger liberty of action. Good-will can inspire a new allegiance which is sorely needed by the State if its aims are to be social. The experience of the war and the years since the war have had much to do with the interest

reopening of the Communist party's demand for affiliation; on the motion to ban the Communists from individual membership in local Labour parties the vote was for 2,870,000, against 321,000. Thus the Communists were repudiated by an overwhelming vote.

that many labour leaders take in the work that a Labour party must do in present-day governments.[19] Labour politics, as Mr. MacDonald has often said, has come out into the open, and never again can Labour refuse to bear its share in the carrying on of the nation's business. The 1925 Labour Party Conference defeated by a very large majority a resolution demanding that no Labour Government be formed unless there was a working majority in the House of Commons. The party did not want to bind the future to a barren policy dictated by no higher principle than Socialist orthodoxy.[20]

A recent comment on the English Labour movement suggestively brings out the point that the failure of industrial struggles on an unprecedented scale after the war has turned men's minds more to the political field.[21] An indication of this may be the Hull Trades Union Congress in 1924, which was the 56th Annual Congress of the trade unions, and was attended by delegates rep-

[19] See the suggestive study of Mr. R. H. Tawney's, *The British Labour Movement* (New Haven, 1925), and the account of "The Labour Party" in the *Labour Year Book 1925*, pp. 9-21, which provides a very full statement of the program and the tactics of the party. Cf. *Labour and the New Social Order* (1918) (Sidney Webb), published by the Labour Party; *The Labour Party's Aims, A Criticism and a Restatement* (1923), by Seven Members of the Labour Party; and Sidney and Beatrice Webb's *A Constitution for the Socialist Commonwealth of Great Britain* (1920). This last is significant for political proposals of its authors and can be taken with Mr. Laski's *A Grammar of Politics* (1925), for Labour commentary on social theory.

[20] By a vote of 2,587,000 to 512,000 the Conference defeated the resolution on minority government moved on behalf of the Transport and General Workers' Union by Mr. Ernest Bevin: That this Conference is of opinion in view of the experience of the recent Labour Government it is inadvisable that the Labour party should again accept office whilst having a minority in the House of Commons. Mr. MacDonald said, "In an absolutely blank political landscape you are asked to say that if you are returned at the next election with 308 members you will take office, but if you have only 306 members you will not. That sort of tactics won't do."

[21] A. Shadwell, *The Socialist Movement* (1925, two vols.), Vol. II, pp. 132 ff. See also Mrs. Townsend's *Creative Syndicalism* (1924), and the interesting novel, *The Wild Men* (1925), by George Blake; and B. G. De Montgomery, *op. cit.*, chap. IV. The fugitive writings of Mr. G. D. H. Cole and other Guildsmen are significant since the war in indicating the lively interest of the militant labor movement in parliamentary action.

resenting 4,328,235 members.[22] The Hull Congress adopted unanimously a resolution offered by the General Council, which constitutes a seven-point program known as the Industrial Workers' Charter. The resolution follows:

That this Congress reaffirms the decisions of past Congresses with regard to necessary and fundamental changes in our social, economic, and political systems, and decides to formulate the said decisions in an Industrial Workers' Charter, and pledges itself to secure by every legitimate means the fulfilment of the objects constituting the Charter, which, subject to such additions as Congress may from time to time approve, shall be as follows:

[22] An indication of the trade union movement's power is to be gathered from the membership of affiliated unions, 1900 to 1925:

	No. of Unions	*Members Represented at Trade Union Congress (in thousands)*
1900	184	1,250
1901	191	1,200
1902	198	1,400
1903	204	1,500
1904	212	1,423
1905	205	1,541
1906	226	1,555
1907	236	1,700
1908	214	1,777
1909	219	1,705
1910	212	1,648
1911	202	1,662
1912	201	2,002
1913	207	2,232
1914	...	....
1915	215	2,682
1916	227	2,851
1917	235	3,082
1918	262	4,532
1919	266	5,284
1920	215	6,505
1921	213	6,418
1922	206	5,129
1923	194	4,269
1924	203	4,328
1925	...	4,343

The membership of the Trade Union Congress since its foundation is shown in the following table, for decennial periods:

	No. of Unions	*Members*
1868	...	118,367
1878	114	623,957
1888	138	816,944
1898	188	1,184,241
1908	214	1,777,000
1918	262	4,532,085
1924 (6 years)	203	4,328,235
1925	...	4,343,000

Information is taken from G. D. H. Cole, *Organized Labour* with its useful tables and charts, from the *Labour Year Book 1925*, and from the *Trade Union Congress Report*, 1925.

(1) Public ownership and control of natural resources and of services—
  (a) Nationalization of land, mines, and minerals.
  (b) Nationalization of railways.
  (c) The extension of State and municipal enterprise for the provision of social necessities and services.
  (d) To make proper provision for the adequate participation of the workers in control and management.
(2) Wages and hours of labour—
  (a) A legal maximum working week of 44 hours.
  (b) A legal minimum wage for each industry or occupation.
(3) Unemployment—
  (a) Suitable provisions in relation to unemployment, with adequate maintenance of the unemployed.
  (b) Establishment of training centres for unemployed juveniles.
  (c) Extension of training facilities for adults during periods of industrial depression.
(4) Housing—
  Provision of proper and adequate housing accommodation.
(5) Education—
  Full educational facilities to be provided by the State from the elementary schools to the universities.
(6) Industrial accidents and diseases—
  Adequate maintenance and compensation in respect of all forms of industrial accidents and diseases.
(7) Pensions—
  (a) State pensions for all at the age of 60.
  (b) State pensions for widowed mothers and dependent children.

This Congress decides that it shall be the duty of the General Council to institute a vigorous campaign in all parts of the country, with a view to mobilizing public opinion in support of the objects of the Charter and their fulfilment.

This Congress further decides that it shall be the duty of the General Council to report to each Annual Trade Union Congress on the extent of the propaganda work carried out and the progress made in relation to the Charter, and no motion having for its purpose the reaffirmation or the deletion of any object contained in the Charter shall be allowed to appear on the Congress Agenda for a period of three years from the date such object was adopted by Congress, unless the motion is, in the opinion of the General Council, of immediate importance.

This Charter can be compared with the trade union program of 1868 and 1900 given in this study, and it is an important commentary on the progress of the Labour movement since 1868. This Charter demands an acceptance of a standard of life for the workman,[23] and it goes much farther than that challenging fact—the movement demands proper provision for the adequate participation of the workers in control and management. Thus the whole problem of the organization of industry is to-day under discussion. And in this connection the following resolution, adopted at the Hull Congress on the motion of the Miners' Federation of Great Britain, seconded on behalf of the Associated Society of Locomotive Engineers and Firemen, is also of note:

This Congress declares:
That the time has arrived when the number of Trade Unions should be reduced to an absolute minimum.
That the aim should be as far as possible, organization by industry with every worker a member of the appropriate organization.
That it is essential that a united front be formed for improving the standards of life of the workers.
And accordingly instructs the General Council to draw up—

(1) A scheme of organization by industry; and

(2) A scheme which may secure unity of action, without the definite merging of existing Unions, by a scientific linking up of same to present a united front.

This united front that is demanded in a "scientific linking up"

[23] My attention has been called to a stimulating analysis made by Miss Theresa S. McMahon of the University of Washington, *Social and Economic Standards of Living* (New York, 1926), who has investigated the possible modifications of standards of living in behalf of social progress. She has made an analysis of the way people want to live, and of the origin and effect of their desires. The point is that a standard of living is in the mind, a conception of the way one wishes to live. Thus it is a complex of psychological factors which are vastly influential in social progress.

is now the special study of the General Council of the Trade Union Congress. Some have seemed to see in the trend of events the break-up of the Labour party and the Trade Union alliance, which since 1900 has given the political movement increasing power. In fact, as Mr. Cole has pointed out,[24] since 1909 when the Miners' Federation joined the Labour party, that party has become "almost as representative of the Trade Union movement as the Congress itself." But the fact that the General Council, representing every phase of the industrial movement, is moving toward the establishment of itself as a centralized authority, able to exert the full power of the trade union movement in applying a national trade union policy, has alarmed some political leaders of the Labour movement. The proposal for the General Council as central authority of the industrial movement is sponsored by the Left wing, and at the Scarborough Congress in 1925 some tactical gains were made by the Left wing of the General Council. The proposal is that the General Council should have its own machinery, its own set of departments, and should have that importance of first position which the industrial movement naturally demands. Yet the General Council's report to the 1925 Trade Union Congress asked for no extension of powers, contenting itself by saying that "valuable experience has been gained and the mining dispute has shown that when the trade union movement is united and determined in defence of the standards of the workers the forces of reaction can be successfully withstood."

The Liverpool Conference of the Labour party in 1925 has been taken to mark a swing to the Right, and the Left wing believes [25] that "the tendencies prevalent at Liverpool show that the Labour party is drifting to political disaster," for it is becoming a new Liberal party and not a "Workers' party." But others believe, as for instance the Labour correspondent of the Manchester *Guardian,* that the expulsion of the Communists means a million votes for Labour at the next election, and possibly victory.[26] Mr. J. Ramsay MacDonald did a great deal to stop

[24] *Organized Labour,* p. 107.
[25] Statement of Mr. A. J. Cook, the militant Miners' secretary.
[26] Manchester *Guardian Weekly,* October 9, 1925, p. 288.

the Left wing advance from the Trade Union Congress at Scarborough,[27] and he claimed that the Liverpool Conference showed "right up to the hilt" that Labour's success depends on "the most complete co-operation" between the political and industrial wings. He does not believe that all differences are corrected, but his faith in an united Labour movement is unshaken. A quarter of a century of progress has not made him less inclined to trust the process of democracy nor to put less faith in Parliament. The political Labour movement is responsive to the large hopes of the Trade Union world for workers' control, and political leaders can be depended upon to make progress toward the "Commonwealth of Labour" as quickly as the industrialists prepare for social control. It is well that the pre-war internal politics of Trade Unionism, which were a chaos of contention between craft and industrial unionism, Syndicalism and Guildism, have passed away. A wider range of ideals determine now the problems of the industrial movement. The future belongs to the workers because they are preparing for it, realizing that only as a new spirit of co-operation among men is the ideal that there is any hope of laying the foundation of the future Industrial Commonwealth in the good society.

[27] Mr. Harry Pollitt said the defeat came because "the Left wing of the Labour party were scared stiff and allowed MacDonald to ride roughshod over them. . . . Not a single Left-winger in the Executive Committee (of the Labour party) dared to burn his boats and warn the 'hero-worshippers' where MacDonaldism was leading to."

BOOK II

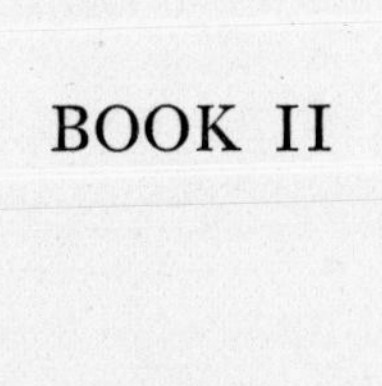

CHAPTER IX

A SURVEY OF FRENCH SOCIAL LEGISLATION

THE law projects introduced in the legislature of 1898-1902 have been the basis of nearly all the social legislation passed by the French Parliament in this century. This fact is largely due to the remarkable quality of a French law project, resisting total annihilation, lying for years before the Chamber or at the door of the Senate, forgotten by a Commission, in its own time re-appearing with fuller life and wider meaning. Again each new legislature offers the opportunity of reviving old measures, and the ease with which a bill may be entered stimulates the zeal of party publicists and propagandists. If it were so easy in the House of Commons to introduce social reform legislation there is little doubt that the records would be as cluttered with a like variety and miscellany of proposals.[1] Yet in the progress of a Bill through many parliamentary sessions an indication of the spread of ideas is given, and the influence upon the Government can be plainly seen in the changed character of many projects and in the acceptance of private members' bills by the responsible leaders. This practice in France and England has been unusually effective with regard to industrial enactments; the history of the old age pensions and social insurance system supplying the outstanding examples.

There is especial interest in the projects of social reform of the Government of M. Waldeck-Rousseau for this Ministry ended an old period and began a new one.[2] There was an opportunity

[1] An authoritative study on certain problems of French government is that of Professor R. K. Gooch, *The Committees (Commissions) in the Chambers (1875 to present time) and Their Influence on Ministerial Responsibility* (Oxford, 1924, Thesis), see especially Introduction, pp. ix-xxxvi, "The French Constitutional System," and his conclusions, pp. 450-474.

[2] Cf. Ernest Charles, *Theories sociales et politiciens, 1870-1898* (1898), for a most suggestive survey of the personalities and politics of this period of French Parliamentary history, especially chap. I, "La Theorie Sociale au Parlement et le Parlementarisme," pp. 1-33; also his *Histoire*

for fresh attack on old problems. The pressure both of public opinion and the influence of organized labour kept constantly reacting on the policies of political parties. Legislation had been increasingly influenced by the earlier Radical and Socialist movement which followed the establishment of the Third Republic. The politics of Radical-Socialists testify to it as well as the effective parliamentary success of the Socialist deputies.[3] It was a time of fruition for the social philosophy of intervention, inspired by the humanitarianism of earlier schools of thought as well as by a widespread industrial deadlock of interests. There was this common bond. If a policy of "sterile parliamentarianism" was reflected in reformistic politics or in the determinism of the doctrine of solidarity[4] as taught by the "elder statesmen,"

psychologique et morale du parlementarisme, 1870-1898 (1898). It is interesting to compare along with this Lowell's *Governments and Parties in Continental Europe* (1896), Vol. I, chaps. I-II, pp. 1-145; J. E. C. Bodley's *France*, 1900 edition, especially the last Preface; and Eugène Pierre, *Politique et Gouvernement* (1896).

[3] Cf. Léon Jacques, *Les partis politiques sous la IIIe République, Doctrine et Programme—Organization et Tactique* (1913); F. Buisson, *La politique radicale* (1909); A. Charpentier, *Le parti radical et radical-socialiste à travers ses congrès*, 1901-1911 (1913), with Preface by F. Buisson. With these may be mentioned post-war books: J. Carrère and G. Bourgin, *Manuel des partis politiques en France* (1924); H. Bourgin, *Le parti contre la patrie* (1924), a record of socialist deputies between 1915-1917, a history of "political secession," M. Bourgin says; and A. Milhaud, *La reconstitution du monde* (1924).

[4] M. Léon Bourgeois' statement in *Solidarité* (1st ed. 1894, 7th ed. 1912), may be taken as a basis of the original idea. To him *Solidarité* appeared in the history of ideas as the development of the philosophy of the 18th century, working out in social and political theory the abstract terms of liberty, equality and fraternity of the Revolution. The inspiration of his life was this theory, the principle of social solidarity. Beginning a brilliant career in the Civil Service, he entered the Chamber of Deputies in 1888, and through many ministries he held an honourable place. He was elected in 1920 President of the Senate. He died in 1925. Of interest is his *Education de la Démocratie* (1897), *Pour la Société des Nations* (1910), and *La Politique de l'Epargue et de l'Hygiène Sociale* (1914). The writings of M. Charles Bouglé early developed this idea; first notably in *Les Idees Egalitaires* (1899) (cf. chap. IV, Part II, pp. 206 ff.); then in *Solidarisme et Liberalisme* (1904), with which compare M. Camille Sabatier, *Le Socialisme Liberal ou Morcellisme* (1904); and more fully in *Le Solidarisme* (1st ed. 1907, 2nd ed. 1924). Cf. Maurice Bourgin, *Les Systemes Socialistes et l'Evolution Économique* (1904), chap. XXIII, pp. 350-388; and for a most sympathetic interpretation, Pic. *op. cit.*, pp. 40-46. It is impossible to consider in this study the writings of M. Duguit on this subject.

there were increasing indications that new powers were forming in the legislatures of 1893-1902.

The Government by introducing the law projects of the Ministry of Commerce and Industry, sponsored by M. Millerand, definitely continued the policy which had been outlined by M. Waldeck-Rousseau in his famous Circular on the law of 1884. The development of the Labour movement since that time was significant in the utilization of that law to promote the economic freedom of the worker;[5] and this, together with the continuous expansion of French industry, had intensified and embittered the struggle between the employers and the employees. Open conflict brought new problems which had to be faced by the Government; the lessening of differences was no less a necessity for the Government than a hope of the new Ministry. The law projects were formulated to meet the most important problems of the French Labour movement and to cope with the larger needs of industrial administration confronting the French nation. Millerand was no mere opportunist nor was he an unbalanced social reformer, and few leaders of nations had stated so definitely as Waldeck-Rousseau their social theory. If they placed too much confidence in the machinery of State control and the efficacy of trade and professional organization, the same spirit had its counterpart in the politics of the socialists and in the syndicalist philosophy of society.

The law projects that were consistently supported and the decrees issued by Millerand while Minister of Commerce and Industry (June, 1899, to January, 1902), constitute a record of achievement of a high order in the effort to use democratic institutions in an industrial civilization as a means to a more just way of living. They indicate his views on the function of the State and toward what type of society its activities were to be directed.

Part I

The Work of Millerand

Millerand first gave his attention to the organization of the staff of administration. A ministerial decree of August 1, 1899,

[5] Cf. *Troisième Congrès Général des Organisations Socialistes Françaises, Compte Rendu*, Lyon, 1901, p. 81, the speech of M. Lagardelle, and pp. 82-83, the remarks of M. Jaurès, quoting the former's article in the *International Socialist Review* (Chicago), May, 1900.

later completed by the decree of October 10, 1900, consolidated in one office, *Direction du Travail,* the work of control and inspection of mines and manufactures, and also the health and security of the workers. By this decree was established the *Division de l'assurance et de la Prévoyance Sociales,* taking over the duties of the department which had had charge before of insurance, pensions and savings banks.[6] The administrative importance of these agencies of control were foremost in the policy of the Government; and by the decrees and letters of instruction on the application of the laws the way was prepared for the creation of the *Ministère du Travail* in 1906.[7] A new office, that of *Enseignement Technique,* dealing with technical and scientific training was created. By this decree the divisions of Commerce and Industry were included under the same administrative head, while a separate office was created to look after problems of personnel and finance of the ministry. The reorganization of the ministry set forth the conscious purpose of using the agencies of Government for a settlement of the problems of French industry and labour. The effort of systematic reform, combined with scientific study of the problems, was revealed in the unity of the law projects which were submitted.

At the beginning of Millerand's ministry three official decrees started lively discussion on the policy of the new administration in all circles—legal, labour and academic. The Decrees [8] of August 10, 1899, are epochal. It is well to remark that while three decrees were issued, they are substantially the same in the conditions they lay down; the first applies to the State, the central government; and the two others concern the departments, cities and charitable institutions of the State. M. Millerand, counting on the support of the Chamber of Deputies and believing that the Senate would oppose his efforts, forestalled their action by means

[6] This new department was charged with organizing and carrying out the law on accidents to workmen of that year, the law of July 1, 1899.

[7] See proceedings of Chamber of Deputies for November 24, 1899, when the Chamber voted the Resolution of MM. Groussier and Lemire, for the creation of the Ministry of Labour; note also Raoul Jay, "Ministère du Travail," *Rev. Hebd.,* May 20, 1911, pp. 344 ff.; Albert Peyronnet, *Le Ministère du Travail, 1906-1923* (1924), pp. 1-8; and B, Malon, *op. cit.,* Vol. II, pp. 169-208.

[8] Dalloz, *Code du Travail,* pp. 125-128.

of a departmental decree.[9] The legality of the decrees has for some time been uncontested,[10] and, in fact, they have become long since a very important part of much existing legislation.

The decrees laid down the conditions upon which the contracts given for public work were governed, and submitted the rules which applied to all of the State enterprises. Millerand stated that if the public powers of the State recognized the need of an industrial reform, they should be the first to prove its utility by putting it into application. This decree required that in all public works the workers should have one rest day a week;[11] that the working day be reduced and that a universal normal working day be fixed;[12] that a minimum wage be established for every category of worker;[13] and that the number of foreign workers be limited.[14] It is only necessary to record the provisions of the Decree to see the broad intention and the principles of legislation upon which it is based. The State defined a power which found further expression in England in the Trade Boards Act of 1909, and, which for France was confirmed by the law of July 10, 1915, establishing a legal minimum wage for home workers.[15]

The important interest of the decree of August 10, 1899, apart from the interpretation of the principles of State action it contained, was the means adopted to carry out its provisions. Administration was centred in the syndicates of the city and department where the work was carried on; the collective contracts entered into by the employers' syndicates and the workers' syndicates were the basis of the decisions and agreements. Where

[9] It is well to note this antagonism which increased among the Socialists very markedly in the early part of the period covered by this study.

[10] Pic, *op. cit.*, p. 659; see pp. 659-663 for a full discussion of the Decrees and their importance.

[11] Art. I, clause 1.

[12] Art. I, clause 4.

[13] Art. I, clause 3.

[14] Art. I, clause 2.

[15] Cf. Pic, *op. cit.*, pp. 82-84; Charles Gide (Editor), *Effects of the War upon French Economic Life*, published by the Carnegie Foundation (1923), pp. 181-184; Barthélemy Raynaud, *Vers le Salaire Minimum* (1913), which has suggestive references to the effect of the laws of 1909 and 1912 in England; E. C. Shepherd, *The Fixing of Wages in Government Employment* (1923), pp. 154-157, France. With M. Gide's work may be found suggestive pages in William F. Gephart, *Effects of the War upon Insurance, with Special Reference to the Substitution of Insurance for Pensions* (1918), especially as the problem of social cost is regarded by the State.

such groups did not exist the mixed syndicates of employers and workers were to determine the basis for contracts of work. This gave the syndicates a new power and importance, not only in their bargaining capacity, but most important of all, gave the authority which the Government recognition of their function of representation in trade interests had made possible. The author of the Decrees pointed out that the first aim of the Decrees was to see that the State, the departments and the municipalities were not unwittingly agents in placing obstacles before the workers. More than that,

> they put upon the workers themselves the control of conditions, gave to the workers' syndicates as well as the employers' syndicates a rôle in the fixing of wages, duration of work and conditions of employment.[16]

Measures were taken to see that the application of the decrees was certain. An administrative commission was instituted four days after to study the conditions of their enforcement in all contracts made in the name of the State. General instructions were sent to all of the offices of the Ministry of Commerce and Industry, especially defining the application of the law to the postal and telegraph service. The contracts given for the Paris Exposition of 1900 by the State were looked after by M. Millerand; and the various departments of the Government gave added instructions where they were concerned in the fulfilment of contracts. These departmental rulings were given to all of the prefects[17] and were made more complete by indications of practical detail. The good effects of the Decrees were in their sanctions, Millerand making it very plain that where the contracts

[16] Millerand's speech at Lille, October 15, 1899, for an interpretation of the Republican Government's efforts to show the masses that their sure support was the Republic which depended upon them for its existence, Lavy, *op. cit.*, pp. 391-399.

[17] It is necessary to keep in mind that the prefect is the nominee of the Minister of Interior and is the most important of the local officials, occupying "a double position, for he is the agent of the central government in regard to those matters of general administration which are thought to concern the whole country, and at the same time he is the executive officer of the department for local affairs" (Lowell, *op. cit.*, Vol. I, pp. 36-37). Cf. Joseph Barthélemy, *The Government of France* (E. T.). J. Bayard Morris (1924), Part VII, pp. 121-159.

were not fulfilled toward the workers the State was to indemnify them directly, and then hold the contractors responsible. While there were no penal sanctions the effective fulfilment of the decrees depended upon the State promptly repudiating a contract where the conditions of the decrees were not met.[18] The effect of this law was not only enhanced by the spirit which the Government showed in outlining the principles of its administration, but it was evidence that the new ministry were in earnest in their efforts of bringing about "peace and social concord." There is no gainsaying the importance of this ideal in the politics of democracy.

Conseils du Travail.

The Decrees [19] of September 17, 1900, and January 2, 1901, creating Labour Councils (*Conseils du Travail*), further outlined the Government policy, indicating even more definitely that the purpose of the ministry was to make the syndicates the working basis of economic and social reform. The Report [20] to the President of the Republic preceding the first decree stated that the principal mission of the *Conseils* should be to inform the Government, the employers and the workers on the actual conditions of work, to promote general agreements between the interests, and to furnish in case of collective conflict, competent mediators to bring forward the good offices of the *Conseils de Prud'Hommes.*[21] In spite of the hierarchical conditions imposed by the discipline of the industrial establishments, the Report stated, it should be possible for the employers and the workers in the same industries and in the same territory to engage in free discussion of their separate and their common interests. This had been the intention of the Government in the earlier legislation, made more necessary, it was pointed out, by the position of the isolated employee and patron. The remedy for this inequality was the syndicate. "To encourage by all means the formation of these corporate associations," the Report continues, "so useful in the progress of social peace, is a task which ought not to be neglected

[18] In the Chamber of Deputies, July 4, 1899, Millerand said that civil action was sufficient to insure observation of the decrees.

[19] Dalloz, *Code du Travail,* pp. 131-134; texts of the decrees published also in *Journal Officiel,* September 18, 1900, and January 5, 1901.

[20] See Lavy, *op. cit.,* pp. 79-82.

[21] Art. II of the Decree.

by a Republican Government." So these later Decrees carried forward the work of unifying the administration of the earlier Decrees; the same purpose guiding in their elaboration "of giving the syndicates a part in the Parliament of Labour," the *Conseil Supérieur du Travail.* "In helping direct to safety the workers who wish to emancipate themselves, we say 'organize yourself.' "[22] The Government thus made plain its friendly purpose.

The Labour Councils were regionally organized and for the districts they represented were to determine the rate of wages and the duration of the working day, governing the contracts made in the name of the State. They were to study unemployment and measures of relief; report to the proper administrative bodies on the distribution and expenditure of public funds to trade organizations; report on the administration of laws and decrees, and make recommendations of change or improvement in labour laws.[23] The legality of the decrees was questioned because they gave the right of public power to purely private organization; and they were attacked also on the ground that they violated the right of universal suffrage, because the professional syndicates were the basis of the electoral system in the Labour Councils.[24] The legality of the decrees was settled by the *Conseil d'Etat* in a decision of February 19, 1904; the plea of the syndicates opposing was rejected, and the decrees instituted to carry out the *Conseils du Travail* declared legal.[25] But the attitude of the Senate[26] (which had passed the proposition of M. Bérenger, providing for election to the Councils on a non-syndical basis and that they should have only a consultative function), resulted in the Chamber refusing to consider the Senate text in the Commission on Labour. This forced the Government to allow the decrees to become almost a dead letter. But the law of July 17, 1908,[27] completed by the Decree of May 10, 1909,[28] constituting the *Conseils Consultatifs*

[22] Millerand, *op. cit.* (Lavy), p. 398.

[23] See Art. 2, clauses 1-6, for prescribed duties.

[24] Millerand replied to these objections in the Chamber of Deputies, November 22, 1901.

[25] Cf. *Bulletin du Office du Travail,* March, 1904, pp. 222-223.

[26] See *Journal Officiel,* Nos. 198, 224, and 462, 1901, for the discussion.

[27] Dalloz, *Code du Travail,* pp. 200-201; D. P., 1908, 4, 69; Bull. Dalloz, 1908, p. 387; and see *Bull. Office du Travail,* June, 1909, p. 691.

[28] Dalloz, *Code du Travail,* pp. 202-205.

du Travail and the rules of their administration, confirmed the principle which the Government had aimed to establish. The Councils are composed of an equal number of employers and workers, and their chief duty is to further the moral and material interests of the trades they represent and to aid the Government by carrying out investigations.[29] At first the Councils were advisory bodies, but the Minimum Wage Act of 1915 [30] gave them the power of determining the minimum wage in their respective districts.[31]

The progress which the State has made in using voluntary and extra-State agencies in the administration of labour law is an outstanding feature of modern administration.[32] The short history of the law just outlined affords a good example. Development of the theory of direct action in politics has brought about a marked change in the problems before modern democracies with regard to the representation of interests in Parliament.[33] Meanwhile the expansion of the consultative bodies in France may be noticed in the service which has been rendered by the *Conseil Supérieur du Travail,* the *Conseils Regionaux du Travail,* the Chambers of Commerce with district and national consultation commissions, and the *Chambres d'Agriculture,* constituted by the law of October 25, 1919, and the decrees of December 25 and February 3, 1920.

Millerand intended the laws and decrees of the Government to be an answer to his adversaries who said that

> the Socialists are men of violence, incapable of using any other means for the triumph of their ideas than brutal revolution; Socialists are those dreamers hypnotised by the chimerical construction of an utopian society; Socialists are those who are creators of hate and civil war, occupied only with fomenting the struggle between classes.[34]

[29] Art. I of the law of 1908.

[30] *Code du Travail,* Art. 33-42, T. III, chap. I; pp. 15-20, Dalloz.

[31] Art. 33 e, 33 f and 33 g of the law of 1915.

[32] For an interesting point of view see Joseph Barthélemy, *Le Problème de la Compétence dans la Démocratie* (1918), chap. IV, section 2, pp. 231-234, "La Participation des non-professionnels aux fonctions publiques." Cf. André Thiers, *La Politique de Demain: Administrative, Financière et Économique* (3rd ed. 1922), and his *Administrateurs et Administrés* (1919).

[33] Cf. Pic, *op. cit.*, pp. 128-129.

[34] Millerand, *op. cit.* (Lavy), p. 399.

He believed that Socialism was intent upon the absorption and disappearance of all classes in a regenerated humanity; that the collectivist program, justifying itself, was becoming more and more each day realized; and, finally, that the "so-called revolutionists were the first to show the example of respect for law and confidence in universal suffrage." [35] Before the first session of the *Conseil Supérieur du Travail,* June 5, 1900 Millerand said the workingmen are henceforth warned that in order to participate through delegates elected from their own ranks in the elaboration of economic reforms which concern them most, it is necessary and sufficient that they enter the ranks of that great army of which the syndicates are the battalions. How can they refuse to do this? By inducing them to do so we believe that we are defending their legitimate interests at the same time that we are serving the cause of social peace in this country.[36]

This was confirmation of his speech outlining the policy of the Government in the Chamber of Deputies, November 23, 1899, when he said that

the best means of bringing back the working masses to the Republic, is to show them not by words, but by facts, that the Republican Government is above everything else the Government of the small and the weak.

Conseil Supérieur du Travail.

The ministerial decree [37] of September 1, 1899, entirely modifying the *Conseil Supérieur du Travail* was a major indication of this purpose, and was one of the most important decisions of the Government with regard to industry. The creation of this advisory body of study and information was under a Decree of January 22, 1891, by the Ministry of Commerce. It had not been of much importance, as its sixty members were nominated by the Minister, with the exception of ten ex-officio members of the Council permanently attached. The members served for two

[35] *Ibid.* Cf. J. Puget, *L'Histoire de la Réforme Électorale,* with Preface by J. Paul-Boncour (1912).

[36] Millerand, *op. cit.* (Lavy), p. 66.

[37] J. O. C. of D., September 2, 1899; the Decree of March 14, 1903 (Dalloz, *Code du Travail,* pp. 137-144), abrogated the Decrees of January 22, 1891, June 9, 1892, September 1, 1899, October 20, 1900, and March 23, 1902, on the organization of the Superior Council.

years. The Council had no fixed time of meeting, its sessions being called by the Minister who determined the objects of the meetings and their duration.[38] There had been lively objection on the part of the Labour leaders to the exclusion of the elective method in choosing the Superior Council; and the Minister of Commerce in 1893, attempted a reorganization of the Council, with a view of including by election representatives of the workers and the employers. In the course of the debate on the Budget of 1899, the reform of the Council in its system of election of membership was voted by more than a hundred majority. Thus the Government was given the opportunity to make a complete change.

In the Report [39] to the President outlining the re-constitution of the Superior Council and interpreting the aim of the Ministry in the application of the Decree, Millerand briefly traced the existing organization of workers' and patronal institutions in France. He referred to the influence of the annual Trade Union Congresses in England, and also the important function of the Royal Commissions in providing information for the Government. He hoped that by the work of the Permanent Commission the Superior Council of Labour would occupy the same place in France. By the Decree of 1891 the Permanent Commission was set up under the Ministry of Commerce, but was changed by the Decree of 1899 to the control of the Council as a whole. The problem for the Government was to initiate the system of election for the Council. While Millerand believed that "universal suffrage ought to be everywhere, in the last resort, the master of public opinion," he had found it best to take professional syndicates as the basis of organizing the system of selection, for both workers and employers had corporate organizations that could be made to function as election groups. The Report admitted that only 500,000 of the workers were represented in the syndicates. Yet it would be very simple for all workers who wished to be represented to organize syndicates of their own, if they did not care to join any of the existing ones. "The Government of the Republic would certainly rejoice to see the workers in greater

[38] Art. 4 of the Decree of 1891.

[39] For this Report, Lavy, *op. cit.*, pp. 69-72, providing ministerial interpretation of the decree.

and greater numbers enjoy the rights conferred by the law of 1884," it was added. The President was assured that the syndicates would not see in the measures of necessary organization any indiscreet curiosity into their private affairs nor any distrust of their development. But, on the contrary, it would be a fresh gauge of progress both for the syndicates and for the nation, that they had been called on to collaborate more definitely, through their membership and professional organization, for a clearly defined economic function.

The Report stated further that the experience of the old Council had shown that it was wise to have members who were not of the "corporate interests," but represented "general interests." This made possible the maintaining of an equilibrium between the two interests that was an essential condition of the functioning of the Permanent Commission.[40] The Superior Council of Labour was constituted of 66 members: 22 delegates each from the employers and workers organizations, as fully representative of their corporate interests in France as was possible; and 22 members from official bodies: the Paris Chamber of Commerce, the Bourse du Travail, professors of the University of Paris, economists and jurists with special competence. The four appointments which M. Millerand made,[41] it is worth noting, as Minister of Commerce and Industry, were Mme. Bonnevialle, a prominent woman socialist and syndicalist, Professor Raoul Jay, professor of Industrial Legislation in the Law Faculty of the University of Paris, M. Victor Legrand, president of the *Tribunal de Commerce de la Seine,* and M. Jaurès, the parliamentary leader of the Socialist party in France.

It was the intention of Millerand to make the Permanent Commission of the *Conseil Supérieur du Travail* a real institution of service. Under the Decree of 1891 it had been controlled directly by the Minister of Commerce and Industry, who named its president, the result being that it had little initiative and no independence. By the Decree of 1899 the Permanent Commission of the Superior Council of Labour was composed of 22 members: 7 delegates each from the workers and employers represented in

[40] The Permanent Commission has two presidents, one from the workers and one from the employers.

[41] J. O. C. of D., May 22, 1900.

the Superior Council of Labour; the Senate and Chamber by a delegate each; the president of the Paris Chamber of Commerce; the vice-president of the advisory council of the Paris Bourse du Travail; a representative of the advisory commission of the workers' co-operative associations; and three officials of the chief public services of France. This was an economic parliament by authority of the State, which elected its own president, carried on investigations, issued reports on legislation, studied problems of administration, and prepared for the Council the agenda of the full sessions. In turn the Government depended on the Council for its policy of social legislation. Inquiries were to be conducted by the Commission, at the request of the Ministry of Commerce and Industry, on conditions of existing laws, relations between workers and patrons, the causes and circumstances of strikes, and all problems affecting the organization of labour and industry. "The *Conseil Superieur du Travail,* thanks to its work (the Permanent Commission), will be able to perform," said Millerand, "the function of the great Royal Commissions of England which study and investigate with painstaking care the problems of the world of labour."

The example of England in its labour organization and in its method of carrying on parliamentary investigation had led this minister to hope for the good effects of a national workers' council in France, and a Permanent Commission of study and investigation at the service of the Government.

A series of Circulars were sent to the Prefects and to all syndicates of patrons and workers, giving complete instructions on the procedure of election for the *Conseil Supérieur du Travail.* It was to meet annually, but special sessions might be called by the Minister of Commerce and Industry. The first session [42] of the reorganized Superior Council was largely given to a study of the proposals for new legislation concerning the *Conseil de Prud'Hommes,* modifications which were carried out in the law of February, 1901. It also committed to the Permanent Commission three subjects of inquiry: (1) municipal and syndical

[42] Cf. Andre Marnet, "La Reforme des Conseils de Prud'hommes," *Le Mouvement Socialiste,* April 1, 1901, pp. 401-416; and for a critical review of the June 3-13, 1901, meeting of the Council, second session, see *Le Mouvement Socialiste,* October 1, 1901, pp. 418-430.

organization against unemployment; (2) conditions of work among persons not protected by existing legislation; and (3) special study of the principles of arbitration. The importance of the second subject was recognized by the Council pronouncing in favour of the intervention of law to assure the health and security of workers and the limitation of the hours of work for women and children and men.[43] It voted that the law of June 12, 1893, on the health and security of workers, the basic law in France, and all the decrees which followed for its enforcement; the law of November 2, 1892, on the work of women and children; and the law of March 30, 1900, on the ten hour day, should apply to all the workers under consideration—*i.e.,* in commercial establishments and small shops. This marked an important development in the theory of State interference, beginning an extension of the protective provisions of legislation for millions of citizens and its end has not been reached. By the law of December 29, 1900,[44] there was manifest the first desire of the legislature in France to extend to commercial employees the protection of health and the security given to other workers. Commercial workers were brought under the administrative control of the labour inspectors, which provisions were more favourably extended by the Decrees of December 28, 1909,[45] October 26, 1912,[46] and June 21, 1913,[47] forbidding certain work to women and children. The extension of the benefits of legislative protection to all workers and all citizens in need of it, a principle established in the twentieth century, is here given support.[48] In the Ministerial Circular of May 17, 1900,[49] completing the law of March

[43] See the Report of the *Commission Supérieur du Travail* (J. O. C. of D., August, 1904), and the extracts and analysis in the September and October *Bulletin du Office du Travail,* pp. 786-797, 863-873.

[44] *Code du Travail,* Liv. II, Art. 76 and 91.

[45] Dalloz, *Code du Travail,* pp. 207-209.

[46] Art. I, clause 5, Decree of 1909.

[47] Dalloz, *Code du Travail,* p. 285.

[48] Cf. *Bulletin du Office du Travail,* Vol. XI, 1904, p. 25; and there may be noted the Report of the Minister of Commerce and Industry, 1901, on the administration of the law of June 12, 1893, *Bulletin du Office du Travail,* Jan., 1903, pp. 13 ff.

[49] This circular is one of the best of the many administrative documents of Millerand's ministry, and, as nearly all of them, gives an adequate historical outline, indicating the unity and continuity of labour legislation.

30, 1900,[50] this principle was defended by Millerand, who pointed out that if there is not unity of administration in applying the laws to all the workers then the condition *status quo* is maintained. The great importance of the law of March 30, 1900, establishing the principle of the ten hour day, was that the State had intervened to fix the hours of labour by statute. This was evident when Millerand affirmed in the Circular that "the regulation of the work of adults is the corollary, the necessary complement of that of the work of women and children." Experience had shown that only on this basis could effective general inspection and administration be obtained.[51] With this in mind he could say that the law "was above all a measure of moralization, of solidarity and of social pacification." [52]

The first session of the *Conseil Supérieur du Travail* further agreed that a day of rest should apply to all workers, in principle, Sunday; that the hours of opening and closing of business houses should be determined by two-thirds majority of those concerned, enforcement to be in the hands of the department or commune police officers; that the requirements of the office of inspection be shown in detail in each establishment, that in the future the supervision of the inspectors might be more effective. The Council also asked for the extension of legislation on apprenticeship,[53] bringing all commercial establishments within the provisions of the law; and the study of the complete revision of the legislation on that subject was given to the Permanent Commission. The interest created by the attempt of practical reforms in legislation dealing with the *Conseil de Prud'Hommes,* continued for a good

[50] The Law of April 23, 1919, establishing the 48 hour week, is the completion by legislation of this earlier Act: see *Code du Travail,* Liv. II, Tit. I, Chap. II, Art. 6-8.

[51] See M. Duboin, *La législation sociale à la fin du XIXe siècle* (Paris, 1900), pp. 14-23; M. Duboin was Advocate General of the *Cour de Cassation,* and this general survey is broad interpretation of the function of the State in an economic régime based on the principle of *solidarité.*

[52] The law of March 30, 1900, was to expire April 1, 1904: see Doc. Parl. Sen. 1903, No. 364 (M. Waddington), and Senate discussion on law March 18, 22, and 24, 1904. See also *Bulletin du Office du Travail,* April, 1904, pp. 364-365, and Doc. Parl. C. of D. 1904, No. 1639.

[53] Cf. Pierre Brizon, *L'Apprentissage, Hier, Aujourd'hui, Demain* (1909), a suggestive book on this subject.

number of years.[54] This special value of leadership in the work of social investigation was noted by the Ministry of Public Works [55] with reference to the Permanent Commission's Report on conditions of work in the transport industries; [56] and in this connection may be mentioned [57] the Report in 1904 on the weekly day of rest as well as that on the notice-to-quit-work law project of that year.

Part II

Administrative Commissions

The *Conseil Supérieur du Travail* is only a consultative and advisory institution, "a national mixed syndicate," Millerand said, possessing technical skill and special competence in dealing with problems which relate to the interests of each group and the whole country. Yet there has not been since 1891 an important project dealing with labour legislation which has not first been discussed and studied by the Council before the debates on it were begun in the Chambers.[58] The Government has first submitted to the Council the proposed legislation dealing with a special subject, which has been a recognition of its duty "to inform itself on the interests of industry, that it might with usefulness fulfil its mission in the work of social co-operation." [59] By the State taking the lead in commanding the services of associative groups within its jurisdiction the better way has been

[54] Cf. *Bulletin du Office du Travail,* April, 1904, pp. 363 ff. "Les Conseils de Prud'Hommes du Senat"; also *Bulletin,* Dec., 1903, p. 1031, for list of law propositions and projects before the Chambers. The Senate in March, 1904, the 1st, 3rd, 4th, 8th and 15th, examined the proposition of the Commission, differing slightly from the text adopted by the Senate on November 26, 1903; it was adopted, sent to the Chamber of Deputies, see J. O. C. of D., March 18, 1904, p. 262. Doc. Parl. No. 1604.

[55] *Bulletin du Office du Travail,* April, 1904, p. 325.

[56] *Bulletin du Office du Travail,* Dec., 1903, p. 990; October, 1903, p. 826; April, 1904, pp. 325-328; and October, 1904, pp. 874-875; the first inquiry of the Permanent Commission and the sessions of 1903-4, are covered in the above.

[57] *Bulletin du Office du Travail,* December, 1904, pp. 1056-1063.

[58] Pic, *op. cit.,* p. 113.

[59] Bry-Perreau, *Les Lois du Travail Industriel et de la Prévoyance Sociale, Législation Ouvrière*" (6th ed. 1921), p. 696.

shown of co-operation and common understanding, which even at this time has led to direct relationships between the organizations of industry and of labour when the State has not been the agent of bringing them together.[60] Distrust of the State often has had a good effect in uniting the two divisions of capital and labour, sharing the feeling together. This works altogether for the good of the State. One thing being done that Governments are concerned with: the common purpose of getting at an agreement is made a social duty.

The creation of consultative and advisory institutions at the service of the Government marks the beginning of a new era with regard to State intervention. It is a democratic effort by the State in France and England to meet the peculiar needs of their people. In England the strength of organization gives the idea its influence, while in France the appeal is to both the industrialists and syndicalists, cursed at times with unreasoning individualism, the evil effects of which are mitigated when the two factions can work together. Employers' associations, workers' federations, and all agencies of trade and commercial and social interests having competence with regard to subjects dealt with by the State through legislation have been called upon to be "councillors of State." This has proved a steadying influence on the Labour movement of France and England. A chance has been given for critical examination of party programs, as well as an opportunity afforded of understanding the inherent difficulties of progress in democracy. A recognition of common responsibilities has been a liberalizing solvent of the class consciousness of the patronal groups. It has begun a wider service of usefulness which the groups within the State can render in organizing and administering the industrial system. Gradually an ideal of common service may transform the whole conception of rights and duties. A common purpose shared by all would mean the surest basis of social peace with justice. That would in time free the State for more congenial duties. This would be an incalculable advantage, for the strain upon democratic institutions, arising from Parliament attempting to organize industry, has often en-

[60] Cf. Etienne Villey, *L'Organisation Professionnelle des Employeurs dans l'Industrie Française* (1923), chap. III, pp. 231-305, esp. pp. 266 ff. on the Superior Council of Labour.

dangered the political well-being of the people by which progress is secured.

The *Conseil Supérieur du Travail* has greatly helped this ideal of unity in national service by the practical aid it has brought to the Government in the formulation of law projects.[61] Chief among these may be mentioned the ones dealing with the control of the conditions of work for shop and commercial employees, 1901 and 1912; of technical and trade education, 1905; on the law of syndicates, 1909; and the payment of a minimum wage to home workers, 1910.[62] This function has been carried on in a

[61] Pic, *op. cit.*, p. 113.

[62] The *Conseil Supérieur du Travail* held eight sessions between 1891-1900; and it is worth noting the Reports and Inquiries of the Sessions from that date. They are published by the *Ministère du Travail et de la Prévoyance Sociale.*

9th Session (1900)—"Enquête sur la législation des conseils de prud' hommes."
10th Session (1901)—"Réglementation du travail dans les bureaux et magasins."
11th Session (1902)—"Apprentissage" and the "Groupes Professionnels du Conseil supérieur."
12th Session (1903)—"Les Caisses de chômage"; "Réglementation du travail dans les industries de transport"; and "Enquête et documents sur le Délai-congé."
13th Session (1904)—"Le Délai-Congé" and "Le Repos hebdomadaire."
14th Session (1905)—"Le Délai-Congé."
15th Session (1905)—"L'Enseignement professionnel" and "Délai-Congé."
16th Session (1906)—"L'Inspection du travail" and "L'Affichage des lois ouvrières."
17th Session (1907)—"L'Organisation du Conseil superieur du Travail"; "La Protection du salaire en cas de faillite ou de déconfiture"; "La Capacité commerciale des syndicats professionnels"; "Les Decrets du 10 août 1899 sur les adjudications"; and "Les Cautionnements versés par les salariés."
18th Session (1908)—No Reports, only *Compte rendu* of Session.
19th Session (1909)—"La Legislation sur les Syndicats professionnels."
20th Session (1910)—No Reports, only *Compte rendu* of Session.
21st Session (1911)—"Rapports sur les Indices des Crises economiques et sur les mesures financieres propres à attenuer les Chômages resultant de ces crises," by the *Commission des crises economiques* (1908-11).
22nd Session (1912)—"La Reglementation du travail des employes," two Reports by Workers' and Patrons' sections of the Permanent Commission.
23rd Session (Nov., 1913)—*Compte rendu.*—1 Vol., XIX—186 p. "Enquête sur la réduction de la durée du travail le samedi" (semaine anglaise); "Enquête de l'Office du Travail," 1 Vol., XVI—259 p. "La réduction de la durée du travail le samedi" (Semaine

more restricted way by two earlier institutions of consultation, the *Conseil Supérieur du Commerce et de l'Industrie* and the *Comité Consultatif des Arts et Manufactures.* The function of these two bodies is to give expert advice and counsel to the Government on matters of commerce and industry, carry on investigations for the Ministry of Commerce, and to aid in a development of national policy with regard to trade arrangements with foreign countries. The *Comité Consultatif des Arts et Manufactures,* created in 1791, but completely reorganized in 1884,[63] now consists of 54 members, nominated by the Minister of Commerce, and of 8 members in their own right. The *Conseil Supérieur du Commerce et de l'Industrie* is a central body representing all France, the members of which are nominated by the President. Its history dates back to 1607. But for all practical purposes it need only be suggested that after the creation of a Ministry of Agriculture in 1881,[64] separate from the Ministry of Commerce, two Councils were formed,[65] the *Conseil Supérieur de l'Agriculture* and the *Conseil Supérieur du Commerce et de l'Industrie,* divided into two sections, Commerce and Industry. There are 32 members in each section, of which number 17 in each are always elected from certain Chambers of Commerce in

anglaise); "Rapports de M. Briat et de M. Pralon," 1 Vol., XXXVII—16 p.
"Age d'admission au service de la clientèle dans les auberges, hôtels, etc." (Rapport de M. Craissac), 1 Vol., X—84 p.
"Allaitement maternel au magasin et à l'atelier," (Rapport de M. Abel Craissac, procès (verbaux, enquêtes et documents.) 1 broch de XX—24 p. (1916).

24th Session (Oct., 1917)—*Compte rendu.*—"Mesures relatives à la démobilisation."—"Allocations de chômage aux démobilisés." 1 Vol., XVII—38 p.

25th Session (Nov., 1921)—*Compte rendu.*—"Rapports; Extension de la loi du 10 juillet, 1915 (salaires à domicile dans le vêtement) à certains travaux non visés dans la loi" (M. Briat).—"Les allocations familiales" (M. Pralon). 1 Vol., XX-76 p.

26th Session (Nov., 1922)—*Compte rendu et rapports.*—"Projet de loi sur les assurances sociales." 1 Vol., XIX—188 p. A majority and a minority report is given.

27th Session (Nov., 1923)—*Compte rendu.*—"Rapport de M. Baudet sur la participation aux bénéfices." 1 Vol., XIX—179 p. (1924).
"Enquête de l'Office du Travail sur la participation aux bénéfices." 1 Vol., VII—129 p.

[63] Decree of March 8, 1884.

[64] Decree of November 14, 1881.

[65] Decree of October 13, 1882.

different parts of the country, that representation may be general for all interests. From this Council, since 1894, there has been formed a Permanent Consultation Commission [66] (*Commission Consultative Permanente*), consisting of 25 members.

The history of such institutions and the *Conseil Supérieur du Travail,* bodies constituted for expert advice, with special duties of consultation and investigation, has often suggested the very important question of the representation of economic interests in Parliament. The advocacy of such a system has most often been founded on the conviction that political institutions are to-day inadequately functioning in the economic régime because of their inherent incapacity to organize life or because of the corrupting influence of class interest. It is often assumed that only by the genius of economic motive can all of life be wholly seen and interpreted. There is no doubt that the human interest in Parliament has been vastly increased and that the efficiency of its legislation has been greatly promoted by the emphasis of this principle. It is a welcome one and as old as the history of assemblies. Yet where there has been no other test of capacity for usefulness and no other criteria but the economic, there has been no advance in the theory of democratic control through legislation and administration. But the increasing acceptance by the modern State of the right of groups within the State to be heard on all questions which concern them, is a proof that democratic Government can use the special services and work through the institutional life of the associations whose interests are not, and need never be, antagonistic to the welfare of all within the State.

The importance of the Government proposal of 1899 and the official sanction it gave to the representation of interests, is indicated in the history of the Decrees which carried on the work of reorganization of the *Conseil Supérieur du Travail.* They are the Decrees of March 14, 1903, January 27, 1904, June 24, 1907, April 30, 1909, July 1, 1913,[67] and January 31, 1921.[68] This is a good example again of the cumulative value of legislative experience, for year by year the administration of the Superior Council

[66] Decree of July 3, 1894.

[67] See Dalloz, *Code du Travail,* pp. 137-144, for Decrees down to 1921, allowing convenient comparison.

[68] Dalloz, *Code du Travail* (*Additions*), pp. 65-71.

has been more effective and its influence in consequence has been greater. A comparison of the Decree of 1899 with the Decree of 1921 suggests the great value of putting upon the statute book sound principles of social legislation. In so short a time validity and new power have been given to the ideal of national interest, which can be protected by group interests, and must be, in a democracy of industry and government.

The *Conseil Supérieur du Travail* is presided over by the Minister of Labour, and the chief secretary of the Labour and Pensions Departments are permanent members of the Council, having the right of discussion but not of voting, and the director of any Government Department, with the consent of the Minister of Labour, may attend the sessions when matters of his department are under consideration. At the present the Superior Council of Labour is composed [69] of 78 members; the patrons and workers each electing 32 delegates; while the 14 remaining members include 3 senators elected by the Senate, five deputies elected by the Chamber of Deputies, one member designated by the Paris Chamber of Commerce, two delegates from the *Conseil Supérieur de la Co-operation,* representing the two sections, Production and Consumption, and three members chosen by the Ministry of Labour from the Institute and the Law Faculty of the University of Paris. The *Conseil Supérieur de la Co-operation* was instituted by the Decree of February 22, 1918, to unify and carry out the administration of the laws of December 18, 1915, on the *Sociétés Co-operatives Ouvrières de Production* and of May 7, 1918, on the *Sociétés Co-operatives Ouvrières de Consommation.* It is evident that the Council of Labour is representative of French national life; is really, by virtue of its being an elective body, as representative as a national council can be of the organized interests of industry and labour. This fact is more evident when it is noted that the 32 members of the two groups are elected by a plan which insures representation of all important national interests.[70] The patronal group is divided into three sections: 22 delegates being elected from the Chambers of Commerce and

[69] Art. 5 of the Decree of 1921, corresponding to Art. 5 of the 1913 Decree.

[70] Art. 2 of the Decree of 1921, corresponding to Art. 1 of the 1913 Decree.

the *Chambres Consultatives des Arts et Manufactures;* two delegates from the *Conseil Supérieur de l'Agriculture,* elected by the Council; and eight councillors *Prud'Homme* from the patrons group. There are two groups of workers' delegates, 24 elected from the syndicates and 8 from the workers' group of the *Conseils de Prud'Hommes.* Both the 22 delegates of the employers and the 24 delegates of the workers represent that many divisions of French industrial organization, set forth definitely in the Decree.[71] The *Prud'Homme* delegates are selected [72] from the five *Conseils de Prud'Hommes* in Paris (two members for each group), and from the Councils in France (six members for each group).

A Permanent Commission is appointed from among the members, which has the duty of carrying on studies in regard to general industrial conditions, the conditions of the workers, and the relations between employers and employees. This Commission presents its findings to the Council and advises as to needed reforms. It can also advise on the matter of strikes or alliances of employers which are formed for the purpose of keeping down wages. Either a single report may be submitted or a majority and a minority report, and these form the subjects for the deliberations of the Superior Council. The Ministers of departments other than Labour often designate a division chief to take part in the sessions of the Permanent Council in the work which particularly concerns their departments.

The purpose of the Government to create a central consultative body, a Parliament of Labour, had been successfully carried out by 1913, for the basis of representation of trade and national labour interest remain unchanged in the Decree of 1921. The *Conseil Supérieur du Travail* was to be the national body, and the Government intended the *Conseils du Travail* to serve as the local institutions.[73] Together these bodies were to co-ordinate the

[71] Articles 8 and 10 of the Decrees of 1913 and 1921.

[72] Art. 7 of the two Decrees. It should be noted that the Decree of July 1, 1913, establishes fully the principle of representation; the 1921 Decree is cited because it is the latest one.

[73] The law of June 21, 1924, codified the laws relating to the jurisdiction, powers, organization, election, etc., of Labor Councils, and more clearly defined the functions of conciliation and arbitration, together with the principle of occupational representation, *i.e.,* joint councils of

plans and put into operation the schemes of social amelioration and labour organization which the Government had committed itself to in the Decrees of August 10, 1899. The major duty of the two Councils was to advise the Government and the parties concerned on the industrial questions for which all shared a common responsibility, and which had to be settled in common. There was little need for argument on the necessity of creating competent agencies for aid in the work of conciliation and arbitration. Millerand pointed out that the law of December 27, 1892, had not accomplished what had been hoped for in bringing together employers and workers for an amicable settling of disputes. But by the general authority of the Superior Council of Labour and the specific power of the Labour Councils in their capacity as agents of conciliation, and under the direction of the two interested parties, it was hoped that a new spirit of self-control and justice might be introduced in the collective agreements of the syndicates.[74]

In introducing the new institution of Labour Councils [75] where "patrons and workers in the same territory could freely discuss their respective general interests and their corporate interests," the Decree stated that "the Government remained faithful to its rôle of peacemaker and arbiter." These two Councils as bodies with advisory and administrative attributes possessed for the State a very great importance and established in French Labour

employers and workers. The laws form Section IV of the labour and insurance code.

[74] A. Millerand, *Politique de Realisations,* Paris (1911), pp 21-26, 150-151, for the views of the author of the Decrees eight years after the Waldeck-Rousseau ministry, on their purpose and significance; and also pp. 17-30, "Le Reglement Amiable des Conflits du Travail," together with pp. 140-152. Cf. Georges Renard, *Discussions sociales d'hier et de demain* (1910), and his *Syndicats, Trade-Unions et Corporations* (1909), for friendly estimate on work of M. Millerand and his reformistic policy. Also Gabriel Seailles, *La Philosophie du Travail* (1923), pp. 1-36, an address reprinted in this volume, on the above title, given at Lille in 1903 and pp. 362-393, on the moral education of democracy, preparing the way of justice.

[75] See the Report of the *Commission du Travail,* by M. Dron, on the institution of the *Conseils Consultatifs du Travail,* for a good history and review of the purpose of the Commission with regard to Labour Councils, J. O. C. of D., June 30, 1908, pp. 632-636, Doc. Parl. No. 1858; also Appendices in Octave Noel's *Le Socialisme et la Question Sociale* (1902).

legislation a new principle of State intervention. Both MM. Millerand and Jaurès interpreted their meaning with these facts in mind. They saw keenly that the evolution of modern industrial society had demanded from the State and from the Labour movement an entirely different answer than the theorists of the early Radical school and the propagandists of that Socialist period were prepared to give. It was their aim at the beginning of the century to give the aid that political methods and institutions could to agencies of control and direction. There was felt the tremendous undercurrent of opinion in the ranks of the capitalists and the labourers toward the new economic order, each side conscious that a desperate struggle for control was going on and each cautious of every step that the Government found necessary to make or was forced to take. The economic movement had to be met. M. Millerand for a time took what refuge a Government ministry could in the attempt at political action and in the use of expert counsel by the State.

"The conditions of work," he said, "become with the development of machinery and of transportation more and more complex; and called daily to intervene for the legal protection of the workers, the Government has need of being informed by important groups, which in their composition assure a competence and a special authority, and to whom it is possible to give certain problems, asking their counsel with the certainty of truthfulness and impartiality."

Taken in connection with the statement just quoted from M. Millerand, the development is remarkable since 1900 of those "important groups, which in their composition assure a competence and a special authority." They furnish the best indication of the scope of the administrative work of the Ministry of Labour in France. The number of Councils, Committees and Commissions which are connected with what are called the "external services" of that department include [76] the

Supreme Council of Public Health.
Supreme Council of Public Relief.
Supreme Commission of Industrial Labour.

[76] *International Labour Directory,* Geneva, 1921, pp. 37-38.

Commission of Industrial Hygiene.
Commission for Codification of Labour Laws.
Supreme Council of Labour.
Supreme Council of Statistics.
Supreme Council of Co-operation.
Supreme Council of Workers' and Peasants' Pensions.
Consultative Council on Disablement.
Commission for Preparing the Distribution of Subsidies to Consumers' Co-operative Societies and Unions of Societies.
Commission on Unemployment Funds.
Commission on Public Employment Offices.
Supreme Council of Economic Dwellings.
Supreme Commission of Savings Banks.
Supreme Commission of the National Fund for Old Age Pensions.
Supreme Commission of Death and Accident Insurance Funds.
Consultative Committee on Insurances Against Industrial Accidents.
Consultative Committee on Life Insurance Societies.
Consultative Committee on Capitalization and Savings Undertakings.
Consultative Committee on Re-insurance and Contract Insurance.
Consultative Council on Mutual Aid Societies.

Chambres de Métiers.

Two outstanding developments in the French economic life since 1918 which directly interpret the changes which have taken place since the war, and yet which are related to the general progress of the labour movement in this century, are the law of July 26, 1925, creating Trade Councils in France, and the Decree of January 17, 1925, establishing a National Economic Council. Both are significant in their conception and in the manner of their administration.

The law of July 26, 1925,[77] established trade councils (*chambres de métiers*) for artisans, both master workmen and journeymen, in the different Departments of France. Master workmen (*maîtres-artisans*) are workers of either sex who work at a manual trade either by themselves or with some member of their

[77] *Bulletin du Ministère du Travail et de l'Hygiène,* Paris, July-Sept., 1925, pp. 299, 300, 113-117, quoted by the *U. S. Monthly Labour Review,* Vol. XXII, No. I (Jan., 1926), pp. 65-66.

family or with journeymen or apprentices, but do not work for an employer. The purpose of the law is to provide through the medium of the trade councils a means of expression for this class of citizens analogous to that of other classes. Merchants and manufacturers can secure through the Chambers of Commerce, a hearing before the Government or Parliament, for the purpose either of registering complaints or giving technical advice, while agriculturalists have a similar opportunity through the Chambers of Agriculture. The skilled workers, however, have up to this time, had no means of representing their interests as a class and it is to remedy this situation that the present law was enacted.

The law provided that the trade councils shall be constituted in accordance with decrees, which may be issued upon the proposal of the Ministers of Labour, Commerce, and Public Instruction, these decrees to be issued after consultation with the interested organizations of the district. There may be one or several trade councils in a Department and each council may be divided into as many sections as seems necessary. The number of members of a Trade Council may not be less than 18 nor more than 36, except in Paris, where there may be as many as 72 members. The councils are composed of two-thirds master workmen and one-third journeymen; to be eligible for membership a person must be at least 30 years of age and have been actively engaged in his trade for at least 5 years, and if he is retired, for at least 15 years. The departmental inspector of technical education, one labour inspector appointed by the Minister of Labour, and one representative of the departmental committee of technical education have the right to membership in the councils, but in a consultative capacity only, and associate members may be appointed from the list of those eligible for active membership who may take part in the meetings of the council but without a vote.

The duties of the councils are to protect the occupational and economic interests of the trades. With this in view the advice of the trade councils should be sought upon all questions having to do with the improvement or development of a trade and upon all general questions interesting the artisan class. Councils may also give advice upon such questions upon their own initiative. The councils are also to participate in the organization of apprenticeship in the different trades under conditions to be fixed by special law. The departmental committees of technical education, provided for by the law of July 25, 1919, must each include four artisans appointed by the trade council concerned and there must be two such representatives on the local committees established in accordance with the terms of the same law.

National Economic Council.

The creation of a National Economic Council[78] in France in 1925 is an extension of a principle of administration which has been stressed with increasing insistence since the end of the war. The Minimum Program[79] of the *Confédération Générale du Travail,* as set forth by the *Comité Confédéral National* in December, 1918, called for the instituting of a *Conseil Economique National,* composed of representatives of different economic groups which should have for its object the orientation of the political and social development of the country and the preparation of bills on economic and social questions to be presented to Parliament for enactment into law. M. Godart, Minister of Labour, appointed a commission, which held its first meeting in July, 1924, to make a study of the way in which "labour, its organization, its initiatives, its aspirations, and the public health which conserves and creates the essential riches of the whole country" should be represented on the council. M. Jouhaux, secretary of the C. G. T., was in charge of the committee which decided that the council should be an autonomous body established through the collaboration of the different ministers to study and seek for a solution of the economic problems of the country. It was further decided that the National Economic Council should have a certain right of initiative in relation to the public authorities, including the authority to bring the results of its deliberations

[78] See the administrative decree, which became effective at once, in the *Journal Officiel,* January 17, 1925.

[79] Accepted by the Lyon Congress in September, 1919, at which time it was decided that the workers themselves would, in spite of the government's inactivity, create an Economic Council of Labour. This *Conseil économique du Travail* was made up of representatives of the C. G. T., the *Fédération nationale des co-opératives,* the *Fédération des fonctionnaires,* the *Union syndicale des techniciens de l'industrie, due commerce et de l'agriculture* (U. S. T. I. C. A.).

before the Government and before Parliament. After the Cabinet considered the proposal and made minor changes, the Prime Minister, M. Herriot, presented it to the President for his approval.

The principal provisions of the decree establishing the National Economic Council are as follows:

It shall be the function of the council to study problems concerning the economic life of the country, propose solutions, and bring its proposals before the public authorities. The council is attached to the office of the Prime Minister and its expenses will be provided for in the budget of the Ministry of Labour.

The council is composed of 47 members, representing the different economic and social groups of the country, as follows: Nine representing the consumers and the general public, selected from consumers' co-operative societies and consumers' leagues, mayors' associations, users of the public utilities, and heads of families; 30 representing labour and industry—(a) intellectual labour and education, (b) management in industry, agriculture, commerce, transportation, the co-operative movement, and the public utilities, (c) salaried employees, *i.e.*, civil servants, technical workers, and general labour in industry, commerce, agriculture, and transportation, and (d) artisans in city and rural trades; and 8 representing capital—(a) industrial and commercial capital, (b) real estate (city and rural), and (c) banks, the stock exchange, and insurance and savings funds. The members shall be chosen from the representative organizations in each class by the Government, through the Minister of Labour, after consultation with the different cabinet officers concerned.

The term of office of the members shall be two years and members must be French, at least 25 years of age, and in possession of full civil and political rights. Women are eligible under the same conditions as men. The council shall meet regularly four times each year for ten days, and extra sessions may be called by the Prime Minister, who is President of the National Economic Council. A permanent committee of ten members shall be elected by the council to take care of current matters between sessions and to insure the carrying out of decisions of the council. A list of experts shall be established, appointed from the different Government departments concerned, from the Superior Council of Labour and the Council of National Defence, and also including the French Government representative at the International Labour Office.

All the ministerial departments, under-secretaries of State, high commissioners, and the competent committees of the Chamber and the Senate will have the right to be represented in the deliberations of the council and its permanent committee. The council will likewise have the right to be heard by the competent committees of either branch of Parliament as well as by the ministers and members of the Government, and to request them to send representatives to the meetings of the council and the permanent committee in case no delegates have been appointed. The Prime Minister shall consult directly with the Economic Council, and the proceedings and decisions of the council in the form of reports or recommendations shall be published in the *Journal Officiel.* Decisions reached by the council must receive a two-thirds vote of the members present, and they shall be transmitted to the Prime Minister who will report them out within one month or ask to have the question reconsidered. The Government shall ask for information from the council on all proposed laws of an economic nature, and every law of an economic order passed may provide for compulsory consultation with the council in regard to the framing of the regulations necessary for its enforcement. The Prime Minister and the ministers of foreign affairs, labour, hygiene, insurance and social welfare, finance, commerce and industry, agriculture, public works, and the colonies will all be associated, as far as the interests of each are concerned, in the carrying out of this decree.

Part III

Labour Organization Within the State

The Syndicate.

The Government projects considered indicate that the syndicates were considered the basis of working class reform and the most useful instrument of progress for labour. An interpellation on unemployment in the Chamber of Deputies, June 1, 1900, gave Millerand the opportunity of saying that he considered syndical organization the dominantly important factor in the problem.

"It is," he said, "the master idea of my administration. Since I have had the honour of being Minister of Commerce, I have considered it indispensable to do everything to stimulate and to facilitate the legal organisation of the syndicates and the *Bourses du Travail*."

It was not only the working class which were to profit by associations; they were "the necessary instrument of education for the employers as well as the workers." [80] With the purpose of encouraging the economic activity of the workers' associations, the Government introduced on November 14, 1899, their project [81] of law on the extension of the rights of the syndicates.[82] The law of 1884 had narrowly defined, said Millerand, the capacities of the professional syndicates and the unions of syndicates. It was the intention of the Government "to extend the capacity of the syndicates and to give the law the sanctions which experience has shown at this time necessary and legitimate." This intention of the Government became increasingly a problem of legislation, for propositions were submitted to the Chamber of Deputies and Senate to sanction more efficaciously syndical liberties and to fortify the authority of the associations. The project of the Government was brought forward by Millerand in 1902 [83] and again 1906.[84] It is certain that the friendly attitude of the Government had good results in stimulating the growth of organized labour, for the number of workers' syndicates increased from 2,361 in January, 1899, to 3,287 in January, 1901; and the membership increased in the same time from 419,761 to 588,832, representing in the former year 76 unions of syndicates affiliating 1,132 syndicates, and the latter year 95 unions of syndicates affiliating 1,533 syndicates.[85] But the most far reaching benefits of the Project Waldeck-Rousseau-Millerand are best shown in the

[80] Address before 78 patronal syndicates of the "Alliance syndicale du Commerce et de l'Industrie," March 6, 1901, Lavy, *op. cit.*, p. 231.

[81] J. O. C. of D., November 14, 1899, Doc. Parl. No. 1185.

[82] See Lavy, *op. cit.*, pp. 229-245, for a full discussion by Millerand of this project, clearly outlining the program of the twenty years following.

[83] J. O. C. of D., October 14, 1902, Doc. Parl. No. 322.

[84] J. O. C. of D., June 12, 1906, Doc. Parl. No. 322.

[85] See Lavy, *op. cit.*, p. 244.

law of March 12, 1920,[86] which embodies almost wholly the earlier text which was first favourably reported [87] by M. Barthou, and from the beginning was considered one of the best solutions of the important question of the juridical personality of the syndicates.[88] The law of 1920 has done away with any shackles which the law of 1884 permitted, especially with regard to the rights of collective action,[89] and has established the complete civil personality of the professional syndicates.[90] The law of 1920 is an indication of the enlarging social rôle of the syndicates,[91] not only in their distinctly economic character but as purposive societies within the State for whom the State has considered it worth while to give special rights and privileges. It is also a larger expression of the State's confidence in the capacity of the syndicates to share in the administration of an industrial society under democratic conditions determined by Parliament.[92] It is progress toward the realization of the political part of the social philosophy of MM. Waldeck-Rousseau, Millerand and Briand who considered, Professor Pic believes, "as socially useful any reform which tended to prepare and make possible the accession of the wage earner to

[86] Dalloz, *Code du Travail* (*Additions*), pp. 10-12; D. P. 1920, 4, 81. Also *Journal Officiel,* March 14, 1920, p. 4179.

[87] Rapport Barthou, for *Commission du Travail,* December 28, 1903, Doc. Parl. No. 1418; also M. Barthou's *L'Action Syndicale* (1904).

[88] Cf. Maurice Cauducheau, *La Reforme de la loi du mars 1884 sur les Syndicats Professionnels* (1911), pp. 229-237; also Pic, *op. cit.,* pp. 354-360.

[89] Articles 4, 5, 6 and 7 of the law of 1884 are modified.

[90] Pic, *op. cit.,* pp. 225-296, for a thorough survey of this law; also Scelles, *op. cit.,* pp. 70-77, and Bry-Perreau, *op. cit.,* Appendix I, pp. 915-924.

[91] Cf. Bry-Perreau, *op. cit.,* p. 915.

[92] See Maxime Leroy, *Les Techniques Nouvelles du Syndicalisme* (1921), and Georges Guy-Grand, *La Democratie et l'Apres-Guerre* (1922), for interesting comment on the change in France, and yet the continuity of the "democratic tradition," as M. Guy-Grand views it. The principal amendments to the law cover changes in the rules governing membership, establishment of certain legal and property rights, and union relations with affectivities affecting labour interests. Civil rights granted to the syndicates include the right to appear in a court of justice and to acquire property, and the protection of the law is guaranteed in all cases of direct or indirect injury to the collective interest of the trade they represent. Regularly constituted trade unions have the right to devise plans for the study and defence of their economic, commercial and agricultural interests.

ownership and control." [93] The modern State has had set before it no more difficult duty.

The employees of the State have demanded protective organization, and this problem in France has been a bitter source of conflict between the Government and the trade unionists. The Council of State in a decree of January 17, 1922, decided that the groups of civil servant employees may not organize into trade unions. The decree in question answered the appeal of the National Union of Excise Agents against a decision of the director of the excise branch of the tax service withholding a list of the personnel of the office for the year 1920.

The decision stated that while the law of 1884 grants legal rights to trade unions, the only associations authorized by the law are those whose exclusive purpose is the study and defence of the economic, industrial and commercial interests of their members. This is considered to limit the authorization to unions of employers or workers as representatives of special interests and does not include civil employees who represent public interests. Benefiting as this latter class does by regulations governing their work and pay and by the control of Parliament, they are obliged in accepting this employment to accept certain obligations and renounce certain rights. This point, so the Council of State held, was further stressed by Parliament in the law of April 12, 1920, which included liberal professions in the scope of trade union activity but not public employees.

The rise of the wage earner, giving increasing economic power to the working class in France, has made this duty most serious. The State has had to take into account the whole relationship of modern industrial organization and the capacity of the workers to direct and control it, as well as to give immediate satisfaction to the claims of the Labour movement for a larger share in the decisions of industry which concern them most directly. The

[93] Pic, *op. cit.*, p. 277, who adds that this is his belief. The Reports on this law are important. Proposed in the Senate by MM. Cheron and Strauss, February 10, 1916, Doc. Parl. No. 37, it was reported in the Senate, March 15, 1917 (Rapport Cheron, Sen. Doc. Parl. No. 81), and in the Chamber of Deputies, September 5, 1918 (Rapport Lauche, Ch. Doc. Parl. No. 4945). Two reports followed, the second Cheron Rapport, December 23, 1919, Doc. Parl. No. 765; and the Rapport Chabrun, March 2, 1920, Doc. Parl. Sen. Ch. No. 453.

Government gave recognition to this feeling in the Decree of July 17, 1900,[94] by means of which the administration of the Bourse du Travail of Paris was put directly under the control of the syndicates who made up its membership.[95] The number of Bourses du Travail [96] in France on January 1, 1899, were 55, representing 1,136 syndicates with a membership of 159,284; and on January 1, 1901, there were 75 Bourses du Travail, uniting 16,630 syndicates with a membership of 276,837. This represents the active or militant organization as they prefer, of French labour at the time. Economic pressure upon the French Parliament was becoming more insistent and the bitter fight between the believers in the Parliamentary method and the extra-Parliamentary school of syndicalism was just beginning to take form. The effort that the Government made to organize industry and prepare syndical organization for larger responsibilities intensified the struggle, but fortunately it helped to define more clearly the issues which were involved and the principles which had to be interpreted afresh.[97]

The "bourgeois ideal of social peace" was not alone in a process of transformation, for the actual program of ministers of Government and the debates of workingmen's congresses proved that the ideal was powerfully at work in all men's minds. In the history of the Labour movement in both France and England it has often been most fully stated in the effort to get rid of strikes, perhaps because popular sympathy can be used by both parties in a dispute. The term "social peace" for a great many has been anathema. At best too often it has been only a negative doctrine. But at the beginning of the century the example of certain young nations making new attempts at the settlement of industrial disputes had a great influence on the policies suggested in the older industrial

[94] J. O. C. of D., July 13, 1900.

[95] Cf. Lavy, *op. cit.*, p. 246-248; Pic, *op. cit.*, p. 295; and Pelloutier, *op. cit.*, pp. 186-195. The Decrees of August 11, 1905, and October 15, 1908, complete the administrative rules.

[96] *Annuaire des Syndicats Professionels,* quoted by Lavy, *op. cit.*, p. 246.

[97] The *Rapport Maginot* (Doc. Parl. 1911, No. 1214), J. O. July 13, 1911, on the *Statut et le Droit d'Association des Fonctionnaires,* includes also the magistral Report of M. Chaigne in 1909 and his supplementary Reports. Together these Reports provide complete Parliamentary record of the question, down to 1911, together with the full text of the Government projects.

communities. In France the Government introduced a project [98] for the regulation of strikes and providing for arbitration. The purpose was stated to be the substitution of a legal régime for the anarchy which then obtained, and to inaugurate a democratic rule of procedure before which the minority would be compelled to submit. A strike was war, declared the Minister of Commerce and Industry. Neither the rights nor the interests of the belligerents would be sacrificed, but there was a higher duty: "We respect them, yet at the same time we safeguard the general and higher interest of society." [99] In presenting the law project on strikes and arbitration, as in the institution of the *Conseils du Travail,* it was said that

> the Government of the Republic continues a work of education and social organization, manifesting its confidence in the organized workers and in the educative value of association, and places its faith in social progress in reason.[100]

The machinery by which Millerand sought to bring about the needed reform was complex and ingenious, but the project was opposed by both labour and capital. Yet the value of it in the history of the controversy of the first decade of this century is very sure, and has exercised a decided influence on all succeeding legislation. The working basis of the law was to be the *Conseils d'Usine,*[101] the beginning of which was in the arbitral sentence of M. Waldeck-Rousseau, October 7, 1899, ending the famous strike at Creusot, one of the principal social disturbances of the last years of the old century.[102] The Government sought to bring together the good effects of all the previous legislation on compulsory arbitration, combining it with a democratic method of administration by the workers themselves. The Shop Councils would be the permanent arbitration boards, a step too advanced for Labour at that time. So was the proposal that the strike vote

[98] J. O. C. of D., November 15, 1900, Doc. Parl. No. 1937.

[99] Millerand's Preface to an *Inquiry* by M. Jules Huret, reviewing the project of the Government and the reaction of public opinion.

[100] See *exposé* of the project, pp. 150-174, Lavy, *op. cit.,* in which M. Millerand gives a full account of the project and the Government's aim.

[101] See *Bulletin du Office du Travail,* 1899, p. 841 ff.

[102] See *Rapport Colliard,* J. O. C. of D., December 27, 1907, Doc. Parl. No. 1418, p. 481.

should be secret and determined by the majority. This project really anticipated several of the major principles of workers' control upon which the greatest value has been placed by the old and the new syndicalist movement.[103] Thus it was not surprising that one of the foremost Syndicalist theorists was, on the whole, favourable to the Waldeck-Rousseau project.[104]

M. Millerand was determined to carry forward the Government project "substituting the authority of law for the hazards of force," which appeared to him the very negation of Republican Government. A house divided against itself cannot stand, and he considered it "the most imperious duty to make every effort to extirpate from France the seeds of hate and the germs of civil war." [105] Little by little, he thought, by the unceasing effort of all men of good will "we shall begin to substitute for the hazards and troubles of the present time a régime of stability, of peace and of increasing harmony." [106] But nine years later he thought "it would be possible without exaggeration to say of the economic regime that it is 'absolutism modified by the strike.'" His conclusion was not the lesson that Labour had learned: "that in the world of economics as in the world of politics it is necessary that absolutism give way to constitutional monarchy." [107] The politics [108] of M. Millerand had undergone a change as great as was evident in the Socialist and Labour movement. The bitterness of the years between 1900 and 1910 had separated the Labour movement from the "economic parliamentarism" of the first Socialist Minister, who had laid the foundation for the future of workers' control and had helped to outline the friendly will of the State. At that time looking back on the formation of the

[103] Rapport Colliard, chap. vii, p. 480-482.

[104] Cf. *Le Mouvement Socialiste,* March 15, 1901, pp. 368-376, and April 1, 1901, pp. 431-444, "L'Exposé des Motifs du Projet de Loi sur l'Arbitrage et la Grève Obligatoires," H. Lagardelle.

[105] Millerand, *Politique de Realisations,* p. 340; see "Les Conflits Sociaux et l'Arbitrage," pp. 303-340.

[106] Millerand in address opening the Creusot pavilion at Paris Exposition, June 29, 1900, where he first outlined the project, see Lavy, *op. cit.,* p. 151; the two full expositions were given July 12, 1900, before the Co-operative Associations, pp. 404-408, and before the 1900 Miners' Congress at Lens, October 7, pp. 409-415.

[107] Millerand, *Politique de Realisations,* pp. 19-20; see *ibid.,* "Le Règlement Aimable des Conflits du Travail," pp. 16-30.

[108] Cf. Millerand, *Pour la Defense Nationale* (1913).

Labour Councils, he thought of them as "the beginning of parliamentarism in industry."

"I know that parliamentarism is not in vogue just now," he added, "but what do you propose to put in its place? By what means will you prevent industrial conflicts, or would you continue the state of things as they are? If so, you are less convinced than I am that it is absolutely necessary to be rid of it all. And I know too, that it is not only the patrons who declare that it is folly to introduce parliamentarism in the workshop, but there are also workers, or those who presume to speak for them. But it is asking no great sacrifice from the two parties: from the employers the giving up of a share of their power, theoretically absolute, and for the workers a renouncing of the method of violence for agreement gained through peaceful means alone." [109]

The Government project was again put forward in 1906,[110] when it was the subject of a most able Report by M. Colliard [111] for the *Commission du Travail*, which favoured the proposal. Three years later a second Report gave again approval.[112] The latest development was in the project [113] of the Minister of Labour, M. Jourdain, and which he and M. Millerand presented in 1920. The experience of the years has made changes, for the main emphasis is now on the obligation of conciliation offers

[109] See Millerand, *Politique de realisations,* pp. 25-26; also his *La greve et l'organisation ouvrière* (1906), and his *Travail et travailleurs* (1908), which fully cover Millerand's aims at the time.

[110] J. O. C. of D., June 12, 1906, Doc. Parl. 14. The text was slightly amended when it was re-introduced; see Colliard Report, 1907, Doc. Parl. 1418, pp. 483-485 (J. O. C. of D., December 27) for the project, and pp. 485-507, for a complete review of existing legislation in all countries on the subject.

[111] *Op. cit.,* above.

[112] J. O. C. of D., June 16, 1910, Doc. Parl. No. 113. A survey of labour law in France and England from the point of view of an outsider is found in the Bulletin of the Department of Labour of the United States, November, 1899, pp. 768-856, by W. F. Willoughby; also the same year, pp. 457-548, a study on "Voluntary Conciliation and Arbitration," by J. B. McPherson, provides partly some of the material from which M. Millerand had to draw for his project, but of course the best survey of the then existing legislation is in the first Colliard Report, pp. 485-507.

[113] J. O. C. of D., March 9, 1920, Doc. Parl. No. 489; and see the *Rapport Lafarge,* J. O. C. of D., July 30, 1920, Doc. Parl. No. 1478.

being made, not upon any acceptance of a compulsory award.[114] It provides that in all establishments, commercial, industrial and agricultural, where twenty or more workers are employed, before there is a stoppage of work there must be an effort by the delegate of the employees (presumably a permanent committee forming the Workshop Committee (*Conseil d'Usine*)) and the management of the works to come to a peaceful agreement.[115] Failing an agreement the dispute is required to be carried before the permanent *Comité de Conciliation;* [116] and if conciliation is impossible, the dispute, by common agreement, can then be arbitrated, and the award is compulsory. It is interesting to note that in public works a strike is forbidden while the hearing is being conducted; [117] an aim that Millerand had in mind from the beginning which was much more effectively stated by M. Briand. From the first draft of the project in 1900 to its statement in 1920 there has been in France a continual discussion on the rights of the State with regard to syndical organization and the part that the State should take in the settlement of industrial disputes. The project of 1900, and the years of discussion through which it has passed, have had a beneficial effect not only on the changed project itself but on the recent law dealing with professional syndicates, that of March 12, 1920. During the years it has been debated in the Chambers and before the *Commission du Travail,* there has been kept to the front of public discussion one of the most serious questions of the relationship of the State with modern industry.[118]

[114] Cf. Bry-Perreau, *op. cit.,* Appendix II, pp. 925-929, for the project; and Pic, *op. cit.,* pp. 925-927.

[115] Art. 2 of project.

[116] The law of 1893 constituted "Conseils de Conciliation et d'Arbitrage"; articles 8-15 of this project give the conciliation procedure, and articles 16-20 provide the arbitration method.

[117] Professor Pic believes this is the most satisfactory provision of the project (p. 927); when the project was first introduced he found it unsatisfactory, and his acceptance of it now indicates a better measure.

[118] M. Bouveri's proposition for the organization of mixed commissions in the mines (J. O. C. of D., September 18, 1917, Doc. Parl. No. 3759), adopted by the Chamber of Deputies, July 2, 1919, can be said to share the principle which the older project has popularized through several legislatures. In this connection the law of March 25, 1919, on the *Convention Collective de Travail,* may be mentioned. The project was introduced in 1910 (Doc. Parl. No. 298), and the law of 1919 is based upon the Report of M. Groussier: J. O. C. of D. S. E., Dec. 5, 1912, Doc. Parl. No. 2334. The significance of this law, M. Pic be-

Conseils de Prud'Hommes

The same function of informing public opinion and inspiring legislative action, which we have just referred to in the history of the two preceding projects, attaches to the laws and decrees which have centred around the peculiarly French institution, the *Conseils de Prud'Hommes,* instituted at Lyon for the first time by the law of March 18, 1806. The four laws of the Third Republic [119] which dealt with the Councils before the Government made the Superior Council of Labour responsible for their reconstitution, were in no way adequate for the duties which it was possible for the Councils to perform.[120] Public opinion and the demands of industry had sought for a long time a complete change of the laws, bringing them down to date and giving new powers to the *Conseils de Prud'Hommes.* The principle which Millerand accepted would extend the jurisdiction of the Councils to include all the workers in the State, commercial and agricultural; and the *Conseil Supérieur du Travail* voted in favour of including within their competence the employees of the State.[121] The long delay in extending the jurisdiction of the *Conseils de Prud'Hommes* was due to the fact that the Chamber of Deputies was favourable to an enlargement of their powers but that the Senate was antagonistic.[122] The law of July 15, 1905, realized a beginning in administrative changes, which were more fully carried out in the law of March 27, 1907,[123] successfully extending the jurisdiction of the *Conseils de Prud'Hommes* to commercial employees. Following this law there were further amendments in procedure

lieves, depends upon the way workers' organizations develop and the extent to which the collective contract can be enforced upon whole trades and over district areas (*op. cit.,* pp. 860-866).

[119] Minor administrative changes represent all of legislative effort: the laws of February 7, 1880, February 23, 1881, November 24, 1883, and December 10, 1884.

[120] See Pic, *op. cit.,* pp. 901-921, for a survey of this institution which is especially attractive for a great many French writers.

[121] The 7th Session (1897) of the *Conseil Supérieur du Travail* considered in an extended report the question of a minimum wage for employees in public works, and the 9th Session (1900) was devoted entirely to the subject of legislation on *Conseils de Prud'Hommes.*

[122] See Pic, "Reforme des Conseils de Prud'Hommes," Rev. Pol. Et. Parl. 1905, for a complete history of the parliamentary debates and the doctrinal discussions which preceded the organic law of 1907.

[123] Dalloz, *Code du Travail,* pp. 160-172; D. P. 1907, 4, 89.

made by the law of November 13-15, 1908[124] (eligibility of women), and of March 8, 1912,[125] before again, by a law of July 3, 1919,[126] important changes allowed the Councils to more effectively fill their essential place in French industrial life. It may be noted further that the law of March 30, 1920,[127] extended the administrative usefulness of the Councils, and that the laws which depend for their usefulness upon the *Conseils de Prud'Hommes* supplying representatives of patrons and employees are another indication of their vitality. The progress of this institution in the twentieth century has been toward a definite inclusion within its jurisdiction of more and more groups of workers. Having competence only in individual disputes, their value must always depend upon the effective co-operation of the parties in industry and in the community. Their growth has proved the attachment of the French for them; their efficacy as an agency of arbitration suited to the needs and temperament of the French patron and worker is manifest.

PART IV

Code du Travail et de la Prévoyance Sociale and the Ministère du Travail et de la Prévoyance Sociale

The progress of legislation dealing with the worker in the countries of Europe rapidly created, says M. Pic, a *droit commun europeen.*[128] The factors of this evolution are complex but the meaning is as important for the Labour movement throughout the world as it is in the history of comparative jurisprudence. The parallel progress of social ideas has only made more secure the hope that they shall have in the future a wider acceptance. From the first two important laws of the Third Republic, that of May 19, 1874 (the protection of children employed in mines

[124] Dalloz, *Code du Travail,* p. 201; Art. 40, pp. 168a-169, law of 1907; D. P. 1908, 4, 102.

[125] Dalloz, *Code du Travail,* p. 279; D. P. 1912, 4, 97.

[126] Dalloz, *Code du Travail,* pp. 407-408; a complete summary of legislation and history can be had in the Rapport Bender, J. O. C. of D., June 4, 1919, Doc. Parl. No. 6248.

[127] Dalloz, *Code du Travail* (*Additions*), pp. 14-15; D. P. 1922, 4, 8.

[128] *Op. cit.*, p. 89.

and manufactures, and forbidding the work of women in mines), and of March 21, 1884 (on the professional syndicates), there had been continuous advance of State intervention. There was in England the example of the Factory Act of 1901, an achievement of great importance in the history of legislation; and in France the counterpart was the proposal for the codification of the workers' laws.[129] There was the necessity of assembling systematically the scattered texts and the various regulations which would give to the workers full information of their rights.[130]

The Ministry of Commerce and Industry, by an Order[131] of November 27, 1901, instituted an extra-parliamentary commission for the codification of the workers' laws. Four years after the commission set to work the Minister of Commerce and Industry introduced two projects, the first dealing with Books I-IV,[132] and the second[133] with Book V of the *Code du Travail et de la Prévoyance Sociale.* Two later projects[134] dealing with Books VI-VII have been deposed but have not been debated. The work of the Commission has greatly helped to bring keen criticism and intelligent study to the subject of labour laws and their function in modern society. The Commission necessarily have had to keep in mind the purpose behind the action of the State. It has done the service, as M. Benoist in his great Report said, of revealing the "double crisis of the State in politics and in economics,"[135]

[129] The best statement of this is in the Benoist *Report,* February 22, 1905, Doc. Parl. No. 2262, on the Government projects; see especially chap. I, pp. 187-207, "L'Evolution du Travail et l'Evolution de l'Etat."

[130] Millerand, *op. cit.* (Lavy), pp. 249-250.

[131] J. O. C. of D., December 2, 1901.

[132] J. O. C. of D., February 6, 1905, pp. 51-134, Doc. Parl. No. 2237; a complete *exposé* together with the Annexes of M. Picard.

[133] J. O. C. of D., February 21, 1905, pp. 171-180, Doc. Parl. 2259; note also J. O. C. of D., December 14, 1903, Doc. Parl. No. 1356, for the earlier Benoist Rapport on the Resolution inviting the Government to submit its project for the *Code du Travail,* which Resolution was adopted December 22, 1905. The two later Reports are invaluable: J. O. C. of D., February 22, 1905, pp. 187-231, Doc. Parl. No. 2262, and J. O. C. of D., April 4, pp. 375-378, Supplementary Report, Doc. Parl. No. 2367.

[134] J. O. C. of D., June 27, 1910, Doc. Parl. No. 183, Report by M. Viviani, bringing the question up to date.

[135] *Op. cit.,* chap. I; and there may be noted the *Bulletin du Office du Travail,* June, 1904, pp. 522-527, "The Codification of the Workers' Laws in France."

There has been the necessity of judging the whole policy of intervention and the obligations which it has brought upon the Government. Just a rapid glance through the first book of the *Code du Travail* with its 107 articles, taking the place of sixteen laws, is convincing testimony of the complex duties that the citizens were willing for the State to assume.[136]

This spirit was given striking endorsement by the Socialist group in the Chamber of Deputies when the Dejeante proposition [137] was introduced dealing with the *Code du Travail*. At the same time they were willing to put varied and conflicting burdens on the State, there was the patent fact that the State was to be subordinated to the professional and economic groups for whom legislation was being proposed. It was yet another contradictory phase of the whole Labour attitude in the early years of the century toward the State. It was proposed that all mixed syndicates be abolished; that syndicates be granted unlimited rights to own and control property; that all *fonctionnaires* be members of the C. G. T.; that a legal working day of three hours be instituted for all workers, including agricultural; that a minimum wage be given for all industry, public and private; that all public services be nationalized or municipalized; that labour inspectors be elected by the workers; and that industry be owned and controlled by the wage earners themselves. The central idea behind this finds a new expression in the syndical organization of to-day [138] and in the *Conseil*

[136] Book I of the *Code du Travail (Conventions Relative du Travail)* became the law of December 28, 1910, completed by the Decree of January 12, 1911; Book II *(Réglementation du Travail)* was promulgated by the law of November 26, 1912, completed by the Decree of November 28, 1912. Codification goes on. Of recent interest is Circular No. 5693, issued by the *Comité Central des Houillères de France. Législation Ouvrière. Loi portant codification des lois ouvrières (Livre IV code du travail et de la prévoyance sociale)* (1924).

[137] J. O. C. of D., Jan. 15, 1903, Doc. Parl. No. 649.

[138] Cf. Maxime Leroy, *Les Techniques nouvelles du Syndicalisme* (1921); Et Martin-Saint-Léon, *Les deux C. G. T.—Syndicalisme et Communisme* (1923); Etienne Villey, *L'Organisation professionnelle des Employeurs dans l'Industrie française* (1923), note especially chap. III, pp. 231-305; Andre Arnou, *La Participation des Travailleurs à la Gestion des Entreprises* (1920), pp. 169-201, on the *Conseils d'Usine* and the *Loi Cheron;* Marc Bourbonnais, *Le Neo Saint-Simonisme et la Vie Sociale d'Aujourd'hui* (1923), introduction, pp. 5-14; and R. Francq, *Le Travail au Pouvoir,* with Preface by Maxime Leroy (3rd ed. 1920), an effort to provide for the organization of industry in the democratic State.

Économique du Travail created by the C. G. T. in 1919. M. Dejeante could not have stated more positively a faith in the syndicalist organization of the State than was recently given for the *Conseil Économique du Travail* by M. Leroy, who believes that "the C. E. T. of the C. G. T. is an invention which, in the near future, will appear as original as that of Parliaments." [139] It is thus interesting to note that what was originally introduced for the purpose of propaganda and debate has become a part of the program of the organized Labour movement in France.[140] The necessity of economic organization has been shown by the very success of political methods in bringing about legislation, yet the limitations of State action have been increasingly apparent as modern industry has failed to satisfy the conscience—and the needs even—of the world of to-day. The development of the administrative powers of the State has brought to industry one of the most valuable lessons for its own control, and in this task the State has done itself no disservice.

By the decree of October 25, 1906, the *Ministère du Travail et de la Prévoyance Sociale* was created, M. Viviani being the lrst Minister in charge of the new State department.[141] He stated that the Government had not only instituted the Ministry of Labour as an important administrative act, but to accomplish a specific social purpose and to inaugurate a new spirit in Government politics. The first responsibility of his Ministry would be the advancement of the interests of social politics, providing a com-

[139] Leroy, *op. cit.*, p. 207; note Guy-Grand, *La Democratie et l'Apres-Guerre,* p. 133, and chaps. II-III, Book I; and Bourbonnais, *op. cit.*, p. 109.

[140] Cf. *Programme d'Action du Parti Socialiste,* pp. 12-20, adopted at the April, 1919, Congress, and the *Programme Minimum of the C. G. T.* (1920), made after the Armistice when the workers "were convinced that the realization of peace was inseparable from social justice"—the opening words of the Program. See Raymond L. Buell, *Contemporary French Politics* (1920), on the French Radical Party and the Unified Socialist Party.

[141] At the beginning of the Millerand Ministry the decree of January 20, 1920, created the *Ministère de l'Hygiène, de l'Assistance et de la Prévoyance Sociales,* and the Briand Ministry which followed continued the two ministries of Labour and of Hygiene. The two decrees of July 20, 1907, and January 27, 1920, outline the administration of the ministries. The Ministry of Health grouped together all the services having to do with health and hygiene that had been previously scattered through five ministerial departments. M. g-L. Breton, parliamentary leader for social legislation, was the first head of the new department of State.

mon reserve of idealism which would unify individual and collective effort.[142] The Parliamentary Reports [143] dealing with the new ministry [144] emphasized the development of the powers of central administration since 1871, the increasing work before Parliament and the problem of Budget expense for social reform. The ministerial statement of M. Clemenceau declared that

in the duty of social justice—another aspect of the fundamental question of the right of all—our concern has been proved by the creation of the Ministry of Labour and Social Welfare, the duty of which will be to co-ordinate all the various efforts that aid and facilitate the progressive realization of solutions for our complex social problems aggravated by the unorganized condition of the working classes and by that kind of spirit which is too often the consequence. It is justice that we seek. No doctrine of justice alarms us, with a free spirit we will judge, undertaking to examine the theories of all, if it is well understood that their success depends upon universal suffrage and republican law.[145]

Government policy has been so far considered mainly from the point of view of the State's purpose in legislation dealing with the organization of labour and of industry within the State, the share of control which it considered necessary to keep to itself, or else safely trust to outside institutions. The State has recognized the corporate life of workers and employers in their syndicates. The organization of the industrial life of France on a

[142] J. O. C. of D., Nov. 9, 1906, pp. 2431-2435.

[143] See Project of Law on creation of the Ministry by MM. Clemenceau and Caillaux, J. O. C. of D. S. E., Nov. 5, 1906, pp. 38-39, Doc. Parl. No. 367; *Rapport Mougeot* on above, J. O. C. of D. S. E., Nov. 6, 1906, pp. 86-87, Doc. Parl. No. 398. Cf. Project of Law presented by MM. Clemenceau and Caillaux on service of the Ministry of the Interior. J. O. C. of D. S. E., No. 27, 1906, pp. 161-162, Doc. Parl. No. 476; also proposition of law on Ministry of Labour presented by M. Abel-Bernard, J. O. C. of D., Doc. Parl. No. 305, 1906, p. 1837.

[144] Cf. *Bulletin du Office du Travail,* Nov., 1906, pp. 1158-1160, for Report to President on the institution of the Ministry, and the Decree of October 25, 1906, the culmination of efforts since M. Blanc in 1849, it was said, first introduced the subject. Other efforts are briefly cited, and the account of passage through Senate and Chamber of Deputies is given in the *Bulletin du Office du Travail,* Dec., 1906, pp. 1267-1268.

[145] J. O. C. of D. S. E., Nov. 6, 1906, pp. 2386-2387. Cf. Paul Fesch, *L'Année Sociale et Economique en France et à l'Étranger,* 1907 (1908), with special reference to the political movement.

basis of good-will reached through common agreement has been the aim of several great law projects which have developed the principle of the representation of interests. This principle whenever clearly defined has given the State an opportunity of interpreting the higher ideal of general interests through a rule of justice, which neglects no interest but gives the highest motives of service to the Governments of democracies. From the law of 1884[146] there was a marked change in the attitude of the French Government toward the associations of workingmen, which change was indicated very early in this century in the law of 1901 on Associations, and equally as definitely in the labour projects which the Ministry committed to social peace, 1899-1902, placed before the French Parliament. The State became friendly; and not only did it put confidence in the representation of organized labour, but based its policies of conciliation and arbitration in syndical strength, giving to the workers a directing administrative power in the carrying out of labour law.

The State fully accepted the syndicates as administrative agents of labour law, responsible partners with the State and with the syndicates of patrons in keeping the industrial system working. It had proposed to give full juridical personality to syndicates and the unions of syndicates, that they might bargain freely, own and control property and carry out their aims unfettered by restrictive legislative interference. The importance of the growth of the functions of the State is indicated in the acceptance by the Government of the syndicates as responsible and representative groups having a corporate life which the laws of the country protected and recognized in its rights. In a comparatively short time both an unfriendly and antagonistic State had found it necessary to use the machinery of labour organization in its own

[146] The law of 1884 permitted the formation without the necessity of obtaining formal Government sanction of trade unions (*syndicats ou associations professionnelles*) consisting of persons following the same or allied occupations, with the object of "the study and defence of economic, industrial, commercial and agricultural interests" (Art. I. Law of 1884: Dalloz, *Code du Travail,* pp. 74-76). The unions might form federations but these did not possess the rights of juristic persons. The law of July 1, 1901, permitted the formation of associations of any kind without any condition as to homogeneity of membership, subject to their pursuing legal objects and abstaining from trading for profit.

service of administration. This necessity implied that the State accepted a new duty toward a large group in society which had slowly gained power. This power was constantly being used to create for labour a new status within the State and in relation to industry, as well as being used to promote the usefulness of the societies united by a common bond of interest for mutual protection. To have longer ignored the associative life of labour as defined by trade unions and syndicates would have precipitated a much fiercer civil conflict than has resulted under the policy of present day Governments. The French Government none too early sought a way out of the warfare which went on daily in industry. At least the effort of legislative interference has made it possible for the State to hear what all groups have to say for themselves, and to judge of their capacity socially to live helpfully in the modern community. Often when this is achieved the State's own duty is more evident.

The duty of the State has determined the efforts toward the organization of the industrial system on a basis of justice.[147] Yet the purpose of the State in creating special rules and confirming special rights with regard to the syndicates has not been at times very clear, nor has the relationship of the State with the associations within it always been genuinely understood. But it can be taken for granted that at the beginning of the twentieth century in France the purpose of the State was friendly. Organized labour's good will was necessary to bring about social peace. Whether or not the two great forces of economics and politics are to share a common ideal for the people of France has been a chief concern of French social politics. Yet the progress of a determined will that democracy shall not be at the mercy of blind economic evolution nor submit to a barren doctrine of class or caste no matter from whence its authority comes, has more than anything else given a basis for the larger hopes of unity and solidarity.

[147] Helping to achieve "harmony between *popular thought* and *objective institutions* upon which a permanent social order must rest," says Professor W. W. Willoughby, in his *Social Justice* (1900), p. 10; cf. *ibid.*, chap. I, Part I, pp. 1-12.

Part V

The State and Social Insurance

The attention given to the organization of labour and the administration of industrial legislation would have little or no interest in this study if it did not reveal a purpose on the part of the Government of France to forward the conditions of successful group action. The syndicate was made stronger for the purpose of making the individual worker more secure, and the conditions which gave power to the larger group of which he was a part made it possible for his own life and happiness to be more fully protected. The freedom of the syndicate gave the worker freedom, the use of which has proved the wisdom of the State's action. The State gave validity to the claims of the workers' associations, recognizing in the larger groups a representative share of the common life of the nation. The aims and ideals of the syndicates have changed as the conditions of industrial life have made necessary a new relationship between the worker and his work, for the individual has been the central figure in the organized labour world. His standard of life has been the personal element in the struggle which has kept alive the spirit of idealism; and the association of all the workers together has been the means whereby a more generous spirit of good will has found a place. The State on one hand has dealt with the workers' associations as representing a substantial group claim for power and recognition in the community. The individual, on the other hand, has pressed his needs for protection and security against the State by the widest appeal to the rights of citizenship and the claims of justice. It is then natural that it is perhaps easier to interpret the purpose of the State with regard to the individual and his welfare than toward the group and its rights; and for this reason the State's aim has often been much more clearly revealed in social legislation than in the more impersonal problem of the determination of the status of trade unions and syndicates.

The history of the old age pension schemes provides in both France and England the most obvious illustration of this principle, for in both countries it was not the controversial issue that syndical organization has been. It has been considered in both nations a necessary institution of social solidarity, of all reforms demanded by democracy the most important. The effort was made in France in 1879 to present a project dealing with old age pensions for industrial and agricultural workers, and from 1890-1900 there were numerous projects and propositions before the Chambers. But in 1901 the Government introduced their project,[148] "creating for more than nine million workers a right to a pension," the principle of which had been approved by the *Commission d'Assurance et de Prévoyance Sociales*.[149] After having voted the law on Associations, then taking up the question of pensions for workers, the Republican Party brought together both ends of its politics and its program, Millerand said. The granting of workers' pensions was "an act of solidarity" on the part of the State, which would protect from feebleness and old age the worker who for thirty years had given to society all that he had of strength and energy.

"It is above all a social debt," he continued, "for it is not possible at the period of civilization which we have reached, when the efforts of solidarity and peace have happily taken among our people a preponderant place, any longer to hesitate to consecrate by law this primordial right, which is the right to life. No, it is not possible that the aged who have done their duty in working all their life, should at the moment when they are no longer able to work, be abandoned by the society which they have served faithfully."

The *Commission d'Assurance et de Prévoyance Sociales* in the sessions of 1902-1906 were too generous for the Senate[150] with

[148] The *exposé* of the project is given in Lavy, *op. cit.*, pp. 191-221, which completely outlines the Government policy as Millerand developed it. Cf. R. Persil and G. Barbier, *Les Retraites Ouvrières* (1906). Introduction by M. Millerand (V-VII), on political importance of subject.

[149] See the two Reports of M. Guieysse, J. O. C. of D., March 9, 1900, Doc. Parl. No. 1502, and J. O. C. of D., November 22, 1904, Doc. Parl. No. 2083; and the *Rapport Fournier*, J. O. C. of D., March 25, 1904, Doc. Parl. No. 1636.

[150] Commenting on the fact that the Senate "is loth to pass laws impregnated with the spirit of State Socialism," M. Barthelemy said: "It retards the laws of so-called workmen's protection. It took four years, three months and one week to consider the proposition passed by the Chamber relative to the weekly holiday. By the same procedure the

regard to old age pensions, but their recommendations were indicative of the importance of the agitation for workmen's pensions throughout the nation. The Commission advocated the giving of pensions at sixty, the general extension of the benefits to include the small farmers and agricultural workers, and the exemption from contribution of all workers receiving less than one franc fifty a day wage.[151] It was estimated that the proposed 1906 project would cost over 400,000,000 francs, which indicated the fate of the measure in the Senate.[152] After the long months in which the Committee on Old Age Pensions sat, it was due to the tireless patience of M. Millerand that in 1905 old age pensions became an active legislative interest.[153] It was he who first made it possible in 1901, as he pointed out in the Chamber of Deputies (June 20) for the problem of old age pensions to be definitely set forth in a legislative text. Along with the income tax measure the project of the Government was not enacted by the legislature of 1898-1902; in 1903 nothing was done, and early in 1904 (March 17) Millerand asked why the bill for workmen's pensions had been dropped. The ministerial announcement of M. Coombes had stated[154] that the insuring of a pension to the workers of industry, of commerce and agriculture, was a problem which imposed itself on all the democracies of the time; and the ministerial declaration of M. Rouvier's Government, following the fall of the Coombes Ministry gave the pledge that the bill for workmen's pensions would be brought to an issue before the

bill concerning retirement pensions was for four years removed from the Chamber's order of the day. As for the Bill of retirement pensions for railwaymen, the Senate kept it for seven years without putting it on the order of the day; so that, passed for the first time by the Chamber in 1897, it did not become law until 1909. Thus when the Senate decides to pass a bill the Chamber hastens to accept it, for fear that once returned to the Luxembourg it may lie there again untouched for years" (*op. cit.*, p. 75).

[151] The Bonnevay amendment.

[152] Cf. Roger Delatour, *Systèmes Financiers de Retraites Ouvrières* (1911), for adequate survey of the financial history and the financial problems of the French system.

[153] A convenient summary of the projects and propositions dealing with old age pensions can be found in the January issue each year of the *Bulletin, Office du Travail,* where a complete record of the year's legislative history is given, note especially for 1903-1906, pp. I-XI, I-XIX, I-XVIII.

[154] *Les Déclarations Ministérielles et les Ministères,* p. 100.

session was ended.[155] The duty could well be borne by the nation in "the social part of a Republican budget," Millerand said earlier, in presenting the Government project. There would be by this law "the expressed recognition of the duty of social solidarity for the first time in French legislation,"[156] he said later, in the general debate of 1905.[157] Like the debate of 1901 the debate of 1905 was a clearing time for all parties and all theories, giving to every shade of opinion a chance of expression.

The official attitude of the Socialists was in the counter proposition[158] of M. Vaillant, based on a non-contributory scheme; Abbé Lemire defended[159] the social theory of his Church and his group; and the example of England was used by M. Charles Benoist[160] to give support to his argument. There is great similarity at that period between the debates in the House of Commons and in the Chamber of Deputies on social insurance, and it is remarkable that the direful prophecies of the politicians of both sides have not come true. The pledge of Governments to the principle was similar in both countries, for even after the sufficient pledges before him, M. Sarrien's ministerial declaration put workers' pensions as foremost in the scheme of reliable reforms;[161] and M. Clemenceau, in the longest ministerial statement[162] of the Third Republic, pledged the Government to promptly pass the law on pensions. But it again found a prominent place in the first ministerial statement[163] of M. Briand, who assured the Chamber of Deputies that he would carry into effect their will. During the long years in which the Senate sought to perfect the measure which the Chamber of Deputies sent

[155] J. O. C. of D., January 28, 1905, p. 63.

[156] J. O. C. of D., November 16, 1905, p. 3287; pp. 3285-3295, entire speech of Millerand.

[157] Besides references given below see J. O. C. of D., Nov. 9, pp. 3095-3105; Nov. 10, pp. 3133-3142; Nov. 14, 15, 16, pp. 3215-3225, 3253-3261; 3285-3295; Nov. 23, 24, 29, 30, pp. 3433-3444, 3449-3461, 3549-3560, 3583-3596; December 1, 6, 7, 13, 14, 15, pp. 3617-3626, 3745-3757, 3777-3788, 3871-3881, 3901-3912, 3935-3946. These pages include the debates entire.

[158] J. O. C. of D., November 8, 1905, pp. 3067-3076.

[159] J. O. C. of D., Nov. 22, 1905, pp. 3395-3407.

[160] J. O. C. of D., Dec. 5, 1905, pp. 3713-3723.

[161] J. O. C. of D., March 15, 1906, pp. 1289-1290.

[162] J. O. C. of D., Nov. 6, 1906, pp. 2386-2387.

[163] J. O. C. of D., July 28, 1909, pp. 2249-2250.

up to them,[164] the country had an opportunity of hearing many of the acute social problems of the nation discussed as well as hearing from the Ministry of France the relationship of the financial policy of the Government to social reform.[165] The old age pension controversy in France and England often involved the Minister of Finance in the debates.

During the first debate in 1901 the Socialist leader Allemane, with other members of the party, introduced a proposition [166] to provide financial resources for pensions by the abolition of inheritances, and this proposition [167] was renewed in the session of 1908. Another indication of the many-sided interest of the agitation was the proposition [168] of M. Maurice Colin, demanding the financial participation of the State in the organization and functioning of the old age pension system. The direct connection between the general system that the State introduced and the several independent schemes with their most interesting development, especially the miners, is discussed later. The text that the Senate finally adopted was far more liberal than many had feared it might be, for benefits had been widely extended, including small farmers and tenants and even shop-keepers; the last mentioned being dropped by the Minister of Finance before the Chamber of Deputies on March 31, 1910, passed the bill by a vote of 560 to 4.[169] It became the law of April 5, 1910,[170] the basic law

[164] See J. O. Sen. Doc. Parl. No. 69, 1906, for the earlier proposition; and for the proposition adopted by the Senate March 23, 1910, see J. O. C. of D., 1910, Doc. Parl. No. 3266, pp. 406-410; and the *Rapport Cuvinot,* given in three parts with annexes, J. O. Sen., 1909, Doc. Parl. No. 104, Part I, pp. 184 ff., Part II, pp. 250 ff., Part III, pp. 375 ff., and Annexes pp. 436 ff.

[165] See especially *Avis* from the *Commission du Finance* on the Old Age Pensions, J. O. C. of D. S. E., 1909, Doc. Parl. No. 253, pp. 85 ff., and J. O. C. of D., June 18, 1909, Doc. Parl. No. 2570, M. Caillaux on the Budget of 1910, pp. 570 ff. Cf. E. Pelleray, *L'Oeuvre financière du Parlement du 1906 à 1910* (1910).

[166] J. O. C. of D., June 18, 1901. For the debates of 1901, see *Journal Officiel,* Chamber of Deputies, of June 5, 7, 11, 12, 14, 18, 19, 21, 25, 26, 28, 29, and July 2-3.

[167] J. O. C. of D. July 10, 1908, p. 800, Doc. Parl. No. 1979.

[168] J. O. C. of D., 1905, pp. 141-145, Doc. Parl. No. 2247.

[169] Cf. The Report of the *Commission d'Assurance et de Prévoyance Sociales,* M. Louis Puech as Rapporteur, J. O. C. of D., March 23, 1910, pp. 414-424, Doc. Parl. No. 3273.

[170] Dalloz, *Code du Travail,* pp. 210-223; D. P. 1910, 4, 49. *Journal Officiel,* C. of D., April 6, 1910, pp. 2998-3003, the text in full. The law

in France on old age pensions and the several developments that are joined with it in the system of social reform of that nation.[171] Two decrees, one by the Minister of Interior[172] and the other by the Minister of Labour and Social Prevision,[173] organized the administration of the law of 1910.

The importance of the system and the popular interest in its administration are indicated by the fact that during the session of 1911 sixteen propositions were submitted for a change in the law.[174] The Government in 1911, through the Minister of Labour, introduced a new project[175] supplementing the law of April 5, 1910, and again in 1912.[176] The law of February 27,

prescribed insurance for practically the entire working population, male and female, rural and urban, receiving in wages less than 3,000 francs a year. The miners and others especially provided for were excluded. Besides the 10,500,000, officially estimated by M. Viviani, Minister of Labour (*Journal Officiel,* March 31, 1910, pp. 1799 ff., for full report on the law by the Minister), provision was made for 6,000,000 to voluntarily insure. These included independent workmen, small employers, peasant proprietors, and other persons, not wage earners, of low income. Employees receiving over 3,000 francs but under 5,000 francs were also included.

[171] Cf. J. Paul-Boncour, *Les Retraites, La Mutualité, La Politique Sociale* (1912), for a convenient survey of the problem including the chief parliamentary speeches of the Minister of Labour and Social Prevision (M. Paul-Boncour at the time) dealing with the administration of the law. See also Report by M. Albert Metin, Minister of Labour and Social Welfare, to the President on application during 1914 of the law of 5 April, 1910-27, February, 1912 (1916).

[172] The Decree of March 24, 1911, Dalloz, *Code du Travail,* pp. 228-232.

[173] Dalloz, *Code du Travail,* pp. 232-276; the Decree of March 25, includes the important ones of August 6, 1912, June 5, 1913, July 26, 1913; and from 1914 began the unusual strain of the War on the whole machinery of social insurance, of which the Decrees issued are witness.

[174] See the two Reports of M. Albert Mètin for the *Commission d'Assurance et de Prévoyance Sociales,* which had in charge the examination of the law of 1910 and its change, J. O. C. of D. S. E., Nov. 14, 1911, pp. 1-16, Doc. Parl. No. 1340, and J. O. C. of D. S. E., Dec. 7, 1911, pp. 16-22, Doc. Parl. No. 1447; and pp. 18-19 for examination of the sixteen propositions. The two Socialist propositions were Doc. Parl. 691 (C. of D. S. O., 1911, p. 80—M. Guesde), and Doc. Parl. No. 1024 (C. of D. S. O., 1911, p. 538—M. Vaillant).

[175] *Project of Law* by M. Renoult, J. O. C. of D. S. E., Nov. 7, 1911, pp. 39-40, Doc. Parl. No. 1270.

[176] J. O. C. of D. S. O., 1912, pp. 1397-1404, Doc. Parl. No. 2039, provides good commentary on the law by M. Leon Bourgeois; and later a good historical sketch is given in Doc. Parl. No. 2271, J. O. C. of D. S. E., Nov. 14, 1912, pp. 78-80.

1912,[177] amending the earlier enactment, made even greater concessions to the workers, who have gradually accepted its provisions and appreciated its benefits. By the Decree[178] of July 16, 1910, was created an *Office National des Retraites Ouvrières et Paysannes,* attached to the Ministry of Labour and Social Prevision but not a part of the central administration of that Ministry.[179]

The attitude of the Socialist Party toward social insurance has been indicated in the counter propositions brought forward from year to year. The general statement was given in the *exposé* of their proposition in 1909,[180] which stated that

> the recognition of the right of the weak, of the poor, of the worker, to an assured existence against all social risk, and the duty corresponding of the society of which he is a member, of assuring the full exercise of this right by legal institutions of guaranty and general social insurance, is the necessary consequence of the idea of solidarity.[181]

The basis of a general system of social insurance has been laid by the old age pensions system and the law of July 14, 1905, on obligatory public assistance to the aged, the infirm and the incurable.[182] This law of public poor relief was preceded by the law of July 15, 1893, on free medical assistance to the poor. A system of general social insurance has been set forth since the War in the

[177] Incorporated with Law of 1919, Dalloz, *Code du Travail,* pp. 210-223.

[178] Dalloz, *Code du Travail,* p. 225. The documentary history of the French system of administration of old age pensions is found in the "Recueil de Documents sur les Retraites Ouvrières et Paysannes" (1912), by the *Ministère du Travail et de la Prévoyance Sociale.*

[179] Art. I.

[180] J. O. C. of D. S. E., December 17, 1909, pp. 216-222, Doc. Parl. No. 2927. This proposition (pp. 222-223) was the same as the one of 1902 (J. O. C. of D. S. E., 1902, p. 257) and was reintroduced in the 10th Legislature (J. O. C. of D., June 13, 1910, pp. 481-491, Doc. Parl. No. 81).

[181] J. O. C. of D. S. E., Dec. 17, 1909, p. 220.

[182] For 1903 debates see J. O. Sen. Nos. 186 and 296; Nos. 43 and 331, 1904; No. 185 and annexes for 1905. See also J. O. C. of D., 1905, Nos. 56, 118, 222, 889; also Doc. Parl. No. 2609, J. O. C. of D., July 10, 1905, pp. 798 ff., for the project of law adopted by Chamber, then sent to Senate and re-submitted by latter to the Chamber; and Rapport by M. Louis Puech for the *Commission d'Assurance et de Prévoyance Sociales,* J. O. C. of D., Doc. Parl. No. 2610, pp. 798-801.

project of the Ministry of Labour (that of M. Daniel Vincent), largely inspired by the system that obtained in the recovered territory of Alsace-Lorraine. The vote on this project constitutes undeniable social progress, a recent writer declared.[183] The attitude of the *Confédération Générale du Travail* is friendly, an indication of the new tactics of the reformists after the War.[184] But the question of expense stands in the way. From 1905,[185] when the duties of public assistance were extended, this problem has been foremost in the discussions of the Chamber of Deputies. The Report[186] of the Commission on the Budget of 1913 declared that the essential principle of social solidarity was constantly in mind, M. Cheron saying that "the principal effort of our last Budgets has been to carry on social reform."[187] The English system has been closely examined, and it has suggested to some that industry cannot stand the cost which is demanded.[188] Yet year by year the major problems of public relief, the raising of standards of health and decency are discussed, and the will of the people to work out a better order of life for all is constantly strengthened.

When the Government first introduced their pensions project it was made clear that in no way would the special rules be abrogated by which already had been established pension funds for the miners by the law of June 29, 1894,[189] and suggested for the railway workers by the project of December 27, 1899.[190] But

[183] Scelle, *op. cit.*, p. 201.

[184] Cf. *Les Travailleurs et les Assurances Sociales: Le Project de Loi. Ses Obligations. Ses Avantages* (1922). Published by the C. G. T., 211 Rue Lafayette, Paris.

[185] See J. O. C. of D., July 6, 1905, pp. 713-714, Doc. Parl. No. 2565, statement of M. Pierre Merlon, Minister of Finance.

[186] J. O. C. of D., March 30, 1912, pp. 466-600, Doc. Parl. No. 1896, by M. Henry Chéron. Cf. M. Caillaux on the Budget of 1910: J. O. C. of D., June 18, 1909, pp. 570 ff., Doc. Parl. No. 2570.

[187] J. O. C. of D., March 30, 1912, p. 1492.

[188] Cf. M. Montchrestien, *Le Problème des assurances sociales en France* (1922), pp. 92-105 on England; chap. III, pp. 108 ff., for criticism of the project of M. Daniel Vincent. Cf. Max Turman, *Problèmes sociaux du travail industriel* (1923); Charles Cestre, *Production Industrielle et Justice Sociale en Amérique* (1921); and Edmond Villey, *L'Etat et le Progrès Sociale* (1923).

[189] Dalloz, *Code du Travail,* pp. 87-98; D. P. 1894, 4, 57.

[190] The *Project Berteaux,* which was voted by the Chamber November 14, 1901, became after years of discussion the law of July 21, 1909.

the purpose of the Government was to extend the principle to all workers, which made it necessary that the system be obligatory if it were to be really adequate to the needs. This feature was contained in the law of 1894, which made it obligatory that in each mine *Caisses de Sécours et de Retraites* be established. The progress of legislation in this direction is to be noted in the law of February 25, 1914,[191] which substituted a *Caisse Autonome des Retraites et des Ouvriers Mineurs,* enjoying civil personality [192] and functioning under the control of the State.[193] The filnancial control of the system is administered by an equal representation of the workers, the employers and the State; six from each, constituting the Administrative Council,[194] the duties of which are set forth by the organic law of April 5, 1910. Every mine worker having reached the age of fifty-five and having worked for thirty years receives from the State a pension.[195] The law of March 9, 1920,[196] prescribed a minimum, 1500 francs for the worker and 750 francs for the widow, toward which the State contributed. In 1914, the allocation of the State was 100 francs.[197] The two laws of July 21, 1909, and December 28, 1911, extend the benefits of the system of pensions to the employees of the French railways. For the employees of the local railways and tramways similar benefits were proposed by the project [198] of law of July 12, 1911, passed by the Chamber of Deputies, July 30, 1913.

The most recent amendment to the original law of June 29, 1894, the miners' old age and invalidity scheme, was the law of December 24, 1923. This law increased the amount of payments

[191] Dalloz, *Code du Travail,* pp. 331-336; D. P. 1918, 4, 203.
[192] Art. I, clause 1, of the Law of 1914.
[193] *Ibid.*
[194] Art. II. The six members representing the State are the director general of the *Caisse des Depots et Consignations,* the director of the *Office d'Assurance et de la Prévoyance Sociales,* two members named by the Ministry of Labour and Social Prevision, one member each named by the Ministry of Finance and the Ministry of Public Works. The administration of the entire law is in the two first named Ministries (Art. 16).
[195] Art. 6.
[196] Dalloz, *Code du Travail (Additions),* pp. 9-10; D. P. 1922, 4, 40.
[197] Art. 8 of the 1914 law.
[198] J. O., July 12, 1911, Doc. Parl. No. 1194; Reported in the Senate by M. Lhopiteau, J. O. Senate, June 13, 1914, pp. 639 ff., Doc. Parl. No. 304.

allowed under the act, but made no changes in the administration of the fund by the Administrative Council described above. The contributory plan of taxes upon wages, a tax paid by employers, and contributions from the State, was kept. The wages of all miners are taxed, but the amount of this tax may not exceed two and one-half per cent of the wages, and the employers are required to pay an amount equal to that paid by the worker. While the State contribution varies it is provided that it cannot be less than one per cent of the total amount of wages paid.

National Insurance Scheme

On March 21, 1921, the French Cabinet approved a social insurance measure drafted by the Minister of Labour,[199] and discussion of this bill, as pointed above, has been going on in France with a great deal of interest. Even before the bill was officially adopted it was decreed that the German social insurance laws should remain in force in Alsace-Lorraine. That is the immediate cause of the comprehensive scheme being advanced at this time, for in all probability such a system would have taken many years to have gained the support that it now has. The present bill is based on compulsory insurance. All French wage workers and salaried employees as well as small tenant farmers (métayers) whose annual income does not exceed 10.000 francs ($1,930) are compulsorily subject to insurance. Farmers and small independent tradesmen below 30 years of age whose annual income does not exceed 10,000 francs may insure themselves voluntarily. Both compulsorily and voluntarily insured persons are to enjoy the same benefits under the law. The insurance grants medical aid in case of sickness or confinement, pecuniary benefits to sick persons or women in confinement, birth allowances, pensions for invalids and persons over 60 years of age, and death benefits to survivors. The funds for paying benefits are to be raised through equal contributions of the insured persons and their employers supplemented by State subsidies. The insured persons are divided into six classes, according to their annual income.

[199] *Document Parlementaires, Chambre, Annexe No. 2369, 1921.*

For the purpose of the organization of the insurance system,[200] France is to be divided into 20 to 25 insurance districts. In each district there is to be established an autonomous insurance fund, which in turn shall establish branch offices in each rural district or in each city with more than 10,000 inhabitants. In addition to the State insurance funds, mutual insurance funds founded by employers' or workers' associations, and establishment funds may be admitted as carriers of the sickness and old age insurance provided they conform to the provisions of the bill. The State insurance funds are, however, to be the exclusive carriers of the invalidity insurance because, as the preamble to the bill says, "private insurance institutions have heretofore neglected this branch of social insurance." A general guaranty fund (*caisse générale de garantie*) is to be created as compensation and re-insurance carrier for all the State insurance and private admitted funds. An insurance office is to be created in each of the insurance districts. This office shall exercise supervision over all the insurance funds in the district. Disputes arising from the insurance procedure are to be decided by the administrative courts to be created at each county seat and at the headquarters of each insurance district. A superior administrative court will sit at Paris to decide appeals from the lower courts.

The financial burden on the State involved in this social insurance system is considerable. The entire costs of administration of the insurance funds and of the insurance offices are to be borne by the State. In addition the State assumes the entire cost of the birth allowances [200a] and grants subsidies to the sickness, invalidity,

[200] A history and a critical analysis of the general social insurance scheme is in *Les assurances sociales* (1924), by H. Gleize; and in *Les assurances sociales* (1924), by M. Degas, the text of the bill as adopted by the committees on insurance and social welfare and the text of proposed amendments are given. Also the majority and minority report of the Superior Council of Labour, the 1922 session, are informative; and see M. Albin Jacquement, *Le problème des assurances sociales en agriculture* (1923), and M. Degas, *Le problème de l'assurance maladie-invalidité* (1922). Two recent studies with discussion are, M. Rey's *Le question des insurance sociales* (1925) and M. Girad's *Éléments de législation ouvrière* (1925).

[200a] The literature on this subject and of State aid in France to large families is abundant and most interesting. See especially the semi-official volume *L'assistance et l'encouragement national aux familles nombreuses. Lois, decrets, circulaires et jurisprudence* (1925), which

old age and maternity insurance. The bill also provides subsidies from the State for the erection of sanatoriums and convalescent homes. The cost to the State of the proposed insurance system during the first year of operation has been estimated at 376,000,000 francs ($72,568,000) by the Minister of Labour. It has been further estimated that during the first 11 years the annual cost to the State would rise to 578,000,000 francs ($111,554,000) and fall to 475,000,000 francs ($91,675,000) after 45 years. The cost of changing from the old age insurance law of 1910-1919 to the new insurance system, which has been estimated at 123,000,000 francs ($23,739,000), is also to be borne by the State. The attitude of organized labour is friendly to the passing of the bill, although there was no representative of the *Confederation Générale du Travail* called in for consultation by the Government. The same opposition in France to the system by the mutual insurance funds (*caisses de mutualité*) was met in England, but the opposition likewise is only with some particulars and not with the general administrative system or the principle.

PART VI

The State and the Conditions of Work

(a) *The Mining Code*

It is important to keep in mind the unusual influence that the mine workers in France and England have had upon the course of labour legislation and social politics. In each country labour organization, politically and administratively, has had new and fresh developments from the miners.[201] The creation of special machinery for the system of miners' pensions and the equal repre-

covers the laws, decrees and circulars relating to family allowances for the period from July 14, 1913, to June 7, 1924. The subject is fully dealt with in the *Annuaire, 1925, Comité Central des Allocations Familiales.* Subjects included are the Central Committee of family allowances, the juridical character of family allowances, with legal opinions, decisions, and decrees concerning such grants and legislation. An administrative decree of July 13, 1923, specified the conditions of employment of workers on State contracts in regard to the payment of family allowances.

[201] Cf. Victor Fere, *Le Mineur, sa condition generale et sa capacité contractuelle dans le droit anglais* (1923), for an exhaustive study.

sentation of workers on the Administrative Council, were only an extension of the principle which was first expressed in the law of July 8, 1890,[202] providing for the election of works delegates for the protection of the miners. Their usefulness has grown and has been given legislative endorsement by increased powers, through the laws [203] of March 23, 1901, May 9, 1905, March 12, 1910, February 13, 1912, December 13, 1912, and the decree of December 19, 1914.[204]

There is no doubt that the growth of this institution was responsible for the friendly reception by the miners of the plans of the Government for a general arbitration system growing out of the creation of *Conseils d'Usine* at Creusot in 1899. For three successive years,[205] 1905-1907, the National Miners' Congress passed resolutions inviting the Government to depose a project of law instituting permanent councils of arbitration for the friendly control of differences relative to the conditions of work.[206]

[202] The French law was derived in part from the English law of 1872 (August 10), Professor Pic believes, *op. cit.*, p. 414; yet the extension of its principles was more effective, apparently, in French law.

[203] *Code du Travail,* Book II, Art. 120-157, include these laws. The complete mining code of France can be found in the *Législation minére et législation ouvrière. Texte des principales lois. Quatrième édition,* Paris, 1920, published by the *Comité Central des Houillères de France.*

[204] See the two Reports of M. Basly for the Commission on Mines, on the project of law adopted by the Senate (J. O. C. of D., 1905, Doc. Parl. No. 2357, p. 372); J. O. C. of D., April 18, 1905, pp. 483 ff., Doc. Parl. No. 2411; and J. O. C. of D., May 15, 1905, pp. 530-532; Doc. Parl. No. 2440, Exposé of proposed legislation. These Reports on Workers' Delegates are supplemented by the Report of M. Baudin for the Commission in Insurance and Social Prevision, on the project adopted by the Senate on the participation of the miners in the pension system, modifying the law of June 28, 1894, as the first project dealt with modifications of the law of July 8, 1890: J. O. C. of D., July 6, 1905, pp. 763-764, Doc. Parl. No. 2568. Note also the Basly Report for the Commission on Mines on the Viviani project of March 12, 1908: J. O. C. of D., February 28, 1910, pp. 197-200, Doc. Parl. No. 3151; and the *Annexes* to *Journal Officiel,* April 18, 1908, and May 26, 1910. Another important Report is that of M. Pelisse for the Commission on Mines, examining amendments and resolutions on the Budget relative to the increase of miners' pensions: J. O. C. of D., November 28, 1907, pp. 311-315, Doc. Parl. No. 1343; this surveys the work of the law of June 29, 1894, March 31, 1903, Article 64 of the Finance Law of April 22, 1905, and Article 66 of the Finance Law of April 17, 1906.

[205] *L'Ouvrier Mineur,* May, 1907, quoted in the Colliard Report, p. 483.

[206] The *Rapport Colliard,* J. O. C. of D., December 27, 1907, pp. 473-507, Doc. Parl. No. 1418, is perhaps the best parliamentary report on the

The extension of the service of the *Conseils de Prud'Hommes* to include the miners was proposed [207] in the session of 1906 by M. Basly, who believed that the cause of labour had been greatly helped by the Councils; and in the next parliamentary session it was proposed to include the agricultural workers.[208] This indicates that the idea of workers' control and responsibility was increasing. The progress of the idea in the ranks of the miners found definite expression in official parliamentary reports and in the numerous propositions brought forward to give directing power with regard to conditions of work to the employees themselves.[209]

The mine workers gave valuable aid with regard to two other important labour problems; [210] for M. Basly introduced first in 1900 the proposition of an eight hour day for mine workers, which he reintroduced in 1906 [211] along with a proposal establishing a minimum wage in the mines.[212] The *Commission du Travail* in 1901 accepted the principle of an eight hour day.[213] The Cham-

conditions of labour and patronal organization with reference to the State's rights of interference in strikes; this Report by the Commission on Labour covers the Millerand project on compulsory arbitration (J. O. C. of D., 1907, Doc. Parl. No. 14), together with propositions having the same object in mind (Doc. Parl. C. of D. Nos. 879 and 971, 1907), and two propositions dealing with the right to strike and the friendly settlement of disputes (Doc. Parl. Nos. 184 and 312, C. of D., 1907). The first general Report was in 1904, J. O. C. of D. S. E., 1904, Doc. Parl. No. 2182.

[207] J. O. C. of D., June 12, 1906, pp. 487 ff., Doc. Parl. No. 33.

[208] J. O. C. of D., March 27, 1907, pp. 282 ff., Doc. Parl. No. 916.

[209] Cf. chap. VIII of the Colliard Report and the 1904 Report on the importance of Workers' Delegates.

[210] A comprehensive survey of propositions and projects dealing with the control of the mines submitted from the first to the ninth Legislature (chap. III, pp. 548-552), is given in the definitive *Rapport Sévaès,* for the Commission on Mines, J. O. C. of D., April 1, 1909, pp. 544-570, Doc. Parl. No. 2431. It reports on the Government project for a new mining code (Ch. Doc. Parl. S. E., 1908, No. 2114), introduced by MM. Barthou, Viviani and Caillaux, and on the proposition of M. Barron (Ch. 1908, Doc. Parl. No. 1174), for the nationalization of mines (chap. VII, pp. 568-570).

[211] J. O. C. of D., June 12, 1906, pp. 486-487, Doc. Parl. No. 486; see *Rapport Janet,* for the Commission on Mines, J. O. C. of D., March 10, 1907, pp. 237-239, and the supplementary report, J. O. C. of D., 1907, pp. 950-951, Doc. Parl. No. 1120, for comment.

[212] J. O. C. of D., June 12, 1906, pp. 484-485, Doc. Parl. No. 29.

[213] See *Rapport Odilon,* C. of D., December 12, 1901.

ber of Deputies confirmed this principle in the debates on the miners' Bill for an eight hour day from pit to return, which was passed following debates on January 29 and February 5, 1902. But nothing else was done by the legislature until the law of June 29, 1905, on the hours of work for miners, which for the first time in French legislation confirmed by statute the principle of the eight hour day. This was extended to all underground workers by the law of December 31, 1913; [214] and the miners by the threat of a general strike secured the enactment of the Durafour law of June 24, 1919,[215] the practical result of which is to institute the seven hour day in French mines.[216] The more general law on the eight hour day [217] of April 23, 1919, was the logical carrying on of the principle of the Decrees of August 10, 1899, and the Law of March 30, 1900 (Millerand-Colliard). The principle was introduced in the administration of the posts and telegraphs first by the Minister of Commerce in his Circular of February 9, 1901, and in the dockyards and naval arsenals by the Circular of M. Pelletan, January 7, 1903. In that same year, November 5, in the debate on the budget, the Government promised to submit a project dealing with the hours of work in all industries. In 1905 the Commission on the Budget submitted a Report [218] asking for supplementary credits to allow the introduction of the eight hour day in the manufactures of the State, the reasons for which had been amply given in that year's budget debate. The action of the Commission was perhaps an inspiration for the Socialists to press harder for a much more comprehensive principle, for both in 1905 and in 1906 M. Vaillant presented for his party their proposition [219] for an eight hour day and a minimum wage

[214] *Code du Travail,* Book II, Chap. II, Sect. II, Art. 9-13, and Book IV, Chap. I, Sect. I, Arts. 159, 160 and 164.

[215] *Code du Travail,* Book II, Chap. II, Sect. II, Arts. 9-13. The proposition of M. Durafour was introduced April 15, 1919 (Ch. Doc. Parl. No. 6013), and was the basis of two Reports, that of M. Drivet, May 27, 1919 (Ch. Doc. Parl. No. 6206), and of M. Colin, June 17, 1919 (Sen. Doc. Parl. No. 263).

[216] Pic, *op. cit.,* p. 555.

[217] Cf. *Hours of Labour in Industry, France, International Labour Office Studies and Reports, Series D, No. 6, 1922.*

[218] J. O. C. of D., July 11, 1905, pp. 801-802, the Report of M. Dulan; and note debate of February 28, 1905, on the budget.

[219] J. O. C. of D., January 13, 1905, pp. 3-6, Doc. Parl. 2198; and J. O. C. of D., November 5, 1906, pp. 61-64, Doc. Parl. No. 375.

for all workers and employees of the State. The attitude of the political leaders of all parties in England on this question was given as an example for the French Parliament.

The Socialist proposals for the workers of the State were supplemented by the proposition of the same year for an eight hour day and a minimum wage to apply for all the workers.[220] The propositions were separately framed that legislative propaganda might be more effective. Both MM. Guesde and Vaillant considered the Chamber of Deputies a very good place in which to carry on Socialist debate and the *Journal Officiel* a very hospitable newspaper for the documents of the party. In 1910 the Vaillant proposition was again introduced,[221] as well as the proposition of a general minimum wage for workers of both sexes, introduced first in 1907 by M. Coutant,[222] and to complete the efforts of the year M. Cuny presented a bill with the same purpose in mind.[223] The temper of the Socialist group in 1907 may be seen in the Coutant proposition for a minimum wage for all workers of both sexes, and it also indicates the dependence of this group upon State action. M. Coutant stated that the basis was laid by no less an individualist than M. Leroy-Beaulieu in his *Traité d'Economie Politique*.[224] The Socialist group declared [225] that it is necessary that the State intervene to assure the workers of both sexes who work to create social wealth a more just division of that wealth.

They were further convinced that it is the duty of the State to intervene to guarantee the standard of living for all members of our democracy.

The Coutant proposition forbade any employer to pay for ten hours' work less than the minimum wage set for the year by the General Councils, in agreement with the *Conseils d'Arrondissement,* after the advice of the Municipal Councils of all France had been given.[226]

[220] J. O. C. of D., November 5, 1906, pp. 58-61, Doc. Parl. No. 374.
[221] J. O. C. of D., November 17, 1910, Doc. Parl. No. 469.
[222] J. O. C. of D., June 11, 1907, pp. 848-849, Doc. Parl. No. 1043; and J. O. C. of D., July 5, 1910, Doc. Parl. 261.
[223] J. O. C. of D., December 5, 1910, Doc. Parl. No. 545.
[224] The citation was p. 484. Cf. Leroy-Beaulieu, *L'etat moderne et ses fonctions* (4th ed. 1911).
[225] J. O. C. of D., June 11, 1907, p. 849, Doc. Parl. No. 1043.
[226] Art. I and II of the proposition Coutant, p. 849.

Thus over a long number of years the principle had been thoroughly discussed,[227] so that in 1909 the Government were forced to accept partially the principle. The proposition [228] of Comte de Mun for a minimum wage in the homework industries was given over to the *Conseil Supérieur du Travail,* the report from which was made in 1910 by M. Honorè. The combined force of all the propositions, from every quarter of Parliament, as indicated by the strange company of M. Vaillant and Comte de Mun, was best seen in the project of the Superior Council of Labour which the Government took charge of on November 7, 1911.[229] But it was November 13, 1913, before the Chamber of Deputies passed the Bill, which was then considered by the commission appointed by the Senate. This Report, March 30, 1914, recommended certain administrative changes. The law of July 10, 1915,[230] provided that a minimum wage should be paid,[231] determined by the Labour Councils [232] set up by the law of July 17, 1908, and the administrative Decree of May 10, 1909. Where no Labour Councils existed two commissions were to carry out the provisions of the law, the *Comités de Salaires* [233] and the *Comités Professionnels d'Expertise,*[234] each being composed of an equal number of representatives of the employers and the workers, chosen by the president and the vice-president of the *Conseils de Prud'Hommes,* who are themselves alternately elected from the two constituent groups.

[227] Cf. Hauriou, *Droit constitutionnel,* pp. 67-68, 101-102, 613-615, for a suggestive statement of the general theory of the "rights of family representation" in politics and economics, together with references to discussion in Chamber of Deputies.

[228] J. O. C. of D., April 2, 1909, Doc. Parl. No. 2453.

[229] J. O. C. of D., November 7, 1911, Doc. Parl. No. 1269; also the *Rapport Berthod* on this project, J. O. C. of D., January 20, 1913, Doc. Parl. No. 2472.

[230] *Code du Travail,* Book I, Art. 33-33n, 99a and 107; see also the Decree of September 24, 1915 (Dalloz, *Code du Travail,* pp. 374-377), the administrative organization of the law, defining the duties of the *Conseils du Travail* and the special Commissions, and the Decree of September 18, 1917 (Dalloz, *Code du Travail,* pp. 389-390), on the "English Week," extending the number of trades to which the law is applicable.

[231] Art. 33d, *Code du Travail,* Book I.

[232] Art. 33e, *Code du Travail,* Book I.

[233] Art. 33f, *Code du Travail,* Book I.

[234] Art. 33g, *Code du Travail,* Book I.

While this law was manifestly inspired [235] by the English law of 1909, its history began with the decrees of Millerand and the law of March 30, 1900, and December 29, 1900, dealing with the work of women and children, and the work of women and children and of men where all three worked together.[236] The continued agitation for the reduction of the hours of work and for a minimum wage was greatly encouraged in both France and England by the fight made for the sweated labourer.[237] There was active support in both the French Senate [238] and Chamber of Deputies for the extension of the principle of the legal limitation of the hours of labour. General agreement on the efficacy of interference [239] with regard to the work of women and children helped to prepare the ground for the much more controversial question of the law regulating the work of adult men. The right of the State to do this was definitely set forth in the law of April 23, 1919, on the eight hour day,[240] which states the general principle of the limitation of hours of work to eight in the day and forty-eight in the week. Progress in this direction was indicated in a Report of the Commission on Labour in 1912,[241] which, while rejecting the Vaillant amendment for an eight

[235] Pic, *op. cit.*, p. 653.

[236] There was in the law of March 30, 1900, "the purpose of reorganising the life of the working family" (Bry-Perreau, *op. cit.*, p. 400).

[237] The Ministry of Labour in 1905 instituted its inquiry, "Le Travail à Domicile dans la lingerie," the first report of which appeared in 1907, and four more volumes in 1909 and 1911, followed by two on the shoe and artificial flower trades in 1913 and 1914. See also the *Rapport Godart* on night work in laundries: J. O. C. of D., March 1, 1910, Doc. Parl. No. 3159, pp. 216-237. Cf. André Mougin, *Le salaire minimum dans la soierie* (Dijon, 1924).

[238] See *Bull. Office du Travail,* November, 1902, for a good summary. In the Senate may be mentioned the proposition passed in 1904 (Sen. Doc. Parl. No. 1639); and in the Chamber of Deputies, the project proposed by the Minister of Commerce and Industry, M. Trouillot, June 14, 1904 (Doc. Parl. No. 1761), which was covered in the excellent *Rapport Chambon,* J. O. C. of D., July 6, 1906, pp. 902-905, Doc. Parl. No. 220.

[239] Note the laws of November 2, 1893, March 30, 1900, July 13, 1906, December 22, 1911, December 31, 1912, June 17, 1913, June 11, August 5 and December 2, 1917, all of which are included under the law of July 23, 1917, in the *Code du Travail,* Book II.

[240] *Code du Travail,* Book II, Chap. II.

[241] See Reports for *Commission du Travail,* M. Justin Godart, on law reducing hours of work of adults to ten in industrial establishments; J. O. C. of D. S. O., 1911, Doc. Parl. No. 967; *Rapport Supplementaire*

hour day, declared that the ten hour day was only a step in the right direction. The advance was made in the project [242] of M. Colliard, the Minister of Labour, and the *Rapport Godart* [243] testified to the progress that had been made since the former report, which the law of 1919 fully confirmed by statute.[244]

This law of April 23, 1919, under which the eight hour day was instituted was preceded by most thorough discussion by a special commission appointed by Clemenceau, and by both the Chamber of Deputies and the Senate. The terms of the law provided that the questions arising out of the application of this principle were to be settled by regulations of the public administration, after consultation with the employers' and workers' organizations concerned. The administrative orders may be issued either on the initiative of the Government or at the request of workers' or employers' associations. They have usually been based on collective agreements already in existence, especially in the metal trades. The law provided that it should be put into effect by decrees of public administration, and a system of administrative orders has been extensively applied under this act, new orders being constantly issued. In November 1922, 24 decrees had been issued covering 2,878,506 workers; 2 decrees, covering banks and insurance companies and electric power companies, had been submitted to the Council of State; 5 decrees, covering 659,000 workers, had been submitted to the employers' and workers' organizations for approval, and 11 decrees covering 884,000 workers were under consideration. Two special laws have been passed for the coal mines [245] and mercantile marine,[246] the latter being abro-

on attitude of the French Chamber of Commerce, J. O. C. of D. S. O., February 1, 1912, Doc. Parl. No. 1619, pp. 61-62, and two supplementary reports (Nos. 1939 and 2051) before June 25, 1912, when *urgence* was declared for the bill.

[242] J. O. C. of D., April 8, 1919, Doc. Parl. No. 5960.

[243] J. O. C. of D., April 10, 1919, Doc. Parl. No. 5980.

[244] Cf. Gaston Tessier, *La journée de huit heures* (1923).

[245] The law of June 24, 1919.

[246] The eight hour day for French seamen was established by the law of August 2, 1919, the regulations governing its application being issued as an administrative order, February 24, 1920. By the decree of September 5, 1922, the law was temporarily suspended, as stated above, but by the administrative decree of March 31, 1925, the three-shift system was established in the French merchant marine (*Bulletin du Ministère du Travail*, Paris, April-June, 1925, pp. 82-92).

gated in 1922 after the failure of the Genoa Conference of the International Labour Organization. By the administrative decree of January 16, 1925, the eight hour day was established for employees on railroads other than engineers, firemen and conductors whose work was regulated. The law of 1919 allowed for supplementary hours and a longer day in occupations in which the work was intermittent, but the decree of 1925 substituted, following the English example, eight hours' presence for eight hours of actual work. In the discussion of the budget of the Ministry of Labour in 1922 in the Chamber of Deputies, the Minister of Labour made the statement the success of the eight hour day in France was assured. The Government has made an effort to carry out its pledges.[247]

The law of December 30, 1924, amends the articles of the French Labour Code (Art. I, Book II) relating to the night work of women and children so as to secure uniformity with the provisions of the convention adopted by the Washington International Labour Conference. The Labour Code fixed the age of children who could be employed in factories, mines, quarries, workshops, etc., of any nature whatever at 13 years. The present law states that children, workers, or apprentices aged less than 18 years, and women, may not be employed at any night work in such establishments. The work between 10 P.M. and 5 A.M. is considered as night work, and it is prescribed that the rest of women and children must have a duration of at least 11 hours. In establishments under the technical control of the Minister of

[247] See two reports by the *Ministère du Travail et de la Prévoyance Sociale, Bulletin de l'inspection du travail et de l'hygiène industrielle, Vingt-septième année* (1919) and *Vingt-huitième année* (1920). These reports give the discussion in Chamber of Deputies and the Senate upon the eight hour day law of April 23, 1919, and the report of the mining commission and the debate on the eight hour day for miners passed on June 24, 1919. See also "Hours of Labour in Industry, France," *International Labour Office, Studies and Reports, Series D., No. 6* (1922); Herbert Feis, "The Attempt to Establish the Eight-Hour Day by International Action," *Political Science Quarterly*, Vol. XXXIX, Nos. 3 and 4, September-December, 1924; G. Guyot, *La loi des huit heures en France et ses consequences economiques* (1922); J. Desplanque, *Le problème de la réduction de la durée du travail devant le Parlement Français* (1918), with extended bibliography; J. Cavaillé, *Journée de huit heures. La loi du 23 avril 1919. L'historique—l'esprit—le mécanisme d'application* (1919); and J. Beaudemoulin, *La loi de huit heures. Enquete sur son application et sur loisirs de l'ouvrier* (1924).

Public Works, the duties of the labour inspectors are assigned to officials, except in case of the railroads in matters of general or local interest which are under the direction of the Minister of Labour.[248]

It is also interesting to record the extension of the law of July 10, 1915,[249] establishing a minimum wage for home workers in the clothing industry. This law provided that its protective clauses could be extended to other industries by administrative decree after consultation of the Minister of Labour with the Superior Council of Labour. For the first time since the enactment a decree dated August 10, 1922,[250] extended the law to other industries employing home labour. The decree ended the controversy regarding the field covered by the original law, for it is specified that the law relates not only to work on clothing but also to other articles of wearing apparel and to linen for personal wear and household use, embroideries, laces, feathers and artificial flowers. Following a demand of the trade unions, the law was made applicable to the manufacture of additional articles of clothing as well as to certain kinds of knitting, making of rosaries, orders, crosses, medals, jewellery, umbrellas, tapestry work, etc.[251] The administrative principle of the original law is maintained, the minimum wage being fixed by the Labour Councils or Wage Committees for the hour or for the day, upon the basis of the average rate paid in the locality to workers of average skill employed in the workshops at the same occupation.

(b) *Extension of Law of Accidents, Eight Hour Day and Weekly Rest Day*

In common with nearly all of the laws of the first fourteen years of the century, the law of July 13, 1906,[252] on a weekly day of rest had a long history. It was accepted in principle by the Chamber of Deputies, March 22, 1902, by a vote of 422-

[248] *Bulletin du Ministère du Travail,* Paris, October-December, 1924, pp. 393, 394.

[249] *Code du Travail,* Liv. I, art. 33 et suiv., 99a et 99b.

[250] Dalloz, *Code du Travail* (*Additions*), p. 109.

[251] Art. I of decree.

[252] *Code du Travail,* Book II, Art. 30-51; the Decrees of August 24, 1906, and July 13, 1907 (Dalloz, *Code du Travail,* pp. 151-152), contain the administrative rules of the law.

10,[253] and as soon as it became a law there was a general effort by private members and by the Government to increase its usefulness.[254] During the session of 1907 there were no less than ten propositions [255] submitted to the Chamber of Deputies seeking to modify the law of 1906; and the law of April 4, 1914,[256] including the central markets of Paris in its provisions, illustrate again the beneficial influence of earlier enactments and the value of once getting upon the statute book the principles of reform. The continuous progress of legislation dealing with the hours of work and the necessary conditions of health and comfort for the worker, a principle of State intervention established in both France and England before any other in labour legislation, is convincing proof that the experiment of legislation is one of the best means of understanding a labour problem.

The extension of the law on accidents to include an ever larger number of workers, as commercial and agricultural employees, and the application of a new principle, that of professional maladies, is a good example in point. England and France have had almost the same history with their law on accidents.[257] The basic law on accidents in France is the law of April 9, 1898,[258] the administrative procedure of which has been changed and improved by the laws of March 22, 1902,[259] March 31, 1905,[260] December 13, 1912,[261] and August 5, 1920.[262] The first extension of this law was to include, with certain reservations, agricultural workers,

[253] *The Rapport Berry,* 1902, is summarized in the later Sèvaés Report, a very substantial and excellent parliamentary document, J. O. C. of D., March 12, 1908, pp. 217-228, Doc. Parl. No. 1578.

[254] See the project of M. Viviani, Minister of Labour, J. O. C. of D., March 31, 1907, pp. 444-446, Doc. Parl. 1007.

[255] These propositions constituted Nos. 385, 406, 440, 631, 864, 865, 891, 892, 895 and 954 of the Parliamentary Documents of that year, for which the *Rapport Sévaès* for the *Commission du Travail* provides an excellent history and commentary.

[256] *Code du Travail,* Book II, Art. 51a-51h.

[257] Cf. Adrien Sachet, *Législation sur les accidents du travail et les maladies professionnelles* (1st ed. 1909, 6th ed. 1921, 2 vols.), Vol. I, pp. 36-43, on England, and pp. 1-25, Introduction.

[258] Dalloz, *Code du Travail,* pp. 103-114.

[259] Dalloz, *Code du Travail,* Law of 1898, Art. 2, 11, 12, 17, 18, 20, 22.

[260] Dalloz, *Code du Travail,* Law of 1898, Art. 3, 4, 10, 19, 16, 21.

[261] Dalloz, *Code du Travail,* p. 281; D. P. 1913, 4, 44.

[262] Dalloz, *Code du Travail* (*Addition*), p. 36; D. P. 1921, 4, 328.

by the law of June 30, 1899.[263] The next important law was that of April 12, 1906,[264] completed by the decree of February 18, 1907,[265] including within its provisions commercial employees; and by the permissive clauses of the law of July 8, 1907,[266] more workers were brought within the scope of its protection.

But it was in the provision for the inclusion of professional diseases within the benefits of the law of 1898 that the marked advance of social legislation with regard to the rights of the worker was seen.[267] The first most thorough effort was in the

[263] Dalloz, *Code du Travail,* pp. 124-125; D. P. 1899, 4, 92. M. Mirman first proposed the further extension to include agricultural workers, December 13, 1900; again in 1904 (C. of D. Doc. Parl. No. 1741) and in 1906 (J. O. C. of D., November 5, Doc. Parl. No. 364). The *Rapport Chauvin* for the Commission on Insurance and Social Prevision reported favourably (J. O. C. of D., February 22, 1907, Doc. Parl. No. 777), but the *Rapport Chaigne* (J. O. C. of D., July 4, 1907, Doc. Parl. No. 1153), for the Commission on Agriculture, was unfavourable because of the financial requirements. With this in mind a new proposition was introduced by M. P. Bureaugard (J. O. C. of D., October 27, 1907, Doc. Parl. No. 127), which was favourably reported (Rapport Chauvin, J. O. C. of D., October 13, 1908, Doc. Parl. No. 2045); taken up again in 1910, it was voted by the Chamber of Deputies May 18, 1915, and following the *Rapport Bienvenu-Martin,* J. O. Sen., April 27, 1920, Doc. Parl. No. 195, it was voted on favourably. The most important feature of this project is the granting of State aid to small farmers. This detailed history is given to emphasize the development of a phase of labour legislation which is important.

[264] Dalloz, *Code du Travail,* pp. 149-150; D. P. 1906, 4, 116.

[265] Dalloz, *Code du Travail,* pp. 159-160.

[266] Dalloz, *Code du Travail,* pp. 190-191; D. P. 1907, 4, 151. It should be noted that the important laws of March 31, 1905, and March 22, 1902, are contained in the law of 1898, along with the laws of March 5, 1917, and October 17, 1919. In the session of 1907-8, five propositions on the law of accidents were introduced: Nos. 127, 1340, 1389 (S. E. 1907), pp. 30, 310, 344; Nos. 1663 and 1737 (S. O. 1908), pp. 306, 422. In 1908-9 there were seven such propositions. See also the Charpentier Report on the law to extend the employees of the State protection (J. O. C. of D., March 17, 1910, pp. 369-372).

[267] Cf. *Bulletin du Office du Travail,* July, 1904, pp. 611-618, *L'Assimilation des Maladies Professionnelles aux Accidents du Travail.* Also Sachet, *op. cit.,* Vol. II, pp. 499-533; and see his *Traité théorique et pratique de la législation sur les accidents du travail et les maladies professionnelles,* Tome III (Paris, 1924), for a commentary on the recent laws on accidents. The last section deals with jurisprudence and legislation on labour accidents (texts of the laws, decrees, etc.) from 1920 to October, 1924). The administration of the law dealing with occupational diseases for the years 1921 and 1922 is surveyed in the

introduction in 1901 of the Breton proposition,[268] sponsored by MM. Briand, Jaurès and Vaillant. Being urged strongly in 1903,[269] it was taken up by the Minister of Commerce and Industry, M. Dubief, and brought forward as a Government measure in 1905 [270] and in 1906.[271] Amended and improved greatly by its progress through the Chambers, the Government project finally became the law of October 25, 1919,[272] extending the law of April 9, 1898, on accidents of work to professional maladies caused by conditions of work in certain industries. The law can be extended to other occupations not specified by administrative decree.

The extension of the law of 1898 to include domestic servants was passed in 1913 by the Chamber of Deputies,[273] but like the proposition to include agricultural workers it was held up by the Senate, until by the law of August 2, 1923, this class of

Bulletin du Ministère du Travail, January-February, 1924, pp. 3-8. The law of October 25, 1919, went into effect January 27, 1921.

[268] J. O. C. of D., December 5, 1901, Doc. Parl. No. 2810.

[269] J. O. C. of D., July 3, 1903, pp. 2032-2053, Doc. Parl. No. 1159. In 1907 this Breton proposition was revised and reintroduced (J. O. C. of D. S. E., 1907, p. 2287 ff., Doc. Parl. No. 2287); and note the *Rapport Breton,* J. O. C. of D., March 22, 1907, Doc. Parl. No. 888, and for 1908 (S. E.) Doc. Parl. No. 2169, p. 201. Also the Report Chauvin and the *Avis* from the Agricultural Committee on professional diseases (S. E. 1908, Doc. Parl. No. 2190, p. 223; and S. O. 1909, Doc. Parl. 2304, p. 125), together with supplementary Report by M. Chauvin (S. O. 1909, Doc. Parl. No. 2507, p. 1177).

[270] J. O. C. of D., May 16, 1905, pp. 532-539, Doc. Parl. No. 2447; and in the 1905 session may be added two other propositions, J. O. C. of D., 1905, p. 530, Doc. Parl. No. 2439, and J. O. C. of D., 1905, p. 407, Doc. Parl. No. 2396.

[271] J. O. C. of D., June 14, 1906, pp. 557-564, Doc. Parl. No. 88. J. O. C. of D., December 1, 1903, Doc. Parl. No. 1336, for the proposition which the Senate submitted to the Chamber of Deputies, which was the basis of the *Rapport Mirman* (C. of D. Doc. Parl., 1903, No. 1337; and the *Rapport Chovet* (J. O. Sen., December 1, 1903, Doc. Parl. No. 299), is a commentary on four propositions sent up by the Chamber of Deputies.

[272] Dalloz, *Code du Travail,* pp. 420-424; and note the administrative Decree of December 31, 1920 (Dalloz, *Code du Travail* (*Additions*), pp. 57-58); J. O. C. of D., Oct. 27, 1919, p. 11973.

[273] Proposition Puglesi-Conti, J. O. C. of D., May 25, 1908, Doc. Parl. No. 1737; two reports were given before it was voted by the Chamber, June 25, 1913, the *Rapport Chauvin,* J. O. C. of D., July 7, 1909, Doc. Parl. No. 2659, and the *Rapport Lairolle,* J. O. C. of D., December 26, 1911.

workers was given protection.[274] Likewise the law of December 15, 1922, extended larger benefits to agricultural workers.[275] The protection of children under thirteen years of age and of apprentices have been the objects sought by propositions introduced.[276] There has been no more general application of a principle of intervention than is recorded in the constant expansion of the law on accidents, which implies in its most recent manifestation, on professional maladies, a very wide social significance and a new obligation on industry which the State has fully supported.

(c) *Housing.*

The history of housing legislation in France, as in England, illustrates the triple co-operation of the State, voluntary organ-

[274] The law of August 2, 1923, extended the provisions of the Workmen's Compensation Act of April 9, 1898, articles 2, 3 and 6 of the law of April 12, 1906, and the law of December 30, 1922, to cover domestic servants, chauffeurs, governesses and porters, and all persons connected with household services.

[275] *Journal Officiel,* C. of D., December 16, 1922, pp. 12014-12016. The law extended the benefits of the accident insurance law of April 9, 1898, to include agricultural workers. The original compensation law which related to workers in industrial enterprises was amended April 12, 1906, to include workers in commercial establishments, and on July 15, 1914, the benefits of the law were extended to forestry workers. The efforts to extend protection to farm workers proved unavailing up to 1922, except that the law of June 30, 1899, made the law of 1898 applicable to agricultural workers in the single case of accidents caused by machinery driven by mechanical power. The law of 1922 on agricultural accidents first passed the French Senate, and it had the support of the Ministers of Agriculture and Labour, who insisted before the joint committees of agriculture and health that the Chamber of Deputies should accept without amendment the text adopted by the Senate. Bibliography is extensive, but see especially J. Bouchet, *Manuel de la législation sur les accidents et les sociétés d'assurance mutuelles agricoles* (1924), written from the experience of an administrator; H. Bourdeaux, *Code des accidents du travail avec annotations d'après la doctrine et la jurisprudence* (*septième édition,* 1924), giving text and decrees from 1898 down through 1923; G. Carrère, *La protection légale de l'ouvrier agricole* (1919). Two worth-while reports from the *Ministère du Travail* are *Contrôle des assurances. Recueil de documents sur les accidents du travail* (1924). *Lois, règlements et circulaires,* and *Exploitations Agricoles. Recueil de documents relatifs à l'application de lois du 15 Decembre, 1922, sur les accidents du travail agricole* (1924), which gives texts and decrees from 1898-1923.

[276] The proposition Doizy, submitted February 1, 1912, adopted by the Chamber January 22, 1914; and the proposition Raynaldi, January 20, 1920.

ization, and the workers or the public.[277] The progress also of public health law is an integral part of the movement in each country; the expression *habitations à bon marché,* says M. Bry,[278] is a bad one, it is rather *habitations hygiéniques.* The creation of special Councils under the control of the Ministry of Hygiene, Assistance and Social Prevision have indicated this. The *Conseil Supérieur d'Hygiène Publique de France* (Decree, June 19, 1906, January 27 and March 31, 1920); the *Commission Consultative d'Hygiène Industrielle* (Order of December 11, 1900); and the *Conseil Supérieur des Habitations à Bon Marché,* Laws of November 30, 1894, and April 12, 1906 (Decrees of January 10, 1907, and May 25, 1913), may be especially mentioned. This last Council was created by the first measure in France dealing with cheap housing,[279] which provided exemption from certain land taxes as well as instituted committees for encouragement of cheap housing in the departments and municipalities. The Act of 1894 was abrogated by the Strauss Act of April 12, 1906,[280] which extended the working of the original Act encouraging associations building cheap houses, and it also included provisions dealing with playing fields and allotments. The Ribot Act of 1908 extended yet further the application of the previous law, and it was intended to encourage large regional societies in the building of small houses.[281] The departments and municipalities

[277] Cf. Pic, *op. cit.,* pp. 957 ff., and Bry, *op. cit.,* pp. 828-848.

[278] *Op. cit.,* p. 829.

[279] See the *Rapport Bonnevay* for the *Commission d'Assurance et de Prévoyance Sociales* charged to examine the project of law modifying and completing the law of April 12, 1906 (No. 1368, S. E. 1911, pp. 254-256), the proposition of M. Sembart (Doc. Parl. No. 1622, S. O. 1912, p. 64), and of M. Marin (Doc. Parl. No. 1773, 1912), J. O. C. of D., March 29, pp. 768-812, for a survey of French and foreign legislation and the reasons for the Government project.

[280] See Strauss Report on the project of law to complete the law of November 30, 1894: J. O. Sen. S. O., March 23, 1905, pp. 329 ff., Doc. Parl. No. 81, and supplementary report, J. O. Sen. S. O., January 23, 1906, pp. 1 ff., Doc. Parl. No. 3. The author was the leader of the better housing agitation. See J. O. Sen., March 18, 1904, on law project of Ministry of Commerce (Doc. Parl. Sen. No. 80); for report on application of law of 1894 see J. O. C. of D., April 2, 1904; for 1902, see *Bulletin du Office du Travail,* June, 1903, pp. 527-531 and p. 480.

[281] See project of law by Minister of Labour modifying law of April 10, 1908, together with exposé of motives, J. O. C. of D., December 2, 1911, pp. 301-302, Doc. Parl. No. 1408 (S. E.); see Report on above by

were authorized to give assistance to the cheap housing movement by (1) granting loans to the housing associations, (2) purchasing bonds of the associations, (3) providing them with land free or at reduced price, and (4) guaranteeing the rate of interest on sums borrowed by such associations. Exemption privileges were extended to plots of ground with an area of not more than seven acres if attached to houses, or ten acres if not so attached. Before this Act was modified by the Law of February 26, 1912, which aimed primarily at meeting the need of the agricultural worker, the law of March 19, 1910, had permitted long term credits for the housing of the agricultural population.[282] The Minister of Labour, M. Renoult, was responsible for the Government project modifying the Act of 1908.[283]

The law of December 23, 1912, amending the law of April 12, 1906, modified the maximum rental value, laid down for the definition of cheap dwellings, and went much further than any previous legislation by creating new bodies known as Public Housing Offices, *Offices Public d'Habitations à Bon Marchè,* for the Departments, and providing for the special work of the *Comités de Patronage des Habitations à Bon Marché et de Prévoyance Sociale.* Up until this measure the State had confined itself to giving financial assistance to the building societies set up by private initiative,[284] but by the law of December 23, 1912, the public authorities themselves were enabled through the Public Housing Offices to take part in the provision of healthy and cheap houses. The former purpose was made plain in the provision that no exemption or reduction in taxation was granted unless the houses constructed met a satisfactory standard of hygiene and sanitation; and the *Comités de Patronage des Habitations à Bon Marché* were empowered to inspect the houses and to

M. Bonnevay, J. O. C. of D., December 21, 1911, pp. 523-525, Doc. Parl. No. 1515 (S. E.).

[282] See J. O. C. of D., February 20, 1904, for Colet Report on the creation of a central credit bank for agriculture (Doc. Parl. No. 1530).

[283] The Ribot Act has been modified by the laws of February 26, 1912, February 11, 1914, and October 28, 1919; the Act of 1906 by the laws of April 10, 1908, July 13, 1911 (art. 3), December 23, 1912, February 11, 1914, July 29, 1916, March 31 (art. 14), April 24, May 17, and October 24, 1919.

[284] The Act of 1906 did not forbid the State to aid, but the tendency of the *Conseil d'Etat* has been resolutely hostile (Pic, p. 959).

issue sanitary certificates. These committees in the Departments consist of 9 to 15 members, 18 for the Department of the Seine; they work in conjunction with the *Conseil Supérieur des Habitations à Bon Marché,* which is under the Ministry of Health.[285]

The parliamentary reports on housing in France, so far as their survey of foreign legislation is concerned, are a history of such legislation in England.[286] This is especially used in the Report of M. Jules Siegfried for the Commission on Health with regard to the project for expropriation for reasons of public health.[287] As in England it has been found necessary for the public powers to aid, and to even actively direct at times, the housing of the people. Each law that has been enacted, however, has included within its scope larger social consequences, the benefits having surely been shared by the community and by the nation. It is class legislation sanctioned by the whole people.

(d) *Post-war Legislation.*

War-acts of course are significant for other reasons, but their history in France is the same as in England. The Rent Moratorium Decree of August 14, 1914, was amended six times; the Act of March 9, 1918, on leases was extended by the Law of October 23, 1919; the Profiteering Act of August 20, 1916, was extended by the Law of October 23, 1919; and all of these were amended and codified in the Act of March 31, 1922, which in turn has been extended to 1926 by the law of December 30, 1923. The Act of September 5, 1922, codified the existing legislation on cheap housing and small properties, the purpose of which

[285] Because of the financial relationship of these Councils to housing and their control by the Ministry of Health with reference to such, the following should be mentioned: *Conseil Supérieur des Caisses d'Epargne* (Law of July 30, 1895), the *Conseil Supérieur des Societes de Secours Mutuels* (Law of April 1, 1898, decrees of February 28, 1898, and May 29, 1905) and the *Conseil Supérieur de l'Assistance Publique* (Decree February 28, 1909). See Art. 75 of the law of 1922 on the Housing Committees and their organization.

[286] See Bonnevay Report (March 29, 1912), pp. 784-786; cf. Gide, *op. cit.* (1921), pp. 271-297. See Pic, *op. cit.,* pp. 448-461, Bry, *op. cit.,* pp. 481-485, and Scelles, *op. cit.,* pp. 140-143, for comments on municipal socialism, with especial reference to English example.

[287] J. O. C. of D., January 19, 1912, pp. 29-46; Doc. Parl. No. 1592; cf. *Avis* from the Committee on the Budget by M. Chéron, J. O. C. of D., July 9, 1912, pp. 1526-1531, Doc. Parl. No. 2152.

is "to encourage the building of cheap and sanitary houses for persons of small means, and in particular workers mainly supported by their wages." The fact of importance from the first Act of 1894 until the latest amending clause is the growing recognition of the conditions which allow larger powers to public bodies [288] to collaborate in the housing of the people, by loans or by subventions. If powers are used unwisely, or not at all, at least the need has been recognized by the legislature. The use of the National Deposit and Loan Fund, as well as other special funds of associations on a mutual or co-operative basis, points the way, M. Pic believes, where the legislature associates the action of all groups in the work of social improvement. The law of March 12, 1920, on syndicates, allowed the important innovation of the use of funds [289] for building houses, buying land for workers' gardens and for purposes of physical education and health.[290] The law of August 27, 1924, authorized the city of Paris to borrow, at a maximum rate fixed by the Minister of Interior, the sum of 300,000,000 francs, for the construction, purchase, or improvement of cheap dwellings.

This survey of the important phases of social legislation in France during the years of the century, with some indication of how earlier legislation has been carried forward, shows that the protective influence of the State has been extended to more and more workers, and that protective power includes nearly all of the problems which concern the working and living

[288] Bry, *op. cit.*, p. 836. This is indicated in the law of October 24, 1919 (*Journal Officiel,* October 26, 1919), amending the law of April 12, 1906, and December 23, 1912, which provided for multiple dwellings (apartments). The State might advance through the mortgage banks not more than 200,000,000 francs, and the Bank of Deposits and Consignations, under Government supervision, might advance not more than 300,000,000 francs to such enterprises. Parliament further authorized provinces and communes to purchase and resell, after subdivision, lands and rural estates, the communes to acquire the lands under the law of April 5, 1884, and the provinces to be limited to the budget prepared by the prefect and especially authorized by the provincial commission (*Journal Officiel,* Nov. 1, 1919). Cf. *Les habitations à bon marché,* the series of *Guides practiques de législation sociale,* by MM. Rendu and Cacheux.

[289] Art. 5, sect. 4, law of 1920.

[290] Cf. Pic, *op. cit.*, pp. 256-257, and Bry, *op. cit.*, pp. 918-919.

conditions of the people. The quaint amusement of the Chamber of Deputies deciding the temperature of the shops wherein Paris fashions are displayed only emphasizes the fact that the modern State has been faced with a complexity of interests with regard to which it is impossible for the legislature to be unmindful.

The long history of the agitation for an eight hour day,[291] a minimum wage and better housing of the people, provides a commentary on the progress of the labour movement in France and England, as well as a good test of the success of the doctrine of State intervention in industry. The labour leaders in England were to give more attention to the problem of the unskilled and common labourer because the whole structure of trade unionism was threatened by the unorganized worker, and in France the doctrinaire syndicalist put his faith in the industrial mob led by the conscious minority. The worker at the bottom of the industrial system had to be protected by the State for his position was a menace to the well-being of the common life. For Labour this worker was an added recruit in the work of overthrowing the capitalistic system. The economic ideals of social justice were gradually extending to all workers the protection of the State and the encouragement of a common organization whose interest was bound up with the interest of each worker. In England the State had recognized since 1891, the principle of a minimum wage for workers, a stipulation which since 1888 the City of London has enforced and which in many cities of England has been progressively carried out. The effects of this recognition on the problem of a minimum wage in industry and the attitude which the Government assumed have been great. Before 1914 the State had committed itself to the principle that there was a standard of life below which it would not allow an individual to fall. It was determined that the costs of industrial progress could not be too heavy nor demand too callously the resources of human life as a sacrifice. The State actually began to judge the industrial system; it began to estimate its tremendous

[291] The Commission on International Labour Legislation of the Peace Conference inscribed first among the objects of international accord "the regulation of hours of work, including the establishment of a maximum working day and week," and they put at the head of the agenda for the first Conference of this organization "the application of the principle of the eight hour day or forty-eight hour week."

costs for the State. This necessarily meant that the State had to actively concern itself with the hours that people worked, the wages that were paid them, and even the work that they were required to do and the manner in which it was required to be done. It had to go farther than it had ever gone before to prevent the degradation of human life by an economic régime which forced the State to provide pensions after a life of work, open free dispensaries and hospitals, tear down insanitary dwelling houses, and by huge subsidies try to make the conditions of life bearable for the great mass of people. It then had to admit defeat before an industrial system founded on profit and exploitation, and begin itself to direct the purposes of this system by prescribing a minimum standard of life. Such an attitude was revolutionary in social theory and politics, but it was the condition of progress, even safety, for the modern State. The insecurity of the people compelled the State to begin the reorganization of all its institutions of control and administration, putting in the first place the individual and his welfare, for upon that depended a hope of social decency for all.

CHAPTER X

SOME POLITICAL ASPECTS OF THE FRENCH LABOUR MOVEMENT

PART I

The General Congresses, 1899-1901, and Efforts for Unity

NEITHER in political or economic organization had the French Labour movement by 1900 kept pace with the industrial progress of the country. One of the most important reasons for the reconstitution of the syndicates, it has been noticed, was to combat the organization of the patrons of France, who have been "out for themselves first, last and all the time." [1] At the beginning unsocial energies were loosed that have continued with almost uncontrolled power. The concentration of the economic resources of France in the hands of the employing class was the result of the uninterrupted industrial development of the nation since the Commune; and this power was more effectively used against the workmen when the employers formed trusts and combines.[2] The one thing left to the workmen with which to fight the employer in his general protective syndicate was the double weapon of economic and political organization.[3] The scientific

[1] Bryce, *op. cit.*, Vol. I, pp. 335-336; also B. G. De Montgomery, *op. cit.*, pp. 5, 9-10.

[2] See articles in *Le Mouvement Socialiste*, "L'Organisation Patronale en France," Nos. 200-204, 1908: July 15, "La Métallurgie," A. Merrheim, pp. 5-25; August 15, *ibid.*, pp. 81-95; Sept. 15 and Oct. 15, "Patronal Organisations," pp. 178-197, 270-277; Nov. 15 and Dec. 15, "Les Comités Régionaux" and "Comité des Forges," pp. 338-362, 408-425; Feb. and March, 1909, "Le Bâtiment," A. Picart, pp. 81-92, 206-215; June and Nov.-Dec., 1909, "Le Métallurgie," A. Merrheim, pp. 431-448, 321-346. The British and American consul reports on French industry since the war are very suggestive; they deal at length at times with internal labour disputes and industrial reorganization. Cf. Sisley Huddleston, "The Economic Revolution in France," *Atlantic Monthly*, August, 1924.

[3] Cf. M. Compère-Morel, *La concentration capitaliste en France* (1913), pp. 45-47; also Paul Louis, *Histoire du socialisme français*, pp. 374-378.

method of industrial and commercial progress by combination and interlocking directorates, suggested to the militant working class of France, as it had earlier to the Trade Unionists of England, the new method of Labour organization.[4]

At the Paris Congress of 1899, M. Lagardelle declared that the Labour movement had reached a period of evolution when new forms of organization and action should be substituted for the old; that the necessities of social evolution made necessary the reshaping of the working class movement.[5] From one of the spokesmen of the revolt which was forming at that time this belief is important. It was a reaction to the "decentralized collectivism" of Jaurès, as well as to the rigid economy of the politics of Jules Guesde.[6] M. Morel endeavoured further to define the problem of the Labour movement of 1900, urging the complete reorganization of the Socialist party from the political and economic point of view. The party had reached the stage of evolution where it was necessary to apply the scientific method,[7] finally looking to that period of transformation in the working class movement of the whole world which would establish the universal Republic, based on equality, justice and solidarity.[8] Throughout the Congress the major problem was the attainment of the unity of the French Labour movement. The *Comité d'Entente* insisted on the importance of a Congress that would bring together for the first time all the political and economic divisions of French Socialism. It should bring about a new era in the diffusion of theories, making more effective all means of propaganda; uniting all who had in common the same principles

[4] See Maurice Bourguin, *Les Systèmes Socialistes et l'Evolution Économique* (1904), for a general statement on the extension of capitalism and the organization "of collective forces which give to the contemporary economic movement its real character" (p. 350); note chap. XV, T. IV, on English trade unions.

[5] Cf. *Compte Rendu, Congrès Général des Organisations Socialistes Françaises,* Paris, 1899, pp. 316-321; the speech of Lagardelle followed Guesde.

[6] Cf. Bourguin, *op. cit.,* pp. 28-40, on Jaurès; pp. 113-134, on Guesde.

[7] The Labour movement becoming "self-conscious" is plainly seen in many such speeches in the French Congresses, and for the same evidence see the presidential address of the 1900 Trade Union Congress, London *Times,* September 5, 1900, p. 10.

[8] Cf. *Congrès Général des Organisations Socialistes Françaises, Compte Rendu,* Paris, 1899, pp. 335-339.

and the same aspirations, believing in "the organization of a new society by the working class." The work of those directing their efforts toward this new social order should not divide the energies of the proletariat. They could unite on the basis of the class struggle, working to bring about "complete social revolution for and by the workers." [9]

The Constitution of the 1899 Congress was the same as that which served for the *Comité d'Entente*: The co-operation and solidarity of all workers; the political and economic organization of the working class as a class party for the conquest of power; and the socialization of the means of production and exchange—that is, the transformation of the capitalist society to a collectivist or communist society. The Congress was composed of delegates from the five Socialist groups which formed the *Comité d'Entente,* delegates from study groups, societies of propaganda and permanent political groups not affiliated in the five large parties.

The order of the day as determined by the Committee was: (1) The class war and the obtaining of public power: (a) By what means, and conforming to the principle of the class war, can the Socialist organizations take part in national, departmental and municipal government? (b) Ways and means of obtaining power: political action, electoral or revolutionary; economic action, strikes, general strikes, boycotting, etc. (2) The attitude of the Socialist party with regard to the various conflicts of the bourgeoisie, militarism, clericalism, anti-semitism, nationalism, etc. (3) Socialist unity, its theoretical and practical conditions; central control of the activity, propaganda and organization of the different Labour organizations.[10]

It was to be expected that a Congress composed of all shades of opinion in the French Labour movement would be a most lively one, but the remarkable thing was that the Congress did succeed in doing a great deal of what it set out to do. This is largely due to M. Jaurès, the master of the Congress, who had the brilliant support of MM. Briand and Viviani, and effective helpers such as MM. Revelin, Carnaud and Champy. Reading the proceedings of the Congress one is impressed that there was a basis for believing that the time had been reached when a will for unity was

[9] *Op. cit., Circulaire de Convocation,* pp. v-viii.
[10] *Op. cit.,* p. vii.

present in the French Labour movement. The Congress performed a service at the time that was effective in shaping future events. The Paris Congress of 1899 seemed to be the nearest approach to a consummation of unity in the Labour movement, due to an overwhelming enthusiasm for unity, and ever since, every French Socialist carries about with him deep down in his heart, the wish for such a national party.[11]

The demand for unity implied a substantial growth in the consciousness of the French Labour movement, a recognition that the time had come for it to play a more important part in the life of the nation. The organization of the Labour movement in the modern democratic State was the problem of the Congress of 1899; and this problem had been slowly forming within the political and economic development of France since the Commune. England and France each had to set itself to this common task, but the preparation of the working class of the two nations for the duty was vastly different.[12] The revolutionary tradition of the French Labour movement was a product of the bitter struggles of its leaders against an unfriendly and hostile State, at no time too secure against revolt. This conditioned the development of the social theory and political practice of the working class. But the heritage of the English Labour movement was greatly different; British Socialism looked back to the idealist Robert Owen with his stress on human brotherhood and not to the realist Karl Marx with his "class war." [13] Frederick Engels wrote in 1886 (the Editor's Preface to the first English edition of *Capital*), that the theory of Karl Marx was the result of a lifelong study of the economic history and condition of England; and that study led to the conclusion that at least in Europe, England is the only country where the inevitable social revolution might be effected by peaceful and legal means.[14] That is only possible where class hatred is a diminishing quality in social progress. Except at a few crises, this has been held to be true of England where there has existed "very little class hatred and no perma-

[11] Cf. Werner Sombart, *Socialism and the Socialist Movement* (6th ed. E. T., 1909), p. 234.

[12] Bryce, *op. cit.*, Vol. I, pp. 297-361.

[13] Cf. Sidney Webb's Presidential Address at the Trade Union Congress, June 23, 1923.

[14] *Op. cit.*, p. xiv (17th ed. 1920).

nent class antagonism, neither is there to-day."[15] Even the rapid rise of a Labour party has not, it may safely be said, tended to create class barriers or promote social strife. At both ends of the social scale there is an equal failure to consider the common good, and if any effort is made to assess the blame the dispossession of one class certainly serves as a mitigating circumstance, while social duty devolving upon the ruling class has often been very lightly held.

A distinguished American student of English Government wrote in the first decade of this century that

> parties in England are by no means divided on class lines, and unless the Labour party should grow in a way that seems unlikely, there is no probability that they will be so divided in the near future.[16]

However the prediction has been made that parties would divide into rich and poor, fighting over the distribution of property,[17] the only durable source of faction, said Madison. This is a very popular view of the class struggle in politics, which has marked the degradation of parliamentary life in the industrial nations.

> The whole of Parliament has become a façade behind which go on the operations of finance capital and the real Government of the country [18]

is a point of view which if long held by responsible groups would tend to destroy responsible legislative life.[19] The acceptance of

[15] Bryce, *op. cit.*, Vol. I, p. 348.

[16] Lowell, *The Government of England,* Vol. II, p. 534.

[17] Cf. G. Lowes Dickinson, *The Development of Parliament During the Nineteenth Century* (1896), p. 163, quoted by Lowell, *op. cit.*, p. 533.

[18] Cf. *Labour and Capital in Parliament,* Vol. III of Labour Research Department Studies in Labour and Capital (1923), p. 6. Cf. The speeches of MM. Cachin and J. Doriot in the Chamber of Deputies, 22-23 August, 1924, published by the *Parti Communiste Français* (S. F. I. C.), "Contre le Plan Dawes et la Trahison Socialiste," No. 5, *Les Cahiers du Militant;* see also A. Friedrich, "Le Plan des Experts et l'Asservissement des Masses Laborieuses," No. 3, *Les Cahiers du Militant* (1924).

[19] Cf. *Financial Times,* Sept. 26, 1921, when there was a difference between the Government and the banks. "Does he, and do his colleagues, realize that 'half a dozen men' at the top of the five big banks could

this doctrine among all classes, that Parliament is a prejudiced tool for special interests, is an outstanding question for modern democracy squarely to meet if the government is to be good. The belief that government can be good has been strengthened by the religious movements which have occurred in England, playing a part in the course of political and social history of England that has no parallel in France.[20] The Wesleyan and Baptist movements "helped to develop many of the moral qualities and sober aspirations which have often distinguished the Labour movement of England from that of the Continent," Trevelyan believes.[21] On the other hand there was the place of the Christian aristocrat, Lord Shaftesbury, who softened "in the manner of his age, as he had softened in its politics the savage logic of the Industrial Revolution." [22] It would be difficult exactly to estimate this heritage of the English Labour movement, but when one recalls the delighted humour of the French delegate [23] to the Trade Union Congress who reported the strange fact that the Congress opened with a sermon (and a bad one, he said!), the point of difference at least is clear.[24]

The main interest just here is that such a background greatly

upset the whole fabric of Government finance by refraining from renewing Treasury bills?" Quoted in *Labour and Capital in Parliament*, p. 6n.

[20] Cf. Margaret Pease, *Jean Jaurès*, with an *Introduction* by J. Ramsay MacDonald (1916), pp. 50-53, 77-79, expressing Jaurès' view on the great disturbance that was caused when he allowed his daughter to receive communion. This was a matter for the whole French Labour movement!

[21] G. M. Trevelyan, *British History in the Nineteenth Century*, 1782-1901, pp. 160-161, 183; see also Dicey, *op. cit.*, pp. lviii-lix. Cf. A. V. Woodworth, *Christian Socialism in the Church of England* (1902), pp. 48-58.

[22] See J. L. and Barbara Hammond, *Lord Shaftesbury* (1924); also, *The Town Labourer*, 1760-1832, chap. xi, pp. 221-246; and note the conclusion, chap. XVI, pp. 320-329.

[23] Cf. Jean Longuet, "Le Congrès des Trade-Unions Anglaises," pp. 467-481, *Le Mouvement Socialiste*, October 15, 1901. M. Longuet, grandson of Karl Marx, has had the usual number of varying points of view on the Labour movement; perhaps his latest is clearly given in *Current History* (New York), "Europe in 1924," July, 1924, pp. 537-542.

[24] Edouard Berth's account of the life of Paul Lafargue in *Le Mouvement Socialiste*, is in point. Lafargue's last statement before suicide is there given. Sorel pointed out that the revival of religious interest in France was largely due to Jaurès.

helps in an understanding of the progress that the Labour movements in France and England have made away from the narrow and embittering doctrine of class war. The extension of that dogma into the parliamentary arena, with all its destructive and anti-social power, was one of the weaknesses of early Socialism. But there has been no surer test of the validity of parliamentary effort than that political ideals of social justice have constantly found a wider hearing. The Kautsky motion which passed the International Socialist Congress in Paris, 1900, was an indication that the Labour movement had set itself resolutely to the task of bringing in the new social order by legal and parliamentary means. The history of the progress of this doctrine can be seen in the workers' congresses in France with their constantly enlarging program of reforms set forth by the political groups. A marked tendency of cumulative reasonableness and a deeper social consciousness of solidarity can be traced from 1900. The two general Congresses of all the Labour groups in France at Paris in 1899 and 1900, provide a contemporary commentary of the attitude toward political action and the growing sense of responsibility which the political Labour movement felt for its share in the common parliamentary life. The resolutions, the speeches, the agenda of the Congresses, show that there was an increasing faith in parliamentary progress; opposition to violence and illegal methods; and a widening of the meaning of class struggle to include the whole of the problem of social and economic emancipation.

The Kautsky motion, which like the *Saint-Mandé Programme* excluded recourse to violence, illegal or revolutionary force, declared that in the modern democratic State, the conquest of political power by the working class cannot be the result of a sudden stroke; but of a long and painful effort of working class organization on the economic and political terrain; by the regeneration physically and morally of the working class; by the gradual conquest of municipal government and legislative assemblies.[25] This is a clear statement of reformistic Socialism at the beginning of the century, and it is not to be interpreted, as parliamentary his-

[25] Cf. A. Zévaès, *Le socialisme en 1912 (Conclusions et Annexes)* (1912), p. 5; a serviceable book which includes more than title suggests; also Albert Thomas, *La politique socialiste* (1913).

tory in France and England has borne out, as the laying down of a too strict doctrine of "political class consciousness." Class conscious Socialists of the Marxian school predominated at this International Congress, but after affirming the class war in economics the Congress decided in view of the position of Millerand, that Socialists might serve in a middle class administration. "It was a significant mark in the evolution of Socialist opinion."[25a] The general strike was voted down; municipal experiment in Socialism was urged; and while the Congress declared against a legal minimum wage[26] its temper was shown in the resolution which was passed in favour of a minimum wage obtained by Trade Union action and by the pressure of Labour opinion on the economic policy of public authorities.[27]

The same problem which the Kautsky motion tried to solve was the first question of the Paris Congresses; the debates centring about the class struggle and the conquest of public powers.[28] This question was the dividing point of the French Labour movement; and it was here that the leaders chose to wage the battle. French Socialism had "the honour and the peril" of bringing to a head the controversial problems of theory and tactics which were prominent in the Labour movement of the industrial nations at the beginning of the twentieth century.[29] The Reformist, Evolutionary or Parliamentary Labour group was opposed by the Revolutionary or Direct Action Group. The speeches of Jaurès at the Congresses in Paris 1899[30]-1900[31] and Lyon, 1901,[32] may be taken as the complete statement of the position of the former group, as opposed to the Guesdists and their varying supporters.[33]

[25a] *Economic Journal,* Vol. 10, Dec., 1900, "International Socialist Congress," J. Ramsay MacDonald, pp. 574-575.

[26] The attitude of the English Trade Unions for years was solidly against this, due to a fear of the legal machinery involved; the changing opinion is noted later.

[27] *Economic Journal, op. cit.*

[28] Part I of Order of the Day.

[29] Zévaès, *op. cit.*, p. 4.

[30] Cf. *Congrès Général des Organisations Socialistes Françaises, Compte Rendu,* Paris, 1899, pp. 54-63, 274-280, 392-393.

[31] Cf. *Deuxième Congrès Général des Organisations Socialistes Françaises, Compte Rendu,* Paris, 1900, pp. 167-169, 253-255.

[32] Cf. *Troisième Congrès Général des Organisations Socialistes Françaises, Compte Rendu,* Lyon, 1901, pp. 77-88, 384-385.

[33] Cf. *Compte Rendu,* Congress, 1899, pp. 175-188, 280-282, 313-316; 1900 Congress: pp. 56, 105, 145, 146; 1901 Congress, pp. 92-95, for M. Lagardelle's speech; note also pp. 382-384, on the De La Porte motion.

M. Jaurès, who constantly sought to bring together the best in the whole of Socialist and Labour thought, based his efforts at these Congresses on two main points: That "political liberties are the essential condition of the working class movement";[34] and that the growth of power by the Labour movement imposed decisive responsibilities.[35] At the first Congress Jaurès asked,

Can it be possible that the working class, with its strong organization to-day, is disinterested with regard to the peril which menaces the Republic? We have all said that the political Republic is the condition of the social Republic; that to bring in social justice, to control in the mines, in the manufactures, the workers must first be in control of the cities. In consequence to strike at political liberty is to menace the hope of the social Republic.[36]

Jaurès assumed as an undeniable fact that the entrance of M. Millerand in the Cabinet of Waldeck-Rousseau was a sign of the strength of socialism.[37] Unlike Paul Lafargue[38] who saw in it "that the Socialist party was able to take over the direction of social affairs," creating a confidence which would insure "the success of the approaching revolution," he held that it involved more of responsibility than peril for the labour movement.[39] M. Jaurès said that Lafargue had "resuscitated and galvanized our old enemy the bourgeoisie," and proclaimed the incapacity of the Labour movement.[40] The entrance of Millerand, for Jaurès, was a strong argument for the unity of the Labour movement. The effect with regard to political influence and economic power was more of control for the worker.[41] M. Viviani strongly

[34] *Congrès Général des Organisations Socialistes Françaises, Compte Rendu,* Paris, 1899, p. 55.

[35] *Op. cit.,* p. 58.

[36] *Op. cit.,* p. 59.

[37] *Troisième Congrès Général des Organisations Socialistes Françaises, Compte Rendu,* Lyon, 1901, pp. 77-91.

[38] *Compte Rendu,* 1899, pp. 110-119; compare M. Lagardelle, pp. 316-321, for two speeches which most nearly provide a statement of those who differed from Jaurès.

[39] Cf. Paul Lafargue, *Le Socialisme et la Conquête des Pouvoirs Publics* (Lille, 1899).

[40] *Compte Rendu,* 1899 Congress, pp. 56, 62.

[41] Cf. *Les deux méthodes,* Conference by Jean Jaurès and Jules Guesde, at the Hippodrome Lillois, published by the *Parti Ouvrier Français* (1900), for a sharp statement of the essential differences in the French

supported Jaurés at the first three Socialist Congresses,[42] urging the Labour movement to face the facts which daily made more necessary preparation for the task of control in the city, the department, the State, convincing all men that it understood the larger interests of France. It should be not only a "party of doctrine, but also a party of action," proving that it was the only possible Government for France.[43]

The *Cas Millerand* gave full opportunity for MM. Briand and Viviani to develop a well-rounded theory of politics for the Labour movement. M. Briand in a speech of antagonizing cleverness and power defended Millerand. To the discomfort of the Guesdists he showed how the expansion of the political Labour movement had largely profited by the evolutionary tactics of Millerand, who had left no one in the dark as to his reformistic convictions. Briand pointed out that the attitude of Guesde and Lafargue had been one of distrust for the deliberative assembly, yet the exigencies of the electoral struggle, especially in their advocacy of the eight hour day and the minimum wage, had forced them to make valuable concessions, successively represented in the electoral program.[44] The lure of the electoral battle and the immediate results often obtained had inspired a lively interest in parliamentary tactics.

Yes, you became interested in these struggles which gave immediate results, and little by little, our militant comrades also became interested in them, took a liking for them to such a degree that they soon came to believe that in order to triumph definitely over the capitalist society nothing was necessary but to storm the ballot boxes. Thus within recent years the country could gain the impression that the Socialist party was no longer a revolutionary party.[45]

Labour movement on the class struggle (pp. 2-3, Jaurès; pp. 10-11, Guesde); tactics and the *Cas Millerand* (pp. 5-8, Jaurès; pp. 13-15, Guesde).

[42] *Compte Rendu,* 1899 Congress, pp. 53-54, 140-146, 168, 405; *Compte Rendu,* 1900 Congress, pp. 191-206; *Compte Rendu,* 1901 Congress, pp. 141-143.

[43] *Compte Rendu,* Paris Congress 1899, pp. 140-146.

[44] *Le Programme du Parti Ouvrier, Ses Considérants, Ses Articles,* was published by Guesde and Lafargue in 1880; also Lafargue was author of *Le Programme Agricole du Parti,* published by the *Parti Ouvier.*

[45] *Compte Rendu,* Congress 1899, p. 155.

The very fact that deviations had occurred in the revolutionary tradition of the party, the *Parti Ouvrier Français* and the *Parti Socialiste Révolutionnaire,* concurring in them, made the share of responsibility for each group the same. The result was that a Socialist Independent entered the Government, free of blame and not liable to censure.[46] The leaders who had objected to that action were chief among those who had recognized the nationalist, clerical and reactionary menace, joining together to form the *Comité de Vigilance.* The force of circumstances and the progress of revolutionary ideas, said Briand, made it "impossible to adapt the old revolutionary thought to the transformation of modern society." [47]

The results of the first general Congress are indicated in the decisions which were arrived at on the questions included in the order of the day. The questions of the conquest of public power and the class struggle were included in two resolutions: the first resolution, that the class struggle did not permit the entrance of a Socialist in a bourgeoisie Government, passed by 818 votes to 634; [48] and the second resolution, which was passed by 1140 votes to 240, declared that all the forces of the party should be given to obtaining power in the city and the department and the State, of all elective offices, which would begin "legally and peacefully the political expropriation of the capitalist class." [49] A democracy that had quite accustomed itself to phrases was satisfied with that pronouncement on the threat of carrying the class struggle into Parliament. It is interesting to note, however, that this first Congress did not disapprove the action of Millerand, due to the skilful directing of the sessions by Jaurès and his supporters. Also there was a solid basis of opposition to the censure of Millerand on the part of a great number of the workers.[50] At each session of the Congress to 1902 at Tours, when it was decided that a Socialist could join a middle class Government on the condition that the Congress gave its assent, the

[46] *Op. cit.,* pp. 158-159.

[47] *Op. cit.,* pp. 156-157, Briand's two speeches at this Congress are of historical value; pp. 151-159, 236-245, *Compte Rendu,* 1899.

[48] *Op. cit.,* p. 409. [49] *Ibid.*

[50] Cf. *Compte Rendu,* Congress 1899, pp. 134, 149, 189-194; 1900 Congress, pp. 94, 97, 98, seq.; and the Congress of 1901 is much more pronounced, see pp. 209, 216, 218, 225.

feeling in favour of Millerand and the strength of the reformistic tendencies in the Labour movement were evident.[51]

The French Labour movement as represented in the first general political Congresses of this century was definitely committed to fighting the battles of organized Labour in the deliberative and legislative assemblies. This belief was joined with the dogma that political expropriation would bring in the Revolution, but it is necessary to take into consideration that in all of the sessions of the Socialist party, as M. Guesde said, such expressions were a return to *logomachie révolutionnaire.* From 1876 to 1900, all the factions of the Labour movement were discarding the use of violence as a method of class warfare; adopting more and more peaceful and legal means of advancing their cause.

> Since the failure of the Commune, that is to say for forty years, the revolutionary method has not had in France a single tentative application, it remains scrupulously isolated in the realm of phraseology; it is nothing more than an exercise of rhetoric.[52]

The entrance of a Socialist Minister into the Government gave rise to great expectations among many people; their belief was strengthened in the electoral and parliamentary machinery of democracy. But the success of the political movement came at the time when Labour was beginning a period of self-examination and criticism, which split wide open the party. Politics became definitely concerned with economic relations. Political organization was secondary in the French Labour movement just when there was an opportunity for it to be used most effectively by the industrial leaders, but those leaders refused at the time to see what advantage was at their hand. In the fierce struggle of the years from 1896-1908, when the economic structure of the French Labour movement underwent great changes, the political party was often forced to consider what was its real function in the

[51] Cf. *Quatrième Congrès Général du Parti Socialiste Français, Compte Rendu,* Tours, 1902, p. 255.

[52] Zévaès, *Le Socialisme en 1912* (Conclusions et Annexes), pp. 9-10; cf. G. de Molinari in *Journal des Economistes,* Jan. 15, 1900, p. 11, "1899": "Our Socialists are quite willing to take their place in a *bourgeois* Government, and when that is the case they show less persistence in transforming the capitalist society. But their programs have not ceased to be terrible."

life of the State and in the fortunes of the working class. Revolutionary Syndicalism and the growing industrial unionism, with a distrust and opposition to the method of politics, had to be seriously reckoned with. The protection of the interests of the working class and the expansion of the ideals of political institutions to include all classes, bringing to the service of the State all the resources of all the people, through the agency of party, was more than ever a necessary duty of the leaders. But there was carried on with unflagging energy an opposition to whatever smacked of politics. Yet it remained for political leaders to indicate forcefully that in the progress of mankind toward a better society there must not be neglected the great balancing power of parliamentary activity; the means which at all times is afforded for a part of the people to discuss before all the people what they imagine they want or have decided that they must have. This is the way democracy often dully and stubbornly teaches that the community good includes the good of the group. For France the discipline of the Labour movement through parliamentary experience has resulted in fuller blessings for the nation than could have resulted in England. In the testing years of revolutionary syndicalism what politics taught economics was not so valuable perhaps as the truth pressed home by economics on politics—in the revolt against the political method of remaking human nature and rebuilding human society—but the common experience which was derived from the clash of each together, constitutes to-day one of the most serviceable contributions to our time of the bitter years of social discord between 1900-1914. The Labour movements of France and England had learned valuable lessons from the hard years of political conflict; they had been taught much by the long and arduous toil of building up professional and trade associations. When the disproportion of life's good things and the work to attain them made many men feel only rebellion against a system of exploitation which left them dispossessed, and against a State which they believed represented that system, it was given to politics to lift the questions of daily subsistence to the level of national greatness. It was for economics to give permanence and stability to the purpose of the people and the State. From this joint effort whatever is abiding in group conflict and industrial disputes has been guarded, kept for the use and good of the nation. Thus slowly the political and economic ideals of social justice serve the needs of men. The power which they have to direct human effort and social aim can be seen in the record of the twentieth century in which with a conscious purpose and a determined will the State has sought to make the good life possible.

Part II

Internal Development:

(*a*) *The Tours Program and the Bordeaux Debates*
(*b*) *Socialist Politics*

The first interpellation on the general policies of the Government in 1900 indicated a common bond between the parties of the Left that was recognized, and at the same time a duty that the Government had accepted.[53] M. Couzy, in whose name the interpellation stood, declared[54] that

we all wish well to the Republic, but not the Drefusyard Republic. But if the country has pronounced positively for the policies of Republican defence, it has also said another thing: it asks at the same time that that defence be not purely passive, it asks that it become active, aggressive and even daring.

Seven months later the second interpellation on general policies was summed up by M. Vazeille, who asked

What will be Republican policy face to face with the Socialist Party? Will it be the policy of fear or the policy of a tolerant attitude?

The Social question was all important, he declared,[55] a belief shared by M. Viviani, who looked back on the fifteen months of

[53] J. O. C. of D., May 23, 1900, pp. 1282-1295, debate entire. Note speeches of M. Waldeck-Rousseau, pp. 1284-1286, and M. Ribot, pp. 1287-1288. The vote for the Government passed by 298-249 votes.
[54] *Op. cit.*, pp. 1282-1283.
[55] J. O. C. of D., Nov. 7, 1900, pp. 1959-1960.

the Government's hold on office, thinking that all inertia by that time should be gone.[56]

"To-day, I hope," he said, "for the honour of all the parties, for the honour of this Parliament, that it is a noble moral battle which commences between ideas. Yesterday it was a struggle against persons, to-day it is a struggle against things. Yesterday it was a defence of the present Republic, to-day it is the organisation of the future Republic."

The practical expression of party attitude was defined in the fourth general Congress (1902) of the *Parti Socialiste Français,* which under the leadership of Jaurès, voted the Program of Tours. This Program[57] sums up in a Declaration of Principles (Part I) and a Program of Reforms (Part II) the majority Socialist attitude of the time.

"Socialism," it declares, "proceeds simultaneously from the movement of democracy and from the new forms of production" yet "between the political régime, the outcome of the revolutionary movement, and the economic régime of society, there is an intolerable contradiction. The irresistible tendency of the proletarians therefore, is to transfer into the economic order the democracy partially realized in the political order. Just as all the citizens have and handle in common democratically, the political power, so they must have and handle in common the economic power, the means of production. They must themselves appoint the heads of work in the workshops, as they appoint the heads of government in the city, and reserve for those who work, for the community, the whole product of work. This tendency of political democracy to enlarge itself into social democracy has been strengthened and defined by the whole economic evolution. Already by winning universal suffrage, by winning and exercising the right of combining to strike and of forming trade unions, by the first laws regulating labour and causing society to insure its members, the proletariat has begun to react against the fatal effects of capitalism; it will continue this great and unceasing

[56] *Op. cit.,* pp. 1961-1963. See speeches of Waldeck-Rousseau, pp. 1964-1966; Ribot, 1966-1967; and Vaillant, p. 1964.

[57] *Compte Rendu,* Tours Congress, pp. 245-252 (Part I); pp. 375-382 (Part II). See R. C. K. Ensor, *op. cit.,* pp. 339-350, for English translation.

effort, but it will only end the struggle when all capitalist property has been reabsorbed by the community, and when the antagonism of classes has been ended by the disappearance of the classes themselves, reconciled, or rather made one, in common production and common ownership.

"How will be accomplished the supreme transformation of the capitalist régime into the collectivist or communist? The human mind cannot determine beforehand the mode in which history will be accomplished. It would be fatal, trusting in the one word revolution, to neglect the great forces which the conscious, organized proletariat can employ within democracy. These legal means, often won by revolution, represent an accumulation of revolutionary capital, of which it would be madness not to take advantage. Too often the workers neglect to profit by the means of action, which democracy and the republic put into their hands. They do not demand from trade unionist action, co-operative action, or universal suffrage, all that those forms of action can give. No formula, no machinery, can enable the working class to dispense with the constant effort of organization and education. The formula of the general strike, like the partial strike, like political action, is only valuable through the progress of the education, the thought, and the will of the working class. The Socialist party defends the Republic as a necessary means of liberation and education. Socialism is essentially republican. It might even be said to be the Republic itself, since it is the extension of the Republic to the régime of property and labour."

Upon the basis of its Declaration of Principles "the Socialist party, rejecting the policy of all or nothing" laid down a program of reforms to be realized:

(1) Democratization of Public Authorities.
(2) Complete Secularization of the State.
(3) Democratic and Humane Organization of Justice.
(4) Constitution of the Family in Conformity with Individual Rights.
(5) Civic and Technical Education.
(6) General recasting of the System of Taxation upon Principles of Social Solidarity.
(7) Legal Protection and Regulation of Labour in Industry, Commerce, and Agriculture.
(8) Social Insurance against all Natural and Economic Risks.

(9) Extension of the Domain and Public Services, Industrial and Agricultural, of State, Department and Commune.
(10) Policy of International Peace and Adaptation of the Military Organization to the Defence of the Country.

Each of the above was subdivided into specific points of reform. To make more plain the industrial program of the political Labour movement and the attitude toward the State there may be considered in detail, numbers 7, 8 and 9. They provide also a commentary on the progress of French legislation.

(7) *Legal Protection and Regulation of Labour in Industry. Commerce and Agriculture:*

(1) One day's rest per week, or prohibition of employers to exact work more than six days in seven.
(2) Limitation of the working day to eight hours; as a means toward this, vote of every regulation diminishing the length of the working day.
(3) Prohibition of the employment of children under fourteen; half-time system for young persons, productive labour being combined with instruction and education.
(4) Prohibition of night work for women and young persons. Prohibition of night work for adult workers of all categories and in all industries where night work is not absolutely necessary.
(5) Legislation to protect home workers.
(6) Prohibition of piece work and of truck. Legal recognition of blacklisting.
(7) Scales of rates forming a minimum wage to be fixed by agreement between municipalities and the working class corporations of industry, commerce and agriculture.
(8) Employers to be forbidden to make deductions from wages, as fines or otherwise. Workers to assist in framing special rules for workshops.
(9) Inspection of workshops, mills, factories, mines, yards, public services, shops, etc., shall be carried out with reference to the conditions of work, hygiene, and safety, by inspectors elected by the workmen's unions, in concurrence with the State inspectors.
(10) Extension of the industrial arbitration courts to all wage workers of industry, commerce, and agriculture.

(11) Convict labour to be treated as a State monopoly; the charge for all work done shall be the wage normally paid to trade unionist workers.

(12) Women to be forbidden by law to work for six weeks before confinement and for six weeks after.

(8) *Social Insurance Against All Natural and Economic Risks.*

(1) Organization by the nation of a system of social insurance, applying to the whole mass of industrial, commercial, and agricultural workers, against the risks of sickness, accident, disability, old age, and unemployment.

(2) The insurance funds to be found without drawing on wages; as a means toward this, limitation of the contribution drawn from the wage workers to a third of the total contribution, the two other thirds to be provided by the State and the employers.

(3) The law on workmen's accidents to be improved and applied without distinction of nationality.

(4) The workers to take part in the control and administration of the insurance system.

(9) *Extension of the Domain and Public Services, Industrial and Agricultural, of State, Department, and Commune.*

(1) Nationalization of railways, mines, the Bank of France, insurance, the sugar refineries and sugar factories, the distilleries, and the great milling establishments.

(2) Organization of public employment-registries for the workers, with the assistance of the Bourses du Travail, and the workmen's organizations; and abolition of the private registries.

(3) State organization of agricultural banks.

(4) Grants to rural communes to assist them to purchase agricultural machinery collectively, to acquire communal domains, worked under control of the communes by unions of rural labourers, and to establish depôts and entrepôts.

(5) Organization of communal services for lighting, water, common transport, construction, and public management of cheap dwellings.

(6) Democratic administration of the public services, national and communal; organizations of workers to take part in their administration and control; all wage earners in all public services to have the right of forming trade unions.

(7) National and communal service of public health, and

strengthening of the laws which protect it—those on unhealthy dwellings, etc.

The Tours Program of principles and reforms provides a good background for the revolutionary and reformist controversy which took place at the Bordeaux Congress (1903) of the French Socialist Party. The Congress was occupied entirely with the Reformist policy of M. Millerand, who attended, defending his action. The debates centred about the questions, whether he should be censured or whether he should be excluded from the party. M. Sarraute, defending Millerand, stated the situation well when he said that it was a problem which began when the Socialist party first came down from the heights of speculation and took part directly in action. The explanation of the deviation from the absolute abstract principle of the class war, of rapid and decisive evolution which led to legal and reformist action, was not to be found in the weakness of individuals, nor in the fascination or the corrupting effect of power. It was to be found entirely in the great fact which dominated modern society, Democracy.

Democracy is, indeed, the denial of the class State. The class State only has a meaning so far as the possessing class is by the very fact of possession the governing class, and the monopoly of property is reinforced by the monopoly of public power. On the contrary, as soon as the State is democratized, and equal rights are admitted for all, whether capitalists or proletarians, as soon as the régime of majorities replaces class obligarchy, and the régime of property qualifications, it becomes contradictory and meaningless to talk of a class State. Political and social institutions are no longer the work and the instrument of the possessing class; they become the work of the majority; they can be steered and guided in the direction of the public interest.

M. Jaurès declared he rejected absolutely the motion of exclusion against Millerand, finding it not only brutal, but unjust and impolitic. Yet he dissented from the oversimplification of the principle of democracy by M. Sarraute, who he thought in a sort of automatic fashion resolved the antagonisms of society. He thought that Sarraute transported himself to the end of political evolution, thinking that political democracy had received its supreme formula—as if political democracy itself could receive its supreme form while it was in contradiction with an economic form, not for its part, penetrated by democracy. Sarraute's mistake was to consider political democracy in the abstract. Just as Guesde erred in positing the class war apart from democracy, Sarraute erred in positing democracy without noting that it is modified, adulterated, thwarted by the antagonism of classes and the economic predominance of one class. Daily the worker was injured in his portion of political democracy, because he did not have his portion of social sovereignty. But it was a mistake to think as Guesde, that the State was exclusively a class State upon which the too feeble hand of the proletariat could not yet inscribe the smallest portion of its will.

In a democracy, in a Republic where there is universal suffrage, the State is not for the proletarians a refractory, hard, absolutely impermeable and impenetrable block. Penetration has begun already. In the municipalities, in Parliament, in the central Government, there has begun the penetration of Socialistic and proletarian influence; and, really, it is a strange conception of human affairs which can imagine any institution whatever, any political or social form whatever, capable of being closed to the influence, the penetration of one of the great social forces. To say that the State is the same—the same closed, impenetrable, rigid State, brazenly bourgeois—under an obligarchic régime, which refuses the proletarians universal suffrage, and under a régime of universal suffrage, which, after all, lets the workers transmit their will even to Government by delegates with the same powers and rights as the delegates of the bourgeoisie itself, is to contradict all the laws of Nature.

Jaurès opposed the easy simplification of Sarraute and Millerand even as he opposed that of Guesde, whom he characterized as being

shut up in an exclusive proletariat, as in a fortress, and one who fights impartially against every party encamped around it: whether they come as friends or foes, he turns his weapons against all quarters of the horizon alike.

He added,

That this policy which I am trying to formulate before the party, a policy which consists in at once collaborating with all democrats, yet vigorously distinguishing one's self from them; penetrating partially into the State of to-day, yet dominating the State of to-day from the heights of our ideal—I acknowledge that this policy is complicated, that it is awkward, that it will create serious difficulties for us at every turn; but am I to suppose that you ever hoped, with your deep practical feeling and high intelligence, that we could pass from the period of capitalism to the organization of Socialism without coming across these difficulties incessantly?

M. Millerand believed that Jaurès paralleled rather too easily what he called the Guesde and the Sarraute conceptions. For himself he declared that his whole policy was limited to retaining that portion of the Socialistic conception which could be assimilated at once.

"I think with you," he said, "that it becomes our duty, I consider our imperious duty, to intrude our ideas, bit by bit, into facts, laws, and customs; the more must we, while realizing peacefully and legally this work of necessarily partial and incomplete construction, show the proletariat simultaneously the complete Socialistic edifice as a whole, and never let it lose sight of the end toward which we march. . . . What is meant by the solidarity of classes? I refer you to Jaurès himself. He showed this morning in a lofty and precise manner, that the Socialist party could take charge on its own account of the general interests of the country, and that there were none of them in which the proletariat itself was not preponderatingly interested. It is understood that the Socialist party, serving and defending the interests of the proletariat, in no way neglects the general interests of the country, but shares in their burden. Is it not, then, clear that it must therefore in every way, under every accessible form, serve those general interests whose care is not separated in its thought from the proletariat's interests?"

The Tours Program and the Bordeaux debates thus mark important landmarks in the history of the French Labour movement. The vote of censure on Millerand's votes in the Chamber of Deputies was passed. At the 1904 Federation of the Seine Socialist Conference he was definitely expelled from the party, and in that same year the International Labour Congress held at Amsterdam urged reconciliation between the *Parti Socialiste Français* and the *Parti Socialiste de France*. Unity was to be based upon the conventional statement of the class struggle; the Socialist party being a purely class party, remaining always fundamentally and irreducibly opposed to the bourgeois class and the State which is its instrument.[58] The first and second Congresses of the *Parti Socialiste* (*Section Française de l'Internationale Ouvrière, S. F. I. O.*) were held in 1905, and the formal unity of the political Labour movement was achieved. At the election of 1906 the number of Unified Socialist deputies increased from 38 to 54, the Independent Socialists from 13 to 22, and in 1910 the number was increased to 76 for the Unified Socialists, while the Independents lost one member. It is thus apparent that unity within the movement added much to the political influence of the party.

But both in Parliament and in the country there was little direction from party leaders. The economic and political situation was reflected in the Vazeille and Lhopiteau interpellation January 14, 1905, on the politics of the Government. The vote on this interpellation forced M. Coombes to resign.[59] M. Paul Deschanel believed[60] that the ministry had not lived up to its powers, that it had ceased to direct the Republican groups, and in fact, had abdicated. MM. Zévaès and Jaurès defended[61] the Government from what they termed the obstructionist manœuvres of the parties of Right, which did not prevent M. Vaillant from saying[62] that

We consider Socialism alone the representative and the true defense of the working class. We are opposed to all bourgeois

[58] Report of the *Commission d'Unification* to the first Congress of the *Parti Socialiste*, pp. 13-15, *Compte Rendu 1er et 2e Congrès Nationaux*, Paris, April 23-25, and Chalon-sur-Saône, October 29-November 1, 1905. The Reports of the two Congresses are printed together.

[59] J. O. C. of D., Jan. 12, 1905, pp. 11-23, and J. O. C. of D., Jan. 15, pp. 27-52, debate entire. The Government escaped by a vote of 289-279, but M. Coombes resigned.

[60] J. O. C. of D., Jan. 14, 1905, pp. 16-19.

[61] *Op. cit.*, pp. 1921 (Zévaès), pp. 46-48 (Jaurès); see Coombes, pp. 31-39, a review of his Ministry and pledges.

[62] *Op. cit.*, pp. 22-23.

Governments, but we assist to-day because of the hope of developing syndical action and organising the working class.

This indication of the divergence of opinion in the Socialist party was not helped by the attitude of the new Rouvier Ministry[63] toward Socialist interpellations, especially with regard to one by M. Augagneur on the strike of the police at Lyon.[64] The Minister of Interior stated that if the Government showed any weakness it would be rendering a bad service to democracy and to the Republic itself.[65] M. Rouvier declared that a strike among officials of a public force would not be tolerated, and at the same time that he recognized both the genius and the vision of the extreme Left, he pledged himself to maintain public order.[66] Six months later an interpellation[67] on the attitude of the Government in industrial conflicts was the occasion of M. Vaillant saying that

I call with reason a Government reactionary which seems to have no other policy than the persecution of the syndicates. But equally with economic growth the workers grow, and with syndical progress the workers' consciousness animates more and more the ranks of the proletariat in larger numbers. The Government seeks to arrest this movement. It cannot be done. It is a movement which it is not possible to check, because it is not artificial, it is profound. The strike supported by Socialism is the method that has great value in the assault on the capitalist system.[68]

A strike in the Government arsenals afforded an opportunity for another Socialist interpellation.[69] In the course of his reply

[63] J. O. C. of D., Jan. 28, 1905, p. 63, Ministerial announcement of M. Rouvier; pp. 64-82 debate on the general policies of the Government.

[64] J. O. C. of D., May 23, 1905, pp. 1815-1823, debate entire; pp. 1815-1818, Augagneur.

[65] *Op. cit.*, pp. 1818-1819 (Etienne).

[66] *Ibid.*, p. 1822.

[67] J. O. C. of D., Nov. 4, 1905, pp. 3008-3027, debate entire. Interpellation signed by Vaillant, Jaurès, Sembat, Rouanet, and Meslier. See speeches of Berteaux, Minister of War, pp. 3014-3019; Sembat, pp. 3019-3023; and Etienne, Minister of Interior, pp. 3023-3024. The Government vote was 444-55, on the order of the day.

[68] *Ibid.*, pp. 3008-3010.

[69] J. O. C. of D., Nov. 17, 1905, pp. 3336-3355, debate entire. See speeches of MM. Thomson and Pelletan, pp. 3343-3346, 3350-3352, the former the Minister of Marine and the latter the ex-Minister, Ferrero,

to M. Jaurès, who stated that there were fifty votes to affirm for the working class the right to strike, the Premier said that

> the Republican party has at all times manifested by its discussions and by its decisions, that it intends to aid all that is legitimate and possible to admit in the hopes of the working class.[70]

This was not the point of view that was taken a few days later by the Socialist leaders' interpellation with regard to Government interference with the Paris *Bourse du Travail*.[71] Renewed Government interference was taken as a sign of strength of the syndicalists. Yet interference was Government reaction, and as such was blamed by M. Vaillant, who said

> we wish at the same time, that the men who threaten this syndical activity, should be well convinced of the solidarity which exists between the socialist and the syndicalist movements.[72]

The anti-patriotic propaganda of the Paris Bourse had been attacked by the Government, to whom M. Sembat said [73]

> You have complained that the anti-patriotic campaign has found an echo among the workers. There is a good remedy: It is to give the worker new reasons to love his country, make it so that he will find in France more of happiness, more of economic well being, more of justice.

pp. 3336-3339; M. Allard, pp. 3339-3342, for Socialists, and Jaurès, pp. 3346-3348. M. Allard said, "It is you yourselves that will end by using and by justifying direct action" (p. 3342), and M. Jaurès declared it was an effort to "exploit the idea of country in the interest of class" (p. 3346).

[70] J. O. C. of D., Nov. 17, 1905, p. 3336; also p. 3348 (Rouvier).

[71] J. O. C. of D., Nov. 28, 1905, pp. 3532-3546; J. O. C. of D., Dec. 2, 1905, pp. 3667-3675; J. O. C. of D., Dec. 9, 1905, pp. 3821-3831, for debates entire on the Paris Bourse du Travail. Cf. Jaurès' speech on Socialist Politics and Internationalism, J. O. C. of D., Dec. 16, 1905, pp. 3992-4002. The interpellations here briefly recorded begin the long fight on the question of Government interference in syndicalist organization.

[72] J. O. C. of D., Nov. 28, 1905, p. 3538; pp. 3532-3539 speech entire. See speeches of MM. Grosjean and Deschanel, pp. 3540-3544, 3544-3546, on revolutionary syndicalism and the anti-patriotic movement represented by *Le Mouvement Socialiste*.

[73] J. O. C. of D., Dec. 2, 1905, p. 3674; pp. 3667-3675 speech entire.

Practical details were added by M. Zévaès pointing [74] out the duty of the Government to pass the weekly day of rest Bill into law, already adopted in principle, the eight hour day, and an arbitration system to prevent strikes.

The union of all Republican forces should be maintained more closely than ever to realize these reforms; the union of all Republicans for the winning of social justice by political liberty.[75]

It was here that M. Jaurès saw the mistake of revolutionary syndicalism opposing democracy, for in the democracy through the working class there was power to fortify political weakness.[76] Just to the extent that the workers organized in syndicates, they would be compelled to carry out the common will of the organized workers through delegates and by mandatories. The politics of democracy would then be absolutely necessary. Yet distrust of democracy was a mistake of, not the force of syndicalism. The latter he wished to bring to the attention of the Government:

"Apart from the inevitable illusions," he said, "as in all new movements, as in all vehement affirmations of a new force, that which remains true, that which is living in revolutionary syndicalism, that which ought to be called to the attention of all Governments, of all deputies, is above everything else this: That the workers aspire more and more to constitute a distinct force, a self-governing force, capable of informing the whole social movement by the integrity of its thought." [77]

It would be puerile to judge such a movement, he added, by "escapades of the pen or words." It would be an error, a singularly imprudent one, to attack this or that phrase pronounced by this or that militant, the important thing being that revolutionary syndicalism was a vast, a profound and a necessary movement in the evolution of the working class.

[74] J. O. C. of D., Dec. 9, 1905, pp. 3821-3823; also MM. Lasies and Jaurès, pp. 3823-3827, 3827-3831.

[75] *Ibid.*, p. 3823.

[76] See J. O. C. of D., Dec. 9 and Dec. 16, 1905, pp. 3827-3831, 3992-3997, two speeches of Jaurès on socialist politics, with special reference to patriotism and syndicalism.

[77] *Ibid.*, p. 3996.

The importance of the syndicalist question from 1906-1910 [78] with regard to employees of the State was foreshadowed in the Ministerial declaration [79] of M. Sarrien, who followed M. Rouvier as Prime Minister. "We are resolved," he said, "to give to the *fonctionnaires* all necessary guaranties against arbitrariness and favouritism." [80] M. Rouvier had definitely made the distinction between workmen (*ouvriers*) who had the same rights in public as in private service, and those agents (*fonctionnaires*) who are intrusted with a share of the public powers.[81] The whole agitation was definitely linked up with social policies, providing an interpretation for the elections of 1906; [82] and for M. Jaurès the famous May 1, 1906, strike was "more than a strike for a shorter day, it became a social manifestation, a social revindication." [83]

[78] Cf. Georges-Cahen, *Les Fonctionnaires, Leur Action Corporative* (1911), chap. III-IV, Part II, pp. 111-117, and Part III, chap. IV, pp. 328-349, for a full account of this important period.

[79] J. O. C. of D., March 15, 1906, pp. 1289-1290; debate, pp. 1290-1300.

[80] *Ibid.*, p. 1290.

[81] J. O. C. of D., Nov. 8, 1905, p. 3081, pp. 3079-3081 entire; and pp. 3078-3090, debate on question of M. Lasies on how the Government interpreted the law of 1884 where officials were concerned (J. O. C. of D., Nov. 4, 1905, p. 3027). One of the first reports was that of M. Marcel Sembat for the Commission on the Budget, examining the budget of the Ministry of Commerce and Industry, with special reference to the postal crisis of 1905: J. O. C. of D., March 5, 1906, Doc. Parl. No. 3046, with which compare Doc. Parl. Nos. 2565, 2672 and 2681. In 1904 two propositions were submitted dealing with the right of association: the Lhopiteau proposition giving ordinary tribunals the right to consider disputes between the administration of the State railways and employees (Doc. Parl. No. 1612, 1904); and the proposition of M. Meunier to complete Art. 6 of the law of July 1, 1901 (Doc. Parl. No. 1749, 1904). Cf. The two Socialist propositions of 1906; the first arising from the postal strike of 1905 to abrogate Articles 414 and 415 of the Penal Code, J. O. C. of D., July 3, 1906, pp. 751-752, Doc. Parl. No. 194; and the other to prevent patronal lock-out, J. O. C. of D., July 3, 1906, pp. 753-754, Doc. Parl. No. 196. These last two propositions were submitted by MM. Coutant, Jaurès, Vaillant, Allemane, and Brousse. The Government project was submitted the day before, J. O. C. of D., July 2, 1906, pp. 716-720, Doc. Parl. No. 158. An *exposé* before the text is given.

[82] See speech of M. Brisson, J. O. C. of D., June 13, 1906, pp. 1935-1936: "The character of this evolution (as seen in the 1906 elections), is not it defined in the expressions of social reform, or social justice, which occur constantly in the programmes, the professions of faith, the discourses, the articles, the journals of all parties?" (p. 1936). Entire debate pp. 1935-1950; Sarrien, pp. 1937-1947; Jaurès, pp. 1947-1950.

[83] *Ibid.*, p. 1948.

The famous debate [84] on the policies of the Government provided for MM. Clemenceau and Jaurès the setting of a six-day debate. M. Zévaès at the beginning again made plain his middle position.

"To realize the end of Socialism," he said, "we appeal to the working class democracy, the rural democracy, to the proletariat of manual work and intellectual work. We repudiate, as unworthy of the great and noble cause of the workers, recourse to anarchist methods and the violence of direct action."

He appealed to the Government to carry out the wishes of the working class with respect to laws of social insurance, protection of young workers, and provide for syndical freedom. The "application of social policies is the only policy worthy of Republican France"; and there were five Bills already passed by the Chamber of Deputies which the Government could definitely take charge of: the law on a weekly day of rest, passed in 1902; the Berteaux law, voted in 1899 and 1901, providing pensions for railway employees; the law forbidding the use of white sulphur in manufacture of matches; the law extending to commercial employees the jurisdiction of the *Prud'Hommes;* and old age pensions. "Let us to our work: economic equality, social justice, and human solidarity." [85]

This was a challenge which M. Clemenceau seemed glad to accept. His defense of the Government was a survey of Republican policies since 1885, and more especially since 1899. "Your accusation is one of words, our response is facts," he said. Briefly he set forth the work done since 1899, mentioning specifically: [86]

(1) The three Decrees of August 10, 1899.
(2) The Decree of September 1, 1899, reorganizing the Superior Council of Labour.

[84] Debate entire: J. O. C. of D., June 13, 1906, pp. 1935-1950; June 15, pp. 1957-1966; June 16, pp. 1971-1982; June 19, pp. 1988-2002; June 20, pp. 2006-2019; June 22, pp. 2025-2038. These debates provided a commentary on the years from 1885-1906. Cf. Debate on the *Report of the Parliamentary Group to the 3rd National Congress of the Socialist Party,* Limoges, 1906. *Compte Rendu,* pp. 37-59.
[85] J. O. C. of D., June 13, 1906, pp. 1941-1943.
[86] J. O. C. of D., June 20, 1906, pp. 2006-2012; pp. 2012-2019, Jaurès reply. The earlier long speeches are: Clemenceau, J. O. C. of D., June 19, 1906, pp. 1994-2002; Jaurès, J. O. C. of D., June 15, 1906, pp. 1957-1961.

(3) The Law of March 30, 1900, on the work of women and children.
(4) The Law of July 1, 1901, on Associations.
(5) The Law of March 14, 1904, creating Public Employment Officers.
(6) The Decree of May 29, 1905, creating the Superior Council on Mutual Aid Societies.
(7) The Law of July 14, 1905, on obligatory public assistance to the poor, the aged, and the incurable.
(8) The Law of November 14, 1905, granting credits for establishing an eight hour day in State shops.
(9) The Law of April 12, 1906, extending the accident law to commercial employees.

M. Clemenceau was intent too upon giving an interpretation of this reformistic policy, an *exposé* of Republican doctrine. Social Democracy, for him, instead of speculating on the Revolution of Marx, should organize and prepare the working class for democracy. The struggle for all reforms in the State aided the working class and helped to transform the institution of the State in a democratic spirit. Quoting [87] from Edouard Bernstein, the German Reformist leader, Clemenceau declared that he was convinced that it was impossible to thwart the evolution of peoples. He therefore attached the greatest significance to the present duty of Social Democracy; to the struggle for the political rights of the workers; to the political activity of the workers in the interest of their class aided by the work of their economic organization. Bernstein had written that at the present time the movement was everything, the final end of Socialism was nothing.

"We are here fully in accord," added Clemenceau. "The final end of Socialism is nothing, and the movement in the direction of social justice is everything. It is votes that talk."

This point of view only confirmed the belief of many Socialists in the impossibility of participation in power with the "association of MM. Briand, Viviani, and Clemenceau." If one wants to find the cause of Parliamentary and Governmental sterility,

[87] J. O. C. of D., June 20, 1906, p. 2010. Bernstein's, *Le Socialisme Théorique et la Social-Démocratie Pratique,* was the source of the quotations.

M. Vaillant said,[88] one can find it in the will to fight in every way and at all times, the Socialist party, the associations of syndicates, and the *Confédération Générale du Travail.* The Nantes strike of 1907 began the first [89] of twelve interpellations [90] in that year on workers' syndicates and the rights of functionaires. The excellent report [91] of M. Colliard for the Commission on Labour, charged with reviewing the various propositions for arbitration of industrial disputes, declared that the increasing number of strikes [92] gave a particular character of necessity to the discussion of the justification of the intervention of the State in collective disputes. Strikes were not due to the growth of syndicates, the example of England and Germany were cited, and the growth of collective bargaining in England was the example to be followed, the Report declared.[93] In France

in nearly all corporations, patrons and workers remain isolated in respective organizations, ignorant one of the other, and full of mutual distrust. In the presence of this inertia what ought the State to do? It is a generally admitted principle that the State ought to observe in all strikes the most strict neutrality. Yet to speak truthfully, the principle of the neutrality of the State is not always carried out in practice and ought not to be because for a long time the State interfered in strikes to the profit of the patrons against the workers.[94]

[88] J. O. C. of D., May 9, 1907, pp. 925-926.

[89] MM. Allemane and Vaillant moved to have a Committee investigate this strike, but were defeated: J. O. C. of D., March 22, 1907, pp. 730-732. The most important interpellation was then offered May 7, on the attitude of the Government to the syndicates: J. O. C. of D., May 8, 1907, pp. 904-921; J. O., May 9, pp. 925-945; J. O., May 11, pp. 947-958; J. O., May 12, pp. 961-970; J. O., May 14, pp. 971-987; and May 15, pp. 989-1013, debates entire. Note speeches of F. Buisson, pp. 914-921; Steeg, pp. 929-933; Paul Deschanel, pp. 936-940; Jaurès, pp. 954-958, 961-970; Briand, pp. 971-981; Ribot, pp. 989-993; Sembat, pp. 993-996; Jaurès, pp. 996-999; and Clemenceau, pp. 1100-1107.

[90] Cf. *Tables Alphabétiques et Analytiques de Chambre des Deputes,* for quick reference to this or any subject before the Chamber. For 1907, Nos. 44, 48, 49, 50, 51, 52, 53, 55, 56, 57, 58, 61.

[91] J. O. C. of D., Dec. 27, 1907, pp. 473-507, Doc. Parl. No. 1418.

[92] *Op. cit.,* chap. I, survey of strikes from 1893-1907.

[93] *Op. cit.,* p. 474. The Reports of the Board of Trade on Rates and Wages were used, especially the Report of 1906, which contained comparative statistics from 1897-1905.

[94] *Op. cit.,* p. 475.

M. Steeg asked the Government to do the just and necessary thing by enlarging the law,[95] M. Paul Deschanel seeing in the struggle one between "legal syndicalism and revolutionary syndicalism" appealed to the Government to use the Republican majority to pass social legislation that was demanded.[96] M. Allemane submitted a resolution that the law of 1884 should apply to the employees of the State.[97] a policy MM. Clemenceau and Briand opposed. But there was no clear-cut Governmental policy.[98] The postal strike of 1909 brought the issue squarely to the front again. The fight, M. Jaurès said,[99] was to give the associations of *fonctionnaires* a place in the Republic; M. Barthou[100] stood firm by his responsibility to Parliament and not to the *fonctionnaires*. Yet the mediocre prestige of Parliamentary power, declared Jaurès, was due to the policy of the Government.[101] His attack

[95] J. O. C. of D., May 9, 1907, pp. 929-933.

[96] *Ibid.*, pp. 936-940. M. Deschanel quoted freely from Pouget's *Bases du Syndicalisme* and *Le Parti du Travail,* the 1906 Congress Report of the C. G. T. (Amiens), and *La Grève Générale. Son But, Ses Moyens, Lendemain de Grève Générale* (1901).

[97] J. O. C. of D., May 9, 1907, pp. 940-945. Two interpellations in 1908 on general politics and the syndicalist controversy carried on the Socialist agitation; J. O. C. of D., April 7, 1908, pp. 885-899, and J. O., June 12, pp. 1156-1170, debates entire. Note speech of Jaurès, pp. 885-889, 896-898; and Clemenceau, pp. 890-896, 1162-1167.

[98] See the Report of M. Jules Jeanneney, J. O. C. of D. S. E., July 11, 1907, pp. 507-534, Doc. Parl. No. 1213 (Annexe I. of the *Rapport Maginot,* 1911), for the first full parliamentary account of the controversy, and pp. 513-519, for development 1901-7; pp. 519-534, the proposed project is given. The great Chaigne Report was presented in 1909 (Doc. Parl. No. 2450, J. O. C. of D., April 2, 1909), and the *Rapport Maginot* (J. O. C. of D., July 12, 1911, Doc. Parl. No. 1214) supplemented the two above Reports. These three Reports provide invaluable documentary study of the period.

[99] J. O. C. of D., May 13, 1909, pp. 1022-1026; answered by M. Barthou, Minister of Commerce and Industry, pp. 1026-1030. See also the debate on the first interpellation on the postal strike: J. O. C. of D., March 20, 1909, pp. 757-772.

[100] J. O. C. of D., March 20, 1909, pp. 772-776.

[101] J. O. C. of D., June 26, 1909, pp. 1661-1669; compare debate J. O. June 19 (pp. 1523-1537), and June 23 (pp. 1577-1581); Briand, pp. 1579-1581. M. Andre Beaunier summed up the politics of 1909 thus, "A Right which no longer counts, an enormous Radical majority, a very resolute Socialist minority. . . . If we examined in detail the biographies of our principal politicians, we should find that they were like the nomads who wandered from country to country driving their flocks before them, never staying in one place and never retracing their steps. Our politicians have travelled

paved the way for the fall of the Clemenceau Government, which was followed by M. Briand's first and second ministries (July 24, 1909-November 4, 1910; November 4, 1910-March 2, 1911). The philosophy of Socialism, he said, was moving on, and the working class struggled not for itself but for all mankind. Because of the languor, the debility, the discouragement, the scepticism of the time, it was necessary to organize a policy of great reforms, vigorous, hardy and progressive. There was the example of Mr. Lloyd George in England and the opposition to him;[102] in comparison to the efforts of that leader he asked what had M. Clemenceau done to achieve large Parliamentary reforms?[103] He asked that the Government not deceive indefinitely the hopes of the working class of the Republic. That was the plea of M. Dejeante:

> In the interest of the profoundly just cause of the working class, in the interest of the Republic, we say to you: Do not continue this system of Government of reaction. It is a peril for the Republic, it is a peril for the country.[104]

A more sober note was struck by M. Buisson who declared that the Government would no longer have the support of the far Left of the Radical party.[105]

The Ministry of M. Briand is important because it had directly to face the problem of the relation of the State with its servants. His efforts were centred upon establishing the firm authority of the State over all public service; yet at the same time he was prepared for the State to assume heavy burdens in assuring a

after this fashion, as forgetful of last night's opinions as pastoral tribes are of the encampments they have forsaken. Thus they have moved on towards the West—I mean towards the Left—more or less quickly, some of them very agile, others dawdling behind. But, leaders or laggards, they will nearly all of them get as far as the last confines of the lowest demagogy." "Contemporary Politics in France," *Nineteenth Century and After*, Vol. 66, November, 1909, pp. 870-886.

[102] J. O. C. of D., June 26, 1909, p. 1669. Special reference to social insurance and the opposition of Capital to financial burdens.

[103] J. O. C. of D., July 16, 1909, p. 2080, pp. 2072-2082, entire; see J. O., July 13, 1909, pp. 2004-2017, Clemenceau's review of his Ministry, and his attack upon the varying politics of Jaurès. The Ministry was defeated on July 21 by a vote of 212-176.

[104] J. O. C. of D., July 3, 1909, p. 1795, pp. 1791-1795, entire.

[105] *Ibid.*, pp. 1795-1800.

just wage and satisfactory working conditions.[106] The railway strike of 1910 he declared was political in motive and revolutionary in character. His Ministerial statement [107] declared that the Government was not unmindful of the evolution of the workers' organization, and the Government project [108] definitely affirmed the right of the State to determine the contract relationship of the employees and the railway companies. M. Briand thus boldly took into his own hands one of the major demands of the Labour movement. The State was to define the conditions of the labour contract, its whole power was to be behind enforcement.

The politics of the next few years centred upon the questions of electoral reform, military organization of the nation, and the Budget.[109] The Parliamentary Reports of the Socialist deputies each year repeat the same detail of interpellations, propositions submitted, and ordinary routine duties done.[110] The Chapter on France, dealing with the Syndicalist movement, will briefly carry forward certain phases suggested in this chapter.

[106] Cf. J. A. Estey, *Revolutionary Syndicalism* (1913), pp. 141-156, and S. P. Orth, *Socialism and Democracy in Europe* (1913), pp. 103-104.

[107] J. O. C. of D., July 28, 1909, pp. 2249-50; see his speech, *ibid.*, pp. 2253-2255.

[108] See *Maginot Report*, pp. 7-19.

[109] See the interesting *L'Action Parlementaire et la Nouvelle Legislature*, with Preface by M. Steeg (1910), a symposium by 25 leaders' opinion on the politics of the time.

[110] Cf. Amédée Dunois, *L'Action Socialiste au Parlement, 1910-1914* (1914), with which may be compared Hubert Rouger's *L'Action Socialiste au Parlement, 1914-1919* (1919). M. Rouger was Secretary of the Parliamentary Socialist group.

CHAPTER XI

SYNDICALISM AND THE FRENCH LABOUR MOVEMENT

PART I

Syndicalism

THE advance of society in the democratic direction had by 1900 transformed the English constitution into something like a democracy,[1] and in France there had been a record of political development toward republicanism.[2] The triumph of democracy has been taken to mean various things: from giving the death blow to the doctrine of parliamentary sovereignty, because democracy begins to put forth the power that had been hers for fifty years,[3] to proving the incapacity of democracy for dealing with the

[1] Dicey, *op. cit.*, p. 48.

[2] This is the well-known thesis of M. Seignobos in his *Histoire Politique de l'Europe Contemporaine: Evolution des Partis et des Formes Politiques* 1814-1896 (E. T. 1904), supported by Viscount Bryce (*op. cit.*, Vol. I, p. 246 ff.), and his later *L'Evolution de la 3e République* (1921); cf. Georges Guy-Grand: *Le Procès de la Démocratie* (1911), and *La Démocratie et l'Après-Guerre* (1923), p. 125 ff.

[3] Cf. Professor C. H. McIlwain's *The High Court of Parliament and Its Supremacy* (1910), Preface, p. xv., with which note Professor A. F. Pollard's *The Evolution of Parliament* (1920) for a strong defence of the principle of democratic evolution of this institution. It may be interesting to note post-war American views: Henry J. Ford, *Representative Government* (1924), Part II, chap. VI, pp. 176–198, "Direct Control with Administration," and chap. XI, pp. 295–309, "Concluding Observations"; Arthur N. Holcombe, *The Foundations of the Modern Commonwealth* (1923), chaps. I-III and XI, and W. W. Willoughby and Lindsay Rogers *An Introduction to the Problem of Government* (1921), chaps. IX and XVII. Also James T. Young, *The New American Government and Its Work* (1915), Introduction, pp. 3-9; F. A. Ogg and P. O. Ray, *Introduction to American Government* (2nd ed., 1925), Part I.; Charles A. Beard, *American Government and Politics* (Revised ed., 1925), Part I. being very suggestive; and W. B. Munro in his *Governments of Europe* (1925), offers a distinctly American point of view on European politics, which in his *Preface* to his

economic organization of society,[4] or else its strange genius for creating the new bondage of the servile State.[5]

At the beginning of the century the labour movements in France and England were at the crossroads. They had to organize their political and economic life within a democratic State, in which political success had brought them parliamentary power. But the fast moving forces of industrial development had given little time for the slow working machinery of the legislature to cope even with actual needs, much less to deal with problems of future control. The political capacity of democracy was challenged. The incapacity of Parliaments to organize the economic life of nations became the basis of an attack against the State. Modern industry had created an anarchy of interests. These interests sought either special favours from the State or else announced their rebellion against authority. The lesser claim of political democracy was implied in the emphasis upon a so-called economic democracy, the "theory of national life replacing the theory of national sovereignty." [6]

Government of the United States (1925 ed.) is explained by his sufficient answer that no man can for many years be associated with the American undergraduate and be anything but an optimist.

[4] Cf. A. Esmein *Éléments de droit constitutionnel français et comparé* [1st ed. 1896, Preface to 6th ed. by J. Barthelemy (1914), 7th ed. prepared by H. Nézard (1921)], Preface to 6th ed.; also H. Lagardelle, "Socialisme ou Démocratie," *Le Mouvement Socialiste* (L. M. S.), Nos. 86, 87, 88, 89 and 91 (1902). Also see M. Jacques Bardoux's Introduction (pp. xviii-xxx) to *Le Bilan de la XII Législature* (1919-1924) (1924), published by the *Société d'Etudes et d'Informations Economiques.*

[5] Cf. Hilaire Belloc, *The Servile State* (1912); cf. M. Beer, *op. cit.*, Vol. I, p. 360, for a comparison of the literary activities of MM. Brunetière, Faguet, Maurras, and Chéradame to the philosophy of Sorel and Lagardelle; Belloc's *The French Revolution* (1911), reveals often what he terms "the nastiness of modern parliamentary life" (p. 56), and he states concisely his central thesis: "to contrast the good 'working' of an institution superficially undemocratic with democratic theory is meaningless. The institution 'works' in proportion as it satisfies that political sense which perfect democracy would, were it attainable, completely satisfy" (*op. cit.*, p. 20). This is a theory of political morals dangerous in the extreme because destructive of democracy's will or even right to self-development —and self-control. Cf. J. Ramsay MacDonald, *Parliament and Democracy* (1920), chap. III-IV. Mr. Belloc's *The Jews* (1922) re-echoes his dictum that "the parliamentary system will not last forever" (pp. 69-94).

[6] Esmein, *op. cit.*, p. 49, referring especially to the theories of MM. Duguit and Charles Benoist; for the former "the personality of the State appears as a pure fiction" (p. 40); pp. 1-64 for full comment.

The revolt against parliamentary progress in the early years of the new century was much more marked in France than in England, though there was common ground in the distrust and the disillusion of political method. In France the work of Millerand found Labour unprepared, just as the Liberal legislation of 1906-1912 made plain the fact that Labour often could not utilize the powers which the State actually forced it to use. Both the measures of Millerand and of the Liberal Ministry educated Labour—and the country—by violence. From 1900 down to the present time the French Labour movement has been at work on the problems which Millerand inaugurated and later forsook; and in England the legislative measures of 1906-1912 yet provide the necessary basis of nearly all schemes of reconstruction. Though Beer considers the theories of MM. Waldeck-Rousseau and Millerand "vitiated by a false idea of social peace and readjustment," they were in some respects far in advance of their time, he adds; and their "premature suggestions of social peace with partnership merely estranged the Trade Unions, and paved the way for an anti-political propaganda." [7] The action of the State in France and England has greatly helped to stimulate the imagination of the Labour movements, if by no other means than convincing proof that there is no magic in the State. This is now a conventional dogma for Labour with the added significance of a definite political experience. Two important reasons for the revolt against parliamentarism were (1) the growth in power of parliamentary socialist groups, and (2) the extension of the collective forces of the economic conflict into larger areas and upon a wider scale by the organizations of patronal and workers' federations. These two factors tended to unite the political and the industrial movements, and each was unprepared, as well as the State or any voluntary agency, to develop a common program. Yet there was the increasing necessity of directing the movements along national lines.

It is apparent to-day that the important reasons for the revolt against parliamentarism at the beginning of this century have an almost equally potent influence with organized labor at this time. The growth in power of parliamentary socialist groups, and the extension of the collective forces of the economic conflict

[7] Beer, *op. cit.*, Vol. I, p. 307.

into larger areas and upon a wider scale is truer in 1926 than in 1900. These two factors tended to unite the political and industrial movements before the war, in spite of distinct contradictory influences within the movements, and that process is going on to-day.

As early as 1893 M. Jaurès had declared that the formation of the Parliamentary Socialist Group was to be the means of making the wage earner the master of economic democracy as he was of political democracy.[8] It was combining with "the economic program of the Socialists the political program of the Radicals,"[9] the coalition which M. Millerand had proposed of the parties of the Left against the parties of the Right.[10] The resolving of the class struggle into political action was the first official decision of the Havre Congress of 1880 under Guesde's influence, and the subsequent history of the party has been more widely to interpret the place of parliamentary socialism.[11] At nearly every stage, often fortunately for the party, it has been a political necessity to support the Government against the Right. Where it has been able to rise superior to the mechanics of the class struggle it has exercised an increasing influence in politics. Thus in the parliamentary history of the French Socialist movement one sees the well-defined tendencies of "dogmatic intransigeance,"[12] as well as an idealism sustained by revolutionary tradition. Against all of this is the background of party expediency and hypocrisy. There is then the story of compromise with the existing political organization which the French and English Socialist movements have in common. Even at this day one can hear M. Cachin, though he is leader of the Communist Parliamentary Group, ridicule the parliamentary régime as "an inferior form of democracy";[13] and, on the other hand, there is

[8] J. O. C. of D., November 22, 1893, quoted by Guy-Grand, *La Démocratie et l'Après-Guerre,* pp. 121-122.

[9] Seignobos, *L'Evolution de la 3e République,* p. 159.

[10] *La Petite République,* February 15, 1892, quoted by Seignobos, *op. cit.,* p. 167.

[11] Cf. A. Zévaès, *Le Parti Socialiste de 1904 à 1923* (1923), pp. 13-46; and J. L. Breton, *L'Unité Socialiste* (1912), pp. 54-87.

[12] Cf. P. Detot, *Le Socialisme devant les Chambres Françaises, 1893-1898* (1903), p. 177.

[13] M. Marcel Cachin, "Démocratie et Soviétisme," *L'Humanité,* August 17, 1920.

the statement of M. Breton that the extension into the political field of the class struggle has caused a marked degeneration in political manners, and has threatened the vitality and the integrity of the Socialist Party. Political organization, Breton declares, is broader than the narrow dogmatism of the economic school.[14]

The compromises which the French labour leaders made reacted more on the political and economic movements of their country than is true of England. The Labour movement in England had more consistently accepted the régime of democracy both in its attitude toward the Government and in the discipline of internal organization. It had accustomed itself to the faith that the pervasive power of public opinion is to bring change by consent.[15] The nineteenth century to one of its leaders was a history of change in opinion and legislation wherein the State tended to become the will of an ever-widening community,[16] with the ideal that the State should be "the most perfect embodiment that is possible of the life of the community." [17] But to a definite group of French syndicalist writers at the beginning of the century there was one important fact in the history of the past century: the antagonism of the State against the working class.[18] The State stood between the progress of the worker and his future control of the means of production. There could be no acceptance of the governmental reformism of Jaurès, or the revolutionary governmental reformism of Guesde.[19] There was from each the insidious danger of social peace within the present order; from

[14] Breton, *op. cit.*, pp. 78, 87.

[15] Cf. *Labour Party* (Sidney Webb), Labour and the New Social Order (1918), and Sidney and Beatrice Webb, *A Constitution for the Socialist Commonwealth of Great Britain* (1920), the latter especially significant with regard to the political proposals of the authors. Mr. Laski's last book, *A Grammar of Politics* (1925), is a stimulating and brilliant commentary on Labour political theory.

[16] Cf. J. Ramsay MacDonald, *Socialism and Government* (3rd ed. 1910), Vol. II, p. 133.

[17] MacDonald, *op. cit.*, p. 92.

[18] Cf. Emile Pouget, *Les Bases du Syndicalisme* (1905).

[19] Cf. M. C. Fages' *Review* of Sorel's *Introduction à l'Economie Moderne* (1st ed. 1903, 2nd ed. 1921), L. M. S., Sept. 1-15, 1905, pp. 87-111. Sorel's *Introduction* (1919) brought down to date his ridicule of *bourgeois* democracy as the safeguard of modern civilization (pp. iii-iv); his conviction remained that "the old revolutionary socialism is infinitely more imbued with the philosophic spirit and more scientific than the hyper-juridical socialism of 'lofty' political reformism" (*ibid.*, p. 397).

such seduction the worker constantly had to be on guard, as much so as from the treachery of the *petit-bourgeoisie* and the opportunism of social reform.[20]

Unwavering opposition was determined against the parliamentary system, for this system implied an already established society, an established political constitution. That society was definitely the bourgeois society. The parliamentary system was the natural product, the result of that form of organization. Naturally from the corruption of this society came the effort of the bourgeois leaders to save themselves. Reformism was only an effort to paralyze the effect of the workers' revolt, a logical sequence of the entrance of socialists into bourgeois governments which could only lead to the "governmentalizing" of the syndicates and the corruption of the labour leaders.[21] The last resource of the bourgeoisie was in a State socialism by industrial legislation;[22] and this only made clearer the tactical error of socialism in attempting the transformation of society through such a perverted means as parliamentarism[23] which could only possibly have the result of bringing about a spirit of reformism which meant a degeneracy of socialist thought. "Socialism to-day becomes philanthropy," Le Bon had written in a letter,[24] a taunt which Lagardelle used after the State socialist program was accepted at Tours[25] (1902)

[20] Cf. Sorel's *Notes additionnelles à "L'Avenir socialiste des syndicats,"* his *Preface* to the Italian translation (1905) of *L'Avenir socialiste des syndicats"* (1898, March and April, in *Humanité Nouvelle*), L. M. S., September 1-15, 1905, pp. 5-16, now pp. 145-151 of Sorel's *Matériaux d'une théorie du prolétariat* (1921).

[21] Cf. Paul Louis, *L'Ouvrier devant l'état* (1904).

[22] Cf. Paul Louis, *L'Avenir du socialisme* (1905), p. 155. M. Louis has rendered the service of providing in his very frequent books not only the history of the socialist and syndicalist movements in France but a satisfactory running account of year-to-year events.

[23] Cf. Sorel, *L'Avenir socialiste des syndicats*, which can be put in his formula which ends the book: "the future of socialism abides in the independent development of the workers syndicates" (p. 133). This significant book with his several *Annexes* and *Préfaces* finds a permanent form in the *Matériaux d'une théorie du prolétariat,* pp. 53-167, being Part I of the book.

[24] Cf. Gustave Le Bon, *Psychologie du socialisme* (1st ed. 1899, 3rd ed. 1902); S. Bourdeau, *L'Evolution du socialisme* (1901), and Emile Faguet, *Le socialisme en 1907* (1907), for a somewhat similar point of view.

[25] Cf. *Quatrième Congrès Général du Parti Socialiste Français,* Tours, March 2-4, 1902, *Compte Rendu,* pp. 375-386; note also the *procès-verbal*

in his disillusioned assertion that "democracy and socialism are one." Believing that democracy was impotent, because it was conservative, to face the economic organization of society, he demanded a revolutionary socialism. He "furnished the theme for young socialism, syndicalist and revolutionary: Duel to the death between socialism and democracy." [26] Revolutionary syndicalism was the answer to democracy. "The program of Tours," wrote Lagardelle, "marks the uncontested triumph of State socialism." [27] This could only mean the unlimited development of the administrative and political services of bourgeois society, for political democracy had neither imagination nor capacity for the task of economic organization. Only in revolutionary syndicalism was there power and authority sufficient to inaugurate a new social movement.

In this study we are interested in revolutionary syndicalism primarily with regard to its effects upon the social politics of France and the organization of the Labour movement. It is as a protest against things as they are and its insistence upon the economic development of the Labour movement, that it may help to illuminate the problems of France between 1900-1914, with reference to our hope of understanding the progress of social justice. The strength of revolutionary syndicalism was marked in the Lyon Congress (1901) of the *Confédération Générale du Travail,* the central organization of the French Labour movement. This Congress denounced the ministerial policy of MM. Waldeck-Rousseau and Millerand. The industrial program of the Government was only a part of the illusion of parliamentarism; an

of the Committee on Programme, pp. 389-403, on which were MM. Briand and Jaurès. This Congress continued, so one chairman said, the not small task of Rabelais, Descartes and Balzac! (p. 41).

[26] C. Bougle, *Syndicalisme et Démocratie* (1908), p. 96. Cf. M. Yves-Guyot, *La Démocratie Individualiste* (1907), of whom (to show how vague the syndicalist statement of democracy was) M. Sorel said he was "almost one of them" (L. M. S. 1907, p. 250); also E. Seillière, *L'Impérialisme Démocratique* (1907), on Rousseau, Proudhon and Marx, and syndicalism as a democratic imperialism.

[27] Cf. H. Lagardelle, *Socialisme ou Démocratie,* L. M. S. No. 87, 1902, p. 684; for the series: No. 86, pp. 625-635; No. 87, pp. 673-687; No. 88, "Ministérialisme et Socialisme," pp. 720-781; No. 89, pp. 774-781; No. 91, pp. 1109-1016, "Political Democracy and Economic Organisation," and pp. 889-897, "Democracy and the Struggle of the Classes"; and No. 95, pp. 1081-1088.

"economic parliamentarism" was not wanted; but reforms which would undermine the foundations of existing society, only obtained independently of parliamentary action. The social revolution—the revolutionary hope of "social transformation"—was the ideal.[28] The Congress of Bourges (1904) was a "prepared success" for the revolutionary syndicalists; reformistic tendencies were represented by a minority; there was little hope for the emancipation of the working class through the bourgeoisie régime. From 1904 to 1906 an intensive campaign was carried on by the militants, and the Amiens Congress (1906) at which the syndicalist Charter [29] was adopted "ended the period of the formation of a theory of syndicalism." [30] Then began the struggle between political and industrial syndicalism, a period of "expanding socialism," so Lagardelle expressed it. The dividing point was on the attitude of the worker toward the State; whether a policy of "reformism," *le socialisme réformiste,* inaugurated afresh by M. Millerand,[31] or "revolutionary syndicalism," *le syndicalisme révolutionaire,* interpreted by the C. G. T., was to be pursued.[32]

[28] Cf. Emile Pouget, *La Confédération Générale du Travail* (1st ed. 1908, 2nd ed. 1910), p. 3.

[29] *XVth Congrès National Corporatif (IXe de la Confédération),* Amiens, 1906, p. 167; cf. *Syndicalisme et Socialisme* (1908), pp. 60-63, and *Le Parti Socialiste et la Confédération du Travail* (1908), pp. 5-6, which provide a general review of the controversy.

[30] Lagardelle, "La Formation du Syndicalisme en France," L. M. S. No. 236, 1911, p. 241 (pp. 241-256 entire); see first part in L. M. S. No. 235, pp. 161-186, and third part in L. M. S. February, 1912, pp. 134-145; also his attempt to state the contribution to working class of socialist-syndicalist period in L. M. S. December, 1911, "Nouveaux Problems," pp. 321-324. Cf. Emile Pouget's four articles on "Le Syndicaliste Congrès d'Amiens," L. M. S. October, November, December, 1906, pp. 26-43, 266-272, 380-393, and January, 1907, pp. 23-53.

[31] Cf. A. Millerand, *Le socialisme réformiste français* (1903), for full statement of this point of view; M. Rappoport, *Socialisme de Gouvernement et Socialisme Révolutionnaire* (1902), issued by *Parti Ouvrier Français;* Felicien Challaye, *Le syndicalisme réformiste et syndicalisme révolutionnaire* (1909), a clear full statement; and Georges Guy-Grand, *La philosophie syndicaliste* (1911), a middle plea between Nationalism and Syndicalism.

[32] M. Sorel's *Réflexions sur la violence* [1906, first in *Le Mouvement Socialiste,* 5th ed. "Avec Plaidoyer Pour Lenine" (1921)], remains the best interpretation of syndical philosophy on "direct action"; a shorter statement is Pouget's in *La Confédération Générale du Travail,* pp. 36-50; (1) The Strike, (2) Boycott and Label, (3) Sabotage, (4) Struggle Against the State, (5) The General Strike.

The chief indictment against the State in the minds of the revolutionary syndicalists was its class conscious aim and origin. The State was conceived as the quintessence of bourgeois domination, its main concern being the exploitation of the working class.[33] Any function that the political State possessed in bringing about the necessary conditions for proletarian control over industry had passed away.[34] The end had been reached in political revolutions, and no further good could be expected from them.[35] The field of politics should be given over to the intellectuals whose true vocation is the exploitation of politics. According to Sorel the rôle of the politician is quite analogous to the courtesan for neither is required to possess industrial aptitude;[36] and somewhat later referring to M. Albert Thomas as one of the "Cardinals of Socialism," he wrote that "the introduction of Catholic manners in Socialism is, up to now, the most clear result of the invasion of the intellectuals."[37]

There is no need of going back further than the Communist manifesto for the popular syndicalist thesis that political power, which came from the State, is merely the organized power of one class for oppressing another. In proportion as anarchy in social production vanishes, the political authority of the State dies out.[38] The moral justification of socialism, for the older socialists so extraordinarily simple, provided a common historical and psychological formula for syndicalism and socialism; that the experience of economic processes has necessarily proved that industrial production be organized and directed by the producing workers. The Amiens Charter declared that the mark of syndi-

[33] Cf. M. Pierrot, *Syndicalisme et Révolution* (1905), and M. Friedeberg, *Le Parlementarisme et la Grève Générale* (1905).

[34] Cf. E. Berth, "L'Erreur Tactique du Socialisme," L. M. S. June 15, 1905, pp. 217-233; and his "Anarchisme Individualiste Marxisme Orthodoxe, Syndicalisme Révolutionnaire," May 1, 1905, pp. 5-35.

[35] Cf. Sorel, *La décomposition du Marxisme* (1st ed. 1908, 3rd ed. 1910), p. 66. It is the view of Elton (*op. cit.,* p. 115) that political illusion survived longer in England than in France.

[36] Sorel, *L'Avenir socialiste des syndicats,* p. 98; cf. Lagardelle's four articles on "Les Intellectuels et le Socialisme Ouvrier," L. M. S. February, March, April, May, 1907, pp. 104-120; 217 ff., 348 ff., 409.

[37] Sorel's *Review* of M. Thomas' *Babeuf: La Doctrine des Egaux,* L. M. S. May-June 15, 1906, Nos. 174-175, p. 173.

[38] Quoted by J. Ramsay MacDonald, *op. cit.,* from Engels' *Socialism: Utopian and Scientific,* p. 86.

calism was to be self-sufficient. Yet the anti-Statism of syndicalism was a very different thing from the anti-Statism of individual anarchism, the pre-syndicalism; the latter transferred authority from the State to the individual, the former did away with it altogether, distributing the power of the State to the syndicate.[39] The political power which represented an inefficient and unscientific State was part of the capitalistic society which, in the natural evolution toward a higher organization of life, would be shuffled off.

This view was inherent in the neo-Marxism which gave a philosophy of action to the syndicalist movement. The bed-rock of Marxism was conceived to be the dissolution of the capitalist society. On that point all Marxians could unite, without entering into the more controversial subject of the means and methods of the dictatorship of the proletariat. Yet at the beginning of the century there seemed no indication that capitalistic society was ready to give itself up to the workers of the world. The leaders of socialism in the constitutional countries had no faith in the remaking of the world because of the increasing misery of the lower classes. There was an universal inquietude in French socialism and in international socialism. The economic period of socialism under Marx was coming to an end.[40] There was the necessity of giving a new meaning with power to *le Marxisme*.[41] Revolutionary syndicalism achieved that end by expanding the scope of Marxian doctrine to include the militant philosophy of the dissolution of the capitalist society by the inauguration of the

[39] Cf. *Syndicalisme et Socialisme,* pp. 9-20 (Arturo Labriola), and the Appendix, "Syndicalisme et Anarchisme," pp. 59-63; also A. Labriola, L. M. S. February 15, 1905, pp. 213-229, "Plus-value et Reformisme," a plea against the philosophy of reformism. The Report of the *Congrès Anarchiste d'Amsterdam 1907* (Paris, 1908), provides a good account of events in France since the Amiens Congress, with regard to Anarchist theory.

[40] Cf. Joseph Hitier, *La Dernière Evolution Doctrinale du Socialisme: Le Socialisme Juridique* (1906), chap. I, pp. 4–15, "La Genèse de la Doctrine Nouvelle," appearing originally in *Revue d'Economie Politique,* March, May and June, 1906; see reply of Sorel, "Le Prétendu Socialisme Juridique," L. M. S. April, 1907, pp. 320-348.

[41] Cf. Sorel, *La décomposition du Marxisme,* Part VI, pp. 60–68; also "Mes raisons du syndicalisme" (appearing originally in the *Rome Divenire Sociale,* March 1-May 16, 1910), pp. 239-286, in *Matériaux d'une théorie du prolétariat.*

régime of the workers. For Sorel this meant the passing from a system of obligation to a system of rights.[42] Socialism having degenerated to mere parliamentarism was to find itself carried on in its entirety in the life of the syndicate. It was only in the syndicate that Marxism would find its practical revivification and its historical equivalent.[43]

The economic basis was the syndicate. The producer was vital, fulfilling the essential organic function, thanks to which society was perpetuated. It was therefore the first duty of socialism to form a society of producers. Just as oppression caused the exploited to group together, so the régime of capitalist production created the syndicate. The syndicate was the natural selection of the most class conscious, the most combative among the workers. For if the class struggle was the whole of socialism, it was possible to say that the whole of socialism was contained in syndicalism, for syndicalism had no other end but the class struggle.[44] But even in the light of this class struggle syndicalism was

more of a means for moral progress than of economic progress. In a world that has lost its taste for liberty, at a time when there is no longer the sentiment for dignity; it makes its appeal to the lively forces of human personality and gives an enduring example of courage and energy.[45]

That gave meaning to the professional associations, the "groups of combat." The syndicates would become the representative organs and directors of the working class; around them would be built the new economic structure of the future. But the syndicates were to have none of the functions of democratizing institutions, nor were they to borrow from the processes of democratic society.

[42] Cf. Sorel's *Review* of F. Lasalle's *Théorie Systématique des Droits Acquis: Conciliation du Droit Positif et de la Philosophie du Droit,* French translation in two volumes by various authors, with Preface by Charles Andler (1904), L. M. S. April 15, 1906, pp. 476-485.

[43] Cf. Sergio Pannunzio, "Le Socialisme Syndicaliste ou l'Individuation du Socialisme," L. M. S. January 15, 1906, pp. 57-71.

[44] *Syndicalisme et Socialisme,* pp. 3-8; this volume is the Report of the International Conference held in Paris, April 3, 1907, and contains the addresses of Griffuelhes, A. Labriola, Robert Michels, Kritchewsky, and Lagardelle.

[45] Lagardelle, *op. cit.,* pp. 52-53.

The economic world was to take nothing from the political world. The principle of majorities, giving a fictitious value of equality to all, was to have no place. The audacious and intelligent minority were to give the impulsion which would bring about the new society. The *droit syndical* opposes, says Pouget, the *droit démocratique*. The organization of a world of workers was to be brought about by a radically different means than that which held together the world of voters, though M. Pouget cheerfully wrote that "the National Syndicate is modelled on the organization of the State which it combats." [46] But with the spirit of self-government within this federalism—the essence, he says, of economic societies in the future—there is the understanding of the profoundly revolutionary spirit of French syndicalism. Electoral socialism would be irremediably hostile, but that could only be expected.

The syndicate was the only adequate form by which this new industrial movement could express its revolutionary spirit.[47] From a stage of industry when the wage earner was a victim used for the greed of an individual or a class he would become a master in his own right, an equal in a society of fellow producers.[48] Economic development had completely changed society; the demands of the economic life were the first and most important factor for people; were fundamental to any progress,

[46] *La Confédération Générale du Travail,* p. 21.

[47] See Fernand Pelloutier, *Histoire des Bourses du Travail, Origine, Institutions, Avenir* (1902), with Preface by George Sorel, and Note by Victor Dave, for the basic statement, often built upon with full acknowledgment by Sorel; cf. D. Halévy, *Essai sur le Mouvement Ouvrier en France* (1901), Part I, pp. 3-98, "Le Syndicat."

[48] Cf. Sorel, *Réflexions sur la Violence*, chap. V, pp. 220–228, "La Grève Générale Politique"; popular accounts are Pouget, *Le Syndicat* (1905), Griffuelhes, *L'Action Syndicaliste* (1908), and *Voyage Révolutionnaire: Impressions d'un Propagandiste* (1910), and Leon Jouhaux, *Le Syndicalisme Français—Contre la Guerre* (1913). The Syndicalist Utopia was written by E. Pataud and E. Pouget, *Comment Nous Ferons la Révolution* (1909). Translated into English by C. and F. Charles, *Syndicalism and the Co-operative Commonwealth, How We Shall Bring About the Revolution,* with Foreword by Tom Mann (1913).

It is interesting to note that Parker Thomas Moon in his *The Labour Problem and the Social Catholic Movement in France* (1921), says that "the scheme of Joint Standing Industrial Councils put forward by the Whitley Committee bears an astonishing resemblance to the scheme of industrial organization formulated many years previously by French Social Catholics," Preface, p. viii.

and to save the worker from the degenerating autocracy of the State, as a producer he must assume control. Only the producers had the right to control and regulate; it was simply an assumption of prejudiced interest that the State could, as an alleged servant of society, interfere. This emphasis upon the economic organization of society represented the progress of anti-political syndicalism, and also revealed the discredit into which the public powers had fallen. At the same time it was a refusal to accept a socialism of party rather than a socialism of class. Yet however much one believed that the political socialist movement had been saved by syndical expansion,[49] as M. Louis did, the warning was given early against the syndicalist exaggeration of attempting through the C. G. T. to reduce the capitalist State by the simple development of *organs corporatifs.*[50] The belief was strong that political action and corporate action complete one another; and though the Congresses of the *Confédération Générale du Travail* from 1901 to 1906 were markedly for revolutionary syndicalism, there was nevertheless a substantial body of reformistic propa-

[49] *L'Avenir du Socialisme,* p. 84; cf. L. Garriguet, *L'Evolution Actuelle du Socialisme en France* (1912), M. Paul Louis' *Le Syndicalisme contre l'Etat* (1910), attempted to show how the Socialist Party got in line with what was usable in the syndicalist program, and how the party adapted itself to the tendencies of that movement. Cf. E. Buisson, *Le Parti Socialiste et les Syndicats* (1907), advising the parliamentary socialists to join the syndicalists and win over the anti-political wing.

[50] Louis, *op. cit.,* p. 184. Both in France and England strong corrective tendencies have operated, such as the co-operative movement of the leagues of consumers, besides definite attempts to provide a wider basis for syndicalist organization. Mr. Beer phrases it thus: "It is not desirable that the ultimate Sovereign body should be either political or industrial. A Trade Union Congress (or a National Syndicate) invested with supreme power would be no less liable to develop tyrannical powers than a State invested with supreme power. It would be in fact a quasi-State, elected on an industrial, instead of a territorial, basis; whereas the real need is for a division of Sovereign power, and a distinct representation of the functions of production or 'making' and consumption or 'use.'" (*Op. cit.,* Vol. I, p. 321). Cf. Paul Leroy-Beaulieu, *Le Collectivisme* (5th ed. 1909), esp. Part IV, "Le Syndicalisme-La 'Nouvelle Ecole.'" The English edition of earlier edition, translated and abridged by Sir Arthur Clay, appeared in 1909, *Collectivism: A Study of the Leading Social Questions of the Day.* A. Emil Davies in *The Collectivist State in the Making* (1914), declared "as organized labour becomes stronger, it is not difficult to conceive a state of affairs when we might be confronted with the tyranny of Labour as compared with the past tyranny of capitalism" (p. xvii), and chap. XXI, "Collectivism and the Labour Problem."

ganda within the ranks of French labour. This was expressed in the Bourges (1904) Congress of the C. G. T. and in the Socialist Party Congress at Châlon in 1905. Though the first two Congresses of this century (Lyon, 1901, Montpellier, 1902) of the C. G. T. condemned compulsory arbitration, the *Conseils du Travail* and all the governmental inventions and policies aimed at parliamentarizing the working class movement and to place it under the dependence of the State [51] there was not so definite a formula in the working class mind as in M. Berth's, that "revolutionary syndicalism transcends the State and will abolish it." [52] It was agreed in Congresses that the State-Patron should be resisted as determinedly as patronal oppression, but from the beginning there was the attempt to interpret the political power of revolutionary syndicalism.[53] For three years the C. G. T. carried on a continuous fight against the old system of employment exchanges, then gaining the victory in 1905, it turned to the agitation for an eight hour day, then the English week, and even later, after anti-militarism, to old age pensions. The continued denial of the "feudal particularism" of revolutionary syndicalism was even one expression of the hope that the leaders had in the unifying power of the economic doctrine of proletariat communism.[54]

The free association of producers was an ideal which inspired the earlier enthusiasm of the leaders of the Bourses du Travail, especially Pelloutier who believed fervently that they had an important part to play in the society of the future which would

[51] L. M. S. August 1-15, 1905, p. 543; the English Trade Unions' reformism is cited as an example to be avoided (p. 542); cf. L. M. S. July 15, 1905, pp. 260-277, "La Campagne Contre la Bourse du Travail," by C. Desplanques.

[52] See his *Review* of H. Roland-Holst's *Generalstreik und Social-démocratie* (Dresden, 1905), L. M. S. pp. 540-541 (pp. 524-541 entire), August 1-15, 1905.

[53] Cf. Lagardelle, "Révolutionnarisme Electoral," L. M. S. December 1-15, 1905, pp. 381-392, on Châlon Congress and political power of revolutionary syndicalism; also, *op. cit.*, A. Morizet, "Les Classification Socialistes Après le Congrès de Châlon," pp. 416-424; and "Les Deux Conceptions du Syndicalisme": (1) *Le Syndicalisme Révolutionnaire,* Victor Griffuelhes, Secretary of the C. G. T., and *Le Syndicalisme Réformiste,* by the secretary of the conservative *Fédération du Livre,* L. M. S. Jan. 1, 1905, pp. 1-41. Cf. Paul Delesalle, *Les deux méthodes du syndicalisme* (1905).

[54] Berth, *op. cit.*

become by the efforts of the workers a superior social order.[55] The revolutionary rôle of the workers' movement, it was thought, at the beginning of the century faced a new enemy in the democratic State. "French syndicalism was born from the reaction of the proletariat against democracy." [56] One who surveyed all the socialist and workers' congresses said in despair, "we are dying of centralization, and the great evil arises from the infection of the workers themselves by this spirit of the State." [57] Sorel agreed. His conclusion was,

> that all revolutionary effort tends to create *free men;* but democratic rulers set themselves the mission of realising the *moral unity* of France. This moral unity is the automatic discipline of producers who would be happy to work for the glory of their intellectual chiefs.[58]

But such degradation was the defeat of the workers' purpose; the great danger which menaced syndicalism was to imitate democracy, for it was far better to content itself for a time with weak and chaotic organizations than to fall under the domination of syndicates who copy the political forms of the bourgeoisie.[59] Such a policy would be fatal to the aims of syndicalism.

The suggestion of the chaotic condition of French syndical organization was accurate. The first Bourse du Travail was opened in Paris in 1887; the first congress of the Fédération des Bourses du Travail was held in 1892, when 14 Bourses were in existence.[60] "The Fédération des Bourses du Travail since 1894," wrote Pelloutier, "has been the only active French organization." [61] The Confédération Générale du Travail [62] had been or-

[55] Cf. Pelloutier, *op. cit.,* chap. VIII, "Conjectures sur l'Avenir des Bourses du Travail," pp. 159-171; cf. Halévy, *op. cit.,* pp. 203-288, Part III, "L'Action Politique."

[56] Lagardelle, *Syndicalisme et Socialisme,* p. 36.

[57] Preface to Pelloutier's *Histoire,* p. 24, quoted by Sorel from M. Ponard, "of whose sound judgment all the world knows."

[58] Sorel, *Réflexions sur la Violence,* p. 268, his italics.

[59] Sorel, *ibid.*

[60] See Paul Delesalle, *Les Bourses du Travail et la C. G. T.* (1910), for short account, and Maxime Leroy, *La Coutume Ouvrière* (2 vols., 1913), for extended critical survey.

[61] Pelloutier, *op. cit.,* p. 159. He was secretary from 1894-1901; from 1901 to 1908 Victor Griffuelhes was secretary of the C. G. T. Their comments on syndical history and organization have a practical significance.

[62] Cf. Leroy, *op. cit.,* Vol. I, pp. 447-478.

ganized in 1895, for the exclusive purpose of uniting the workingmen, in the economic domain and by bonds of class solidarity, in the struggle for their complete emancipation, and to put to an end the disorganization which penetrated their ranks under cover of the political spirit. The need of an independent spirit in the struggle against "the bourgeoisie and democratic State," which characterized French syndicalism and gave to the Confédération Générale du Travail its originality in the international working class movement, began in the organization of the Fédération des Bourses du Travail in 1892.[63] The later Confédération Générale du Travail aiming at freedom from all governmental tutelage, State or municipal, took the syndicate—the group of workers—as the base; the next inclusive group was the Federation of Syndicates and the Union of Syndicates; and the third stage of organization was the Confédération Générale du Travail, the group of Federations and Unions.[64]

At each stage the autonomy of organization is complete: the Federation and Unions of syndicates are autonomous in the Confédération; the syndicates are autonomous in the Federations and Unions; and the workers are autonomous in the syndicates.[65] This ideal of unity in the French trade union movement, constituting a theory of workers' self-government, began its development at the Limoges Congress (1895), when the C. G. T. was inaugurated. Following several years of dispute the Fédération des Bourses du Travail at the Montpellier Congress (1902) joined the Confederation, and there began "the heroic period" of syndicalism, down to 1908.[66] It was asserted at this time that the intellectual leaders of the syndicalist movement were afflicted with the "nostalgia of heroism." [67]

Within the heroic period of 1901 to 1908, whatever place the intellectuals may have had,[68] the workers themselves were articu-

[63] Delesalle, *op. cit.*, pp. 6-7.

[64] E. Pouget, *La Confédération Générale du Travail*" (1910), pp. 3-36, for principles upon which the C. G. T. were organized.

[65] Pouget, *op. cit.*, p. 4.

[66] Lagardelle, "La Formation du Syndicalisme en France," L. M. S. No. 235, Sept.-Oct., 1911, p. 161 (161-186 entire).

[67] Cf. C. Bougle, *Syndicalisme et Démocratie* (1908).

[68] See E. Berth's *Review* of Sombart's *Sozialismus und Soziale Bewegung* (6th ed., 1908), in L. M. S. May 15, 1908, pp. 389-397, and J. B. Severac's *Review* of C. Bougle's "*Syndicalisme et Démocratie* (1908), L. M. S. Dec. 15, 1908, pp. 471-475, for denial of the intellectuals' dictation.

late. The revolt against a benevolent State was made in the name of freedom; for the attack was against a socialism of the State, when formally expressed, because it limited economic development and was nothing more than a perpetuation of capitalism. The marching order of the new working class was from parliamentarism to socialism, until all State influence had disappeared and the syndicate was the means of control.[69] "All socialism of the State can do," said M. Fages, "is to substitute a new for an old slavery," and, "socialism must not be under the tutelage of the State and its *fonctionnaires*."[70] "Direct action, struggle against the bourgeois State and democracy," M. Delesalle wrote, were the points which a militant never lost sight of; and the working class demanded financial and political freedom from each.[71] For Marx, it was believed, the organization of the economic society meant destruction of the State, yet by 1908 the doctrine of "revolutionary evolution" was acclaimed as his significant contribution to social theory.[72] Social revolution would not be the work of a day; it was dependent first upon the proletariat being able to take over the succession of capitalism. It was therefore a patient and long work which the working class imposed on itself. The workers did not hope for the miracles of the Commune. They had no utopias all ready to be introduced by decree of the people. They well knew that to realize their true emancipation, and at the same time achieve the most noble order toward which society directs itself by its own proper economic forces, they would have to go through long struggles and the whole cycle of historical progress, which transformed circumstances and men. Practical action, creating institutions

[69] Cf. A. Labriola, "Du Parlementarisme au Socialisme," L. M. S. December, 1905, pp. 296-313; and his *Reforme e Revoluzione Sociale* (Lugano, 1906), contained his chief contributions to the syndicalist movement through the *Mouvement Socialiste*.

[70] C. Fages, "La Crise Socialiste," L. M. S. April 15, 1906, pp. 377-389; cf. "La Crise Révolutionnaire du Socialisme Français," Eugene Fournière in *Revue Socialiste*, June and July, 1905, reviewed by H. Lagardelle, L. M. S. October 1-15, 1905, pp. 252-264.

[71] "Les Bourses du Travail et Leurs Difficultés Actuelles," L. M. S. March 15, 1908, pp. 161-170.

[72] Lagardelle, "Apropos de Marx," L. M. S. March 15, 1908, pp. 194-201. Marxism as a theory of action meant three things: (1) the preponderance of working class institutions; (2) anti-Statism and its corollary anti-patriotism; and (3) revolutionary evolution (p. 196).

and ideas, came before all. That alone was revolutionary. Thus the proletariat would manifest their power by acts and not by words. It was by this daily method that there would be little by little produced revolutionary institutions and ideas, which became their aim, and at the possible moment, the society in their own image. It was to that Marx appealed—revolutionary evolution! [73]

There was little room for this doctrine in the political socialism of reformism, even though, as with M. Guesde, the class struggle theory of parliamentary action was followed out. Each day revolutionary enthusiasm became less on the democratic terrain. Revolutionary syndicalism gave a new vigor to socialism, but its purpose was not to be diluted through weary political manœuvres; but was rather defined through the general strike, which expressed "the resurrection of the people, becoming conscious of itself, of its complex personality, of its spiritual unity." [74] While the German or English working class movements were only adaptatations to bourgeois society, the French working class movement was a movement of absolute negation and creation. The parliamentary régime had corrupted France, for when democracy triumphs the politicians become masters of the day. The Clemenceau Ministry appeared the most typical example of this decomposition of democracy. It was contemporaneous with the high tide of revolutionary syndicalism in 1906, which gave a freshness, a daring to the criticism of revolt. It did not matter that M. Deschanel condemned in the Chamber of Deputies the narrowness of syndicalist conceptions of work; [75] the conviction of the leaders was that the great problem which agitated the nation was that of the organization and liberation of work. Syndicalism then became a theory which gave to the workers' professional organizations, animated by the revolutionary spirit, the real meaning of social transformation. It was a *workers' socialism,* said Lagardelle. By its conception of the class struggle it opposed itself

[73] *Op. cit.*, p. 200.

[74] E. Berth, "Marchands, Intellectueles et Politiciens," L. M. S. March 15, No. 196, 1908, p. 221; also his three other articles under this title Nos. 188, 191 and 192, 1908. Cf. "Le Droit de Grève," Report of the Conference in Paris (1909), at which MM. Gide, Barthélemy and Perreau spoke. The editor of the series wrote that Socialism tended to reduce itself to Syndicalism and Syndicalism itself found perfect expression in the strike.

[75] J. O. May 9, 1907, pp. 936-938, quoted by G. Beaubois in "L'Etat, les Partis, et le Syndicalisme," L. M. S. Aug.-Sept. 15, 1907, pp. 113-127.

to all pure *corporatisme,* of which the English Trade Unions furnished the type; by its emphasis on proletarian institutions it separated itself from parliamentary institutions; and by its care for positive creations and its distrust of ideology it was differentiated from traditional anarchism. It was taken for granted that it was impossible to change the nature of the State. This was proved by Briand, Millerand, and Viviani, and the cause was in the imitation by parliamentary socialism of the process of democracy. Syndicalism did not think democracy capable of providing new values; it was little more than a régime of demoralization which exalted the human person.

It was the principle of *indirect action* of democracy that syndicalism denounced as corruptive of human personality. The representative system supposed by definition that the citizen was powerless. He was powerless because he was incompetent.[76]

His incompetence arose when he was detached from real conditions of life, having to pronounce, not on the problems which came under his hand and made up the matter of his existence, but on that whole body of vague questions which were designated under the name of "general interest" and which ignored him. This helped to explain the development of the tradition of anarchism in syndicalism; but what anarchism combated in syndicalism was its pragmatism and anti-intellectualism. However, syndicalism was born of the worker's experience and not his theories. It distrusted dogmas and formulas. Its method was realistic. Anarchism was *anti-parliamentary;* syndicalism was *extra-parliamentary;* it recognized only the producer, ignoring the citizen, while anarchism relegated economics to a second place. But if for the accomplishment of its own proper tasks the parliamentary means were not the best, it permitted, outside the syndicate, the independent worker to utilize political parties for other work. Syndicalism was not chained to any dogma.[77] Yet syndicalism was not a socialism of institutions; it was created in the struggle which made the selection of the militant worker for the work of revolutionary socialism.

[76] H. Lagardelle, "Les Caractères Généraux du Syndicalisme," L. M. S. June 15, 1908, pp. 426-436; cf. G. Beaubois, "La Décadence Démocratique," L. M. S. pp. 341-354.

[77] Lagardelle, *op. cit.*

This cannot be mere democratic reform, for "the conciliation of reformism and syndicalism is not possible." [78] Though the demands of political democracy in some countries may have forced the Socialists at times to discharge the political functions of the bourgeoisie, there was the more important problem of what the future society is to be. While socialism cannot be definitive, it is the power which is to create the new order. It must be more than the advance guard of bourgeois democracy.[79] The modern democratic State fits in well with the capitalist order, in fact, better than the ancient State; and because the parliamentarians have systematically refused to study economic questions, the workers are driven to create a world of their own. "We come not as founders of a new school or purveyors of dogma," said Lagardelle, "we are simply disquieted men, who, in the desert of our epoch, are seeking the sources of fresh and abundant life. The good will is our means. For the rest, we leave it to destiny." [80]

Such a statement suggests the view that an act of faith was at the basis of revolutionary syndicalism, faith that in the proletariat was the hope for the recreation of society.[81] But M. Sorel denied this, because the superiority of the proletariat was acquired in the class struggle; it was the only class animated by the spirit of war, and, in consequence, the only one which was virile and capable of progress.[82] On this basis Sorel appealed to M. Bergson to direct his theory to the service of the social movement; [83]

[78] *Ve Congrès National du Parti Socialiste* (S. F. I. O.), Toulouse, 1908, *Compte Rendu,* p. 274 (Lagardelle); pp. 252-274 for his long address on syndicalism and socialist politics.

[79] Cf. E. Szabô, "Politique et Syndicats," L. M. S. No. 207, Feb. 15, 1908, pp. 108-129. He points out the contradictory attitude of A. Labriola, candidate for Parliament in Italy, Lagardelle in the Unified Socialist Party, and Michels in Germany for democratic liberty (p. 108).

[80] "Classes Sociales et Parti Politique," L. M. S. July-August, 1909, pp. 5-25.

[81] Cf. E. Dolleans, *Le Caractère Réligieux du Socialisme* (1906); appeared originally in *Revue d'Economie Politique,* June, 1906; Charles Maurras, *Le Dilemme de Marc Sagnier: Essai sur la Démocratie Réligieuse* (1907); Bernard Allo, *Foi et Systèmes* (1908), a study in which Bergson is omitted; and A. Fouillée, *La Pensée et les Nouvelles Ecoles Anti-Intellectualistes* (1911).

[82] Sorel, L. M. S. November, 1906, pp. 282-293.

[83] See Sorel's series of articles on Bergson's *Creative Evolution* in L. M. S. Nos. 191 and 193, 1907, pp. 25 ff., 478 ff., and Nos. 194, 196, 197, 1908, pp. 34 ff., 184 ff., and 276 ff. The last (pp. 276-294) is the special

and at the same time he was grateful to William James for inspiring a new interest in religion,[84] an interest which he would utilize for proletariat unity in the myth of the general strike. It was patent that political socialism was not the best expression of the class struggle. The final period of its vitality, says Lagardelle, was expressed by Guesde in the Chamber of Deputies, June 16, 1896, when he said,

> take guard when socialism begins to disappear, you will then have no defence against individual reprisals and the assaults of groups. Socialism is the best lightning-conductor (*paratonnerre*) against the workers' revolt.[85]

Jaurès expressed another phase of reformism when he said that it was necessary that the struggle cease between the Government of the Republic and the working class. The disaffection of the working classes thus had stronger economic reasons.[86] Formerly the revolt was against the State as an oppressor, it was now against the State as a benefactor. It was therefore the duty of French syndicalism to destroy for the working class the State-superstition, proving that the State remained the same under the various aspects it assumed, an oppressive and external mechanism to life. The last incarnation of the State was also the death of the State.[87] In its place was the syndicate, the natural organ of the class struggle; that was the first fundamental idea of syndicalism.[88]

appeal. See also the symposium in L. M. S. on "Influence de la Philosophie de M. Bergson," April, July-August, November (1911), January and February (1912), and J. B. Severac, *William James,* February, 1911, pp. 142-144.

[84] Cf. Sorel's *Review of Science et Réligion dans la Philosophie Contemporaine* (1908), L. M. S. May 15, 1908, pp. 388-389. A suggestive study is M. Ernest Seillière, *Le Péril Mystique dans l'Inspiration des Démocraties Contemporaines* (1918); and see Parker Thomas Moon's *The Labor Problem and the Social Catholic Movement in France* (N. Y., 1921), and Denis Gwynn, *The Catholic Reaction in France* (1925).

[85] Lagardelle, "Les Origines du Socialisme Parlementaire en France," L. M. S. No. 214, Oct., 1909, p. 193, quoted; pp. 170-193 entire; L. M. S. Nos. 213, 215-216, pp. 81-99, 241-264, for the first and third articles of series.

[86] Pelloutier, *op. cit.*, p. 66.

[87] Lagardelle, *op. cit.*, p. 260.

[88] *V*e *Congrès National du Parti Socialiste* (S. F. I. O.), Toulouse, 1908, p. 255 (Lagardelle).

PART II

The Reaction on Politics

The success of continued syndicalist appeal to the economic basis of working class progress had a definite political response beyond reviving the Socialist party. M. Ribot, in the Senate, November, 1909, declared:

I guard my convictions, but the more I reflect the more I am convinced that the great political struggles are for a moment finished and that the combats we see are only skirmishes of the advance guard. On the other hand social questions take daily a more important place. There is a deep aspiration in all those men (workers) who have our equality of law and share with us popular sovereignty, toward liberty and well-being, toward a diminution of labour and also an increase of dignity. We are not able to be unconcerned. The egoism of class has always been a fault; to-day it would be unpardonable; it would be suicide.[89]

Yet the reaction of socialist politics upon the economic policies of syndicalism created, from 1909 on, the crisis of "domestication," [90] The emphasis upon revolutionary evolution anticipated the general reaction toward reformistic syndicalism, and the ministry of M. Briand did not check its opportunistic tendencies. The function of revolutionary syndicalism was then conceived to be to orient politics toward economics; for in all countries, as it was thought England pointed the way, the political struggle was an economic struggle. Workers' representation would be the extension to Parliament of direct syndical action.[91] Parliamentary action by labour representation became nothing more than the extension and integration of direct action. This recalls the earlier counsel

[89] J. O. Sen, November 6, 1909, p. 868, quoted by A. Merrheim to prove the value of eight years of agitation, in his *La Crise Syndicaliste,* L. M. S. Nov.-Dec., 1909, p. 298 (pp. 290-304 entire).

[90] See symposium by leaders in L. M. S. January, April, August-September, 1910, pp. 57-65, 262-275, 116-122; also A. Merrheim, "La Parlementarisation du Syndicalisme," L. M. S. April, 1910, pp. 241-249, against the scheme of a "Fédération Nationale du Travail."

[91] Cf. Sergio Pannunzio, "Syndicalisme et Représentation Ouvrière, L. M. S. May-June, 1910, pp. 320-337.

of M. Sorel himself: It is up to the syndicalist to choose the political candidate who seems less bad, having regard to the time and place, or not to choose at all.[92]

But the attitude toward socialist politics had changed, even if for industrial socialism the problem remained the same in 1910 as it was in 1900: Was socialism to be of the workers or of political parties?[93] Lagardelle could say in 1910 that one believed less and less in the creative force of the State and the magic of parliamentarism.

> It was not so ten years ago. The primacy of politics over economics seemed incontestable; democracy was the dogma of dogmas. We spoke a premature language. But events came to our aid. Traditional socialism began to decompose with a disconcerting rapidity. I do not know of any period more sad than the beginning of the twentieth century. Instead of a conquering, heroic, regenerated movement for which we had waited, there was a small parliamentary party, trafficking in politics, disreputable in its abdications. Neo-Marxism was the base of criticism and affirmation. It was our duty (Lagardelle and Sorel) to prove that syndicalist socialism was a movement issuing from democracy.[94]

> But syndicalism was never conceived as a new school[95] with its dogmatics and its inflexible formulas. It appeared as a suggestive movement of new ideas, soliciting from thought an original work, provoking necessarily varied reflections and always revisable. In the full decadence of democracy syndicalism furnished the elements of social renewing. It represented the revolt of economic society against political society, the insurrection of labour against incompetence and parasitism, the struggle of *nation against the State*.[96]

This revolt against the State had an interesting development, when MM. Sorel and Berth decided in 1910 to join with the group of the *Action Française* in the publication of a neo-mon-

[92] Cf. Sorel, "Le Décline du Parti Socialiste Internationale," L. M. S. February 6, 1906.

[93] Cf. H. Lagardelle, *Le Socialisme Ouvrier* (1910).

[94] Lagardelle, *op. cit.*, the Preface.

[95] Cf. Sorel, *La Décomposition du Marxisme*, p. 63.

[96] Lagardelle, Preface to J. Gaumont's *L'Etat Contre la Nation* (1911), on "La Politique Syndicaliste."

archist monthly, *La Cité Française.* Sorel's appeal[97] was "to all who sense the vanity of democratic declarations." But this apostacy had hardly any more effect than confirming the fact that the economic movement of the French working class had deeper roots than in the theorizing of the gourmets of social theory.[98] While the neo-monarchist indictment of democracy might share the revolutionary syndicalist opposition to reformism, it was hardly just to the ordinary workers[99] to say that their nerves have need of powerful excitations, their artistic sensibilities suffer a painful revulsion before all philistinism, against all bourgeois spirit of shop keeping.[100] After the abdication of Sorel and Berth it was yet true for revolutionary syndicalism that the fetish of the representative régime was fought, and that its duty was progres-

[97] See *Prospectus* of *La Cité Française,* in L. M. S. January, 1911, pp. 52-53; *ibid.,* Lagardelle, "Monarchistes et Syndicalistes," pp. 52-55; *op. cit.,* July-August, 1912, pp. 101-106, his "Les Enemis de Rousseau"; and January, 1912, pp. 65-69, his "Proudhon et les Neo-Monarchistes." Cf. George Valois, *La Monarchie et la Classe Ouvrière* (1910); the author was one of the founders of the ill-starred *La Cité Française.*

[98] Cf. E. Berth, *Guerre des Etats ou Guerre des Classes* (1924), for a recent survey of these tendencies, which may be compared with his *Méfaits des Intellectuels* (1914); also *Les Derniers Aspects du Socialisme* (1923), a revised and augmented edition of *Les Nouveaux Aspects du Socialisme* (1908), presents more forcefully and definitely the author's point of view. In common with nearly all syndicalist writers M. Berth brings together whatever he has written under a title which may have no relation to a great deal of the book.

[99] Professor Sombart wrote in 1907, that "the hold of the Syndicalists on the masses has not had the result of raising the social faith of the masses to a higher level, or filled them with a desire for a higher form of social warfare. The Syndicalist leaders are mistaken if they imagine that the masses understand the new teaching as they themselves do. The masses regard it as a revival of the old ideas of revolution, so dear to their hearts. There can be little doubt that in the adoption by the masses of syndicalist doctrines we may perceive the old dislike which the French spirit entertains of all progress, of the weary daily task in the parliamentary and trade union struggle. No matter what the leaders of the movement may say to the contrary, syndicalism has taken the place of antiquated Blanquism in the hearts of the impatient Frenchmen. It is, therefore, not a step forward but a step back to old forms of social warfare" (*op. cit.,* p. 237). Cf. George Weill, *Histoire du Mouvement Social en France* (1st ed. 1904, 2nd ed. 1911), pp. 378 ff.

[100] Werner Sombart, *Sozialismus und soziale Bewegung* (9th ed. 1920), p. 75; cf. Michel Ralea, *L'Idée de revolution dans les doctrines socialistes: Etude sur l'Evolution de la Tactique Révolutionnaire,* Preface by C. Bouglé (1923), pp. 360–390, chap. II. "Une Renaissance du Voluntarisme Revolutionnaire."

sively to reduce the domain of politics to its normal proportions. The syndicalist charter of Amiens remained, for it was more of an historical description than a reflection of the present. It was a view of the future, when the workers' syndicalism would become a general syndicalism and in many ways penetrate the whole of French society.[101] It was the formula which could express the evolution of the real France from authoritative to liberal democracy.[102] The old Liberalism was anti-State too, but syndicalism was a spontaneous revolt against an impotent administration and government. "The revolt against the State by the workers robbed the State of its magic." On the eve of the first general strike in 1909, M. Aulard, historian of the French Revolution, stated that it was the most important social fact which had happened in France since 1789. The decline of the former traditions of "authority and parliamentarism and Statism is in France the prelude of a dawn and not a twilight"; and there is a growing force of liberalism "because of the elemental conditions of social justice" to which syndicalism has directed the thought of "the free spirit of France which is always living." [103]

The autocracy of parties as a hindrance to the workers' development was not less condemned by revolutionary syndicalism than the autocracy of the State.[104] So while syndicalism was less antagonistic to political socialism in France, it is also true that there was a much broader outlook on the function of a workers' party. While M. Vaillant could truthfully say at the Saint

[101] Cf. Jules Sageret, *La doctrine du syndicalisme intellectuel* (1921), pp. 14-36; and G. Tessier, *Le statut legal des employés* (1924).

[102] Lagardelle, "La Critique Syndicaliste de la Démocratie," L. M. S. Feb., 1911, pp. 81-86; also "Les Difficultés du Syndicalisme," L. M. S. September-October, 1912, pp. 161-164, and "Cynisme et Décadence," L. M. S. July-August, 1909, pp. 76-80. Cf. R. Michels, *Zur Soziologie des Parteiwesens in der modernen Demokratie* (Leipzig, 1911); Charles Brouilhot, *Le Conflit des doctrines dans l'economie politique contemporaine* (Paris, 1908); and M. Bourdeau, *Entre deux servitudes* (1908). The socialist movement of the period is fully analyzed in the above.

[103] Cf. Lagardelle, "La Démocratie en France," L. M. S. December, 1912, pp. 321-332, and January, 1913, pp. 13-29.

[104] See Lagardelle's *Review* of Ostrogorski's *La Démocratie et les Partis Politiques* (French edition, 1912), L. M. S. November, 1912, pp. 313-318; the English situation and the Prime Minister's remarks in the House of Commons, April 26, 1911, on parties, is referred to, cf. R. Michels, "La Composition Aristocratique des Partis," L. M. S. January, 1911, pp. 21-33, and February, 1911, pp. 87-97.

Quentin Congress in 1911, that "one is always occupied in France with formulas, unfortunately it is a quite French malady with which we are infected,"[105] that Congress set itself primarily to the work of organizing municipal socialism.[106] Nevertheless, M. Compère-Morel in the debate on the Parliamentary report, while recognizing the value of utilizing parliamentary struggles, in a resolution he moved, affirmed that the socialist deputies are the representatives of the party of opposition fundamentally and irreducibly opposed to the whole of the bourgeois class and to the State which is its instrument.[107] Yet three years before the report of the Committee of 34 on the General Action of the Party,[108] declared that the Socialist Party, party of the working class and of the Revolution, pursues the conquest of political power for the emancipation of the proletariat by the destruction of the capitalist régime and the suppression of classes. The campaign manifesto of 1914 appealed to the citizens of France to affirm with the Socialist Party the necessity of full social justice—before the defaultings of pretended democrats incapable of any hardy and vigorous reformistic action.[109] The annual conference of the Bourses du Travail and the Federations in 1911 considered mainly the questions of old age pensions, the eight hour day, and the

[105] *VIIIe Congrès National du Parti Socialiste,* April 16-19, 1911, *Compte Rendu,* p. 318 (pp. 318-336 entire). Municipal socialism as the means of a better standard of life, "according with the principles of social evolution," for all the people, was his plea (p. 336).

[106] *Op. cit.,* pp. 86-92, Report of Municipal Commission and the program; pp. 442-444 for resolution on program and tactics for municipal elections; and pp. 250-345, for speeches of MM. Milhaud, Guesde, Lafargue, Compère-Morel, and others on municipal socialism. The progress of ideas and the social significance of the aims of political socialism can be judged in these extended debates. The significance of syndicalism in bringing discussion down to administration is significant.

[107] *Op. cit.,* p. 209.

[108] *Ve Congrès Parti Socialiste* (S. F. I. O.), 1908, Toulouse, *Compte Rendu,* pp. 484-485, the Report, made by Jaurès (485-488); see also Jaurès' speeches, pp. 81 ff., 311 ff., 377 ff., and the extended one of Lagardelle, pp. 252 ff. Two five-hour speeches on democracy for one Congress.

[109] "Le Parti Socialiste (S. F. I. O.) Manifesto, 1914," L. M. S. March-April, 1914, pp. 215-217; pp. 217-236 campaign documents; and J. B. Severac, "Le Parti Socialiste et les Prochaines Elections Législatives," L. M. S. January-February, 1914, pp. 39-44, and "Les Elections Legislatives et le Parti Socialiste," May-June, 1914, pp. 319-333.

English week.[110] At any rate the gain of 34 members in the Chamber of Deputies between 1910 and 1914[111] indicated that the electoral tactics of the party had not failed to profit from the continued controversy among the ranks of the workers.[112] Political socialism had increased its party strength, if it had not materially raised its prestige with the workers and in the nation at large.

The address of M. Jouhaux, secretary of the C. G. T., at the 1913 Trade Union Congress was a commentary on the effect of the political movement on French trade unionism. We desire, he said, that the trade unionist shall be a progressive factor in our social status; he has been so trained that, even if he be a passive factor to-day, he becomes an active factor to-morrow, and our endeavours are directed toward developing in him the principles of direct action. It was recognized that the worker in his task of organization and his struggle to secure rights which properly belong to his class, was moved by diverse aspirations. His action sometimes was wanting in singleness of aim and the spirit of continuity. It lacked logic. Not infrequently it reached a state when between its practice and its theory there was a great gulf fixed. Often he was forced by circumstances to listen to dictates remote from the pretensions of his declared policy of autonomy and independence. His daily practice revealed little rectitude, and to all appearances the general tendency of direct action or syndicalism bore in itself the seeds of its own dissolution, and that the people must recognize the necessity for that permanent delegation of functions and powers represented by the modern State. To appreciate this more allowance must be made for the influential power wielded by institutions of Government and the employing classes. Between the employer class and the State and the wage earner there was a state of war, and so long as victory was for the stronger the workers must see to it that

[110] See "La Conférence des Bourses du Travail et des Fédérations," June 22-24, 1911, L. M. S. July-August, 1911, pp. 124-131.

[111] For the declaration of the Socialist deputies in Chamber of Deputies, June 1, 1914, see L. M. S. May-June, 1914, pp. 387-389.

[112] See *XIe Congrès National du Parti Socialiste,* Amiens, January 25-28, 1914, *Compte Rendu,* pp. 162-241, 269-387, for extended debates of this Congress on electoral tactics, and pp. 424-427 for the text of the resolution on *la tactique électorale* by the Resolutions Committee, offered by Jaurès.

strength shall be theirs. Till that end was achieved the proletariat must alternately impose its will and submit to compromise, which, in most cases, would never assume the form of a definite treaty. "Agitation," "Strikes," "Sabotage," "Boycott,"—were the weapons of the workers, even the forms themselves of direct action. With each, as with all, it was the worker who decided for himself. So, too, it was by means at his disposal, by his function and his rôle that he decided the nature of his activities and his method of fighting. But by the method pursued by the Confederation both social and corporate benefits had been obtained for the workers.

To-day, in a nation of ardent temperaments, more than 600,000 rebels are enrolled under its banner against the existing order of things. Opposed to these are but eight organizations of workers, to whom direct action is unacceptable. This infinitesimal minority apart, it is the method which impels the great mass of our workers. It has welded them into unity; it has created in them a common interest and a common aspiration, which has united and coalesced the men for the final combat—the general strike of expropriation, which will replace in the hands of the workers the instruments of production.[113]

Part III

The Contribution of Syndicalism

There is little to be gained from this survey of revolutionary syndicalism if it is isolated from the whole of the effort of modern France to understand its needs and to express its hopes. It was a contradictory, vague, and often meaningless search for industrial freedom. It was a human thing, very much so, despite the "sublimity" which brilliant writers superinduced upon it. When it is remembered how nonchalantly Congress after Congress resolved upon a new world, how clearly seen were the liberties of that experience for men who worked and had never tried to escape from it, but in their own milieu dared to think a better world could be made, the meaning for a study of social justice is plain. Men have the capacity for political ideals, for economic ideals, and

[113] Léon Jouhaux, *Report of the 46th Annual Trade Union Congress*, Manchester, 1913, September 1-6, pp. 257-260.

it is social treason to go on with Governments and an industrial régime which do not give full opportunity for their expression. However productive cynicism is for picturesque literary brilliance, it is a barren doctrine for democracy. It may steady but it will not sustain politics for long. There is good humour in comparing the high disdain of the syndicalist for paltry politics on one page, then turn to the next and see his endorsement of a six-point legislative program. But it only means a larger interest. Then there is M. Jouhaux in 1913 blandly giving the old platitudes of syndicalism, and all the time working through his ordinary trade union machinery. But he uses freely imaginative phrases that would embarrass an English trade union executive, because nearly always words mean the same no matter how often used. M. Jouhaux too could help to frame a peace treaty for Labour,[114] signed by leaders of "proud bourgeois democracies," whom, cursing as he went down into his grave, M. Sorel saw "cynically triumphant." [115]

The all-rounded view of syndicalism was early demanded by the leaders who had helped to shape the movement, if the far-reaching effects of its influence in France were to be understood.[116] The analytical method was not enough, the whole view must be taken. It was not sufficient to dismiss socialist thought as bankrupt and Marxism as "a trap for socialism." [117] Rather the division of

[114] Cf. Justin Godart, *Les Clauses du Travail dans le Traité de Versailles* (1920); J.-L. Puech, *La Tradition Socialiste en France et la Société des Nations,* with Preface by Charles Gide (1921); Achille Viallate, *L'Impérialisme Economique et les Rélations Internationales pendant le dernier Demi-Siècle,* 1870-1920 (1923); and Prof. E. Mahaim, *Le Droit International Ouvrier* (1913).

[115] Sorel, *Reflexions sur la Violence,* p. 454, the concluding words of his "plaidoyer pour Lenine."

[116] Cf. Lagardelle's reviews of A. Acht's "Der Moderne Französische Syndicalismus" (Jena, 1911), L. M. S. December, 1912, and of L. Levine's, "The Labour Movement in France" (1912, N. Y.), L. M. S. March-April, 1913. Professor W. Y. Elliott's study *The Pragmatic Revolt in Politics* (Oxford, 1923, Thesis), and Professor W. R. Dennes' *The Method and Presuppositions of Group Psychology* (Oxford, 1923, Thesis), are worthwhile contributions to this whole field of discussion.

[117] Vladimir G. Simkhovitch, *Marxism Versus Socialism* (1st ed. 1913, 3rd ed. 1923), p. 287, also pp. 185-224; cf. J. S. Nicholson, *The Revival of Marxism* (1920), pp. 35-47, *The State According to Marx.* See *Historical Materialism and the Economics of Karl Marx* (1914), *Introduction* by A. D. Lindsay; Charles A. Beard, *Cross Currents in Europe To-Day*

social democracy into right and left groups over the question of organization and control was not only a significant demonstration of the inadequacy of that Marxian analysis which resolves all social conflict into a struggle of classes [118] but of all analysis which does that, and from which social action arises. It is not necessary to stress the anti-social tendencies of the syndicalist glory in the class struggle, for its own literature is full of contradictions on this subject. It is one of the mystical adventures of socialist theory and has no need for dogmatics. But the contribution of syndicalism helped to interpret the new industrial forces which had spread fear and hopelessness in the lives of millions of working people. Syndicalism as a protest is significant because of its freshness in defining anew old hopes. That socialism should gradually change from a class movement into a social movement,[119] is no more remarkable than that all class conscious institutions, education, religion, music, and all class conscious groups should have forced upon them the futility of this attitude. The genius of resolving social conflict into the antagonism of classes is not a class possession. Syndicalism is made clearer when it is considered as a movement which comes between two historical phases. Whether or not it represents the lively basis of human groups in the future, when political parties, and the socialist party, born only as transitory creations, will be condemned, it does form an indestructible link between that period of history which is just ending and that which lies just beyond the horizon of the people.[120]

The reluctance to give up the Marxian notion that the main antagonists are labour and capital is a common possession. Syndicalist thought omitted, no less than more conventional propaganda of political groups, a whole-rounded view of national life. The differences which separate political society from economic society exist, but the mistake is to think them far greater than they are.

(1923), chaps. VI-VIII, pp. 163-181, esp. chap. VIII. "Socialism and the Labour Movement"; M. Beer, *op. cit.,* Vol. II (1920), p. 202; and H. J. Laski *Karl Marx* (1922).

[118] Cf. Franklin H. Giddings, *Introduction* to Louis Levine's *Syndicalism in France* (2nd revised ed. 1914), p. 18.

[119] Montgomery, *op. cit.,* p. 284, "The tendency of modern socialism toward democratization is remarkable."

[120] Louis, *Histoire du Mouvement Syndical en France, 1789-1910* (2nd ed. 1911), p. 282, also pp. 269-282, *La Doctrine du Syndicalisme.*

It is impossible to reverse the laws of psychology and of organization which govern the world, and the continued stress upon the economic and juridical self-sufficiency of the group against the State, necessarily brought revolutionary syndicalism face to face with facts with which it was unprepared to deal.[121] Millerand put too much weight upon State machinery, and the syndicalist opposition was a healthy symptom; yet with all their emphasis upon economic organization the C. G. T. and the Labour movement had a like incompetence for creative organization. But the effort to grapple with the direction of economic interests and to relate them to the national life developed tremendously the consciousness of French Labour. It developed in many an understanding of the processes of society. In France it was truer than in England that

> for too many citizens socialism is limited to the expression of discontent, the cry of suffering, the half-mystical confidence in the establishment of a new order of things. Its historic foundations, its ineluctable character; its relations with the capitalist system have not always been well known.[122]

That condition was true in 1900 and it was true in 1914, but with the difference that definite problems had been faced in the French trade union world and in the French Parliament during the intervening years. The life of the ordinary worker had been related to large issues. Human life had more meaning. Daily work was more significant. The individual possessed a new worth in the groups to which he belonged, and the State through all the years had to concern itself with the welfare and the happiness of the people. If it were true that the State had been robbed of its magic there was no loss to its real purpose.

The growth of revolutionary syndicalism in France came at a time when the reaction against parliamentary reforms was at its height, the French Labour movement suffering from a bad case of nerves and depression. There was felt to be no hope in the

[121] Cf. Sergio Pannunzio, "Le Droit Syndical et la Notion d'Autorité," L. M. S. July-August, 1912, pp. 81-96, No. 2 *op. cit.*, September-October, 1912, pp. 188-198, and his "Syndicalisme et Souveraineté," L. M. S. July-August, 1913, pp. 59-73; also R. Michels, "L'Oligarchie et l'Immunité des Syndicats," January, 1913, pp. 90-96.

[122] Louis, *Histoire du Socialisme Français* (1901), p. 299.

fruitful policy of working class participation in the electoral struggles; that all had been gained that was possible. It was a revolt against the reformistic tendency of the political Labour movement, which had not kept pace with the needs nor led the hopes of the working class. Neither had it freshly stated the contribution to the nation as a whole of the working class. The revolt was against the State, representing the impotency of the political leaders. The incapacity of political parliaments to organize the economic life of nations accounted for the spread of administrative syndicalism and the doctrine of economic organization, demanding a revolt away from State tutelage.[123] The challenge was to the purpose of the State and the power of the State to make its purpose plain. Thus the social basis of this revolt[124] had an equal significance with the economic necessity which compelled many of the freshest minds in the Labour movement to declare that political dry rot was intolerable, and that economic progress made inevitable a realignment of loyalties, the validity of which the State must recognize. Syndicalism at this point made a valuable contribution to the social theory of this century.[125] Its tediously vague polemics about the antagonism between democracy and syndicalism really have no meaning, so far as this study can take account of them, for the present concern is to know that in the period men were trying to state more clearly what they conceived the conditions of freedom to be. Democracy is not defeated because men catch only glimpses of its enlarging meaning in human life. But it is helped by every movement which brings more definitely to a place of first importance the individual and his rights within the community, and how in the

[123] Cf. Esmein, *op. cit.,* Preface p. xv. Also Thomas-Garrigue Masaryk, *Les Problèmes de la Démocratie,* Preface by M. Albert Thomas (1924), chap. IV, pp. 65-96, "Syndicalisme et Démocratie."

[124] Cf. Harold J. Laski, *Authority in the Modern State* (1917), chapter on "Administrative Syndicalism," pp. 321-387. "There is probably no epoch in social history where organized resistance to State decision has not its roots in some deep grievance honestly conceived. . . . It (administrative syndicalism) is not a revolt against society but against the State. It is not a revolt against authority but a theory of it which is, in fact, equivalent to servitude" (pp. 386-387).

[125] Cf. C. Bouglé *La Sociologie de Proudhon* (1912); his *Chez les Prophètes Socialistes* (1918), pp. 185-246, "Marxisme et Sociologie"; and his Preface to *Proudhon et notre Temps* (1918), a valuable collection of essays by various writers.

modern State these rights are related to the freedom of all the people. The syndicate was the basis in the beginning of the industrial life of the worker, and it sought to promote widely his aims and interests. Whether or not revolutionary syndicalism has greatly helped the individual French worker to use his associative freedom more effectively yet remains to be seen. But it is true that the importance of the rank and file of the industrial workers and the collective power of the organized groups are to-day more widely understood. There is no movement of reform which omits to take account of the worker as he is, and it is impossible for any program of social consequence to disregard the aspirations of Labour.[126] It is for the future to direct nobly the ideal of justice which can finally win the allegiance of all men as they prepare in mind and heart for the good society.

[126] The syndicalist literature is abundant but the following may be noted since the war: Leon Jouhaux, *Le Syndicalisme et la C. G. T.* (1920); Pierre Paraf, *Le syndicalisme pendant et après la guerre* (2e éd., 1923); Martin Saint-Leon, *Syndicalisme ouvrier et syndicalisme agricole* (1920); Emile Cazalis, *Les positions sociales du syndicalisme ouvrier en France,* with which can be joined M. Valdour Jacques' *L'Ouvrier agricole* (1919) and *La vie ouvrière* (1919); C. Metton, *Un village syndical* (1920); and Pierre Hamp, *La peine des hommes. Les métiers blessés* (5e éd., 1919). See preceding and following chapters for further references.

CHAPTER XII

THE FRENCH LABOUR MOVEMENT SINCE THE WAR

THE leaders of the French Labour movement joined determinedly their countrymen when the war became a cruel necessity of patriotism. The Syndicalists and the Socialists supported whole-heartedly the whole war program of the nation, and M. Jouhaux, leader of the *Confédération Générale du Travail,* received the appointment as the representative of French Labour at the Peace Conference. In France as in every nation the five years of the war set the peoples to thinking of what the world might be like after the struggle and what the needs of the nation would be. It was easy to believe that tremendous changes could take place. This spirit found expression in the demands of Labour for fairer conditions of work and for control of industry, and even the abolition of the wage system. In 1920 the National Federation of Agricultural Labourers, forming a central body by the amalgamation of four agricultural organizations, decided that wages were to be accepted only as for an intermediary stage and as "a kind of anachronism." In December, 1918, the confederal committee of the C. G. T. published a program of minimum demands, which represented a compromise between the moderates and the extremists of the industrial movement.[1] This minimum program is as significant of the politics of the Labour movement in France as it is of the new demands of the workers for control in industry. In publishing the program the International Labour Office at Geneva announced that it did so because of its value as an indication "of the development of working class ideas, and of the formulas on which organizations may decide at times to base their actions."

[1] *Programme minimum de la C. G. T.* (1919), published by the C. G. T., 211 Rue Lafayette, Paris, with which can be compared two other reports issued by the C. G. T., *Les travailleurs et les assurances sociales* (1923), and the *Rapport Rey sur les assurances sociales* (1923).

[2] Studies and Reports, Series A, No. 19, International Labour Office, Geneva, *The Minimum Program of the General Confederation of Labour*

The minimum program reflected the crisis of the world following the armistice, for it gives the place of first importance to problems of peace. But in that crisis the solution rested exclusively upon the labouring classes, it was asserted; and that though it was not sufficient to change the political order by making the revolution—production must be increased—immediate reforms should not be an abdication of the ideal of the revolution; on the contrary it was to prepare for the new order. The program asked for the creation of a League of Nations, the abolition of protective tariffs, the end of economic wars, the creation of an international office of transportation to divide raw materials among nations, and general disarmament. It also asked that the individual liberties suspended during the war be re-established. This phase of the program dealt directly with problems growing out of war conditions.

The economic and social reforms under "the Rights of Labour" in the program are of interest. It demanded that labour be no longer treated as a commodity, that the equality of the two sexes be recognized, that an unlimited right of combination be recognized, and that collective bargaining regulate wages and conditions of labour. Freedom of speech and of the press and the inauguration of political amnesty were asked for. It asked for an eight-hour day in commerce, industry and agriculture, and for the prohibition of night work in bakeries, etc., and in any industry in which women, or children of less than eighteen years, are employed. It asked that the compulsory school period be prolonged to fourteen years. (The program with regard to the National Economic Council has been noted above.) The program also insisted that property is a trust, held by individuals for the good of society, and that the nation should watch over the exercise of property rights which owe their value to the protection of society. As has been pointed out in an able way,[3] a very important part of the

in France (1921); also in same Studies and Reports, Series B, No. 8, *A Demand for Workers' Control in France* (1921), which gives text of correspondence between the French Federation of Metal Workers and the Association of Metallurgical Industries in regard to establishment of workers' control in that industry.

[3] See B. G. De Montgomery, *op. cit.*, pp. 50-54, and R. L. Buell, *Contemporary French Politics* (1920), chap. VIII. Both are valuable studies for history and for competent criticism.

program, which in reality marked the difference between this program and that of the Socialists, was concerned with State control in industry. The C. G. T. recognized that it would not be desirable for the State to extend its industrial activities too far, but that control should be exercised in the industries which still permit the play of initiative and competition. In the production of necessaries the State should strictly control the conditions of labour and the division of profits. The State must intervene wherever and whenever private monopoly gains control of raw materials, products, or organizations, or where collective property is exploited for the advantage of monopolists. The State then must appropriate it for society, establishing "its social right to collective wealth and to the means of producing or exchanging it." But public monopolies should not be operated by the old centralized Statism, but the utilization of collective property and monopolies should, so far as possible, be taken over by the departments, co-operative societies, by decentralized and autonomous groupings of producers, consumers and government officials. The C. G. T. also demanded measures against alcoholism, poor housing, and adequate protection by law for evils of unemployment and disability. Approval was expressed with regard to an unified system of social insurance at the cost of the State, and the necessity was emphasized for the extension and improvement of the laws relating to safety and health in all kinds of manual industries. Finally the minimum program of the C. G. T. declared for the abolition of all taxes and duties on the necessaries of life, as food, clothing, light and fuel.

Before briefly carrying forward the story of the industrial movement through the C. G. T. Congress of 1925, attention may be given to the program of reforms advocated by the Unified Socialist Party, *Parti Socialiste* (*Section Française de l'Internationale Ouvrière*). While this is not the place to give extended political history, it is well to point out certain post-war developments. In the Parliament elected in 1919 the Radical party, accustomed to power in the days before the war, found itself in the minority groups. The coalition of the Sacred Union (*Union Sacrée*), formed in 1914 as a war measure, continued through the

Viviani ministry,[4] the Briand, Ribot and Painlevé ministries, but during 1917, personal antagonism became too strong for coalition, and the Clemenceau ministry, which finished the war and negotiated the peace, contained no members of the Unified Socialist party. The election of 1919 was a war election, and the French people were still absorbed in the passion of that terrible era. The formation of the *Bloc National Républicain* marked the beginning of the bourgeois coalition against the Socialists. The time was opportune for the forces of conservatism to unite, so a coalition was formed by combining the middle groups, Right and Left Centre, into the *Bloc National.* This was a combination of all Republican groups (Moderate Republicans, Left-Centre, Moderate Democrats), against the Unified Socialists. The general election of 1919 gave a victory to this combination of parties, though the working of the new electoral law of 1919 did not serve to make the Unified Socialists feel that they had their just representation.[5] The victory of 1919 was a conservative triumph, and for five years the coalition held fairly well together. But in 1924 at the general election the National *bloc* was faced by an organized combination of the parties of the Left, a *bloc des Gauches.* In all but about a dozen departments they united their forces in a single list, the *Cartel des Gauches* label. Included in this combination were the Radicals and Radical-Socialists, the Republican Socialists, and the Unified Socialists, comprising the whole of the effective opposition to the National *bloc* except the extreme Left wing, the Communists as always uncompromising.

[4] Viviani in his *As We See It* (translation by T. R. Ybarra, London, 1923), gives a vivid account of the events leading up to the war and the French view. M. René Viviani formed his ministry June 13, 1914, and reorganized it August 26, 1914, as a coalition ministry, including prominent Socialist leaders. In October, 1915, M. Briand formed his fourth ministry, being followed in March, 1917, by the fifth ministry of M. Alexandre Ribot, which in turn gave way in September, 1917, to M. Paul Painlevé's ministry, which lasted only until November, 1917, when M. Clemenceau's ministry assumed power. His cabinet included no Unified Socialists, no Socialist-Republicans, no conservative Republicans, no monarchists. The Ribot and Painlevé ministries contained no Unified Socialists because they refused to enter.

[5] See *Appendix III* in Sait, *op. cit.,* for the text, and Munro, *The Governments of Europe,* chap. XXIV, and Barthélemy, *The Government of France,* chap. IV, for changes since 1919. Cf. Esmein, *op cit.,* pp. 223-273.

The National *bloc* were not closely united as in 1919, and their popular appeal to the country was not nearly so effective. In the old Chamber in April, 1924, the National *bloc* (counting Monarchists and Catholic Conservatives) could muster a maximum of about 370 votes, the Left *bloc* about 150 to 175 votes, with the Communists on the extreme Left. In the new Chamber of Deputies which met in 1924 the divisions according to the *communiqué* issued on May 14 by the Ministry of Interior were as follows: National *bloc,* including Conservatives, Republican Entente, Republicans of the Left, and Democrats of the Left, 264; Left *bloc,* including Radicals, Radical-Socialists, Republican Socialists, and Unified Socialists, 276; Communists, 29. The following table gives an approximate account of the Chamber representation in 1914, 1919, and 1924. It is notorious of course that party lists vary.

	1914	1919	1924
Republicans of Left	7	133	125
Radical Socialists	257	143	127
Republican Socialists	30	27	39
Unified Socialists	101	68	101
Communists	...	6	29
Progressists	36	133	130
Liberal Action	32	69	
Conservatives	27	31	26

It is interesting to note that though the United Socialist representation fell from 101 to 68 in the 12th Chamber of Deputies, 1919-1923, the party polled 300,000 more votes in 1919 than in 1914; the vote in 1914 being 1,400,000, and in 1919, 1,700,000. The Socialist vote in 1914 was 16 per cent of the total vote, in 1919 it was 25 per cent, and in 1924 the *Cartel des Gauches* gained control of the Chamber of Deputies. Dr. Shadwell well says that in the sum it was a general move toward Socialism, but rather of the Centre than the extreme Left;[6] however, the large gain by the Communists cannot be overlooked. In the present Chamber they have the same numerical strength that the British Labour party had in 1906.

There is no definite way to sketch what M. Herriot has termed the "topographical" position of French political parties. The

[6] *The Socialist Movement,* Vol. II, p. 107.

regular groups in the Chamber of Deputies have varied since 1919 to the present time from ten to seven, and there is always the likelihood that both the labels of factions and the number of groups will change. There are now three Socialist groups, the Unified Socialists, the Republican Socialists, and the Radical Socialists. The Unified Socialists are the most numerous, maintaining a policy of parliamentary isolation, and carrying on the orthodox formal program of socialist propaganda. The Republican Socialist group, in the Chamber brilliantly represented from the time it was formed in 1910, by leaders like Millerand, Viviani, Briand and Painlevé, is of a less radical stripe; and there is the Radical Socialist party, which holds, so M. Herriot points out, a position in French politics somewhat analogous to that of the Liberal party in England.[7] He adds with caution that ideas, like flowers and fruits, vary with the latitude. Lord Bryce broadly took French political groups as subdivisions of four types of political opinion—first, the Monarchists; secondly, the Moderate Republicans (sometimes called Liberals); thirdly, the Advanced Republicans, cherishing the traditions of the First Revolution; and lastly, the Socialists, whose professed aim is an economic reconstruction of society. The groups might from time to time dissolve, or unite, or re-form, but were sure to be different from year to year.[8]

Professor Sait in 1920 believed that the time was ripe for party consolidation, because the leaders of all parties spoke of the futility and incoherence of Parliament and its incapacity for any prolonged enterprise of reform.[9] Jean Jaurès gave utterance to an accepted fact that Parliament suffers from "its ambiguous parties and fluctuating program, its confused and hesitating majorities." It is held by Professor Munro that there has been a well-defined tendency for all the parties except the extremists (the *Action Française* and the Communists) to coalesce

[7] See his article in *Foreign Affairs,* Vol. II, No. 4 (June, 1924), pp. 558-570, "The Program of Liberal France." Professor Sait's discussion of French parties is very suggestive, *op. cit.,* chap. X., pp. 327-380; and see the valuable chapters in Buell, I-II-IV-VI; the *Annexes* to Zévaès' *Le Parti socialiste de 1904 à 1923,* and the programs given in the *Manuel* by MM. Carrère and Bourgin, are illustrative of recent events.

[8] *Modern Democracies,* Vol. I, pp. 252-253. Cf. Lowell, *Government and Parties in Continental Europe,* Vol. I, pp. 104-142.

[9] *Op. cit.,* Chap. X, a very clear statement.

into two opposing blocs.[10] The question of party groupings is important both in France and in England, and it can be seen in 1926 that in both countries a general election, perhaps several, must take place before there is any marked change in the present party divisions. It is certain that to-day there is not the cock-sure faith that parliamentarism has passed, as was stated when M. Millerand formed his ministry, and in England there is work yet for the Mother of Parliaments to do. There is a very interesting statement with regard to French social theory by M. Herriot who believes that there is a constructive program for a liberal France, a State recognizing duties. He speaks particularly of the attitude of the Radical party and the State, but his views may be taken as indicating a substantial body of French opinion.[11] With regard to social questions, the Radical party is firmly attached to the principle of private property. But it believes that the best way of supporting the principle lies in combating its abuse, a thought often emphasized by Mr. Lloyd George. A due regard for individual property rights, says M. Herriot, does not preclude assigning the State its share in national resources. An industrial State which was itself a producer would not find itself obliged to demand so much in taxes. He would be glad to see the State take control of the railways and of organizations which are indispensable to the country's well-being.

M. Herriot definitely points out his position with regard to the problem of the control of government by economic units.

It would be a very grave error to let political policy be ruled by autocratic economics—a tendency unhappily observable in many countries. We see at this very moment (1924) in France to-day

[10] *Governments of Europe*, pp. 502-503. "The French party system will veer more and more towards that of England and America. The groups may continue in name at any rate; but it is altogether likely that most of them will merge definitely and with an increasing degree of permanence into the two great blocs, Right and Left" (p. 510).

[11] The attack upon the Herriot Government by M. Millerand stirred bitter feelings in France. The chief opportunity was given Millerand at the banquet of the Ligue Républicaine Nationale in December, 1924, which was quickly met by a rejoinder from the executive committee of the Radical and the Socialist-Radical party. The committee declared he had violated his pledge as President, and therefore held up to the reprobation of republicans "the man who, after betraying all his doctrines and all his friends, has become to-day the banner-bearer of reaction, and is trying,

a group called the *Union des Intérêts Economiques* which has raised a considerable sum for fighting the parties of the Left. *The day when economics dominates politics will mark the end of democracy.* Democracy presupposes a moral and reasonable system of continuous arbitration between individual citizens. If economic interests should succeed in securing a dominion, Marx would be right. The democratic "balance" would then be destroyed, to give place to a permanent social conflict. The class spirit of the capitalists would then quite justify the class spirit of the workers. Materialism and economic fatalism would emerge triumphant over the idealism which is the foundation of democracy.[12]

Social life then is not static, it is dynamic. A democracy does not mean, therefore, an arrangement for reducing all men to the same level, but rather an order of things which, placing all citizens under the conditions most favourable to their development, permits the humblest to rise to the heights by his energy and by his virtue.

In this political survey it is well to make plain the fact that there is not the unity in the French Labour movement that characterizes the English Labour movement. The French Socialist party is in the main limited to political action, though many of its adherents staunchly support the General Confederation of Labour, the militant branch of the movement. Each branch of the Labour movement is independent or autonomous; that is, there is no stable tie connecting the trade union, socialist, and co-operative groups and they do not meet except in special definite cases to plan their policy. The British Labour party has been often pointed to by Frenchmen as an example for the French Labour movement, but unless the movement toward permanent blocs of the Right and the Left continues definitely there is little prospect of the Labour movement becoming strongly unified. Of course the vote of the Socialist party has nothing to do with the members' cards issued by the party organization, for in 1920 there were 160,000 members' cards issued, yet in the November, 1919, elections, nearly 2,000,000 votes were cast for socialist candidates.

in order to gratify his spite, to disturb the work of external peace and internal restoration." The Ligue Républicaine Nationale was nothing more than the Bloc National repudiated by the electors.

[12] *Op. cit.*, pp. 568-569, his italics.

Thus there is interest in the social and economic program of the Unified Socialists drawn up in April, 1919, not only because it is a comprehensive post-war statement but because it represented a compromise between the majority and minority elements, somewhat like the minimum program of the C. G. T. with which it has much in common.[13]

The war had divided the socialist ranks, and there was no Jaurès to lead the way toward unity. To the natural love of factional strife was added the stupid propaganda of the Bolshevists who seem to have no understanding of any country. But the Unified Socialists adopted in the Paris Congress of April, 1919, a program which in parts was as pontifical as any penned before 1914. The war did not lessen the pompous rhetoric of a *Programme d'Action.* The war, it declared, had proved on all essential points Socialist doctrine and had justified Socialist action. The war proved that socialism was not a utopia, but it was the sole solution for the overwhelming problems which the war produced. It also proved that the class struggle was the fundamental law of society, and there was no safety save in International Socialism. So the social revolution became the final aim of the socialist world. Such a revolution is nothing more or less than the "substitution of a collectivist régime of production, of exchange and of consumption for the present economic régime, founded on private property, an economic order which belongs to a last period of history. The social revolution would fulfil the work of the French Revolution by effacing the hereditary privileges of property and the hereditary servitudes of Labour.

The future would determine whether this revolution should be by the legal transmission of power under the pressure of universal suffrage, or by a movement of force. "The Socialist party does not confuse revolution with violence. . . . It ardently desires that its victory be accomplished in peace. . . . But the proletariat

[13] The following studies are illustrative of post-war French Socialism: Gabriel Hanotaux, *La démocratie et le travail* (1920); Edgard Milhaud, *La marche au socialisme* (1920), and his *Les fermiers generaux du rail* (1920), both dealing with "industrialized nationalization"; and of value is the volume by Paul Durand, *Les organismes sociaux officiels en France. L'état et le problème social,* III (1923), giving the official organizations dealing with social affairs, the ministries and bureaux with varying duties, etc.

cannot renounce any means of combat which will forward the conquest of political power; the form of the revolution will finally depend . . . upon the nature of the resistance opposed to it."

There was work to be done while awaiting the revolution, and the party was urged to continue its effort to reform present society so that the transition to a new social order would be less difficult. The political program,[14] standing for the complete organization of labour, asked for the revision of the Constitution so that it will be based on (1) universal suffrage of both sexes, (2) direct consultation of the people, (3) right of popular initiative, (4) integral proportional representation by regions, (5) a single legislative assembly, (6) administrative decentralization, (7) the incompatibility of the holding of legislative office by heads of public business enterprises affecting the State and the cost of living, (8) creation of economic Chambers to study and organize national and regional production, (9) reorganization on an industrial basis of all public services and State monopolies.

The problem of economic reconstruction, discussed in the program under this heading, allowed opportunity for indictment of a "capitalist war," and for the suggestion of a post-war policy for France. Asserting that Germany could not pay for the damages inflicted upon France the Socialist party urged that the difference be raised by (1) State seizure of excess profits, (2) conscription of fortunes, (3) a tax on capital and on increasing wealth, (4) the strict collection of income tax, (5) the establishment of new monopolies, (6) State participation in every sufficiently centralized industry, (7) the nationalization of the railways, and all other means of river and land transportation, of the great steel factories, of water power, of refineries, of banks, of insurance, and the manufacture of alcohol. This is seen to be a much more inclusive plan of government ownership than the plan which the Radical party under M. Herriot advocated.

Under the heading "Immediate Reforms" certain principles concerning the place of Labour in the State were outlined. The program first presented demands, concerning the organization of labour: (1) the suppression of unemployment by means of em-

[14] *Programme d'Action du Parti Socialiste,* published as a separate pamphlet by the party at its headquarters, 142 Rue Montmartre.

ployment bureaus, (2) increase of social insurance, (3) the protection of the health and security of workmen, (4) the reduction of hours of work, (5) the fixation of a minimum wage based on the normal cost of living, (6) the control of the importation of foreign goods and the equality of wages for the same, (7) the unreserved recognition of syndical liberty. Secondly the program made proposals concerning agricultural labour: (1) the extension of laws of industrial labour to agriculture, (2) alleviation of the tenant system, (3) co-operative organization of small proprietors and tenants for production, sale of products, purchase of seed, machinery, and insurance. The program dealt thirdly with problems of social welfare: (1) rigorous protection of mothers and children, by the medical control of children, the creation of nurseries, school sanatoriums, and open-air colonies, (2) the fusion of all education, free and compulsory, under national control, "permitting, by a series of selections and specialization, the utilization to the best end of the social interest, of the variety of individual aptitudes." Finally the program dealt with measures concerning the well-being of the workers: (1) the general expropriation of insanitary property, (2) the creation by the communes, with the aid of the State of a public housing service, (3) immediate use of public funds for construction of healthful lodgings, (4) the organization by the departments, the communes and of the co-operatives of a public food service, (5) the public organization of leisure, by sports, theatrical representations, art and culture.

The program that the Unified Socialist Party adopted was declared to be based upon international organization and peace. Modern civilization had created among all nations an inescapable solidarity, and the party demanded that the League of Nations be provided with sanctions capable of assuring its authority. Especially important must the economic functions of the League become in controlling an equitable distribution of raw materials. The program of 1920 closed with the following typical French Socialist rhetoric:

> There will be true equality only when the sole recognized distinction between men shall be that of their social value. True justice will exist only when the sole property recognized in men will be

that which arises from man's own labour; when the tithe levied by the employer upon the employee, by the proprietor of the soil upon the tenant, shall have disappeared with the form of property of which it is the direct expression. There will only be true harmony when the activity of each man shall be applied to his natural task and the commonwealth of the soil is exploited for the good of all.

The Socialist party therefore calls upon all labourers to assist by their efforts in this beneficent evolution of history. It calls upon them to assist in the work of social regeneration which is its end and object. The general interests of the nations, and those of entire civilization, are indissolubly linked with our own. Heirs to the benefit of every effort of organization which has developed in the world, we must ourselves realize a program, the accomplishment of which a fallen bourgeoisie and a covetous capitalism would not even dare to attempt.

The policy of reformism was continued in the Congress held at Strasbourg in February, 1920. Violence was repudiated, and the attitude of the party with regard to a capital levy, State monopolies for the production of luxuries, financial partnership of the State in all sufficiently centralized enterprises, socialization of railways, shipping and mines, waterpower, banking and insurance was redefined in the resolution dealing with the *politique intérieure*.[15] But at this time the influence of the Red International at Moscow was plainly seen, and there was every reason to expect another disruption in the French Socialist party. At the Strasbourg Congress three views were represented with regard to the international policy of French socialism.[16] First, the view of the old majority that membership should be retained in the Berne Internationale; the second view, held by the new majority, under Jean Longuet, for adhesion to the old Internationale provided that it moved toward the Left; and the third view, that of the advanced group who were for adhesion to the Third Internationale. By a vote on an indecisive motion the old majority

[15] Cf. *Compte Rendu 17e Congrès National,* Strasbourg, 1920, pp. 562-564.

[16] *Compte Rendu, 17e Congrès National,* Strasbourg, 1920, pp. 564-567, for resolution on international policy. The remarks and speeches of Cachin, Frossard, Longuet, Loriot, Renaudel, Lefebvre, and others are indexed fully in the Congress *Compte Rendu.* The Communists out-talked the Congress by good measure.

won out by 894 against 757, yet 270 votes were cast at the Strasbourg Congress for the Loriot motion for adhesion to the Third Internationale. Between the Strasbourg Congress in February and the Tours Congress in December, 1920, the Bolshevists won over a majority of the party. The faction under the leadership of Cachin and Frossard, who had gone to Moscow in 1920, won out in the Tours Congress when they moved a resolution in favour of the Red Internationale, which was carried by 3,208 votes to 1,022.[17] This Congress marked the formation of the French Communist party, *Parti socialiste, Section française de l'Internationale communiste.* Since that date the Communist party and the Unified Socialist party have had about the same number of adherents. The Communist party is of course affiliated with the Red Internationale, the Socialist party with the Hamburg International (L. S. I.). In the Chamber of Deputies the Unified Socialist deputies far outnumber the Communist deputies, the number being 101 and 29 respectively in 1926. The Cachin-Frossard resolution declared for the direction of the proletariat of the world by the Communist Internationale, and in a series of *Thèses* set forth the militant French labour theory. This elaboration in 1920 gave no new interpretation to the theory of the dictatorship of the proletariat, the absolute denial of the State as anything but a servant of the dominant class, and Parliament as an essential bourgeois machine of oppression, incompatible with the proletarian régime, *"la République des Conseils de travailleurs."* The syndicate was the first necessity of working class organization, the basis of the militant movement which would make real the social revolution. But even to the Communist party peace was the first essential of carrying out a policy of international solidarity, and so the first duty of the proletariat was to force the bourgeois governments of the world to make peace with the United Republic of the Russian Soviets. This naturally led to a clear statement that the international policy of the proletariat was to be based on the policy of the Communist Internationale. It was not sufficient to give accord to the general principles of Marxist socialism, but the authority of the practical revolutionists of Moscow must be the guide in laying down the tactics for prole-

[17] *Compte Rendu, 18e Congrès National,* 1920, Tours, pp. 563-595, for resolutions of this Congress.

tarian revolt. Experience had shown that the collaboration of communists and reformists was incompatible with revolutionary action.

The policy of participation in the Government has been steadfastly rejected by the Socialist party, and there seems little prospect of change in the immediate future. Immediately after the decisive defeat inflicted on M. Poincaré and the Bloc National by the Cartel des Gauches in 1924, the Socialist party decided not to enter the Government, but to support M. Herriot's Socialist-Radical Cabinet. M. Herriot, in return, undertook to push a program which included the abolition of "decree-laws," a general amnesty, reinstatement of the railwaymen who had been dismissed for striking, the abolition of the Vatican Embassy, the strict enforcement of the Separation Law with regard to religious associations, certain important measures of fiscal reform and social insurance, and the reduction of the period of military service to one year.

The Grenoble Socialist Congress of February, 1925, was called upon to review the results of the eight months of co-operation with the Government, and, secondly, to decide whether it was to be continued or not. The leaders had been severely criticized for serving the Government too well, but it was also recognized that leaders like MM. Léon Blum, Renaudel, and Compère-Morel had carried through a good part of the program of the Socialist party. This was instanced in the Wheat Control Bill which passed the Chamber of Deputies, and in the promise of M. Herriot to push on with the new Military Law and social insurance measures. But the Left Wing were anxious to prove that the party was not getting what it should in return for their support of the Government, and to make clear what everyone knew, that the policy of the Government was not the policy of the Socialist party. M. Léon Blum, the leader of the party, made the chief speech of defence of the policy of co-operation. To those who criticized the lack of differentiation between the Socialists' policy and that of the Government he replied that the more successful their policy was, the less it showed, because that meant that the Government had adopted it. He deprecated, however, being represented as the "Eminence grise" of the Government, and declared that whole weeks sometimes passed without his ever seeing M.

Herriot in private. A sharp departure from the policy of support, now that they had started it and accustomed the working classes to it, would be dangerous, because they would necessarily leave a mass of stragglers and baggage behind. He doubted whether the British Labour Party's tactics of crushing Liberalism between the reactionary and Labour groups would succeed in France. M. Blum asked for a unanimous vote. He was followed by M. Jean Longuet, Karl Marx's grandson, who bitterly attacked M. Herriot's policy with regard to foreign affairs, especially toward Germany, and called for a more active and separate Socialist propaganda.

The vote of the Congress of Grenoble was in favour of the continued support of the Herriot Government. The majority resolution by which the Socialist Congress conveyed its decision to support the Government marked the conditions of the support significantly. The resolution insisted on the connection of the party with its origins. It "does not give up its traditional and necessary position as a class party"; and the Parliamentary group was recommended to be "particularly scrupulous on all questions with regard to which the party is in the position of a trustee for the Internationale." The attitude of the party toward the practical policy of the Government left no doubt that in matters of social policy the Government was to be pressed, as it had always been, but more insistently. Measures against the high cost of living, the army reorganization scheme, and the National Insurance Bill were part of the program of "effective action" which M. Renaudel had included in the resolution. The resolution meant that the party must be the author or instigator of a strong social policy, or it cannot live. Mention of the more revolutionary objects toward which some sections of the party lean were avoided.

The Grenoble Congress implied that M. Herriot would have difficulties ahead in both foreign and domestic affairs. His Government was to fall because the Chamber of Deputies with growing impatience seemed unwilling to allow strong executive policy, and the Socialist party has done nothing to strengthen the cause of constitutional government in France by a helpful, vigorous policy of parliamentary co-operation. The fall of M. Briand's last Government (March, 1926) indicates again a fatal weakness in French politics—the failure of Parliament to share responsibility in governing at a time when France sorely needs a strong directing power. The truth of Professor Sait's remark on France is apt, that democratic government has suffered enough already from the incompetence of representative assemblies, and from their perverse hostility to the growth of a stable authority in the executive.

That French Socialism is hopelessly confused needs hardly be suggested, and it is well now to end this chapter on the post-war Labour movement with a survey of the industrial labour movement. It is well known that the most distinctive feature of the French Labour movement is Syndicalism, represented in the *Confédération Générale du Travail.* In 1914, the C. G. T. had approximately 500,000 members; while by 1920 the membership was given at 2,000,000. The C. G. T. Congress of 1919 was held at Lyons, in which over 2,000 syndicates, representing more than 2,000,000 members, took part. This Congress forms one of the most important landmarks in the French Syndicalist movement, not only because the working class in France had never before been represented in such large numbers at any Labour Congress, but also because the principles of modern Syndicalism were laid down in a comprehensive way. This Congress declared the aim of Labour to be complete supremacy, "the other factors of society are only subordinate or parasitic." Syndicalists claimed the whole political as well as economic power of society. They could not use the *bourgeois* State or adopt parliamentary methods; but they aimed at the control of society by Labour because economic not political conditions were the fundamental concern of men. They demanded the socialization of transport, mines, water-power, and banks, as the Socialists did. But the State was not to be the agent of control, but rather the independent groups of workers, wherein producers as well as consumers would be represented.

The General Confederation of Labour met in 1920 at Orleans, and here again the discussion of the congress revolved about the methods and policies of the organization as interpreted by the "moderate" and the "extremist" elements. M. Jouhaux led the moderates, and MM. Frossard and Cachin, editor of *L'Humanité* led the extremists. This congress, in the vote on the resolutions, gave a decided vote for the moderates, the majority resolution receiving 1,479 votes against 602 for that of the minority group. The resolution of the majority group reaffirmed the Amiens Charter, which holds that their revolutionary aim is "more than ever incompatible with existing institutions, with capitalism and its political expression." The immediate aims of the C. G. T. were stated to include control of commerce and industry and the industrialized nationalization of vital industries. The work of the International Labour Office in its endeavour to secure legislation for the protection of the worker was indorsed. The resolution further expressed the indignation of the congress against the French Government, stating that it "is the servile tool of reaction all over the world." Complete solidarity with the Russian revolution was voiced and the need for continual agitation for the total restoration of peace, the independence of the Soviet Republic, and free self-government in Russia. The closing paragraph of the majority resolution was as follows: "For these reasons the congress declares that the constitutional basis of the C. G. T., the principles of autonomy which it has hitherto maintained, and its methods of action, are in strict accordance with the present needs of the struggle, with the improvements to be realized and with the revolutionary powers to be attained. The C. G. T. proclaims once more before the whole world its ideal of economic liberation by the abolition of the wage system."

The 1920 congress attracted a great deal of attention, partly due to the disastrous general strike in 1920, called by the Left Wing, which completely failed, and partly because the Government had watched closely the leaders of the Labour movement. The comment of *Le Temps* on the 1920 congress is an interesting indication of post-war thought.[18]

In spite of the victory of Longuet and his branch of the party, the C. G. T. remains to-day, as it was yesterday, a formidable organization for social war. Furthermore, the entire program of syndical demands is there to show that the C. G. T. will renounce nothing of its revolutionary ideals; the nationalization of essential industries and means of exchange, the control by workingmen of industry and commerce so as to wrest from employers

[18] See the able article in the *U. S. Monthly Labour Review,* Vol. XII, No. 2 (February, 1921), by Anice L. Whitney, in which periodical literature is fully used.

their authority, the suppression of salaries, and complete solidarity with the Russian revolution—such are the essential points of a program which is considered as a thing to be put into immediate realization. It is very difficult to understand why after all Moscow repudiates the C. G. T. since the latter is striving by its own means, which are not the least dangerous, to prepare the way for the brutal realization of the dictatorship of the proletariat.

L'Humanité, the Communist daily, rejoiced that the highest official of the Socialist party, M. Frossard, not only spoke there but spoke in the name of the revolutionary minority, showing, the paper said, that in the future "revolutionary socialism will refuse to efface itself before 'reformist' trade-unionism."

The annual congress of the C. G. T. met in July, 1921, at Lille, the date being advanced from September, as the confederal bureau announced, because the situation within the labour organizations brought about by Bolshevist propaganda had to be considered, for united syndical action had become impossible. The opponents on the outside said that the confederal bureau merely wanted to bring about the immediate separation of the two parties within the C. G. T. The majority resolution reaffirmed the general principles laid down in the Amiens Charter, which all succeeding congresses had passed and which maintained that syndicalist action had for its purpose the abolishing of all classes, abolition of the wage system, and control by the workers of social activity. The minimum program of the C. G. T. therefore was stated to be reconstruction of the devastated regions, industrialized nationalization of the great public utilities, social insurance, labour control, and resistance to efforts of employers to reduce wages and increase hours of labour conformably to the Charter of Amiens which states that syndicalism ought to work for the increased well-being of the workers by the realization of immediate improvement in their condition. The adherence of the C. G. T. to the Amsterdam Internationale was maintained.

The "revolutionary" resolution of the minority party stated that it was essential that the C. G. T. should return to the principle of revolutionary syndicalism which was expected of it by the union members as well as by the militants. The resolution quoted the Amiens Charter, indorsing direct action as a means for bringing about immediate betterment of workers while stating that the ultimate aim is capitalist expropriation, and urged that the Congress of Lille should go on record as condemning collaboration of classes, stating that in the pre-revolutionary period the principal rôle of syndicalism is to present consistent opposition to the forces of capitalism. The resolution further stated that since syndicalism is by its origin, its character, and its ideals a revolutionary force it ought to represent "the maximum effort of the labour unions to destroy the capitalist régime and to realize the proletarian revolution." The resolution maintained that the C. G. T. should withdraw from the Amsterdam Internationale and give its adherence to the Red Trade Union International.

The majority resolution passed by a vote of 1,572 against 1,325 votes for the minority resolution. This congress showed that there was a decided swing to the Left in revolutionary sentiment. It was seen that a break must come in the C. G. T., and when in September, 1921, the National Committee of the C. G. T. expelled all members who were found guilty of working for the disintegration of the Syndicalist movement, the way was wide open for the revolt of the Left wing. Accordingly a congress of the extremists was held in Paris, December 22nd to 24th, 1921, at which time the National Committee of the C. G. T. was condemned, and a number of important syndicalists and Federations of syndicates declared themselves independent. In February, 1922, the extremists formed a new party under the name of the *Confédération Générale du Travail Unitaire* (C. G. T. U.) with a membership of 350,000. Thus the industrial movement was divided in the same way as the Socialist parties.[19]

The first general meeting of the C. G. T. since the Lille Congress of 1921 was held in Paris, January 30-February 2, 1923. This congress was attended by over 700 delegates, representing 1,423 unions, 25 federations, and 34 departmental unions. The question of labour unity, which had agitated the ranks of labour

[19] M. Jules Sageret in his *La doctrine du syndicalisme intellectuel* (1921), says that the only concrete reality attached to the word progress, is the progress of human activity so prodigiously developed by the economic revolution, and thus is it important to note that the C. G. T., in spite of its divisions, is more cohesive than the Socialist Party. His thesis is that the foundations are more sound to-day than before, its logic for social organization inevitable (pp. 30-36).

since the extremists in the Confederation seceded in December, 1921, forming the C. G. T. U., came up before the congress. A letter from the executive committee of the C. G. T. U. expressed the desire of this organization for syndical unity and unity of action. The letter proposed that a confederal congress composed of delegates from the two organizations should be called for the purpose of considering a program of national and international action. While waiting for the actual co-ordination of the syndical organizations the committee of the C. G. T. U. advocated common action against the menace of war by all syndical organizations favouring the class struggle. The committee to which this proposition was referred for consideration decided upon a categorical refusal of the demand for unity upon the basis of the C. G. T. U. proposals because of their adherence to the Moscow Internationale. The committee believed, however, that it was possible to secure fundamental unity within regularly confederated syndicates, the syndicates retaining all their rights on the condition that the decisions of the national congress should be respected. After long debate the congress adopted a resolution in practical agreement with the committee, basing its refusal to call a joint meeting of the two organizations on the fact that since the C. G. T. was the central organization of the labour movement any steps toward unification should take place within the C. G. T. itself. The problem of a Left wing industrial movement has brought both the French and the English Labour movements some of the hardest questions of policy since the armistice.

At this Paris congress the questions of economic policy were put in the form of committee resolutions, contrary to the French custom. The questions were social insurance, family allowances, the tax upon wages, trade union rights of civil employees, nationalization and monopolies, labour control in industry, and the eight hour day.

The committee on the eight hour day presented a unanimous report which the congress was asked to adopt without discussion. The resolution urged the united action of all syndicates to oppose efforts to abolish the eight hour day, which, it stated, had been openly attacked, and was in danger of being set aside for a long period of time unless the working class should intensify by every means the propaganda in favour of it. As one means of accomplishing this result workers everywhere were urged to stop work whenever attempts against it were imposed. An amendment insisting that the eight hour day fulfils all the needs of national and international production was accepted and the resolution was adopted unanimously.

The congress also went on record as opposed to the transfer of State monopolies such as transportation services, posts, telegraphs and telephones, arsenals, etc., to private industry, and declared for the policy of "industrialized nationalization," which was first advocated by the economic council of the C. G. T. shortly after the formation of the council in 1920. It was decided to intensify the campaign for nationalization and to endeavour to obtain financial control of management immediately in all public services in order that modern methods of accounting might be instituted and political influence eliminated. A resolution was also introduced protesting against Government refusal to recognize the right of Government employees to belong to trade unions.

The problem of placement of workers was declared by the congress to be intimately connected with that of foreign labour and that no solution of the latter problem could be expected without a methodical and rational organization of the French labour market. The establishment of a system of closely associated employment offices under a national bureau was advocated, these offices to be under the direction of persons qualified in the scientific placement of workers.

Since the war the custom of paying family allowances has grown rapidly in France and a special study of the question has been carried out by the C. G. T. The 1923 congress considered at length this question, and went on record as opposed to the practice of paying family allowances on the ground that the extra allowance affects the basic wage and gives the employer an unfair advantage. In spite of this fact, however, the C. G. T. believes that while the nation should be concerned with childhood and the family, this should properly be the concern of society and not of the employer. To secure this protection to the family a scheme of social insurance covering the allowances for and care of children was outlined, to which the employers should be compelled to contribute but which should be managed by official committees composed of representatives of the different interests.

The congress advocated in the matter of workers' control, labour and syndical direction of hiring and firing; syndical agreements concerning wages, hours of labour, discipline, and all other questions relating to the industry or trade concerned; the application of social laws and the rights of labour which have been juridically established by usage. The congress favoured a social insurance system which would provide old age, sickness, invalidity, and maternity insurance, all of which are in the Government proposal, and it also considered that unemployment insurance should be included. It was proposed that social insurance should be one of the principal claims of the working class and that constant propaganda should be carried out until the law was passed. A comprehensive system of apprenticeship was drawn up providing for the extension of compulsory school attendance to 14 years of age, modification of the primary education program and the subjects of study relating to industry, agriculture and commerce.[20]

Such a program would strike the English worker as on the whole a very conservative one, and he would not find much opposition from the employers in directly putting into effect such a social plan. It is far from being the well-rounded industrial program of the British Labour movement, and it is remarkable that meaningless phrases about the "social revolution" should so clutter up the record of French congresses. But it is a hopeful sign that the French Labour movement is facing the problems of industry and labour with a more determined will to understand them, and is working out schemes of reform and of control. This spirit is certainly indicated in the national congress of the C. G. T. held at Paris, August 26-30, 1925. The congress was attended by 800 delegates, representing 1,728 unions, 36 federations, and 85 departmental unions. The program of the congress called for the consideration of the following questions: Wages, covering methods of payment, bonuses, gratuities, family allowances, etc.; social laws, including social insurance, the eight hour day, workmen's compensation, and labour inspection; foreign labour in

[20] Cf. *L'Apprentissage. Examen général des divers problèmes posés par l'apprentissage du point de vue de l'intérêt de la classe ouvrière* (Paris, 1924). In this a short account of the work of the *chambres de metiers,* organized by the Chambers of Commerce, and trade councils is given.

France; a unified school system; workers' control; vacations with pay; and various questions relating to trade union organization.

The question was once again put forward of union with the extremists in the C. G. T. Unitaire. Letters from the executive committee of the C. G. T. U. which were read to the congress urged the holding of a joint conference for the purpose of bringing about the union of the two organizations. The debate upon the question brought out no new material, and the committee to which the proposition for an interfederal congress was referred offered a resolution stating that the only way that trade union unity could be achieved was through the return of the communist branch of the C. G. T., that the adherence of this branch to the Moscow Internationale had subordinated the trade union movement to a political party and that there was as yet no evidence that the C. G. T. U. had abandoned its attempt to destroy the labour movement. This resolution received a majority of the votes cast.

The economic program adopted by committee resolutions at the 1925 congress differs very little from that outlined at the Congress at Lille in 1923. The report of the committee on vacations with pay for workers, was unanimously adopted, and this report stated the paid vacations were absolutely indispensable for the physical and moral health of all workers. A resolution relative to compensation for industrial accidents and occupational diseases advocated the following amendments to the present law: Extension of the law to cover all wage earners; no exemption as at present for accidents due to natural forces or other causes; increases in compensation for serious accidents and in the payments made to orphans and other heirs in case of death; vocational re-education by the insurer, of workers obliged to change their occupation as a result of accident; application of the law to all industrial diseases instead of, as at present, to certain diseases caused by lead and mercury poisoning. Special consideration was also demanded for workers who had suffered industrial injury before the law went into effect and for the injured of the devastated or occupied sections of the country whose compensation had been computed on a lower wage scale. In the matter of social insurance the congress advocated extension of compulsory insurance to all wage earners without regard to the amount of their wages, elimination of payment of premiums by those earning small wages, establishment of a minimum pension corresponding to the cost of living for the transition period before the law becomes fully effective, continuation of payments to those pensioned because of old age, and other recommendations relative to the administration of the pension funds. The congress also voted for the protection of women and children through better medical and surgical care and payment of maternity and nursing allowances.

With regard to education in France it has been often pointed out that the nation achieved a high degree of civilization at an early date, and it harbours institutions bearing the imprint of every sort of régime. Monarchical creations like the Collège de France stand cheek by jowl with Revolutionary creations such as the Ecole Normale Supérieure and with creations of the Third Republic like the Universities. It is highly important in France to reorganize the school system. The 1925 congress gave considerable attention to the question of workers' education, and it considered that the present school system was inadequate for the needs of the children of the workers. An entire reorganization of the educational system so that children of labouring people would have an opportunity to secure a higher education and so that there would be a general leveling up of the scale of culture of the entire working class was recommended. Education can make for justice in a democracy, and no better security against class warfare can be had than a trained citizenship, but for too long education has been a class institution.

France has had a hard struggle since the war to maintain a high standard of living, and the condition of the franc has often imperiled the savings of thrifty folk and has made the cost of living a daily political problem. The congress of 1925 declared that, although no fixed rule should be established in regard to wages, the lowest rates of the least skilled workers should amount to a sum sufficient to satisfy all the needs of a family living in a civilized society. This minimum wage should be established by the Economic Labour Council and by the regional councils, and a system should be established by which wages generally should be adjusted to the changes in the cost of living. The congress again set forth the principle, always endorsed by the C. G. T., of equal pay for men and women for equal work.

Other resolutions passed by the congress included one relating to the labour inspection service which advocated the appointment of labour delegates designated by the unions to report infractions of rules by employers, more rigid application of the eight hour law, and establishment of labour and syndical control in the matter of hiring and firing, in syndical agreements affecting wages, hours of labour, discipline, and all other questions relating to the industry or trade, and in the application of social laws and labour rights which have been juridically established by usage.

The industrial program outlined above indicates substantial growth in the Labour movement of France.[21] It is reformistic and is dependent in a good part upon the action of Parliament. But the contradiction of the syndicalist philosophy of distrust of the State and the formation of a list of immediate reforms through parliamentary action is not at all disconcerting to the average syndicalist. What this distrust of the State suggests with regard to the problem of constitutional morality is discussed in the final chapter which follows, in which an attempt is made to summarize some of the ideals of social justice for the individual and for the community. At this time there is abundant reason for hope that the syndicalist movement will contribute to the development of ideals of the good life, and that the industrial movement will again freshen the whole outlook of social politics. There is less stupidity to-day than ever before in the Labour movement of France, simply because problems are being attacked honestly on the plane where the workingman lives. That ideals

[21] Number and membership of employers' and workers' organizations in France, January 1, 1923, 1924, and 1925.

	January 1, 1923		January 1, 1924		January 1, 1925	
Organization	Number	Members	Number	Members	Number	Members
Employers'	5,970	423,732	6,210	434,833	6,596	496,360
Workers'	6,540	1,809,052	6,597	1,804,912	7,072	1,846,047
Mixed (employers' and workers')	193	32,458	194	32,161	196	32,331
Agricultural	8,260	1,187,587	8,633	1,204,946	9,041	1,222,534
Total	20,963	3,452,829	21,634	3,476,852	22,905	3,597,272

Information is from the *Bulletin du Ministère du Travail et de l'Hygiène,* January-March, 1925, July-September, 1925, and quoted in the *U. S. Monthly Labor Review,* November, 1925, and January, 1926.

of workers' control are clearer than they were in 1900 and 1914 is due to the fact that regard for human life has taken on a new meaning. The challenge of ideals of the good life has met industry at every hand, and more men are determined that human welfare must be above all else the concern of industry and of trade and of government. Writing just before the days of 1914 one competent critic of French industrial history saw that the process of social readjustment which was going on all over the world would lead in France to a more or less catastrophic collision of the discordant elements which her political and economic history had brought into existence.[22] That process goes on to-day in 1926. It is a process which believers in democracy are hopeful is making for progress. Men who see in France of to-day no hope of stable government, no respite from the charnel house of industrial discord, forget how slowly democracy learns its best lessons. Reaction, revolution, and violence seem the interminably tedious story of peoples. So to-day the short cut of violence is attractive to many. But there are many, many more who take their stand in defence of the doctrine of evolution and, through evolution, of progress. It is plain, as M. Herriot has stated, that this sort of wisdom is sadly lacking in the allurement of pretty nonsense. "Man, we know very well, and especially the Latin type, orients himself above all by shibboleths. Possibly error is actually more attractive than truth. But that is no reason for surrendering to it."[23] And then M. Herriot expresses the hope, shared by all who love France, that athwart all varieties and shades of opinions men will hold firm to the pursuit of the democratic tradition of France, that France will shine, not by the power of her arms but by the nobility of her ideal, and that she will keep her traditional aspect of kindness, of justice, and of generosity.

[22] Levine, *op. cit.*, p. 222. [23] *Op. cit.*, 570.

CHAPTER XIII.

CONCLUSION

PART I

Social Justice and the Individual

THE preceding chapters have indicated some of the main criticism of the social system of England and France in this century. This criticism, it has been seen, brought about an organized effort to maintain better standards of life for the people, an effort in which the State has taken a leading part. Both the attitude of the State and the program of groups within the State have shown that there has been a growing insistence on a juster distribution of the good things of life. With this demand there has come a sounder criticism of the means necessary to attain the desired end. The result has been that the ideal of a good community has become more real as the conditions which make it possible have been sought by more people. The social ideal has not made less the individual duty in helping to realize a good society, but the duty of the individual has become a more conscious factor in the welfare of the community at the same time that his capacity for sharing a great ideal of human good has become more evident. He has demanded from the institutions which he has used and created more of service to the common good. The individual has not become lost in the institution. But, in fact, the good citizen to-day has a larger responsibility for a good order of society than ever before, simply because there is more of freedom for purposive individual effort directed toward the common good of all. Social progress has helped to free good men for better service to their fellowmen, because the rights of the individual have been increasingly protected at the same time that the ideal of the highest good for all has been given a more definite meaning in legislation. This is one of the encouraging signs that democracy has the creative power to overcome besetting difficulties, for the rendering of better service by men anxious to aid their generation is a proof that the will for a good society is an enduring factor making for social justice. This will for a good society has set men to thinking of the institutions about them and through which they express their will.

Criticism of the social and economic system in modern democracies has greatly helped in defining the problem of politics. The problem cannot be formally or definitely put, yet there is much to be gained from the fresh contributions made by competent students of public life on the times in which they live and work. There is a better understanding to-day of what democracy in the West is, because there has been some effort to find out what democracy in the West wants. Oftentimes the problem for some of the ethical basis of the State has made the practical contribution of bringing light to bear on the question of sound individual idealism with regard to group loyalties. And yet again, some by the effort to form an international organization have been directed to the closer study of community good will. Thus by strange ways are men taught lessons in politics. The State itself, since becoming what Bryce called "an engine of reform," has been to a school of politics which has not as yet very clearly set forth its philosophy.

The constant criticism of social institutions (definitely set out in this study in the chapters on legislation), institutions which daily affect their lives, is one of the surest proofs of the capacity of men for political society. It makes it possible to formulate a freely creative conception of the State. It is also a test of the will of men to change the form of old institutions which do not fit their needs, and of their desire that new ones shall be developed which are more in accord with their aspirations. This is to-day, so Mr. Hobson believes, the attitude of most politically-minded persons in the Western World toward the State and its government; and that while the State and the Government are thought to be a very disagreeable necessity, they are more necessary than ever before.[1] Thus the problem

is one of envisaging the State as a creative power using its distinctively political faculties to help man as skillfully as possible in

[1] See the *Contemporary Review,* October, 1925, for Mr. J. A. Hobson's article, "The Transformation of Politics," a study of Mr. Laski's book.

making the best of his life in the material and moral environment in which he finds himself, and to help in adapting that environment to the better achievement of his purposes.

The outstanding reason for belief in the political capacity of men is that they have constantly sought to re-define what justice is in their daily life of work and in the social control of their institutions. The exercise of this capacity for justice is the source of happiness for good men, and it is the foundation of order in the State. As they have aimed for justice they have found their duty as citizens. And this aim has unified the functions of political democracy as it has tended to bring all good men toward a standard of excellence in service for the public weal. Justice as a social ideal directing legislation and informing administration has done more than all else to make clear just what the function of law is in modern society. The popular sanction has been impressive whenever men have felt justice at stake.

The capacity for using and enjoying the freedom which political communities have made possible has joined the life of the citizen with that of the State, giving him an opportunity of fulfilling at its best his own life at the same time that a common destiny is being worked out for all. That at times he has felt a conflict of loyalties which might threaten allegiance to the most inclusive society of which he is a member—the State,—has broadly served to lift the issues of lesser relationships to a higher level. Thus the expanding idea of political action and the capacity of men to change political organization have continually helped to interpret a loyalty to the State which has been expressed in a keener sense of individual duty and in a wider vision of the possibilities of collective action. As political power has become less concentrated the ideals of human solidarity have had more significance because they have been shared by more people. The growth of a common purpose in which more men are eager to add their part has expressed this fact, and the moral growth of the purpose of the State is shown by the fact that it can command the highest service from those who believe its will to be for the good. The individual that so believes will go outside his own interests for the sake of common interests.[2]

[2] Professor Bosanquet wrote that "the basis of State regulation is the emergence of aspects of common interest in the system of particular in-

Thus by the example of the good citizen the minimum standards which society can enforce are gradually raised, and the aims which go to create a common purpose become sanctioned by an actively approving political community which has learned its best lessons from individuals whose ideals go far beyond the ordinary *minima* of social conduct. The beneficial effect of these ideals is to move forward the whole limits of moral conduct for the community. The good citizen is thus the builder of the good society, which in turn makes possible for him a fuller freedom of life.[3]

Thus is joined that idea of social good, which for all democratic government is a principle of legislative action, and which, as Mr. Hobson has suggested, is fundamental for most modern thinkers, and the ideal of individual good. Together these two ideas form the major problem of politics: How the common good is to be served by making the highest individual excellence possible. Because this good is social the major burden is upon politics to make its implications plain. After you have defined the needs of the individual as an "economic man" there is the necessity of understanding him as a citizen, and it is here that the larger duty of politics is most felt. The good life to be sure is an economic ideal, and too it is an ideal which demands the good political society for its fulfillment. Thus when the relations of the State and the individual are considered there is an ideal of the good society and there is the ideal of the good individual. Social good is the comprehensive thing that is in mind. But what is it that makes for social good in this world? For Mr. Laski there is no directly operative social or "general" will making for this good. The doctrine of Rousseau, of Hegel, of Green and Bosanquet, he will have nothing of. The social good consists in and emanates from the co-operative wills of individuals, each finding his own good in the common service.[4] He seeks to associate the intelligence and

terests" (*The Philosophical Theory of the State,* 1st ed. 1899, 3rd ed. 1920, p. 257).

[3] In this sense M. Hauriou says that "the State is an organisation which moves toward personification" (p. xiii), and the progress of civilisation is the development of a tradition which holds that "society is a moral fact, the essential problem is that of good and evil" (*Principes de droit public,* pp. xxii-xxiii). The later quotation is the thesis of his *Science sociale traditionnelle* (1896).

[4] In his recent study, *A Grammar of Politics* (1925), Mr. Laski has given a most suggestive treatment in his first chapter on the purpose of social

will of as many active-minded men and women as possible in the processes of political and industrial government. This association cannot be made by the mere process of choosing representatives. Neither can it require that ordinary citizens or workers shall decide issues which involve expert knowledge which lies outside their experience. If self-government is to be real, it must imply some fairly regular participation in the activities that constitute government, whether in politics or industry. At present, the so-called democracy which the citizens of the Western nations are supposed to possess, says Hobson, is almost as unreal as that which capitalism denies to them as workers. The nature and causes of its unreality are obvious. In order to be a real citizen in a community two things are necessary, knowledge and some active functions within each. A great centralized machinery of government, concentrating initiative and power both legislative and executive, leaves to the ordinary citizen no function but that of empty consent.[5]

The problems of democracy have led the most hopeful of political scientists to doubt whether ideal justice can be completely established in the sovereign States of modern times. But there can be small ground for dispute in what Professor Holcombe gives as his conclusion about the ideal commonwealth,[6] that "those who seek the fullest and most complete justice must demand a commonwealth organized on a far broader basis than the contemporary capitalistic and nationalistic States." Their aspirations, he believes, were most adequately voiced by Woodrow Wilson before the tomb of Washington at Mt. Vernon on July 4, 1918, when he said: "What we seek is the reign of law, based upon the consent of the governed and sustained by the organized opinion of mankind."

organization (pp. 15-35). To him what we call the State is "simply a source of ultimate reference which makes a decision upon grounds that it deems adequate" (p. 34). Further, "the power of government is the right of government in the degree to which it is exercised for the end of social good" (p. 36). This means "that the quality of any State will depend upon the degree to which men consciously seek to give the State the import of the meaning they find in their lives" (p. 37). So, "the State is thus a fellowship of men aiming at the enrichment of the common life" (p. 37).

[5] Hobson, *op. cit.*

[6] Arthur N. Holcombe, *The Foundations of the Modern Commonwealth* (1923), p. 478. Chapters VI and VII on "Justice" and "Liberty" are rich in suggestion.

I

So with regard to the individual social justice is a positive ideal, providing both the inspiration and the method of progress toward security. Social justice considers collective action as an achievement of common purpose, which implies individual action at its best; for collective action should always be a wise means of largely increasing individual freedom. The good society for the individual is thus impossible without a collective good will. It is then apparent that the ideal of the common good is really the development of a belief in the capacity of the individual and the acceptance by the community of finer values for a judgment of human nature. Thus a basis for believing in the principles of social justice is afforded by the changed attitude toward the individual and his worth. Society had to be better for the better individual; and the most prosaic of legislation in this century has contained revolutionary doctrines with regard to the ordinary citizen and his importance. Professor Muirhead has written [7] that even in England, while the legal and political reforms of the early nineteenth century may seem to have been inspired by utilitarian ideas, it may well be doubted whether the underlying principle of the social movement which began toward the middle of the century, and is the most characteristic feature of the present time, does not owe more to the Kantian principle of the sacredness of humanity in each than to the Benthamite doctrine that each was to count as one, and nobody as more than one.

This changed attitude toward human nature has given a new meaning to justice. The claims of citizenship have been more broadly interpreted, and the State has put great confidence in the loyalty of good men who share with the large community the purpose of community well-being. Social justice, enlarging the whole concept of welfare as the aim of the State, gives first place to the ethical claim of individuals and groups for conditions which make living the good life possible. We have seen in this study that the needs which arise when men live together in communities and daily work to earn their living have been considered largely; economic and political relationships have become part of the moral

[7] J. H. Muirhead, *The Elements of Ethics* (1921 ed.), pp. 135-136.

problem of personal development and the creation of the good society. It is not with the economic man alone nor with the political man that the community is most concerned, and from time to time the emphasis turns from one to the other. But steadily the purpose grows that the individual in all his relationships and with all his needs must be understood. Any lesser view is inadequate for politics or for ethics. Neither society nor the individual can be over-simplified for the convenience of a system of psychology or to prove the orthodoxy of a political dogma. Yet steadfastly through the confused debates of parliaments and workers' congresses one conviction stands, and it is part of the ideal upon which social justice builds the hope of the future. This conviction is, that the individual is good. The legislation that has been considered must then be judged with regard to its effect on the welfare of the individual, the protection of his rights; and it is thus true that the good State is one which actively cooperates with the individual in advancing the cause of the highest good. With this assumption we can say that social justice gives first place to the good life in the development of the idea of welfare in economic doctrine and political theory. Legislation and democratic administration are convincing proof that democracy means to create the conditions which will make possible for all citizens the living of the good life. That essential duty the community has accepted.

This ideal of the good life is not a sterile sort of individualism, nor does it neglect the very important fact that the group life of the community must be good even as the individual is good. It would be idle to overlook the conflicts which go on between industrial sections of the labour movement, almost as intense as that struggle which divides the employer and the employee, yet it is just at this point that the ideal of social justice becomes an unifying power in the community. Social justice interprets a purposive social will which is determined upon achieving a moral, and, therefore a voluntary social solidarity. Social justice is then, not a mechanical creation, but it is a belief in the possibilities of just living among men. It does not accept a view of social solidarity which is conditioned by the blind forces of economic evolution or by the pre-determined caprice of social forces within society which bend men to an acceptance of an ordered unity. But it is rather that we believe that good is either social or it is not good at all. "Social good is thus such an ordering of our personality that we are driven to search for things it is worth while to obtain, that thereby we may enrich the great fellowship we serve." [8] But the acceptance of the fact of organized social purpose through the State does not in any way commit one to the belief in a directly operative social or "general" will making for social good, a view that immediately suggests the great names of Rousseau, of Hegel, of Green and Bosanquet. But rather we can find a closer agreement in the view that the social good consists in and emanates from the co-operative wills of individuals, each finding his own good in the common service. Here, if anywhere, is an ethical basis for politics. It does not prevent one from being in substantial agreement with the view that "the State is not that all-inclusive organic context of social relations and institutions which Bosanquet has hypostatized into a general will." Yet, as the question has been put, what is to prevent the political community from extending its sphere in all directions—from becoming omnicompetent? It is, as Mr. Elliott has so well pointed out, the fact that political purpose is limited to safeguarding the conditions of the good life. That means a qualified individualism, not simply social atomism or negative protection. So that the State can play an active rôle in providing a justice which will "hinder the hindrances" to the good life—to use T. H. Green's phrase. Upon this claim rests the essential right of the State to be judge in its own case, *i.e.*, to be sovereign.[9]

From a somewhat different point of view the problem of sovereignty has been put thus:

Only in the State can the life of man be fully lived; it is essential to the State that it enact laws and issue commands, and it is essential that these laws and commands be obeyed by every citizen. What, then, must be sovereign in a State if a man is always to be able to feel it is his duty to obey the State, however intrinsically wrong may appear to him the things it commands him to do? For the State exists to make the moral life possible, that is, to make it

[8] Laski, *op. cit.*, pp. 24-25.

[9] See Mr. W. Y. Elliott's review of Mr. Norman Wilde's *The Ethical Basis of the State* (Princeton, 1925), in the *Nation* (New York), Vol. 121, No. 3140, September 9, 1925.

always possible; the State is, therefore, so far defeating its own ends if its citizens have to choose between being put in prison and acting as moral cowards. It is obvious that individuals will often think that what is commanded by the law or by the government is not the best course in this particular instance, and yet if the State is to stand the law must be obeyed. Clearly, then, the whole fabric of society, of which the law is a part, must be seen to guarantee something of such infinite value that no citizen can ever seriously think of failing to maintain that fabric.[10]

And the conclusion reached by the writer is worth noting:

Obviously the State does not exist as something abstracted from the individuals which compose it, for its reality lies in them as theirs lies in it. But just because the State is itself an individual we cannot say abstractedly what it ought to be any more than we can say abstractedly of a man what he ought to do. We can only speak abstractedly of an abstraction. Since the State is an entity, we study it and judge it, but our judgment is misleading if it be taken to imply that the State might have been otherwise. To say that its constitution has improved is the same as to say that it has advanced to a higher level—it has realised more fully the true obligations of its citizens to one another and to itself. The history of its development is the history of "the march of God upon earth."[11]

It is then of a great deal of importance to find out what the State sanctions in the rendering of service to the citizen. That will indicate at what level of consciousness the State as the world spirit appears.

The conflicts between groups with the same industrial outlook and between groups with real dividing issues of interest make necessary the development of this will for a voluntary solidarity; for there are destructive forces which would, if uncontrolled and undirected, wreck any hope of stable political organization and make impossible any hope of a saner social life. This ideal of solidarity has been interpreted on the principle of social justice so far as the conscious direction of political minded societies has

[10] C. R. and Mary Morris, *A History of Political Ideas* (1924), pp. 159-160.

[11] *Ibid.*, p. 176. Cf. Franklin H. Giddings, *The Responsible State*, pp. 36-48, and Professor Coker's comments cited hereafter.

been toward welfare. And the idea of solidarity has given the sanction required for the collective action of the State, which has meant in democracy the State realizing more definitely its purpose. The acceptance of a State-purpose has made more clear what is the will of the people, and the growth of higher conceptions of right and duty has enlarged the scope of what may be achieved for the common good.

The purposes which have been sanctioned by the State have compelled new allegiance from men of good will, who have felt the unifying power of the State to bring all lesser good and conflicting loyalties together. They have believed that only the State can establish a comprehensive social economy which ensures that no good thing be forfeited or lost. By so doing the State re-asserts a moral supremacy which challenges detractors who condemn it as either impotent or as prejudiced. The will for the highest good and the sharing of a common purpose with men of good will have remade the State. A State with this ideal cannot become a servile State, for freedom is the condition of its service; and if democracy has the capacity to develop ideals of the good life under conditions of freedom it is not likely that for long it will lack imagination to escape the obvious perversions of political organization which defeat the purposes of freedom. The building up of definite means of control by legislation, education, self-government and public opinion have helped to promote the belief that mankind can control its social destiny. The achievements of social institutions have directed study to the forces which make for the good society, and if we assume that a good society can be judged by the product turned out, the judgment which social justice renders would more and more tend to give recognition to rights of personality and direction to the efforts of the community.

2

The idea of progress is closely joined with the development of State-purpose, the central idea of which—the State serving a common moral ideal of justice and goodness—has authority as an increasing desire for a good life on the part of more people gives a power to public opinion which in turn enforces its decisions through the instrument of the law. The significance of the idea of progress has been realized by those who see in the process the working of an unifying principle which would bring together in a consistent whole all social effort.[12] This study suggests that the ideal of social justice is that unifying principle, which, as it unites the purpose of the individual with the State for the achievement of a common end, the highest good, more fully defines what is the nature of the good State and the good individual. That there is an interdependence between the two in the fulfilment of this moral purpose becomes increasingly important as the power to conceive justly high aims is afforded to the individual and the State through experience and the will which shapes their aims toward the fullest social good. One eminent authority on this point says that

the dependence of State machinery on the requirements, feelings and opinions of society becomes even more apparent when we proceed to examine the *aims* of the State. The question as to the aims of the State is a necessary complement to the question concerning the nature of the State.[13]

[12] Cf. J. B. Bury, *The Idea of Progress* (1918), who suggests that a "science of society" is a very modern idea, and "in England this idea was still a novelty when Mill's *System of Logic* appeared in 1843" (p. 307). L. M. Bristol's *Social Adaptation* (1914) supplies a general survey of the contribution of sociology to this idea, which can be judged more fully in the writings of Lester F. Ward, Thomas Nixon Carver and E. A. Ross. "A dynamic study of society gives rise to problem of progress" (Bristol, p. 20), is, in general, the point of view. The contribution of Professor H. E. Barnes to the literature of this field is fresh and significant, see especially his *The New History and the Social Studies* (1925), chap. VIII. pp. 470-518, and his chapter "Some Contributions of Sociology to Modern Political Theory" in *Political Theories: Recent Times* (1924), pp. 357-402. The reading lists given are extensive. Also *The History and Prospects of the Social Sciences*. Edited by H. E. Barnes (1926).

[13] Sir Paul Vinogradoff, *Outlines of Historical Jurisprudence*, Vol. I, (1920), p. 93, his italics. Professor Bosanquet said "the State is the condition of organized good life for the inhabitants of a certain territory," p. 144 in *The International Crisis in its Ethical and Psychological Aspects* (Oxford, 1915) from his essay "Patriotism in the Perfect State," pp. 132-154. With this essay may be compared Mr. A. D. Lindsay's essay, "The State and Society" in *The Theory of the State* (Oxford, 1916), pp. 92-108. Mr. Lindsay in his essay "Political Theory" (pp. 164-180, in *Recent Developments in European Thought*, 1920, ed. by F. S. Marvin), has insisted that the organized force of the State be the expression of men's settled and permanent will to maintain their common interests and

When we thus understand the aims of the State to be for the highest good, loyalty to the State makes the closest bond between the citizen and the political community a moral one. This highest good assumes a State that is positively concerned with justice for each individual and for all groups within its jurisdiction. Social justice, or in this instance, the notion of corporate justice, corresponds in its turn to the belief that the corporate social organization, the State, held in equilibrium by the constitutional system,

> is the highest type of organisation because it is the image of the human personality, which is the image of God. The divine right of the king was the monarchical principle; the divine right of the people was the revolutionary principle; and the divine rule of the corporate life nationally organised, of which the individuals are participant members, is properly the constitutional principle.[14]

The effect upon the individual is—in the ideal—that

> we learn to think of our political conduct in terms of the vast reverberation of consequences on thousands and millions of lives, great and lowly, present and to come.[15]

Not that the average citizen and trade unionist concerns himself with the difference which a professor of political science may see between the democratic or humanitarian view and the metaphysical view of the State.[16] But what is important is the faith that this

safeguard the conditions of the good life. He concludes that "If we consistently follow out Green's dictum that will, not force, is the basis of the State, we shall be anxious that the political organization to which we render obedience shall follow the actual ramifications of common interests and of men's willingness to co-operate" (p. 179).

[14] Hauriou, op. cit., p. xii. A much more extended interpretation of the social philosophy of M. Hauriou can be found in his *Précis de droit constitutionnel* (1923); especially pp. 42-52, for statement on the ideals of justice as determined by individual or collective action, and his incisive attack upon the "collective conscience" as the determining factor in collective evolution (p. 45); also pp. 191-194, for his five bases of modern democracy with his emphasis on the moral qualities determining political and social progress.

[15] L. T. Hobhouse, *The Metaphysical Theory of the State* (1918), p. 136.

[16] Hobhouse, *op. cit.*, p. 137: "Here precisely lies the issue between the two views of the State. In the democratic or humanitarian view it is a means. In the metaphysical view it is an end. In the democratic view it is the servant of humanity in the double sense that it is to be judged by what

citizen has in the political community and the confidence which the groups within its control have in the common rule of justice which its sovereign power enforces. This faith and confidence are what is essential if economic and political privileges are to be destroyed, giving the workers access to "the moral assets of the State." [17]

We would apply the same test of loyalty to the State for the group that is applied for the individual; and by this test the social value of the group may be determined, as in the phrase of T. H. Green it is for the individual, by "the power to make a common good his own." [18] Not only has this test when applied to individuals and to group action not delimited the moral ideal of a perfect State, but it has in reality given it a new birth of freedom. It has been made plain that democracy has the insight to comprehend a conception of the highest good and is capable of making great sacrifices for its realization. "If the great majority of persons," M. Duguit declares, "do not have an opinion on what constitutes social solidarity, they have a sentiment, vague perhaps, but deep and real, of social solidarity, which gives a positive base to the rule of law." [19] Even the tragic blunders of associative action, where public interest has often suffered from the sharp intensity of a conflict of group interests, have shown that

> what makes and maintains States as States is will and not force, idea of a common good, and not greed or ambition; and that this principle cannot be overthrown by the facts of self-interest in

it does for the lives of its members and by the part that it plays in the society of human kind. In the metaphysical view it is itself the sole guardian of moral worth. In the democratic view the sovereign State is already doomed, destined to subordination in a community of the world. In the metaphysical view it is the supreme achievement of human organisation."

[17] See Harold J. Laski, "The State In the New Social Order," *Fabian Tract No. 200* (1923), p. 3. See Mr. Laski's article in the *Harvard Law Review,* Vol. XXXIX, No. 7 (May, 1926), "Judicial Review of Social Policy," pp. 832-848, for an interesting comment on a most significant phase of State action.

[18] *Principles of Political Obligation,* p. 351.

[19] Léon Duguit, *Traité de droit constitutionnel* [3 vols. Vol. I (2nd ed. 1921)], p. 55; also pp. 47-56, "Le sentiment de la socialité et le sentiment justice." The positivistic philosophy of law of M. Duguit and his belief that organic social solidarity is the necessary source of law is fully given in *Traité de droit constitutionnel* (2nd ed. Vol. III). "La Théorie Genérale De L'Etat" (suite et fin) (1923).

ordinary citizens, or of selfishness in those who mould the destinies of nations.[20]

We have thus tried to lay a basis for the loyalty of the individual and the group to the State, and we believe that this can be done by showing that the will of the State is for the good society and that its action has promoted the aims of the good life. This study has often pointed out the dependence of the State upon the co-operation of voluntary administrative boards and the honest good will of groups before which the State laid particular problems to be solved. Between the individual and the State we see no fundamental conflict of purpose, and a view of the State which would to-day maintain the reality of this conflict completely fails to estimate the moral advance of mankind in raising the standards of individual duty and of collective responsibility. There is implied a possibility of separating between individual and social interests, which must be denied; but "this does not mean that individual and social interests may not conflict, but that there are no individual interests with which society is not concerned."[21] There is no such thing as a "wage fund theory of choice";[22] and this critic, writing in 1910, at the high point of Liberal legislation, in which the State was a pioneer of reform, declared, that "actually if the State action is at all sensible, my opportunities for action and therefore for choice, are greatly increased."[23] Three years later when the reaction against parliamentary interference had had full literary denunciation as well as definite economic and industrial consequences, one who had helped to make articulate an important phase of the revolt wrote that "the liberty-fund theory is as untenable as that of the wages-fund."[24] "The State exists and

[20] Bosanquet, *op. cit.*, pp. 273-274.

[21] See A. D. Lindsay, *Introduction* (1910) to "Utilitarianism, Liberty, Representative Government," by John Stuart Mill, p. xxii.

[22] *Op. cit.*, examining the principle of Lord Hugh Cecil's *Liberty and Authority* (1908), which Mr. Lindsay stated thus: "The only moral worth is in choice and spontaneity: government action destroys choice and therefore destroys moral worth" (p. xxiii). A general social outline of this thesis is in Lord Hugh Cecil's *Conservatism* (1912). The Writings of Sir J. A. R. Marriott, especially his *Ethics and Economics* (1924) provide a recent apology for Conservatism.

[23] Lindsay, *op. cit.*, p. xxiii.

[24] Cf. G. D. H. Cole, *Introduction* (1913) to "The Social Contract and Other Essays," by Jean Jacques Rousseau, p. xxxvi.

claims our obedience," he further stated, "because it is a natural extension of our personality." [25]

In the search for freedom and in the hopeless confusion of conflict which has often arisen, as we have seen in this study, we believe that it has been evident that the State is a necessary instrument of promoting the highest good of the individual of good will. The history of parliamentary struggles between 1900 and 1926 proves that the State is not a prejudiced tool of predominant economic or social groups. But by its power of lifting the issues of the day to a higher level of national importance it educates the nation in tolerance and leads the way toward good will. The incompetent State is as unthinkable to-day as the omnicompetent State. But a far wider range of choice is allowed democracy. It is not necessarily limited either to the dilemma expressed in a homely phrase during the syndicalist debate of 1912 in the House of Commons, when a member confessed, "I would far rather be governed by Tom Mann than by Mr. and Mrs. Sidney Webb." [26] Hardie put the case for Labour more bluntly when he said "to dogmatize about the form which the Socialist State shall take is to play the fool." [27] The State would be what the people made it, and

> as the political education of the working class progresses, and they begin to realise what are the true functions of the State, their power will be extended in an increasing degree in the direction of transfiguring the State from a property-preserving to a life-preserving institution.[28]

The attitude of the individual toward the State, as we have considered the new regard for human nature which an ideal of justice makes possible, can be one of loyalty based on the moral appeal of the State that it will help in the fulfilment of the good purposes of the individual. This naturally involves a new estimate of the power of mutual loyalty between the individual and the State to change conditions for the good of society. It demands an individualism of good will acting in freedom, and it also demands a

[25] *Op. cit.*, p. xxxix.

[26] Parl. Deb. H. C. 5 S. March 27, 1912, Vol. 36, p. 537; pp. 535-544, speech entire (Ormsby-Gore).

[27] J. Keir Hardie, *From Serfdom to Socialism* (1907), p. 96.

[28] Hardie, *op. cit.*, pp 23-24.

good will from the State inspired by a conception of service for the common good. The years between 1900 and 1926 witnessed the development of this spirit, the good effects of which continue on even in a world that has seemed particularly callous to the needs of reconciliation. Ideals of the good continue to stir individuals to their best work, and the community will gradually be fashioned in the image of the good man. The State cannot be unconcerned about the good society, nor is it, nor will it ever be again. There has been too commanding a challenge from all groups within the State that the conditions of life be juster, that more opportunity be allowed for the fulfilment of the best that is in mankind. It is the insistence of society on the satisfaction of the demand for the good life that gives importance to the struggle for a higher standard of life. It is thus certain that more and more the ideal of social justice will demand a social morality which will enable the community to get the best out of all individuals and thereby help to bring in the full creative spirit of the good community.[29]

This conception has suggested to one writer the classical period when the State

> was not conceived as a kind of necessary evil to be tolerated for the sake of order and security. On the contrary the Greeks attributed a positive aim to the State; it exists not merely to facilitate association, but to shape it: to help reasonable and strong-minded men in the pursuit of *welfare*. This is the proper sphere of the State, because the task of finding true welfare is out of the range of individual effort, but within the range and power of a political association.[30]

Part II

Social Justice and the Community

The importance of the individual in a study of social justice has been made clear, and the significance of the good individual raising the standards of social action has been stressed. There is now to be considered the demand of justice for the community as a

[29] Cf. Rollo Walter Brown, *The Creative Spirit* (1925).

[30] Vinogradoff, *Outlines of Historical Jurisprudence,* Vol. II. "The Jurisprudence of the Greek City" (1922), pp. 13-14, his italics. Cf. J. L. Stocks, *Aristotelianism* (1925), pp. 103-118, "The City."

whole, which is a test of the moral progress of society. In this regard it is well to note that the ultimate goal of social justice is the well-being of all the people. That is the basis of believing in a theory of progress for democracy, and, so far as the ideal of the common good can find a definite place in economic doctrine and political theory, social justice provides the ideal which can unify the forces making for progress in democracy. It lays down a principle by which private action and public policy may be judged. The principle applied is: does individual action or public policy help or hinder in the realization of social good for the whole of the people? Is the good society brought nearer to the world as it is to-day?

The interpretation of the principle is not easy, because of the complexity of modern social, political and industrial organization, which creates the sharpest problems of personal and social duty. And at the same time a process of re-definition and re-valuation goes on with reference to the rights of the group, the State and the individual. Conflicts grow out of this complexity so serious and far-reaching in their consequences that the existence of governments is threatened; devastating effects of group warfare and class conflict at times almost overcome the constructive will of democracy to control and direct itself.

Such a condition of anarchy shows the need for a body of principles based on the ideal of social justice, which would tend to unify the aims of all within the community. The need becomes more evident when one considers the conflicts of industry, of trade, of groups which have become so powerful that their uncontrolled activity and collective selfishness—or, equally destructive, their unconscious social blindness—bring conditions approaching social anarchy and intolerable social discord. The attempt by the State to adjust conflicts fairly has made more definite the obligation of the State, yet it has shown that the administrative and legislative capacity of government have not been equal to the need. But the effort of the State and of industry and of labour to adjust themselves to these questions is significant of a will for justice, and constitutes a rough idea, as they conceive it, of a system of social justice. The attempts have been awkward, often useless, even provocative of social disturbance, yet behind the whole movement of these great social, political and economic forces has been at work the ideal of equitable relationships. If it has been often unconscious and less often clearly understood, it has meant at any rate an effort to bring about a socially just order of living. Rights have been more widely recognized, social duties of groups made more definite, and in settling the differences arising from conflict there is more willingness to consider the general good. From such considerations it becomes a conviction that the higher the social and ethical organization of the State, as reflected in the demand of just relationships, the clearer is the ideal of social justice.

It is apparent then that, though the problem for the State in intervening is a moral one where the good of the community is concerned, there is a danger of the State defeating the purpose for which it originally is justified in taking action. This is made plain when the ethical basis upon which the political community co-operates with the individual is kept constantly to the front. It is a problem of freedom. It is ever present, for the individual is in relationship at all times with other individuals and with lesser groups within the large community. The State, representing the community good, must carefully determine where intervention can promote the aims of freedom. So it is that the adjustment of conflicting interests, protecting some and restraining others, carrying out principles of State control and discipline, is the problem of social justice. It constitutes also a moral problem for the State, for justice is the name for the moral obligation of the State, as distinct from the individual, with respect to the task of adjusting conflicting interests. "Since the State has this to do, it must find out how to do it. What *ought* the State to do with respect to these conflicts and how *ought* it to do it? These are the questions of social justice". [31]

[31] See T. N. Carver, *Essays in Social Justice*, Harvard University Press, Cambridge (1915), pp. 9-10. The problem of social justice, Professor Carver believes, "has to do with the internal economy of the nation rather than with its external relations. As to the individual, it has to do with his external relations with his fellow citizens rather than with his internal adjustments. Since the first duty of the State is to be strong in order that it may live, and since it must adjust the conflicting interests of its citizens, it follows that its duty is to so adjust these conflicting interests as to make itself strong. It must repress and discourage those interests of its individuals which conflict with its own, and it must support and encourage those which harmonize with its own. That is justice. In the most general terms, therefore, justice may be defined as such an adjustment of the

Therefore it has been one of the necessary aims of this study to note how far State action, with reference to the accepted ideal of social justice, has been a factor making for a good social order, in the first quarter of this century. It has been necessary to see to what extent the principles of social justice have been embodied in positive law and expressed in public adiministration, becoming the rule of justice enforced by the community.[32] The rule of justice defined in positive law has been taken to mark the progress of law from "contract to community," [33] which, stated by another, means that "welfare as the aim of the State supposes the closest interdependence between social and political organization." [34] We have seen how this has been carried out in the modern State, for it has been evident that the principles of social justice are to be realized through institutions, and as the growth of democracy has gradually increased the functions of the State social control has been administered through new institutions.

4

With the increase of the functions of the State the problem of a good social order has been more insistently the supreme task of the modern democratic State. And, while the moral obligation of the State, the old problem of justice, is no new doctrine, the pressure for immediate reform has often made it impossible to understand the validity which it has come to have in the present social order. Yet a better social system is being realized within the State, because this century began with knotty problems of distributive justice stirring the imagination of economists more than

conflicting interests of a nation as will interfere least with, and contribute most to, the strength of the nation" (pp. 9-10). Professor Carver's point of view, we believe, is an overemphasis of the economic basis of social justice and its relation to the strong State.

[32] Cf. Carver, *op. cit.*, p. 10. The rules of justice "may emanate from the sovereign group, called the nation, in which case they take precedence, in practice over all others, or they may emanate from indefinite and intangible groups called "the community," "society" or even "civilization" or "Christendom," in which case they become effective as they are embodied in positive law and are enforced by the sovereign group.'

[33] M. T. Follett, *The New State* (1918), pp. 122-133. The idea is more fully developed in her *Creative Experience* (1924).

[34] Vinogradoff, *op. cit.*, Vol. I, p. 97.

any other problem to consider "the uncertain permanence of our present social ideals." [35] But it has not been alone the demand for economic justice, in itself at times a subtle weapon to defeat larger hopes of the working class and to postpone finer social blessings, that has brought nearer the ideal of human good to the ordinary every day person. And yet the enthusiasm for reform has largely consumed the energy of those who have been concerned in the realization of a juster order. There have been too few "whose main concern is not with applications but with principles, not with institutions but with the ends that they serve." [36] This has caused a breakdown in a reasoned ethical insistence on reform that at times almost stops the advance of idealistic forces in social politics. But it is evident that whenever there is a renewal of interest in the ethical foundation of relationships the moral problem of State-purpose is revived, and there is a wider interpretation of the principle of justice which finds expression in many new directions. This fact gives substance to the belief that there is and that there must be such a thing as social justice, an ideal which demands that all the people share in the good things of life. The human appeal of this ideal formed part of the Treaty of Versailles, which declared that "conditions of labour exist involving such injustice, hardship and privation to large numbers of people as to produce unrest so great that the peace and harmony of the world are imperilled," and that "universal peace can be established only if it is based on social justice." [37]

Such a formal demand as that set forth in the Treaty of Versailles indicates the movement of reform which has produced a body of positive law and formulated policies of intelligent social administration, all of which indicate both the necessity of mankind controlling its social destiny and the consciousness of its power to do so. Social justice takes account of this consciousness of power

[35] Alfred Marshall, *Principles of Economics* (8th ed. 1920), p. 46; also Book I, chap. IV. "The Order and Aims of Economic Studies," which reproduces a section from a "Plea for the creation of a curriculum in economics and associated branches of political science," addressed to the University of Cambridge in 1902; and note *Appendix C*, pp. 770-780, "The Scope and Method of Economics." Cf. F. W. Taussig, "Alfred Marshall," *Quarterly Journal of Economics,* Vol. XXXIX, No. I. November, 1924, pp. 1-14.

[36] L. T. Hobhouse, *The Elements of Social Justice* (1922), p. 13.

[37] Treaty of Versailles, Part VIII. Section I. "Organisation of Labour."

which has become to-day a practical problem in government, for the people use the power given to them to experiment along economic lines. This experiment has helped to bring out into the open the struggle for control which goes on between groups within the State, and it has been necessary for the central authority to take an active part in deciding what the aims of control shall be. This struggle has often failed to bring to the front the best aims in social organization, but it has served the purpose of showing that social warfare rather than social justice has too often been the condition of progress. Thus the institutions created by modern industrial society lack a spirit of unity, and their competition has often been self-destructive, but they are necessarily the institutions through which the new spirit of good will is to be expressed. That spirit is to be the deciding factor in determining who is to hold power in the future when the ideal of communal good is developed from the conflict of interests and sustained by an effective moral public opinion.[38] If the source of this power abides in opinion, and if democracy is capable of controlling its social destiny, there is great reason for directing the opinion of mankind to a study of those principles by which a good society can be told from a bad society. The effort to understand these principles may bring a wider appreciation of the need of an unity or aim among men of good will who seek a common ground for social action in their purpose of bringing in the good society. The importance of a unifying principle has been emphasized by Professor Hobhouse in his *Elements of Social Justice,* where he says, that

[38] Cf. Bertrand Russell, "Sources of Power," Part III. *The Freeman* (N. Y., 1923): "Tradition and habit, strong as they are, are diminishing forces in our kaleidoscopic world. This opinion becomes the decisive factor in determining who is to hold power in the future." An extension of this thesis can be found in Bertrand and Dora Russell's *Prospects of Industrial Civilisation* (1924); and in his *What I Believe* (1925), there is an interesting discussion of the good life (chap. II) and the possibilities of its achievement. Mr. Russell's *Education and the Good Life* (1926) is a very stimulating discussion of what individual and social life may become, freed from fear and its tyranny; note especially Part I, pp. 15-83, and chap. XIX. "In one generation," he says, "if we chose, we could bring the millennium" (p. 316). "A generation educated in fearless freedom will have wider and bolder hopes than are possible to us, who still have to struggle with the superstitious fears that lie in wait for us below the level of consciousness. Not we, but the free men and women whom we shall create, must see the new world, first in their hopes, and then at last in the full splendour of reality" (p. 318).

the only valid principles are those that emerge out of our experience, and the function of the highest generalizations is to knit our partial views together in a consistent whole. That our social efforts suffer from lack of articulate statement and rational coherence is only too palpable. To promote unity of aim among men of good will and lay a basis of co-operation between those attacking different sides of the social problem is a practical problem of the highest importance.[39]

It is then apparent that when just principles of social organization are known and have sufficient sanction to become expressed in law, the obligation so to express them is upon the State and the community, the powers of administration and control.

What ought the State to do? What ought the people to approve in the way of social control, what schemes of social control, what social institutions, what systems of economic organization, production, distribution *ought* to meet the approval of the masses of the people? This is the real question of social justice.[40]

There is always this *oughtness,* for the moral obligation of the State compels it to apply principles of justice which promote the well-being of the whole people. This brings us nearer to the truth that social justice always implies, that

social and political institutions are not ends in themselves. They are organs of social life, good or bad, according to the spirit which they embody. The ideal is to be sought not in the faultless un-

[39] *Op. cit.,* Preface.

[40] Carver, *op. cit.,* p. 32, his italics. Professor Carver's *The Present Economic Revolution in the United States* (1925) states fully his belief that it is just as possible to attain equality under capitalism as under any other system; that the inequalities which exist under it are due to disturbing factors that are easily removable and are not due to the nature of the system itself (p. 7). Western democracy has been told to produce, to produce, and then again to produce. For what reason? That we may all finally become little capitalists? That is a dangerous way to teach democracy the meaning of possessing in common all good things. The essential work before democracy is to direct the purposes of industry, to re-define the aims of production, and finally to prepare industry in spirit for the service of all. It is inevitable that social incentives for profit-making shall become less in a democracy intent upon economic justice, and it would be well for the politics of our democracy to prepare in its special way for that change in the motives of industry which present day economics hopefully forecasts.

changing system of an institutional Utopia, but in the lore of a spiritual life with its unfailing spring of harmonious growth unconfined. But growth has its conditions and the spiritual life its principles . . . the sum of which we call Social Justice.[41]

We may then say, having in mind the duty of the State and the needs of the great community, that in the common good of the whole people is that social freedom which is the ideal of social justice, and that this ideal is powerful enough to direct the purposes of common effort.

Mr. A. D. Lindsay in his penetrating way has suggested [42] how constantly the practical successes of democracy have been due to the impulsion given by the appeal to the fundamental facts and ideals of human relationship of which the abstractions of Rousseau and Marx are the expression, and how much they depend for further achievement on the inspiration of that appeal. It is an old story, he says, that the essence of the demand for justice is a demand for equality, and that the equality which justice demands is not by any means easy to define; it does not consist in men getting equal amounts of anything.

It is always equality of men as members of society, and any distributions of rewards or portions or rights which is to be just must be relevant to and determined by the end of society. To try to discover a system of economic reward which should be just in itself is to assume that the only purpose and end of society is economic.
But it is also an old discovery that equal justice can be given to all members of a society only if the end that society pursues is such that it can be shared. There are certain purposes which society may make its own which are in their nature competitive. The demand that such ends should be equally shared by all is necessarily unrealizable—but the fact that it is so is a criticism not of the demand for equality but of the end which will not support the demand. *The demand for abstract justice is seldom as abstract as it appears.* It accepts the valuations of existing society, and

[41] Hobhouse, *op cit.*, p. 13.
[42] His *Karl Marx's Capital* (1926), pp. 124-125, my italics. Cf. also his essay on "Political Theory" in *Recent Developments of European Thought* (edited by F. S. Marvin, 1920), pp. 164-180, and note the chapter by Professor F. W. Coker in *Political Theories: Recent Times,* "Pluralistic Theories and the Attack Upon State Sovereignty," pp. 80-119.

demands that the things at the production and preservation of which society seems most to aim, should be available to all members of society. If the demand fails, the failure is the condemnation of the ends. *The demand for abstract justice is the touchstone of the purposes of any given society.*

V

The power of this ideal is proved by the fact that however difficult the task has been to establish principles of social justice there has been no lessening of the effort to attempt it. The need has shown insistent duties, the claims of which have strengthened the will of democracy to overcome difficulties by political organization where it can be serviceable. The illusion of parliamentarism has been estimated, but there has been no abandonment of the ground gained by the common endeavour to raise the standard of life. There has been more of determination that it should be sustained and extended. And at the same time that there has been a growth of political consciousness in group movements, scientific study has contributed to the ways by which the level of human existence can be lifted, and politics have helped to socialize the knowledge of economic investigation.[43] Reflected in the extension of political democracy the will of the people has defined the functions of the modern State, which in turn show the degree to which this will is organized and the faith of the citizens in the State's capacity for social control. This faith is a condition of working out principles of democracy through a society dedicated to these principles; and, though perils and evils have been many, the will of the people expressed through the State has been known more fully. As it has been better known the conviction has been sure that the will of the people is for the good society. Only on this assumption can be fully understood the years of struggle by which the hope of the good society has been more intelligently expressed.

The question finally raised by this study is, How are faith in democracy and hope for the order of society it can produce related

[43] Cf. Hobhouse, *The Metaphysical Theory of the State,* pp. 11-25, "The Objects of Social Investigation."

to social justice? They are related so far as the ideal of social justice helps to account for the reasonableness of the faith, and sustains the conviction that democracy and social justice are compatible. It has been important to inquire into the kind of society and the type of citizen that an industrial civilization has produced in the modern State. This has been done in this study mainly by reference to what the governments were forced to do to protect their citizens and their standard of life, and this has afforded some insight into the aims behind protection which the State and the groups within the State have held. The attempt has been made to see just how effective politics and industry have been in creating "the good society" and the "good individual," by applying an ideal of community good which we have called the ideal of social justice. In considering what has been done there has been at times an ideal of the common good that was placed in the future, in "the new order." But this has given insight into present aims, for the ideal of the common good of the future must be based on principles which mankind have found necessary in the present day conception of a system of justice. This ideal of social justice has become more definite, because enlarging demands have interpreted social needs and defined the ideals of social progress under conditions of freedom—a freedom that recognizes the rights of the individual, the new power of community life, the rights of groups within the State, and the right of the State to express the common purpose for the highest good of all.

We have been too indifferent to the problem of freedom in our industrial civilization, and we are just now beginning to understand the importance of high social ideals in the work of the State. The aims of the State are everywhere under the test of an ethical ideal. Politics and economics and ethics are being called upon to contribute toward an understanding of the citizen of to-day. This understanding is needed as the political purpose of the modern State is more clearly set forth. This purpose has to-day a commanding power when its aims are just, and these aims look not only to the rule of justice in the present order, but provide for all men the incentive to believe in an order in which the creative will for justice is a more natural and a more generous compulsion upon all men. The ideal of the common good is more and more the determining influence in the politics of democracy, and this ideal as it is honestly sought after will give insight into the present aims of the State and of the groups within the State. The co-operative will of the State is more fully defining what is needed to bring about the conditions which will make possible the living of the good life, and this is convincing testimony of democracy's capacity to use ideals. Democracy, determined upon ideals of the good life, will not fail to challenge the devotion of all who believe in a freedom under law wherein the best that is in men can be developed. Then as men learn to use their freedom wisely they will build together on earth the good society. They will build this good society because they have learned that as members of a political society their real freedom is in the common life, and out of this common life all there is of freedom for the individual must come.

NOTE ON BIBLIOGRAPHY

This study is based upon parliamentary debates in England and France, and upon the reports of the workers' industrial and political congresses. The volumes of Hansard and the *Journal officiel de la République francaise* report fully the proceedings in the House of Lords and the House of Commons, the French Senate and Chamber. The volumes of each house are separately published, and this is also true of the parliamentary papers and committee reports. In connection with the legislative proceedings the important parliamentary papers between 1900 and 1926 have been used, and they provide a body of rich material for the student of social politics. The House of Commons papers and the French *Rapports* are not included in the bibliography due to the regard for space, but they can be quickly referred to in the chapters dealing with legislation. The hearings, the preliminary reports and the conclusions of Select Committees and Royal Commissions are published, and the more important of these have been noted in the text. Likewise a complete record of the reports of the *Conseil Supérieur du Travail* since 1900 has been given. This body has had an increasing influence on French social legislation, due to the support the Government has given it. The service that it gives corresponds in some degree to that rendered by the great Royal Commissions in England. The yearly reports of the department of state dealing with labour, health, commerce and trade, finance and local government provide a vast amount of source material for investigation. Of special significance in England are the reports of the Local Government Board, the Board of Trade, the Ministry of Health, and the Ministry of Labour. The duties of the old Local Government Board have been largely given over to the Ministry of Health, and these reports since 1920 are very suggestive. The *Ministry of Labour Gazette* gives a weekly account of labour and industrial affairs, indicating the progress of legislation and the administration of public business. The yearly reports in France of the *Ministère du Travail et de l'Hygiène* are important, and the monthly *Bulletin du Ministère du Travail et de l'Hygiène* contains the chief current accounts of French legislation and administration. The reports in France and England of the factory inspectors provide perhaps the best review of administration. The publications of the departments of state can be easily secured, and the list since 1900 indicates the wide range of interests.

The reports of the Trade Union Congress, the Labour Party, the

Confédération Générale du Travail, the *Congrès Général des Organisations Socialistes Françaises* (S. F. I. O.), the *Parti Communiste Français* (S. F. I. C.) are published yearly and can be obtained from their respective headquarters. The *International Labour Directory*, published annually at Geneva, is of service in providing correct addresses.

The material on the parties is abundant in England, and in France some very creditable histories have been written. This material is fully given in the bibliography which follows. The yearly conferences of the parties are worth noting, and the proceedings are published in report form. The Labour party is unusually active in pamphleteering and of real value are the reports of the Fabian Research Committees, the Labour Research Department, and the Trade Union Congress. The *Labour Year Book* is indispensable, and is of increasing value in furnishing information. The *Annual Register* in England, and the *Annuaire du Parlement* (since 1898) provide a review of each year's events. Both countries have a notable group of *Quarterlies* and *Reviews*, and the student of England and France should know the best of them. Finally, mention should be made of the splendid service rendered by the International Labour Office (League of Nations), for in their *Studies and Reports Series* the student has an account of social legislation and its administration in all countries.

The author gives this selected bibliography not as in any way a definitive one, but in the hope that it may suggest the vast material that is ready for the student of social politics. Some of these books are decidedly inferior books, a good many are now only of value in pointing out the issues of the past. It is difficult for one to judge in a period of twenty-five years what is the abiding, and what forces a hundred years from now will prove to have been the determining influences in our time.

Selected Bibliography[1]

Ashley. W. J. *The Economic Organisation of England* (1914).
Ashley, Anne. *The Social Policy of Bismarck: A Critical Study with a Comparison of English and German Insurance Legislation* (1912).
Adams, George Burton. *Constitutional History of England* (1922).
Addison, Rt. Hon. Christopher. *The Betrayal of the Slums* (1922).
Aldridge, Henry R. *The National Housing Manual* (1924).
Aayle, A. *The Houses of the Workers* (1924).
Annual Register.

[1] Where the place of publication of an English book is London, and where Paris is the place of publication of a French book, only the date of publication is given. All books not published in these two places are noted.

Andrews, Irene Osgood. *Economic Effects of the War upon Women and Children in Great Britain* (1918).

Alden, Percy. *Democratic England* (1910), *The Unemployed, A National Question* (1905), with preface by Sir John Gorst.

Atherley-Jones, Judge. *Looking Back: Reminiscences of a Political Career* (1925).

Allo, Bernard. *Foi et systèmes* (1908).

Al-Sanhoury, A. A. *Les restrictions contractuelles à la liberté de travail dans la jurisprudence anglaise* (Paris, 1925).

Arnold-Foster, H. O. *English Socialism of To-day* (1908).

Arnou, André. *La participation des travailleurs à la gestion des entreprises* (1920).

Bardoux, Jacques. *L'Angleterre radicale 1905-1913 : Essai de psychologie sociale* (1913).

Book of the Labour Party, The. (3 vols., 1925). Edited by Herbert Tracey.

Blanshard, Paul. *An Outline of the British Labour Movement* (1923), With Introduction by Arthur Henderson.

Buisson, F. *La politique radicale* (1909).

Buisson E. *Le parti socialiste et les syndicats* (1907).

Bourgeois, Léon. *Solidarité* (1st ed. 1894, 7th ed. 1912), *Education de la démocratie* (1897), *Pour la société des nations* (1910), *La politique de l'épargne et de l'hygiène sociale* (1914).

Bouglé, Charles. *Le idées égalitaires* (1899), *La sociologie de Proudhon* (1912), *Solidarisme et libéralisme* (1904), *Chez les prophètes socialistes* (1918), *Le solidarisme* (1st ed. 1907, 2nd. 1924), *Syndicalisme et démocratie* (1908), *Proudhon et notre temps* (1918), a preface to essays by various writers.

Barthélemy, Joseph. *Le gouvernment de la France* (1919). English translation by J. B Morris (1924), also a new French edition in 1924. *Le problème de la compétence dans la démocratie* (1918).

Brizon, Pierre. *L'apprentissage, hier, aujourd'hui, demain* (1909).

Barthou, Louis. *L'action syndicale* (1904).

Bourbonnais, Marc. *Le neoSaint-Simonisme et la vie sociale d'aujourd'hui* (1923).

Beaudemoulin, J. *La li de huit heures. Enquête sur son application et sur les loisirs de l'ouvrier* (1924).

Beard, Charles A. *American Government and Politics* (1925 ed.), *The Economic Basis of Politics* (1922), *Cross Currents in Europe To-day* (1923).

Beer, Max. *History of British Socialism* (2 vols., 1916-1920.)

Berthiot, M. *Cours de législation du travail et notions de législation ouvrière et industrielle* (2nd ed. 1921).

Barker, Ernest. *Political Thought in England from Spencer to To-day* (1915).

Barnes, Harry Elmer. *The New History and the Social Studies*

(1925), *Political Theories: Recent Times* (1924), with Merriam and others; *Sociology and Political Theory* (1923), *The History and Prospects of the Social Sciences* (1926), Editor.

Bourgin, Georges. *Manuel des partis politiques en France* (1924).

Bourgin, Maurice. *Les systèmes socialistes et l'évolution économique* (1904).

Brown, W. Jethro. *The Underlying Principles of Modern Legislation* (1st ed. 1910, 6th ed. 1920).

Bryce, James (Viscount Bryce). *Modern Democracies* (2 vols., 1921).

Bry, Georges. *Les lois du travail industriel et de la prévoyance: législation ouvrière* (6th ed. revised by E-H. Perreau, 1921).

Batut, Guy de la, and George Friedmann. *A History of the French People* (1923), with Introduction by Henri Barbusse.

Buell, R. L. *International Relations* (1925), *Contemporary French Politics* (1920).

Berth, Edouard. *Les derniers aspets du socialisme* (1923), the revised edition of *Les nouveaux aspets du socialisme* (1908); *Guerre des états ou guerre des classes* (1924), *Méfaits des intellectuels* (1914).

Bouedeaux, H. *Code des accidents du travail avec annotatins d'après la doctrine et la jurisprudence* (7th ed. 1924).

Bourdeaux, S. *L'évolution du socialisme* (1901), *Entre deux servitudes* (1908).

Belloc, Hilaire. *The Servile State* (1912), *The French Revolution* (1911), *The Jews* (1922).

Brouilhot, Charles. *Le conflit des doctrines dans l'économie politique contemporarine* (1908).

Bury, J. B. *The Idea of Progress* (1918).

Bristol, L. M. *Social Adaptation* (1914).

Breton, J.-L. *L'Unité Socialiste* (1912).

Barnes, Harry. *Housing, the Facts and the Future* (1923).

Barrault, M. *Le droit d'association en Angleterre* (1908).

Blum, Leon. *Les congrès ouvriers et socialistes français* (2 vols., 1896-1900).

Brown, Rollo Walter. *The Creative Spirit* (1925).

Bosanquet, Bernard. *The Philosophical Theory of the State* (3rd ed. 1920), *The International Crisis in its Ethical and Psychological Aspects* (Oxford, 1915), his essay "Patriotism in the Perfect State."

Bosanquet, Mrs. Bernard. *The Poor Law Report of 1909* (1910).

Bodley, J. E. C. *France* (1900 edition).

Barker, J. Ellis. *British Socialism: An Examination of its Doctrines, Policy, Aims, Practical Proposals* (1908).

Behrens, E. Beddington. *The International Labour Office (League of Nations). A Survey of Certain Problems of International Administration* (1924).

Bowley, A. L. *Livelihood and Poverty* (1915), with A. R. Burnett-Hurst; *The Nature and Purpose of the Measurement of Social Phenomena* (1915).

Barnett, Canon, and Mrs. S. A. *Towards Social Reform* (1908).

Beveridge, Sir William. *Unemployment, A Problem of Industry* (1909).

Bouchet, J. *Manuel de la législation sur les accidents et les sociétés d'assurance mutuelles agricoles* (1924).

Cannan, Edwin. *Theories of Production and Distribution* (3rd ed. 1920).

Cardoza, Benjamin N. *The Nature of the Judicial Process* (1921).

Carver, Thomas Nixon. *Essays in Social Justice* (1915), *The Present Economic Revolution in the United States* (1925).

Carlyle, A. J. *Wages* (1912).

Carrère, G. *La protection légale de l'ouvrier agricole* (1919).

Carrère, J. *Manuel des partis politiques en France* (1924).

Carnegie Report on the *Physical Welfare of Mothers and Children, England and Wales* (2 vols., Liverpool, 1917).

Charnay, Maurice. *Les Allemanistes* (1912).

Clark, John J. *Social Administration Including the Poor Laws* (1922), *Local Government of the United Kingdom* (1922), *Outlines of Local Government* (4th ed. 1920), *Outlines of Central Government, Including the Judicial System of England* (1925, 2nd. ed.).

Clynes, J. R. *Industrial Negotiations and Agreements*, a Foreword by Mr. Clynes to this volume published by the Trade Union Congress and the Labour Party (1923).

Cole, G. D. H. *Organised Labour* (1924), *The World of Labour* (1913, 1917, 1919 editions), *William Cobbett* (1925), *Robert Owen* (1925), *Social Theory* (1920), *The Future of Local Government* (1920), *Labour in the Coalmining Industry 1914-1921* (1923), *Trade Unionism and Munitions* (1923), *Workshop Organisation* (1923), *Chaos and Order in Industry* (1920), *The British Labour Movement* (3rd ed. 1924), *Introduction* (1913) to Everyman's edition of Rousseau's *Social Contract.*

Compère-Morel, M. *Pourquoi nous sommes socialistes* (1913). This is a volume in the series edited by M. Compère-Morel in the *Encyclopéde Socialiste Syndicale et Coopérative de L'internationale Ouvrière. La concentration capitaliste en France* (1913).

Cleveland-Stevens, Edward. *English Railways, Their Development and Their Relation to the State* (1915).

Cox, Harold. *The Failure of State Railways* (1925).

Cohen, Joseph L. *Insurance Against Unemployment* (1921), *Social Insurance Unified and Other Essays* (1924).

Charles, Ernest. *Théories sociales et politiciens, 1870-1898* (1898).

Histoire psychologique et morale du parlementarisime 1870-1898 (1898).

Cauducheau, Maurice. *La réforme de la loi du mars 1884 sur les syndicats professionnels* (1911).

Cestre, Charles. *Production industrielle et justice sociale en Amérique* (1921).

Cavaillé, J. *Journée de huit heures. La loi du 23 avril, 1919. L'historique—l'esprit—le mécanisme d'application* (1919).

Challaye, Felcien. *Le syndicalisme reformiste et syndicalisme révolutionaire* (1909).

Cazalis, Emile. *Les positions sociales du syndicalisme ouvrier en France* (1920).

Cecil, Lord Hugh. *Conservatism* (1912), *Liberty and Authority* (1908.)

Davis, W. J. *A History of the British Trades Union Congress* (2 vols., 1910-1916).

Da Costa, Charles. *Les Blanquistes* (1912).

Dicey, A. V. *Law and Opinion in England* (1st ed. 1905, 2nd. 1914), *Law of the Constitution* (8th ed. 1915).

Delemer, Adolphe. *Le bilan de l'étatisme* (1922), with Preface by M. Jacques Bardoux; *Le bilan de la XIIe législature (1919-1924)* (1924). Published for the *Société d'Études et d'Informations Économiques.*

Dalloz. *Code du travail et de la prévoyance sociale.* The 1923 edition cited in this book.

De Molinari, G. *Le mouvement socialiste et les réunions publiques avant la révolution du 4 Septembre, 1870* (1872).

Detot, Paul. *Le socialisme devant les chambres françaises 1893-1898* (1902).

Dimnet, Ernest. *France Herself Again* (Tr. 1914).

De Ruggiero, Guido. *Modern Philosophy*, translated by A. H. Hannay and R. G. Collingwood (1921).

Duboin, M. *La législation sociale à la fin du XIXe siècle* (1900).

Duguit, Leon. *Le droit social, le droit individuel et la transformation de l'État* (1st ed. 1908, 3rd ed. revised with a new preface, 1922); *Traité de droit constitutionnel* (2nd ed. 4 vols. 1921-25): Vol. I.—*La règle de droit—Le problème de l'État;* Vol. II-III.—*La théorie générale de l'État;* Vol. IV.—*L'organisation politique de l'État français.*

Durand, Paul. *Les organismes sociaux officiels en France,* III: *L'État et le problème social* (1923).

Drake, Barbara. *Women in Trade Unions* (1920), Labour Research Department, Trade Union Series, No. 6.

De Montgomery, B. G. *British and Continental Labour Policy* (1922).

Davies, A. Emil. *Why Nationalisation is Inevitable* (1925), *Land*

Nationalisation, The Key to Social Reform (1921), with Dorothy Evans; *The Collectivist State in the Making* (1914).
Drage, Geoffrey. *Trade Unionism* (1905).
Delatour, Roger. *Systèmes financiers de retraites ouvrières* (1911).
Degas, M. *Les assurances sociales* (1924), *Le problème de l'assurance maladie-invalidité* (1922).
Desplanque, J. *Le problème de la réduction de la durée du travail devant le Parlement Français* (1918).
Dunois, Amédée. *L'action socialiste au parlement, 1910-1914* (1914).
Delesalle, Paul. *Les deux méthodes du syndicalisme* (1905), *Les bourses du travail et la C. G. T.* (1910).
Dolleans, E. *Le caractère réligieux du socialisme* (1906).
Dennes, W. R. *The Method and Presuppositions of Group Psychology* (Oxford, 1923, Thesis).
Effects of the War upon French Economic Life (1923), edited by Charles Gide, published by the Carnegie Foundation.
Elton, Godfrey. *The Revolutionary Idea in France, 1789-1871* (1923).
Ensor, R. C. K. *Modern Socialism* (3rd ed. 1910).
Emmet, Lord. *Nationalisation of Industries: A Criticism.*
Elliott, W. Y. *The Pragmatic Revolt in Politics* (Oxford, 1923, Thesis).
Esmein, Adhémar. *Éléments de droit constitutionnel français et comparé* (7th ed., 2 vols., 1921).
Estey, J. A. *Revolutionary Syndicalism* (1913).
Fabian News.
Fabian Research Department Reports, of which the one edited by Sidney Webb, *How To Pay for the War* (1916), is an example.
Fesch, Paul. Editor of *L'Année Sociale et Économique en France et à l'Étranger,* published for 1907 and 1908.
Faguet, Emile. *Le socialisme en 1907* (1907).
Fere, Victor. *Le mineur, sa condition générale et sa capacité contractuelle dans le droit anglais* (1923).
Follett, M. T. *The New State* (1918), *Creative Experience* (1924).
Foa, E. F. *The Law of Landlord and Tenant* (6th ed. 1924).
Finer, H. *Representative Government and a Parliament of Industry* (1923).
Fisher, H. A. L. *The Republican Tradition in Europe* (1911).
Foignet, Renè, and Emile Dupont. *Manuel élémentaire de législation* (4th ed. 1921).
Fouillée, A. *La démocratie politique et sociale en France* (2nd ed. 1910), *La pensée et les nouvelles écoles anti-intellectualistes* (1911).
Fournière, Eugene. *Les théories socialistes au XIX, siècle* (1904).
Fournal, Etienne. *Le moderne Plutarque ou les hommes illustres de la IIIe République* (1923).

Francq, R. *Le travail au pouvoir* (3rd ed. 1920), with preface by Maxime Leroy.
Ford, Henry Jones. *Representative Government* (1924).
Friedeberg, M. *Le parlementairisme et la grève générale* (1905).
Gettell, Raymond G. *History of Political Thought* (1925).
Gide, Charles. *Les institutions de progrès social* (1st ed. 1900, 2nd. 1921).
Grice, J. Watson. *National and Local Finance* (1910), Preface by Sidney Webb.
Guyot, Edouard. *Le socialisme et l'evolution de L'Angleterre contemporaine (1880-1914)* (1913).
Gleason, Arthur. *What the Workers Want, A Study of British* Labour (1920).
Guèsde, Jules. *Quatre ans de lutte de classe à la chambre, 1893-1898* (2 vols., 1901).
Gooch, Robert Kent. *The Committees (Commissions) in the Chambers (1875 to present time) and Their Influence on Ministerial Responsibility* (Oxford, 1924, Thesis).
Gunn, J. Alexander. *Modern French Philosophy: A Study of the Development Since Comte* (1922), with Foreword by Henri Bergson.
Greenwood, J. H. *The Theory and Practice of Trade Unions* (1911), with preface by Sidney Webb.
Griffuelhes, Victor. *L'action syndicaliste* (1908), *Voyage révolutionnaire: Impressions d'un propagandiste* (1910).
Gwynn, Stephen W., and Gertrude M. Tuckwell. *The Life of Sir Charles W. Dilke* (2 vols., 1917).
Gwynn, Denis. *The Catholic Reaction in France* (1925).
Green, John Richard. *A Short History of the English People*, revised and enlarged with *Epilogue* by Alice Stopford Green (1916).
Gordon, Alban. *Social Insurance: What it is and What it Might Be* (1924).
Griffith-Boscawen, A. *Fourteen Years in Parliament* (1907).
Gephart, W. F. *Effects of the War upon Insurance, with Special Reference to the Substitution of Insurance for Pensions* (1918).
Gaumont, J. *L'État contre la nation* (1911), with preface by H. Lagardelle on "La Politique Syndicaliste."
Guy-Grand, Georges. *La démocratie et l'après-guerre* (1922), *Le procès de la démocratie* (1911), *La philosophie syndicaliste* (1911).
Gleize, H. *Les assurances sociales* (1924).
Girad, M. *Éléments de législation ouvrière* (1925).
Guyot, G. *La loi des huit heures en France et ses conséquences économiques* (1922).
Georges-Cahen, M. *Les fonctionnaires, leur action corporative* (1911).

Garriguet, L. *L'évolution actuelle du socialisme en France* (1912).
Godart, Justin. *Les clauses du travail dans le traité de Versailles* (1920).
Giddings, Franklin H. *The Responsible State* (1918).
Hammond, J. L., and Barbara. *Lord Shaftesbury* (1924), *The Town Labourer (1760-1832), The New Civilization* (1917), *The Rise of Modern Industry* (1925).
Hauriou, Maurice. *Principes de droit public* (2nd ed. 1916), *Leçons sur le mouvement social* (1899), *Précis de droit administratif* (10th ed. 1921), *Précis de droit constitutionnel* (1923), *Science sociale traditionnelle* (1896).
Haldane, Lord (R. B.). *Education and Empire* (1902), Introduction to *Schools and the Nation* (1914); *The Problem of Nationalisation* (1921), with Introduction by R. H. Tawney and H. J. Laski.
Hanotaux, Gabriel. *Contemporary France* (4 vols., 1903-1909), translation by J. C. Tarver of *Histoire de la France contemporaine; La démocratie et le travail* (1920).
Hassall, A. *The French People* (1902).
Henderson, Archibald. *George Bernard Shaw* (1911).
Hardie, J. Keir. *The Case for the Labour Party* (1909), *John Bull and His Unemployed* (1905), *My Confession of Faith in the Labour Alliance* (1909), *From Serfdom to Socialism* (1907).
Hammond, M. B. *British Labour Conditions and Legislation During the War* (1919), Carnegie Foundation, British Series Report.
Hetherington, H. J. W. *International Labour Legislation* (1920).
Humbert, Sylvain. *Les Possibilistes* (1911).
Hutchinson, Keith. *Labour in Politics* (1925).
Hitier, Joseph. *La dernière évolution doctrinale du socialisme: Le socialisme juridique* (1906).
Halévy, Daniel. *Essai sur le mouvement ouvrier en France* (1901).
Hobson, J. A. *Free Thought in the Social Sciences* (1926), *Work and Welfare: A Human Valuation* (1914), *The Evolution of Modern Capitalism* (1902), *The Crisis of Liberalism* (1909), *The Industrial System* (1909).
Hobson, S. G. *National Guilds and the State* (1920).
Hobhouse, L. T. *Democracy and Reaction* (1904, 2nd ed. 1909), *Social Evolution and Political Theory* (1913), *Liberalism* (1911), *The Metaphysical Theory of the State* (1918), *The Elements of Social Justice* (1922).
Hope, James F. *History of the 1900 Parliament* (1908).
Holmes, Oliver Wendell. *Collected Legal Papers* (1920).
Holyoake, George Jacob. *Sixty Years of an Agitator's Life* (1893).
Howell, George. *Trade Unionism, New and Old* (3rd ed. 1900).
Holcombe, A. N. *The Foundations of the Modern Commonwealth* (1923).
Humphrey, A. W. *A History of Labour Representation* (1912).

Hutchins and Harrison. *History of Factory Legislation* (1903).
Hamilton, Mary Agnes (Iconoclast). *Margaret Bondfield* (1925), *J. Ramsay MacDonald: The Man of To-morrow* (1922), *J. Ramsay MacDonald (1923-1925)* (1925).
Hoare, H. J. *Old Age Pensions* (1915).
Hayes, Carlton H. *British Social Politics* (1913).
Hamp, Pierre. *La peine des hommes. Les métiers blessés* (5th ed. 1919).
Hyndman, H. M. *England For All* (1881), *Socialism Made Plain*, by the Social Democratic Federation (1883).
Ilbert, Sir Courtenay. *The Mechanics of Law Making* (N. Y., 1914), *Legislative Methods and Forms* (Oxford, 1901).
Industrial Unrest and the Living Wage: Lectures Given at the Interdenominational Summer School at Swanwick, July, 1913 (1913).
Industrial Council: Report on Enquiry into Industrial Agreements (Cd. 6952, 1913).
Industrial Unrest: A Practical Solution (1914). The Report of the Unionist Reform Committee, with Introduction by F. E. Smith.
Independent Labour Party. Reports and Pamphlets.
Jay, Raoul. *La protection légale des travailleurs* (2nd ed. 1910).
Jacques, Léon. *Les partis politiques sous la IIIe République* (1913).
Jacques, Valdour. *L'ouvrier agricole* (1919), *La vie ouvrière* (1919).
Jacquier, Paul. *La limitation légale de la journée de travail en France* (1902).
Jacquement, Albin. *Le problème des assurances sociales en agriculture* (1923).
Jaurès, Jean. *Études Socialistes* (1908), *Idéalisme et matérialisme dans la conception de l'histoire* (Lille, 1901), debate with Paul Lafargue, Paris, 1895, including his reply.
Jèze, Gaston. *Cours de science des finances et de législation financière Française* (6th ed. 1922), *Le Budget* (1910).
Judge, Mark H. Editor of *Practical Socialism: A Remonstrance* (1908), Papers of the British Constitution Association.
Joseph, H. W. B. *The Labour Theory of Value in Karl Marx* (1923).
Jouhaux, Léon. *Le syndicalisme français—Contre la guerre* (1913), *Le syndicalisme et la C. G. T.* (1920).
Kirkup, Thomas. *History of Socialism* (5th ed. revised and largely rewritten by Edward R. Pease, 1913).
King, O. Bolton. *The Employment and Welfare of Juveniles* (1925, London).
Keeling, Frederick. *Child Labour in the United Kingdom: A study of the development and Administration of the Law Relating to the Employment of Children* (1914).
Kirkaldy, A. W. *Economics and Syndicalism* (1914).
Labour Annual, and *Reformers' Year Book*, published 1896-1908, an unofficial publication.

Labour Year Book, 1916 on, an official party publication of great value
Labour and the New Social Order (1918) (Sidney Webb).
Labour Party *Handbook of Local Government for England and Wales* (1920).
Labour Party's Aims, A Criticism and a Restatement (1923), Seven members of Labour Party.
Labour Party *Annual Conference Reports*, published since 1900.
Labour and Capital in Parliament (1923), Volume III of Labour Research Department Studies in Labour and Capital.
Lavy, A. *L'oeuvre de Millerand: Un ministre socialiste (Juin 1899-Janvier 1902)* (1902).
Leacock, Stephen. *The Unsolved Riddle of Social Justice* (1920).
Levasseur, E. *Histoire des classes ouvrières et de l'industrie en France de 1789-1870* (1st ed. 1867, 2nd ed., 2 vols., 1903-04), *Questions ouvrières en France sous la troisième République* (1907).
Loria, A. *Verso la giustizia sociale* (1st. ed. 1904, 2nd 1908).
Lowell, A. L. *The Government of England* (2 vols., 1st ed. 1908, new ed. 1917), *Greater European Governments* (1st ed. 1918, revised 1925), *Governments and Parties in Continental Europe* (2 vols., 1896).
Low, Sir Sidney. *The Governance of England* (1st ed. 1904, revised ed. 1914).
Leroy, Maxime. *La coutume ouvrière: Syndicats, Bourses du Travail, Fédérations professionnelles, Coopératives, Doctrines et Institutions* (2 vols., 1913); *Les techniques nouvelles du syndicalisme* (1921).
Leyret, Henry. *De Waldeck-Rousseau à la C. G. T.—La Société et les Syndicats* (2nd ed. 1921).
Lowe, B. E. *The International Protection of Labour* (1921).
Les associations ouvrières encouragées par la deuxième République (Décret du 5 Juillet, 1848) (Paris, 1915). Volume IV of studies edited by the *Comité des Travaux Historiques, Scientifiques.*
Les associations professionnelles ouvrières (Vol. I, 1899, Vol. II, 1901, Vol. III, 1903, Vol. IV, 1904), published by the official historian of the *Office du Travail.* An indispensable documentary history.
Les déclarations ministérielles et les ministères (du 4 Septembre, 1870, au Ier Janvier, 1914) (1914), edited by Gay Lavaud.
Les travailleurs et les assurances sociales: Le projet de loi. Ses obligations. Ses avantages (1922). Published by the *Confédération Générale du Travail*, 211 rue Lafayette, Paris, whose pamphlets are all of interest with regard to social policy in France.
Législation minière et législation ouvrière. Texte des principales lois. (4th ed., Paris, 1920), published by the *Comité Central des Houillères de France.*
Laski, H. J. *A Grammar of Politics* (1925), *The State in the New*

Social Order (1923), Fabian Tract No. 200; *Karl Marx* (1922), *Authority in the Modern State* (1924).

Lafargue, Paul. *Le socialisme et la conquête des pouvoirs publiques* (Lille, 1899).

Le Bon, Gustave. *Psychologie du socialisme* (1st ed. 1899, 3rd ed. 1902).

Lagardelle, H. *Le socialisme ouvrier* (1910), *Syndicalisme et socialisme* (1908).

Levine, Louis. *The Labour Movement in France* (N. Y., 1912), second edition as *Syndicalism in France* (1914), with preface by Franklin H. Giddings.

Louis, Paul. *Histoire du socialisme en France depuis la Révolution jusqu'à nos jours* (1925), *Histoire du socialisme Français* (1901), *Histoire du parti socialiste en France, 1871-1914* (1922), *Histoire du mouvement syndicaliste en France, 1789-1910* (2nd ed. 1910), *L'ouvrier devant l'État* (1904), *L'avenir socialiste des syndicats* (1905), *Le syndicalisme contre l'État* (1910).

Leroy-Beaulieu, Paul. *Le collectivisme* (5th ed. 1900). Sir Arthur Clay edited an earlier edition, *Collectivism: A Study of the Leading Social Questions of the Day* (1909).

Lindsay, A. D. *Karl Marx's 'Capital'* (Oxford, 1926), *Introduction* (1910) to Everyman's edition of Mill's *Essays, Historical Materialism and the Economics of Karl Marx* (1914), *Political Quarterly*, Nos. 1 and 4, 1914; his essay "The State and Society, in *The Theory of the State* (Oxford, 1916), his essay "Political Theory" in *Recent Developments in European Thought* (1920), edited by F. S. Marvin.

Land Enquiry Committee, The Report of (2 vols., 1914).

Liberal Land Committee, The Report of (2 vols., 1925), I, *Land and the Nation*, II, *Towns and the Land.*

Loch, C. S. *Old Age Pensions: A Collection of Short Papers* (1903).

Lloyd George, David. *The People's Insurance* (1911), *Coal and Power* (1924), the Report of an Enquiry presided over by Mr. Lloyd George, with Appendix on "Housing Conditions in Mining Areas," by R. A. Scott-Jones; *The People's Budget* (1909).

Lowther, the Rt. Hon. James William (Viscount Ullswater). *A Speaker's Commentaries* (1925).

Marx, Karl. *Capital.* Translated from the third German edition by Samuel Moore and Edward Aveling and edited by F. Engels (17th ed. 1920).

Marriott, Sir J. A. R. *The English Constitution in Transition, 1910-1924* (Oxford, 1924), *Economics and Ethics* (1923).

Mallet, Bernard. *British Budgets, 1887-1913* (1914).

Mallock, W. H. *Social Equality* (1884), *Property and Progress or a Brief Inquiry into Contemporary Social Agitation in England* (1884).

Mann, Tom. *Memoirs* (1923).
Mess, H. A. *Factory Legislation and its Administration, 1891-1924* (1926, London).
Malon, Benoît. *Le socialisme intégral* (2 vols., 1890-94).
Métin, Albert. *Les traités ouvriers: Accords internationaux de prévoyance et de travail* (1908).
Mahaim, E. *Le droit international ouvrier* (1913).
Morley, John (Viscount). *Recollections* (2 vols., 1917), *Life of Gladstone* (3 vols., 1903).
Massaryk, Thomas-Garrigue. *Les problèmes de la démocratie* (1924), preface by Albert Thomas.
Munro, W. B. *The Governments of Europe* (1925).
Millerand, Alexandre. *Politique de réalisations* (1911), *Pour la défense nationale* (1913), *La grève et l'organisation ouvrière* (1906), *Travail et travailleurs* (1908), *Le socialisme réformiste français* (1903).
Michels, Robert. *Zur Soziologie des Parteiwesens in der modernen Demokratie* (Leipzig, 1911).
Metton, C. *Un village syndicale* (1920).
Milhaud, Edouard. *La marche au socialisme* (1920).
Muirhead, J. H. *The Elements of Ethics* (1921 ed.).
Morris, C. R., and Mary. *A History of Political Ideas* (1924).
Masterman, C. F. G. *The Condition of England* (1909).
Mansbridge, Arthur. *An Adventure in Working-Class Education* (Being the Story of the Workers' Education Association, 1903-1915) (1920), *University Tutorial Classes* (1913).
Mantoux, Paul. *Lectures on the History of the Nineteenth Century* (Cambridge, 1902), *La Crise du Trade-Unionisme* (1903), with Maurice Alfassa.
Maitland, F. W. *Life and Letters of Leslie Stephen* (1906), *The Constitutional History of England*, edited by H. A. L. Fisher (Cambridge, 1908).
Moon, Parker Thomas. *The Labour Problem and the Social Catholic Movement in France* (1921).
Marshall, Alfred. *Principles of Economics* (8th ed. 1920).
Money, Sir Leo Chiozza. *The Triumph of Nationalisation* (1920).
May-Holland, *The Constitutional History of England* (3 vols., 1912 edition by Mr. Francis Holland).
Milner, Lord. *Questions of the Hour* (1923).
Morley, Felix. *Unemployment Relief in Great Britain: A Study in State Socialism* (1924).
Marlin, E. *Le chômage involuntaire et la législation anglaise* (1924).
Morin, M. *La situation juridique des Trade Unions en Angleterre* (Caën, 1907).
Montchrestien, M. *Le problème des assurances sociales en France* (1922).

Maurras, Charles. *Le dilemme de Marc Sagnier: Essai sur la démocratie réligieuse* (1907).

MacDonald, J. Ramsay. *Parliament and Democracy* (1920), *The Socialist Movement* (1911), *Socialism and Government* (2 vols., 3rd ed. 1910), *Socialism and Society* (1905), *Margaret Ethel MacDonald* (1st ed. 1912, 5th ed. 1920), *The Social Unrest, Its Cause and Solution* (1913), *A Policy for the Labour Party* (1920).

MacGregor, D. H. *The Evolution of Industry* (1911).

Macrosty, H. W. *Trusts and the State* (1901).

McDougall, William. *Ethics and Some Modern World Problems* (1924).

McG. Eager, W., and H. A. Secretan. *Unemployment Among Boys* (1925).

McMahon, Theresa. *Social and Economic Standards of Living* (1925).

McIlwain, C. H. *The High Court of Parliament and Its Supremacy* (1910).

Nicholson, J. S. *Historical Progress and Ideal Socialism* (1894), *The Revival of Marxism* (1920).

Noel, Octave. *Le socialisme et la question sociale* (1902).

Orléans, M. Louis Philippe de. *Les associations ouvrières en Angleterre* (1869), translated by Nassau J. Senior and edited by Thomas Hughes, *The Trades' Unions of England* (1869).

Ogg, F. A., and P. O. Ray. *Introduction to American Government* (1925 ed.).

Orry, A. *Les Socialistes Indépendants* (1912).

Orth, S. P. *Socialism and Democracy in Europe* (1913).

Osborne, Walter V., and Mark H. Judge. *Trade Unions and the Law* (1911).

Ostrogorski, M. *La démocratie et les partis politiques* (French edition, 1912). (English edition, revised, 2 vols., N. Y., 1922).

Pease, Edward R. *History of the Fabian Society* (1916, new ed. 1925).

Pease, Margaret. *Jean Jaurès* (1916), Introduction by J. Ramsay MacDonald.

Pelloutier, Fernand. *Histoire des bourses du travail, origine, institutions, avenir* (1902), with preface by Georges Sorel and Note by Victor Dave.

Political Quarterly, 1914-1916, edited by W. G. S. Adams.

Pound, Roscoe. *Law and Morals* (1924), University of North Carolina Press.

Paraf, Pierre. *Le syndicalisme pendant et après la guerre* (2nd ed. 1923).

Pic, Paul. *Traité élementaire de législation industrielle. Les lois ouvrières* (5th ed. 1922).

Paul-Boncour, M. *Le fédéralisme économique* (1900), with preface by M. Waldeck-Rousseau; *Le syndicats de fonctionnaires* (1905), with preface by M. Anatole France; *Les retraites, la mutualité, la politique sociale* (1912).

Pollard, A. F. *The History of England* (1912), *The Evolution of Parliament* (1920).

Pollock, Sir Frederick. *History of the Science of Politics* (1st ed. 1890).

Poor Law Reports of 1834 and 1909.

Property: Its Duties and Rights, Historically, Philosophically, and Religiously Regarded. Essays by various writers with Introduction by the Bishop of Oxford, Dr. Gore (1st ed. 1914, 2nd 1915).

Puech, J.-L. *La tradition socialiste en France et la société des nations* (1921), with preface by Charles Gide.

Price, T. W. *The Story of the Workers' Educational Association (1903-1924)* (1924), with Introduction by R. H. Tawney.

Pigou, A. C. *Wealth and Welfare* (1912), *Lectures on Housing* (Manchester, 1914), with Seebohm Rowntree.

Pratt, E. A. *Trade Unionism and British Industry* (1904).

Pierre, Eugène. *Politique et gouvernement* (1896).

Pierrot, M. *Syndicalisme et révolution* (1905).

Peyronnet, Albert. *Le ministère du travail, 1906-1923* (1924).

Puget, J. *L'histoire de la réforme électorale* (1912), with preface by J. Paul-Boncour.

Persil, R., and G. Barbier. *Les retraites ouvrières* (1906), with introduction by M. Millerand.

Pelleray, E. *L'oeuvre financière du Parlement du 1906 à 1910* (1910).

Pouget, Emile. *Les bases du syndicalisme* (1905), *La confédération générale du travail* (1st ed. 1908, 2nd 1910), *Le parti ouvrier* (1908), *Le syndicat* (1905), *Comment nous ferons la révolution* (1909), with E. Pataud, translated by C. and F. Charles, *Syndicalism and the Cooperative Commonwealth, How We Small Bring About the Revolution* (1913), with foreword by Tom Mann.

Rait, Robert S. *Memorials of Albert Venn Dicey: Being Chiefly Letters and Diaries* (1925).

Raphael, Gaston. *Walter Rathenau, ses idées et ses projets d'organisation économique* (1919).

Rappaport, Charles. *Jean Jaurès, L'Homme, Le Penseur, Le Socialiste* 1st ed. 1916, 2nd 1925), *Socialisme de gouvernement et socialisme révolutionaire* (1902) issued by *Parti Ouvrier Français*.

Rey, M. *La question des assurances sociales* (1925). M. Rey is author of the report on social insurance by the C. G. T.

Redgrave's *Factory Acts* (12th ed., London, 1916), by Charles F. Lloyd, revised by W. Peacock.

Reynauld, Paul *M. Waldeck-Rousseau* (1913).

Raynauld, Barthèlemy. *Vers le salaire minimum* (1913).
Report of the Industrial Conference, Balliol College, April 6-10, 1922.
Reformers' Year Book, combined with the *Labour Annual,* published from 1896-1908, the files of which have a good deal of valuable information.
Robinson, James Harvey. *The Mind in the Making* (1921).
Roberts, Harry. *Constructive Conservatism* (1913), with an Introduction by L. S. Amery, M.P.
Reeves, Mrs. Pember. *Round About a Pound a Week* (1913).
Redslob, Robert. *Le régime parlementaire* (1924).
Rees, J. F. *A Social and Industrial History of England, 1815-1918* (19—.)
Rose, Frank H. *The Coming Force: The Labour Movement* (Manchester, 1909).
Rowntree, B. Seebohm. *Land and Labour: Lessons from Belgium* (1910), *Lectures on Housing,* with A. C. Pigou, (Manchester, 1914); *Poverty: A Study of Town Life* (1901), *How the Labourer Lives* (1913), with May Kendall.
Russell, Bertrand. *Principles of Social Reconstruction* (1916), *Roads to Freedom: Socialism, Anarchism and Syndicalism* (1st ed. 1918, 3rd ed. 1920), *Prospects of Industrial Civilization* (1924), with Dora Russell; *What I Believe* (1925), *Education and the Good Life* (1926).
Renard, Georges. *Discussions sociales d'hier et de demain* (1910), *Syndicats, trade-unions et corporations* (1909).
Rendu and Cacheux, MM. *Les habitations à bon marché,* in the series of *Guides pratiques de législation sociale.*
Rouger, Hubert. *L'action socialiste au parlement, 1914-1919* (1919).
Ralea, Michel. *L'idée de révolution dans les doctrines socialistes: Étude sur l'évolution de la tactique révolutionnaire* (1923), with preface by Charles Bouglé.
Saulière, A. *La grève générale: de Robert Owen à la doctrine syndicaliste* (1913).
Sabatier, Camille. *Le socialisme libéral ou morcellisme* (1904).
Sait, Edward M. *Government and Politics of France* (1921).
Seignobos, Charles. *L'Évolution de la 3me, République, 1875-1914* (1921), Vol. VIII, *Histoire de France contemporaine depuis la Révolution jusqu'à la Paix de 1919,* Ernest Lavisse, editor; *Histoire politique de l'Europe contemporaine: évolution des partis et des formes politiques 1814-1896* (E. T. 1904).
Scelle, Georges. *Le droit ouvrier* (1922).
Schloss, D. F. *Insurance of Unemployment* (1909).
Seailles, Gabriel. *La philosophie du travail* (1923).
Seillière, Ernest. *Le péril mystique dans l'inspiration des démocraties contemporaines* (1918).
Schatz, Albert. *L'entreprise gouvernementale* (1922).

Shaw, G. B. Introduction to 1908 edition *Fabian Essays in Socialism*, Preface to *Back to Methuselah*, Appendix to Pease's *History of Fabian Society*.

Smith, Constance. *The Case for Wages Boards* (1906).

Smith, F. E. (Earl of Birkenhead). *Industrial Unrest, A Practical Solution: The Report of the Unionist Social Reform Committee* (1914). The committee members were W. J. Ashley, J. W. Hills, and M. Wood.

Smith, J. H. *Collectivist Economics* (1925).

Soltau, R. H. *French Parties and Politics* (1922).

Sombart, Werner. *Sozialismus und soziale Bewegung* (Jena, 1908, 9th ed. 1920).

Soutter, F. W. *Recollections of a Labour Pioneer* (1923).

Sorel, Georges. *Matériaux d'une théorie du prolétariat* (2nd ed. 1921). Contains the prefaces written for Italian books, and fugitive pieces. *Introduction à l'économie moderne* (1st ed. 1903, 2nd 1921); *Réflexions sur la violence* (First appeared in *Le Mouvement Socialiste*, 1906, 5th ed. "Avec Plaidoyer Pour Lenine," 1921); *La décomposition du Marxisme* (1st ed. 1908, 2nd 1910); *L'avenir socialiste des syndicats.*

Spender, J. A. *The Life of the Rt. Hon. Sir Henry Campbell-Bannerman* (1923). *A Modern Journal: A Diary for the Year of Agitation, 1903-1904* (1904).

Stewart, William. *J. Keir Hardie: A Biography* (1921, Introduction by J. Ramsay MacDonald.

Shadwell, A. *The Socialist Movement* (2 vols., 1925).

Scott, J. W. *Syndicalism and Philosophical Realism* (1919).

Shepherd, E. C. *The Fixing of Wages in Government Employment* (1923).

Sutherland, William. *Old Age Pensions in Theory and Practice* (1907).

Sells, Dorothy. *The British Trade Boards System* (1923).

Snowden, Philip. *Labour and National Finance* (1920).
Labour and the New World (1921).

Shallard, S. D. *Has Liberalism a Future* (1909).

Stoddart, Jane T. *The New Socialism* (1909).

Siegfried, André. *L'Angleterre d'aujourd'hui, son evolution économique et politique* (5th ed. 1924).

Saint-Leon, Et-Martin. *Syndicalisme ouvrier et syndicalisme agricole* (1920).
Les deux C. G. T.—syndicalisme et communisme (1921).

Sachet, Adrien. *Législation sur les accidents du travail et les maladies professionnelles* (1st ed. 1909, 2nd ed. 1921, 2 vols.).
Traité théorique et pratique de la législation sur les accidents du travail et les maladies professionnelles (1924, third volume in series).

Steeg, M. *L'action parlementaire et la nouvelle législature* (1910), being a symposium by 25 leaders with preface by M. Steeg. *Syndicalisme et Socialisme* (1907). This volume contains the report of the international conference held in Paris, April 13, 1907. Compare with this the report of the *Congrès Anarchiste d'Amsterdam,* 1907 (Paris, 1908).

Sageret, Jules. *La doctrine du syndicalisme intellectuel* (1921).

Simkhovitch, Vladimir G. *Marxism Versus Socialism* (1st ed. 1913, 3rd ed. 1923).

Stocks, J. L. *Aristotelianism* (1925).
Patriotism and the Super-State (1920).
The Voice of the People (1920).

Vinogradoff, Sir Paul. *Outlines of Historical Jurisprudence* (2 vols. 1920-22).

Villiers, B. *The Opportunity of Liberalism* (1904).
The Socialist Movement in England (1908).

Vabre, Albert. *Le droit international du travail.*

Vaillant, Edouard. *Le Chômage à Chambre* (1905).

Vandervelde, Émile. *Le parti ouvrier belge* (1925).

Villey, Étienne. *L'organisation professionnelle des employeurs dans l'industrie française* (1923).

Villey, Edmond. *L'État et le progrès social* (1923).

Valois, George. *La monarchie et la classe ouvrière* (1910).

Viviani, René. *As We See It* (Translation by T. R. Ybarra, London, 1923).

Towler, W. G. *Socialism in Local Government* (1908).

Trevelyan, G. M. *British History in the Nineteenth Century, 1782-1901.* (1922).
Lord Grey of the Reform Bill (1910).

Tables Alphabétiques et Analytiques de Chambre des Députés, reference index of all subjects before the Chamber of Deputies; and of Senate, a similar index.

Tillyard, Frank. *The Worker and the State* (1923).

Townsend, Mrs. *Creative Syndicalism* (1924).

Tuckwell, Gertrude. *Women in Industry from Seven Points of View* (1908) with six others.

Tawney, R. H. *Minimum Rates in Chainmaking Industry* (1914).
Minimum Rates in Tailoring Trade (1915).
The Sickness of an Acquisitive Society (1920).
The British Labour Movement (1925).

Toynbee, Arnold. *The Industrial Revolution of the Eighteenth Century in England,* (1st ed. 1884), with *Reminiscence*—by Lord Milner in 1894 edition.

Thiers, André. *La politique de demain: administrative, financière et et économique* (3rd ed. 1922).
Administrateurs et administrés (1919).

Turman, Max. *Problèmes sociaux du travail industriel* (1923).

Thomas, Albert. *La politique socialiste* (1913).

Tessier, G. *Le statut légal des employees* (1924), *La journée de huit heures* (1923).

Watson, A. *A Great Labour Leader, Being the Life of the Rt. Hon. Thomas Burt, M.P.* (1908).

The Case for the Factory Acts (1902), *Introduction to Problems of Modern Industry* (1902), *English Poor Law Policy* (1910), *A Constitution for the Socialist Commonwealth of Great Britain* (1920).

Webb, Sidney and Beatrice. *The History of Trade Unionism* (1920 ed.). *Industrial Democracy* (1st ed. 1897).

Sidney. *Socialism in England* (1890).

Beatrice. *My Apprenticeship* (1926).

Wells, H. G. *Outline of History* (1920 ed.).

Wallas, Graham. *Human Nature in Politics* (1908), *The Great Society* (1914), *Our Social Heritage* (1920).

Waldeck-Rousseau, René. *Discours parlementaires de Waldeck-Rousseau.*

Watney, Charles, and James A. Little. *Industrial Warfare; The Aims and Claims of Capital and Labour* (1912).

Willoughby, W. W. *Social Justice* (1900), *The Fundamental Concepts of Public Law* (1924), *An Introduction to the Problem of Government* (1921), with Lindsay Rogers.

Williams, T. G. *The Main Currents of Social and Industrial Change, 1870-1924* (London, 1925).

Wolf, Humbert. *Labour Supply and Regulation* (1923).

Woodworth, A. V. *Christian Socialism in the Church of England* (1902).

Weill, George. *Histoire du mouvement social en France* (1st ed. 1904, 2nd 1911).

Yves-Guyot, M. *Politique parlementaire et politique atavique* (1924).

Young, J. T. *The New American Government and Its Work.*

Zéavès, A. *Le socialisme en France depuis 1871* (1908), *Les Guesdistes* (1911). M. Zéavès has edited the series of histories of the French parties written by MM. Da Costa Charnay, Humbert, Orry, and Breton. *Le parti socialiste de 1904 à 1923* (1923). *Le socialisme en 1912 (conclusions et annexes)* (1912).

INDEX